The Plays of
Eugene O'Neill

LITERATURE AND LIFE SERIES
(Formerly Modern Literature and World Dramatists)

Selected list of titles:

Complete list of titles in the series available from the publisher on request.

THE PLAYS OF EUGENE O'NEILL

A New Assessment

VIRGINIA FLOYD

Frederick Ungar Publishing Co. / New York

To my mother and the memory of my father

Copyright © 1985 by Frederick Ungar Publishing Co., Inc.
Printed in the United States of America

Design by DAVID LUNN

Library of Congress Cataloging in Publication Data

Floyd, Virginia.
    The plays of Eugene O'Neill.

    (Literature and life series)
    Bibliography: p.
    Includes index.
    1. O'Neill, Eugene, 1888–1953—Criticism and interpretation.
I. Title. II. Series.
PS3529.N5Z6427 1984   812'.52   84-8874
ISBN 0-8044-2206-0
ISBN 0-8044-6153-8 (pbk.)

Acknowledgments

I am grateful to the Collection of American Literature, the Beinecke Rare Book and Manuscript Library, Yale University as legatee of the Eugene O'Neill Collection for permission to use quotations from O'Neill's works and photographs of the dramatist, his family, and productions of his plays, and to The Estate of Carl Van Vechten. I am indebted also to Bryant College for the sabbatical leave provided me in spring 1983; to my colleagues, Stanley Kozikowski and Vera Krieger for their encouragement; to my fellow scholar Tom Olsson of the Royal Dramatic Theatre for his assistance; to Philip Winsor, my editor at Ungar, for his guidance and advice; and to beloved members of my family for their support and enduring patience with my persistent quest for the quintessential O'Neill.

Contents

Illustrations follow pages xxvii, 173, 369, and 499.

Illustrations

Chronology

16 October 1888   Eugene Gladstone O'Neill born at Barrett House, a New York City hotel, to James and Ella O'Neill.*

1888–95   Spends first years with parents on actor-father's theatrical road tours and at family summer home in New London, Connecticut.

1895–1902   Attends St. Aloysius Academy for Boys in the Riverdale section of the Bronx (five years); and De La Salle Institute in New York City (two years).

1902–1906   Attends Betts Academy, a nonsectarian private school in Connecticut.

1906–07   Attends Princeton University; suspended for prank before examinations in June; no incentive to return.

1907–08   Works as secretary in a New York mail-order business; interest in anarchism and Nietzsche grows.

1908–09   Sets out for Honduras on gold-prospecting trip arranged by father two weeks after marriage on October 2, 1909, to the pregnant Kathleen Jenkins.

1910   Returns from Honduras, tours with father in *The White Sister*; Eugene Jr. born in May; sails to Buenos Aires in June on *Charles Racine*; arrives in Argentina in August; becomes destitute after quitting jobs with American companies.

---

*Some information in this chronology is taken from "Cycles," O'Neill's arrangement of the significant events in his creative and personal life in a pattern of seven-year cycles. The complete "Cycles" record appears in *Eugene O'Neill at Work* (New York: Frederick Ungar, 1981), pp. 385–387.

1911   Returns to New York on the *Ikala* in April; lives at Jimmy the Priest's, a waterfront saloon-hotel; ships for Southampton as seaman on the American Line's *New York* in July and returns on the *Philadelphia* in August.

1912   Attempts suicide in January at Jimmy the Priest's; joins father's *The Count of Monte Cristo* vaudeville tour in New Orleans; returns to summer home in New London and becomes a reporter for the *Telegraph* in August; is divorced by Kathleen; enters Gaylord Farm Sanatorium on Christmas Eve for treatment of tuberculosis.

1913–14   Reads works of Strindberg and others during confinement in sanatorium and decides to become a playwright; after release in June 1913, while recuperating at family home and at the Rippins' house, where he boarded, he writes a vaudeville sketch, *A Wife for a Life*; eight one-acters, *The Web, Thirst, Recklessness, Warnings, Fog, Bound East for Cardiff, Abortion,* and *The Movie Man*; and two long plays, *Bread and Butter* and *Servitude*.

1914–15   Enters Baker's English 47 class at Harvard in September; completes one year of the playwriting course and two extant plays, the one-acter *The Sniper* and the four-act "The Personal Equation."

1915–16   Goes to Greenwich Village in the fall and spends unproductive year there; absorbs atmosphere at the Hell Hole, which is used later in work; travels in June 1916 to Provincetown where two plays, *Bound East for Cardiff* and *Thirst*, are staged by an amateur group, known later as the Provincetown Players; writes three-act farce-comedy *Now I Ask You* and one-acter *Before Breakfast*; returns to New York in the fall with the Players; group opens The Playwrights' Theater and stages *Before Breakfast* on December 1 and all but one of O'Neill's plays in next four years; completes two short stories: "Tomorrow" and "The Movie Man," adapted from earlier play.

1917–18 Moves to Provincetown where he writes three of the *Glencairn* plays, *In the Zone*, *The Long Voyage Home*, and *The Moon of the Caribbees*, and *Ile* in winter-spring 1917; completes a short story, "The Hairy Ape," and a novelette, "S.O.S."; meets Agnes Boulton, a fiction writer, in fall while attending rehearsals for plays in New York; returns to Provincetown with Agnes and marries her April 12, 1918; that year he completes four one-acters: *Shell Shock, The Rope, The Dreamy Kid*, and *Where the Cross Is Made*; the three-act *Beyond the Horizon*; and the first draft of *The Straw*, an account of his stay at Gaylord.

1919 Spends winter at wife's home in West Point Pleasant, New Jersey; records many ideas for plays but writes little of value; completes *Chris Christopherson*, which fails and is later rewritten as *Anna Christie*, and a revised version of *The Straw*; moves to new home in Province-town, Peaked Hill Bars; leaves this isolated summer home for rented house in Provincetown where son Shane is born October 30.

1920 Receives Pulitzer Prize for *Beyond the Horizon*; abandons the one-acter for longer forms, writing *Gold, Anna Christie*, and *Diff'rent*; begins, with *The Emperor Jones*, the experimental plays of the 1920s; father dies on August 10.

1921–22 Gains international acclaim for expressionist works *The Hairy Ape* and *The Emperor Jones*; wins Pulitzer Prize for *Anna Christie*; writes *The First Man, The Fountain*, and *Welded*; mother dies on February 28, 1922; purchases Brook Farm in Ridgefield, Connecticut, for winter home.

1923–27 Writes major works of the 1920s: the controversial plays *All God's Chillun Got Wings* and *Desire Under the Elms*; and *Marco Millions, The Great God Brown, Lazarus Laughed*, and *Strange Interlude*; brother Jamie dies November 8, 1923; daughter Oona born May 14, 1924; moves to Bermuda at the end of 1924 and purchases a home, Spithead, there in 1926; spends summer and fall of 1926 at Belgrade Lakes, Maine, where he meets Carlotta Monterey, with whom he later falls in love; sells Brook Farm in 1927; leaves Agnes, his children, and Spithead in November 1927, ostensibly to discuss the Theatre Guild's productions of *Marco Millions* and *Strange Interlude*, but decides not to return to family.

1928–31 At the height of his fame and popularity in America in 1920s; receives Pulitzer Prize for *Strange Interlude*; after play opens, elopes with Carlotta on February 10, 1928, on the Southampton-bound S.S. *Berengaria*; begins *Dynamo* at Guéthary, France; sails in October with Carlotta on the S.S. *Andre Lebon* for Singapore, Saigon, and Shanghai; returns to France in January 1929; finishes *Dynamo* in April and works for the next two years on *Mourning Becomes Electra*; Agnes reluctantly obtains divorce; he marries Carlotta July 22, 1929; *Dynamo* is pronounced a failure by the critics; returns to New York on May 17, 1931; attends rehearsals in fall for trilogy, which is an artistic and critical success.

1932–33 Moves to Sea Island, Georgia, in April 1932 and into newly built home, Casa Genotta, in June; except for the month devoted to the autobiographical *Ah, Wilderness!*, an immensely popular comedy, works continuously on *Days Without End* from February 1932 to December 1933; notes in Work Diary twice for this period: "return toward Catholicism."

1934–38 *Days Without End* is a critical failure when it opens on January 7, 1934;* ordered in March to take a six-month rest to prevent nervous breakdown; makes notes in December 1934 for "Calms of Capricorn series," which eventually becomes eleven-play Cycle; works on

*O'Neill precedes the entry for each subsequent year in the "Cycles" from 1934–35 to 1944–45 with the notation "No Prod." No play was staged in New York until the 1946 production of *The Iceman Cometh*.

Cycle for next two years until ill health prompts him to leave Georgia for the West Coast; in Seattle in November 1936 when notified of Nobel Prize award; hospitalized from December 27 to March 2, 1937, in Oakland, California; resumes the Cycle plays in June and works on them for next two years; settles in December 1937 in newly built home, Tao House, in Danville, California.

1939–43 Conceives first idea on June 6, 1939, for two greatest plays, *The Iceman Cometh* and *Long Day's Journey into Night*; interrupts work on them to develop ideas for three antitotalitarian plays, "The Visit of Malatesta," "The Last Conquest," and "Blind Alley Guy," and to recuperate from periods of depression caused by concern about the war; begins the "By Way of Obit" series but completes only *Hughie*, in September 1941; resumes work on the Cycle but finishes only *A Touch of the Poet* and a typescript for *More Stately Mansions*; tremor in hands makes it impossible to continue writing; completes final play, *A Moon for the Misbegotten*, in 1943.

1944–47 Moves to the Hotel Fairmont in San Francisco after sale of Tao House in February 1944; depressed by failing health and inability to write; leaves West Coast on October 17, 1945, and settles in New York; plans two productions with the Theatre Guild, *The Iceman Cometh*, which opened on October 9, 1946, and *A Moon for the Misbegotten*, which closed during its road tour in 1947 before reaching Broadway.

1948–51 Relinquishes all hope of ever writing again; moves to Boston and returns to the mystical sea; purchases home in Marblehead, Massachusetts, and lives there, unobtrusively, until hospitalized in February 1951; breaks with Carlotta but reconciles in May; laments suicide of son Eugene in September 1950.

1951–53 Lives last two and one-half years at the Hotel Shelton in Boston, isolated from friends by Carlotta; destroys unfinished Cycle plays; illness debilitates his body, increases his dependence on wife; death comes, hastened by his deep longing for release from life.

27 November 1953   Dies at the Hotel Shelton and is buried in a private ceremony at Forest Hills Cemetery.

Introduction

The year 1988 marks the centennial anniversary of the birth of Eugene O'Neill, America's foremost dramatist. It seems particularly pertinent, as this centurial date draws near, to assess the contribution this solitary figure has made to American drama, culture, and thought. During his lengthy artistic career, O'Neill functioned as national archivist, social critic, and moral guide. He held a mirror up to American society in a period bracketed by World War I and World War II and became its conscience. Yet the dramatist transcends the barriers of time and place. As the poet of the human heart, O'Neill bears a message for all men of every era.

In the past, the O'Neill canon seemed to be the exclusive domain of a coterie of scholars. This book is an introductory study designed to bring contemporary students and general readers to an understanding of Eugene O'Neill, the man and playwright. The volume contains an interpretive analysis of the fifty plays O'Neill completed. Each of these is a self-contained unit, comprehensible in and of itself. Collectively, the dramas chronicle the birth of a playwright, tracing the thirty-year span, 1913–1943, of development from amateur to craftsman to creative artist.

For a twenty-five-year period, 1918 to 1943, O'Neill recorded his ideas for plays in a collection of notebooks, developing the more promising concepts into scenarios and drafts for dramas. Some of these he finished and published; others he worked on from time to time but eventually decided he could never write; some he apparently never gave up hope of being able to complete. In the 1930s the dramatist began sending his notebooks and manuscripts to the Beinecke Rare Book and Manuscript Library at Yale University for safekeeping. Carlotta Monterey O'Neill added others to the O'Neill collection after her husband's death in 1953, many with the stipulation that they be restricted for twenty-five years. In March, 1978, I was given permission by Donald Gallup, curator of the Collection of American Literature, to edit this material for publication. O'Neill's handwriting, miniscule at all times, was nearly illegible during his last creative years, 1939–1943. After transcribing the hundreds of pages of notes and editing and annotating this material for a scholarly publication, *Eugene O'Neill at Work* (Frederick Ungar, 1981), I decided that a new evaluation of the plays was badly needed and prepared this companion volume for contemporary devotees of O'Neill.

This study incorporates the knowledge gained from close examination of O'Neill's notes and notebooks and offers a new, comprehensive assessment of the playwright and a fresh, more perceptive interpretation of the extant body of his work. No other dramatist of modern times so exposed the secret recesses of his soul, and those of his parents and brother, as has O'Neill in the many ideas for plays he recorded and in some instances developed in the 1918–1943 period. Frequently, he mutes the harsh portraits found in the first notes and scenarios when he writes the final drafts of plays. Yet it is necessary to go back and reflect on the glimpses the author provides of the four O'Neills in the formative stages of creation in order to comprehend fully the extremely personal nature of the dramas and to understand the man himself. O'Neill had one tale to tell in his work: his own tortured, convoluted life story. His relationship to his mother, father, brother, wives, children, and friends is dramatized in endless variations in the canon. Because all human lives pivot around the same types of familial ties and friendships,

O'Neill's work assumes universal dimensions. He speaks
the common language of the heart, expressing the longings of all mankind to love and be loved, to belong, to
determine the why of existence. Because this language is
readily understood by people of all classes and races,
O'Neill has become an international playwright, respected and produced in countries throughout the world.

Yet, despite his universality, the dramatist was
uniquely American in his depiction of and response to
life. His plays are distinctly nationalistic in the historical
perspective they provide of people living in a particular
cultural and social milieu, a capitalist society subtly gov-
erned by Puritan principles that decree a demanding
work and moral ethic. As O'Neill perceives and records
the phenomenon, the drive to attain wealth and to maintain the aura of respectability and morality distorts and
dichotomizes the American nation and character.

On the national level, the capitalist system, which is
predicated on the expansion of a highly industrialized,
technological society, created two diametrically opposite
classes: the wealthy, rapacious exploiters and the poor,
downtrodden exploited. O'Neill sounded his first major
clarion call to social revolt in 1921 in *The Hairy Ape*,
which depicts, through one individual, Yank, the dislocation, disillusionment, and destruction of Americans in the
early twentieth century who were victimized by the highly technological system they had, by their own excruciat-
ing efforts, helped create. In subsequent plays, such as
Desire Under the Elms and *Mourning Becomes Electra*,
the author showed the disastrous effects of material prosperity and a life-denying Puritanism on two New England
families, the Cabots and the Mannons. Throughout the
1920s and 1930s O'Neill was constantly rewriting the
"Modern Faust Play," an idea for a drama he had in 1927,
depicting the American character as having sold its soul
for material prosperity. He stated: "We've squandered
our souls by trying to possess something outside it." The

primary purpose of the eleven-play Cycle he attempted in the 1930s was to dramatize the long two-hundred-year drive of a single American family, the Yankee Harfords, to appropriate unto themselves the vast treasures to be attained by exploiting the land and their fellow man, particularly the immigrant hordes that arrived after they had established their economic, political, and social supremacy. The title O'Neill assigns the Cycle, "A Tale of Possessors Self-Dispossessed," reveals his revulsion from American greed and indicates the kind of punishment meted out to the avaricious accumulators of wealth: moral and spiritual impoverishment. The author points out the underlying theme of the Cycle, which, in one sentence, sums up for him "the whole secret of human happiness": "For what shall it profit a man if he shall gain the whole world and lose his own soul?"

On the personal level, the dualistic pursuit of exterior prosperity and inner self-realization produce a schism within the individual. O'Neill demonstrates this split in man through the materialist businessman–idealist poet dichotomy, sometimes manifested in one character, such as Simon Harford in *More Stately Mansions*, or in two opposing figures, such as the businessman William A. Brown and the artist Dion Anthony in *The Great God Brown*. The subsequent struggle for dominance waged within or between individuals illustrates the American dilemma and the central focus in the O'Neill canon: man's attempt to retain his humanity, dignity, and personal identity in an impersonal, highly mechanized, disruptively selfish society. His depiction of the American dilemma makes O'Neill extremely relevant today. Countless young people are being trained in universities throughout the country to excel in business and computer technology. They are beset by the same problems O'Neill's heroes face when they attempt to retain their touch of the poet, their humanity, and dignity. The technology may be new, but man is again relegated, like Yank, to functioning as an extension of the machines he has developed. Having evolved into a more sensitive, thinking creature than Yank, modern man is even more desperate in his search to belong and to give his life meaning.

O'Neill should not be classified merely as American. He continuously stressed his identity as an Irish-American. His Irish heritage exerted the strongest single influence on him as man and playwright. Former President John F. Kennedy's statement of self-identification applies, in part, to O'Neill: "a Roman Catholic and third generation Irish American with the Puritan spirit and legacy." In 1946, the playwright told his son Eugene that "the one thing that explains more than anything about me is the fact that I'm Irish and strangely enough it is something writers who have attempted to explain me and my work have overlooked." How precisely did his Irishness affect him? One of the major premises in his work is the concept that family fate is rooted in the past, in one's collective racial and individual heritage. The difficulties encountered by James O'Neill, the author's father, as a young, uneducated immigrant-laborer, left the elder O'Neill hopelessly flawed for life. His subsequent miserliness supposedly was the cause of the morphine addiction of his wife Ella, who became totally absorbed in her secret, selfish world, from which her sensitive son Eugene was barred. He was constantly haunted by his mother, a woman whose flawed character destroyed the man but nourished the playwright.

The consequences of O'Neill's Irish heritage are threefold. First, it formed his personal character. Deeply introspective by nature, sensitive, and moody—qualities exacerbated by his mother's indifference and his own feelings of lovelessness and loneliness, the author became a true Black Irishman in mind and spirit. When God apparently failed to heed the young man's prayers to cure his mother, leading him, in despair, to abandon the ardent Catholicism of his youth, O'Neill suffered serious guilt feelings and began a lifelong search to replace his once-meaningful religious faith. After completing *Days Without End*, whose renegade Catholic hero returns to the faith of his youth, O'Neill stated: "All of my plays, even when most materialistic, are, for me, in their spiritual implications, a search and a cry in the wilderness." Finally, the rejection his Irish family experienced by snobbish, wealthy Yankee New Londoners led him to identify throughout his life with the outcasts and victims of discrimination. He depicts his closest lifelong friends, a group of pitiful misfits, whom his wife Carlotta sarcastically called his "blood brothers," in *The Iceman Cometh*, which he identified as perhaps "*the* best" play he had ever written. His affection for the work, he says, "is not wholly inspired by nostalgia for the dear dead days 'on the bottom of the sea.' " There are moments in the play, he remarks, "that suddenly strip the secret soul of a man stark naked, not in cruelty or moral superiority, but with an understanding compassion which sees him as a victim of the ironies of life and of himself. Those moments are for me the depth of tragedy" (letter of July 17, 1940, to Lawrence Langner). O'Neill seems, unwittingly, to have singled out one of the outstanding traits of his work: an "understanding compassion."

Between 1907, after his expulsion from Princeton, and 1912, prior to his confinement in a sanatorium for tuberculosis, O'Neill was a homeless vagabond and outcast, plunged in a personal shipwreck of alcoholic dissolution. He seemed ill-equipped to become a playwright. In the first years he learned his craft through a process of trial and error, laboriously forging the early primitive melodramas from his own personal experiences and familial relationships. Lacking a formal, advanced education, he became a voracious reader, absorbing the theories of Nietzsche, Jung, and Freud and studying the techniques of European dramatists: Strindberg, Ibsen, Synge, Hauptmann, Kaiser, and Toller. He developed a unique philosophy of life, a strange hodgepodge of the tenets of Irish Catholicism, elements of Irish and Eastern mysticism, the political concepts of Proudhon and other anarchists, and observations derived from reading and contact with family members and friends. O'Neill continuously expanded his dramatic horizons, going from the one-acters of 1913–1919 to multi-act plays in the 1920s, to trilogies in the late 1920s, to the Cycle in the mid-1930s. He also experimented with theatrical devices: masks, choruses, interior-exterior sets, and thought asides. Through his own herculean efforts he managed to transform the American theater, directing it away from the frivolous romanticism and crude melodrama of the late nineteenth and early twentieth centuries and into the current international mainstream of serious tragedy. Tennessee Williams observed that "O'Neill gave birth to the American theatre and died for it."

What, in turn, did the American theater do for him? In the 1920s and early 1930s O'Neill won national recognition and acclaim and three Pulitzer Prizes. While the plays were frequently criticized for weaknesses of plot, language, and style and occasionally banned in some cities for "obscenity," they were, at least, produced. O'Neill was theatrically alive. However, in 1934 he became a dramaturgic pariah, a playwright in search of a theater in this country after the unsuccessful production of *Days Without End*. He was disappointed that "no one grasped its Faustian undertheme." What particularly irked him was the unfavorable reviews the play received. In his letter of February 14, 1934, to Kenneth Macgowan, he states, "It holds audiences tensely and silently all thro' to six to ten curtain calls nightly at the end. . . . And yet the critical jackasses have the nerve to say the technique doesn't come off! If we could get people in the theatre, I really believe now this play could be a success—but the reviewers keep too many away, that's the trouble. It's alive for those who go."

O'Neill withheld the release of *Long Day's Journey into Night* in his lifetime and deliberately delayed the production of *The Iceman Cometh* until 1946. Except for the premiere of this drama and the unsuccessful road tour of *A Moon for the Misbegotten* in 1947, there was no major production of the plays in this country from 1934 until May 8, 1956, when *The Iceman Cometh* was again staged. In a record the author kept, labeled "Cycles," listing the significant events in his creative and personal life, he begins each entry for the years 1934 to 1945 with the words: "No Prod[uction]." Ironically, during this same period, O'Neill's works were produced and applauded in theaters throughout the world. In 1949 Carlotta O'Neill told Dale Fern that "most people here have forgotten Eugene O'Neill ever wrote for the American theatre! Europe still remembers & Japan!"

O'Neill died not in 1953 but a decade earlier. His wife states that when he "had to quit his job—*he died*—& life, since then, has been a hell for him" (letter of October 23, 1953, to Fern). In 1945, after the couple sold their home in California and moved into a hotel-apartment in San Francisco, the dramatist longed to return to Sea Island, Georgia, and told Langner: "What is imperative, so the doctors tell me, is that I must have complete rest in my own environment—that is sun, swimming—All the things that I have been deprived of for years." In 1948 O'Neill returned to his native terrain, New England— not to New London but to a seaport town resembling it, Marblehead. Like his characters in *The Iceman Cometh*, he still retained one final dream: to resume his work. On December 4, 1948, with his "hand petering out of control," as he remarks, he wrote to Dudley Nichols, in his last handwritten letter, "And now at last, with everything to the last book in place (or nearly so) we can sit back and rest a while, and I can hope to start writing plays again."

O'Neill's health deteriorated in the next years and so did his relationship with Carlotta. When, in February

1951, he fell outside their Marblehead home and broke his leg, she reportedly refused to help him. He was discovered later by someone else and taken to the hospital. For some strange reason, perhaps a deliberate choice of his own personal nemesis, O'Neill agreed to a reconciliation with Carlotta that spring even though they had quarreled bitterly. He followed the example of one of his most tragic characters, Lavinia Mannon, who immured herself with the ghosts of her parents and brother within the Mannon home, and spent the last two years of his life isolated in a Boston hotel. His condition became progressively worse. Carlotta described the "insidious disease" as a "degeneration of the nerve tissue" and said that it affects "the muscles and slowly kills all coordination between the brain & the muscles. Hence, he starts to get out of bed in the normal way & falls on his face! He always walks with a stick, even to the bathroom. . . . His tremor has become so bad again it is most difficult for him even to eat solids alone" (letter of October 15, 1953, to Fern). The illness was not epilepsy, she remarks, "but a 21st cousin to it."

While O'Neill never mentioned the theater during his last months and "the Nobel and Pulitzers," according to Carlotta, meant "nothing to him—now," he took comfort in the fact that he had retained his integrity during his long career as a playwright. Carlotta states that the month before he died, when she was preparing him for sleep, "he began to recite Austin Dobson's 'In After Days':

> In after days when grasses high
> O'er the stone where I shall lie,
> Through ill or well the world adjust
> My slender claim to honor'd dust,
> I shall not question nor reply.
>
> I shall not see the morning sky;
> I shall not hear the night-wind sigh;
> I shall be mute, as all men must
> In after days!

> But yet, now living, fain would I
> That some one then should testify,
> Saying—"He held his pen in trust
> To Art, not serving shame or lust."
> Will none?—Then let my memory die
> In after days!

Then he looked at me & repeated (so quietly), 'He held his pen in trust to Art, not serving shame or lust.' "

    The final line could serve as O'Neill's epitaph. His single lifelong passion was his work. All else was sacrificed to it. Other world dramatists may excel him in lofty lyric power or philosophical discourse. None, however, surpass him in the sheer magnitude of the men and women who people his plays. O'Neill understood the human psyche, its baseness and its greatness, as few other writers have. And though he was always "a little in love with death," it is life he celebrates in his plays, not some fanciful version of it but the tragic, comic, splendiferous reality of it. He tried to awaken the noblest aspirations of a growing nation to foster its pursuit of the high ideals of the early founding fathers. He cared about his country and his countrymen. He urged them not to live on the surface of life but to search both within the self to determine an inner behind-life force and without for the secret of life "beyond the horizon." In his work he tried to contribute to this discovery. "The theatre," he said, "should be a source of inspiration that lifts us to a plane beyond ourselves as we know them and drives us deep into the unknown within and behind ourselves. The theatre should reveal to us what we are." He adds: "Holding the mirror of a soul up to a nation; it is time we returned to this if only to prove that the theatre still has a soul unsullied by contact with appearances."

    O'Neill is America's primordial and premier playwright. To date, there has not been any dramatist to equal him. Tennessee Williams comes closest to him in characterization, depicting the broken, tragic misfits of life.

Introduction

Arthur Miller concerns himself, as did O'Neill, with the social problems that afflict us, but he could hardly be classified as the spokesman for the poor and the down-trodden. No one has usurped O'Neill's place in the American theater. He carved out the path in the wilderness; others followed. He himself summed up one facet of his contribution to it in a letter to Russel Crouse written shortly after he was awarded the Nobel Prize. He had received congratulations from dramatists all over the world "but none from home front playwrights with the exception of Edward Sheldon, Sam Behrman, & Geo. Middleton." O'Neill states: "Few, if any of them, have ever had the decency to admit that my work had ever meant a thing to American drama or to them, or that my pioneering had busted the old dogmas wide open and left them free to do anything they wanted in any way they wanted (not that many of them have had the guts to try anything out of the ordinary—but they could have)."

One purpose of this study is to document O'Neill's "pioneering" efforts on behalf of American drama. The book is divided chronologically into four periods, following the author's classification of his ideas for plays in his four notebooks. The introduction that precedes each section provides pertinent information about the author's life, activities, and attitudes to enable readers to comprehend the autobiographical nature of the plays within the segment. Each individual unit contains a synopsis of the plot of the play to allow the reader to visualize what happens on stage and a commentary on its origin, style, and merit. Following each of the major chronological divisions is a list of the ideas the dramatist conceived during that period and recorded in his notebook. The entire contents of these notebooks, containing these ideas and an annotated discussion of other notes, scenarios, and early drafts for plays, appear in *Eugene O'Neill at Work* (see the Bibliography for a complete listing of material Yale made available to me). I have used information from this book to explicate the plays and to show the manifold autobiographical interconnections linking all the dramas. Only when these notebooks and the early notes and manuscripts are studied in conjunction with the plays themselves is it possible to comprehend fully O'Neill, the man and playwright. What they reveal is that O'Neill's life and his work are fashioned out of the same fabric.

Eugene O'Neill was not pretentious or given to self-aggrandizement. He was a simple man, a deeply compassionate man who had reverence for all living things. He was a Black Irishman who fell in love with words. He used those words to articulate the sorrows of his life and those of mankind. Often he stumbled; occasionally he succeeded, and when he did, he added new luster to the American theater, which he, through his efforts, single-handedly transformed. The primary goal of this book is to shed new light on this frequently misunderstood artist and to make his work more accessible and comprehensible. Herman Melville chastised nineteenth-century Americans for their neglect of another New England son, Nathaniel Hawthorne, and said: "Let America prize and cherish her writers. Let her glorify them. For how great the shame, if other nations should be before her, in crowning her heroes of the pen!" In the past, Americans have at times been remiss in honoring and producing O'Neill's works. It may be that a new generation of theatergoers will render America's only dramatist to be awarded the Nobel Prize the homage he deserves. To this new generation of O'Neill devotees this book is dedicated.

The Plays of
Eugene O'Neill

Ella Quinlan O'Neill

James O'Neill

Eugene, Jamie, and James O'Neill, circa 1898, New London

Fledgling playwright, 1914, New London

Inscription: (cross my heart)—Jan. 1, 1914
New London, Conn. Water—39° snow
"The uniform I wore
Was nothin' much before
An' rather less than 'arf o' that behind"
(Removed from Gaylord Farm Sanatorium file)

Painting by William L'Engle called "Lord Christ O'Neill" shows some leading figures of the Provincetown Players, 1920
Top, Terry Carlin
Second Row: Susan Glaspell, William L'Engle, Robert Edmond Jones
Third Row: Agnes Boulton O'Neill, Eugene O'Neill, William Zorach, Ida Rauh, Wilbur Daniel Steele
Fourth Row: Thelma Sirien, Madeleine Iselin
Fifth Row: Bobby Harriman's monkey, R. Benjamin

Credit:
Photograph by George Yater

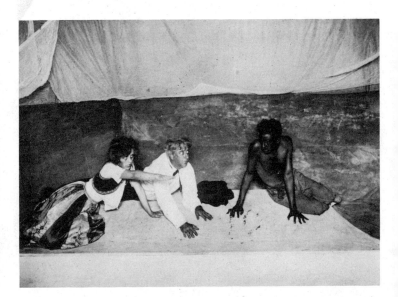

Thirst, The Wharf Theatre, Provincetown, Mass., August 1916. The Dancer, Louise Bryant; The Gentleman, George Cram Cook; The Mulatto Sailor, Eugene O'Neill

Bound East for Cardiff, The Wharf Theatre, Provincetown, Mass.,
July 1916. Seaman, John Reed, Yank (in lower bunk), George Cram
Cook; Driscoll, Frederick Burt

The Long Voyage Home, The Playwrights' Theatre, New York, 1917.
Olson, Ira Remsen; Freda, Ida Rauh; Fat Joe, George Cram Cook

1. The Sea-Mother's Son: Early Plays And Beginnings

Throughout his life Eugene O'Neill felt homeless, as though fate did not know exactly where to place him. When he speaks through his most accurate self-portrait, Edmund Tyrone in *Long Day's Journey into Night*, he reveals his affinity for the sea. Reminiscing about a night on the trip to Buenos Aires on a Squarehead square-rigger, Edmund says:

> I became drunk with the beauty and singing rhythm of it, and for a moment I lost myself—actually lost my life. I was set free! I dissolved in the sea, became white sails and flying spray, became beauty and rhythm, became moonlight and the ship and the high dim-starred sky! I belonged.

To O'Neill, as both creator and created, the sea assumes mythic proportions. It was there he found a purpose for his own aimless life and gained a perception of the mysterious behind-life force he incorporates in his plays. He surrendered to the sea, and it in turn marked his mind indelibly. In 1927 he started "The Sea-Mother's Son," which he identified as a "series of plays based on autobiographical material." The 1928 notes he made indicated that the dramas would unfold in a series of flashbacks. The self-portrait, a forty-year-old man, "lies in the hospital at the point of death." He overhears the doctor's words: he alone must make the choice between life and death. The man examines his old life, the important episodes and influences that molded him. In the end he decides to say yes to life, "to conquer his death wish, give up the comfort of the return to Mother Death."

O'Neill gave up this specific plan to dramatize his life and seems to have merged it, consciously or not, with two autobiographical plays of the early 1930s: *Ah, Wilderness!* and *Days Without End*. It is significant to note that he was apparently unaware that in actuality he had long ago started "The Sea-Mother's Son," that his preceding plays were invariably woven from the fabric of his life.

O'Neill had an auspicious beginning as the son of James and Ella O'Neill. He was born at the Barrett House, a family hotel at the corner of Forty-Third Street and Broadway. His father was the son of an Irish immigrant who had deposited his wife and eight children on American soil and returned alone to Ireland. In 1867, after years of deprivation and sacrifice, James made his acting debut at the National Theatre in Cincinnati. He worked hard to eliminate his Irish brogue and mannerisms and became a respected Shakespearean actor. In 1874, when he was only twenty-eight, James O'Neill was considered to be the equal of Edwin Booth, then the finest actor in the country. The two alternated the leading roles in *Othello*. In 1883, in a move he would later regret, James abandoned serious drama for more lucrative melodrama, wasting his talent for the next fifteen years in a romantic swashbuckler, *The Count of Monte Cristo*, a dramatization of Dumas's novel.

The future playwright's maternal grandparents, the Quinlans, also fled to America to escape the consequences of the famine years in Ireland. Thomas Quinlan eventually settled in Cleveland. Prospering, he lavished his money and attention on his only child, Mary Ellen, who shortened her name to Ella, and sent her to a private boarding school, St. Mary's Academy in South Bend, Indiana. The young woman reciprocated by adoring her father and ignoring her jealous mother. O'Neill gives his

mother this particular background in the early notes for
Mourning Becomes Electra and *Long Day's Journey into
Night*. Christine Mannon and Mary Tyrone, who are
clearly portraits of Ella O'Neill, have inordinate attach-
ments for their fathers, both of whom at their deaths leave
their daughters independently wealthy.

Ella Quinlan's tragedy commenced with her decision
to marry James O'Neill. As a young woman, she was a
hopeless romantic. She played the piano moderately well
but dreamed of becoming a famous pianist; she observed
the pious nuns at school and imagined herself as one of
them. Her father died, and she became infatuated with
his handsome friend, the actor James O'Neill. When they
married on June 14, 1877, she was seventeen and he was
thirty-one.

A line in *Long Day's Journey into Night* that O'Neill
later deleted suggests why the marriage was doomed. The
mother, conversing with the maid, Cathleen, says of her
husband: "14 years older—was great mistake—more like
father—." In each of the plays in which the hero's parents
are portraits of James and Ella, the marriage is described
as a mistake. There is an initial physical attraction that
may continue even after the marriage has deteriorated
badly, but it is usually one-sided: the wife is able to
manipulate her sexually enslaved husband. The effects of
exposure to the ensuing love-hate relationship on any
offspring can be devastating. Such children are fated to be
maimed for life; so too were the sons of Ella and James.

In the first years of her marriage Ella's romantic
nature enabled her to survive the endless parade of dingy
hotel rooms in the towns she toured with her husband,
even after the birth of her first son, Jamie, in September
1878. After her second son, Edmund, was born, she left
her sons in the care of her mother. In 1885, while she was
away, Edmund became ill and died. Ella never forgave
herself, or her husband, or Jamie, whom she accused of
deliberately infecting Edmund. Ella feared having an-

other child after Edmund's death. Being devout Catholics, the couple probably practiced sexual abstinence. James persuaded his wife to replace their lost child, and in 1888 Ella had her third son, Eugene.

It was a difficult birth, as the baby weighed over ten pounds. James O'Neill was later accused of miserliness and negligence by his sons for hiring a cheap doctor who prescribed the morphine for Ella that began her twenty-five-year addiction. The question asked in real life, as in *Long Day's Journey into Night*, is: how did the mother become addicted so easily and for so long? By the time Eugene was born she had grown weary of the continuous travel, the lonely hotel rooms, the drunken condition of her husband when he finally returned each night from the theater. She no longer had Jamie to care for; he had been put, at the age of seven, in a boarding school. There was a nurse to help with Eugene until he too was sent away. In the child's early years the mother was there, but often she was like a disembodied spirit, her mind flickering like the light of a candle. She was one of life's wounded. It is impossible to discern which of her qualities most affected her husband and sons: her detachment, which consequentially increased her desirability; her mental anguish, which inspired pity and sacrifice; or her ability to instill guilt, which aroused self-accusation and pain. Without doubt, Ella O'Neill exerted the greatest single influence on her sons. She may have been addicted to morphine, but they were addicted to her.

Ella was a failure as a housekeeper, but, as she and her sons complained in later years, James O'Neill neglected to provide her with the kind of home that would bring the family the respectability and prestige she craved. In the early 1880s James bought a summer home in New London, where he hoped to rest for a few months between theatrical seasons. This house, which James kept until 1920, the year of his death, became the only permanent home the family ever had. He did not realize in the beginning that he and his family would never be accepted by the snobbish, wealthy New London Yankees, who prided themselves on their Puritan lineage. A man like James O'Neill would be anathema to them: he was an actor, and worse, he was Irish. What annoyed the Yankees most was the fact that he refused to settle in east New London with other Irishmen; he had bought a home deep in Yankee territory on Pequot Avenue. Of Ella, it can be asked: Did her addiction make it impossible for her to make and keep friends or did the rejection by New Londoners merely plunge her deeper into her world of morphine?

The sons returned each summer, after their schools closed, to the house on Pequot Avenue. To Eugene, this period with his mother made up for the previous months of unhappiness and loneliness. When he walked a few steps from the house and crossed the road, he was on the shoreline of Long Island Sound. Looking out on the far horizon, he saw the start of the sea. The fair-skinned Ella sat in the gazebo, as Deborah Harford would in *More Stately Mansions*, while her son played on the shore or gazed seaward.

Eugene went to Catholic schools for seven years, exposed first to the regime of strict but well-meaning nuns at St. Aloysius Academy for Boys and later to the sterner Christian Brothers at De La Salle. The young boy was pious, sensitive, and highly impressionable. He was thoroughly indoctrinated in the tenets of Catholicism and in the details of its practice as specified in the catechism, which he learned by rote. Unfortunately, what these harsh religious educators recommended was discipline, a relentless system of crime and punishment; what the young Eugene needed was love and understanding, someone to assuage his loneliness.

As Eugene grew older, as his brother Jamie's influence over him became stronger, he grew more and more

cynical about his faith, his father, and life in general. He
insisted on transferring to a secular private school, Betts
Academy, in 1902. There is perhaps some interconnec-
tion between the events of this period. After Ella was
thwarted in an attempt to commit suicide by jumping off
the pier near the house, an act of despondency that
occurred when she had depleted her supply of morphine,
Eugene could no longer be sheltered and was told the
truth about Ella's condition. He prayed ardently for his
mother's deliverance; when it was not forthcoming, he
informed his father of his intention never to go to church
again. This verbal renunciation of Catholicism was a futile
gesture. The words he assigns a self-portrait, the renegade Catholic hero of *Days Without End*, apply to himself: "Once a Catholic, always a Catholic."

   The Catholic faith is an integral part of the Irish, like
some primitive ancient code that has been indelibly im-
printed in the racial consciousness. The reverse side of
the coin is the Irishman's hatred of the British. The second possibly engendered the first. In their seven centuries of devastation, the English robbed the Irish of their
homes and land, their livelihoods and civil rights—
everything but their faith. To this the Irish clung during
the dread days of the famine and in the better life they
sought in the new world. For the Irish who settled in New
England, it seemed as though they had scarcely left Ireland in one respect: they found themselves again ostracized and scorned by the Yankees, descendants of the
Puritan English. Normally, when attacked from without,
the Irish Catholics, strengthened by their faith, tended to
form close family ties for solace and refuge. In the case of
the O'Neills, however—first the sons and then the
parents—loss of faith in the efficacy of external worship
preceded loss of faith in each other. Alienation from God
led to alienation within the family. Moral dissolution
followed in the wake of spiritual and personal isolation;
drink, drug addiction, and, in the case of the sons, visits to

whorehouses, become methods of escaping the reality of life.

The rejection of Catholicism was perhaps a rebellion against James the father rather than God the Father on Eugene's part. The break with Catholicism at an early age left O'Neill with a case of arrested development. Theologically, he was frozen in time with an adolescent concept of the dogmas of his religion, which were simplistically broken down in the catechism he studied. The emphasis on mortal sin, penance, and redemption manifests itself in O'Neill's explanation of his work: "In all my plays sin is punished and redemption takes place." He luxuriated in the mysticism of the Irish, in the symbols of Catholicism. He used the concept of the cross in *Welded* and *Days Without End* and the crucifixion in "The Last Conquest." His preoccupation with confession and forgiveness forms a recurring motif in a number of plays. In *A Moon for the Misbegotten*, Josie, a virgin, assumes the pose of the Madonna Mary in the *Pietá*, holding the corpselike Jamie throughout the night. Perhaps the emphasis on the Virgin Mary, Christ's mother, the quintessential saving figure in Catholicism, explains why Irishmen like Eugene and Jamie O'Neill venerate their mothers. Here is where the second great influence on O'Neill, Irish Catholicism, merges with the first.

All the components for what O'Neill became as man and playwright are found in his early life and family. Each real person and event has its corresponding equivalent in the fictive world. Jamie boasts in *Long Day's Journey into Night* that he contributed to his brother's education, and so he had. Jamie was, as his brother would label him in his last play, the most misbegotten of the O'Neills. While Eugene, highstrung and sensitive, resembled his mother in appearance and nature, Jamie was nerveless and had the build and features of an Irish peasant like his father. He resented the fact that Eugene was Ella's favorite.

Jamie's single obsession in life was his mother, a

fixation that ultimately destroyed him. He became a hopeless alcoholic, a drifter who could not hold a steady job, a parasite living on a small allowance meted out to him by his father or the pittance paid for some minor service performed when he accompanied the elder O'Neill on a theatrical tour. As his brother did later, Jamie fell victim to both the Oedipal and the Madonna–whore complex. He could associate love only with the mother and sex solely with the prostitute. The mother being forbidden, Jamie frequented whorehouses, particularly in the Bradley Street area, which was called the Barbary Coast of New London. Not content with his own debauchery, Jamie saw to it that his brother was taken, at the age of fifteen, to a bordello. The sordid experience becomes part of the biography of Charles Marsden in *Strange Interlude*.

The young O'Neill spent less than a year in college. He entered Princeton in the fall of 1906 but did not apply himself to his studies. Carousing one night the following spring with a group of his fellow students, he reportedly threw an Anheuser-Busch beer bottle into the window of the university president, Woodrow Wilson. O'Neill was merely suspended, but he had no desire to continue his studies and decided to leave Princeton. He seems to have been more anxious at that time to explore the political ramifications of anarchism and to learn firsthand about life and living it than to theorize about it.

It seemed at times that the youth was destined to follow in Jamie's dissolute footsteps. The two brothers frequently went out drinking together during the eighteen-month period Eugene worked as a secretary for a New York firm. While there, the young man met Kathleen Jenkins, a refined, sheltered girl, who fell deeply in love with him and threw caution to the winds by having an affair with him. O'Neill had, according to that day's standards, compromised Kathleen; worse, he had gotten her pregnant. The situation would be dramatized later in

Abortion, *Before Breakfast*, and *A Touch of the Poet*.

Disregarding the advice of his father, the youth did the honorable thing and married Kathleen in October 1909. He abandoned her a few days later, however, reluctant to assume the burdens of married life. James hustled his son off with friends who were sailing to Honduras to prospect for gold. When he wrote to his parents from Honduras on November 9, he was enthusiastic about the country and the prospect of making good. By Christmas, however, "sick from rotten food" and desperately lonely, he told his parents: "God got his inspiration for Hell after creating Honduras, a Siberia of the tropics." He re-created the gold-prospecting camp as the setting of his first short sketch, *A Wife for a Life*. O'Neill was scheduled to remain in Honduras until June, but at that time he was sailing on the *Charles Racine* for Buenos Aires, having spent three months as assistant manager touring with his father's production of *The White Sister*. His motive for this voyage, like the trip to Honduras, was to escape responsibility: Kathleen had given birth in May to a son, Eugene Jr.

In the account he provided Barrett Clark of the stay in Argentina, O'Neill said that he worked "in the draughting department of the Westinghouse Electrical Company, in the wool house of a packing plant [Swift's] at La Plata, in the office of the Singer Sewing Machine Company in Buenos Aires."* He stated he then shipped out, although no proof exists, on a ship headed for Durban, South Africa. In Buenos Aires, he knew "a lengthy period of complete destitution," spent "on the beach."* In *Bound East for Cardiff*, some of his experiences, such as attending the moving pictures at Barracas and drinking at the Sailor's Opera, become part of Yank's recollections on his deathbed.

O'Neill sailed in April 1911 for New York, where he

---

*Barrett H. Clark, *Eugene O'Neill* (New York: Robert M. McBride and Co., 1926), p. 5.

lived for a period at Jimmy the Priest's, a waterfront
hotel-saloon frequented by sailors. In July he shipped out
on the American Line's *New York*, bound for Southampton. The author makes use of the New York–Southampton voyage in *The Hairy Ape*; the Great General Strike,
which occurred while he was in England, becomes the
focal point of "The Personal Equation." By the time of his
return trip in August on the *Philadelphia*, he had become
a good friend of one of the stokers, Mike Driscoll, a
brawny Irishman, whom he re-creates in the four *Glencairn* plays, in "The Personal Equation" as O'Rourke, in
Chris Christopherson as Mickey Devlin, and in *The
Hairy Ape* as Yank. The other sailors he knew, Smitty,
Cocky, and Olson, reappear in the *Glencairn* series.

O'Neill was happy at sea, even though the work was
tedious and the discipline severe. Among the rough, uneducated seamen, he learned lessons about the value of
friendship, sacrifice, and integrity. But he also became
dissolute in the days and nights on shore, drinking beyond the level of sociability. A few weeks after the *Philadelphia* docked, he went back to Jimmy the Priest's and
retreated completely from the real world. He used his
small allowance from his father to drink himself to oblivion and to pay for his insect-infested room upstairs. In
The Iceman Cometh he calls this saloon "Harry Hope's"
and portrays his friends Jimmy Byth and Major Adams as
Jimmy Tomorrow and Captain Lewis. Jimmy the Priest's
also becomes Johnny the Priest's in *Chris Christopherson*
and *Anna Christie*, and his real-life sailor-friend, Chris
Christopherson, emerges as a central character in both.

Unlike authors who live in a particular place to absorb its atmosphere for use later, O'Neill was truly one of
the lonely, homeless, hope-forsaken outcasts who appear
in *Iceman*'s "Bottom of the Sea Rathskeller," the "End of
the Line Cafe." According to George Jean Nathan, "there
were times when he went on benders that lasted a whole
month and times when he slept next to the bung-hole of a

whiskey barrel at Jimmy the Priest's and when Jimmy, the Proprietor, coming to work the next morning, found the barrel one-eighth gone."*

In December, in order to provide his first wife, Kathleen, with evidence of infidelity needed for a divorce, O'Neill went to a seedy hotel room with a prostitute, where, according to plan, he was "discovered" *in flagrante delicto*. The sordid experience depressed him; guilt for having abandoned wife and child weighed him down. In January 1912, in his room at Jimmy the Priest's, he took the supply of Veronal he had accumulated in an attempt to commit suicide. He was rushed to Bellevue Hospital by Byth and Adams. The two managed to get fifty dollars from James O'Neill for emergency treatment and went on a drinking binge. On hearing the story, their recovered friend demanded his cut of the money. The suicide attempt is depicted in the one-acter "Exorcism," which O'Neill later destroyed.

James also sent his son funds to join him in New Orleans, where he was appearing in a vaudeville tour of *The Count of Monte Cristo*. Eugene joined the company, playing a minor role, and returned with his family to New London in the spring. There, with the help of his father, he obtained a job as a reporter for the *Telegraph*, a local newspaper. He also had a poetry column, which featured his own mediocre rhymes. That summer he courted Maibelle Scott, a local girl whose family lived about a block from the O'Neill home. He portrays the romance in the 1932 autobiographical *Ah, Wilderness!* and telescopes other, more important events of 1912 for that one fatal day in August in *Long Day's Journey into Night*: Ella O'Neill's return to drugs after recently being pronounced cured and her younger son's discovery that he has tuberculosis.

On Christmas Eve O'Neill entered Gaylord Farm Sanatorium for treatment of tuberculosis. Under strict

The Intimate Notebooks of George Jean Nathan (New York: Knopf, 1932), p. 31.

orders to rest, he had the opportunity, for the first time in
his life, to devote himself entirely to reading and to the
authors his father castigates in *Long Day's Journey*:
Nietzsche, Zola, Ibsen, and, his favorite, Strindberg. The
superstitious see some significance in the events of 1912
and believe that the Swedish playwright's mantle of greatness passed at his death that year to the young American,
who asserted that reading the works of Strindberg inspired him to write. O'Neill relates the story of his stay
and his relationship with a fellow patient, Kitty MacKay,
whose love for him was not reciprocated, in the 1918 *The
Straw*. Of this period in his life he states:

> It was at Gaylord that my mind got the chance to establish
> itself, to digest and evaluate the impressions of many past
> years in which one experience had crowded on another
> with never a second's reflection. At Gaylord I really
> thought about my life for the first time, about past and
> future.*

Pronounced cured in June, O'Neill returned to New
London to spend the summer with his family. In the
recuperation period that summer, he completed *A Wife
for a Life*, a vaudeville sketch, and two one-acters, *The
Web* and *Thirst*. When Ella and James departed for the
fall theatrical season, their son moved across the street to
room with the Rippins. In the past, whenever Ella was
without a cook, the O'Neills took their meals at the Rippins' boarding house. Between the fall of 1913 and the
spring of 1914, O'Neill wrote four new one-acters, *Recklessness*, *Warnings*, *Fog*, and *Bound East for Cardiff*, and
one four-act play, *Bread and Butter*. The following summer he finished two more one-acters, *Abortion* and *The
Movie Man*, and a three-act play, *Servitude*.

In July the dramatist sent a letter to Professor
George Pierce Baker, asking permission to enter his English 47 class at Harvard. He stated as his goal "to be an

*Clark, p. 12.

artist or nothing." Touring with his father, he had learned the rudiments of stagecraft. Now he would discover how to structure a play. Throughout his career, the dramatist adhered to the principles Baker taught: recording the original idea, writing a scenario, and, to add "meat" to this skeleton, setting down dialogue for a first draft. The young author was not able to create anything of worth during that academic year. In the fall he wrote "Dear Doctor," a one-act adaptation of a short story. This and two second-semester plays, "The Knock on the Door" and "Belshazzar," he destroyed. *The Sniper* and "The Personal Equation" survived.

Although Baker urged his promising student to return for the second part of the course, which focused on full-length works, O'Neill followed a destructive, rather than a creative, path the next year. He moved to New York in the fall of 1915, not to Jimmy the Priest's again but to the equally dismal Golden Swan in Greenwich Village. Called the Hell Hole by irreverent patrons, the establishment offered furnished rooms upstairs. Nathan described O'Neill's attitude to friendship:

> Once he has made a friend for himself, that man remains a friend, in his eyes, until Hell freezes. In all the world I suppose that there are not more than five men at the very most whom O'Neill really regards as friends, and at least three of these are relics of his early more or less disreputable days in Greenwich Village and the adjacent ginmills.*

The three close friends of this period were O'Neill's roommate, Joe Smith, a black gambler, and Terry Carlin and Hippolyte Havel, former anarchist radicals; they are depicted in *The Iceman Cometh* as Joe Mott, Larry Slade, and Hugo Kalmar. The Hell Hole became, with Jimmy the Priest's and the Garden Hotel, part of the composite that formed the play's setting.

The regular patrons at the Hell Hole included

*Nathan, p. 32.

thieves, prostitutes, and a famous gang of criminals called the Hudson Dusters. The Dusters, who were Irish, took an interest in the young O'Neill, feeding and protecting him. He aligned himself with both the underworld habitués of the Hell Hole and with its political radicals, the IWW's and the anarchist group. If some of O'Neill's ideas for plays in his 1918–1920 notebook had materialized, these people would have been immortalized. Among the titles for the projected "Gunman Series" are "The Pig of the Hell Hole" and "The Dirty Half-Dozen," the latter perhaps another name for the Dusters.

In June O'Neill accompained Terry Carlin to Provincetown, Massachusetts, then a remote fishing village, described by O'Neill as "hard to get to and get out of," and frequented in summer by a small group of writers. A few of these, led by Susan Glaspell and her husband, George Cram Cook, had formed an amateur theatrical company the previous summer to produce the plays members had written. Hoping to repeat their success, they sought new plays to open the 1916 season. Carlin told Glaspell that O'Neill had a trunk full of plays, and the dramatist was asked to read one to the group. Glaspell recalls that after the work chosen, *Bound East for Cardiff*, was presented to the group, "we knew what we were for." The group, later called the Provincetown Players, staged this first sea play on July 28 in its makeshift theater, located appropriately on the wharf. This first O'Neill production, which was proclaimed a tremendous success, was followed in August by *Thirst*, with the bronze-tanned author playing the West Indian sailor.

Across the street from O'Neill's residence lived the art colony's most interesting couple: John Reed, a correspondent, whose later visit to Russia during the height of the revolution resulted in *Ten Days That Shook the World*; and Louise Bryant, an independent, plucky writer, who was as intelligent as she was beautiful. For the first time in his life O'Neill fell hopelessly and recklessly in love. As a friend of Reed, he was prevented by his sense of honor from telling Louise he loved her. She took the initiative, however, and the two began a secret affair. It continued into the fall when the trio returned to Greenwich Village with the Players, who opened their New York theater on Macdougal Street. It continued after Louise's marriage to Reed and throughout the month Reed was hospitalized at Johns Hopkins in Baltimore. O'Neill used Louise as the model for Lucy Ashleigh in his uncharacteristic comedy, *Now I Ask You*, which he started shortly after they met. In it, he mocks the shallow talents and sensibilities of the bohemian artists he had met in Provincetown and in Greenwich Village. He completed a short story, "Tomorrow," focusing on the tragic life of his friend Jimmy Byth, which was published in *Seven Arts Magazine*, and *Before Breakfast*, another scathing analysis of marriage, his first play to be staged in New York. This and all of his plays of the next four years, except *In the Zone*, were premiered at The Playwrights' Theatre by the Provincetown Players.

In Provincetown O'Neill found a spot close to the sea congenial to him. He returned there in January 1917 and in the next months wrote *In the Zone, The Long Voyage Home*, and *The Moon of the Caribbees*, using his sea experiences and friends; *Ile*; another short story, "The Hairy Ape"; and a novelette, "S.O.S." In the fall he returned to New York for the production of three sea plays and met Agnes Boulton, an attractive woman who supported herself by writing short stories for pulp magazines. Friends remarked on Agnes's resemblance to the lost love, Louise Bryant. O'Neill may not have noticed the physical similarity, but he was impressed by the fact that because both he and Agnes were writers, they had something in common. More important, he was extremely lonely and seemed willing to compromise with life and settle down. When he returned to Provincetown in January, Agnes accompanied him. They were married on April 12, 1918.

The year in Provincetown was even more productive

than his first year at the Rippins' home. Perhaps his
creativity in both cases was the result of his contentment.
In his letter of February 4, 1919, to Jessica Rippin, he
compares the two places:

> Hearing the waves all the time, I was often reminded of the
> winter at your mother's when I first started my pen-push-
> ing in earnest. At any rate, I've never worked harder or
> with pleasanter surroundings than I did those *cold* months
> in the Packard. Your family gave me the most real touch of a
> home life I had had up to then—quite a happy, new
> experience for an actor's son! I've never forgotten to be
> grateful to all of you for it.

By the sea, leading a well-regulated life—work, exercise,
reading—O'Neill prospered and completed four one-acters, *Shell Shock*, *The Rope*, *The Dreamy Kid*, and *Where
the Cross Is Made*; his first full-length play to be staged,
Beyond the Horizon; and an early version of *The Straw*.

In November O'Neill attended rehearsals in New
York for *Where the Cross Is Made* and then went with
Agnes to spend the winter in her home in West Point
Pleasant, New Jersey. Although the house was only a
short distance from the sea, which in the past had always
inspired him, the author was restless and his output was
slim: the outlines for three one-acters, which he destroyed, the revised *The Straw*, and *Chris Christopherson*, which failed in tryouts in Atlantic City and Philadelphia.

James O'Neill gave his son and his new wife a home
on the outskirts of Provincetown as a wedding gift. Isolated and surrounded by miles of sand dunes, Peaked Hill
Bars had been a life-saving station that had been remod-
eled by its previous owner, Mabel Dodge, a former mistress of John Reed. The summer of 1920 was spent making
the seaside home livable, but O'Neill began the one-acter
"Exorcism" before he and Agnes moved on September 10
to a rented house in Provincetown where he finished the
play. On October 30 O'Neill's second son, Shane, was

born. This child, unlike his half-brother, would, in his formative years, know his father. Ultimately, however, both sons would share the same tragic fate.*

After the failure of "Exorcism" in the spring of 1920, the dramatist abandoned one-acters for longer forms; he would not return to them until he wrote *Hughie* twenty years later. The year 1920 marked the end of an era for O'Neill. In an interview he remarked:

> I am no longer interested in the one-act play. It is an unsatisfactory form—cannot go far enough. The one-act play, however, is a fine vehicle for something poetical, for something spiritual in feeling that cannot be carried through a long play.†

In his first six and one-half years of writing, the dramatist achieved two different kinds of resurrection. The first was his own personal metamorphosis. He could have gone in either of two directions in June 1913 upon his release from Gaylord: back to the self-destructive life of drinking and dissolution he had known at Jimmy the Priest's (and would experience again briefly in 1915–1916 at the Hell Hole) or on to a new path of meaningful creativity. Fortunately for the sake of the American theater, he chose the latter course. To O'Neill more than to any other person goes the credit of salvaging and transforming, irrevocably, the American theater. He not only revolted against the old techniques, forms, and characterizations but also gave birth to the new, providing both the philosophical manifesto and the practical application of it in his plays. He did not come to this all at once; the transition, professional as well as personal, was gradual.

---

*Both of O'Neill's sons committed suicide: Eugene on September 25, 1950, and Shane on June 22, 1977. The playwright's daughter Oona married Charlie Chaplin in 1943 and bore him eight children.

†*New York Herald-Tribune*, November 16, 1924.

In 1913 when be began to write, O'Neill had a basic understanding of the stage at that time, the poorly crafted melodramatic milieu of his father. He saw both its limits and its potential. Working with Baker taught him discipline; he learned how to structure his material. O'Neill's greatest advantage as a fledgling dramatist was having the Provincetown Players on hand to stage the early plays as he envisioned them. Edna Kenton, the Players' representative, remarks:

> But there is no doubt at all that, had he not had our Playwrights' Theater and our experimental stage to use always precisely as he wished to use them, he would have reached Broadway by quite another road and with quite other plays. . . . No other American playwright has ever had such prolonged preliminary freedom.*

Over half of O'Neill's dramas, nineteen short and seven long plays,† were written before 1920, and twelve of them had either ocean settings or sea-related elements. O'Neill lived by the sea, in New London or Provincetown, while working on all of the early plays except the two extant dramas done for Baker's class. For good reason, he called himself "The Sea-Mother's Son." The sea mesmerized and inspired him. It represented what he labeled the "behind-life force," the power that controls the fate of man, benevolent when its codes are followed, malevolent when betrayed. In *The Long Voyage Home* and *Bound East for Cardiff*, Olson and Yank contemplate leaving the sea for the land, the ultimate betrayal, and must be punished. Olson is shanghaied, and Yank has a fatal accident. As he lies dying, he recalls earlier sea voyages and accepts the inevitable: burial at sea rather than on land. Only when man enters into the ceremonies

---

*Clark, p. 20.

†*Chris Chistopherson*, which was begun in Provincetown in 1918 and revised and renamed *Anna Christie* two years later, will be discussed with the plays of the 1920s.

of the sea can he find peace and forgiveness. Death for Yank becomes the loving embrace of the Sea-Mother.

O'Neill "maternalizes" the sea, making it mysterious, dark, and demanding and merging it mystically with his own mother. The subtitle he gives to "The Sea-Mother's Son," the projected autobiographical series of the late 1920s, "The Story of the Birth of a Soul," can be applied to the early body of his work. The first plays trace the evolution of an artist and mark the stages of the author's personal development. In discovering his ability to create dramatically, O'Neill was himself created anew. His gift became his tragic nemesis; when he was physically no longer able to write, his creative soul died.

The purpose of presenting O'Neill's personal data at the beginning of each of the four sections of this book is to prepare the reader to recognize the autobiographical characters, motifs, and themes that are woven throughout the canon. The dramas in the first section (1913–1919) contain portraits of friends, family, and self: the husband and wife in conflict, modeled on James and Ella O'Neill (*Ile, Recklessness, Warnings*); the self-centered wife who destroys her artist-husband in a marriage that is, like the author's, a mistake (*Bread and Butter, Before Breakfast*); and three other self-portraits: the tubercular writer (*The Straw*), the irresponsible youth who impregnates and destroys a girl (*Abortion*), and the suicidal failure ("Exorcism").

The most revealing pre-1920 work is *Beyond the Horizon*. In depicting the four Mayos, the author unconsciously draws his first tentative sketch of the O'Neill family unit. The work contains patterns that recur in later dramas: the father-son conflict; the struggle between the poet-idealist and the businessman-materialist; the closeness of two brothers and the destruction, ultimately, of the younger by the older. *Beyond the Horizon* divides the early and middle periods. Coming at the end of the first, it represents the culmination of the author's efforts to develop his craft, expanding it from vaudeville sketch to one-acter to successful full-length drama. Ushering in the second, it brought a Pulitzer Prize and national fame, which until that time had eluded him. As the new decade began, O'Neill was America's leading dramatist; in the 1920s "The Sea-Mother's Son" would belong to the world.

1.   A Wife for a Life

Eugene O'Neill launched his career as playwright with the short vaudeville sketch *A Wife for a Life*,* written shortly after his release on June 3, 1913, from Gaylord Farm Sanatorium. During his five months of confinement and treatment for an illness doctors diagnosed as tuberculosis,† he read a number of plays, particularly those of Strindberg, and decided to write for the theater. This early sketch, however, contains no clues, no subtleties of plot or arresting characterizations, to indicate that its author would one day equal or surpass the dramatists who inspired him. Two men meet, talk, and part. Nothing happens, yet everying is irrevocably changed. As he does throughout the canon, O'Neill shows in this brief sketch the ineffable role fate plays in the lives of men.

The two central characters in *A Wife for a Life* are the Older Man, who is about fifty, and his partner, Jack (John Sloan), the Younger Man, who is in his early thirties. The sketch is set in a gold-mining camp in the Arizona desert and opens with the arrival of Old Pete, an unsuccessful

---

*O'Neill made a notation on the title page of *The Web*, identifying it as his first play. He then adds an afterthought: "To be scrupulously exact, for the record, 'The Web' is *not* the first thing I wrote *for the stage*. I had some time before dashed off in one night a ten minute vaudeville skit, afterwards destroyed. But this was not a play. In fact, my friends in vaudeville crudely asserted it was not a vaudeville skit, either! It was nothing. And 'The Web' *is* the first *play* I ever wrote." The author seems to have forgotten that *A Wife for a Life* was copyrighted on August 15, 1913. When the copyright expired, the skit was published in the unauthorized *Lost Plays of Eugene O'Neill* (New York: New Fathoms Press, 1950).

†In a letter to Lee Simonson in early 1938, O'Neill implies that the diagnosis was incorrect: "The Docs now tell me that X-rays show no evidence whatever of my ever having T.B.!"

prospector, who brings a telegram for Jack. Thinking that it pertains to business, the Older Man opens the telegram and reads its cryptic message: "I am waiting. Come." Only later does it become apparent to the Older Man that his own wife, Yvette, sent Jack the message.

Gradually, through dialogue and asides, the past is reconstructed. Six years earlier Jack had been prospecting in the mountains of Peru and had gone to a small mining camp near the frontier of Ecuador to reoutfit. There he fell in love with the young wife of an absent, alcoholic mining engineer, who apparently "realized she could never love him and was trying to drown the memory of the mistake he had made." Yvette loves Jack but refuses to leave with him, saying she must keep her marital vows. The husband returns and hears rumors about his wife's infidelity. Doubting her innocence and seeking vengeance, he sets out in pursuit of the lover. A year later the paths of the two men cross in the Transvaal, where Jack risks his own life to save the life of the husband, the Older Man. Neither realizes the true identity of the other, and the two become friends and partners. When the play opens, they have been working the claim in Arizona for four months.

After his return to the camp, Jack, who has been panning dirt from the upper end of the claim, announces he has discovered large quantities of gold. In a toast, in which "the two Prodigals welcome the fatted calf," he says: "Here's to the Yvette mine!" The Older Man realizes his abandoned wife is the woman of Jack's dreams. He fingers his gun: "Nothing seems alive about him but his eyes, staring horribly." The Younger Man attempts to convince his partner, who is cynical about the virtue of women, that the woman he loves has never been unfaithful to her husband. Jack produces the letter she sent the morning he left Ecuador. The Older Man peruses it: "I must keep my oath. He needs me and I must stay. To be true to myself I must be true to him." In the six-year period that followed, she has sent Jack only one other letter, which reached him the previous year in South Africa. In it, she stated she would wait another year for her husband. If he failed to return, she would be legally free and would send for Jack.

Although he realizes that the lover, as well as Yvette, is innocent, the Older Man, when alone, attempts to burn the telegram. Some inner emotion that is stronger than his desire for vengeance overwhelms him: "My God I cannot!" Jack is ecstatic when he reads the telegram and makes plans to leave immediately to meet Yvette in New York. The Older Man never reveals his terrible secret. Alone, he says: "What tricks fate plays with us. . . . God grant they may both be happy—the only two beings I have ever loved. And I—must keep wandering on. I cannot be the ghost at their feast." He sits down by the campfire, buries his face in his hands; then "with a whimsical sadness" he says: "Greater love hath no man than this that he giveth his wife for his friend."

The plot of *A Wife for a Life* is simplistic, melodramatic, and at times improbable. Yet basic motifs in this crude first effort were to be more carefully developed in later dramas. Although sketchily drawn, Jack, a partial self-portrait, is O'Neill's first split hero: the romantic dreamer and materialistic businessman. The words "dreamily," "dream," and "dreaming" are applied to Jack when he speaks of Yvette. Yet after he tests the new prospect and finds "a small heap of bright yellow particles" at the bottom of the pan, he talks excitedly about becoming rich and organizing a company. The Older Man, haunted by his past and his ill-treatment of his wife, is the precursor of Captain Bartlett in *Gold*. When he sees the yellow particles, he feels them possessively with his fingers: "O' course gold; just as I suspected."

The Older Man is O'Neill's first portrait in a gallery of unloved husbands: Ephraim Cabot in *Desire Under the Elms*, Ezra Mannon in *Mourning Becomes Electra*. Like their wives, Abbie and Christine, Yvette had married an older man for money, not love. In these and other plays, such as "The Guilty One," *Dynamo*, *Long Day's Journey into Night*, and "Blind Alley Guy," the two people trapped in a loveless union are thinly disguised portraits of O'Neill's parents.

While *A Wife for a Life* has autobiographical characters and elements, the author was not subconsciously depicting his parents' marriage but that of James Findlater Byth, James O'Neill's press agent, whom the younger O'Neill met in 1907. Byth and the young O'Neill became friends and were particularly close in 1911–1912 when both roomed at Jimmy the Priest's in New York. When the despondent O'Neill tried to commit suicide there in 1912, Byth aborted the attempt. Byth is depicted as "Jimmy, the roommate" in the 1919 one-acter "Exorcism," the dramatist's recreation of this incident, and as James "Jimmy Tomorrow" Cameron in the 1939 *The Iceman Cometh*.

Jimmy Tomorrow, the final portrait of Byth, attributes his alcoholism to his wife's infidelity. Serving as a war correspondent in South Africa during the Boer War, he had returned from the front to their home in Cape Town to find his wife in bed with one of his best friends. In the last act, however, he confesses he only used her adultery as an excuse to drink. "Why Marjorie married me, God knows. It's impossible to believe she loved me. She soon found I much preferred drinking all night with my pals to being in bed with her." The Transvaal, where the Older Man and Jack had met, is mentioned in *The Iceman Cometh*: General Wetjoen, a Boer commando leader, reminisces about the "old days in Transvaal."

While Byth was never actually a war correspondent in South Africa as he asserted, his narration of his unhappy marriage obviously made an indelible impression on O'Neill, who re-creates the tragedy in *A Wife for a Life*, his first play, and two decades later in *Iceman*, one of his last plays. Similar terms are used to describe the Older Man and Jimmy Tomorrow. Of the former, O'Neill writes, "His face is the face of one who has wandered far, lived hard, seen life in the rough, and is a little weary of it all. Withal his air and speech are those of an educated man whose native refinement has clung to him in spite of many hard knocks." Jimmy "has a face like an old well-bred, gentle bloodhound's." His "forehead is fine, his eyes are intelligent and there once was a competent ability in him. His speech is educated." His "manners are those of a gentleman." Byth's age in 1913, forty-seven, approximates that of the Older Man. While O'Neill derived details of the camp setting and of panning gold from his own experience when he was in Honduras prospecting with Fred and Ann Stevens, the true inspiration for *A Wife for a Life* is his friend Byth.

On June 6, 1913, three days after O'Neill's release from Gaylord Farm Sanatorium, Byth committed suicide, leaping from the window of his room at Jimmy the Priest's.* O'Neill must have learned of the tragedy while he was recuperating at the family home in New London. That summer, probably in July, he wrote *A Wife for a Life*. It can be assumed that O'Neill remembered Byth on subsequent anniversaries of his death. His first concept for *The Iceman Cometh*, the "Jimmy the Priest's idea," is dated June 6, 1939.

---

*Don Parritt dies in the same manner and place in *The Iceman Cometh*.

2.   *The Web*

O'Neill wrote his first "Play in One Act," *The Web*,* in
the fall of 1913, after leaving Gaylord Farm Sanatorium.
Originally entitled "The Cough," the work seems to have
had as its early focus the tubercular condition of its heroine, Rose Thomas. As the story evolved, she became ever
more deeply ensnared within the inexplicably tangled
design spun by indifferent forces controlling her life. In
the early one-acter a web is an obvious symbol of man's
hopelessly trapped condition. In later plays, the author
takes a more subtle approach: the cage imagery in *The
Hairy Ape*, the room that becomes increasingly smaller in
All God's Chillun Got Wings, the stone wall crushing the
Cabots in *Desire Under the Elms*.

   The Web is set in a squalid room on the top floor of a
Lower East Side rooming house in New York on a rainy
summer evening. Rose, a prostitute, makes a futile effort to
disguise the terrible toll illness has taken on her face
before she goes out on the streets that evening to work.
Twenty-two, but looking thirty, she is "in an advanced
stage of consumption"; her face is "deathly pale with
hollows in under the eyes, which are wild and feverish."
Throughout the play, a chronic cough serves as a reminder of her condition.

   The hard expression of Rose's face softens when she
glances, protectively, at the bed where her small child
lies sleeping. The child is a source of bitter contention
between Rose and her pimp, Steve, the cause, according
to him, of their being "broke all the time." Steve, O'Neill's

*The one-acter was never copyrighted or produced. It was pub-
lished in August 1914, one of five of O'Neill's earliest efforts, in
Thirst and Other One-Act Plays (Boston: The Gorham Press).

first villain, is "flashily dressed, rat-eyed, weak of
mouth." His face betrays "the effects of drink and drugs."

In their first confrontation, Rose asks Steve to be
allowed to stay in that evening. She reminds him of "all
the coin" she has given him that morning and begs for a
few dollars for a doctor's visit. Sullenly, Steve, an inveterate gambler, confesses he lost the money earlier in a
game at Tony's and viciously accuses Rose of "holdin'
out": "D' yuh think I'm a simp to be gittin' yuh protection
and keepin' the bulls from runnin' yuh in when all yuh do
is to stick at home and play dead?" He would have reason
to complain, Rose replies, if she were like Bessie, who has
"enough salted to leave" her pimp, Jack, Steve's friend.
Steve argues that Bessie should be beaten, to warn "all
youse dolls."

Anger and Steve's present condition (he is "full of
booze and hop") embolden Rose; she threatens to replace
him: "There's many others I kin git." Steve becomes
vindictive and bullies her: "git dat brat outa here in a
week" or "I'll have yuh pinched and sent to the Island.*
The kid'll be took away from yuh then." Rose pleads with
him: "For the love of Gawd lemme keep her! She's all I
got to live for. If yuh take her away I'll die. I'll kill myself."
When Steve renews his threat, Rose attacks him physically. He retaliates by hitting her in the face and knocking
her down.

A number of elements in this early one-acter reappear in the 1939 *The Iceman Cometh*. Like Steve, Rocky,
the pimp-bartender, believes his "baby dolls" Margie and
Pearl are "holdin' out." He also slaps his "goils" in the face
when they call him a pimp and warns them: "Lay off me or
I'll beat de hell—." Both Steve and Rocky are corrupt
grafters, paying protection money to policemen in the
area. Steve threatens to put Rose "in the cooler" if she
refuses to work for him. In the first notes for the last act of

---

*O'Neill refers to Blackwells Island (where Yank is incarcerated
in *The Hairy Ape*).

Iceman, Rocky, who "looks now like a minor Wop gang-ster," plans to use his conections to punish Margie and Pearl when they go on strike. He tells the police sergeant to "pick up the girls if they do any more trade—I'll show them where they get off without any protection." In addition to the parallel situations and the approximate years of the settings, 1912 and 1913, O'Neill uses similar expressions and identical words—"yuh," "youse," "dat," "retoin"—to reflect the same socioeconomic level of the prostitutes and pimps.

Rose is rescued when Tim Moran, a gangster who is hiding from the police, pushes his way into the room. "He is short and thick set, with a bullet head, close-cropped black hair, a bull neck, and small blue eyes set close together." His face, while a "criminal type," is "redeemed by its look of manliness." When Tim points a revolver at the cowardly pimp and orders him from the room, Steve slinks out, swearing to get revenge.

In the strange scene that follows, two lonely misfits of society instinctively perceive in the other a ray of hope and confess the sordid details of their wasted lives. Rose recalls the number of times she tried to break the pattern of her life. Each menial job ended disastrously. Once, while a housekeeper, she was fired when a male dinner guest recognized her and informed his hostess of Rose's past. She laments: "They—all the good people—they got me where I am and they're goin' to keep me there." Tim's recollections are equally grim. Sent to a reform school as "a kid" after getting mixed up in a robbery with older fellows, he could find no employer willing to hire him upon his release. He then "stole again to keep from starving." Most of his life has been spent in jail, where he learned to be a yeggman. Two weeks ago he "broke out" and robbed a bank. While "hiding out" in the room next to Rose's, he had overheard her conversation with Steve. Risking capture, Tim determined to rescue Rose from her pimp.

When Tim discovers that Rose's one hope for a cure
is a move to the country, he gives her a "large roll of
money." Rose protests: "Yuh don't know how rotten I
am." Earlier Rose had told him she never kissed her
child, fearing she would communicate tuberculosis. Disregarding possible danger to himself, Tim takes Rose in
his arms and kisses her: "That's how rotten I think yuh
are. Yuh're the whitest kid I've ever met."* All the hardness in Rose's face vanishes; it "is soft, transfigured by a
new emotion."

Repeatedly in later plays, O'Neill suggests that love
or the close bond of friendship and understanding has the
power to transfigure two desperately lonely people whose
paths fatally intercept, even briefly. They experience
what Robert Browning calls "the perfect moment"; in
O'Neill it has connotations of salvation as well as of exhil-
aration. Erie Smith, "a small-fry gambler" in the 1940
one-acter *Hughie*, resembles Tim Moran. Erie has blue
eyes and appears to be short: "his big head squats on a
neck which seems part of his beefy shoulders." Throughout the play the lonely Erie tries in vain to make friends
with the new hotel Night Clerk. Only at the end of the
play are these two isolated men able to transcend the
barriers of indifference and reach out to each other. At
that moment, "beatific vision swoons on the empty pools
of the Night Clerk's eyes. He resembles a holy saint,
recently elected to Paradise." Erie's "face lights up with a
saving revelation."

Tim promises to come to Rose in the country "when
it's safe." At last, it seems, the web is broken; there is
hope now for Rose. Her eyes are "full of happy tears."
Visible for some moments at the open window leading to

---

*To kiss or not to kiss a tubercular victim in O'Neill's plays is a
sign of nobility or cowardice. In *The Straw* the shallow Fred
Nicholls shrinks from kissing the infected Eileen Carmody. The
"whitest kid" concept, signifying the ultimate acceptance, is
used later in *All God's Chillun Got Wings*; the white Ella Harris
calls Jim, her black husband, the "whitest man that ever lived."

the fire escape, the exit Tim intends to use to avoid
capture, is Steve's face, which contorts with rage when
the lovers embrace. A noise in the hall prompts Tim to
dash toward the window. When he nears it, Steve shoots
him, throws the gun into the room, and disappears. As
Rose cradles the head of the dead man against her breast,
a policeman and two plainclothesmen enter. The money
designed to save her life now ironically destroys it. Discovering the roll of bills in her hand, the men accuse Rose
of killing Tim. "She reads her own guilt in every eye" and
ceases her protest of innocence.

The child begins to cry. Rose, knowing she is
doomed, soothes it in a "dull, mechanical tone." There is
no hope, no way out of the cruel maze. Life is, as she
remarked earlier, "a bum game all round." A strange
phenomenon occurs. Rose "seems in a trance. Her eyes
are like the eyes of a blind woman. She seems to be aware
of something in the room which none of the others can
see—perhaps the personification of the ironic life force
that has crushed her." Speaking of her child, she asks the
"unseen presence in the room": "I suppose yuh'll take her
too?" Rose's first line—and that of the play—was "gawd!
What a night! What a chance I got!" In the closing scene
she stretches "both arms above her head and cries bitterly, mournfully, out of the depths of her desolation,"
addressing her words "to the air": "Gawd! Gawd! Why
d'yuh hate me so?" As the policeman leads Rose out of the
room, the child cries "Maamaaaa!" The First Plainclothesman "cuddles her on his lap with elephantine playfulness" and says: "Mama's gone. I'm your Mama now."

Rose, O'Neill's first heroine, is beset by a wide range
of misfortunes: tuberculosis, an illegitimate child, dire
poverty, a treacherous pimp-lover. In spite of these
seemingly contrived afflictions, the excesses of a fledgling
playwright, she emerges as a credible tragic figure.
O'Neill makes the reader care about her, sympathize with
her. Like many later characters in the canon, she is help-

lessly split, an early Cybel (*The Great God Brown*), masked and unmasked: the prostitute, street-wise, hard, tough, distrustful of others, versus the woman, maternal, soft, loving with her child and Tim.

In contrast, Steve is a one-dimensional character. His sole function is to serve as the avenging adversary, thus sealing Rose's doom. He is depicted as the epitome of evil: selfish, cowardly, devoid of any redeeming characteristics. The Irish Tim Moran is pursued by law officials for crimes considered by society to be far more serious than Steve's, yet O'Neill portrays the yeggman as sensitive, selfless, and concerned. Steve and Tim resemble the two thieves crucified with Christ on Calvary: one vengeful, the other compassionate. Viewed another way, Steve is another Judas, for he betrays Rose by summoning the police. Rose, a repentent, redeemed Mary Magdalen, is the first of many prostitutes in the canon: Min, Belle, Pompeia, Fat Violet, the tarts in *Iceman*.

The gambler and yeggman in the early one-acter are prototypes for underworld figures in later dramas. Walter White, the central character in O'Neill's unfinished last work, is a Hitler-like American gangster. Criminal types and references abound in other works: *The Dreamy Kid, The Iceman Cometh, Hughie*. In his 1918–1920 notebook the dramatist recorded an idea for a "Gunman Series." Twenty years later, in 1940, he outlined a series of monologue plays, "By Way of Obit," which, like *Hughie*, the only one completed, contain underworld references.

The question obviously arises: what prompted the playwright to focus consistently on characters and situations from the underside of life? Incidents in his own life may have contributed to his choice. Shortly before writing *The Web*, O'Neill had lived for almost a year at Jimmy the Priest's, which housed an assortment of low-life figures. He had heard stories about colorful New York characters from his brother Jamie. The source of inspiration for *The Web* is unimportant. The fact that the dramatist chose to set this play of doomed lovers against an underworld backdrop is significant. In this, his first developed work, O'Neill conveys in a moving way a sense of man's unutterable loneliness, the hopelessness of his struggle against fate. It would be difficult to find more appropriate symbols of man's alienation and his estrangement from society than those used in *The Web*: the prostitute and the gangster. They are the first, but not the last, in O'Neill's gallery of outcasts.

3. *Thirst*

In *Thirst** O'Neill demonstrates for the first time his concept of the sea as a malevolent force affecting men adversely and as having a mystical power over them. Labeled a "tragedy," the one-acter depicts the hopeless struggle of three shipwrecked people to survive on a life raft. Dying of thirst and sinking rapidly into madness, they long only to be rescued. They perish at the end solely because they prey on each other. After their loss of humanity, the sea asserts itself and claims them as its own.

The specific references to the clothes of the characters is the first indication of their disparate social levels. The West Indian mulatto wears a blue seaman's uniform. The middle-aged Gentleman, a first-class passenger, is clad in an evening dress reduced by the sun and water "to the mere caricature of such a garment." The young blond-haired Dancer is dressed bizarrely "in a complete short-skirted dancing costume—of black covered with spangles." At her throat a diamond necklace glitters. It is apparent "she must have been very beautiful before hunger and thirst had transformed her into the mocking spectre of a dancer."

At the outset of the play, the oppressive tropical heat and an obsessive fear are just beginning to goad them into madness. The sun "glares down straight overhead like a great angry eye of God." Its blue color merges "into a

*O'Neill dates the play "(1913) (New London, Conn. Fall)" in the longhand draft. In the "Cycles" he lists it with works written at the O'Neill summer house, prior to his move to the Rippins' home. When he went to Provincetown in June 1916, the author brought with him the five plays published in *Thirst and Other One-Act Plays*. *Thirst*, the second of O'Neill's plays to be staged, was presented by the Provincetown Players in August 1916.

black shadow in the horizon's rim." Close to the raft, sharks cut the water in lazy circles. In spite of their common plight, the three are separated by social and psychological barriers. The Gentleman and the Dancer huddle weakly on the right side of the raft, commiserating with each other. The Gentleman calls the sailor opposite him "our companion in misfortune. God knows we are all in the same pitiful plight. We should not grow suspicious of one another."

Eventually, the inner strength of the black sailor instills fear in the Gentleman and the Dancer. Why, they wonder, is he stronger than they? Here for the first time O'Neill uses a theory that will be found in later works: that representatives of a particular ethnic group, usually a deprived, exploited social class, are superior, physically, morally, or both, to the possessors of wealth, position, and power. For example, blacks (Brutus in *The Emperor Jones* and Jim in *All God's Chillun Got Wings*) are dipicted as being superior to whites (Smithers and Ella); the Irish (Sara Melody in *A Touch of the Poet* and *More Stately Mansions* and Phil Hogan in *A Moon for the Misbegotten*) soundly defeat haughty aristocratic Yankees (Deborah Harford and T. Sedman Harder, Standard Oil millionaire).

The Gentleman and the Dancer are portrayed as materialists; both had returned to their staterooms immediately after "the crash" to retrieve valued objects: he his wallet, she her diamond necklace. The sailor thought only of saving his sole possession: life. His present predicament is merely one new hardship imposed on him by an indifferent fate. Having remained close to his primitive roots, he is in harmony with nature. While the Gentleman and the Dancer cry out in vain to a dead God, fashioned in their likeness and long-absent from their mausoleum churches, the sailor "croons a monotonous negro song" to the sharks. When asked its meaning, he says: "It is a charm I have been told. It is very strong. If I sing long enough perhaps they will not eat us." The Dancer is strangely disturbed by the "dirge," as she calls it: "I have heard many songs in many languages in the places I have played but never a song like that before." She is even more upset by the profound, breathless silence that ensues when the sailor ceases to sing; then the world seems to her "emptier than before" and more frightening.

While most of the play's dialogue is assigned to the Gentleman and the Dancer, their speeches are frequently monologues; each recounts incidents that occurred before and after the shipwreck to the self-absorbed other. The Gentleman expresses his belief that the ship's captain had wanted to make a quick passage across the Atlantic to New York and had followed "a course but little used." The route apparently brought them close to the equator. The Gentleman speaks of "these seas" as being full of coral islands, adding: "it was probably an uncharted coral reef the steamer hit." The description of the crash, "that horrible dull crack," and the aftermath, the crowds of people "fighting to get into the boats," is an accurate account of the tragedy of the *Titanic*, which sank after crashing into an iceberg on its maiden voyage across the Atlantic in 1912, the year before O'Neill wrote *Thirst*. The commanding officers of the British liner were reportedly guilty of negligence because they ignored messages warning them of imminent danger. In *Thirst* the captain is also responsible for his ship's destruction. The Dancer recalls seeing him, his face "pale and drawn like the face of a dead man," shoot himself on the bridge.

The Dancer fainted shortly after this incident. While she remembers someone kissing her, perhaps the young English officer "with the great dark eyes," she cannot recall who saved her life. The Gentleman, who swam to the safety of the raft after his overcrowded boat capsized, believes the officer ordered the sailor to take her away from the ship on the raft, intending to join her later. The

sailor refuses to answer any questions. There is a feeling
that he himself might have saved her on his own initiative.

Initially, the Gentleman and the Dancer cling to the
slight hope that a passing ship will rescue them. When
none appears, the Dancer weeps despairingly: "My God,
this is horrible to wait and wait for something that never
comes." For one brief period she experiences a revival of
hope. Her sick mind tricks her senses, and she imagines
that she hears water running over stones on a cool green
island. The Gentleman brings her back to the world of
reality, saying: "The blind sky will not answer your appeals or mine. Nor will the cruel sea grow merciful for any
prayers of ours."

In his despair, the Gentleman gets, and transmits to
the Dancer, a "mad fixed idea" that the sailor has a flask of
water hidden under his jersey. With all hope of external
help gone, water symbolizes the only means of survival to
the Gentleman and the Dancer. She exclaims violently:
"We will kill him then. He deserves to be killed." The
Gentleman knows that they are too weak physically to
seize the flask by force and suggests cunningly that she
trade her diamond necklace for the water. When she
rejects this plan, he warns her that she will take the
necklace to the sharks: "For my part I would sell my soul
for a drop of water."

Convinced finally, the Dancer drags herself over to
the sailor and offers him the necklace, explaining its great
value, in exchange for water. He responds "I have no
water" and pushes her hand away. She returns to her
place and plans a new strategy: "I have still one card to
play. It has never failed me yet." She makes an absurd
effort to improve her appearance, braiding her hair,
pinching her cheeks. The Gentleman guesses her scheme
and believe she is selfishly abandoning him; he mocks
her: "Dance, dance, Salome." The Dancer crawls back to
the sailor, puts her arm around his neck, and offers him
her body "that men have called so beautiful." For one

moment her voice arouses some latent passion within him; but abruptly he "turns to the sharks," repeating his words: "I have no water!" Calling him a "black animal" and a "dirty slave," she "clutches the sailor with both hands at his throat." He takes her hands from his neck and says quietly: "Leave me alone! I have no water."

The Dancer stands for the first time, infused with a surge of strength. "The last string has snapped. She is insane."* She retreats to the safe world of the past, reliving an earlier incident in her theater dressing room and imagining that the cue has come for her to perform. She commences to sing and then to dance wildly "like some ghastly marionette jerked by invisible wires." Suddenly she falls back on the raft and dies. The sailor looks relieved, "as if some perplexing problem had been solved for him." He takes out his knife and sharpens it: "We shall eat. We shall drink." Horrified, the Gentleman pushes the Dancer's body into the water. In the ensuing struggle, both men fall into the sea. Shortly, the sharks circle no loner. The sun is again likened to the "great angry eye of God." At the beginning of the play the glaring sun was an omen, a warning to man. The reference to it at the end is a grim reminder that God will not be mocked by man. O'Neill's message in *Thirst* is clear: when man turns on his fellow man and breaks the bond of common humanity that links them, he contrives his own moral and physical destruction.

At the top of the first page of the handwritten draft of the play, O'Neill wrote "'Hunger' or 'Thirst.'" Later, probably when the one-acter was completed, he drew several lines through the word "Hunger." This first title, however, suggests that the dramatist might have con-

---

*The Dancer is the first of a multitude of women who, when last seen, are mad or totally irrational. Mary Tyrone in *Long Day's Journey into Night* is the best example, but other Ella O'Neill-like portraits resemble her: Ella Harris in *All God's Chillun Got Wings*, Deborah Harford in *More Stately Mansions*, Annie Keeney in *Ile*.

sidered using greed as the motivating force leading to the characters' downfall. The diamond necklace apparently would serve the same purpose in this play as the "treasure" in *Gold* and the farm in *Desire under the Elms*. In describing the empty raft "floating in the midst of a great silence" at the close of the play, O'Neill adds a supernatural element: "The eerie heat waves float upward in the still air like the souls of the departed." Justice, administered by the vengeful sea, the nemesis of an angry God, has been served. The only remnant of the holocaust, the diamond necklace, the symbol of man's acquisitive, perfidious nature, lies upon the raft "glittering evilly in the blazing sunshine."

Thirst resembles O'Neill's first two works in that it contains a triangular two men–one woman relationship. Although the woman in *A Wife for a Life* is an offstage character, she is a palpable force onstage. The Gentleman in *Thirst*, like the "villains" in the other two plays, the Older Man and Steve, becomes obsessed with the idea that he has been betrayed and seeks revenge. The trapped heroines of *The Web* and *Thirst*, finding themselves doubly assaulted, by a man and by an implacable life force, rebel but are inevitably destroyed. There is in these two plays an experienced or visible manifestation of the supernatural: the "unseen presence in the room" in *The Web*, the "eerie heat waves" in *Thirst*. O'Neill's first three works incorporate the same themes: waiting for the eagerly anticipated event that will bring change or salvation; greed or materialism versus romanticism or close association with nature; betrayal and revenge; hope versus despair (the Dancer, who dreams of reaching the safety of land, says: "I must not think or despair will kill me").

In subsequent works O'Neill consciously experimented with monologues and thought asides. In these early, inferior plays, the apprentice playwright used them unconsciously as a means of revealing the conflicts of the characters. The Older Man and Jack in *A Wife for a Life*, Rose and Tim in *The Web*, the Gentleman and the Dancer in *Thirst* appear to be conversing with each other; actually they are verbalizing their inner thoughts and frustrations and attempting to rationalize and understand their pasts. All are caught in an encircling web and cry out for help to God, some perceived life force, be it the air, the sea, the cruel sun. The pattern established in these early plays emerges in later works: man, haunted by his past, victimized by the forces of fate and his own nature, struggles in pursuit of a goal. In his despair, he is buoyed sporadically by a vague impossible hope. Ultimately, however, he cannot escape his doom, often the punishment incurred for an act of betrayal; dying physically or psychologically, he is nearly always redeemed.

4. *Recklessness*

Recklessness, written in fall 1913,* is a domestic tragedy.
The one-acter's setting, a "summer home in the Catskills,
New York" on a "warm August night," possibly reflects
O'Neill's lazy recuperative period, following his release
from Gaylord in June, when he stayed with his family in
New London. The two central characters, Arthur and
Mildred Baldwin, are partly fictitious, partly autobio-
graphical, a first probing glance at James and Ella O'Neill.

When the play opens Mildred sits alone in the Baldwin library, a "typical sitting-room of a moderately
wealthy man with little taste." She wears a low-cut grey
evening dress and is a "tall, strikingly voluptuous-looking
young woman of about twenty-eight. Her hair is reddish-
gold, almost a red, and her large eyes are of that dark
greyish-blue color which is called violet." With her is the
family chauffeur, Fred Burgess, a "tall, clean-shaven,
dark-complected young fellow of twenty-five or so with
clear-cut, regular features, big brown eyes and black
curly hair."

The two kiss passionately. Mildred begs Fred to take
her away that evening before the return of her husband,
who has been away on a racing car tour for two weeks.
Fred reminds her they lack the funds to escape. Baldwin
will never give her a divorce, preferring to keep her
"bound to him in name for years—just for spite." Mildred
responds that even though Baldwin has never "known
what the word 'husband' ought to mean," she "can't think
him the devil in human form" Fred believes him to be.

*The revised, handwritten script of *Recklessness* is dated
"11/25/13." The one-acter was never produced. It was published
in August 1914 in *Thirst and Other One-Act Plays*.

She longs for "one more night" with her lover and hopes something will detain her husband: "I kept thinking of how he would claim me—force his loathsome kisses on me." When Fred "groans in impotent rage," she entreats him to "save me that degradation." They are completely absorbed in each other and fail to notice the appearance of Mildred's maid, Gene, who stands in the doorway to the verandah. Like Steve looking through the window at Rose and Tim in *The Web*, Gene glares at the lovers, "vindictive hatred shining in her black eyes."

At the sound of a powerful motor, Fred leaves. Arthur Baldwin enters. He is "a stocky, undersized man of about fifty. His face is puffy and marked by dissipation and his thick-lipped mouth seems perpetually curled in a smile of cynical scorn. His eyes are small with heavily dropping lids." He gazes possessively at his wife and brags about his success on the racing tour. Fretfully, he complains about a problem he had with the steering gear of his car on the hill leading to their home. "I had to creep up here. If I'd gone fast your hubby would be draped around some pine tree now."

After Mildred goes upstairs, her maid, Gene, "a pretty young woman of twenty-one," enters and informs Baldwin his wife is having an affair with Fred. The triangular structure of O'Neill's first works expands in *Recklessness* to a rectangular configuration. Here two supposedly betrayed parties seek vengeance. Gene admits, under harsh questioning, that she loves Fred and wants "to get even with Mildred." She exclaims: "I'll teach him to throw me over the way he did." Gene shows Baldwin a letter, arranging an assignation, that his wife has sent to Fred. Baldwin wonders why Mildred carelessly committed the message to paper; she should have telephoned or summoned Fred to the house. Fate, once again, plays an important role in the lives of O'Neill's characters: Gene states that the garage telephone had been out of order until that morning. To the outraged husband, the maid describes the secret meetings of his wife and Fred, how she had followed Mildred to the garage "several different nights." Gene's revenge is that the lovers will know who had "spoiled their fun."

Alone, Baldwin gazes at his auto coat and at the garage telephone. They "seem to suggest an idea to him—a way for his vengeance." He telephones the chauffeur, telling him to rush to the village to get a doctor for Mildred. "Her life's in your hands. Turn the car loose! Drive like hell!" The motor of the racing car is heard. Then the stage is darkened to suggest a time lapse of one-half to three-quarters of an hour.

As the lights go up, the telephone rings. Baldwin responds with "mocking compassion" to the news that Fred has been killed in an accident. He rings the electric bell for Mary, the housemaid, who is sent to summon Mildred. Cruelly, he wants to see his wife's reaction when she sees her dead lover. Mildred enters fearfully. She resembles Mary Tyrone in the last act of *Long Day's Journey into Night* and wears "a light blue kimona and bedroom slippers of the same color. Her beautiful hair hangs down her back in a loose braid."

Baldwin pretends to have told Fred about the faulty steering wheel and to be disturbed that the chauffeur took the car out that night. Fred, he says, is careless, "absolutely reckless, especially with other people's property." After playing a prolonged cat-and-mouse game with his wife, Baldwin takes out the letter and mocks her: "You are a novice at this game, my dear. Take the advice of a hardened old sinner—in the years and loves to come never write any more letters." He refuses at first to divorce her and then perversely announces he will supply the evidence she needs and free her. He asks his now-grateful wife if, in truth, she married him for his money. She admits she has never loved him, that her parents forced her into the marriage. Mildred puts her arms around his neck and kisses him, saying: "I do love you now." He thanks his wife for "that Judas kiss" and tells her she shall have Fred.

Three men enter the room carrying the battered body of the chauffeur. Mildred sways and faints. Her husband "pushes the button of the electric bell" and, with the housemaid, carries Mildred to her room upstairs. After Baldwin returns, the maid rushes in, begging him to go upstairs: "I think she's gone mad, sir. She's pulling out all the drawers looking for something. . . ." Her words are interrupted by "a dull report" from upstairs. The husband's face hardens; then he says calmly: "Mrs. Baldwin has just shot herself. You had better phone for the doctor, Mary."

Recklessness, with its two violent deaths to illustrate the theme of crime and punishment, is another example of O'Neill's early use of the melodramatic. In his badly seamed plot, he relies heavily on chance: Gene's discovery of the letter to establish proof of guilt, the badly contrived accident, the disposal of the chauffeur in a readily available faulty car. The characters, however, are more fully developed than previous ones and are more plausibly motivated. Apparently, the sources of O'Neill's inspiration account for the more realistic handling of material.

Shortly before writing *Recklessness*, O'Neill read the plays of Strindberg. Because of its many similarities to *Recklessness*, *Miss Julie* was certainly among them. The same social distinctions exist between the erring lovers in both plays: Julie, the aristocrat, is mistress of an estate; Jean, dressed in the livery of a valet, is her social inferior. Like Mildred, Julie goes to her servant's room and begins a forbidden affair. Both women, lacking money, are trapped when they try to flee hastily with their lovers before the return of a betrayed authoritative figure. In *Recklessness* the absent husband appears early in the play and seeks revenge; in *Miss Julie* the Count, Julie's father,

remains an offstage character, although he does return
before the drama ends.

The two symbols that represent the Count and ter-
rify the valet, the bell and the telephone, play ominous
roles in *Recklessness*. There is also in each play "the other
woman," a servant and former mistress of the valet/chauf-
feur. Had there been a confrontation between Julie and
her father, he would probably have mocked her as Baldwin taunts Mildred: "It takes courage to proclaim oneself
the mistress of one's chauffeur—to play second-fiddle to
one's maid." Both heroines go mad in the final scenes and
commit suicide. The major difference between the two
plays is that O'Neill is more even-handed, meting out a
retributive violent death to the man involved in the illicit
relationship. The valet survives in the Strindberg play.

In Mildred and Arthur Baldwin there are early traces
of the autobiographical mother and father figures of later
plays, couples who are trapped in bad marriages that are
frequently called "a mistake." Mildred's words to her
husband, expressing their incompatibility, are later
echoed by Ella O'Neill–like wives: "We are not the same
age. We do not look at things in the same light—we have
nothing in common." In the first notes for *Long Day's
Journey into Night*, Mary Tyrone pawns her jewels to buy
the drugs that will allow her to escape temporarily from an
unhappy marriage. In *Recklessness* Mildred plans to sell
her jewels to escape permanently from a disastrous union.
Arthur Baldwin's favorite occupation, attending racing
car meets, like James Tyrone's acting profession, takes
him all over the country. Baldwin says to his wife ac-
cusingly: "You never seem to care very much about touring around with me."*

---

*O'Neill seems to have had his family's summer home in mind
when he conceived the play's setting, which resembles the
Tyrones' living room in *Long Day's Journey into Night*. The time
of the action in the two plays is August. In both settings there are
windows on two sides of the room and doors leading to a porch or
verandah. Identical pieces of furniture are described: along the
walls of the rooms are two bookcases, a small wicker table, a

Recklessness is basically the story of a wife's betrayal of her husband and its consequences. The same first scene, in which the wife complains to her lover about the return of a sexually repulsive husband, reappears years later in *Mourning Becomes Electra*. Adam Brant, like Fred, is infuriated by the thought that the hated husband will possess the woman he loves, Christine Mannon. Mildred is a younger version of Christine, who has the same "voluptuous figure," "violet blue" eyes, large mouth, and a "lower lip full." Christine's hair is "partly a bronze gold"; Mildred's is a "reddish-gold."*

In the *Electra* trilogy, a daughter, Lavinia, suspects her mother's infidelity and follows Christine to the place of assignation. Armed with proof of her mother's guilt, Lavinia, like Gene, seeks revenge, finding justice in Christine's suicide. In *Strange Interlude* a son, Gordon Evans, discovers his mother, Nina, and her lover, Edmund Darrell, embracing. The boy "appears in the doorway at rear and stands for a moment in a passion of jealousy and rage and grief, watching them." In the early notes for *Strange Interlude* O'Neill calls the betrayed husband Art Truesdale, the first name being the same as that assigned the wronged husband in *Recklessness*. There is a lingering suspicion, derived from the early manuscript notes and the actual published versions of the plays, that Ella O'Neill was either unfaithful to her husband or that her author-son believed her to be guilty of

---

desk, and a divan/couch. In *Recklessness* both the left and the far side look "out on the verandah." "A heavy oak table stands in the center of the room" and on it is an "electric reading lamp wired from the chandelier above." The floor is of "polished hard wood with a large darkish colored rug covering the great part." In *Long Day's Journey* the porch "extends halfway around the house." The hardwood floor is "nearly covered by a rug, inoffensive in design and color. At center is a round table with a green shaded reading lamp, the cord plugged in one of the four sockets in the chandelier above."

*It should be noted that most portraits of Ella O'Neill either have, or once had, some shade of red hair. In the early notes for

infidelity. Usually cautious about autobiographical reve-
lations in his early plays, O'Neill gives his own name,
Gene, to the maid, who from "the doorway" observes
Mildred with Fred with "vindictive hatred" in her eyes.

In their last confrontation, Baldwin tells Mildred
that he feels "conscience-stricken" for leaving her "so
much alone this summer." He suggests that if they
economize "a bit by letting Fred go" she could stay at a
"more fashionable resort." Mildred desperately tries to
persuade him to allow the chauffeur to remain, saying that
she enjoys motoring. In *Long Day's Journey* James Tyrone complains about the waste involved in keeping an
automobile: "You used to ride in it every day, but you've
hardly used it at all lately. I paid a lot of money I couldn't
afford, and there's the chauffeur I have to board and
lodge." Mary argues that Smyth was "only a helper in a
garage and had never been a chauffeur" and that he makes
money from excessively high repair bills. "Something is
always wrong. Smyth sees to that."

If O'Neill's parents did have such discussions about
their chauffeur and their repair-prone car in the summer
of 1912, the time of the action in *Long Day's Journey into
Night*, these elements might have filtered into their son's
consciousness the following year when he wrote *Recklessness*. The play should be evaluated for its dramatic value
and not for its autobiographical revelations when its place
in the canon is assessed. In characterization, *Recklessness*
marks a significant development over earlier one-acters,
The Web and *Thirst*. As for plot, a weakness here, O'Neill
was to spend years mastering its intricacies. His strength
as a dramatist was his characters. Ironically, the more
autobiographical they became in subsequent plays, the
more realistic were their lives and actions and the author's
total creative vision.

Mourning Becomes Electra, Christine's hair is a "dark reddish
brown." Mary Tyrone's was "a rare shade of reddish brown."
Deborah Harford in *A Touch of the Poet* has "red-brown hair."

5.   *Warnings*

The 1913 *Warnings** is derivative, containing elements found in the two works that preceded it. The first scene, set in the home of an unhappily married couple, the Knapps, suggests that *Warnings* will be, like *Reckless-ness*, another domestic drama. The second scene, how-ever, which occurs at sea on the S. S. *Empress*, would provide an appropriate introduction for *Thirst*. Having hit a derelict vessel, the ship is sinking; its passengers are set adrift in lifeboats at the end of the play. In *Thirst* the captain, whose negligence causes the shipwreck, shoots himself on the bridge; in *Warnings* the wire operator Knapp, whose deafness leads to his ship's destruction, also ends his life with a revolver.

In this early work, O'Neill calls the Knapps James and Mary, names he assigned his own parents nearly thirty years later in the autobiographical *Long Day's Jour-ney into Night*. There is a ten-year age difference between the husband and wife in both plays, but the Knapps do not resemble the Tyrones physically. Mary Knapp, a shrew, is a "pale, thin, peevish-looking woman of about forty, made prematurely old by the thousand worries of a pen-ny-pinching existence." She has "brown hair thickly streaked with gray," a "thin-lipped mouth," which "droops sorrowfully at the corners," "faded blue eyes," and a "plaintively querulous" voice. Because her hus-band's occupation has kept him at sea much of their married life, she has had to assume total responsibility for

---

*The revised handwritten script of *Warnings* is dated "1913." The author probably wrote it in December 1913 immediately after he finished *Recklessness*.

raising their five children,* whose ages range from the fifteen-year-old Charles to the year-old baby. Mary Knapp is unable or unwilling to discipline her children. They quarrel continually whenever they appear onstage together: Lizzie, eleven, and Sue, eight, in the opening scene and Charles and Dolly, fourteen, when they enter later.

The purpose of the long first scene, which constitutes two-thirds of the play, is to provide the motivation for Knapp's fatal decision to sail on the S. S. *Empress*, even though he knows his condition endangers the lives of the crew. The Knapp dining room reflects the family's poverty. The drab furnishings affect the occupants adversely; the children, with their sallow complexions and shabby clothes, are irritable. The teenagers, Charlie and Dolly, seek to escape the home's oppressiveness through outside interests deemed illicit by their mother. Dolly accuses Charlie of carrying on with "that red-headed Harris girl." Charlie retaliates by saying he has seen his sister hiding in hallways "with that Dutch kid whose father runs the saloon in the next block." The rigid Puritanical mother gives Charlie "a crack over the ear with her open hand" and threatens to whip Dolly if she is caught in "dark hallways with young men again."

Mrs. Knapp awaits her husband's return from a visit to the doctor, bitterly resenting the ear specialist's five-dollar fee. Her words about her husband's illness (he "has a bad cold") will be repeated later by Mary Tyrone in her discussion of Edmund's sickness. Neither woman wants to face the consequences of a more serious diagnosis by a doctor. To Mrs. Knapp, any threat to her husband's job is a threat to the economic survival of the family. She is in a highly agitated, nervous state by the time her husband returns home.

---

*Five children are listed in the *dramatis personae*. An elder son, named Jim like the author's older brother, no longer lives at home.

Knapp is a "slight, stoop-shouldered, thin-faced man of about fifty." He is "almost completely bald with a thin line of gray hair extending over his large ears around the back of his head." His face is a "sickly yellow," his mouth "large and weak." Charlie, "in his best bellow," tries to cheer his depressed father but succeeds only in waking the baby. After scolding Charlie, the mother goes out to quiet the child. A pathetic scene follows, one that reveals the close bonds between father and son. Charlie is a totally different person, more considerate and sensitive, with his father. The son asks for a new suit as the only one he owns "is full of patches and holes" and the kids laugh at him. "A look of pain" distorts Knapp's features; he promises to buy a "fine new suit with long pants" when he returns from the next trip. When Knapp turns his face to hide his emotion, Charlie clumsily "pats his father on the back."

Alone with her husband, Mrs. Knapp complains about the disgraceful behavior of Charlie and Dolly. Knapp says mildly: "Where's the hurt? They're only kids and they've got to have some fun." Mrs. Knapp switches the target of her attack when she is told the specialist's report: her husband might go stone deaf at any moment. Statements in Mrs. Knapp's tirade against doctors will be repeated later by Mary Tyrone* in *Long Day's Journey into Night*: "All those doctors make things worse than they really are. He's just tryin' to scare you so you'll keep comin' to see him." Bitterly, Mary Knapp says that the doctor wants "to keep you comin' to him. I know the way they talk."

Knapp resolves to do the honorable thing: inform his employers about his condition and give up his job. His wife calls him a fool and reminds him angrily how impossi-

---

*The events depicted in *Long Day's Journey* occurred in the summer of 1912, the year before O'Neill wrote *Warnings*. Ella O'Neill's lamentations about her son's sickness would still be fresh in his memory.

ble it has been in the past for him to find work. She says, "Your salary is small enough but without it we'd starve to death. Can't you think of others besides yourself? How about me and the children?" Then she asks herself: "Why did I ever marry such a man? It's been nothin' but worryin' and sufferin' ever since." In desperation, Knapp cries out: "For God's sake let me alone. I'll go. But this is going to be my last trip. I got to do the right thing."

Scene 2 opens two months later. The door of the wireless room on the boat deck of the S.S. *Empress* is open, revealing "Knapp bent over his instrument." The ship is sinking; its bulkhead cannot hold "more than half an hour—an hour at most." The passengers have assembled, awaiting the order to leave in the lifeboats. Captain Hardwick prods the confused Knapp, seeking replies to the urgent messages he had sent earlier requesting help. The Captain tells Mason, the first officer, that Knapp is behaving strangely; the operator's only response during the interrogation is: "I haven't heard a thing yet, sir." Knapp has given an accurate assessment of his condition; the "sudden stroke" the doctor predicted has left him stone deaf. Finally, he blurts out his story, sobbing bitterly: "I was hoping against hope. . . . I wanted to give up the job this time but she wouldn't let me. She said I wanted them to starve—and Charlie asked me for a suit."

One of the passengers, Dick Whitney, wireless operator of the *Duchess*, is recruited. He sends a message to the nearest ship, the *Verdari*. Its crew had sighted the derelict vessel on the previous day and had sent a warning to all vessels in the area, including the *Empress*. Enraged at the loss of his ship, the Captain orders Whitney to write out the message, stressing the "warnings we didn't get," and to give the paper to Knapp. The sorrowful Knapp stares at the message "with wild eyes and pale twitching features." The Captain motions Knapp to follow him and the others. Alone, Knapp whispers: "God! It's my fault then!" He sees the boats being lowered and despairingly stumbles to the wireless room, takes a revolver from a drawer, and shoots himself. Whitney returns, shouting: "They're waiting for you." He sees Knapp's body, exclaims: "Good God," and rushes astern terrified.

In *Warnings*, as in all his early plays, O'Neill presents a character trapped by the circumstances of his life and by his own nature. While Knapp is purposely given an obvious physical defect, he is also flawed psychologically. A weakling, he lacks the courage to assert himself, to follow his convictions. Like Rose in *The Web*, he is one of the sacrificial lambs trampled ruthlessly by stronger predators. And, like Rose, Knapp is motivated by the love of a child and the entreaty of a partner to continue a distasteful, morally destructive line of work.

Warnings marks a slight step forward in technique, an expanding of dramatic horizons. For the first time in his work, O'Neill uses two settings, the Knapp home and the S.S. *Empress*, and a hero who struggles to free himself from the sea. Knapp does not have the type of love-hate relationship with the sea that plagues later sailors in the canon. He does, however, betray the code of the sea, the silent law that binds each sailor, in honor, to protect the lives of fellow crewmen. Knapp seems singularly isolated from the other sailors of the *Empress*, however. When the captain asks if the operator's erratic behavior might be the result of drinking, the first officer states: "I never saw him touch a drop—even on shore." A sailor who is always sober is suspect, an anomaly in O'Neill.

The first scene in *Warnings* seems more plausible than the second, its dialogue more believable and representative of the characters portrayed. Even the real villainess of the play, Mrs. Knapp, a woman who goads her husband into committing an unconscionable crime, has a softness in her nature when she is not worried about finances or plagued by quarreling children. When her husband returns from the doctor's, she kisses him and pulls out an armchair for him, remarking sadly that he looks worn out. Here, as in the other early works, O'Neill has a problem portraying women. They are often one-dimensional caricatures rather than well-developed flesh-and-blood figures. His first attempt to depict children is successful. He captures their speech patterns, their contrariness, petulance, and vindictiveness. His first scene between a father and son is particularly moving; similar confrontations in later plays will be fraught with suspicion, accusations, and hatred.

The first scene serves a definite purpose: to introduce the moment of truth on the ship when Knapp realizes the consequences of his fatal mistake. The second scene seems anticlimactic. The crewmen are wooden, emotionless. Given the fact that they are on a ship that is "listing pretty badly" and they will soon be adrift in lifeboats, the officers of the doomed ship respond calmly to their plight. There is no sense of alarm, no concern voiced. O'Neill again relies on chance to develop his plot by having a second wireless operator conveniently on board to transmit the information about earlier warnings from the *Verdari*, thereby affixing the blame to Knapp. He is the sole credible figure in the scene, particularly at the end when he is haunted by guilt. Once again, O'Neill's dramatic world ends with violence. After pressing the trigger, Knapp "falls forward on his face on the floor before his instrument."

There is no hope in Knapp's world. The true warnings, O'Neill seems to say, are those inner signals one's conscience emits, urging right behavior in a chaotic universe. Because of weakness, Knapp failed to heed all the warnings in his life. His deafness is an appropriate metaphor for his bankrupt condition.

In late 1918, five years after completing *Warnings*,*

---

*See Peter Egri's discussion of *Warnings* and its similarities to Conrad's "The End of the Tether" in "The Short Story in O'Neill's and Chekhov's One-Act Plays" in *Eugene O'Neill: A World View*, edited by Virginia Floyd (New York: Frederick Ungar, 1979), pp. 125–132.

O'Neill rewrote the play as a short story entitled "S.O.S."
In this work, John Lathrop, a wireless operator like
Knapp, is told he is going deaf, but he insists on making
one more trip on the S.S. *Rio Grande*. He does not hear
the warning that his ship is nearing a German warship.
The American ship is sunk; its crew is captured by Germans. John risks his life to send a message to a second
American ship. He is killed by the Germans but proclaimed a hero by his rescued fellow crewmen.

6. *Fog*

Fog is the third of O'Neill's early playlets* to focus on a catastrophe at sea. *Warnings* closes with the crew and passengers abandoning the sinking S.S. *Empress*. *Fog*, like *Thirst*, opens shortly after a shipwreck. The author manipulates fate in these early one-acters; its manifestation, the sea, exerts a stronger determining influence over his characters than their own inner natures. In the first plays fate is external, imposed; in the later works character is fate.

While the dramatist's List of Plays† indicates that *Fog* was completed in early 1914 after *Warnings*, internal evidence suggests that its composition date is closer to that of *Thirst*. The initial situation in both *Fog* and *Thirst* is identical: two men and a woman are adrift in a lifeboat on a merciless sea. The characters in both one-acters are stereotypes representing different social levels rather than flesh-and-blood figures. A foreigner, a Polish immigrant woman, occupies the socioeconomic level corresponding to that of the West Indian sailor in *Thirst*. The two other central characters in *Fog*, like those of *Thirst*, signify different classes; they also profess distinct philosophies of life: one is an idealistic poet, the other a materialistic businessman.

---

*In March 1914 James O'Neill arranged to have *Fog* and four other one-acters (*The Web, Thirst, Recklessness,* and *Warnings*) published by the Gotham Press of Boston. *Fog* was produced in January 1917 at The Playwrights' Theater.

†O'Neill compiled a complete record of his works, titling it "List of all plays ever written by me, including those I later destroyed, giving where and when they were written." The record appears in my *Eugene O'Neill at Work* (New York: Frederick Ungar, 1981), pp. 388–393.

Little care is given to individualizing the characters in *Fog*. The woman is never described. Throughout the play she sits huddled at the end of the boat, "one arm over her face concealing it." The two men are caricatures; their dialogue is stilted, didactic. There is a forced, strained quality about the play. Its sole *raison d'etre* is to provide O'Neill with a vehicle to express his philosophical beliefs. The spokesman of the play, the poet, is a self-portrait, the author's first. He is identified at first only as the "dark man" and is later described as having an oval face "with big dark eyes and a black mustache and black hair pushed back from his high forehead." The businessman is sketchily drawn; he has a "round, jowly, clean-shaven" face and an "imposing double chin."

O'Neill tries to inject a supernatural element into his description of the setting for *Fog*, as he had in *The Web* and *Thirst*. The lifeboat drifts off the Grand Banks of Newfoundland in dense fog following the sinking of the *Starland*. "The surface of the water is shadowy and unreal in its perfect calmness. A menacing silence, like the genius of the fog, broods over everything." The Poet and the Businessman sit close together in the middle of the boat. The woman opposite them clutches a white bundle containing the body of her small son, who has died quietly while sleeping. The pompous, self-confident Businessman ignores the plight of the miserable woman and talks about his "country place on the Connecticut shore." Symbolizing the indifference of the wealthy to the poor, he may be O'Neill's first portrait of the millionaire Edward Harkness, whose estate was located on this shore, a few miles from the O'Neill home in New London. Harkness is depicted later as Harker in *Long Day's Journey into Night* and Harder in *A Moon for the Misbegotten*.

Fog contains strong statements protesting social and economic inequities. The Poet tries to awaken the social consciousness of the Businessman, predicting the unhappy fate of the Polish child had he lived. Defensively, the Businessman says: "I'm not responsible for the way the world is run." In a speech reflecting O'Neill's personal views, the Poet responds: "We—the self-satisfied, successful members of society—are responsible for the injustice visited upon the heads of our less fortunate brothers-in-Christ because of our shameful indifference to it. We see misery all around us and we do not care. We do nothing to prevent it."

In *Long Day's Journey into Night*, which depicts the dramatist in 1912, a year and a half before he wrote *Fog*, James Tyrone attacks his writer-son for his "Socialist anarchist sentiments." In *Fog* the Businessman, when he discovers that his companion is a writer, remarks: "I knew you weren't in business when I heard those Socialistic ideas of yours. Beautiful idea—Socialism—but too impractical—never come about—just a dream." Another autobiographical link is established with the revelation of the Poet's ardent death wish prior to the shipwreck. Determined to go down with the *Starland*, he had hidden in the steerage to avoid being rescued by the steamer's officers. When he discovered that the Polish woman and her child had been overlooked by rescuers, the Poet lowered a lifeboat and left the ship, concerned only with aiding them. In saving them, the Poet also saved himself, spiritually as well as physically. He tells the Businessman: "I think all that happened to me is an omen sent by the Gods to convince me my past unhappiness is past and my fortune will change for the better."

Recalling the mother's screams when she discovered that her child had died, the Poet regrets the sufferings his "reckless life-saving" had inflicted on the woman. He takes off his ulster and covers the sleeping woman with it. With the coming of light, the "bundle of white clothes can be seen to be a child four or five years old with a thin, sallow face and long black curls." The body is rigid; "the eyes are open and glassy." Keeping in mind the play's mystical ending, O'Neill stresses the fact that the child is indeed dead.

A huge white mass drifts toward the boat, towering above it. The Businessman is relieved when he discovers the "horrible phantom of the sea" is, in reality, an iceberg. As the lifeboat is oarless, the men have no means of rowing to a safer position. Their frustration is compounded when they hear the whistle of a steamer whose officers are searching the area for survivors of the stricken *Starland*.

O'Neill uses the rescue scene to demonstrate the moral superiority of the Poet, who warns the Businessman not to signal the steamer's officers; for he would, by this act, jeopardize the lives of those on board: "We can die but we cannot risk the lives of others to save our own." Angrily, the Businessman responds, "I'm not going to be left here to die on account of your damn fool ideas." He is about to call out when the Poet forces his hand over the man's mouth, stifling the cry for help. The two struggle; the lifeboat begins to rock dangerously. The Poet raises his right fist threateningly, and the Businessman mutters vengefully, "I'll get even with you, you loafer." He panics when a piece of the iceberg breaks off and splashes into the water. "Insane with fear of this new menace," the Businessman is about to throw himself into the water, but the Poet restrains him. The Businessman "weeps like a fat child" and says: "You want to die. Do you want to kill me too, you murderer?" Almost immediately, there is the sound of other voices. A lifeboat from the steamer approaches. With salvation at hand, the Businessman regains "his self-assured urbanity" and asks his companion to forget the unpleasantness between them. The Poet's face is "drawn and melancholy as if uncertain of the outcome of this unexpected return to life."

The steamer's third officer asks, "Where's the kid?" He explains: "If it hadn't been for the kid crying we would have missed you—weird too it sounded with everything so quiet and the fog so heavy. . . . That's how I was able to shape such a direct course for you. I was steering by the sound." Unable to decide "whether the Officer is fooling or not," the Businessman looks at him with an expression of "annoyed stupefaction on his face." The Poet tries to awaken the mother and discovers that she is dead. When he informs the rescue crew that the child has been dead for twenty-four hours, the officer calls him a madman and turns to the Businessman for a rational explanation. He, however, verifies the Poet's statement, leaving the officer to conclude that "he has two madmen to deal with instead of one."

Choosing to remain with the dead while the lifeboat is towed back to the steamer, the Poet looks at their still white faces "with eyes of great longing." The remarks of the Businessman, now safely on the steamer's lifeboat, can be heard. The officer's words close the play: "What you have just finished telling us is almost unbelievable."

Unwittingly, O'Neill in his last line expresses the average person's reaction to *Fog*. It is, without doubt, the weakest of the five early one-acters published in *Thirst and Other Plays*. The outcome of the conflict between the two central characters is predictable: the noble, idealistic artist achieves a moral victory over the greedy, material-istic businessman. The play is significant in that it reveals, through the obviously autobiographical Poet, O'Neill's social views at the time of the play's composition. He was to refine and redefine the artist-businessman conflict in later, more successful, plays, but nowhere is the bat-tleline as decisively drawn as in *Fog*. Perhaps the play fails for this reason. It seems to have been written solely for its social statement. There is no subtlety of characterization or plot.

The attempt to instill the play with a supernatural dimension through the description of the fog and the mirac-ulous cry of the child fails. In *The Web* Rose's "addressing the unseen presence in the room" as she rages against her fate is believable. In *Fog* the child's cry becomes a *deus ex machina*, an easy way to resolve the play's conflict. Never again would O'Neill rely on such a blatantly simplistic device. The play is undoubtedly O'Neill's most immature one-acter. Yet for all its flaws, *Fog* is unique in that in it O'Neill voices for the first time a concept that pervades much of his work: that "we—the self-satisfied, successful members of society—are responsible" for injustice visited upon the heads of "our less fortunate brothers-in-Christ because of our shameful indifference to it." One of the most significant messages in O'Neill's work is that all men are brothers. Throughout the canon, rejection of the tie that binds people together leads to alienation, despair, and, in some instances, death. When *Fog* was written, O'Neill was indeed merely a poet, a man seeking to come to terms with the injustices of the world. The play, however, brought him one step further on the road to Parnassus.

7.   *Bread and Butter*

O'Neill dates *Bread and Butter*, his first full-length drama, "1913–14."* Like *Warnings*, it appears to be, at the outset, a family play. The focus in each work, however, narrows eventually to one family member, who struggles in vain to achieve a goal. While the tone and atmosphere of the first scene of *Warnings* bespeak impending tragedy, in the first act of *Bread and Butter* the good-natured banter and teasing of siblings and the rivalry between the idealistic John Brown and his pompous older brother Edward, clearly a buffoon, suggest the unfolding of a comedy.

Elements of setting and characterization in *Bread and Butter* will be duplicated later in the 1932 comedy, *Ah, Wilderness!*, a semiautobiographical family play. The early drama is set in Bridgetown, Connecticut.† O'Neill obviously had his own hometown, New London, and his family's summer house in mind for these locales. Had *Bread and Butter* been written after *Ah, Wilderness!*, it could have been considered a sequel to it, a continuation of the saga of a sensitive youth's attempt to become a creative artist. At the end of the latter, the seventeen-year-old Richard Miller, a budding poet, is about to begin his freshman year at Yale University. At the conclusion of the first act of *Bread and Butter*, the twenty-two-year-old John Brown, a recent graduate of Princeton, sets out for New York to become an artist. The creative aspirations of

---

*The copyright date is May 5, 1914.

†O'Neill calls the small-town Middletown in the notes he made in 1934 for the sequel to *Ah, Wilderness!*, which would have taken up the story of the Miller family fifteen years later.

both young men are jeopardized by their infatuations with hometown sweethearts, pampered daughters of dry-goods merchants (Maud Steele in *Bread and Butter*, Muriel McComber in *Ah, Wilderness!*).*

When *Bread and Butter* opens, John's future is being decided by his father, who manages his home and family as he operates his hardware store: with detached, businesslike efficiency. Like James Tyrone, he is proud of his humble origin, of his transformation from uneducated farmhand to successful businessman. He had refused to send his two older sons, Edward, thirty, and Harry, twenty-five, to college, deeming their education a waste. After graduating from high school, both had gone to work at the hardware store. They feel slighted because John, the obvious "pet of the family," has gone to college. Edward also bitterly resents the fact that Maud prefers John to him. Edward has proposed to her and been rejected. Harry questions Edward's motive for desiring the marriage, implying that he is impressed "by the fact that her dear daddy is overburdened with coin" and that her family is "socially spotless."

John bears a strong resemblance to his creator; he has a dark complexion, black hair, and "large dreamer's eyes, deep-set and far apart in the oval of his face." His mouth is "full lipped"; "his nose straight and thin." Like Eben's two older brothers in *Desire Under the Elms*, Edward and Harry both have qualities of Jamie O'Neill, the dramatist's brother. Edward, the pompous social climber who is jealous of John and considers him a threat to his political aspirations, represents the proud, sober side of Jamie, who cringed when wealthy New Londoners saw him cutting the hedges dressed in old clothes. The dissipated, Mephistophelean Jamie is reflected in the amiable Harry, who is "given to beer drinking, poker parties, and kelly pool."

---

*Both are portraits of a New London girl, Maibelle Scott, a merchant's daughter, whom the young O'Neill met in 1912, the year before he started *Bread and Butter*, and believed he loved.

The focal point of the first act is John's career choice. When he returns from the Steele home, Harry calls him a "prisoner of the bar" and says: "Speaking of futures shall I communicate to you the reverend judge's (indicating his father) sentence regarding yours? He has sentenced you to a lifetime of delightful idleness—You are condemned to be a lawyer." The young Eugene must have been subjected to a similar decision-making session with his parents, for the courtroom scene is repeated in later works. In the Prologue to *The Great God Brown*, Billy Brown stands before his parents, who are determining his future, "like a prisoner at the bar, facing the judge." His father wants him to be an architect, his mother a lawyer. In a first draft of the play, the fate of Dion Anthony, another portrait of Jamie O'Neill, is decided by his parents in the same manner. Dion is also described as "a prisoner at the bar"; the judge in the Brown household is the dominant mother, whereas the father in the Anthony household "sits in the rocking chair of judgment."

Edward cannot conceal his resentment when his father insists that John go to law school. Even the easygoing Harry allies himself momentarily with Edward and denounces John for pulling "that lily of the field stuff." John, for his part, vehemently rejects his father's decision and announces his intention to go to an art school in New York. His father agrees to let him go only after Maud's father assures Brown that John can become a financial success as a commercial artist. Brown gives his son a year to prove himself.

At the end of the first act, Maud envisions the "oodles and oodles of money" John will make in New York, the hundreds of dollars he will get for each magazine cover he does. Contemptuously, John throws the magazine she holds in the wastepaper basket. He will, he declares, do "finer things than that."

When Act II opens, John has been living for a year and a half in a New York studio with three roommates:

Steve Harrington and Babe Carter, fellow art students, and Ted Nelson, a writer. Babe has fallen in love with John's sister Bessie but is vehemently disliked by old Brown. After John leaves for the railroad station where he is to meet his father, the master of the art school, the elderly Eugene Grammont, who serves as the hero's father figure and the author's spokesman, comes to the studio. Grammont says that John shows "promise of becoming a great artist," but he denounces the young man's father and Maud, fearing these "worshippers of the golden calf, these muddy souls will exert their power to hold him to their own level." Upon their return, old Brown tells John that he will disown his daughter if she does not give up Carter; he denounces John's argument that Bessie has a duty to herself" as "damned rot" believed only "by a lot of crazy Socialists and Anarchist[s]."*

In the first act Brown seemed to be merely a concerned father, a man who, while he rules his family firmly, acts in the best interests of his children. In the second act he is a vicious, hard-hearted villain. He is shocked by John's paintings and by his friends: "drunkards, old lunatics, and women of the streets." He gives his son an ultimatum: "You either come home with me in the morning or you needn't look to me for help in the future."

Act III opens four months later on a hot Sunday afternoon in July in John's New York studio. Having refused to go home, he has taken a job checking sugar bags and barrels on the docks to support himself. His face is haggard and dissipated; his efforts to work creatively have been futile for the past months. His roommate Ted also lacks the creative impulse and complains, "I'm always

---

*James O'Neill must have voiced similar sentiments to his son Eugene. In later autobiographical plays, such as *Long Day's Journey* and *Ah, Wilderness!*, fathers accuse their sons of being socialists and/or anarchists. In this early play the father rails at the son for his paintings, particularly those of nude dancers; later fathers find fault with the books their sons read.

going to start that play—tomorrow. They ought to write on my tombstone: The deceased at last met one thing he couldn't put off till tomorrow."*

Mrs. Brown and Maud come to New York and beg John to return home. Maud lists the things her father is willing to give John after their marriage: a new home, a good job in his store, and one free afternoon a week to continue his painting. John scornfully rejects Steele's gifts. The two young people quarrel; Maud leaves but returns and sees John sobbing. There is a tearful reconciliation, and he promises to go home for her sake.

Two years have passed when the last act opens. The sitting room of John's new home in Bridgetown is oppressive, a drab environment for an artist. Maud, who has become a prim, irritable shrew, complains to Edward about the hardships she endures. Edward has been elected mayor of the town and seems destined to become a congressman in Washington. Maud despises her husband, but out of spite, she will not divorce him. Later, when she is alone with John, she rejects his request for a divorce and his promise to give her "all the evidence" she would need.†

Bread and Butter contains elements that are clearly

---

*Ted Nelson is another view of James Byth, O'Neill's journalist friend, depicted as "Jimmy, the roommate" in the 1919 "Exorcism" and "Jimmy Tomorrow" in the 1939 *The Iceman Cometh*. Like his first recreation of Byth, the Old Man in *A Wife for a Life*, who is cynical about the virtue of women, Ted is a "pitiless dissector of women's souls." Ted maintains that he and John must have purchased the alcohol they are drinking "down on the water front" the previous evening. The friendship between O'Neill and Byth grew when they lived at the waterfront saloon, Jimmy the Priest's. In Act IV Ted is a successful drama critic on a Chicago newspaper. Byth had also worked for a time in the theater.

†O'Neill is probably recalling a personal experience. To provide his first wife, Kathleen, with evidence of infidelity, he had gone

Strindbergian. The struggling young artist here resembles the sculptor Bertel Thorvaldsen, who leaves home
and lives with fellow bohemians in Strindberg's first play,
I Rom. This play may not have been translated and made
available to O'Neill before he wrote *Bread and Butter*,
but the fact that both dramatists in their first year of
writing explore the same theme makes the similarities
between the plays even more remarkable. The battle of
the sexes in the last act of *Bread and Butter* shows the
definite influence on O'Neill of Strindberg's *The Dance of
Death*. John says to Maud that life could "still hold something pleasant if we've only the courage to break our
chains. . . . Is there any reason in God's world why we
should be confined together like two cats in a bag?" Later
he remarks: "We're two corpses chained together. . . .
Death is the only cure for this marriage."*

John's sister Bessie visits him and tries to give her
brother a new incentive for love and for work. She tells
him how successful his three former roommates have
become. He informs her of the "tragic irony of fate"; the
day before his marriage, he received a check from *Col-
per's Weekly* and an offer to do some illustrating for the
magazine. For Maud's sake he had not answered the
letter.

After Bessie leaves, John shows his resolve to change
his life when he "picks up the bottle as if to pour out a
drink; then puts it down again with an exclamation of
disgust." At this point Maud enters the room, "her face
twisted with rage." She has been eavesdropping and
makes wild accusations about Bessie's relationship with
Carter before their marriage. John calls her a "devil of a

to a hotel with a prostitute, having previously arranged to be
caught by a "witness."

*In *The Dance of Death* Alice speaks of her marriage to the
Captain: "We are welded together—we can't escape. Once we
did separate—in our own home—for five years. Now only death
can separate us. We know it, so we wait for him as the deliverer."

woman"; he attempts to strangle her, and, failing in this, rushes out of the room and upstairs. The silence of the house is "broken by the muffled report of a revolver."

Bread and Butter is a dismal failure that splits into three disorganized parts, corresponding to the three conflicts of its hero: his struggle in Act I against the provincial forces of home and family; his inner artist-businessman dichotomy in Acts II and III; the battle of the sexes in Act IV. O'Neill combined all these elements more successfully a decade later in *The Great God Brown*. In this the mask becomes the symbol of the artist's alienation. Only when wearing it is Dion Anthony, another failed artist, accepted by his wife and family. Like John Brown, Dion can say: "I am an artist in soul." The point O'Neill makes in both plays is that there are forces at work—selfishness, greed, materialism—to crush the soul of the artist, to weigh him down. The external representation of these forces manifests itself, at times, in something as simple as a name. In *Bread and Butter* Carter says: "Even his name—John Brown! Isn't that the hell of a name for an artist? Look better at the top of a grocery store than at the bottom of a painting. The only thing recorded in the Book of Fame about a John Brown is that his body lies moldering in the grave." O'Neill assigns the name Brown to the central character in *The Great God Brown*, the businessman William A. Brown, whose prosaic soul has artistic longings. At the end of the play, after Brown has assumed the mask of Dion Anthony, the businessman and artist merge, a feat denied John Brown in *Bread and Butter*.

8. *Bound East for Cardiff*

In the late winter of 1914 O'Neill began a play he called *Children of the Sea*. The second version was given the title *Bound East for Cardiff*.* The one-acter has the distinction of being the first of O'Neill's works to be produced. While vacationing at Provincetown in the summer of 1916, O'Neill was approached by the Provincetown Players and asked to give a reading of one of his works. The drama selected, *Bound East for Cardiff*, was enthusiastically received by the group, and by the audience when it was later staged on July 28, 1916.

As the title implies, a ship, the British tramp steamer *Glencairn*, is making its way to Cardiff, having set sail several weeks earlier in New York. The setting is the seamen's forecastle on a foggy night shortly before eight o'clock. Lying on one of the bunks is a sailor named Yank, who has been injured in an accident. He does not fear death itself, only the thought of dying alone. Alternating between states of consciousness and unconsciousness, he clings desperately to his sole last wish: to have his friend, Driscoll, remain at his bedside. Driscoll, "a brawny Irishman with the battered features of a prizefighter," rages inwardly because he can do nothing to alleviate Yank's suffering. The other sailors also stand by helplessly; all mouth sincere but awkward words of encouragement and cheer. Depressed, the men seem anxious to begin their watch. When the bell tolls eight times, they stumble numbly out into the oppressive fog. To Driscoll, who should also respond to the summons, Yank says in "an agony of fear": "Don't leave me, Drisc! I'm dyin'." Driscoll has no intention of abandoning his friend.

*The copyright date is May 14, 1914.

The inept captain and the second mate enter; the former takes Yank's temperature and discovers that he has a fever. In response to Driscoll's plea for help, the captain only shakes his head: "I can't do anything else for him. It's too serious for me. If this had only happened a week later we'd be in Cardiff in time to—."

When the two friends are alone again, Driscoll declares wildly that he will not let Yank die. The latter is philosophical about death: "It can't be no worser'n this." He enumerates all the hardships of a sailor's life, stressing its loneliness. One dream, he confesses, has sustained him: that he and Driscoll would eventually settle down on land one day in Canada or Argentina and buy a farm. Driscoll says that he, too, has had that dream. From this point on, the room and its furnishings seem remote and misty to Yank. Dreamily, he relives the good and bad times he and Driscoll shared the last five years. One particular memory chills him: he had stabbed a man at Cape Town. Although he "ain't never had religion," Yank fears God will hold it against him. Then he reasons, "They say He sees everything. He must know it was done in fair fight, in self defense." Driscoll says, reassuringly, that if he had a record as good as Yank's, "I'd not be afraid av the angel Gabriel himself." Yank disposes of his next pay, asking Driscoll to "divvy up with the rest of the boys."

In the early version of *Children of the Sea*, Driscoll asks: "But have ye no relations at all to call your own?" Yank replies: "The old lady died when I was a kid, and the old man croaked when I was fourteen; the old booze got him. I've got two brothers but to hell with them! They're too respectable to want news of me dead or alive." Yank, having suffered the indignities of fate all his life, longs in the depths of his soul to die in dignity: "Why should it be a rotten night like this with that damned whistle blowin' and people snorin' all round? I wish the stars was out, and the moon, too; I c'd lie out on deck and look at them, and it'd make it easier to go—somehow."

Yank realizes the end is near. Suddenly, he "stares

straight in front of him with eyes starting from their sockets" and inquires, "Who's that?" When Driscoll asks whom he means, Yank whispers, "A pretty lady dressed in black." Yank dies and Driscoll makes the sign of the cross, sinking to his knees: "his lips move in some half-remembered prayer." Cocky, one of the sailors, comes in and announces, "The fog's lifted." He gazes at Yank's motionless body with a look of awed recognition of what has occurred.

Internal evidence suggests O'Neill did not write *Children of the Sea* and *Bound East for Cardiff* at two distinct time periods. The latter is merely a revision of the former, even though the titles are dissimilar. When later plays were revised, their titles seldom changed drastically, as in this case, and the evolutionary process was clearly discernable. The *dramatis personae* is the same in the two versions except that in the first version the Swede is called "Oleson" rather than "Olson"; the accordionist is identified simply as "a Norwegian" rather than as "Paul"; and a first mate, not a second mate, accompanies the captain to the forecastle. In the early version the steamer is not given a name, and Driscoll is described as "a red-headed giant." The action in both is the same throughout. The ending of the second version is a little tighter. In the first script Yank bleeds from the mouth after his death, and Driscoll begins the "Our Father" twice but can only remember the first line.

The care O'Neill took in writing *Bound East for Cardiff* demonstrates his awareness of the value of this play. It was his first true success. All the elements—characters, setting, language—come together in a symmetrical whole. O'Neill knew the sea and the life of a sailor. The setting is strikingly realistic; the small details, such as the sea chests, the light, and the oilskins, are effectively drawn. The dialects of the sailors are believable. Surprisingly, in such a short work, the men are given individualizing traits and attitudes. They are not merely part of a background crowd.

These are men the dramatist had known at sea. One of the most remarkable things about this play is the sailors' spirit of camaraderie. Throughout the work they commiserate with one another in an effort to cope with their miserable lot. For the first time in his work, O'Neill's social statement becomes an integral part of the fabric of a play. The men complain about the food on "this rusty lime-juicer," which Scotty calls "a starvation ship." Davis adds: "Plenty o' work and no food—and the owners ridin' around in carriages!"

Yank's vision, the "pretty lady dressed in black," is far more believable than the mystical elements in the earlier *Thirst* and *Fog*. When writing this new sea play, O'Neill could not resist the temptation to include at least a passing reference to a shipwreck. Driscoll reminisces about the night "the auld Dover wint down." He and Yank managed to get into one of the boats. They drifted for seven days with scarcely any food or water. "Twas Yank here that held me down whin I wanted to jump into the ocean, roarin' mad wid the thirst. Picked up we were on the same day wid only Yank in his senses."

Most of the characters in *Bound East for Cardiff* appear later in three other sea plays: *In the Zone* (1917), *The Long Voyage Home* (1917), and *The Moon of the Caribbees* (1918). Because of their similarities, these three plays and *Bound East for Cardiff* are classified as one unit, bearing the title the *Glencairn* series.

9. *Abortion*

O'Neill turned from his sea experiences, used in *Bound East for Cardiff*, to those of his personal life in his next one-acter, *Abortion*.* The focus of this work is the inability of a young man, Jack Townsend (a self-portrait), to cope with guilt. Jack has callously cast aside a poor trusting young girl whom he impregnated. It has been a loveless affair on his part, and he has merely used her selfishly. O'Neill is probably dramatizing the anguish he himself experienced after his loveless affair with Kathleen Jenkins. His brief stay at Princeton apparently inspired details of the setting, a student's study "on the ground floor of a dormitory in a large eastern university of the United States." It is an early evening in June during commencement week, and the students are honoring Jack, the captain of the baseball team, for his role in winning the championship game.

In the opening scene Jack's mother and nineteen-year-old sister, Lucy, return to the study with his roommate, Donald "Bull" Herron, "a huge swarthy six-footer with a bull neck and an omnipresent grin." An ominous note is struck when Joe Murray, a young fellow of eighteen, appears and asks for Jack. O'Neill uses physical qualities here to delineate different social classes. Herron, a gigantic "All-American tackle," is extraordinarily healthy looking, while the slight, stoop-shouldered Murray has the "large feverish black eyes, thin lips, pasty complexion, and the sunken cheeks of a tuberculosis victim." Herron haughtily disposes of Murray, telling him to wait elsewhere.

After his entrance, Jack becomes "visibly uneasy"

*The date of the copyright is May 19, 1914.

when told a "townie" has tried to see him. Because of his
athletic ability, Jack, "a well-built handsome young fellow
about twenty-two years old," has "become a figure of note
in college circles and is accustomed to the deference of
those around him." He is obviously spoiled by his parents
and adored by his beautiful, dark-haired fiancée, Evelyn
Sands, who takes delight in the thought that Jack belongs
exclusively to her: "He is *mine, mine!*" In view of later
revelations, Evelyn's words of adulation are ironic. She
tells Jack that his conduct on the field symbolizes "the way
you would always play, in the game of life—fairly, square-
ly, strengthening those around you, refusing to weaken at
critical moments, advancing others by sacrifices." Jack
promises to conform to this ideal, pointedly adding "in
the future."

Alone with his father, a distinguished, well-pre-
served, somber alumnus of the university, Jack loses his
self-assurance. Townsend says he was glad the son came
to him for help when he "got in this trouble with Nellie
Murray," but he is dismayed now that Jack has not responded to the note the young woman wrote after her
abortion five days earlier. Asked if he is certain he was the
father of the aborted child, Jack admits that he has played
the "scoundrel all the way through"; he would like to
reply in the negative. "To even think such is an insult to a
sweet girl. For she is a sweet, lovely girl in spite of
everything, and if I had loved her the least particle, if I
had not been in love with Evelyn, I should certainly have
married her."

The father wonders aloud why his son had the affair.
He is reminded of his own indiscretion as a student by his
son and "stares at the floor in moody retrospection." He
comments: "We've retained a large portion of the original
mud in our make-up. That's the only answer I can think
of."

Jack.   That's it! Do you suppose it was the same man
                 who loves Evelyn who did this other thing! No,
                 a thousand times no, such an idea is abhorrent.

> It was the male beast who ran gibbering through
> the forest after its female thousands of years
> ago.

Townsend. Come, Jack, that is pure evasion. You are responsible for the Mr. Hyde in you as well as for
the Dr. Jekyll. Restraint—

When Jack attempts to place the blame on society, his
father remarks: "Save your radical arguments for the
younger generation."

The snobbish Townsend cannot understand why his
son became involved with a poor working-class girl; an
upper-class young woman, he believes, would never have
had a premarital sexual relationship. Jack assures his father
that the girl's family knows nothing of the abortion. She
has a silly, unsuspecting widowed mother, a brother who
is only home on weekends, and two sisters, who are both
under ten. Jack believes that he has paid for his mistake
through his "glance into the abyss." The older man attempts to bury the unpleasant past. Cheerfully, he shakes
hands with Jack: "All's well that ends well. You've learned
your lesson."

Townsend goes out to watch the parade just as Murray returns and informs Jack that his sister is dead. He
accuses Jack and his "dirty skunk of a doctor" of murdering his beloved sister. Like Mary Tyrone in *Long Day's
Journey into Night* and Ella O'Neill in real life, Nellie has
had a "faker of a doctor." Jack has behaved like a coward,
and Murray intends to make him pay for his actions, even
if he has "to go to hell for it!" He will not allow Jack to
"get away with that stuff" and "marry some goil" of his
own kind.

The tragic news has a profound effect on Jack. "His
eyes are haunted, full of despair, as he vainly seeks to
escape from the remorse which is torturing him." According to Murray, after Nellie's death, the negligent doctor
had given the brother "blood money" to keep quiet. Jack's
eyes light "up with a gleam of hope"; he offers Murray

"ten times as much" if he will agree not to punish the innocent: his parents, sister, and Evelyn. The offer infuriates Murray. He pulls a revolver from his coat pocket, but the physically stronger Jack takes it from him. Murray leaves, threatening to call the police. As the parade passes the windows of the study, Jack can hear the students wildly chanting his name. He cries out: "No! No! For God's sake!" He picks up the revolver and "presses it to his temple. The report is drowned by the cheering."

Evelyn enters, and like the spurned wife in *Bread and Butter*, she discovers the body of another of O'Neill's unfortunate heroes. The self-inflicted single shot is the most popular method of committing suicide in the canon. Nearly two decades later, both Christine and Orin Mannon shoot themselves. In an early draft of *Days Without End*, John Loving attempts to shoot himself before a statue in church.

The common motive for most of the suicides in O'Neill's dramas is guilt. Usually the central character has committed some heinous crime and cannot endure the accusations of his conscience. Neither the author nor his characters punish the wrong-doer; he punishes himself. Earlier Murray had asked Jack why he hadn't answered Nellie's letter: "Yuh knew she was sick and never answered it. She might'a lived if she thought yuh cared, if she heard from yuh; but she knew yuh were tryin' to git rid of her." Although O'Neill had married Kathleen Jenkins when he discovered she was pregnant, he abandoned her after the ceremony and sailed for Honduras. His guilt is manifested in his work; throughout the canon, from these early one-acters to the late dramas, such as *A Touch of the Poet* and the unfinished "The Visit of Malatesta," young women are seduced and impregnated by men who either subsequently abandon them or reluctantly marry them.

Abortion is an inconsequential effort. Like many of the early plays, it is merely a cathartic indulgence. The inclusion of taboo topics such as abortion in these works indicates that O'Neill was clearly ahead of his time. Usually, however, he was prompted to insert them not to revolt against Puritanical codes but to assuage his own guilt-ridden conscience.

10.   *The Movie Man*

The Movie Man, the final effort of O'Neill's first year as
fledgling dramatist,* appears to be, on the surface, a
traditional melodrama. A handsome American hero,
Henry (Hen) Rogers, aids a beautiful young Mexican
woman, Anita Fernandez, in rescuing her father from a
firing squad and the vindictiveness of the villain, General
Virella. *The Movie Man* is more than mere melodrama;
subtitled "A Comedy in One Act," it is a satire on war, the
media's coverage of it, and the film industry.

Rogers and a photographer, Al Devlin, both representatives of Earth Motion Picture Company, are filming
a one-sided version of an ongoing revolution in Mexico.
Billeted in a house in a large town in northern Mexico,
they are in the protective custody of Pancho Gomez,†
commander-in-chief of the Constitutionalist Army. In exchange for money, guns, and ammunition, Gomez has
agreed to give Rogers exclusive rights to film the campaign being waged to conquer the countryside and, ultimately, Mexico City. The bungling, alcoholic General
Gomez utters no stirring revolutionary slogans. He is
more concerned with appeasing his aide, General Virella,
who wants his enemy, Ernesto Fernandez, shot, than in
planning his overall battle strategy. The more scotch that

---

*The copyright date is July 1, 1914. O'Neill mistakenly included
the play among those he wrote in 1916 while in Provincetown.
Clark also believed that it was written in 1916, listing it as one of
four destroyed dramas.

†The prototype for Pancho Gomez is probably Francisco "Pancho" Villa, who tried to overthrow the repressive President
Victariano Huerta in 1913. Villa's enemy, Emiliano Zapata, also
led a revolt against the regime.

Rogers pours into Gomez, the nearer Mexico City becomes—theoretically.

When the play opens, Rogers and Devlin banter
good-naturedly, vexing the Mexican soldier who stands
guard at Gomez's field headquarters. Their only interest
is in obtaining good action shots of all the battles. Devlin
is annoyed that General Virella had recently attacked the
enemy before the camera had been set up to photograph
the assault. Whatever his faults, Virella is concerned for
the safety of his men; he asks: "Shall my glorious soldiers
be massacred waiting for your machine?"

The movie makers seem indifferent to the moral
implications of the execution at sunrise the following day
of Fernandez, "a good fellow," who had been educated in
the United States.* They plan to request that the event be
postponed until later in the morning because the light will
be better at that time. Rogers tells Devlin, "It'll make a
great picture. Be sure and get it." O'Neill stresses the
efforts the movie makers undertake to exploit the sensa-
tional elements of the struggle, and, in doing so, he
anticipates the extensive and frequently objectionable
media coverage of subsequent wars. The dramatist also
attacks Americans who think they can, with impunity,
manipulate or destroy governments of other countries,
particularly those to the south of the United States.

Later, after Rogers meets Anita, he tries to save her
father by striking a bargain with Gomez, who wants to
launch a major attack that night. Rogers reads a clause in
the contract stipulating that Gomez is "to fight no battles
at night or on rainy days or at any time whatsoever when
the light is so poor as to make the taking of motion pictures
impracticable." Gomez is reminded of the great debt he
owes the American:

> Who buys and sends you most of your ammunition, eh?
> Who pays you and the other Generals and the Germans in

---

*Fernandez is probably a portrait of Venustiano Carranza, who
became president of Mexico after President Woodrow Wilson
ordered a military intervention.

charge of your artillery—the only men who savvys how to
use the guns right—eh? Who has promised to see that you
get siege guns for Mexico City? . . . And, above all, who
has promised to help you become President when you reach
Mexico City?

When Gomez threatens to have Rogers shot, the
American replies: "Nix on that rough stuff! You wouldn't
dare. You've got to keep on the right side of the U.S.A. or
your revolution isn't worth the powder to blow it to—
Mexico." Gomez asks to be allowed to break the contract
this once. "The plan is fine, the town will be ours, my
soldiers will steal and no more grumble against Gomez.
Tomorrow I will shoot all the prisoners for your pictures, I
promise eet." The price Rogers demands in return for his
concession is the life of Fernandez. Gomez "twirls his
mustache"; if he frees Fernandez he will have to shoot
General Virella: "Mexico ess to es-small for those two
humbres—both alive."

After they have struck a bargain, Gomez pulls a flask
from his pocket, and, using words that were to be immortalized in the film *Casablanca*, says to Rogers, "Here
ess looking at you!" The General has no integrity; the two
Americans are brash and overbearing. Neither shows any
compassion for those involved in the struggle until Rogers
becomes enamored of Anita. He is motivated not by
justice but by lust when he says to her, boastingly, "I'll
save your old man if I have to start a revolution of my own
to do it." Anita invites Rogers to her home, "the first
Hacienda beyond the hill," the next day and assures him
he will be like her "father's son" to the family. After
Rogers extracts the promise of another type of relationship with her, he commences a Spanish dance and concludes the play with a few bars of "Mexico, my bright-
eyed Mexico."

The Movie Man is an extremely short, immature
work. The setting, characters, and plot are barely established before the one-acter is brought to an abrupt
close. Although he satirizes the "movie man," O'Neill's

primary purpose in writing the one-acter seems to have been his desire to make an antiwar statement.* He does so subtly here in a comedy. Later, during World War I, he was to write two tragedies, *The Sniper* and *In the Zone*. In the early 1940s, during World War II, he began but did not complete three antitotalitarian plays. Unlike his insensitive hero in *The Movie Man*, O'Neill was deeply concerned about the cruelties of men perpetrated against each other while justifying their actions in the name of an honorable war.

---

*In his introduction to the collection of O'Neill plays, Lawrence Gellert suggests that the author presages World War I: the play was completed before the assassination of Archduke Ferdinand at Sarajevo. Gellert writes: *"The Movie Man* is O'Neill early caught in a rare, playful mood—he banters and ridicules the foibles of Hollywood. And the most remarkable thing about it all is that actually O'Neill could anticipate from the shadowy embryonic form at this writing . . . 1914, the swollen monstrosity to come." *The Movie Man* was included in the *Lost Plays of Eugene O'Neill* (New York: New Fathoms Press, 1950), p. 9.

11. *Servitude*

O'Neill labelled *Servitude*, written in the late summer of
1914,* "A Play in Three Acts." A photograph of the dramatist taken at this time reveals that he could have used his
own mirrored reflection to describe his hero, David Roylston, a successful playwright and novelist: "He is a tall,
slender, dark-haired man of thirty-five with large handsome features, a strong ironical mouth half-hidden by a
black mustache, and keenly-intelligent dark eyes." He
wears a white shirt and black bow tie. Unfortunately, the
character's insensitive attitude to women seems to reflect
his creator's at this particular period in his life. Roylston
talks and writes about enlightenment and freedom for
women, yet he encourages his own wife to live, as the title
implies, in servitude.

At the beginning of the first act, Roylston is shown
working in a comfortable study in his house at Tarryville-
on-the-Hudson, New York. He is, from all appearances, a
wealthy man; working for him are a man-servant, Benton;
a gardener, Weson; a chauffeur; and, assuredly, offstage
maids. Two classes of people inhabit the terrain O'Neill
creates in his early plays: the destitute misfits who struggle to survive but are ultimately crushed by fate, and the
ultra-rich, frequently socially prominent, powerful individuals, who are overly attached to their possessions.
While the latter are usually castigated and eventually
shown to be shallow, greedy, and morally bankrupt,
O'Neill seems somewhat envious of them in the early
plays. There is in him the same wistful longing Mary
Tyrone displays as she observes the wealthy Chatfields in
Long Day's Journey into Night.

---

*The date of copyright is September 23, 1914.

Benton, whose sole distinguishing feature is a badly crossed eye, which gives him "a look of sly villainy," announces the unexpected arrival of Ethel Frazer. Although he professes to be working intensely on his latest play, Roylston is flattered and agrees to see the woman, believing her to be a frustrated writer needing his advice. He is visibly impressed by Ethel's striking beauty. She possesses the physical attributes O'Neill admires most and bestows on many of his heroines: "Her complexion is pale; her eyes large, expressive, dark; her hair black and wavy; her figure inclining a little toward voluptuousness." The daughter of a deceased, wealthy lawyer, "the baby and pet of the family," she has left her husband, a Wall Street broker, eight months ago, after seven years of marriage, proclaiming to have been liberated by Roylston's novels and plays. His novel, *The Street*, an exposé of Wall Street brokerage houses, has showed her that everything her husband "was interested in was so shallow" and that their life "together was the merest sham." His heroine in his play *Sacrifice*, Mrs. Harding, who leaves her husband after being "awakened," is her inspiration.

Lacking specific training for a job, Ethel learned typing and shorthand, and she bought a plain black dress, apparently the prerequisite in O'Neill's mind for obtaining a secretarial position. The working world shocks her sensibilities: "The men were all such beasts and the women I had to come in contact with were so unintelligent and ordinary." After repulsing the advances of her employer, whom she had considered a gentleman until his display of passion,* she was fired. Ethel then goes to Roylston's

---

*In an early draft of *Anna Christie*, Anna, who is also a secretary, loses her job when she spurns an ardent employer, a gentleman. O'Neill's women have a narrow range of employment opportunities. They usually live within the safe confines of a husband's or father's home or earn their living as prostitutes. Most are completely dependent on men. Infrequently portrayed are women like Eleanor Cape, in *Welded*, a free-spirited, independent actress, who balks at the marital restrictions imposed by her husband.

home, seeking his assurance that she is "on the right path." Roylston's wife and two children are in New York to attend the theater and are not scheduled to return until the following afternoon.

Ethel has missed the last train to the city and is stranded in Roylston's country estate. He invites her to stay in his home that night and offers her a job typing for him. She must, he says, put aside the "worn-out code of ethics" and prove she is truly liberated. Asked how his wife would react to her presence, Roylston speaks contemptuously of her; his work comes before any family relationship. At the end of the first act Ethel confesses that she deliberately missed the train in order to test Roylston, to see if he has the courage of his convictions. The writer's passions are aroused by this woman; after she ascends the stairs, he finds that he can no longer continue working on his manuscript.

During the second act, which opens at nine the following morning, Ethel discovers gradually that her idol has feet of clay. Benton informs her that Roylston enjoys being pursued by mobs of women and callously reads parts of their letters to his wife. Alice Roylston returns unexpectedly; she wants to consult the family doctor about her daughter's illness the previous evening. She assumes that Ethel is the special woman her husband has been meeting in New York, the one who "had left her home to work out her salvation."

In one of the most improbable scenes O'Neill ever wrote, Alice reveals all her secret inadequacies to her supposed rival and offers to move out, stating that Ethel is more entitled to live in this home than she. The wife reveals that she had been her father-in-law's secretary and that Roylston had married her eleven years earlier because he thought "he had to." The father then angrily disinherited the son, and Alice took a secretarial position by day to support the family and typed her husband's manuscripts at night. The nobility and purity of this woman's love for her husband prompt Ethel to exclaim: "How

much you have taught me! Happiness, then, means servitude?" The wife responds: "Love means servitude; and
my love is *my* happiness."

Roylston enters and assumes that his wife is not at all
jealous to discover that a strange woman had spent the
night in their home. He salutes his "Angel of Trustful-
ness" and says mockingly: "My dear Alice, you really are
the perfect wife." Ethel informs Roylston of his wife's
suspicions that she is his mistress and the author of the
letters Alice has read. Roylston coldly tells his wife that
she has insulted him and his friend and that he will move
out of the house to avoid living "with a wife who is also an
evil-minded spy." Alice begs her husband's forgiveness
and asks him to allow her to leave, thus giving him his
freedom. The curtain falls as she rushes out of the room.

There is no time lapse between the second and third
acts. Roylston, in an amazing display of arrogance, acts
like the wounded party; he feels betrayed because his
wife read letters foolish women sent him. He has no
understanding of how much pain he inflicted on her every
time he arrogantly displayed them. Now that his faith in
his wife is shattered, he says, he will have "to hunt a new
illusion." The man is so dense that he fails to comprehend
Ethel's pointed remarks that she, too, has become disillusioned—in him. His cruel vanity, she remarks, "has
torn off the mask." She now sees him merely as an egotist
"whose hands are bloody with the human sacrifices he has
made—to himself!"

Ethel explains the lesson she learned from his wife.
Using details from the story Alice had told her earlier,
Ethel reminds him of all the sacrifices his wife has made
for him throughout the years, stressing those made immediately after their marriage when he was struggling to
become an established playwright. After a few of Ethel's
illuminating speeches, Roylston is completely transformed—unbelievably so. The penitent exclaims: "Poor
Alice! What a woman she is!" He claims that the sin for
which Alice blames herself is his. He rhapsodizes about

the finer, happier future that will be his and Alice's: "Servitude in love, love in servitude! Logos in Pan, Pan in Logos! That is the great secret—and I never knew!" Feeling that her mission, to open his eyes and her own, has been accomplished, Ethel says she will now return to her husband. She will go back "to the chains which have suddenly become dear to me."

The doorbell rings, and George Frazer enters, looking haggard and grief-stricken. Seeing the two of them alone in the room he suspects the worst and pulls a revolver out of his pocket. Roylston wonders aloud when this "ludicrous melodrama will end." (It is a question any audience viewing this play would be tempted to repeat.) Frazer despondently throws down his gun and a dramatic reconciliation occurs. Ethel kneels before her husband, swears she is innocent, and says she loves only him. Frazer takes his wife in his arms and kisses her. At that precise moment Alice enters carrying a small suitcase. She is stunned to see the couple embracing. Ethel shakes hands with Alice, expresses her desire to be friends, and exits with Frazer.

Roylston enters for the second reconciliation. He admits for the first time that he is not as liberal in his thinking as he is in his writing. Fearful of the scandal his presence in the house the previous evening might create, he spent the night at a roadhouse. His pride prevented him from defending himself earlier. He kneels before his wife and promises her "a lifelong honeymoon."

Servitude has no merit whatsoever. The characters are mere caricatures: the wronged wife and her proud husband, the alleged "other woman" and her suicidal, jealous husband. The plot seems a pastiche of incidents and characters from Ibsen's plays. Mrs. Harding, the heroine in Roylston's play, *Sacrifice*, resembles Mrs. Alving, the awakened wife in *Ghosts*. Ethel's walking out on her husband seems a weak imitation of Nora's action at the conclusion of *A Doll's House*. Alice's jealousy of her writer-husband's new secretary mirrors Hedda's of Thea at the end of *Hedda Gabler*. In his "List of Plays," O'Neill records the title "Solitude" where *Servitude* should have been inserted. He seems either to have forgotten he had written this play or to wish he had not done so.

12.   *The Sniper*

The Sniper heads the 1915* entries of works written for Professor George Pierce Baker's English 47 class in O'Neill's "List of Plays."† Set in a shell-shattered cottage "on the outskirts of a small Belgian village," it is the dramatist's strongest protest against the war then raging in Europe. It would be wrong, however, to view the one-acter as merely an antiwar statement, for it goes beyond silent, broken bodies and ruined lives and questions the benevolence of a God who allows such manifestations of man's barbarity.

As the curtain rises, Rougon, an elderly Belgian peasant, carries the dead body of his son Charles into the bombed wreckage that was once their home. Laying the young soldier's body on the floor, he moans to himself "like a wounded animal." The village priest enters and tries to console Rougon with pious platitudes: "Pray to God for strength. We must all bow ourselves before His will."

Gradually, the earlier tragic events of the day are revealed. Charles had discovered that the Germans were planning a major offensive that would threaten those he

*The play was copyrighted May 13, 1915, and staged at The Playwrights' Theater on February 16, 1917.

†The last 1915 entry reads: "(Title Forgotten)—(One Act Adaptation of Short Story) Harvard—English 47 (Room on Mass. Ave., Cambridge)." Clark identifies the play as "The Dear Doctor," a one-act farce dramatized from a Black Cat story. O'Neill describes the plays he wrote for Baker as "rotten" and adds, "But it's rather funny about the one-acter. We thought it was slick enough for vaudeville, but when I began to see about the rights I found the story I'd based it on was stolen from a successful vaudeville sketch" (Clark, *Eugene O'Neill*, p. 18).

loved. He convinced his mother; his fiancée, Louise; and her family to leave that morning for Brussels. His father stubbornly remained behind, deeming it cowardly to flee. Having promised his son that he would not use a carefully concealed old rifle, although he fervently wished to do so, Rougon hid in the well on his property when the battle commenced. He saw his son laughing with his comrades after the Germans were beaten back. But suddenly "one of their devilish flying machines" attacks. Rougon watched helplessly while his barn burned and the roof of his house tumbled in. Then he saw his son fall, and he rushed to him, "but it was too late."

Rougon is portrayed in the beginning of the play as a man whose faith in God, while somewhat shaken by his son's death, is still strong. He possesses a vital inner belief that goes deeper than such outward symbols as the large black crucifix hanging over the door. Until today, his son had been his sole purpose for living; now only the thought of his wife, Margot, sustains him and restrains him from committing a rash deed. Rougon longs to avenge the young inexperienced soldiers, who died so senselessly: "With my little rifle in there I could pick off more Prussian swine than a whole regiment of youngsters like my poor Charles."

The priest calms Rougon and persuades him to swear "before God who watches over us" that he will not resort to violence. The priest kneels beside Charles, intoning a prayer in which the words "Infinite justice, Infinite love, Infinite pity," stand out "from the general mumble of sing-song sentences." The irony of this "futile prayer penetrates the sorrow-numbed brain of Rougon and proves the last straw." The father weeps bitterly, asking: "Why did not God take me instead?"

A young German captain enters and tells the priest that the town's inhabitants must not commit any acts of violence against German soldiers. "Civilians caught with arms will be immediately shot." After the soldier leaves, Jean, a young boy who had gone that morning with Rougon's wife to seek safety, enters. The priest calms the trembling, frightened youth and draws from him his gruesome story. After traveling some distance, the group found itself caught in crossfire and flanked by the dead and wounded of both armies. "Then everything around blew up." Jean was hurt. When he rallied, he saw the dead bodies of the villagers "all around." To leave no doubt as to the fate of Rougon's wife and his son's fiancée, O'Neill describes the former as having "a big hole" in her chest and the latter as having "a hole in her head." Jean had found his way home "like one in a trance."

When Rougon hears the German troops approaching, he rushes to get his rifle and positions himself at a breach in the wall. He fires one shot for his wife, one for Louise. Immediately, German soldiers swarm the room and form a firing squad. The German captain tells Rougon that if he has a prayer to say, he should do it quickly. The prisoner responds, "I want no prayers." The priest begs him to make his peace with God. Rougon spits on the floor: "That for your God who allows such things to happen."

The play is a melodramatic tableau, relying heavily on visual elements: the gutted house and its apparently meaningless religious images, the German gunmen, the dead son. It also makes excessive use of coincidence. Rougon is left Job-like, having lost everything he cherishes in a quick succession of events. Jean arrives precisely at the moment the German officer leaves; he finishes his story just as the troops march by. For a touch of irony, Charles dies on the day he was to have been married.

Rougan is credible at times as the grieving father, first seeking answers and finally justice; the priest is hopelessly one-dimensional. He does not respond in a normal, believable manner to Rougon's grief. But perhaps the author deliberately portrays the priest as ineffectual.

The entries in O'Neill's Work Diary for the war years, 1939–1943, demonstrate how utterly he detested the inhumane, barbaric forces that threatened freedom and civilization. The antiwar sentiments he expressed so eloquently during World War II reflect those he dramatized in World War I. The despair O'Neill manifested in the early 1940s mirrors Rougon's in the last scene of *The Sniper*. To O'Neill, the priest, who looks "down with infinite compassion at the still bodies of father and son," might represent some kind of God-equivalent. If this is so, the prospect is disturbing. Rougon, tried beyond human endurance, needs and deserves not a methodical bookkeeper-God but a compassionate, loving, and forgiving Father-God.

13.   *The Personal Equation*

In the spring of 1915, while he was a student in Professor George Pierce Baker's English 47 class, O'Neill completed the four-act "The Personal Equation."* With justification, the author maintained later that the plays he wrote for Baker "were rotten." He described "The Personal Equation" as "a rambling thing about a seamen's and firemen's strike."† The drama is more than a treatise on strikes; it is an important personal document revealing O'Neill's attitudes, political philosophy, and affiliations in 1915, one that provides insights into his relationship with his parents and friends.

"The Personal Equation" was the dramatist's strongest defense to date of anarchism. Most of its central characters are involved with the movement. Its hero is Tom Perkins, a radical activist for a group called both the I.W.U., the Independent Workers' Union, and the IWE, the International Workers of the Earth. A self-portrait, Tom has "large intelligent eyes" and is "handsome in a rough, manly, strong-featured way. His manner is one of boyishly naive enthusiasm with a certain note of defiance creeping in." He is in his early twenties, as O'Neill would have been in 1911, when the play is set. Tom's background resembles the author's: one year that he "wasted in college"; a round-trip voyage on an ocean steamer made with a pal, duplicating the writer's journey to Ar-

---

*The author identified "The Personal Equation" in the "List of Plays" as the last work written for Baker in the spring of 1915. The drama has never been copyrighted, published, or produced. The only extant copy, a typescript, is in the Theater Collection of Houghton Library, Harvard University.

†Clark, p. 18.

gentina on the *Charles Racine*; the crossing of the Atlantic in 1911 and arrival in England during the General Strike.

The model for the play's heroine, Olga Tarnoff, was the woman the author admired most in his youth, Emma Goldman, prominent anarchist and editor of the radical *Mother Earth*. Like Goldman, Olga is of Russian descent, delivers radical speeches in Union Square, advocates birth control and free love, and is violently opposed to war. In one of her first statements, Olga calls on men "not to shoot their brother men for a fetish of red, white, and blue, a mockery called patriotism." The speech is ironic, for at the end of the play a father will shoot his son for a far less important cause than patriotism. Olga is an attractive young woman with "strong, fine features, large spirited black eyes, slender supple figure."

When the play opens, Olga and Tom are shown in the Hoboken headquarters of the I.W.U. awaiting the arrival of Hartmann, their anarchist leader.* He had given Tom, who is an assistant cashier for the Ocean Steamship Company, strike pamphlets to distribute among the crew of the *San Francisco* when the ship arrived from Liverpool. For this misdeed, Tom was fired this morning. He dreads the task of conveying this information to his father, "a poor servile creature living in constant fear of losing his job." For thirty years he has been "in the same little rut" as second engineer for this steamship company.

The son rebels against everything his father repre-

---

*Although a Sadakichi Hartmann is listed among Goldman's friends in New York in the early twentieth century, the character in the play is actually a portrait of the Czech anarchist Hippolyte Havel, one of O'Neill's best friends in his Greenwich Village period. Havel became Goldman's lover in London in 1899, returned with her to the United States, and worked for her on *Mother Earth*. He was also the model for the anarchist Hugo Kalmar in *The Iceman Cometh*. Hartmann and Kalmar are described in similar terms. Each man has "long black hair," dark eyes which "peer near-sightedly from behind a pair of thick-rimmed spectacles," a head "too large for his body." Each dresses in black and wears a white shirt and a "flowing Windsor tie."

sents, although his radical friends believe that his love for
Olga rather than anarchist ardor prompted him to join the
movement. Having lived with Olga for six months, he
now asks her to marry him. She rejects "enforced servitude": "Do you want a signed certificate proving I am
yours—like a house and lot?" When the couple discusses
children, Olga insists she would kill herself rather than
have a child. "To me the birth of a child is a horrible
tragedy." If Tom created a better world, she would "be
proud and not ashamed to bear children."

Hartmann enters and announces the possibility of
war breaking out in Europe. Olga becomes belligerent. If
working men of all nations refused to work or to bear
arms, she insists, foolish leaders would have no one to
fight for them. Remembering Tom's previous stint as a
stoker on an ocean steamer, Hartmann asks him to disguise himself and ship out as Fred Donovan, a stoker, on
the *San Francisco*, the finest ship of the Ocean Steamship
Company, which controls the ship combine known as the
Ship Trust. Olga, traveling as a second-class passenger, is
told to meet Whitely, the I.W.U.'s contact in Liverpool,
who will give her dynamite* that Tom will use to destroy
the ship's engines. To inspire his followers, Hartmann
repeats the words of Danton: "It is necessary to dare, and
again to dare, and still again to dare."† Tom shudders at
the prospect that his father, the second engineer for the
San Francisco, will recognize him. As the first act closes,

---

*Emma Goldman became involved with the treacherous Donald
Vose, son of an anarchist friend, after he used dynamite to
destroy the *Times* building in Los Angeles. Vose betrayed his
coconspirator, Matthew Schmidt, who was charged with the
crime. In "The Personal Equation" one of the stokers is named
Schmidt. Vose was depicted later as Don Parritt in *The Iceman
Cometh*.

†O'Neill's obsessive interest in the French Revolution is manifested in his gallery of ardent Jacobins: Ramsay Fife in the notes
for *Dynamo*, Evan Harford in *A Touch of the Poet*, and Richard
Miller, a self-portrait, in *Ah, Wilderness!* The latter character
views Carlyle's *French Revolution* as a "great book"—especially

he expresses his determination to see the project through to its conclusion.

The second act seems like a scene in one of O'Neill's domestic dramas. It is set in the Perkinses' sitting room in a small home in Jersey City. It is 9:00 P.M. Elements in this scene foreshadow the last act of *Long Day's Journey into Night*: a father, consoled by alcohol, plays cards while he waits for his son to come home; the son, who returns reluctantly, accuses his father of lack of understanding. Thomas Perkins resembles James Tyrone in one respect, a physical feature that reappears in O'Neill's portraits of his father: he is "half bald but an unkempt fringe of thin grey hair straggles about his ears." He wears "ill-fitting shabby clothes."*

The father has revealed his attitude toward Tom in his earlier conversation with his friend Henderson, the first engineer of the S.S. *Empress*,† and in his remarks to his belligerent Irish housekeeper, Mrs. Allen, a middle-aged shrew with sharp features and an unpleasant, rasping voice. She chastises Perkins for "always findin' excuses" for Tom and for making sacrifices, sweating "in a dirty engine room to send him through school." O'Neill crossed out an autobiographical section after the word "school": "and a year in college. And what did he do in college I'd like to know? He never went back I notice." Also deleted is Perkins's response: "He didn't want to."

As in *Long Day's Journey into Night*, the son here "isn't like" his father; "he takes after his mother," who,

that part "about Mirabeau—and about Marat and Robespierre." In 1938, twenty-three years after he wrote "The Personal Equation," O'Neill developed an idea for a play on Robespierre, encompassing the personal and political rise and fall of the French leader.

*In *Long Day's Journey into Night* James Tyrone's grey hair is "thin with a bald spot like a monk's tonsure." His suit is "threadbare," for he believes in "wearing his clothes to the limit of usefulness."

†In the 1913 one-acter *Warnings*, the S.S. *Empress* had sunk a derelict and had then been sunk herself.

according to Henderson, "neverr perrmitted ye to call your soul your ain." The mother died when Tom "was a little chap." Because Perkins, like James O'Neill, was "away most of the time," Tom has been sent to boarding schools. The father tells Henderson: "I haven't seen much of him." The author deleted a later statement in which the father again compares his son and wife: "He is a good son—only he's different. It's just his way—like his mother." Perkins has failed not only to become president of the company, his wife's great plan for him, but also to be promoted during his thirty years of service. Yet he is utterly devoted to the sea, the company, and, above all, his beloved engines.

In their scene together, Tom informs his father of his relationship with Olga: that they are living together as "comrades." The son also admits that he is a member of the I.W.E. and that he will dynamite his father's engines if necessary to cripple the Ocean Steamship Company, a "thieving line" run by the "biggest financial bandits in Wall Street or in the country," the "greatest gang of crooked capitalists in the world." The father rejects Tom's argument that the seamen are underpaid and overworked; he is disturbed to discover that Tom has been discharged in disgrace, but, in a conciliatory gesture, he offers him money. Tom spurns the money and says: "I've tried to think of you as my father,* tried to feel like a son toward you, but it's time to give up the pretense. You're in one world and I'm in another." After the son departs, the father breaks down and sobs sorrowfully.

When the third act opens, two weeks have elapsed. The first scene is set in the firemen's forecastle of the *San Francisco*, now docked in Liverpool. Assembled are O'Rourke, "a giant of a red-headed Irishman"; Cocky, a

---

*The son's words here, supposedly spoken in 1911, resemble those of Edmund Tyrone a year later in *Long Day's Journey* when he denounces his father and says "I've tried to make allowances." He also asserts: "I hate your guts!"

squat, broad-shouldered, pasty-faced man; Harris; and
Schmidt. The stokers express their opinions of two events
that are occurring that evening on shore: a meeting of the
officers of the union to discuss a possible strike against the
shipowners and a dinner given for the officers of the *San
Francisco* by her owners to celebrate their successful
efforts to avoid a strike. The contrast is made between the
men dining lavishly at the banquet and the stokers "dyin'
wid the heat and thirst in this stinkin' rat's hole." Drunkenly singing "Whiskey Johnny," Hogan, a stoker, comes
on board. He waves a newspaper and announces a "bloody
war wid the Dutchmen is comin'." When Hogan and
Schmidt argue and go outside to fight, the men follow,
delighted that the war has already started.

Olga, dressed in men's clothes, comes into the forecastle and warns Tom that they can expect no support
from the union leaders, who have decided not to strike.
They have been bought off by the shipping companies and
have "crawled behind patriotism," using the excuse that
"beloved Brittania might become involved in a great
war." The young woman's attitude has changed considerably in the last two weeks. Discovering that she is pregnant, she adopts a maternal tone and tells Tom: "I'll bring
up our child with a soul freed from all adorations of Gods
and governments if I have to live alone on a mountain top
to do it." She begs Tom to abandon the plan to dynamite
the engines. Whitely enters and tells them that the man
scheduled to bring the dynamite has been arrested. He
now wants to prevent the *San Francisco* from sailing the
next day and to promote a strike on board that he hopes
will spread to other ships. When Whitely describes the
treachery of the union leaders, the stokers become enraged and offer to help Tom smash the ship's engines.
Olga alone has some reservations—and a premonition of
tragedy.

Scene 2 shows Perkins in the engine room guarding
his beloved engines. He takes up a revolver and points it

at the approaching stokers. Seeing his son, the second engineer chokes with emotion, but still he warns the crowd that he will shoot the first man who touches the engines. Tom laughs contemptuously at the man who has been a coward all his life. Perkins issues a second warning to his son, but Tom begins smashing the face of a gauge with his iron bar. The report of a revolver is heard. Struck in the head, the son "pitches forward on his face and lies unconscious."

When the fourth act opens in a Liverpool hospital, three weeks have passed. Tom's mind has been shattered. He will be "like a little child for the rest of his life." The doctor tells Olga: "There is little hope for his reason—*but*—there is always a hope!" Ironically, Tom's father has been promoted to chief engineer for the stand he took when the men mutinied. He tells Olga that he never meant to fire the revolver. The two struggle for the right to take care of Tom in the future. Finally, in desperation, Olga discloses that she will soon have a child: "If you do not let me have Tom, I will kill it." The two are eventually reconciled and agree to take care of Tom together. Melodramatically, Tom wakes and holds out one hand to Olga, the other to his father. Convinced that his son has forgiven him, the father departs.

Whitely tells Olga of his resolve to enlist now that war has broken out. He assures her that Kropotkin himself and all the socialists and syndicalists are united to crush German militarism. Olga ponders the efficacy of Tom's sacrifice and decides it was worthwhile. Her final statement expresses her determination to pursue the goals of anarchism: "Long live the Revolution!" With a stupid smile on his face, Tom mimics her: "Long—live—the Revolution!"

Professor Baker was correct when he remarked that his pupil needed a second year of work, that he could not, after one year, "manage the longer forms." If staged, "The Personal Equation" would require five different settings.

The plot is predictable; most of the characters are stereotypes: the noble father, the rebellious son, the reckless,
bomb-throwing radicals. The dialogue becomes, in places,
an anarchist diatribe. "The Personal Equation" was, however, a worthwhile experiment in the area of full-length
drama on O'Neill's part, becoming one more link in the
vast dramaturgic chain he forged.

Despite its deficiencies, the work is one of the author's most important plays, not as a piece of dramatic
literature but as a revealing personal testament. It demonstrates his social concerns, anticipating issues he raised
six years later in *The Hairy Ape*. In both dramas, stokers
are depicted as oppressed victims, shipowners as greedy,
corrupt capitalists. In the early play Tom speaks of having
seen "the contrast between us grimy stokers and the first
class cabin people lolling in their deck-chairs." *The Hairy
Ape* illustrates the conflict by showing the stokers in the
firemen's forecastle in the first scene and the wealthy
Mildred Douglas on the promenade deck in the second.
O'Neill's friend Driscoll is the model for Yank in *The
Hairy Ape* as well as for O'Rourke in "The Personal Equation." The latter, after his fight with Schmidt, wants to
make himself presentable when he hears Olga is approaching the forecastle. Her appearance among the stokers foreshadows Mildred's visit to the stokehold in *The
Hairy Ape*. Anarchist propaganda permeates both plays;
each of them has one scene set in the headquarters of the
I.W.W.

Sporadically throughout his life O'Neill manifested
his adherence to anarchism, believing it to be a means to
achieve social and economic equality. Citing formative
influences on him for 1907–1908 in the "Cycles," he
writes: "M.O. Grey—his studio—anarchism." His most
accurate self-portraits share his political beliefs: the radical Richard Miller in *Ah, Wilderness!*, the "Socialist anarchist" Edmund Tyrone in *Long Day's Journey*. The central character in "The Visit of Malatesta," an unfinished

work of his last creative years, is a portrait of the famous Italian anarchist hero Enrico Malatesta. As late as 1946, in his last big interview, prior to the premiere of *The Iceman Cometh*, the author called himself a "philosophical anarchist."

"The Personal Equation" is a valuable document because it provides insights into O'Neill's relationship with his parents in 1915. He portrays Tom, his self-portrait, as being victimized, even destroyed, by his father. The unanswered question remains: Why is the young hero's mother dead? Mother and son are described as being similar, as are all the autobiographical mothers and sons in the canon. The author seems reluctant at this time to present a portrait of his mother; he did not do so until he wrote *Ile* in 1917. The important biographical element in "The Personal Equation" is the frightful loneliness of young Perkins's early life. His brief relationship with Olga is cut short, and he is plunged forever into the isolation of madness, as the terrifying last scene suggests. The remark the doctor makes in the last act about his patient probably applies also to O'Neill: "He doesn't seem to have any relatives alive. It's a pity. He might have been different if he had had the influence of a home. As it is, there's no trace of who he is or where he came from. He's one of those strange human strays one sometimes runs across."

14. Before Breakfast

*Before Breakfast** was apparently written in July 1916
after O'Neill's arrival in Provincetown in late June and
before the premiere of *Bound East for Cardiff*. No single
source inspired the play's subject matter, the wife who
literally nags her husband to death. Three distinct elements appear to merge and motivate the play.

Shortly after his introduction to the amateur players,
O'Neill made a quick assessment of the type of plays the
group favored, noting the emphasis on man–woman relationships in such works as Susan Glaspell's *Suppressed
Desires* and Neith Boyce's *Constancy*. He had not as yet
fallen in love with Louise Bryant, and he perceived the
man–woman relationship, at that time, to be fraught with
tragic Strindbergian overtones. Even the device used to
dramatize the story, the monologues, is borrowed from
the Swedish playwright.† The monologue contains several autobiographical references. The marriage of the
Rowlands is actually a highly imaginative treatment of
O'Neill's brief involvement with Kathleen Jenkins. Like
Strindberg, he could be ruthless in making people and
events in his own life serve a dramatic purpose, callously
distorting people and events.

Before Breakfast is set in the kitchen–dining room of

---

*The play was first staged at The Playwrights' Theater on De-
cember 1, 1916. It was published that month in *The Provincetown Plays* (Third Series), by Frank Shay, one of the Players.

†Clark describes *Before Breakfast* as "a technical stunt in the
manner of Strindberg's *The Stronger*." During the lengthy monologue in each of these plays, the words of the one actor speaking
"skillfully suggest a dramatic background" (*Eugene O'Neill*, p.
49).

the Rowlands' dingy flat. It is about 8:30 on an early fall
morning. Mrs. Rowland, the only onstage character in the
play, is "in her early twenties but looks much older."
Physically, she is a slattern. Her toilet is "slovenly"; her
drab-colored hair is bunched up in a "mass on top of her
round head." She is "inclined to a shapeless stoutness."
Her face is "characterless, with small regular features and
eyes of a nondescript blue. There is a pinched expression
about her eyes and nose and her weak, spiteful mouth."
Mentally, she is a small-minded, sadistic, vindictive
shrew.

The woman yawns, mutters to herself, and looks
furtively at the bedroom door before opening a kitchen
closet, taking a bottle of gin out of its hiding place, and
pouring herself a large drink. Her next secretive movement, after downing the shot, is to search the pockets of
her husband's coat and vest. In the latter she discovers a
letter. As she reads it, her face registers emotions of
hatred, rage, and "triumphant malignity." The wife punctuates her remarks with a shrill cry, "Alfred," in an attempt to rouse her sleeping husband. Bitterly, she attacks
him for playing the gentleman and loafing "around bar-
rooms with that good-for-nothing lot of artists from the
Square" while she goes out to sew every day to support
them. Once she is certain he is out of bed and dressing,
the wife starts to berate the man for his appearance; he
should shave if he expects anyone to give him a job. She
hands him a bowl of hot water. "He reaches his hand into
the room for it. It is a slender hand with sensitive fingers.*
It trembles and some of the water spills on the floor." She

*O'Neill played the husband in the 1916 production. The de-
scription of Edmund in *Long Day's Journey*, the most accurate
self-portrait in the canon, contains a reference to this character's
hands, which are "noticeably like his mother's, with the same
exceptionally long fingers. They even have to a minor degree the
same nervousness. It is in the quality of the extreme nervous
sensibility that the likeness of Edmund to his mother is most
marked."

implies he has delirium tremens. The previous day he pawned his watch, their last possession of value, and went on a drinking spree. A serious fight erupted when he returned home that night.

Facts about their relationship, its origin and its present status, surface. He had been "the millionaire Rowland's only son, the Harvard graduate, the poet, the catch of the town." He had gotten this woman pregnant and been "honorable enough to marry" her. Apparently he had not sought financial help from his father, who later "died owing everyone in the world money." Ironically, the child, the cause of this unfortunate union, was born dead.

The wife's words gradually reveal the full tragedy of her husband's situation: he foreswore the woman he really loved to form this union that duty decreed. Mrs. Rowland pokes her head into the bathroom and gloats, "How about Helen?" The look she receives leaves her "half frightened." She continues her tirade, accusing him of objecting to her taking a "little something to keep up" her spirits and of running "after all these silly girls that think you're such a wonderful, misunderstood person—this Helen and the others."

Only at the end of the play does the audience learn that Helen is pregnant. The wife asks tauntingly, "What is she going to do—have the child—or go to one of those doctors? That's a nice thing, I must say." She works herself up to a state of supreme indignation and tells her husband: "You can't get a divorce from me and you know it." Helen deserves to suffer, she asserts, as she is "no better than a common streetwalker." There is "a stifled groan of pain from the next room." The wife thinks her husband has merely cut himself shaving, but then she hears something dripping and goes to the doorway. Her face is "transfixed with horror." When she discovers her husband has cut his throat with the razor, she turn wildly to the other door, opens it, and "runs shrieking madly into the outer hallway."

The ending here is identical to that of *Bread and Butter*. Both wives, after driving their husbands to suicide, rush from their homes. Like Maud Steele in the earlier play, Mrs. Rowland is a selfish, insensitive woman. Whereas John Brown is an aspiring artist, the husband here writes poetry and stories "no one will buy." There are two kinds of conflicts involved in these plays: the obvious battle of the sexes, which the female wins, and the businessman–artist struggle. Both wives are daughters of grocers and represent to O'Neill the mercantile, provincial force that destroys the creative artist.

A comparison of *Bread and Butter* and *Before Breakfast* shows the strides O'Neill made in his craft in two years. In 1916 he is able to compress the story he earlier needed four acts to tell into a short one-act monologue. O'Neill's style is deft in *Before Breakfast*. He maintains a serious tone throughout the tragedy. The comic elements in the first act of *Bread and Butter* are incongruous in view of the later tragic aspects. *Before Breakfast*, however, contains striking examples of melodrama: the destructive, unloved wife; the melancholic, noble, trapped husband; the understanding other woman; the incidents of plot, climaxing in the inevitable suicide. The dramatist will present the same characters and plot in later plays but never again in such a succinct manner.

15. Now I Ask You

Now I Ask You is O'Neill's earliest extant full-length comedy.* In it, he takes up the theme of an earlier three-act drama, *Servitude*: a woman's twofold desire to realize her potential as an individual and to escape the slavery of the marriage bond, which the heroine of *Now I Ask You* calls "the most despicable of all the laws of society." While the 1914 domestic drama becomes a preachy, boring tract, the comedy provides plausible insights into the causes and effects of a young woman's dilemma and shows her rebelling against the traditional role society would have her play.

Unlike Ethel Frazer, the sheltered, one-dimensional, cardboard heroine of *Servitude*, Lucy Ashleigh is a healthy, energetic, aware young woman, who mistakes "herself for the heroine of a Russian novel" and affects a depressed, pallid exterior. She is a slender, beautiful girl with large eyes, "which she attempts to keep always mysterious," and brooding lips, which she "compresses to express melancholy determination." She is, in actuality, "an intelligent, healthy American girl suffering from an overdose of undigested reading." Her contradictory appearance reflects her inner dichotomy: she is an introverted closet conservative but an extroverted, vocal rebel.

Lucy's father is a sedate, portly, bald, sixty-year-old prosperous businessman who is extremely annoyed with

---

*Called a "Three Act Farce-Comedy" in the "List of Plays," the play was conceived in the summer of 1916 during O'Neill's stay in Provincetown. He put it aside when he returned to New York that fall and revised it in March and April of the next year after his return to Cape Cod. The copyright date is May 23, 1917.

his daughter's "insane faddism," her "half-baked theories," and the collection of bohemians she adopts and
brings home periodically: a tramp poet, a long-haired
sculptor, a "yogi mystic in a cerise turban." Mrs. Ashleigh
is "a handsome white-haired woman of fifty" who proves
to be an amazingly modern, truly wise, liberated woman
"with a keen sense of humour."

Lucy's perplexing dual nature is illustrated in her
choice of friends, wild Greenwich Village artists such as
Leonora Barnes and her lover, Gabriel Adams, and her
choice of a husband-to-be: the sensible, likable businessman Tom Drayton. He, like his creator at this time, is far
more sensitive to the needs of a woman than David Roylston, the supposed emancipator of women, in *Servitude*.
The difference is easily explained.

Events occurring in the two-year period between the
plays brought O'Neill emotional and intellectual maturity. Friends he made in Greenwich Village in 1915—
writers, artists, former anarchist activists such as Terry
Carlin and Hippolyte Havel—and those he met in Provincetown in the summer of 1916, the nucleus of the new
amateur theatrical group, had a profound effect on the
aspiring dramatist. He knew he did not want to write for
the traditional commercial theater, but he had only a
vague perception of the type of new theater he wished to
create to replace the old. O'Neill learned his craft by
doing. He attended all rehearsals of his dramas and
played minor roles in three of them (*Bound East for
Cardiff, Thirst,* and *Before Breakfast*). His experiences in
staging his own work gave him a new perspective, leading
him to revise and reshape his current work and his approach.

O'Neill had only to use his powers of observation that
first summer in Provincetown for the plot and characterization of *Now I Ask You*. His own personal romantic
situation probably provided the inspiration for it. He fell
in love that summer with Louise Bryant, who was living

with John Reed, a radical socialist and later a defender of the Bolshevik revolution. The triangular relationship became the substance of the plot for *Now I Ask You*. O'Neill looked at Louise Bryant, and Lucy Drayton (nee Ashleigh) was born. The two have a number of shared attributes, including physical appearance. Louise contributed a drama entitled *The Game* to the Provincetown Players' repertory. Lucy is a would-be playwright. Louise was obviously influenced by Reed and his anarchist friends, particularly Emma Goldman. Lucy's father calls his daughter "our lady anarchist." Louise lived with Reed that summer and seemed reluctant to marry him. Lucy, like her prototype, finds herself attracted to two men: Tom Drayton, a good-looking, trusting individual like Reed, and Gabriel Adams, an impoverished poet with long black hair, a thin, intelligent face, and "big soulful eyes." Louise was involved with both O'Neill, the poet-playwright, and Reed in the summer of 1916.*

In *Now I Ask You* O'Neill experiments with structure, using it to convey meaning. He devises a Prologue to create suspense and to add an element of mystery, which is only resolved in the Epilogue. The Prologue, set in the library of the Drayton home, shows Lucy alone. Hearing Tom and Leonora come down the stairs, she hides in the next room. Tom calls her name. Receiving no response, he leaves the house in disgust with Leonora. The sound of a car door closing is heard. Lucy returns to the library, walks to a table, takes a revolver from the drawer, and raises it to her temple. The curtain is lowered as a shot is heard.

---

*Their affair began that summer and continued through the fall after Louise's marriage to Reed and during the month, mid-November to mid-December, that Reed spent at Johns Hopkins Hospital in Baltimore. The house that Reed purchased in Croton-on-Hudson seems to have provided the model for the "house in a fashionable New York suburb" within easy driving distance of Greenwich Village.

The first act, a flashback to an evening in June four
months earlier, opens in the living room of the Ashleighs'
home in Gramercy Park, New York City. The time is the
present. As in a number of O'Neill's plays, parents are
shown in a first scene discussing their offspring's rebellious nature and future. The parents here, as elsewhere,
have opposing opinions on nearly every subject. Mr.
Ashleigh criticizes Lucy for her "indecent" conduct "for
the past year since she left college." Mary Ashleigh defends their daughter, saying, "She is tomorrow, I am
today, and you, my dear Dick, are yesterday." She firmly
believes that Lucy's fiancé will effect a change: "The meek
lamb will succeed where the roaring lion has failed."

Ashleigh retreats from battle when Lucy's friend,
Leonora, arrives. The young woman wears a painter's
smock and sandals on her bare feet. Small, pale, and
anemic-looking, she has bright, restless eyes and thick
blond bobbed hair. She looks scornfully at the family
portraits on the wall and mutters: "Philistines! Chinese
ancestor worship." An advocate of free love, she ridicules
Mrs. Ashleigh's rationale for Lucy's marriage ("she is in
love") as "mid-Victorian sentimentality." She deposits
her wedding gift for Lucy, a futurist painting entitled the
"Great Blond Beast," explaining, "You know, Nietzsche.
It is the expression of my passion to create something or
someone great and noble—the Superman or the work of
great art." Introduced to Tom, "a tall, blond, finely-built
man of about thirty with large, handsome features,"
Leonora brashly tells him he attracts her physically and
that he resembles the idea she portrays in her painting.

Alone with Tom, Mrs. Ashleigh advises him to pretend to take Lucy and all her "extravagant poses" seriously after their marriage the next day. Opposition would
only trigger rebellion; he must play the neophyte, for
Lucy is intent on converting him. Neither the mother nor
Tom is prepared for Lucy's latest pose, "Strindberg's
daughter of Indra," when she enters. Inspired perhaps by

ideas presented at the anarchist meeting the previous evening, Lucy calls off her marriage because "it would be the meanest form of slavery." She is bewildered, however, when Tom suggests that they live together. Reason prevails, and Mrs. Ashleigh persuades Lucy to "sacrifice" herself for Tom: to go through with the ceremony but to make their marriage "a model of all that's best in free love." Lucy draws up a contract: she must not be forced to have children and must be allowed to have lovers. Recalling Mrs. Ashleigh's advice, Tom agrees to live with her "in the true comradeship of a free man and woman."

Three months elapse. Lucy, as Act II opens in the Drayton's library, resembles Ibsen's Hedda Gabler. Both women, having recently returned from their honeymoons at the beginning of the plays, are bored; longing for "a vital purpose," they turn to other men, writers in each case. Lucy has been spending considerable time with Gabriel while her husband is working. Although he is living with Leonora, Gabriel flirts openly with Lucy, who foolishly believes he is the only one who understands her.

Gabriel's interest in Lucy is a pretense; he and Leonora are parasites, seeking free meals and entertainment. When Leonora asks him how his affair "with the Blessed Damozel" is going, Gabriel says he wishes Lucy "knew the wisdom of silence." She has seen *Hedda Gabler* "for the Nth time," and he is forced to play the "drunken gentleman with the vine leaves in his hair." When he is alone with Lucy, Gabriel begs to be allowed to take her away "to the castles in the air, to the haunt of brave dreams." Just as he bends to kiss her hand and proclaim his love, Tom enters and sees them, "an expression of anger coming over his face." After Gabriel sheepishly leaves, Tom reproaches his wife bitterly. She reminds him of their contract and the clause allowing her to have a lover.

Tom complains to Mrs. Ashleigh, who is visiting the couple, about Gabriel's continual presence: "He's around

the house more than the cat is. Wherever I go I find him."
The mother suggests that Tom "turn the tables" and
pretend he has fallen in love with Leonora, "the little Nietzsche lady—Gabriel's Leon. You shall be her Great Blond
Beast." Feeling rejected by Gabriel, Leonora responds
eagerly to Tom's advances, thus arousing Lucy's jealousy.

Act III takes place a month later at 7:00 P.M. The
four young people have assembled in the Drayton library
and are trying to decide what to do that evening. Leonora
suggests they motor to New York and take in "some
perfectly shocking burlesque." Tom agrees to go with her
after Lucy and Gabriel decline to go; and, when Leonora
complains about having nothing to wear, he suggests she
borrow one of Lucy's gowns. As soon as the theatergoers
go upstairs to dress, Lucy and Gabriel, consumed with
jealousy, begin to quarrel. He assures Lucy that Tom and
Leonora are having an affair and are planning to elope that
evening. The two admit they do not love each other.
When Gabriel confesses he is actually married to Leonora, that they had kept their union a secret to avoid
seeming provincial to their Greenwich Village friends,
Lucy laughs hysterically. She sends Gabriel away and
begins to sob violently.

Mrs. Ashleigh enters but has little compassion for
Lucy. She reminds her that the terms of the contract give
Tom, as well as herself, freedom to conduct affairs. Melodramatically, Lucy assures her mother that Leonora is
Tom's mistress and that she will leave the house the
following day. She refuses to heed her mother's explanation that Tom is merely acting, and she flees to the adjoining room. Leonora, looking attractive in Lucy's gown, and
Tom come down the stairs. At this point the Prologue is
again enacted. The car is heard, Tom and Leonora leave
the house. Lucy takes out the revolver, and the sound of a
shot is again heard.

Three minutes elapse before the Epilogue. Another
shot is heard. Lucy drops the gun and "crumples up and

falls to the floor." The other four characters enter. Tom
stares at his wife and exclaims: "She shot herself!" Then
he grins and opens the gun: "It's never been loaded."
Both young women throw themselves into the arms of
their respective mates. The chauffeur enters carrying a
flat tire that had noisily blown out. "There is a roar of
laughter" when the young people realize how the shot
originated. Leonora points to the tire and exclaims dramatically: "General Gabler's pistol! Fancy that, Hedda."

   Now I Ask You is seriously flawed. Its characters are
shamelessly manipulated, responding to their creator's
cue rather than to rational motivation. The plot is an
ill-conceived caricature of Ibsen's *Hedda Gabler*. The
tragic potential of the Prologue becomes a travesty in the
Epilogue with O'Neill's ridiculous explanation for the
sound of the shot. While the scheme is faulty, the fact that
the author strives to create a comedy at this time in his life
is significant. The effort reflects his cheerful, almost
happy, frame of mind.

   Upon his arrival in Provincetown, the dramatist met
a strange assortment of highly individualized, and, in
some instances, eccentric amateur artists. He experienced the intoxicating triumph of success when his first
plays, *Bound East for Cardiff* and *Thirst*, were staged
and lavishly praised. The most important determinant in
the author's life that summer was his attraction for the
flamboyant Louise Bryant. O'Neill continually used
events in his own life as subjects for his plays. The fact that
he could step back, appraise his hopeless position in the
Reed–Bryant relationship, and transform the triangle
into farce suggests that his involvement with Louise and
her subsequent rejection of him did not devastate him.

   The play also indicates O'Neill's attitude to his two
Scandinavian mentors. Ibsen is disrespectfully satirized
throughout the play—from the Prologue, showing the
Hedda-like heroine attempting to shoot herself, to the
closing line of the Epilogue, referring to General Gabler's

pistol. Strindberg is treated with more respect. When Lucy makes her first appearance in the play, she assumes the pose of his tragic literary heroine, the Daughter of Indra. The Strindbergian battle of the sexes, used later by the author to depict serious marital problems, is reproduced here humorously in the foolish heroine's struggle to retain her identity in marriage. *Now I Ask You* provides a rare respite in the somber O'Neill canon. The author did not produce another comedy until the nostalgic *Ah, Wilderness!* in 1932.

16.   In the Zone

In the Zone seems to have been the first of four sea plays
O'Neill completed in the winter of 1917* and the second
of the one-acters that would later be labeled the S.S.
Glencairn series.† The action in *In the Zone* takes place in
the forecastle of the British tramp steamer *Glencairn*
shortly before midnight one night in the fall of 1915.
Seven of the nine seamen in the cast appeared in the
earlier play, *Bound East for Cardiff*. The deceased Yank
is replaced now by Jack and the easy-going Olson** by "a
squat, surly-faced Swede" named Swanson.

When the play opens, five of the seamen "are in their
bunks apparently asleep." One of them, Smitty, stealthily
gets up and pulls out a suitcase from under a bunk. At that
moment Scotty wakes, and Davis, carrying a pot of hot
coffee, appears in the doorway. Both men watch Smitty
suspiciously. After unlocking his suitcase, Smitty takes
out a "small black tin box," which he hides under his
mattress. He slides the suitcase back and returns to his
bunk.

Davis rouses the men and angrily chastises Paul
upon discovering that a porthole near his bunk is open.
"What's the use o' blindin' the ports when that thick-head
goes an' leaves 'em open?" After Davis informs the men

*The play was staged by the Washington Square Players on
October 31, 1917.

†Clark states that Frank Shay's theatrical group, the Barnstorm-
ers, brought four of O'Neill's sea plays together in 1924 under
the title *S.S. Glencairn* (*Eugene O'Neill*, p. 49).

**In *The Long Voyage Home*, which precedes *In the Zone*
chronologically, Olson is shanghaied and sent to almost certain
death on a dangerous trip around Cape Horn.

that the ship entered the war zone three hours earlier, they begin to talk fearfully of submarines and torpedoes. The risk, Driscoll states, is not worth the "twenty-five percent bonus." Scotty, glancing at Smitty, speaks of "German spies and the dirty work they're doin' in the war."

Smitty, a sensitive dreamer, goes out to see the bo'sun. The seamen have long regarded him an outsider. Driscoll calls him a "bloody gentleman," Scotty "his Lordship." Cocky complains: "Be the airs 'e puts on you'd think 'e was the Prince of Wales." It takes little effort on the part of the mean-spirited Davis, when he describes Smitty's "black iron box," to arouse the suspicions of the men. Smitty's failure to return and his posture "on the hatch starin' at the moon like a mon half-daft" convince Cocky that he is "keepin' 'isself clear of us like 'e was afraid."

To Davis, the evidence is conclusive. Smitty possesses no money or coins. Nevertheless, he keeps the black box locked when he knows the forecastle harbors no thief. He does not look like an Englishman, although he professes to be one, and "he talks too damn good" to be English. His real name is probably Schmidt, not Smith. He had known little about a seaman's duties two years ago when he joined the crew. What Davis resents most is Smitty's reluctance to discuss his personal life and "that sly air about him 's if he was hidin' somethin'." Smitty, he now maintains, must surely have opened the porthole to signal "any sub that was watchin'."

Fearful that the black box contains a bomb, the men submerge it in a bucket of water. There is only one way to deal with the "black-hearted thraitor," Driscoll says. "I'll choke his rotten heart out wid me own hands, an' over the side wid him." Davis adds: "An' no one the wiser. He's the balmy kind what commits suicide."

When Smitty enters, the men pin and tie his arms behind him. Smitty resists, and seeing his submerged belongings, he indignantly objects to this invasion of privacy. Driscoll becomes the chief prosecutor, hurling cruel epithets at Smitty. He threatens to kill Driscoll if the box he now holds is opened. The men throw Smitty to the floor; Driscoll puts a "big wad of waste" into his mouth and secures it with a handkerchief.

The men are mystified and disappointed to see that the box holds only a black rubber bag containing a small packet of letters. Smitty's "muffled groan of rage and protest" convinces the relentless Davis that the letters contain a coded message. He urges Driscoll to read one letter. In it, a young woman named Edith tells the recipient, Sidney Davidson, how much she loves him, but that he must prove he really intends to settle down while she is away at singing school before she "can agree to live out" her life with him. Davis presses Driscoll to read on in pursuit of the hidden code. The latter reads all the letters to himself until he reaches the last line of the final letter, in which Edith tells Smitty she never wants to see him again. He betrayed her trust while she was away by continuing his alcoholic way of life after he had promised to reform. Driscoll unties Smitty, who covers his face with his hands and weeps inwardly. The men are so ashamed of themselves that they cannot look at one another. They slink off to their bunks, crawl in, and cover themselves with their blankets.

In the Zone was well received by American audiences, who were troubled by the war in Europe and concerned for their loved ones endangered by it. Clark praised the play in an article in 1919, but O'Neill disagreed with his high estimate of it and stated:

> It is too facile in its conventional technique, too full of clever theatrical tricks, and its long run as a successful headliner in vaudeville proves conclusively to my mind that there was something "rotten in Denmark." At any rate, this play in no way represents the true me or what I desire to express. It is a situation drama lacking in all spiritual import—there is no

big feeling for life inspiring it. . . . I consider *In the Zone* a conventional construction of the theater as it is.*

While O'Neill was aware of the "clever theatrical tricks," having conceived them, audiences did not find them obtrusive. In these years of formation and transition, each play marks a step forward. Except for two brief statements, O'Neill does not describe the characters in the play, yet two strong portraits emerge: Driscoll, the thick, stubborn Irishman who attempts to disguise his ignorance by his bullying, boastful bravado; and Davis, the frustrated, spiteful American who will persecute an obviously innocent man to gain standing with his peers.

Nevertheless, *In the Zone* lacks one essential quality: the deep feeling for the sea that is manifested by sailors, even if it is a mixed love–hate attitude, in the other *Glencairn* plays. O'Neill acknowledges the flaw, for he tells Clark that the play "might have happened just as well, if less picturesquely, in a boarding house of munition workers." The realization subsequently produced a work of rare beauty, one that captures the majesty and power of the sea, in the later *Glencairn* one-acter *The Moon of the Caribbees.*

*Clark, pp. 41–42.

17. *Ile*

Whereas *In the Zone* could have been set on land, the
action of *Ile** could only occur at sea. The caprice of the
sea serves as a catalyst, influencing the behavior and
minds of the characters. In the game of chance waged in
the one-acter, the obsessed Captain Keeney pits the fate of
his wife, his crew, and himself against the unknown forces
of the implacable sea. He triumphs in the end, but his is a
pyrrhic victory: all that a wise man would cherish has
been destroyed.

When the play opens, the steam whaler *Atlantic
Queen* has been locked in ice for a full year, stuck in it, as
the steward states, "like a fly in molasses!" The ship's
captain plays a waiting game, hoping for the break in the
ice that will allow him to get to the whales and return
home with a ship full of oil. It is an early afternoon in June
1895, the final day of the sailors' two-year contract. The
men are on the verge of mutiny and the food supply is low,
yet the captain, like a man possessed, refuses to retreat.

Curtains cover the portholes in the captain's cabin.
The only light entering the room comes through the
skylight; it is "sickly and faint, indicating one of those gray
days of calm when ocean and sky are alike dead." Two
objects seem oddly out of place in the austere, masculine
environment: a woman's sewing basket on the sideboard
and a small new organ. The conversation between the
elderly steward and the young cabin boy as they remove

---

*In the "List of Plays" O'Neill places *Ile* immediately before *The
Long Voyage Home* and *The Moon of the Caribbees* among works
written in "1917, Winter." *Ile* was first staged on November 30,
1917, at The Playwrights' Theater and published in May 1918 in
The Smart Set.

dishes from the table provides the exposition. The boy hopes that the captain will turn south now that the ice in that direction has broken. The steward calls Keeney a "hard, hard man" and fears that the captain is "mighty nigh losin' his senses." He says:

> Who but a man that's mad would take his woman—and as sweet a woman as ever was—on a stinkin' whalin' ship to the Arctic seas to be locked in by the rotten ice for nigh on a year, and maybe lose her senses forever—for it's sure she'll never be the same again.

The men respect Mrs. Keeney, whose softening influence on her husband has made their lot easier on this trip. She recognizes no one now but her husband and does nothing but sew all day and cry to herself.

The sailors depart quickly when the captain, a man of forty, enters the cabin. "His face is massive and deeply lined, with gray-blue eyes of a bleak hardness, and a tightly clenched, thin-lipped mouth. His thick hair is long and gray." Tom Slocum, his tall, rangy, thirty-year-old second mate, comes in and warns the captain that the men are ready to mutiny.

The officers are interrupted when the door leading to the Keeney's sleeping quarters opens and the captain's wife appears. She is "a slight, sweet-faced little woman primly dressed in black. Her eyes are red from weeping and her face drawn and pale." Nervously, she raises the curtain of a porthole. Seeing the clear water behind the ship, she asks to be allowed to go on deck to see the sun, "her face transfigured with joy." The captain fears the mood of the men and commands her to stay below and to leave him alone with the second mate.

Keeney takes out his revolver, not to use, he says, but to frighten the men. Slocum uses several arguments to persuade the Captain to change the ship's course: the food is getting low, the men could make trouble in the courts if they are forced to work beyond the two-year agreement; when these arguments fail, he cites Mrs.

Keeney's failing health. The captain is determined to stay
the course and states:

> It ain't the damned money what's keepin' me up in the
> Northern seas, Tom. But I can't go back to Homeport with a
> measly four hundred barrel of ile. I'd die fust. I ain't never
> come back home in all my days without a full ship. . . . I got
> to git it in spite of all hell, and by God, I ain't agoin' home till
> I do git it!

A group of seaman, led by Joe, a harpooner, approaches the Captain. Joe threatens mutiny, but "Keeney's
fist shoots out to the side of his jaw." The men pull out
their knives but are confronted by revolvers. The captain
warns them that he will shoot the first man he sees
"shirkin'" his duty. After the men leave, the captain
discovers that his wife has entered the room and has been
watching the scene before her in horror. He reminds her
that he had been reluctant to take her on the voyage. She
tells him of her loneliness during the first six years of their
marriage when he was at sea.

> I used to dream of sailing on the great, wide, glorious ocean.
> I wanted to be by your side in the danger and vigorous life of
> it all. I wanted to see you the hero they make you out to be
> in Homeport. And instead—All I find is ice and cold—and
> brutality.

When his wife implores him to take her home before
she goes mad, Keeney tells her to go to bed: "You got fever.
Your eyes look so strange like." He tries to reassure her that
in a month or two, "three at the most," he will have his "ile"
and then "pint for home." She reminds her husband that
if they turned back and started home, they would be there
to celebrate their wedding anniversary. When all other
appeals fail: his love for her, her record as a good wife, she
makes one last wild effort: "I'm going mad. I can feel the
threat in the air. I can hear the silence threatening me—
day after gray day. . . . I'm afraid. For the love of God,
take me home." A "tremendous struggle" is going on
within him. Finally, "his iron spirit weakens" and he says:

"I'll do it, Annie—for your sake—if you say it's needful for ye."

Suddenly, the Second Mate enters and announces that the ice has broken to the north. The men, he says, are "meek as lambs" and will cooperate. Defeated, Mrs. Keeney begins "to laugh hysterically." She sits down at the organ and plays a hymn. Keeney looks into her eyes, but she only "stares up at him with a stupid expression." He thinks his wife is merely trying to deceive him. "I've got to git the ile. Answer me! You ain't mad, be you?" The Mate calls out saying a school of whales has been sighted; the boats have been lowered. The Captain's face grows "hard with determination." The wife has lost all hold on reality; she sways to the rhythm of the hymn and plays "wildly and discordantly as the curtain falls."

Keeney is a man with a single passion: he must maintain his reputation as "first whaling captain" in Homeport. All else, including the lives and welfare of his wife and crew, is subordinate. Ruthlessly he has driven his men onward, controlling them by the sheer force of his brutal determination. O'Neill uses the word "hard" over and over to describe this stern New England Yankee, the prototype for such figures as Ephraim Cabot in *Desire Under the Elms* and Ezra Mannon in *Mourning Becomes Electra*. In one way or another each of these men has, in some way, destroyed his wife. The woman in each of the three plays bears a distinct resemblance to Ella O'Neill.

Like the autobiographical Mary Tyrone in *Long Day's Journey into Night*, Mrs. Keeney sinks deeper and deeper into a dazed unawareness as the play progresses. In the beginning her husband is able to awaken her from her dreamlike state; at the end he is as helpless as James Tyrone to penetrate the wall of oblivion the wife erects. Keeney bought his wife an organ, hoping to placate her; he is resentful when she does not play it. Similarly, James Tyrone complains when his wife fails to make use of the car he has purchased and the chauffeur he has hired.

Annie is weary of the years of isolation and wants to "hear a woman's voice talking to me and be able to talk to her." Mary wishes there were "some woman friend I could talk to—not about anything serious, simply laugh and gossip."

Annie has a habit of passing "her hand across her eyes"; Mary's hands constantly "flutter up to her hair." Both women mention their wedding anniversaries, Annie with "a rapt smile," Mary with "a rapt, tender, girlish smile." The two seem almost to will their nonrational states as if to spite their husbands. Annie warns Keeney near the end, "My memory is leaving me—up here in the ice." When he persists in remaining in the Arctic, she stares up at him at the end with a "vague smile on her lips." Mary Tyrone at the end of *Long Day's Journey*, after numerous morphine injections, says: "It's terrible, how absent-minded I've become. I'm always dreaming and forgetting." At the close, she "passes a hand over her forehead as if brushing cobwebs from her brain—vaguely." The two have the same self-effacing manner, the same tolerant attitude to their bullying, self-centered husbands. Both women reminisce nostalgically, joyously about a month of June in the past.

It is Captain Keeney's pride that destroys his wife and any possibility they may have of living a happy, normal life; it drives him to wrest from the sea the spoils he needs to maintain his reputation. The image of the ship locked in ice approximates the captain's heart bound in pride. While the sun is eventually able to penetrate the ice, its symbolic equivalent, Mrs. Keeney's love, is powerless to dissolve her husband's hardness of heart.

Ile is O'Neill's finest early one-act play. All the elements—plot, setting, dialogue—are masterfully woven to form a unified, coherent pattern. David and Annie Keeney are strongly drawn, believable characters. One of the most profound scenes in all of the early work is the horrific view of Mrs. Keeney, totally lost in madness at the close of the play, swaying "to the rhythm of the hymn" as she plays the organ. The same quality of utter abandon and despair will not be matched until the final scene of *Long Day's Journey* when, after Mary Tyrone clumsily plays a Chopin waltz, she remains detached and oblivious of her family.

18. *The Long Voyage Home*

The Long Voyage Home* continues the saga of the seamen of the S.S. *Glencairn*, although only four characters from the earlier one-acters, Olson, Driscoll, Cocky, and Ivan, appear here. Unlike any of the other plays in the series, *The Long Voyage Home* is set entirely on land: "a low dive on the London water front." Nevertheless, the sea is a living presence to the sailors; it becomes a malignant force to the man who betrays it.

The two villains of the play are introduced immediately: Fat Joe, the proprietor of the saloon, "a gross bulk of a man" with a "red, bloated face and little piggish eyes," and Nick, a crimp, a shabbily dressed young fellow with a pasty face, a weak mouth, and shifting, cruel eyes. It is after 9:00 P.M. and Joe demands to know why his place is deserted when he pays Nick to lure sailors to it. Nick defends himself: he boarded the *Glencairn* when it docked that afternoon, and the men promised to stop in. He also saw the captain of the *Amindra*, a ship that will sail "at daybreak ter-morrer."

Nick needs Joe's help and his "drops"; he intends to shanghai a sailor for the *Amindra*. He explains why this action is necessary.

> The capt'n an' mate are bloody slave-drivers, an' they're bound down round the 'orn. They 'arf starved the 'ands on the larst trip 'ere, an' no one'll dare ship on 'er. I promised the capt'n faithful I'd get 'im one, and ter-night.

Nick has chosen his prey, one of the four two-year men of the *Glencairn*, who had just been paid off. The sound of boisterous singing is heard in the street. Nick looks out

---

*The play was first staged on November 2, 1917, at The Playwrights' Theater. It had been published the previous month in *The Smart Set*.

and informs Joe triumphantly that the men have arrived.

The seamen are not described in the earlier work, *In the Zone*, but they are here:

> Driscoll is a tall, powerful Irishman; Cocky, a wizened runt of a man with a straggling gray mustache; Ivan, a hulking oaf of a peasant; Olson, a stocky, middle-aged Swede with round, childish blue eyes.

Olson is "perfectly sober," but the others are "very drunk." Driscoll remembers that he has been in this saloon before and was stripped of his last shilling while sleeping. Joe protests; he runs an honest place. Driscoll good-naturedly forgives him and orders Irish whiskey for Cocky, Ivan, and himself. Pointing at Olson, Cocky says mockingly, "An' a glarse o' ginger beer fer our blarsted love-child 'ere." Olson's plans for the future upset Cocky: "A-saivin' of 'is money, 'e is! Goin' back to 'ome an' mother. Goin' to buy a bloomin' farm an' punch the blarsted dirt, that's wot 'e is! (Spitting disgustedly) There's a funny bird of a sailor man for yer, Gawd Blimey!" Driscoll defends the Swede, saying he would do the same if his own mother were alive—"maybe."

Joe signals Nick that the toughs are behind the door at the left. When Driscoll sees the two men whispering, he accuses them of conspiring against the seamen. Nick assures him that he was only trying to get "gels" for the men. Cocky rejects Joe's "gels": "They'd fair blind yer, they're that 'omely. None of yer bloomin' gels fur me, ole Fatty. Me an' Drisc knows a place, down't we, Drisc?" When Joe's "gels" enter, Cocky calls them " 'orrible." Freda is "a little, sallow-faced blonde"; Kate is "stout and dark." Driscoll lays claim to Kate: "A good Irish name, but you're English by the trim av ye, an' be damned to you." Freda sits beside Olson, and when he takes out a roll of notes to pay for drinks, "Joe, Nick, and the women look at the money with greedy eyes."

As the sailors, who have been drinking continually since their arrival, stagger to the next room with Nick and

Kate to dance, Freda begs Olson to stay and talk with her. Olson, one of the world's last great innocents, believes Freda's statement that she too was born in Stockholm. Olson states that he is finished with the sea forever. He plans to return to the family farm and to his mother and brother. "I have plenty money, now. I go back with two years' pay and buy more land yet; work on farm. (Grinning) No more sea, no more bum grub, no more storms— yust nice work."

Driscoll and Cocky return, supporting Ivan, who is "in the last stage of intoxication." Driscoll doesn't trust Ivan "in this hole as drunk as he is, an' him wid a full pay day on him." He drags Ivan out to their boardinghouse, saying that he and Cocky will return shortly. Freda coaxes Olson back to the table while Joe and Nick stand by the bar whispering. Nick then blocks the Swede's view of the bar while Joe "pours the contents of the little bottle into Olson's glass of ginger beer."

Freda attempts to distract Olson and asks him about his mother. His desire to see his eighty-two-year-old mother before she dies has prompted him to abstain from alcohol. He had resolved to go home in the past but had always succumbed to temptation and spent his money. "So dis time I say to myself: Don't drink one drink, Ollie, or, sure, you don't get home." Freda is "moved in spite of herself," yet she proposes a toast to encourage him to consume the drugged drink. "Success to yer bloomin' farm an' may yer live long an' 'appy on it. Skoal."

Joe's two toughs enter and sit waiting for Olson to collapse. One of them laughingly mentions the *Amindra*. Olson warns the men angrily about "dat damn ship— worse ship dat sail to sea. Rotten grub and dey make you work all time—and the Captain and Mate wus Bluenose devils." When he discovers that the ship is headed for Cape Horn, Olson says: "Py yingo, I pity poor fallers make dat trip round Cape Stiff dis time year. I bet you some of dem never see port once again." After Olson falls to the floor unconscious, Freda takes the roll of money from his pocket and furtively puts one note "into her bosom." Joe tells his men to get Olson to the *Amindra* before the sailors return. Then he turns to Freda, demands the money she took, and strikes her. Kate enters and helps Freda to the next room.

When Driscoll and Cocky return, Joe pretends that Olson has gone out with Freda. Driscoll remarks that he is glad Olson is sober, as "she'd have him stripped to his last ha'penny." He then asks for whiskey, "*Irish* whiskey," as the curtain falls.

Just before Yank dies in *Bound East for Cardiff*, he tells Driscoll that he wants to leave the sea and "git a farm." Olson makes a valiant effort to realize Yank's dream. O'Neill condemns both men not only to failure but to punishment. Over and over in these and later plays, he suggests, the sea will always reclaim its own, in either a living or actual death. When Olson reappears again as Chris Christopherson in both the play of that name and in *Anna Christie*, he will be shown as having learned a valuable lesson about "dat ole devil sea." He lives on an old tugboat in safety, but eventually he finds himself lured back to the sea.

Because he actually knew the models for Olson, Driscoll, and the other seamen and because he understood their way of life, O'Neill is able to achieve a kind of realism in the sea plays that his other early works lack. The incidents leading to Olson's betrayal and capture seem to be contrived, yet all the elements—characters, actions, dialogue—work together to make the drama plausible. The ending lacks the dramatic intensity of the last scene of *Bound East for Cardiff*. In both, however, fog and fate mysteriously intertwine, and always in the presence of a woman. When Olson stands in the doorway wondering whether to follow his departing friends, Freda tells him to close the door as she is "freezin' to death wiv the fog." Olson obeys and his fate is sealed. In the earlier play, the fog lifts just as Yank sees the "pretty lady dressed in black" and dies.

19. *The Moon of the Caribbees*

No other American one-act play evokes the beauty of the sea quite like *The Moon of the Caribbees*. It was O'Neill's acknowledged favorite among his early works,* his attempt, as he told Barrett Clark, to achieve a "higher plane of bigger, finer values." Whereas the other works in the *Glencairn* series depend on characters, plot, or action for their dramatic impact, *The Moon of the Caribbees* relies primarily on mood. It is O'Neill's eulogy to the sea.

The entire cast of seamen depicted in the first *Glencairn* one-acter, *Bound East for Cardiff*, including Yank, reappear here. Joining this group are firemen and other crew members of the *Glencairn* and the West Indian women who come aboard. The action takes place on the main deck of the British steamer "at anchor off an island in the West Indies. The full moon, half-way up the sky, throws a clear light on the deck."

The men are shown resting after their day's work when the play opens. "A melancholy negro chant, faint and faroff, drifts, crooning, over the water." The music, which Driscoll calls "keenin'," depresses them. Smitty, a "young Englishman with a blond mustache," is particularly downcast. Cocky slaps him on the back, saying: "Down't be ser dawn in the marf, Duke. She loves yer."†

---

*The date on the longhand draft of the play is "3/20/17." It was first published in August 1918 in *The Smart Set* and first staged on December 20, 1918, at The Playwrights' Theater.

†The action in *Bound East for Cardiff*, *The Long Voyage Home*, and *The Moon of the Caribbees* takes place before the outbreak of World War I. O'Neill includes a reference here to Smitty's girl in anticipation of her farewell note to him in *In the Zone*. The

Driscoll tells the men that he has persuaded the native woman to bring back rum enough for all of them when she returns that night. The captain has given her permission to sell fruit to the men but has ordered her "to bring no booze on board." To drown out "the mournful singing of the negroes on shore," Driscoll sings a chanty, "Blow the Man Down." He is about to begin a third stanza when the rumboat approaches, bearing, the soloist says hopefully, "foine West Indy rum wid a kick in ut loike a mule's hoind leg."

Cocky, described as "a wizened runt of a man with a straggling gray mustache," has the same high expectations here about women that he had in *The Long Voyage Home*. He is afraid the other "gels" will be as "bloomin' ugly" as the first woman he sees. "Looked like a bloody organ-grinder's monkey, she did. Gawd, I couldn't put up wiv the likes of 'er!" One of the firemen, Paddy, "a squat, ugly Liverpool Irishman," calls Cocky a "squint-eyed runt" and taunts him: "Ye'll be lucky if any of thim looks at ye." Cocky reaches for his sheath knife, but Driscoll appears, bearing a pint bottle of rum for the men to sample.

Five women board the ship with their leader, Bella, "the oldest, stoutest, and homeliest." Driscoll says that "two swate little slips av things" have been sent to the captain, that "gray-whiskered auld fool, an' the mates— an' the engineers too, maybe. The rist av thim'll be comin' for'ard whin she comes." Cocky calls the captain a hypocrite; when the ship set sail, he had looked like "a bloody ole sky pilot" standing on the bridge waving to his crying wife and children. Cocky is reminded that he has bragged of having a woman and children weeping for him "in iviry divil's port in the wide worrld." Driscoll explains the

author makes little effort to interconnect the four one-acters. The fact that the characterizations of individual seamen remain consistent throughout these plays strongly suggests O'Neill met all of them while at sea.

arrangements. If the men buy a bottle of "Somethin'," they must write "tobacco" or "fruit" and the price on a piece of paper, sign it, and give it to the women, who will later be reimbursed by the captain.

Four women appear: Bella, Susie, Violet, and Pearl, "the youngest and best looking," who has already won the heart of Yank. Bella warns the men not to drink on deck. Four men sign their names and go into the forecastle. Paddy ignores the line and grabs a bottle out of Pearl's hand. Yank, her protector, questions Paddy, who says sullenly that he cannot write. Yank warns him: "There ain't goin' to be no welchin' on little Bright Eyes here— not when I'm around." Paddy defiantly takes a drink "in the full moonlight" before going inside. Bella gathers the girls around her and heads for the safety of the forecastle.

Pearl lingers to talk to Smitty, who sits staring into space. "Come ahn in, pretty boy. Ah likes you." He goes in for a bottle and returns immediately, shuddering "as if flinging off something which disgusted him." Smitty complains to the Donkeyman, an old gray-headed man with a kindly, wrinkled face, about the music from shore that is heard once again in the still night. " 'Tain't sich bad music, is it? Sounds kinder pretty to me—low an' mournful—same as listenin' to the organ outside o' church of a Sunday." Smitty confesses that it is not the music but the "beastly memories the damn thing brings up" that upset him. The Donkeyman says he has had his share of bad times in life and, like Smitty, always resorted to getting drunk to forget. He believes a "gel" is the cause of the young man's sorrow. "An' she said she threw you over 'cause you was drunk; an' you said you was drunk 'cause she threw you over."

Davis and Violet come out of the forecastle and go off together into the dark. Pearl appears and approaches Smitty, who pushes her proffered hand away coldly. Smitty seems like a gentleman to her when compared to the other crude men. The woman disgusts him, but, with the bottle now nearly consumed, he suddenly laughs wildly and pulls her to him. At that moment Yank appears. At first he is shocked to see Smitty and Pearl together. Then he says: "Pals is pals and any pal of mine c'n have anythin' I got."

The revelers in the forecastle make their way out onto the deck. Only Bella is "absolutely sober," and she tries, in vain, to quiet the drunken sailors. Driscoll embraces Bella and joins the three other couples dancing. When Cocky and Susie near the hatch, Paddy sticks his foot out, and the couple falls flat on the deck. Enraged, Cocky attacks Paddy; all the others join in the battle. A knife flashes in the moonlight. A scream is heard. The men rush to the forecastle and enter, leaving Yank and Driscoll, their clothing torn, standing beside the still form of Paddy when an officer appears. He discovers that Paddy has a slight shoulder wound and commands the seamen to "take him aft." He then notices the group of women huddled together. Seeing an empty rum bottle, he angrily orders them off the boat.

Smitty and the Donkeyman are alone on stage. Once again, in the silence, the melancholy music "drifts crooning over the water." The Donkeyman opens the door to his cabin and tells Smitty: "You can't hear it in the fo'c's'le —the music, I mean—and there'll be more drinks in there, too." Smitty rises wearily and enters the forecastle. "There is silence for a second or so, broken only by the haunted, saddened voice of that brooding music, faint and far-off, like the mood of the moonlight made audible."

When Barrett Clark praised *In the Zone*, O'Neill expressed his preference for *The Moon of the Caribbees*: "The spirit of the sea—a big thing—is in this latter play the hero." Against this background of eternal, sad beauty, he continues, Smitty's gestures

> of self-pity are reduced to their proper insignificance, his thin whine of weakness is lost in the silence which it was mean enough to disturb, we get the perspective to judge

him—and the others—and we find his sentimental posing much more out of harmony with truth, much less in tune with beauty, than the honest vulgarity of his mates.*

After seeing *The Moon of the Caribbees,* Clark disagreed with the author. To Clark, the rhythmical prose did not seem to evoke "the spirit of the sea" but rather "the spirit of man's loneliness in the presence of nature." One of the most serious charges Clark levels against O'Neill is that he "leaves too much to the director and the stage-carpenter: for drama which is poetic in conception must be poetic in execution."

Having envisioned this richly symbolic play, O'Neill realized that it could not be staged in the same way as his earlier, realistic works such as *The Long Voyage Home.* While he did depend on scenic designers to establish the proper setting for the drama he conceived, it is the play itself that is the jewel rather than its setting. The visual setting is but one element; sound, the distant melancholy chant, is another; lighting, the moonlight illuminating the sky, is yet another. These elements establish the mood, embellish the illusion created. The mainstay of the play is the characters, their camaraderie, the countless vignettes, the myriad tales told through the fleeting fragments of dialogue, of past hopes and present despair, of bitter rivalries, like that of Paddy and Cocky, and enduring friendship, like that of Driscoll and Yank.

O'Neill knew the worth of his method; the poet in him labeled *The Moon of the Caribbees* his favorite early work. More significant than all other achievements of the play, he does here, in a tentative, probing way, what he was to do often and with greater success in the future: he shows the impelling, inscrutable behind-life forces at work in the lives of men.

*Clark, p. 43.

20. *Shell Shock*

Shell Shock* represents another attempt on O'Neill's part to dramatize the traumatic effects of World War I on American soldiers. *The Sniper*, the earlier war play, focuses on the fighting in Europe. A bereaved Belgian civilian who has lost his wife, son, and home retaliates against the invading Germans. In *Shell Shock*, the war is brought home to America: three soldiers who have recently returned from Europe try to forget the nightmares of combat and resume normal civilian life. The play concentrates on the plight of Jack Arnold, the soldier most seriously affected by the war, and the attempts his fellow officers make to cure him of shell shock.

The play is set in "the grill of the New York club of a large Eastern University" (Harvard) on a hot afternoon in September 1918.† The exposition is provided by Robert Wayne, "a young man of about thirty dressed in the uniform of an officer in the Medical Corps," and Herbert Roylston, a "brawny young fellow of twenty-seven or so, clad in the uniform of a first lieutenant of the infantry." The latter "bears the marks of a recent convalescence from serious illness." His eyes seem "shadowed by the

---

*In his 1918–1920 notebook, O'Neill lists two alternate, but canceled, titles: "Butts" and "A Smoke." In the "List of Plays" the author, apparently forgetting the assigned title *Shell Shock*, calls the one-acter "At Jesus' Feet." The copyright date for this work, which was written in early 1918, is May 5, 1918. *Shell Shock* was never produced, nor was it published until its inclusion in the 1972 collection of early plays, *Children of the Sea*, edited by Jennifer McCabe Atkinson.

†The dramatist's drawing of the set and his first idea for the play appear in my *Eugene O'Neill at Work* (pp. 11–12). O'Neill provides no explanation for setting the play in September 1918, approximately seven months after its composition date.

remembrance of pain, witnessed and not by them to be forgotten."

The two men, who now meet by chance, have spoken only once before, when they were introduced by a mutual friend, Jack Arnold. Wayne was Jack's roommate at Harvard. Roylston fought with and was saved by Jack in France. He was wounded when his unit tried to capture a Bosche trench. Jack came out into that "no man's land" and rescued him. Wayne had been told that Jack risked his life to retrieve the body of a *dead* officer. Roylston explains what had really happened. He had lain motionless for three days and nights on the battlefield. In frustration he screamed out loudly in the darkness. Somehow he managed to pull himself together and stand up. He was struck in the chest immediately by a German bullet. At that moment, when he fell to the ground, Jack ran toward him, through a hail of enemy bullets, and pulled him back to safety. The exploit was but one of a "whole caboodle of such stunts" to Jack's credit.

Because of the experience he gained in France treating victims of shell shock, Wayne had been transferred back to the United States after shock patients "commenced to be sent home in appreciable numbers." When Wayne says he suspects Jack will soon become one of his patients, Roylston is surprised and says: "Jack's made of iron. I've seen him in the trenches and I know. If he'd been shot or gassed or—but shell shock—Bosh!" Wayne continues his story: Jack was wounded in the leg and sent to a hospital. A Doctor Thompson wrote to Wayne, saying that Jack "had been invalided home" because he showed signs of a nervous breakdown. The doctor underlined the three words in his postscript: "Watch Arnold—cigarettes."

Roylston leaves the grill but promises to return to thank Jack for saving his life. Wayne is alone only a few minutes when Jack enters. His description indicates that he has a serious disorder. His eyes have a

> strained expression of uncertain expectancy as if he were constantly holding himself in check while he waited for a

mine to explode. His hands tremble a little. He has a queer
mannerism of continually raising the fore and middle fingers of his right hand to his lips as though he were smoking
an invisible cigarette. He wears the uniform of a major of
infantry.

Wayne greets Jack like a friend, but before long he begins
analyzing him like a patient. Jack begins to manifest
symptoms of illness almost immediately. He borrows cigarettes from Wayne continuously throughout the play. He
takes a few puffs of each cigarette, extinguishes it, and
then "carefully puts the butt into a pocket of his uniform."
Noticing that he is being observed, Jack apologizes for his
"devilish habit." Pressed for an explanation, he mutters:
"It's the silence. That does it." He then describes the
continuous sound of guns and bursting shells heard in the
trenches; "even the night is goaded into insomnia by the
ever-lasting fireworks."

Wayne deliberately changes the topic of conversation and mentions he has just seen Jack's old friend Roylston. Jack is stunned, for he had thought his friend was
dead. He recounts his experiences at Chateau Thierry.
His company had been cut off from the rest of the army;
no supplies reached it. Whereas some men cried out for
food and water, all Jack craved "was a smoke—and not a
one." He relives the agony of the trenches: the continual
bombardment by enemy shells, the horrible "screams of
the wounded," the orders he had given his men forbidding them to rescue those lying out in "No Man's Land."
Recalling that Roylston had given him a cigarette before
the battle began, Jack, driven to desperation by desire,
makes his way out to where his friend lies. He remembers
nothing of what happened next.

Aided by Wayne's probing questions, Jack works
through his problem for the first time. He recalls now that
he had heard Roylston's scream and had realized he was
alive. "That's why I went over—to save him—Herb—not

the damned cigarettes." Wayne dismisses Jack's case: "You're cured already." Roylston returns and embraces Jack, thanking him for saving his life. He offers him a cigarette. Jack refuses, saying: "Never another! A pipe for mine for the rest of my life!"

If judged only by its style, *Shell Shock* seems to precede, rather than follow, the *Glencairn* series. The sea plays succeed because O'Neill drew from his own experiences to produce them. Jack Arnold, the central character in *Shell Shock*, is given some of the author's attributes: his age, description, and occupation: "a scribbler." The dramatist could not, however, relate to his hero's war experiences, which seem to be hollow summaries of newspaper accounts. He should have selected a more convincing premise and motive for Jack's mental condition. It seems hardly likely that a man as disturbed as Jack could be cured in such a short period of time.

The entire plot of the play is shallow and not worthy of the effort put into it. O'Neill obviously mulled the idea over in his head for some time before writing the one-acter, as he recorded the original concept earlier in his 1918–1920 notebook. Nevertheless, the play is a failure, and not an interesting one at that. There is nothing about the characters, setting, or theme that marks a step forward for the author. Wisely, he decided not to allow it to be staged.

21. *The Rope*

In its first printing in 1919 and in subsequent publica-
tions, *The Rope** was included among the plays of the sea.
While the action of the play takes place on the New
England coast in an old barn whose doorway looks "out
over the ocean," the land exerts a stronger influence on
the characters than the sea. The old Bentley farm is
heavily mortgaged and unproductive. Nevertheless, the
Bentleys, like the Cabots in *Desire Under the Elms*, lust
to possess the land. The farm could possibly become
profitable again, but even more important, a fortune in
gold has been hidden somewhere on the property.

The Rope is a study of greed. It shows how the
inordinate desire to possess wealth warps the natures of
the four adult characters: Abraham Bentley, his son and
daughter, Luke and Annie, and Annie's Irish husband,
Sweeney. Also interwoven into the one-acter are two
minor motifs that become major themes in later plays: the
father–son/daughter conflict and the New England Yankee–Irish Catholic struggle for dominance. As in many of
O'Neill's studies of a family, each of the four members has
contributed in some way to the group's unhappy situation.

Annie's statements to her father at the beginning of
the play—he merely injects appropriate Biblical quotations between her remarks—provide the exposition.
Bentley has been "shoutin' Scripture" all his life, but, like
many husbands in the O'Neill canon, he had "druv" his
wife to death with his "naggin', and pinchin', and miser
stinginess." Bitterly, Annie reminds him that her mother
"wasn't cold in the earth" before he was "down in the port

*The longhand draft is dated "3/1/18." The Playwrights' Theater
presented the first production of the one-acter on April 26, 1918.

courtin' agen—courtin' that harlot that was the talk o' the whole town!" Annie was forced to marry Pat Sweeney to escape the machinations of her cruel stepmother, who turned Bentley against his daughter. She calls the father a hypocrite for labeling her a sinner because she had married a Papist, "after not bein' at Sunday meetin' yourself for more'n twenty years!"

Whereas Bentley destroyed his first wife by the meanness he "done to her all her life," he was himself undone by his second. He ruined the farm, according to his son-in-law, by "sellin' everythin' to buy that slut new clothes." Throughout the six years of the marriage, the stepmother had been "the shame of the whole county," going "with this farmer and that, and even men off the ships in the port." Finally she deserted Bentley, leaving a son she claimed was his: five-year-old Luke. Bentley had mortgaged the farm for one thousand dollars in gold, and his wife informed him that "he could support Luke on the money he'd got." Annie had moved back home with her husband to help raise the child.

When he was sixteen, Luke stole one hundred dollars from his father and ran away from home. Before he left, Luke had taunted his father about the theft and laughed when Bentley "was took crazy and cursed him." He had "only laughed harder" when the father hung a rope in the barn and told him to "hang himself on it when he ever came home agin." The rope is the dominant symbol of the play. "About five feet long with an open running noose at the end," it hangs from the edge of the loft twelve feet from the floor. After Luke's betrayal and departure, the old man became unhinged. The rope is an obsession with him, and he returns to the barn frequently to make certain it is still there.

Bentley is a "tall, lean, stoop-shouldered old man of sixty-five." He walks aided by a cane. "His face is gaunt, chalky-white," his eyes "peer weakly from beneath bushy, black brows. His mouth is a sunken line drawn in under his large, beak-like nose." Annie is a "thin, slovenly, worn-out looking woman of about forty with a drawn, pasty face." Her husband is a "stocky, muscular, sandy-haired Irishman" with an "expression of mean cunning and cupidity about his mouth and his small, round, blue eyes." The couple's child, Mary, is a "skinny, over-grown girl of ten with thin, carroty hair worn in a pigtail." The child's face is "stupidly expressionless." She is described as being "half-witted" like her grandfather.

The play opens just before sunset on a day in early spring. Bentley enters the barn, discovers his grand-daughter, and drives her out, muttering: "Out o' my sight, you Papist brat! Spawn o' Satan! Spyin' on me!" When Annie comes in and urges him to return to the house to take his medicine, the old man strikes her "viciously over the arm with his stick." Sweeney enters, calling Annie a lazy slut for not having prepared his supper. Told of the attack on his wife, he "advances toward Bentley threateningly." The old man curses him, and Sweeney "instinctively crosses himself" and draws back; regaining his courage, he says, "Spit curses on me till ye choke. It's not likely the Lord God'll be listenin' to a wicked auld sinner the like of you."

Sweeney orders Mary, who is terrified of her father, to take the old man to the house. He then tells his wife he has gotten Dick Waller, a lawyer, drunk in an effort to find out how Bentley had disposed of the mortgage money in his will. The lawyer informed him that there was no cash and that Bentley has left the farm to Luke. If Luke does not return in two years, the court will declare him legally dead, and Annie will inherit the farm. Since his marriage, the Irishman has supported the family by working as a carpenter, a job he detests. He also hates Bentley and would choke him if he were not Annie's father. His dream is to find the thousand dollars. He would stock the farm and work it, "an' in a few years we'd be rich." The doctor has warned Annie that Bentley will be "a real lunatic" after his next attack. Sweeney wants to discover the hiding place of the money before he goes mad.

The couple is startled when Luke appears in the doorway, holding Mary by the hand. His face reveals a dual nature, a quality found in many characters in O'Neill's plays. He has a "good-natured, half-foolish grin" and a "certain devil-may-care recklessness and irresponsible youth in voice and gesture. But his mouth is weak and characterless; his brown eyes are large but shifty and acquisitive." Annie gives Luke a "venomous look of hatred"; Sweeney scowls at him. Only Mary is pleased to see him. Luke gives the child a silver dollar and invites her to go to the edge of the cliff where they can "chuck some stones in the ocean same's we useter." Mary wants to throw the silver dollar: "It's flat 'n' it'll skip." Seeing that the idea aggravates her greedy parents, Luke agrees and takes the child to the cliff.

Fearing Annie's inability to conceal her hatred of Luke, Sweeney tells his wife to go to the house and break the news of her brother's return to Bentley. Luke "needs to be blarneyed round to fool him an' find out what he's wantin'." Sweeney extends his hand in friendship to Luke, who is cautious and suspicious, and offers him a drink. The two sit down. Luke sees the rope and becomes infuriated when he recalls his father's command to hang himself. He promises to "git back at him" and "git every cent he's got this time." He wants only his father's money, not the farm. When Luke leaves this time, he will not return.

Bentley enters "in an extraordinary state of excitement, shaking all over, gasping for breath, his eyes devouring Luke from head to foot." The old man chants a passage from the parable of the Prodigal Son, the father's words of welcome, "bring forth the best robe," and concludes by saying: "For this my son was dead, and is alive again; he was lost, and is found." Overjoyed, Bentley touches his son's arms and chest as though trying to

convince himself he is not dreaming. He finds it nearly
impossible to talk, but he manages to utter: "Luke—
hang." Luke stands on a chair, puts the noose around his
neck, and pretends he is going to jump. When the old
man nods his head vigorously, Luke becomes vicious and
calls him a "stinkin' old murderer." He shakes him furi-
ously and sends him sprawling on the floor. Sweeney
intercedes and leads Bentley out to safety. He then returns to resume his conversation.

Believing that his father wants him dead, Luke
promises to "git even" that night. If his father refuses to
tell where the gold is hidden, he will make him talk. He
picks up a chisel. "We'll just shove this into the stove till
it's red hot and take off his shoes and socks and warm the
bottoms of his feet for him. He'll tell then."

As the men turn to leave, Mary enters and begs to be
allowed to swing on the rope. Her father forbids her to do
so. Not wanting her to witness the attack on her grandfather, Sweeney orders her to stay in the barn. Luke
promises Mary that "ter-morrer" he will give her a hand-
ful of "bright things." Later Mary stands on a chair under
the rope and pulls it. The rope falls to the floor; a dirty
grey bag is tied to the end of it. The child pours the
contents into her lap: a glittering pile of fifty twenty-dollar
gold pieces. She picks up some coins, runs to the cliff, and
throws them into the sea. Laughing shrilly, she returns
for more gold pieces as the curtain falls.

The Rope is probably the longest and best developed
of O'Neill's early one-acters. The exposition is lengthy,
but the revelations of the past provide information
needed to understand the motives and actions of the
characters, such as Luke's misjudgment of his father's
command to jump and the son's subsequent vengefulness
and cruelty. The father-son conflict in other works becomes tinged at times with violence, but in no other play
does a son's hatred provoke him to perpetrate the type of
torture Luke devises for his father at the end of *The Rope*.

The scene is chilling, terrifying. Seemingly, O'Neill's goal in devising it is to show the viciousness of a person motivated solely by greed.

The play is O'Neill's strongest indictment in the one-acters of materialism. Old Bentley had beaten his son when Luke was growing up; he had humiliated Sweeney over the years, ridiculing his Irish Catholicism. However, nothing he did in the past warrants the physical punishment these brutal men contemplate. Ironically, it is Bentley's uncharacteristic display of human emotion, of which his son and son-in-law are incapable, that dooms him. When he urges Luke to hang on the rope, Bentley does not want to punish his son but, literally, to shower wealth upon him. As revolting as the old man is, he is, at the end, redeemed and ennobled by love.

To Barrett Clark, *The Rope* is the "bitterest and in some respects the most mature play" of O'Neill's pre-1918 work. He labels Bentley "one of those hard, militant-Christian New Englanders, like Ephraim in *Desire Under the Elms*."* There are so many valid comparisons that *The Rope* seems but a prelude to the 1924 drama. The miserly Ephraim hides his money, which is later used by his sons to escape the farm. He is also accused of working his second wife to death and denounced for marrying a woman who is called a whore, a term applied to Abbie in *Desire Under the Elms*. Like Bentley, Ephraim has weak eyes and cannot see that his wife is unfaithful, that the son she produces may not be his. Both fathers favor their last-born children and make them their heirs.

As he did in his next play, *Where the Cross Is Made*, O'Neill in *The Rope* took a situation from a long play he had already devised and condensed "it into the one-act form" because he wanted a short work for the Provincetown Players. In the same period when he worked on *The Rope*, the author wrote an eighteen-page scenario for a play entitled "The Reckoning." In its first scene, a father,

*Clark, p. 48.

Stephen Donohue, and his stepdaughter, Bessie, have a bitter quarrel, one similar to the argument between Bentley and Annie. In "The Reckoning" the Irish father, who is described as "half-witted," threatens Bessie's Yankee lover if he does not marry her. In *The Rope* Sweeney, the Irish son-in-law, threatens the feeble-minded Yankee Bentley. What is significant is the fact that O'Neill expanded "The Reckoning" into a four-act play entitled "The Guilty One" in 1924, the same year he wrote *Desire Under the Elms*, which seems to have had its roots in the earlier one-acter, *The Rope*.

22. *Beyond the Horizon*

Beyond the Horizon, which won the Pulitzer Prize, established O'Neill's reputation as one of America's foremost dramatists. Prior to this play, he had completed four other full-length works, but none had ever merited a production. When *Beyond the Horizon* was staged,* audiences, accustomed to only brief flashes of the author's insights into human nature, were overwhelmed by his ability to sustain and develop believable characters in a multi-act work.

A number of O'Neill's earlier themes coalesce in *Beyond the Horizon*: the necessity of the dream to sustain man, the wife-husband and father-son conflicts, the contrasting value systems of the idealist poet and materialist businessman, the lure of the land versus that of the sea. A new element, however, is suggested by the play's title: that one must engage in the quest to find the ultimate meaning of life, to discover the mysterious behind-life force that lies just beyond the horizon. A seemingly inconsequential incident inspired an early idea for the play. One day when the dramatist was sitting on the beach at Provincetown, a small, feeble-minded boy of six who had "formed a deep affection for him" wondered aloud " 'what was beyond the Point, and what beyond the sea, and what beyond Europe?' 'The horizon,' announced O'Neill. 'But what,' persisted the lad, 'is beyond the horizon?' "†

*The play opened at the Morosco Theater on February 2, 1920. It has two copyright dates: June 7, 1918, and August 5, 1918. O'Neill's second wife, Agnes, states that he "had very nearly finished *Beyond the Horizon*" at the time of their marriage on April 12, 1918 (Agnes Boulton, *Part of a Long Story*, New York: Doubleday, 1958, p. 111).

†Clark, p. 14.

Two months after *Beyond the Horizon* opened,
O'Neill revealed the origin of the play's plot in a letter to
The New York Times. During his trip to Buenos Aires in
1910, O'Neill befriended a Norwegian seaman who re-
gretted leaving his family farm to go to sea. At the precise
time he was searching for a new theme for a play, the
author says, he thought of the sailor and asked himself:

> "What if he had stayed on the farm, with his instincts? What
> would have happened?" But I realized at once he never
> would have stayed. . . . It amused him to pretend he craved
> the farm. He was too harmonious a creature of the God of
> Things as They Are. . . . I started to think of a more in-
> tellectual, civilized type from the standpoint of the above-
> mentioned God—a man who would have my Norwegian's
> inborn craving for the sea's unrest, only in him it would be
> conscious, too conscious, intellectually diluted into a vague,
> intangible wanderlust. His powers of resistance, both moral
> and physical, would also probably be correspondingly wa-
> tered. He would throw away his instinctive dream and
> accept the thralldom of the farm for—why, for almost any
> nice little poetical craving—the romance of sex, say.

The man who craved the farm but went to sea becomes
Andrew Mayo; the sensitive intellectual who sacrificed
his dream of the sea for the "romance of sex" becomes his
younger brother, Robert.

In contrast to the one-acters, which usually have a
single, simple set, *Beyond the Horizon* has in each of its
three acts one scene inside the Mayo farmhouse and
another outside. Appropriately, the play begins and ends
on a road that seems to be "winding toward the horizon
like a pale ribbon." The scene opens at twilight on a day in
May. Shown sitting on a fence, reading a book, is Robert
Mayo, "a tall slender young man of twenty-three. There is
a touch of the poet about him expressed in his high
forehead and wide, dark eyes. His features are delicate
and refined, leaning to weakness in the mouth and chin."
He is joined by his brother, who returns from the fields.

Andrew "is twenty-seven years old, an opposite type to Robert—husky, sun-bronzed, handsome in a large-featured, manly fashion—a son of the soil, intelligent in a shrewd way, but with nothing of the intellectual about him."

Robert is obviously a self-portrait. He is given not only O'Neill's physical characteristics but also some of his biographical background, having spent a year at college and experienced a long illness. Although he is close to his parents and brother, he feels something calling to him from beyond the horizon.

The brothers have different natures and opposite attitudes to the land and sea. Whereas Andrew is "wedded to the soil," Robert hates the farm. To the practical older brother, life at sea is merely a means of accumulating wealth: "There are great opportunities for a young fellow with his eyes open in some of those new countries that are just being opened up." The sea, to Robert, holds "the beauty of the far off and unknown." He longs to explore "the mystery and spell of the East."

Andrew has convinced himself and his family that Ruth Atkins, the girl next door, intends to marry him. Ruth, however, prefers the romantic Robert and sets out to win him. She is a healthy, pretty girl of twenty, but a suggestion of duplicity mars her appearance: her features are marked by an "underlying, stubborn fixity of purpose hidden in the frankly-appealing charm of her fresh youthfulness. She wears a simple white dress." Ruth's white dress, like Mildred's in *The Hairy Ape*, signals a manipulatively virginal, but willfully destructive, nature.

Forced to care for her petulant, invalid mother now that her father has died, Ruth envies Robert's freedom. Asked why he is leaving, Robert tells her the origin of his dream: how he was often pushed, as a child, in his chair to a window by his mother, who wanted to get him out of her way. He speaks poetically of the promise he made himself then to follow the winding road that led to the sea. Saying she understands, Ruth "snuggles close against his side." He puts his arms about her and admits his second reason for going is because he loves her. She confesses she loves him and "throws her arms about his neck." Robert cannot believe he must sacrifice the sea to have Ruth. Whenever he shows signs of leaving her to pursue his dream, Ruth sobs and begs him to stay. He succumbs to her pleas and promised sexuality, consoling himself with the thought that love might be "the secret beyond every horizon." Ruth takes his hand to lead him homeward, but "his eyes are fixed again on the horizon." Finally, he throws "off some disturbing thought" and follows her.

Scene 2 is set in the sitting room of the Mayo home at about 9:00 that evening. Sixty-five-year-old James Mayo "is his son Andrew over again in body and face." Whatever resemblance Robert has to his family "may be traced" to his mother, Kate, fifty-five, who "retains a certain refinement of movement and expression foreign to the Mayo part of the family." With the couple are Andrew and Kate Mayo's brother, Captain Dick Scott, a "typical old salt," who narrates a sea yarn but gets little reaction from the family. Andrew, disturbed by his brother's failure to return from escorting Ruth home, goes out to the barn. Scott asserts that Andrew would make a "good strong sea-farin' man," but Mayo says that his son is a "born farmer." He favors the marriage between Andrew and Ruth as it would join the Mayo and Atkins farms and "make a jim-dandy of a place." The widowed Mrs. Atkins "needs a man, a first-class farmer, to take hold o' things; and Andy's just the one."

Upon his return, Robert informs his parents of his plan to remain home and marry Ruth and to take an interest in the farm in the future. Andrew enters, and, while deeply hurt, he congratulates his brother. He tells the family that he wishes to sail in Robert's place. Outraged, old Mayo argues that Andrew does not really want to leave: "You're riled cause your own brother's got Ruth 'stead o' you, and——" Andrew interrupts, saying that he hates the farm and is weary of working "like a slave without getting a word of thanks for it." His father raises his arm as though to strike Andrew: "You're no son o' mine—no son o' mine! You can go to hell if you want to! Don't let me find you here—in the mornin'—or—or— I'll throw you out!"

Alone with his brother, Andrew admits that his real reason for leaving is jealousy; he cannot cope with seeing Ruth and Robert together. Robert laments the evening's tragic events and looks about "as if his vengeance were seeking the responsible fate." The first act closes with Andrew assuring his brother that everything will work out.

Three years have elapsed when the second act opens. It is shortly after noon on a hot summer day. Two women are seated on opposite sides of the table in the Mayo sitting room: Mrs. Mayo, whose face has "become a weak mask wearing a helpless, doleful expression of being constantly on the verge of comfortless tears," and Mrs. Atkins, a pale-faced woman "with hard, bright eyes." Confined to a wheelchair for many years, she has "developed the selfish, irritable nature of the chronic invalid." She taunts Ruth endlessly for marrying a man who has failed utterly as a farmer. To Mrs. Mayo, Robert has been the victim of bad luck in the two years since his father's unfortunate death. Cruelly, Mrs. Atkins says it was "God's punishment" for old Mayo's refusal to forgive his older son. She believes that only Andrew's expected return from the sea can save the farm. Even Mrs. Atkins's two-year-old grandchild, Mary, is not exempt from her wrath, for the youngster is sickly like Robert. Everyone appears to be unhappy in this wretched household. Ruth, who has had to assume some responsibility for running the farm, in addition to caring for her fretful child and complaining mother, has become a bitter drudge. Her face has lost its youthfulness and freshness and become "hard and spiteful." Her only hope is that Andrew's return will change her miserable life. Robert has aged considerably; his eyes are "dull and lifeless," and his lips "drawn down at the corners" in an expression of resigned hopelessness. He has only two joys in life: love for his daughter and delight in his books. The first arouses his wife's jealousy; the second leads him, Ruth asserts, to neglect the farm.

Whenever Ruth talks longingly of Andrew's return, Robert thinks enviously of his brother's life at sea. He curses the once-beloved hills: "They're like the walls of a narrow prison yard shutting me in from all the freedom and wonder of life." During their quarrel, Ruth tells Robert that their marriage was a mistake and that she hates him; she has always loved Andrew. Her husband can leave the farm any time he wants now, for Andrew will be home soon to run it properly. Two sounds bring the argument and the scene to an end: the child's frightened whimpering from the bedroom and Andrew's cry from the road announcing his arrival.

The second scene takes place the next morning on top of a hill on the farm overlooking the sea. Robert stares out toward the horizon, his face pale and haggard. Andrew's face, in contrast, is deeply tanned. "The old easygoing good-nature seems to have been partly lost in a breezy, business-like briskness of voice and gesture." Like Marco Polo in the later play *Marco Millions*, he seems, after his years of travel, to have become a selfish materialist and to have lost his capacity to love; emotion has been stifled by greed. He confides that he had not been gone from home long before he reached the conclusion that he had never loved Ruth.

Andrew intends to leave the sea and to go to Buenos Aires, where a man can prosper in the grain business. Robert refuses the offer of a loan for a thousand dollars. All he asks of his brother is that he refrain from telling Ruth that he no longer loves her, realizing that the truth would shatter her.

Ruth appears. In an anxious attempt to look young, she has put on a white dress and "shows she has been fixing up." Insensitive to her feelings, Andrew tells her of his plan to go to Argentina. Shocked, she reminds him of the love he once professed for her and is about to express her love for him when he says he is over "that silly nonsense." Andrew, who will sail the next day on a steamer bound for Argentina, promises, "I won't come back with empty hands next time."

Act III opens on an October morning five years later in the Mayo sitting room. The shabby room has an atmosphere of "habitual poverty." Ruth, dressed in mourning, sits by the stove. Her hair is streaked with grey; her pale face "has the stony lack of expression of one to whom nothing more can ever happen, whose capacity for emotion has been exhausted." Robert, "his face and body emaciated," comes out of the bedroom and mocks the order to remain in bed issued by his doctor, whom he labels "a country quack." He asks to read the telegram announcing his brother's arrival that morning with a lung specialist.

For a brief moment Robert manifests his jealousy: "Andy's made a big success of himself—the kind he wanted. And now he's coming home to let us admire his greatness." Immediately, Robert is sorry for his words and speaks sorrowfully of his daughter's death eight months earlier: "Our last hope of happiness! I could curse God from the bottom of my soul—if there was a God." Wildly he begins to ramble on about his new plan to shake off the curse of the farm and to settle down in the city where, he believes, he could make his living as a writer. This now becomes Robert's new dream.

Ruth is alone when Andrew arrives. He has changed considerably. "His face seems to have grown highstrung, hardened by the look of decisiveness which comes from being constantly under a strain." There is a "suggestion of ruthless cunning" about his eyes. Doctor Fawcett, who accompanies him, goes into Robert's room. Shaken by his brother's deterioration and filled with remorse, Andrew asks Ruth why she has not kept him informed of matters.

Ruth lists all the tragedies that have beset them: the deaths of Mrs. Mayo and of Mary, the unending problems with the farm.

Again Andrew shirks family responsibility and informs her that he cannot remain home to help with the farm. He has just lost all but ten or twenty thousand dollars in a foolish speculative venture. Several times he had been "almost a millionaire—on paper." He will have to return to Argentina to recoup his losses.

The doctor reports his conclusions: Robert's "lungs are terribly affected"; he is dying, and nothing can be done to help him. There is only "that last chance—the miracle." As soon as the doctor leaves, Robert enters. He has eavesdropped but seems unperturbed by the hopelessness of his condition. He manifests a strong death wish: "Now that I'm sure what's happening I can say kismet to it with all my heart."

Pressed by Robert for details of his success, Andrew boasts of his integrity during the first four years in the grain business. Then, he confesses, he took to speculating. Robert blames the change he detects in Andrew on this moral aberration. In perhaps the most important speech of the play, denouncing the man who sells his soul for material things, Robert exclaims:

> You—a farmer—to gamble in a wheat pit with scraps of paper. There's a spiritual significance in that picture. . . . You used to be a creator when you loved the farm. You and life were in harmonious partnership. . . . But part of what I mean is that your gambling with the thing you used to love to create proves how far astray— So you'll be punished. You'll have to suffer to win back——

Robert suggests the form that punishment could take when he asks his brother to promise to marry Ruth. Andrew humors him and leads him into the bedroom urging him to sleep.

Ruth then recounts the details of what happened five years ago, of her admission to Robert before Andrew's last arrival that she loved Andrew. Andrew is shattered when he thinks of how Robert must have suffered. He concludes that there is only one way to bring Robert peace before his death: Ruth must convince her husband that she never loved Andrew; she had merely spoken in anger. Ruth goes to the bedroom door but discovers that Robert is not there.

Scene 2 is set on the road where the play opened. Robert staggers in, falls into the ditch, and then makes an effort to crawl to the top of the bank where he can see the sunrise. Ruth comes in and kneels beside Robert; she cradles his head in her lap. Andrew clenches his fists "in an impotent rage against Fate." There is no bitterness in Robert's last words, only joy. He feels free at last to "wander on and on—eternally!" He hears the old voices calling from beyond the hills and exclaims: "I've won to my trip—the right of release—beyond the horizon!"

At Robert's death, Andrew castigates Ruth: "You damn woman, you coward, you murderess." Then, remembering his own culpability, he begs her forgiveness. His groping last words to Ruth suggest an attempt on his part to comply with Robert's wishes. Ruth, her mind dulled by this latest tragedy, is totally lost in another world "beyond the further troubling of any hope."

Beyond the Horizon is a transition play. It is O'Neill's first successful full-length drama, and as such it presages his experimentation in the 1920s with increasingly longer forms. However, there is a sense of finality at the conclusion of the first and second acts that impedes the flow of action. The author has not completely discarded the method of the one-acter. Eventually he became aware of the connecting weblike pattern in his work. In 1931, George Jean Nathan stated that *Beyond the Horizon*, as O'Neill "himself now sees it in retrospect, was essentially a trilogy arbitrarily compressed within a single, regulation-length play." Nathan reprimanded "superficial critics" for failing to recognize in the trilogy structure of O'Neill's *Mourning Becomes Electra* "a natural outgrowth of a seed that has been in his work since first he began to write."* Nathan also commented on the impulse toward trilogy in the natural unit formed by three of the one-acters of the *Glencairn* series. Unconsciously, the dramatist created in the sea plays a set of characters whose physical descriptions, personalities, and experiences remain constant.

The long lapses of time, the three-year and five-year periods, sharpen the division between the three acts of *Beyond the Horizon*. The characters change dramatically in the time spans, making it necessary for the dramatist to reintroduce them each time. There is a kind of finality about the conclusion of each act: a reconciliation and new understanding between the two brothers in the first act, between Ruth and Robert in the second, and between Ruth and Andrew in the third.

Thematically, *Beyond the Horizon* emphasizes two of O'Neill's central preoccupations in the early one-acters: the sea and the family, particularly man–woman relationships. Implied is the concept that one of these elements can be as destructive as the other, as he proves in other dramas. Yet nowhere in the canon, even in the earliest efforts, is a man defeated solely by his environment or external circumstances. He is always brought down by some inner flaw, usually greed or a form of betrayal: of the sea, of the life-sustaining dream, or, most crucially, of a person.

Beyond the Horizon marks a turning point in O'Neill's career, for in it he tried to incorporate what he called an "interesting technical experiment": the division of each of the three acts into interior and exterior scenes. Critics failed to give O'Neill credit for what he terms his "departure in form in search of greater flexibility." He told Barrett Clark that the whole play could have been laid in the farm interior and been "tight as a drum a la Pinero. Then, too, I should imagine the symbolism I intended to

The Intimate Notebooks of George Jean Nathan, p. 198.

convey by the alternating scenes would be apparent even from a glance at the program."*

O'Neill had presented glimpses of his family members in his earlier one-acters. For the first time, however, with the four Mayos he creates a family unit closely resembling the four O'Neills. James Mayo, a kindly but quick-tempered Celtic farmer, is an early approximation of James Tyrone—O'Neill, son of a bog-trotter Irish peasant. Like Tyrone, Mayo seems more attached to his sickly poetic son and antagonistic to his sturdy older boy, whom he eventually orders out of the house. The closeness of the Mayo brothers foreshadows that of Edmund and Jamie in *Long Day's Journey into Night*. Mr. Mayo boasts, "You wouldn't believe how them boys o' mine sticks together. They ain't like most brothers. They've been thick as thieves all their lives, with nary a quarrel I kin remember."

The family resemblances are the same in both plays: the father is the older son "over again in body and face"; the younger son's refinement and sensitivity can "be traced" to his mother. Mrs. Mayo and Mrs. Atkins, as they are depicted in Act II, seem to signify the two sides of Ella O'Neill. The former wears a "weak mask" of helplessness and is constantly on the "verge of comfortless tears." She represents Ella the defenseless victim, who is powerless to resist the onslaughts of "the things life does to us." Mrs. Atkins is the aggressive victimizer, who, because of her chronic sickly condition, can attack others with impunity.

Ruth's condition in Act III foreshadows that of Mary Tyrone in the last act of *Long Day's Journey*. Both move like dazed, disembodied sleepwalkers. Mary is described as absent-minded, preoccupied, impersonal. She regards her husband "without recognition," "without either affection or animosity." The word "dully" prefixes twenty-two of Ruth's speeches in the first scene of the last act. Among

*Clark, p. 53.

the other qualifiers are "without feeling (emotion/inter-est)" and "indifferently" (used thrice). In the final lines of the play, Ruth's mind sinks back into a spent calm; Mary is lost in a "sad dream" in which she evokes memories of the past.

Beyond the Horizon contains concepts O'Neill explored at length in later plays. For example, in *Desire Under the Elms* two men and a woman are trapped on a bleak farm and caught up in a triangular relationship. Each has unfulfilled desires and contributes, unwittingly, to the destruction of the others. The hero of *Marco Millions* sets out innocently, like Andrew, to make his way in the world but becomes in time a rapacious capitalist. In *The Great God Brown* Dion Anthony and William A. Brown, who are described as brothers, represent, like Robert and Andrew, the idealistic poet and the materialistic businessman. *Welded* and a number of later plays focus on a Strindbergian love-hate marital relationship.

Two major themes in *Beyond the Horizon* recur in many subsequent plays: the necessity of the dream to sustain a man and his quest to discover the mysterious behind-life force wherein lies the secret to the meaning of life. Robert's death illustrates the need for the dream; his suffering provides him with insights into the purpose of existence. Trapped by life, he is unable to discover what lies beyond the hills, the sea. The wealth Andrew pursues is rejected; the love Ruth promises is denied him. The play becomes the odyssey of Robert as he turns within himself to discover the core of meaning; he discovers at the end that the enduring reality is suffering. Through it, he is redeemed. In O'Neill happiness through love is rarely realized. Frequently, love represents the dictates of fate in man's life and the trials of marriage become the means of his redemption.

In Act III Robert says, "Only through contact with suffering, Andy, will you—awaken." What O'Neill implies here is important for understanding later works.

Suffering brings not merely salvation hereafter but also peace. At the end Robert mumbles, "Only through sacrifice—the secret beyond there—." Mustering his strength, he points to the horizon where the sun merges with the tops of the hills.

23. *The Dreamy Kid*

The inspiration for *The Dreamy Kid** came from a story
O'Neill heard, and he attempted, at first, to reproduce it
in narrative form. While in New York in April 1918, the
author contacted some of his former drinking companions
and reminisced with them about the past. According to
his wife, Agnes, he got the idea for the one-acter during a
conversation with Joe Smith, his old friend at the Hell
Hole. She described Joe as "the boss of a Negro underworld near the Village," a man whose "tales were startling."†

    In May the couple returned to Provincetown, where
O'Neill "did a page or so of the short story, then put it
aside—decided it should be a one-act play." Agnes believed it was the name "Dreamy" that ignited her husband's imagination: "I remember Gene speaking that
name almost lovingly and then laughing. Negro gangster
named Dreamy—so Joe had spoken of him. *Why*
Dreamy?"** To a man who would stress the importance of
the pipe dream in many of his plays, the name proved
irresistible. It was the name Mammy Saunders had given
her grandson Abe as a baby when the two sat under a
willow tree and his big eyes chased "de sun flitternin' froo
de grass." It signifies the one side of man that society
cannot touch or corrupt, the spiritual side of Dreamy that
triumphs when all else collapses.

---

*The Playwrights' Theater produced the play on October 31,
1919. It was published in *Theatre Arts Magazine* in January
1920.

†Boulton, p. 135.

**Boulton, p. 176.

Somehow, as the years passed, the child's eyes lost their dreaminess, which was crushed by the harsh realities of his life on the streets of New York. He is a gangster when the play opens. His "eyes are shifty and hard, their expression one of tough, scornful defiance. His mouth is cruel and perpetually drawn back at the corners into a snarl." Occasionally, but only in the presence of his grandmother, he displays flashes of his former self. The focus of the play is Dreamy's psychological split and his strange superstitious streak, which finally forces him to manifest his true nature at the end of the play.

The one-acter opens shortly after midnight on an early winter night in Mammy's bedroom, located upstairs in a house in New York City. The ninety-year-old woman, whose face is "furrowed by wrinkles and withered by old age and sickness," has a premonition that she will die that night, but she stubbornly refuses to do so until her grandson arrives. Assured by her daughter, Ceely Ann, who finds it impossible to conceal her grief, that Dreamy is coming, she drowses off. Ceely's central concern throughout the play is to keep Mammy from discovering that Dreamy is not "de mos' innercent young lamb in de worl'."

Irene, Dreamy's girl friend, enters, looking for him. She is a "young, good-looking Negress, highly rouged and powdered, dressed in gaudy, cheap finery." Ceely tells this "street gal": "Git back ter yo' bad-house whar yo' b'longs!" and reproaches the absent Dreamy for keeping company with this type of woman and for being the boss of a gang—"fightin' wid white folks, an' totin' a pistol in his pocket." Ceely refuses to believe the warning that Dreamy is in danger. Irene leaves to continue her search.

Later Dreamy enters, clutching a weapon in his pocket and looking furtively out into the hallway to make certain no one is following him. He is furious with Ceely for sending word that Mammy is "croakin' "; she seems, to him, merely to be sleeping. Ceely has jeopardized his safety, as he is being hunted by the police for killing a white man the previous evening in an act of self-defense. Dreamy says that the man told folks "he was gwine ter git me for a fac'."

To save himself now, Dreamy should leave immediately, but some mysterious force prevents him from going. "With superstitious fear" he explains what prompted him to risk the visit:

> But when I heerd it was old Mammy croakin' and axin' ter see me, I says ter myse'f: "Dreamy, you gotter make good wid old Mammy no matter what come—or you don' never git a bit of luck in yo' life no mo'."

Mammy wakes, and "in an ecstasy of happiness," she makes him promise to stay until she dies. The years "roll away" for the old woman. She recalls the death of Dreamy's mother, Sal, and says the only good she has done "in de sight er de Lawd, hit's dat I raised yo' fum a baby." She is seized by a "sudden religious ecstasy" and, thinking she hears the blessed angels singing, exclaims: "Bless Gawd! Pity dis po' ole sinner."

Dreamy is angered when Irene returns, for he thinks "de bulls" will be shadowing her. He asks: "Is you pinin' ter git me kotched an' sent to de chair?" The young woman tells him she has overheard "Big Sullivan from de Central Office" order his men to stake out the house. A plainclothesman now watches the front of the house. Dreamy can still escape out the back door. She warns him: "It's de cooler for you certain if you stays here. Dey'll git you like a rat in de trap." To Ceely, Irene has confessed that she would "go ter hell for Dreamy." She proves her love by stating her desire to stay with him even if "dey kills" her. In spite of his brutal stance, Dreamy obviously returns her love. To save her from herself, he strikes Irene and forces her out of the room.

Fearing that her grandson will abandon her, Mammy rouses herself and threatens him: "If yo' leave me now, yo'

ain't gwine git no bit er luck s'long's yo' lives, I tell yo' dat!"
Dreamy is overwhelmed by his dilemma: if he remains he
will surely be captured; if he goes, a dying woman's curse
will haunt him all his days. He is trapped by his ties to this
dying woman, by the ancient religious spell she casts
upon him. Feeling he must remain or be doomed, Dreamy
says "with gloomy fatalism": "Dey'd git me in de long run
anyway—and wid her curse de luck'd be agin me."

In the last scene of the play, O'Neill uses the thought
aside to emphasize the contrast between Mammy's perception of Dreamy as the wide-eyed innocent child and
the man he has become. Although each of them is conscious of the presence of the other, they speak at cross-
purposes. Mammy relives the past and sees him as a baby
again, "jest a-dreamin' an' a-dreamin'—an' dat's w'en I
gives yo' dat nickname—Dreamy." Her grandson sees that
there are three plainclothesmen outside and that they are
converging on the house. He vows they will not take him
alive. Mammy calls him to her side. The terrible split in
him is manifested in his last act. He sinks down on one
knee beside the bed. The old woman clutches his left
hand in a death grip; his right hand holds the revolver he
will never use. Mammy's last words, "Lawd Jesus,"
merge with the sound in the hallway. The trap is sprung.

The Dreamy Kid ranks with *Ile* as the best of O'Neill's
one-acters. It is not, however, included in anthologies as
frequently as the popular *Ile*. The central figures of the
two plays, Captain Keeney and Dreamy, are determined
to pursue a course of action. They must wrestle with their
consciences when ailing women, both in desperate situations, beg them to relinquish the goal. The Captain,
motivated by pride, ignores the request; Dreamy,
prompted by love and superstition, complies.

Like *Ile*, *The Dreamy Kid* succeeds because its char-
acters and plot are credible. O'Neill had roomed with Joe
Smith at the Hell Hole and had other black friends in
Greenwich Village. In the play he shows his awareness

not only of the exterior characteristics of blacks, such as appearance and dialect, but also of their inner qualities and conflicts. Dreamy, like Brutus Jones in *The Emperor Jones*, whom he vaguely resembles, has killed a white man when his life was threatened. Similarly, Dreamy flees but is trapped and destroyed in the end, partly because of his superstitious beliefs.

There are two forces at work affecting Dreamy: his heritage, symbolized by his aged grandmother, that preserver of an ancient culture, and his environment, represented by the policemen who, in the name of society, assault the very stronghold where the cultural symbol lies dying. O'Neill suggests here the existence of the racial problem but offers no solution. He does not explain how his central character lost the dream in his eyes. This he will attempt to do in his portraits of blacks in the completed and contemplated plays of the 1920s.

24.   *Where the Cross Is Made*

Where the Cross Is Made, O'Neill's last one-act play of the sea, was written a few months after he completed *The Rope*. In the summer of 1918 the dramatist began making notes for the multi-act sea play *Chris Christopherson*. Finding himself "stumped," he put this work aside and began *Where the Cross Is Made*,* which resembles *The Rope* in some aspects.

The central character, Captain Bartlett, like Abraham Bentley in *The Rope*, bears a Biblical first name, Isaiah. He too has a son and a daughter, Nat and Sue, and is a widower. Bartlett is also viewed as being insane, for he is obsessed by the idea that he knows the secret location of a treasure that would enrich him and his family. The sons in both plays devise plans to betray the fathers: Luke at the end of *The Rope*, Nat at the beginning of *Where the Cross Is Made*. They are both motivated by greed. Nat also wants his father to abandon his illusions and enter the real world. To that end, he persuades a Doctor Higgins from the nearby asylum to come to the house in an attempt to convince the physician that the Captain should be committed.

Nat, at age thirty, is one of life's walking wounded: "His right arm has been amputated at the shoulder." His

---

*O'Neill was living in Provincetown at the time with Agnes Boulton, a writer, whom he had recently married. Agnes was experiencing creative difficulties that summer on her current project, a short story entitled "The Captain's Walk." According to Agnes, her husband liked the premise of her story and transformed it into *Where the Cross Is Made* (Boulton, *Part of a Long Story*, p. 192). The longhand draft of the one-acter is dated "1918, fall." The Playwrights' Theater offered the first production of the play on November 22, 1918.

sleeve "hangs flabbily or flaps against his body as he moves." He has "a shock of tangled black hair." His face is "long, bony, and sallow, with deep-set black eyes, a large aquiline nose, a wide thin-lipped mouth shadowed by an unkempt bristle of mustache." Some aspects of this description apply to O'Neill. Nat has also been to sea and is currently writing a book.

Doctor Higgins is ushered into a room that the Captain has furnished to look like a ship's cabin. It is early one evening in the fall of 1900. The only light in the room is the stream of moonlight that creeps in through the portholes. Nat takes a lantern from the sideboard, saying he wants to convey all the facts to the doctor, "and for that light is necessary. Without that—they become dreams up here." Except for the trips he makes upstairs to the roof, which he has rigged up to look like a ship's deck, the Captain has not left the room in three years. The doctor must see for himself "the mad way he lives."

Nat provides the play's exposition as he relates the events of the past. Seven years ago the Captain's whaling ship left port. Four years later he was shipwrecked, with six of his men, on a tiny island in the Indian Ocean. On the island, the men found the hulk of a Malay war prau containing two chests that the dazed sailors thought held gold and precious jewels. When they realized that they were going mad from hunger and thirst, the men buried their loot and drew a map marking the treasure "where the cross is made." The crew was rescued, but only three of the men, besides the Captain, remained alive: Silas Horne, the mate; Cate, the bosun, and Jimmy Kanaka, a Hawaiian harpooner.

The survivers returned home with the Captain, who then mortgaged his house to outfit a schooner, the *Mary Allen*, which he named for his wife. He intended to return to the island for the treasure with his men but was unable to do so because his wife was dying. His derangement dates to the moment when he heard that the *Mary Allen*

was lost "in a hurricane off the Celebes with all on board
—three years ago." The Captain refuses to believe that
the ship sank. Nat remarks, "He *knows*, Doctor, he
knows—but he won't *believe*. He can't—and keep living." To convince the doctor that his father is deluded, the
son displays a bracelet made of paste and brass that the
Captain brought back from his voyage.

Nat explains other details of the family's situation.
The mortgage, the price of the Captain's folly, is to be
foreclosed. Nat and his sister, Sue, who is to be married
soon, will have to move, but they will not be able to take
their father with them. The son says that his father might
recover if he were "away from the sight of the sea." The
doctor has to leave, but he promises to return that night to
take the Captain to the asylum.

Shortly after the doctor goes, Sue, a "tall, slender
woman of twenty-five, with a pale, sad face framed in a
mass of dark red hair," enters and wants to know who had
been there. She discovers the bargain Nat has struck with
Old Smith, who holds the mortgage. Apparently aware of
the terms of the will, in which the Captain leaves the
home to Nat, Smith has offered him two thousand dollars
for the house and permission to stay on as caretaker if the
son succeeds in getting the Captain committed. Sue is
horrified: "You know he'd die if he hadn't the sea to live
with." She had planned to have her father and brother
live with her after her marriage. Nat is outraged: "Would
you saddle your young husband with a madman and a
cripple?"

Nat holds two grudges against his father. First, he
had forced Nat to go to that "damned sea," the sea "that
robbed me of my arm and made me the broken thing I
am!" When Sue begs Nat, for their mother's sake, not to
commit their father, Nat replies: "Stop! She's—dead—
and at peace. Would you bring her tired soul back to him
again to be bruised and wounded?" While committing his
father seems one way to settle old scores, Nat is motivated

mainly by his desire to escape the mad game his father plays with him: "whispering dreams in my ear—pointing out to sea—mocking me with stuff like this!" He takes the fake bracelet from his pocket and hurls it into a corner. "It's too late for dreams now. It's too late! I've put them behind me tonight—forever!" Horror-stricken, Sue responds: "You've sold him! Oh, Nat, you're cursed!"

Like a man demented, Nat pulls out the treasure map from his pocket, stating that the lure of wealth has for years stood between him and life, driving him mad. He knew "it was all a dream," but he couldn't kill it: "God forgive me, I still believe! And that's mad." Asserting that his father has stolen his brain, Nat sets fire to the treasure map, believing this act will free him from the father's spell.

At that moment Captain Bartlett comes into the room. "He bears a striking resemblance to his son, but his face is more stern and formidable." His hair is pure white. "Bushy gray brows overhang the obsessed glare of his fierce dark eyes." As insane as he is, the Captain seems to be aware of Nat's plan. He is "in a state of mad exultation" and curses his son for turning traitor: "mockin' at me and sayin' it's all a lie—mockin' at himself, too, for bein' a fool to believe in dreams, as he calls 'em." The old man maintains that the *Mary Allen*, "loaded with gold," has just returned and dropped anchor. He tells his son to look out the porthole; he will see the red and green light that signals the ship's return. Nat succumbs to his father's madness. Convinced that he sees the signal, Nat follows his father to the roof and repeats the old man's words of welcome to his crew.

Sue looks out into the harbor and sees nothing. Later she tells Nat that he is doing the right thing by humoring their father when no ship exists. Nat turns on Sue and calls her "a blind fool." The Captain returns, his face transfigured with the ecstasy of a dream come true." Mentally, he traces the movements of his men from the ship to the path leading to the house.

> The sound of the wind and sea suddenly ceases and there is
> a heavy silence. A dense green glow floods slowly in rhyth-
> mic waves like a liquid into the room—as of great depths of
> the sea faintly penetrated by light.

For every imagined happening that Nat's feverish
brain projects, Sue has a rational explanation: the green
glow is moonlight; the sound on the stairs is only rats
running around. The Captain is positive that his men are
approaching; he goes to the door to welcome them. His
mad dream becomes a reality: the forms of Silas Horne,
Cates, and Jimmy Kanaka glide noiselessly into the room.

> The last two carry heavy inlaid chests. Strands of seaweed
> are in their hair; their eyes stare frightfully wide at nothing.
> Their flesh in the green light has the suggeston of decom-
> position. Their bodies sway limply, nervelessly, rhythmi-
> cally as if to the pulse of long swells of the deep sea.

Horne gives a piece of paper to the Captain, who
motions to the figures to follow him up the stairs to the
roof. Doctor Higgins comes in and goes up to the roof with
Nat. The two return carrying the Captain's dead body.
"Heart failure," says the doctor. Sue begs her brother not
to touch the body, but Nat, "as if in a trance," forces his
father's clenched fingers open and removes "a crumpled
ball of paper." Triumphantly, he holds up the map and,
disregarding the vision of the returning sailors, wildly
announces his "mad, solemn decision" to seek the treasure. Sue laments the loss of father and brother as the
curtain falls.

The play is given an incredible ending. Once again,
as he did in *Fog*, O'Neill relies entirely on the supernatural for his conclusion. Through it he conveys the
power of the cherished dream. The Captain is in part
motivated by greed in his desire to reclaim the treasure,
but he is compelled primarily by his mad obsession to
realize his dream. Its spell is so overwhelming that his
normally clear-headed son succumbs to it. Bartlett is lost
to the illusionary world; his daughter inhabits the realm of

reality. The focus of the drama is the struggle of each for the soul of Nat, who totters precariously on the periphery of insanity. Just before the visionary appearance of the dead sailors, he takes his sister's hand and cries out hysterically: "Save me! Save me!"

O'Neill states that he never "really valued *Where the Cross Is Made*. It was great fun to write, theatrically very thrilling, an amusing experiment in treating the audience as insane—that is all it means or ever meant to me."* In early 1920 the dramatist expanded the story narrated in *Where the Cross Is Made* into a four-act play entitled *Gold*. He asserts that the one-acter did not inspire the longer play but that "the reverse is the real truth." In writing the second version of Bartlett's story, O'Neill changed the focus of the original work; the longer play does not stress a man's obsession with realizing his dream but rather his desire to possess wealth. The title of the early play implies that a man's dream can prove to be his cross, his destruction; the later work suggests that his desire for wealth can be his curse.

---

*Clark, pp. 47–48.

25. The Straw

Stephen Murray in *The Straw**, like Robert Mayo in *Beyond the Horizon*, is a self-portrait. Both have O'Neill's physical traits, his characteristics, and his consumptive condition. The author seems to have written two scenarios for his life in these plays. In *Beyond the Horizon*, the more fictional account, he is the twenty-three-year-old Robert Mayo, the man with "a touch of the poet about him," who dreams of going to sea but stays home to marry his childhood sweetheart. He sacrifices himself for others, neglects his serious lung condition, and dies with his dream unfulfilled but untarnished. In *The Straw*, the more accurate biography, he is Stephen Murray, a small-town newspaper reporter with a desire to become a creative writer who is a patient at Hill Farm Sanatorium in Connecticut.† The specific year of the action of the play is not given, but it probably corresponds to the period O'Neill spent at Gaylord Farm Sanatorium in Wallingford, Connecticut: December 24, 1912, to June 3, 1913. Chronologically, the action of *The Straw* follows the discovery of Edmund Tyrone, a self-portrait in *Long Day's Journey into Night*, set in August 1912, that he has tuberculosis.

---

*The date of the copyright is November 19, 1919; that of the longhand draft is "(1918–19) fall–winter."

†During the period O'Neill wrote these plays, 1918–1919, he seems to have been obsessed with his own mortality, with his two apparent brushes with death in 1912: his failed attempt to commit suicide early that year at Jimmy the Priest's and his subsequent discovery that he had tuberculosis, then considered fatal. In the "List of Plays" the author indicates that he began "Exorcism," in which he recreates himself and the suicide attempt, after completing the revised text for *The Straw*.

O'Neill completed *Beyond the Horizon* in the early summer of 1918. According to his wife, Agnes, he then reminisced about the period he spent at Gaylord and a girl there whom he had almost forgotten. When the author entered the first idea for *The Straw* in his 1918–1920 notebook, he clearly identified himself with the protagonist, calling him Eugene, rather than Stephen, Murray. The nearly forgotten prototype for the girl is Kitty Mac-Kay, a patient who fell in love with the young O'Neill. She is called Norah O'Brien in the early notes and Eileen Carmody in the final version. The name "Nora" is assigned to one of Eileen's sisters in the published text. Heading these notes is a line indicating two possible titles for *The Straw*: "The Matter of a Pound or the Laughing Sailor." The latter suggests that O'Neill might have intended to inject his own experiences as a seaman into Stephen Murray's biography.

In the early notes the play opens in the sanatorium on a day in spring; in the final version the first scene is set in the kitchen of the Carmody home in Waterbury, Connecticut, in late February. Bill Carmody waits for the doctor, who is upstairs examining his ailing daughter, Eileen. The father is a heavy-set, muscular man with a harsh mouth, selfish, cunning eyes, and the red, purple-streaked complexion of a chronic drinker. Like James Tyrone in *Long Day's Journey into Night* he has the Irish immigrant's superstitious belief that tuberculosis is fatal and a miserliness that makes him reluctant to hospitalize Eileen. Similarly, Carmody contributed to his wife's physical condition; she had died the previous year, a victim of neglect and overwork. Both fathers berate their offspring for reading: Carmody attributes Eileen's sickness to it; Tyrone, his son's moral dissolution. As in so many family plays, there is a line drawn here between family members: eight-year-old Mary, the delicate youngest child, always has her "nose in a book" and resembles her sister Eileen and their mother. Fourteen-year-old Billy is a "replica of his father," as are Nora, eleven, and Tom, ten.

Carmody refuses to allow Eileen to go to Hill Farm Sanatorium when Doctor Gaynor informs him she has consumption because of the fee, seven dollars a week. "I'll not have a penny saved for me old age—then it's the poorhouse!"* The father acquiesces only after the doctor says that a charitable organization will pay half of the medical expenses. The doctor seems to get more cooperation from Eileen's fiancé, Fred Nicholls, whose easygoing smile is contradicted by the "petty, calculating expression" of his eyes. After graduating from business college, Eileen had gotten a job as a stenographer in the firm where Nicholls works as a bookkeeper, but she had to relinquish the position to take care of the children when her mother died. Home responsibilities, the doctor asserts, are "the main cause of her breakdown." He assures the young man that Eileen can be cured in six months. Nicholls is horrified when he discovers that tuberculosis is extremely contagious.

The second scene takes place a week later in the reception room of the sanatorium's infirmary. Seated before the fireplace is thirty-year-old Stephen Murray, whose pale, lined face is "jaded and worn for one so young." His eyes look tired "but can quicken instantly with a concealment mechanism of mocking, careless humor whenever his inner privacy is threatened. His large mouth aids this process of protection by a quick change from its set apathy to a cheerful grin of cynical good nature." His manner is "nervous, inquisitive, alert." He tries to convince his nurse, Miss Howard, that he is not sick like the other patients and says cynically, "I suppose it's that pipe dream keeps us all going."

Eileen, a lovely but extremely thin girl of eighteen,

---

*In *Long Day's Journey into Night* James Tyrone cries "poorhouse to Hardy," the doctor treating Edmund, when he is told his son must be hospitalized.

arrives. She has a wavy mass of dark hair, sweet, pierc-
ingly direct eyes, and a heavy Irish jaw, which contrasts
with the delicacy of her features. With her are her father,
who has "very evidently been drinking," and Nicholls,
who wants only to accomplish this "necessary but dis-
agreeable duty" as quickly as possible. As they depart, the
older man curses the sanatorium; the younger man callously provokes Eileen to tears. Alone with the girl, Murray attempts to console her by describing life at the sanatorium as being "like heaven." To cheer her, he describes
his dream: he wants to write short stories. When Eileen
encourages him, Murray asks her to "play the critic" and
tell him "where they're rotten." He holds the confused
girl's hand, and she agrees to do so. Eileen leaves, and the
act closes with Murray toasting the absent girl with a glass
of milk and parodying lines from the *Rubaiyat* of Omar
Khayyam:

> A glass of Milk, and thou
>   Coughing beside me in the wilderness—
> Ah—wilderness were Paradise enow!*

For the first scene of Act II, O'Neill uses the outline
he sketched for *The Straw* in his 1918–1920 notebook.
The doctor, his assistant, and the visitor from the south of
the country become, respectively, Doctor Stanton; his
assistant, Doctor Simms; and Mr. Sloan, "a visitor,"
whose "endowments have made the Hill Farm a possibility." The inquiries of Sloan elicit from the doctors information O'Neill wishes to convey to an audience. The
patients, who will soon file into the assembly room to be
weighed, appear to be progressing satisfactorily. At the
end of six months, however, those who fail to respond to
treatment are labeled "hopeless" and sent, if poor, to one
of the State Farms. The staff is "strictly anti-Cupid." Any
intimacy between patients is considered an obstacle to
getting well.

---

*In the autobiographical *Ah, Wilderness!*, the lovesick Richard
Miller, another self-portrait, recites the actual lines of the poem.

In the four months that have passed, Eileen has grown stouter. But her face, in spite of its healthy color, is depressed. For the last three weeks she has scarcely eaten, as she knows that Stephen, who "has filled out solidly," will soon be discharged. He has sold his first story and plans to continue his writing in New York. He attributes his success to Eileen's encouragement. O'Neill employs a device here, which is to be used later in the Marco Polo–Princess Kukachin relationship in *Marco Millions*, to demonstrate a man's insensitivity to a woman's love. Eileen gazes into Stephen's eyes "as if imploring him to comprehend" her love for him. "Lowering her eyes in confusion," she remarks: "If you can't see—." She conceals her feelings, however, even when she learns that she has lost three pounds and Stephen has gained the same amount, thus making him eligible for release the next day.

The next scene is set at midnight at the crossroads near the sanatorium. Disregarding the nurse's warning not to exert herself, Eileen has summoned Stephen to a meeting in the woods. At first he ignores her feelings for him and speaks only of his future plans. Told that Eileen has broken her engagement to Nicholls, Stephen, not wanting to become involved with her, remarks callously: "You must get one of the right sort—next time." Recklessly, Eileen puts her arms around him and says that love "has made me happier than I've ever been—." Stephen kisses her and promises to come back. Perhaps in time, she reasons, he will discover that he loves her. She will pray "God to make it so." Her words—"I'll hope—I'll hope—till I die!"—haunt Stephen, and he clenches his fists "in impotent rage at himself and Fate."

When Act IV opens, four months have passed. Eileen, her face pale and drawn, is confined to an isolation room in the infirmary. She gazes out of the window at the bleak October scene, deriving no pleasure from the visit of her father and Mrs. Brennan, the crude housekeeper whom Carmody married two weeks earlier. Shortly after they leave, Stephen arrives. He is thin, pale, and dissipated. One glance assures Eileen that he has not returned because he loves her. She pretends not to remember anything she said on that ill-fated night four months earlier.

Nurse Gilpin calls Stephen aside and tells him that Eileen is dying: "She's given up hope. She hasn't wanted to live any more." The nurse asks him to pretend that he loves Eileen to make her last days happy. Later, when he declares his love to Eileen and tells her that they will marry and go away together, Stephen experiences a true "awakening—a revelation." At the end of *Beyond the Horizon* Andrew Mayo seeks to prolong his brother's life by planning a trip to Arizona. Stephen tells the nurse that he intends to take Eileen to the far west. He sees the negative look in the nurse's eyes and exclaims. "Oh, why did you give me a hopeless hope?" She responds that there is "some promise of fulfillment—somehow—somewhere—in the spirit of hope itself." The play ends with Eileen forgetting her own condition and telling the kneeling Stephen that she will take care of him in the future.

The Straw contains the strongest expression, prior to 1920, of one of the major themes in O'Neill's work: the need for the dream. For Eileen the hopeless hope is that Stephen will love her; for him, it is, at the end, that she will be cured. The title of the play indicates the fragility of the dream. Forced to relinquish the dream, the individual will, like Eileen, decline unto death.

In *The Straw* O'Neill presents an extremely unfavorable portrait of himself: self-centered, self-serving, insensitive. He leaves unanswered the question: did he in real life contribute, by his indifference, to the demise of Kitty MacKay, the prototype for Eileen Carmody? Was he merely exaggerating his own experiences for dramatic purposes as he had done in the past and would do many times in the future? *The Straw*, which O'Neill identifies as one of his favorite plays, is merely an exercise in self-indulgence. It remains one of the author's most sentimental and least effective works. When it was first staged at the Greenwich Village Theatre on November 10, 1921, the audience found it depressing and morbid.

Throughout O'Neill's life the straw imagery assumed special significance to the author, as well as to his characters. At the end of his career he was working on an antitotalitarian play in which the forces of good struggle valiantly to defeat the forces of evil. The play, known finally as "The Last Conquest," was tentatively called "More Straw for the Drowning." The personal hope expressed first in *The Straw* becomes in the later work a universal hope for mankind.

IDEAS: 1918–1920 NOTEBOOK

Honor Among the Bradleys

The Signature

The Trumpet

Exorcism

The Straw

Silence

Shell Shock

Chris Christopherson

Play of a Small Town*

The Little Things

Man of 45*

The Old Game*

Beyond the Horizon Sequel*

T.B. Sailor*

Man and Wife*

Monologue*

Nickel Poolroom*

Play of Family*

I Spy

The Old Fisherman*

Reincarnation*

Jim and Self*

Forty Years

Sailor's Snug Harbor

Series: Jimmy the Priest Series

Sanatorium Series

Gunman Series

German Spy*

His Master's Eyes*

Spanish Sailor*

Titles listed here in regular type indicate an idea not developed or published. Titles in *italics* indicate that the idea was ultimately published.

*O'Neill provided no titles for a number of ideas. Key words, taken from these ideas and summarizing their central focus, are used as working titles where so indicated by an asterisk.

O'Neill at his home in Bermuda, 1926.
Inscription: "To Carlotta with my love, Gene." "This is a corner of Spithead—coral rocks—and the sea—and my grinning self."

Eugene and Carlotta O'Neill at Chateau du Plessis, France, 1929, shortly after their marriage

The Hairy Ape, Provincetown Playhouse, New York, 1922. Yank,
Louis Wolheim; Mildred Douglas, Carlotta Monterey

Yank's encounter with Mildred in Tairov's production. Kamerny
Theatre, Moscow, 1926

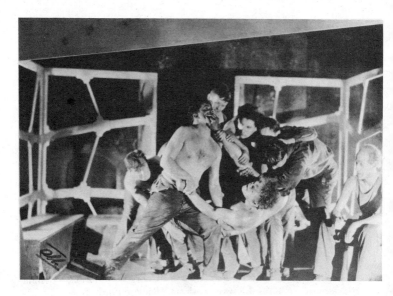

American version of stokers in forecastle

Stylized Russian view of men in forecastle

Anna Christie, New York, 1921 Chris Christopherson, George Marion; Anna, Pauline Lord

Lazarus Laughed, Pasadena Community Playhouse, Pasadena, Calif., 1928. Unmasked, Lazarus (Irving Pichel) and Miriam (Lenore Shanewise) stand before Tiberius Caesar (Gilmor Brown).

2. The Mariner's Horizon

The Mariner's Horizon: Experimental Plays and Maturation

The 1920s were a period of extraordinary growth for Eugene O'Neill. The decade began, appropriately, with the production on February 2, 1920, of *Beyond the Horizon*, the author's first full-length drama to be staged. Its title suggests the progressive visionary journey he had undertaken as an artist. Technically, he would expand the horizon of the American theater by introducing to it experimental devices—masks, choruses, complex multiple sets—and forms—the nine-act play, the trilogy. Thematically, he would extend his artistic range, offering deeper insights into his own personal life and experiences and going beyond these narrow confines to present ideas that had social and political dimensions.

Five of the first seven plays completed in the early 1920s, like half of those written in the prior period, have either ocean settings or sea-related elements. As in the first period, O'Neill derived inspiration from his own surroundings as well as from his former experiences at sea. From 1920 to 1927 he lived near the ocean for part or all of each year. For the first two years of the decade, while residing at Provincetown, he wrote *Gold* and *Anna*

Christie, both of which use a shipwreck to advance the plot. These two plays, however, do not, technically, belong with the works of the 1920s; they are holdovers from the first period. *Gold* is a four-act expansion of the 1918 one-acter *Where the Cross Is Made; Anna Christie* is a reworking of the 1918 *Chris Christopherson*.

The early 1920s were dominated by four domestic dramas, *Diff'rent, The First Man, Welded,* and *All God's Chillun Got Wings*, whose central focus is a complex man-woman relationship. *Welded* and, to some extent, *The First Man* mirror O'Neill's own marriage at that time to Agnes Boulton. In the former, the playwright-husband, a self-portrait, demands that his wife, an actress, share his idealized concept of their marital union. In the latter, Curt Jayson forbids his subservient secretary-wife to have a child. His desire, when she does become pregnant, to live "the old, free life together," probably reflects O'Neill's suppressed annoyance over the birth of his son Shane on October 30, 1919, a year before he began *The First Man*.

When a wife becomes destructive, like Ella Harris in the 1923 *All God's Chillun Got Wings*, she is no longer a portrait of Agnes but of Ella O'Neill, the dramatist's mother. Not until after Ella's death on February 28, 1922, did the author allow himself to portray his mother as victimizer in his work. In his next two plays, *Desire Under the Elms* and *The Great God Brown*, the central figures, Eben Cabot and Dion Anthony, lament the deaths of mothers who were victimized by their husbands. While writing the former in 1923 at his home in Ridgefield, Connecticut, O'Neill, like Eben, felt his mother's spirit haunting him. He used this rural locale for his description of the Cabot farm. The dramatist spent each winter from 1922 to 1924 at Ridgefield and each summer of these years at Peaked Hill Bars.

After the success of the multi-act *Beyond the Hori-*

zon, O'Neill sought to express his ideas in other forms. Content and form were stunningly wed in late 1920 in *The Emperor Jones*. To develop this "Long Play—Eight Scenes," he abandoned normal modes used by American dramatists and looked to European experimental theater techniques. In a most fortunate stroke of luck, O'Neill decided to incorporate expressionistic techniques in *The Emperor Jones*. The realism of its opening and closing serves as a frame for the six expressionistic scenes that dramatize the deteriorating mind and condition of Brutus Jones. The new mode is used later to allow setting to reflects the minds of characters in *Diff'rent* and *All God's Chillun Got Wings*.

In a three-week period in December 1921 O'Neill completed his second major expressionistic work, *The Hairy Ape*. He tells Macgowan in a letter on December 24, the day after finishing the eight-scene drama:

> It seems to run the whole gamut from extreme naturalism to extreme expressionism—with more of the latter than the former. I have tried to dig deep in it, to probe in the shadows of the soul of man bewildered by the disharmony of his primitive pride and individualism at war with the mechanistic development of society.

Just as O'Neill borrowed an appropriate method from European dramatists for *The Emperor Jones* and *The Hairy Ape*, these two plays, in turn, repaid the debt and made him famous throughout the continent. The author continued his experimentation in the 1920s, using masks in *The Great God Brown*, masks and choruses in *Lazarus Laughed*, soliloquies and asides in *Strange Interlude*, multiple settings depicting various nations and cultures in *Lazarus Laughed* and *Marco Millions*, an innovative scenic plan for an electrical generating plant in *Dynamo*.

Europe with its avant-garde theaters was able to accommodate the new drama. Desiring to stage his plays as he envisioned them, O'Neill joined forces in 1923 with Kenneth Macgowan, a theater critic, and Robert Jones, a scenic designer, to found the Experimental Theatre. In their three seasons of collaboration, they produced *Welded, All God's Chillun Got Wings, Desire Under the Elms*, and *The Ancient Mariner** in 1924; *The Fountain* in 1925; and *The Great God Brown* in 1926. Even so, the author was disappointed with the setting in *Desire* and the masks in *Brown*; he despaired of finding a theater he could give his "best to in every way." He had a backlog of massive plays the Experimental Theatre could not possibly mount: *Marco Millions, Lazarus Laughed, Strange Interlude*. In August 1926 he told Macgowan, "In fairness to a friend, I think you should set me free to submit L[azarus]' to the [Theatre] Guild now."

When the triumvirate dissolved, O'Neill began his long association with the Theatre Guild. It presented the premiere of every play staged in the author's lifetime, with one exception: *Lazarus Laughed*, which was done at the Pasadena Playhouse on April 9, 1928. The Theatre Guild's first production, offered on January 9, 1928, was *Marco Millions*, a historical play that was more difficult to stage than its earlier counterpart, *The Fountain*.

O'Neill made a change in his private, as well as his professional, life in early 1928. On February 10 he sailed for Europe on the S.S. *Berengaria* with Carlotta Monterey, believing that his second marriage, to Agnes Boulton, could not be salvaged. In late 1924 the playwright had moved to Bermuda with Agnes and had purchased a new home, Spithead, there in 1926. The couple spent the summer of 1926 at Belgrade Lakes, Maine, where Carlotta was vacationing. She had met the dramatist in 1922, while playing the role of Mildred Douglas in *The Hairy*

---

*O'Neill adapted Coleridge's poem as a pageant play in 1923, adding only a few words and stage directions. The Provincetown Players' production of the pageant play was not successful. It opened on April 6, 1924, and ran for only thirty-three performances. The dramatization was published in the *Yale University Library Gazette*, Donald Gallup, ed. (New Haven, 1960), pp. 61–86.

Ape. Throughout the 1920s O'Neill felt beset by family responsibilities and resented the distractions that interfered with his creativity. The household steadily increased; Oona was born on May 14, 1924. The author's first son, Eugene Jr., and Agnes's daughter, Barbara, both offspring of earlier marriages, were frequent visitors.

The quiet sanctuary offered by the cool, detached Carlotta was welcomed as an alternative to the noisy home with the harried, distracted Agnes. Children, however, did not ruin the marriage; there was something fundamentally wrong with it. When Agnes at first refused to give her husband a divorce, he wrote a spiteful letter on September 21, 1928, to Macgowan, saying that the relationship never had any permanent basis in truth. "I'll bet, if I hadn't had alcohol to close my eyes whenever I began to look at her—alcohol & work which would account for 95% of the time—I wouldn't have stayed married to her for a year."*

In 1928 O'Neill abandoned Agnes and their two children. He had, at the outset of the decade, experienced another type of loss. In what seemed like rapid succession, his father died in August 1920, his mother in February 1922, and Jamie in November 1923. These deaths were followed, in the next two decades, by a series of portraits in plays of the O'Neill family. In 1924, the dramatist collaborated with Agnes on "The Guilty One," a development of an eighteen-page scenario, "The Reckoning," written in 1918.† In the latter a pregnant woman tricks her lover, Jack Gardner, into believing he has

---

*O'Neill has an undeserved reputation as a lifelong alcoholic. It should be noted that he stopped drinking in 1926 and had probably no more than two lapses in later years.

†The sole copy of "The Reckoning" is in the Theatre Collection of Houghton Library, Harvard University. The extant fragment of "The Guilty One" is at the Beinecke Rare Book and Manuscript Library, Yale University.

murdered her stepfather and forces him to marry her. Years later she threatens to take their son from her husband, now a wealthy New England businessman, if he does not run for Congress. The man calls his wife, whose description is similar to Mary Tyrone's, "a fiend of a woman who has ruined his life and whom he hates from the bottom of his soul." Discovering the truth, the son labels the mother "mad" and her deceit "fiendish." "The Reckoning" is obviously a veiled version of *Long Day's Journey into Night*; in it, Mary Tyrone is described as "a fiend of a woman" by her husband and "hard and cruel" by her son.

The "perfect" son of the scenario becomes, in "The Guilty One," an irresponsible drunkard who has gotten the heroine, Mildred Lord, pregnant. He scorns his mother, an elusive specter in the household, but loves his father, Jim Smith, an early portrait of James Tyrone, who tells his son, "I've lived twenty-two years of hell, Jud. Because—of a mistake. Life was mine, then!" The autobiographical characters depicted in these two works are presented in different guises in subsequent plays: the selfish, deceitful mother who destroys her husband and betrays her son by allowing him to be sent away from her; the father who regrets the choices he has made—in his profession and his marriage, which is a "mistake"—and who is made to feel "guilty" by his wife; the rebellious, dissipated son, who resents his mother's betrayal and cannot have a normal, loving relationship with a woman; the woman is often—like Mildred here, Ada in *Dynamo*, and Dora in "Blind Alley Guy"—merely an object of sexual desire to be seduced.

After completing "The Guilty One," in which he depicts his parents and himself, O'Neill devoted his creative efforts to portraying his brother, Jamie. The author had, because of his ambiguous feelings for his parents, turned to his brother for companionship, affection, and guidance. The 1918–1920 notebook contains an idea for a "long play—Jim & self—showing influence of elder on younger brother." In April 1924, five months after his brother's death, he resumed work on *The Great God Brown*, developing an "idea for doing it with masks" and using the Faust-Mephistopheles concept. One of O'Neill's dominant themes is man's good–evil dichotomy. In some plays the duality is represented by one figure; in others by two opposite characters. *The Great God Brown* is a strange combination of both. There is the "good" William A. Brown and the "bad" Dion Anthony, who is, however, split, wearing Pan-Mephistopheles masks to conceal his ascetic face. Dion, who becomes dissipated, drinking and frequenting whorehouses, is clearly a portrait of Jamie O'Neill, who is described as Mephistophelian in the late autobiographical plays, *Long Day's Journey into Night* and *A Moon for the Misbegotten*. He is referred to several times as "brother" by the "good" Brown. In time Brown begins to imitate Dion and assumes his mask when Dion dies. The agony of sharing the dead "brother's" burden proves to be too much for Brown; he dies but as "Dion Brown"—Man; Mephistopheles and Faust, Jamie and his brother, are one.

O'Neill was obsessed with the Faust theme, the idea that in America a man's soul was "always for sale." In 1927 he made a notation for a "Modern Faust Play" that would depict the American character, as he perceived it, as having sacrificed the spiritual for the material things of life. The concept of "the duality of Man's psyche" reverberates throughout his work. The best example in the 1920s is the ascetic artist, Dion Anthony, versus the materialistic businessman, William A. Brown. *Beyond the Horizon* in the early period focused on the plight of Robert Mayo, the doomed dreamer-poet. O'Neill planned a sequel, "a long play—taking up the 'Beyond the Horizon' situation where that play leaves off—'the play of Andrew.' " *Marco Millions* could be considered a continuation of the story of Andrew, the businessman who journeys to distant places to make his fortune. He would have become, in time, as spiritually deformed as Marco, given O'Neill's attitude to men who seek possessions. In *Marco Millions*, the Kaan says of the American-like Marco, "He has not even a mortal soul, he has only an acquisitive instinct."

Two major motifs emerge in O'Neill's plays in the 1920s: autobiographical reminiscences of his parents, brother, and friends, and of his relationship with his wife Agnes; and societal concerns: the exploitation of the worker by capitalism (*The Hairy Ape*), the destructive effects of greed (*Desire Under the Elms, Marco Millions, The Great God Brown*), political oppression by totalitarian rulers in historical plays (*The Fountain, Lazarus Laughed*), and racial injustice (*The Emperor Jones, All God's Chillun Got Wings*). The author mounted a personal crusade in the 1920s to combat racial bigotry.

Ever mindful of the prejudicial attitude of wealthy Yankee New Londoners toward his own Irish family, he planned a number of plays depicting discrimination. His first two plays with black protagonists, *The Dreamy Kid* (1918) and *The Emperor Jones* (1920), did not deal specifically with the black man's plight in white America, nor would his 1921 idea, "Honest Honey Boy," the "tragicomedy of Negro gambler" (based on the life of Joe Smith, O'Neill's roommate at the Hell Hole in 1915). Joe emerged in 1939 as the black gambler Joe Mott in *The Iceman Cometh*. In 1923, in *All God's Chillun Got Wings*, O'Neill painted a grim picture of how racial bigotry destroys the self-esteem of an intelligent black man and reduces him to an inferior in the eyes of his white wife. From 1927 to 1934, O'Neill worked intermittently on a play, tentatively titled "Bantu Boy," depicting the "Negro's whole experience in modern times—especially with regard to America." In it, a noble African chief who is drugged and transported to the United States as a slave proves to be superior to his white captors.

In the 1928 *Dynamo*, two motifs merge: autobiography and the subordinate theme focusing on the dangers of worshipping technology. The hero, Reuben Light, possesses his creator's physical traits and a "duality in character": his boyish nature conflicts with a "demonic cruel spirit." His mother, forty-five, "a religious fanatic," and his father, fifty-five, "a meek unassuming soul," are portraits of O'Neill's parents. Their marriage has been "a loveless affair."

Mrs. Light encourages her son to become a businessman rather than a minister and, like Mary Tyrone, tells him "sly tales of the real privations she has had to undergo." She betrays him, however, by revealing a confided secret to her husband. Reuben rejects his parents' Old Testament God and leaves home. He gets a job at a power plant and begins to worship the great Mother Dynamo, identifying the machine with his mother. In an effort to be united with his mother, he builds an altar before the dynamo and climbs to its core, where he is seemingly "crucified." O'Neill describes the "real plot" as the story of "Reuben's psychological mess over his father and mother's betrayal and how he at last deifies and finds her again."

While *Dynamo* was a critical failure, its immediate predecessor, *Strange Interlude*, which O'Neill called his "woman's play," was a theatrical and financial success. The dramatist had made giant strides in the 1920s to master his craft. For good reason he was able to say in a 1935 letter to Leon Mirlas, "I do think *Welded* and *The Fountain* are inferior work. Also *The First Man* and *Gold*." He wrote these early works quickly and carelessly. Discussing the choice of act or scene divisions for *The Fountain* in his letter of April 8, 1921, to Macgowan, the playwright states: "I have no rule either one way or the other. I always let the subject matter mould itself into its own particular form and I find it does this without my ever wasting thought upon it. I start out with the idea that there are no rules or precedent in the game except what the play chooses to make for itself." *Desire Under the Elms* was completed in about six weeks in 1924. The dramatist went to the other extreme in the late 1920s, devoting two entire years, 1926 and 1927, to *Lazarus Laughed* and *Strange Interlude*. In a letter to Macgowan dated August 7, 1927, O'Neill speaks of the latter, saying he wrote two separate versions of a scene "and tore them up before I got started on the really *right* one! The point is my stuff is much deeper and more complicated now and I'm also not as easily satisfied with what I've dashed off as I used to be."

Encouraged by the success of *Strange Interlude* and determined to expand his creative powers, O'Neill contemplated a grand opus in 1927, "The Sea-Mother's Son," described as "one of those timeless Big Things," having "ten or more *Interludes* in it." He planned two trilogies, "Myth Plays for the God-forsaken," composed of *Dynamo* and *Days Without End*, which he completed; "It Cannot Be Mad?," which remains in scenario; and *Mourning Becomes Electra*. In 1929, after a decade of experimentation, O'Neill uttered a cry of emancipation "for good":

> No more sets or theatrical devices as anything but unimportant background. . . . To read "Dynamo" is to stumble continually over the sets. . . . Greater classical simplicity, austerity combined with the utmost freedom and flexibility, that's the stuff! (Letter to Macgowan, June 14, 1929).

Dynamo, finished in 1928, marks the halfway point in O'Neill's writing career. Of the fifteen plays written in the 1920s, two, the expressionistic *The Emperor Jones* and *The Hairy Ape*, were artistic triumphs in this country and abroad; three controversial works, *Anna Christie*, *Desire Under the Elms* and *Strange Interlude*, won popular acclaim by the public. The other ten can be classified as either moderate successes or failures. O'Neill's favorites of his early plays were *The Great God Brown*, *The Hairy Ape*, *Lazarus Laughed*, and, in the one-act category, *The Moon of the Caribbees*. He won his first Pulit-

zer Prize in 1920 for *Beyond the Horizon*; his third came at
the end of the decade, for *Strange Interlude*.

O'Neill had, in the 1920s, expanded not only his own
artistic technique but also the dramatic possibilities of the
American theater. In the second half of his career, he
would simplify technique. As he circled closer and closer
in the 1930s to his family home and the full story of the
four O'Neills, the dramatist disposed of the trappings of
the 1920s.

26. *Gold*

Gold was written in 1920,* but it is a holdover from O'Neill's early period. It seems to be a multi-act expansion of the 1918 *Where the Cross Is Made*, yet O'Neill states:

> The idea of *Gold* was a long play one from its inception. I merely took the last act situation and jammed it into the one-act form. . . . I mention this only because I know how impossible it is to expand a natural short play into a long one, and would hardly make such a futile mistake. *Gold* was always full length to me.†

Actions narrated in the one-act *Where the Cross Is Made* are dramatized in the four-act *Gold*. As its title suggests, *Gold* contains a lesson on the destructiveness of an acquisitive nature; greed is the catalyst for a man's descent into madness.

The first act of *Gold* is set on a barren island in the Malay Archipelago. Cast on to its shore are the shipwrecked survivors of the whaler *Triton*: Captain Isaiah Bartlett and five of his crew. The sun blisters the earth with unrelenting cruelty, creating "a quivering mist of heat-waves which distorts the outlines of things, giving the visible world an intangible eerie quality." Reality becomes blurred; to the sun-crazed, thirsty men a box of worthless metal junk is a chest of precious treasure.

As in *Thirst*, the desire for water merges with greed and makes murder necessary: good and evil forces emerge. The innocent victims are Butler, who had been shang-

---

*The date of the first draft is "winter 1920"; that of the copyright, July 27, 1920. *Gold* premiered at the Frazee Theater on June 1, 1921.

†Clark, p. 47.

haied to serve as cook on the voyage, a middle-aged man
with a "halo" of dirty thin gray hair circling his head; and
the ship's boy, fifteen-year-old Abel. The chief of their
tormentors is Captain Bartlett, a gray-haired, huge-
framed man with a jaw frozen in "implacable stubbornness" and dark eyes obsessed by madness. His followers
are his boatswain, Silas Horne, whose face is "marked by a
lifetime of crass lusts and mean cruelty"; Ben Cates, a
bestial brute with a stupid face and "greedy pig's eyes";
and an impetuous young islander, Jimmy Kanata, whose
belt holds a menacing sheath knife.

Butler protects young Abel and shares with him the
precious water in a concealed flask. The other men have
not had water in three days; deliriously they make plans to
dispose of their "gold." The Captain promises his men
"Rum, and wine, and women" for the rest of their lives.
He himself dreams of going home and remaining there,
an idea that carries with it a curse, as in the O'Neill canon
abandoning the sea is tantamount to betraying it. Bartlett
wants to buy gifts for his wife that will "make the damn
neighbors open their eyes." He promises to go to church
with his wife as she has prayed he would.

Infuriated when Butler states that the treasure is
only brass and pieces of glass, the Captain accuses him of
wanting to steal the booty. An approaching trade schooner is sighted. To avoid sharing the wealth with his rescuers, the Captain decides to bury it, draw a map showing
its location, and return in a schooner to reclaim it. Horne
suggests that Butler and Abel will inform others of the
existence of the treasure. The Captain wrestles with his
conscience when Jimmy says, "Me kill um quick." Like
Pilate, Bartlett absolves himself of responsibility: "I
couldn't prevent—." Jimmy boasts: "I fix um."

> Bartlett doesn't answer, but stares at the treasure. Horne
> makes violent motions to Jimmy to go. The Islander stares
> at his master's face. Then, seeming to read the direct com-
> mand there, he grunts with satisfaction, and pulling his
> knife from his sheath, he goes stealthily off left.

Screams and a dying groan are heard. Twice Bartlett mutters: "I spoke no word." The act closes with the Captain on his knees in front of the chest, fingering the "gold" before he buries it. His eyes are fixed "in an ecstatic vision."

Act II opens six months later in an old boat shed on the wharf of the Bartlett home, located on the California coast. The Captain has changed drastically. His hair is white, his face deeply hollowed. His jaw expressed "defiant determination, as if he were fighting back some weakness inside himself, a weakness found in his eyes, which have something in them of fear, of a wishing to avoid other eyes." He plans to return to the South Seas the next day but admits to his three men that he is haunted by the ghosts of Butler and Abel. The Captain has asked his pious wife, Sarah, to christen the newly outfitted schooner, the *Sarah Allen*, for good luck, but she refuses to do so.

The Bartlett family appears in Act II. The Captain's wife is described in conflicting terms. Physically, she shows signs of "premature old age" and walks "feebly with the aid of a cane." Inwardly, however, she is strong; a resolute spirit flashes from her eyes. While Nat, the Captain's son, retains many of the physical traits attributed to him in *Where the Cross Is Made*, he is eighteen in *Gold*, rather than thirty. He works in the designing department of a local shipyard but longs desperately to go to sea with his father. Sue, his pretty twenty-year-old sister, has large blue eyes, reddish-brown hair, and a vital, "nervous strength about her." In this version, her fiancé, Danny Drew, an officer on a freight steamer, returns home after a four-month absence.

To Danny, Sue describes the serious rift between her parents. When her father first returned "with those three awful men," he spoke of becoming a millionaire but seemed normal mentally. Then the Captain bought the schooner. That night something happened, Sue says, between her parents. Her mother was ill the next morning and has been growing sicker each day since. The Captain no longer sleeps in the house and enters it only at mealtimes. No one in the family can understand why he wants to give up whaling for trading on the Islands.

Later Bartlett confronts his wife and threatens to take Nat with him if she does not christen the ship. Terrified, Sarah agrees. Accused of driving her husband from her bed, she says that his conscience has driven him away; his ravings in his sleep have convinced her that he has committed a wrong. She urges him, unsuccessfully, to confess his sin "to God and men" and to accept his punishment: "Forget that gold that's cursed."

Act III is set at dawn the following morning on a cliff overlooking the wharf. The *Sarah Allen* has just been christened. The Captain speaks of good luck that is certain to come, but Jimmy warns him that his wife has cast a spell on the ship. "She catch strong devil charm for schooner." Mrs. Bartlett had collapsed after the ceremony and was taken home. She now asks to see her husband before he sails. Sue begs her fiancé to sail in her father's place. In a totally improbable act, the young man boards the ship and sails off on a six-month voyage. The Captain returns and angrily shakes "his clenched fist at the sky as if visualizing the fate he feels in all of this." He cries out: "Curse ye! Curse ye!" His wife appears and tells him that the ship is cursed. "I thank God He's saved you from the evil of that voyage, and I'll pray Him to visit His punishment and His curse on them three men on that craft you forced me to give my name." She then raises her hand "as if calling down retribution on the schooner."

The setting for the fourth act duplicates the nautical decor of *Where the Cross Is Made*. The Captain's room on the upper level of his home looks like his ship's cabin. In the opening scene Sue converses with the family doctor, who calls the Bartlett home a "house of mad dreams." She is dressed in mourning, having suffered two tragedies in the past year: the death of her mother and the loss of her fiancé, who reportedly drowned when the *Sarah Allen* sank. He has, however, been miraculously saved. Stabbed by Horne and Cates, Drew was left for dead in a native settlement. The sailors resumed their voyage but perished later when the schooner went down.

The Captain, refusing to believe that the *Sarah Allen* is lost, spends most of his time on the walk of the roof, waiting for the ship's return. Doctor Berry wants Sue to commit her father to an asylum. If the Captain ever faced reality, the doctor states, "the shock of it would kill him. That darn dream of his has become his life." Sue is the demented man's "one connecting link" to the real world. Nat, however, has become as obsessed with the dream as his father.

Later, when the others have gone, the Captain comes down from the roof. His madness is most apparent "in his eyes which seem to stare through and beyond objects with a hunted, haunted expression." He takes out a map and relives the past, conjuring up the ghosts of those he has wronged. He reaches out to strangle Butler: "Ye lie! Is it gold or no?" He speaks reassuringly to his wife: "I spoke no word, I swear to Ye!" Nat enters, sees the map, and exclaims, "Confess." Like Luke, the greedy son in *The Rope*, he fears that his father will die "without ever speaking." Relieved, the Captain narrates the events that followed the shipwreck, including details of the murders. Nat's statement, "They deserved what they got," earns him his father's praise: "Ye be true son o' mine."

Bartlett looks out the porthole and announces the arrival of the *Sarah Allen*. His face is "transfigured by the ecstacy of a dream come true." Nat's face is transfixed by a "possessed expression." Sue comes in; a kind of exorcism occurs as she tries to draw both men back from the brink of madness. Over and over, Sue begs her father to free Nat and tell him the truth. Finally, he says despairingly, "after a tremendous struggle": "Nothin' there, boy! Don't ye believe! . . . And I lied to ye, boy. I gave the word—in my mind—to kill them two. I murdered 'em in cold blood." The dream is difficult to relinquish. Bartlett is

overcome "by the old obsession." His body quivers "with
the effort he makes to force this sustaining lie out of his
brain." Then the old man clutches the map, the symbol of
his mad dream, and tears it up. Life seems suddenly to
ebb from his body, and he dies.

O'Neill uses a concept in *Gold* that will reappear in
later plays: that when the dream dies, so too does the
dreamer. Yet although the dream may indicate, indeed
induce, madness, it is the only refuge one has from the
real world. In *Where the Cross Is Made* the crazed Captain Bartlett, who is still caught up in the spell of the
dream at the end, apparently dies from the exultation of
the final delusion: realizing it. In *Gold* the Captain dies
when the dream is shattered. While O'Neill adamantly
maintains the necessity of the dream, he also seems to
suggest that there is something self-destructive in the act
of harboring it.

Critics have denounced *Gold*, with justification. It
resembles the melodramas in which James O'Neill starred
and against which his son rebelled. The characters are too
strident, too easily categorized as good and evil. The plot
lacks originality and seems pieced together, perhaps because O'Neill is working backward from the preconceived
fourth act, which formed the substance of the earlier
Where the Cross Is Made. In his attempt to write the
full-length play, he pilfers ideas from *Thirst* for the first
act, from his plays having a marital conflict for the second,
and from *Where the Cross Is Made* for the final act. The
borrowing is not confined to his own work. In his descent
into madness and his subsequent death, the Captain resembles Strindberg's Captain in *The Father*. Both men
have a destructive obsession and are thwarted by their
wives.

Barrett Clark writes that "*Gold* somehow does not
'come off.' But what a magnificent epic idea." He views
Captain Bartlett as a heroic figure, "potentially a Balzacian giant." He states: "I suspect that the dramatist was
simply not equal to his theme. The plays look like the

dramatization of an idea, not a living organism."* Rather than "Balzacian," Bartlett is Faustian. The subtly inter-woven motif in *Gold*, which O'Neill used repeatedly in later plays but does not seem to have verbalized here, is: "What does it profit a man if he gains the whole world and loses his soul." Bartlett is a man who is not only possessed: he is obsessed. Over and over, he shows that he will risk damnation for the treasure: "I be sailin' out as I planned I would in spite o' all hell!" He disregards his wife's warning that the "curse o' God" is on the voyage. *Gold* can be classified as a play that does not "come off." Perhaps its most unforgivable fault is that it is boring and tedious. Yet it contains seminal material that will take root later.

---

*Clark, pp. 59–60.

27. Anna Christie

Anna Christie, like its heroine, is a play gone wrong. In its three-year germination period, 1918–1920, O'Neill struggled to find a central focus. His perception of the characters and plot shifted several times. What began as a light-hearted tribute to his friend Chris Christopherson emerged, finally, as a tale about the tribulations of a prostitute, a pseudo-tragedy with a happy ending. A source of embarrassment to the author in his lifetime, the play is merely an interesting failure today.

In the summer of 1918 O'Neill jotted down an idea for a sea play entitled *Chris Christopherson*."* Finished in the spring of 1919, it opened the following March in Atlantic City but was so flawed that the New York premiere was canceled. O'Neill doggedly revised the work the next summer, changing its emphasis from Chris to his daughter, Anna, and its title from "The Old Davil" to *Anna Christie*.†

The first act depicts a waterfront saloon, Johnny the Priest's, an early re-creation of Jimmy the Priest's, where O'Neill and Chris frequently drank together. A squat, broad-shouldered man of fifty, Chris has light blue eyes that twinkle "with a simple good humor," a "childishly self-willed and weak" mouth, and a "thick drooping, yel-

---

*O'Neill's first concept in the 1918–1920 notebook reads: "Chris. Christopherson—captain of coal barge—long play with all action taking place on the barge."

†*Chris Christopherson* is dated "winter/spring 1919." *Anna Christie* was completed on September 18, 1920, and copyrighted as "The Ole Devil" on November 29, 1920. The Theatre Guild staged the revised four-act *Anna Christie* on November 2, 1921.

low mustache."* With him is his live-in companion, Marthy, a coarse, unkempt middle-aged woman, who, after "camping with barge men the last twenty years," looks the worse for the experience. "But there still twinkles in her bloodshot blue eyes a youthful lust for life which hard usage has failed to stifle."

Larry, the bartender, gives Chris a letter sent by his daughter, Anna, announcing her impending visit. The old man is overjoyed by the news; he has not seen her in fifteen years, since she "vas little gel in Sveden five year ole." She was brought to Minnesota by her mother to live with cousins on a farm. To protect Anna from "dat ole davil, sea," Chris decided that she should remain with her relatives when his wife died. He is apprehensive about Marthy's reaction to the news that Anna will live with him on the barge; he would like Marthy to leave the barge but doesn't want to hurt her. She understands his predicament and good-naturedly volunteers to "beat it."

After Chris goes out to eat, Anna arrives.

> She is a tall, blond, fully-developed girl of twenty, handsome after a large, Viking-daughter fashion but now run down in health. . . . Her youthful face is already hard and cynical beneath its layer of make-up. Her clothes are the tawdry finery of peasant stock turned prostitute.

This Anna is entirely different from the prim Puritanical daughter in *Chris Christopherson*, a former secretary from Leeds, England, who speaks with an English accent and is dressed in a tailor-made British suit. The early Anna is a virginal, wide-eyed innocent who drinks tea rather than whiskey. The dual concept O'Neill has of his heroine explains the two Annas of the final version: the sickly, hard prostitute of the first act and the "healthy transformed" sea lover of the second.

---

*Ollie Olson, the Swede in the *Glencairn* series, is described in similar terms. O'Neill depicts other seamen from the series in the early *Chris Christopherson*: Devlin, and Mickey, another portrait of Mike Driscoll.

Anna sits down near Marthy and orders a whiskey.*
The two women "size each other up." When Marthy says
she has got Anna's "number," the younger woman replies: "You're me forty years from now." The two make
friends, and Anna relates her past: the first sexual experience at sixteen forced upon her by a cousin; the next two
years in St. Paul as a nurse; the period in a "joint" that was
raided and the subsequent thirty days "in the cooler"; and
finally the stay in a hospital, the result of "being caged
up"† in jail. Bitterly, she accuses the men in her life for
her downfall and hates "em all, every mother's son of
'em!"

Tactfully, Marthy leaves when Chris returns. He
kisses his daughter nervously; her "brilliant clothes, and,
to him, high-toned appearance, awe him terribly." The
old man explains that he did not return home to Sweden
because he always spent his passage money on alcohol.
"Dat ole davil Sea" is to blame. He vows never again to
"gat yob on sea."** Anna accepts his invitation to remain
on his barge until she recovers, and she asks for a drink.
Fearing that alcohol might be too strong for a "young gel,"
he suggests "yinger-ale—sas'prilla." Anna laughs hysterically. Her relief is obvious at the end of the act: she has at
last found a safe refuge from life.

Ten days have passed when Act II begins. Father and
daughter are on the barge, the *Simeon Winthrop*, an-

---

*Her speech was heralded as the Swedish Greta Garbo's first
words in a talkie in a movie version of the play. Two other
Scandinavians, Ingrid Bergman, a Swede, and Liv Ullman, a
Norwegian, later portrayed Anna on the stage.

†Anna is a direct descendant of Rose, the prostitute in *The Web*.
Both women are hopelessly trapped by the circumstances of
their lives.

**O'Neill states that when Chris was his room-mate he was out of
work, wouldn't go to sea and spent the time guzzling whiskey
and razzing the sea. In time he got a coal barge to captain. He
died in 1917 when he accidentally fell overboard and drowned.

chored off Provincetown. It is late evening, and a dense fog shrouds the barge. Anna looks radiantly healthy, and, like Edmund in *Long Day's Journey into Night*, loves the fog. She feels cleansed of her past and happier than at any other time in her life. Disturbed by her ardor for the sea, Chris describes the toll it has taken on their family: his father, uncle, two brothers, and two sons.

Chris has a premonition of impending disaster. Suddenly, from the fog comes a cry for help. Four survivors of a shipwreck, who had spent the last five days in a small open boat, are rescued. Only one, Mat Burke, a tall, burly Irishman,* can walk without help. His face is "handsome in a hard, rough, bold, defiant way. He is about thirty, in the full power of his heavy-muscled, immense strength." Making the sign of the cross, he thanks Anna for the drink she offers and tells her that she reminds him of a "mermaid out of the sea come to torment" him. Mat assumes that she is the "square-head's woman" and tries to kiss her. Anna gives him a blow that sends him sprawling on the deck and informs him reproachfully that she is Chris's daughter. She lies about her occupation and says she is a governess. Mat apologizes for mistaking her "for the like of them cows on the waterfront. . . . I'm a hard, rough man and I'm not fit, I'm thinking, to be kissing the shoe-soles of a fine, dacent girl the like of yourself."

Mat describes himself as a stoker who has shoveled a "million tons of coal." He speaks of his loneliness, his desire to return to Ireland, his distaste for the wicked women he has met in the world's ports. What he wants most is a little house and a fine girl like Anna to marry. It was the will of God, he insists, that brought him through

---

*In the early *Chris Christopherson* the young hero is Paul Anderson, an American Swede from Minnesota, a second mate of the *Londonderry*, and a pompous, vain womanizer. Here the barge is rounding Cape Cod when it is struck by the *Londonderry*, which is bound for Argentina. Chris is forced to work as a sailor to pay for their passage and to watch helplessly while Anna and Paul fall in love.

the storm to her. Chris enters and watches the couple
jealously. Enraged, he orders his daughter to go to bed.
She ignores the command and assists Mat to the cabin.
Alone, Chris shakes his fist at the sea: "Dat's your dirty
trick, damn ole davil, you! But py God, you don't do dat."

A week has passed when Act III begins, and the
barge is docked in Boston. Anna sits in the cabin reading,
while Chris, gloomy and uneasy, pretends to be occupied
with chores. Breaking the silence, he advises his daughter
to ignore seamen and to marry someone who can give her
a house in the country. She wishes he could see the little
home in the country he had her live in until she was
sixteen. Anna reveals her love for Mat but says she will
never marry him. "Two years ago—I'd have jumped at
the chance." Now she "ain't good enough for him."

Chris is alone when Mat comes in, dressed in a cheap
new suit and determined to marry Anna that day. To Mat,
Chris has "swallowed the anchor," allowed his fear of the
sea to turn him into a coward. What the family needs now
is an Irishman to "put guts in it so that you'll not be having
grandchildren would be fearful cowards and jackasses the
like of yourself!" The father throws himself, knife in hand,
at the younger man, who grasps the Swede like a child and
sends the weapon into a corner.

Anna comes in and demands to know the cause of the
fight. Hearing that it was Mat's admission to Chris of his
love for her, she is deeply moved and admits that she
returns his love. After kissing him, however, she says
goodbye. The Irishman accuses Chris of filling her ears
with "bloody lies." The men quarrel bitterly. In an outburst of fury, Anna relates her story. She turns to Chris,
asking why he had not visited her after she had written
describing how cruelly she was treated. It was, she says,
one of the cousins "that you think is such nice people—
the youngest son—Paul—that started me wrong. It was
none of my fault. I hated him worse'n hell and he knew it.
But he was big and strong—(Pointing to Burke)—like

you!" As Anna continues her narration, Mat groans and clenches his fists; Chris puts his hands over his ears to drown out the words. "I was in a house, that's what!—yes, that kind of a house—the kind sailors like you and Mat goes to in Port." Chris weeps; Mat fumes.

The most moving passage in the play is Anna's speech to Mat that alternates between resignation and pitiful pleading. She asks him if he would laugh if she told him that the sea had changed her, that she viewed him as a man different from any other in her life, that she has been made clean because of her love for him. In utter despair, he laments the black shame of his life, loving a woman "the same as others you'd meet in any hooker-shanty in port." Mat puts his curse on her "and the curse of Almighty God and all the Saints." The father shakes his fist at the sea, cursing it for casting up "dat Irish fallar." First Mat, then Chris, rushes out to get "dead rotten drunk." At the end of the act even Anna seeks the release of alcohol.

Two days have passed when Act IV begins. Chris enters, bleary and bedraggled after his long drinking spree. He is startled to see Anna's suitcase and dismayed by her plan to return to New York to resume a life of prostitution. Assuming the blame for what happened to her and saying he wants only her happiness, he begs her forgiveness. As a gesture of his sincerity, he has signed up to ship out the next day on the *Londonderry*: "Ay tank if dat ole davil gat me back she leave you alone den." What has happened is "nobody's fault! It's dat ole davil, sea!" To Anna, Chris "ain't right" and she will never blame him for "nothing no more." She discovers the revolver he had bought to use to kill Mat and confiscates it. The old man kisses her and goes off to bed.

Mat returns. His clothes are torn; his face is marked with bruises from the fights he has had "on his 'bat.' " His eyes reflect a "wild mental turmoil," an "impotent animal rage baffled by its own abject misery." When Anna raises the revolver she holds, Mat says he would welcome death: "it's a rotten dog's life I've lived in the past two days since I've known what you are." Ashamed of the love that binds him to her, he begs Anna to say that she lied about her past. She urges him to "forgive what's dead and gone—and forget it." All his life he has been picking up a new girl in every port. She asks: "How're you any better than I was!" He announces that he is leaving the next day for Cape Town on the *Londonderry*. She is amused for a moment by the irony of the situation: her father and Mat sailing on the same boat.

Mat longs desperately to find an excuse to accept her. It comes with her assurance she hates all the men of her past and loves only him. From his pocket he takes a small, cheap crucifix given to him by his mother and asks Anna to "swear an oath" that she has loved only him. She does so and promises to forget her badness and "never do the like of it again." A sudden thought comes to him: "Is it Catholic ye are?" Her negative response creates doubt, but in a wild burst of passion he embraces her: "I'd go mad if I'd not have you!" They will be married the next morning "in spite of the devil!"

When Chris joins the couple, the animosity between the men flares briefly and then quickly dies as Anna urges the two prospective shipmates of the *Londonderry* "to kiss and make up." Mat worries about Anna being left alone but then brightens, promising Chris a grandchild. The old man has a "sober premonition" as he considers the thought that he and Mat will ship on the same boat. He fears the "ole davil sea" will "do her vorst dirty tricks." Mat gloomily agrees with him. Anna alone is buoyant and manages to lift their spirits with a proposed toast to the sea. The play closes with Chris looking out into the fog-filled night and saying: "You can't see vhere you vas going, no. Only dat ole davil, sea—she knows!"

In the last scene of *Chris Christopherson*, two young sailors goad Chris to murderous anger with a detailed description of Paul Anderson's wicked ways with women and their assurance that he intends to marry Anna. He lunges wildly at the lover with his sheath knife, determined to kill him. Anna steps between the men, and her father tries to stab himself but is prevented from doing so by Anderson. The characterization in this early draft is disastrously inconsistent: Chris is a warm, jolly lovable man in the first half of the play—perhaps a perfect re-creation of the old friend O'Neill knew so well—but in the second half he is a jealous, suspicious, irrational maniac capable of murder.

Anna is more seriously flawed dramatically than Chris in the early version, precisely because she was conceived of as flawless. The author depicts her as perfect physically and morally, a doll figure rather than a realistic flesh-and-blood woman, unlike any other female he had portrayed before or, possibly, had ever met. Agnes Boulton describes her husband's efforts in the winter and spring of 1919 to breathe life into his aloof heroine and to make her convincing. She states: "I used to secretly wonder how old Chris had ever come to have such a daughter. She didn't like herself either, it seems, and even then was secretly rebelling and a year or so later became a prostitute."*

The early concept of Anna, the perfect woman, is the antithesis of the tough, cynical prostitute in the first act of *Anna Christie*. The author, unfortunately, attempts to merge the two Annas in later acts. Little effort is made to motivate her conversion, her sudden emergence as a purified woman, which is attributed vaguely to the sea in Act II and to love in Act IV. The strong, cynical side asserts itself briefly in the third act when she firmly denounces her father and lover, but the toughness dissolves into all-forgiving penitence in the last act.

O'Neill's difficulty in creating a credible Anna stems perhaps from the fact that the Swedish heroine was an

*Boulton, *Part of a Long Story*, p. 278.

imaginary figure. His portraits of Chris and the characters at Johnny the Priest's are true-to-life, perhaps because he had simply to evoke them from memory. His wife, Agnes, states, "Old Chris—how real *he* was! It was Chris Gene really knew and loved, and old Marthy too—and the bums and outcasts in the first act down at Johnny the Priest's saloon on South Street in lower New York."*

The second, and equally serious, weakness of *Anna Christie*, deriving probably from its uncertain characterization, is its plot. The change of title, from *Chris Christopherson* to *Anna Christie*, signifies the shift in focus sought by the author. The emphasis of the former play was Chris and his relationship with his daughter; that of the latter, Anna's inner conflict and destiny. The father–daughter clash becomes a minor theme. Both plots seem faulty at the core. O'Neill creates a flawed tragic heroine and two complex secondary male figures, all held captive to an avenging sea by their superstitions and premonitions. Trapped by the inevitability of fate and their own natures, the three are doomed to tragedy.

Yet O'Neill gives the play a contradictory happy ending. In a letter in 1920 to George Jean Nathan, he suggests that audiences look beyond the final reconciliation of Mat and Anna to the brooding sea that seethes outside. "The happy ending is merely a comma at the end of a gaudy introductory clause, with the body of the sentence unwritten," O'Neill remarks. "In fact, I once thought of calling the play *Comma*." He concludes by saying: "all of them at the end have a vague foreboding that although they have had their moment, the decision still rests with the sea which has achieved the conquest of Anna."

The makeshift happy ending haunted the author for years. On May 8, 1932, he wrote to Langner, suggesting that the Theatre Guild revive *Anna Christie* with "the last act played as I obviously intended in the writing not the

*Boulton, p. 279.

conventional happy ending as directed by Hoppy—I could heighten the sea-fog-fate uncertainty atmosphere by slight cutting and rewriting."* In the Nathan letter he speaks of "the trappings of theatre" inhibiting "sincerity of life," the necessities of plot influencing characteriza-tion. When he began the two-year period devoted to *Chris Christopherson–Anna Christie,* O'Neill had not developed the skill to manipulate the intricacies of plot while sustaining believably motivated characters. The 1920s would see this integration. O'Neill gave the world a flawed *Anna Christie,* but it is one of his most interesting failures.

---

*On July 29, 1941, he makes the same suggestion to Langner and remarks: "I couldn't sit through it without getting the heebie-jeebies and wondering why the hell I ever wrote it—even if Joan of Arc came back to play 'Anna.' "

28.   *The Emperor Jones*

The new O'Neill, the craftsman who was to revolutionize
the American theater in the 1920s in his experimental
period, emerges in *The Emperor Jones*.* In it, the author
moves beyond anything he had previously attempted in
an effort to integrate form and subject matter. He blends
expressionism with realism to dramatize the tragedy of
the deposed despot Brutus Jones, whose flight for freedom, which becomes a personal quest for self-identity,
takes him to his death.

O'Neill's use of expressionism in *The Emperor Jones*
had two effects: first, it brought him into the mainstream
of the European experimental theatrical movement; second, it established his international reputation. Directors
in Sweden, Germany, and other countries on the continent took note of the young American and began producing his dramas. O'Neill claims not to have been influenced by the European movement. *Jones*, he states, "was
written long before I had ever heard of Expressionism."
He apparently had not read German expressionists, such
as Kaiser and Toller, before beginning *The Emperor Jones*
and probably came to the new mode by way of Strindberg, who also provided the impetus for Central European dramatists. There is a marked similarity between
the flashing dream sequences showing Brutus Jones moving back into his personal and racial past and those depicting the Daughter of Indra journeying forward into her
mortal life in Strindberg's *A Dream Play*.

The Emperor Jones relies primarily on expression-

*O'Neill dates the longhand draft October 2, 1920. *The Emperor
Jones* was first staged at The Playwrights' Theater on November
3, 1920.

istic settings for its effectiveness. The drama begins and ends with realistic scenes in the present, but its six intervening scenes are played out in the hero's wild, distorted mind, as his convoluted trip through the forest takes him back further and further into the past. Reality becomes distorted fragments filtered through Jones's consciousness as he enacts his thoughts in dreamlike reveries. The first scene is set in a spacious room in the Emperor's palace "on an island in the West Indies as yet not self-determined by white Marines." Everything in the room—walls, tiles, pillars—is white, an appropriate blank background for the statement-making "dazzling, eye-smiting scarlet" throne of the arrogant, brutal despot. It is late afternoon, the last day of the Emperor's reign.

Jones, a powerfully built, middle-aged black man, enters. His face displays "an underlying strength of will, a hardy, self-reliant confidence in himself that inspires respect. His eyes are alive with a keen, cunning intelligence. In manner he is shrewd, suspicious, evasive." He wears an outlandish uniform: a blue jacket decorated with brass buttons and gold braid and bright red trousers with a light blue stripe down the side. A pearl-handled revolver in its holster and patent leather boots with brass spurs resemble the gear of an outlaw of the American frontier and clash with the attempt to ape the finery of European monarchs. "Yet there is something not altogether ridiculous about his grandeur. He has a way of carrying it out."

With Jones is Smithers, a white Cockney trader about forty years old. His "naturally pasty face" has been transformed by the sun to a "sickly yellow, and native rum has painted his pointed nose to a starling red." His expression is one of "unscrupulous meanness, cowardly and dangerous." He is clearly portrayed as the black man's inferior. Jones, in his two years on the island, has learned the language of the natives and taught some of them English. Smithers has been there ten years and still cannot com-

municate verbally with them. The former forged his way
from a lowly stowaway, after his escape from an American
jail, to emperor. He had been Smithers's employee, doing, as he says, "de dirty work fo' you—and most o' de
brain work." During a revolution Jones had seized power
after surviving an assassination attempt by Lem, a native
chief. When Lem's hired killer, standing only ten feet
away, failed to shoot Jones, the people fell to their knees
as though it were a "miracle out o' de Bible." Jones told
the superstitious natives that only a silver bullet could kill
him.* His revolver contains five lead bullets and one
"silver baby," "his rabbit's foot," which he intends to use
to kill himself "when de time comes."

Jones has exploited his subjects and plundered the
island, using the lessons he learned "listenin' to de white
quality talk" during his ten years as a Pullman porter. He
has hidden his wealth in a foreign bank and plotted the
route he will follow to escape through the forest while
pretending to be hunting. He plans to make his way to the
forest's edge and to travel through the woods to the coast,
where a French gunboat will take him to Martinique.
"And dere I is safe wid a mighty big bankroll in my jeans."

Smithers assumes that Jones will not return to the
United States, having escaped from prison there, but the
Emperor is fearless and boasts of his exploits. He implies
that he killed a black man in a gambling dispute and his
cruel white prison guard, an overseer, when he was "wuk-
in' de road." Smithers suggests, maliciously, that it may
be time for Jones to run away again, for the palace guards
and servants are conspiring with Old Lem to depose him.

The low, vibrating sound of a tom-tom is heard. "It
starts at a rate exactly corresponding to normal pulse

---

*An old circus man told O'Neill a story "current in Hayti con-
cerning the late President Sam. This was to the effect that Sam
had said they'd never get him with a lead bullet; that he would
get himself first with a silver one." The author states: "This
notion about the silver bullet struck me, and I made a note of the
story" (Clark, p. 57).

beat—72 to the minute—and continues at a gradually accelerating rate from this point uninterruptedly to the very end of the play." According to the trader, the natives are " 'oldin' their 'eathen religious service." "They'll 'ave their pet devils and ghosts 'roundin' after you." Jones is contemptuous of the natives' ceremony. "As a member in good standin' o' de Baptist Church," he feels protected against their "devil spells and charms." Reminded that he has ignored that church for the past years, Jones reasons: "It don't git me nothin' to do missionary work for de Baptist Church." The scene closes with Jones's departure for the woods "with studied carelessness."

The mood of the play shifts in the next six scenes as Jones makes his way through the jungle into the past and self-awareness. Here the technical devices of expressionism—lighting, setting, sound—are used to project the Emperor's visions, to reveal his state of mind. The scenes form one prolonged dramatic monologue, part dialogue when he addresses his "ha'nts," part soliloquy when he talks to himself.

In *Long Day's Journey into Night* O'Neill equates the weather and Mary Tyrone's mind; as the fog increases so too does her drug-induced haziness. In *The Emperor Jones* he achieves the same effect using lighting, going from the blazing sunlight of the first scene, where the hero's mind is clear, to the moonlight "merged into a veil of bluish mist" in the seventh scene, where fear undermines his sanity.

It is not yet dark in the second scene when Jones reaches the Great Forest. He eyes the deep wall of darkness before him with a sense of foreboding and tries to cheer himself with the expectation of food. He searches in vain, however, for the "tin box o' grub" he has hidden previously. From the forest creep black, shapeless "Little Formless Fears" with glittering eyes. They emit a "low mocking laughter" and squirm menacingly toward him. Terrified, he takes out his revolver and fires, sending the creatures back to the woods. The power of the gun gives him self-confidence and he boldly enters the forest.

The moon in the third scene casts an "eerie glow" on the small triangular clearing Jones has reached. The blackness of the woods resembles "an encompassing barrier." The tom-tom beats a trifle louder now. Jeff, a middle-aged black man in a Pullman porter's uniform, crouches in the rear of the triangular space, casting dice with the "mechanical movements of an automaton." Jones freezes in fear. "Day tol' me you done died from dat razor cut I gives you." In his frenzy, he pulls out his revolver and fires at the specter and then plunges into the underbrush.

A dirt road, glimmering ghastly and unreal in the moonlight, splits the stage diagonally in Scene 4. Jones stumbles into view, his once-splendid uniform ragged and torn. He throws off his jacket, leaving himself naked to the waist, and his spurs, the "frippety Emperor trappin's." Terror returns and the fear of "ha'nts"; then he remembers the Baptist parson's assurance that "no such things" exist. He measures that new-found mainland religion against the old cult of the island and asks: "Is you civilized, or is you like dese ign'rent black niggers heah?" A small group of black convicts enters, each with one leg shackled to a heavy ball and chain. A white prison guard, armed with a Winchester rifle and a heavy whip, follows. In stylized movements the prisoners work on the road. The once-proud Emperor responds "subserviently" "in a hypnotized stupor" when forced to join the gang. The guard lashes him viciously with his whip, and Jones angrily shoots the "white debil." Instantly, the vision fades and he plods onward.

Whereas Jones retreats into his personal past in the first expressionistic scenes, in the next three he regresses into the collective consciousness of his race, the *Spiritus Mundi* Yeats speaks of in "The Second Coming." In Scene 5 the moon outlines a circular clearing in the woods. Jones throws himself on his knees and pleads: "Lawd Jesus, heah my prayer!" A confession of his three crimes follows: the two murders and the theft of all he could extort from the natives. Fervently, he prays to be delivered.

A crowd, dressed in Southern costumes of the 1850s, converges on the clearing: planters, an auctioneer, a group of "young belles and dandies who have come to the slave-market for diversion." Their movements are "stiff, rigid, unreal, marionettish." A group of slaves is appraised by planters. Jones is forced to stand on the auction block. He glares with "raging hatred and fear" at the auctioneer and the planter who is buying him and fires two shots at them. Jones rushes off, maddened by fear and the progressively louder beat of the tom-tom.

In the sixth scene the trees form an arched enclosure, resembling the dark "hold of some ancient vessel." Jones, lamenting the wasted bullets, cringes: "Lawd, it's black heah! Whar's de moon?" His pants are so tattered that "what is left of them is no better than a breech cloth." Two rows of figures sit shackled in despairing attitudes; the slaves row rhythmically in unison. Compelled against his will, Jones begins to sway in movement with the others. The light fades and the tom-tom accelerates.

No time elapses before the next scene. The wail of the slaves is heard offstage. Rough boulders rise to form an altarlike structure at the edge of a great river. Jones is now totally deranged. His eyes have an "obsessed glare"; his movements resemble those of "a sleepwalker or one in a trance." The place seems familiar to him. An old Congo witch doctor, carrying a charm stick, begins to dance and to chant before the altar. In pantomime he mimics Jones's flight from spirits and tries to placate "some implacable deity demanding sacrifice." Jones, "completely hypnotized," joins in; the "meaning of the dance has entered into him, has become his spirit." Salvation necessitates appeasement; "the forces of evil demand sacrifice." Realizing that he must become the sacrifice, Jones begs for

mercy. The head of a crocodile emerges from the river, its
eyes devouring him. The witch doctor motions him toward
the monster. Obediently, Jones crawls forward. Suddenly, he breaks the spell, reaches for his revolver, and fires
his last bullet at the crocodile. The tom-tom asserts its
"revengeful power."

The last scene, like the second, occurs at the forest's
edge. It is dawn. Lem, an "old savage of the extreme
African type," enters, followed by his soldiers and by
Smithers. The latter mocks the native chief's optimism
about finding Jones. At the sound from the forest, Lem
motions his men, who have melted down their money to
fashion silver bullets, to enter. Several shots are heard;
the tom-tom ceases abruptly, at the very moment, presumably, that the Emperor gives up his spirit. The natives emerge from the woods carrying Jones's body, and
Smithers voices his admiration: "Silver bullets! Gawd
blimey, but yer died in the 'eight o' style." Even in death
Jones evokes awe and respect. He had died as he desired,
perpetuating the myth that made him emperor.

The Emperor Jones is the first of many attempts
O'Neill made in the 1920s and 1930s to depict the plight of
blacks in America. Granted, Jones does exploit his own
people. The narrated betrayal, however, is overshad-
owed by the dramatized examples of white oppression:
the cruelty of the white guard to the chained convicts, the
sale of human beings as slaves, the forced voyage on slave
ships of innocent people uprooted from their African
homes. O'Neill elaborates on all of these details in a
projected work in 1927, "Bantu Boy," the full-length
study of the life of one such victim. Like Jones, the central
figure would endure harrowing treatment in America and
finally makes his way back to his roots, in Africa, at the
end.

A second dominant motif that emerged in the 1920s
and is illustrated in *The Emperor Jones* is the Faust
theme. Jones is a man who clearly has sold his soul for

material possesion: "I'se after de coin, an' I lays my Jesus on de shelf for de time bein'." The "debils" pursue him until he surrenders his soul in death. He commits his first crime, Jeff's murder, in a squabble over money and succumbs to greed and the lure of "white quality talk," assuming the role normally played by white oppressors as he exploits his black subjects. He expiates his crime later when he undergoes the demeaning experiences of his race, the humiliation on the auction block, the confinement in the hold of a slave ship crossing the Atlantic.

Somewhere along the route from porter to Emperor, as he emulates the ways of whites, Jones loses sight of who he is. He rejects his black identity and heritage and scorns the garments of the natives, the loincloth worn by Lem. The royal trappings become the embodiment of Jones' pseudo-self; by shedding them piece by piece, he strips away the layers of veneer of white society. After witnessing the historical tragedies of his race, he is reduced to a tattered breechcloth. Appropriately, the seventh scene is set in Africa. Having denied his cultural roots, Jones must make amends there.

Jones's long night's journey into the past is a religious quest as well as a personal search for identity. During the assimilation process in white America, Jones lost not only his black culture and values but also his native beliefs. The only remaining traces are his superstitions. He has adopted the God the white man fashioned into his own likeness, yet he abandoned even this God in his pursuit of wealth. His own conscience and the witch doctor pronounce him guilty and condemn him to be sacrificed to the crocodile god. At the moment that Jones begins his penitential crawl toward the open jaws and prays for deliverance, he remembers the silver bullet. Ironically, the crocodile god proves to be his undoing. Shooting it brings him death, for the noise alerts Lem and his men to his location. The death of the crocodile god sends the witch doctor hurrying away. Jones lies with "his face to the ground, his arms outstretched," in the symbolic position of the crucified Christ, suggesting that he has, through his suffering, atoned and found redemption.

The Emperor Jones was a landmark drama, not only in conception but also in production: a black actor, Charles Gilpin, was permitted for the first time to enact the leading role in a New York drama. The play was a critical and popular success, and the critics attributed considerable credit to Gilpin for his brilliant portrayal of Jones. Years later, in an interview in 1946, O'Neill said: "As I look back now on all my work, I can honestly say there was only one actor who carried out every notion of a character I had in mind. That actor was Charles Gilpin." *The Emperor Jones* signaled a coming of age of the American theater. Its triumph convinced O'Neill that audiences would accept experimental works and plays focusing on the controversial racial problem in America. The two elements, technique and the until-then taboo topic, would merge and emerge two years later in *All God's Chillun Got Wings*.

29. Diff'rent

Diff'rent* is a grim reminder to Americans of their Puritan heritage, of the dark period in the past when the joy of life was sanctimoniously crushed by harsh moral codes in the name of a tyrannical God. It is one of the three distinctly Puritan New England plays O'Neill worked on in the 1920s, in which he attacked the hypocritical religious hangover that had persisted to that time. In it, a primly scrupulous, narrow-minded woman, Emma Crosby, rejects her fiancé, Caleb Williams, because of his single sexual indiscretion. The consequential ripple effects of her prudery destroy them both.

Because its central characters are products of their class and culture, *Diff'rent* can be labeled a naturalistic play. Victims of their heredity and environment, the characters are denied the possibility of change. Naturalism enables O'Neill to project a theme that permeates his work: the impossibility of escaping the past. Had New Englanders not evolved into the stiff, repressed individuals he depicts in the Puritan plays, O'Neill implies, their society would have had fewer moral aberrations. The whorehouse thrives where men's forbidden fantasies outstrip their allowed real-life options. What evolves for O'Neill is the tantalizing question: Is evil a power in itself or merely a force that conflicts with the perceived good?

In the small details of his description of Emma and Caleb, O'Neill depicts their duality, the struggle waged

---

*The play was completed on October 19, 1920, and first produced at The Playwrights' Theater on December 27, 1920. Clark states that *Diff'rent* "was not received very favorably." O'Neill found the "poor press" reassuring and said: "I had begun to think I was too popular to be honest" (Clark, *Eugene O'Neill*, pp. 66–67). The drama's original title was "Thirty Years."

between their natures and the laws of their society.
Emma is a slender girl of twenty. Her soft blue eyes, the
only attractive feature of her plain face, have an "incongruous quality of absent-minded romantic dreaminess
about them." In contrast, her mouth and chin are "heavy,
full of self-willed stubbornness." The word "incongruous,"
meaning inappropriate as well as inharmonious, is significant in view of Emma's inexplicable transformation in
Act II. The romanticism this repressed woman craves and
denies herself in the first act becomes an abnormal travesty of love in the second.

Caleb, about thirty, has dark eyes, a bronzed face,
and a "mouth obstinate but good-natured." There is,
however, a rigid quality to his body. His whole attitude is
"wooden and fixed as if he were posing for a photographer; yet his eyes are expressively tender and protecting
when he looks at Emma." His wooden, fixed stance, like
the sober, black "Sunday best" clothes both he and Emma
wear, reflects his exterior conformity to the standards of
his society, an indication of what that society has done to
this emotionally restricted but potentially passionate
man.

The same rigidity is detected in the setting, the
parlor of the Crosby home, located in a seaport village in
New England. It is afternoon on a day in spring in 1890.
The room is drab, "small and low-ceilinged." The dark,
stiff furniture is oppressive. The books on the table, "a
bulky Bible" and volumes that look like "cheap novels,"
signify the conflicting traits of the characters.

Emma plans to marry Caleb, a captain on a whaling
ship owned by her father, in two days. She is certain that
Caleb, during his recent two-year voyage, has remained
faithful to her because he is "diff'rent from the rest." She
wants to be considered "diff'rent, too—not just the same
as all the other girls hereabouts"; her goal is to make them
"a married couple—diff'rent from the rest." Caleb promises to do his best, but he is clearly disturbed: "I'm scared

you'll want me to live up to one of them high-fangled heroes you been readin' about in them books."

The fantasy world Emma creates is shattered when her brother Jack relates the story Caleb's crew "has been tellin' the whole town." Because of one of one of those wry twists of fate that are common in O'Neill's work, Caleb's ship had been blown off its course in the South Seas during a tempest. He put in at one island for water but remained on board while his men went ashore and cavorted with the native women. Desiring to play a joke on Caleb, the men told a beautiful "brown gal" that the captain had sent for her and wished her to swim to the ship. None of the men knew "what happened between 'em." She took "an awful shine to Caleb" and stood on the beach "howlin' and screamin' " as the ship set sail. When she swam after it, the men had to "p'int a gun at her and shoot in the water near her afore the crazy cuss gives up and swims back to home, howlin' all the time."*

Emma's stubborn nature, nourished by her perverse illusions and New England Puritan mentality, asserts itself. She refuses to marry her fiancé. His sister, Harriet, who is engaged to Alfred Rogers, argues that her friend should have fallen in love with a minister, not a sailor. "If you're looking for saints, you got to die first and go to heaven." Old Captain Crosby, a powerful sixty-year-old man, asks his daughter what she wants in a husband: "a durned, he-virgin sky-pilot?" Boasting that he himself knows "them brown females like a book," he concludes that his daughter is not crazy but that if "she ever got religion that bad, I'd ship her off as female missionary to the damned yellow Chinks."†

---

*This woman resembles the African, "savage and superb," who pursues Kurtz in *Heart of Darkness* by Conrad, whose sea novels made a deep impression on the young O'Neill.

†In the late unfinished comedy "The Visit of Malatesta," a father complains that one daughter is a "high brow" and "wants to be a nun in Tibeta. With the Chinks. And her a good Catholic. Can you beat it!"

In one revealing moment, Emma, when alone, looks around the room "as if she longed to escape from it." Her face betrays "the conflict that is tormenting her." Later, Caleb tries to explain the transformation he had experienced in "them Islands," where "it's purty all the time" and you "git feelin'—diff'rent. And them native women—they're diff'rent. . . . and at night they sings—and it's all diff'rent like something you'd see in a painted picture."

Caleb expresses sorrow for what occurred. He did not believe Emma would let "a slip like that make—such a diff'rence." There is nothing he can do if she "ain't willin' to take me that way I be." He reminds Emma, who pledges to "stay single," that she is human and "liable to make mistakes." He vows never to marry any woman but her and to wait until she changes her mind, "thirty years if it's needful!"

In *Diff'rent*, as in *Mourning Becomes Electra*, O'Neill contrasts the cold, barren New England environment, where people repress their emotions and sexual feelings, and the exotic South Sea Islands, where primitive natives dance "naked and innocent—without knowledge of sin." The trilogy's heroine, Lavinia Mannon, who possesses Emma's dual nature, manages to escape to the "Blessed Isles"; in the last play she is reborn and set free of her inhibitions. Emma Crosby has been transformed too when the second act of *Diff'rent* opens, but the change is not caused by natural means, as it is in Lavinia's case.

Emma's face is masklike. She has made a desperate effort "to cheat the years by appearances." There is an "absurd suggestion of rouge on her tight cheeks and thin lips, of penciled make-up about her eyes. The black of her hair is brazenly untruthful." She wears a frilly white dress and "resembles some passé stock actress of fifty made up for a heroine of twenty."

The newly decorated Crosby parlor has a "grotesque

aspect of old age turned flighty and masquerading as the most empty-headed youth." The curtains are orange, the rugs garish-colored, the wallpaper cream and pink. Standing by the Victrola is Benny Rogers, Caleb's twenty-three-year-old nephew, a coarse, cocky army private recently returned from France. After his father and uncle Jack drowned, he and his mother moved in next door with Caleb, whom Benny calls "a darn stingy, ugly old cuss." Slyly, Benny flatters Emma, pretending to believe she is young and to be jealous of his uncle. Emma makes a fool of herself in pursuit of youth and the romance that has eluded her. She looks at Benny "ardently and kittenishly" and is particularly pathetic when she goads him to tell her about French girls and their wicked ways. Deprived of information on sexual matters all her life, she craves a glimpse of the dark, unknown, forbidden pleasures that lie beyond her world.

In a later scene Harriet warns her son Benny that she has told Caleb, just returned from a voyage, about the money Benny has stolen from her, the frequent trips he makes to "that harlot, Tilly Small," and the "sneakin' way" he is making a fool out of Emma. Defensively, he asks: "How can I help it if she goes bugs in her old age and gets nutty about me?" His hatred of his uncle flares up, inflamed by his mother's assurance that he will never receive another penny from her or Caleb. Harriet hopes to reconcile Emma and Caleb. Maliciously, vengefully, Benny promises: "She'll never marry the old cuss—I'll fix that!" To this end, he informs Emma that he has been thrown out of his home. When invited to stay with her, he says: "let's me 'n' you git married, Emmer—tomorrow, eh? Then I can stay." Emma embraces him fiercely and accepts, "if I'm not too old for you." Benny escapes out the back door before his uncle enters.

Caleb has changed little in thirty years except that his hair is nearly white and his face wrinkled. He is repelled and shocked by the "garish strangeness" of the

Crosby parlor. His face "wears its set expression of an emotionless mask but his eyes cannot conceal an inward struggle, a baffled and painful attempt to comprehend, a wounded look of bewildered hurt." He is repulsed by Emma's appearance. He looks at her "as if he were seeing her for the first time, noting every detail with a numb, stunned astonishment." When she bursts into tears, he apologizes, "looking at her with the blind eyes of love."

Emma ignores his humble plea to marry him and berates him harshly when he accuses Benny of "sneakin' thievery" with her. Told of the marriage scheduled for the following day, Caleb, horrified, swears to prevent it, threatening either to kill his nephew or to buy him off. He then sees the hopelessness of the situation: "Folks be all crazy and rotten to the core and I'm done with the whole kit and caboodle of 'em. I kin only see one course out for me and I'm goin' to take it." If she *is* "diff'rent from the rest o' folks," he states, "it's just you're a mite madder'n they be!"

Benny, having eavesdropped, callously plans to "beat it" if Caleb will "dig in his jeans for some real coin." Emma utters a tortured moan. Mercilessly, he rejects and ridicules her. When she tells him to get out, he calls her an "old hen" that "oughta been planted in the cemetery long ago." Emma collapses, looking "horribly old and worn out. Her face is frozen into an expressionless mask." When Benny goes to the barn to investigate strange noises his mother has heard, Emma moves about the room, mechanically taking down the curtains and pictures, dropping them in a pile in the middle of the room. She pushes the rugs to the center. Breathlessly, Benny returns and announces that Caleb has hung himself in the barn. He asks Emma to go over to console his mother and leaves. With an "outburst of wild grief," Emma whispers; " 'Wait, Caleb, I'm going down to the barn.' (She moves like a sleepwalker toward the door in the rear as the curtain falls.)"

Emma Crosby is a tragic figure, a victim of her Puritan environment and her own nature. She loses her only chance for happiness because of her willfulness and her tragic flaw, an overweening pride. The desire to be "diff'rent" reflects her need for the esteem and approval of those in her society who demand perfection. She is a product of that same culture that produced the scientist Aylmer in Hawthorne's "The Birthmark," who is married to a woman flawed by a small blemish on her cheek. Although she is perfect in every other way, the husband keeps making experiments until he finds a way to make the mark fade. His "honorable love—so pure and lofty" will accept nothing less than perfection. Purified, the wife dies.

Caleb, like the wife in Hawthorne's tale, is nearly perfect. Fearful of revealing any blemish that will repulse Emma, he masks his emotions and tries to hide his inner self. Like Margaret later in *The Great God Brown*, Emma is in love with an illusion, an exterior mask, and refuses to see the man Caleb truly is. The meaning of the play revolves around the interpretation of the word "diff'rent." Emma wants a man who is "diff'rent," not only from others in their society but from what he actually is. The play is about hypocrisy, a person's willingness to accept the other masked, and about identity, the ability to perceive one's own and the other's true nature. The clownish makeup Emma flaunts in the second act is an example of the mask one wears to conceal the inner self, not only from the other but, as Pirandello suggests in *Henry IV*, from the self. *Diff'rent* is a repulsive play, as is the dark side of man when he refuses to accept the other person as he is, whatever that may be.

Ironically, Emma's makeup-mask enables Caleb to see the shallow, silly person Emma truly is. He is a man with a single dream: that the pure, noble Emma is "diff'rent." Only after Caleb's death does she realize that his love for her remained untarnished while hers for him was flawed. She had demanded the spiritual, nonsexual love idealized in her Puritan society. She cannot, however, reconcile the ideal with the reality of her own passionate nature. Her suggestive behavior with Benny in Act II shows how abnormal restrictions pervert normal sexuality. When pent-up emotion is finally unleashed, it spends itself and its possessor. O'Neill will repeat the same situation again in the second Puritan play, *Desire Under the Elms*. The only difference here is that Abbie, unlike Emma, is free of Puritan inhibitions and able to express her sexual desires.

Diff'rent is not a great or even a good play, but it is an important play for several reasons. First, it contains the seeds of the two later New England Puritan plays, *Desire Under the Elms* and *Mourning Becomes Electra*. O'Neill also experiments in it with the mask, expressed not as a separate removable identity, as in *The Great God Brown*, but as the face in repose, as in *Mourning Becomes Electra*. There is also the fleeting introduction here of the dream motif: the concept that a man dies when his dream does. Finally, O'Neill shows in *Diff'rent* a marked improvement in his handling of his characters. Here they do not seem to be manipulated by their author but by the normal outside forces of their lives. Inexplicably, being thus motivated, they seem to act on their own, as if O'Neill had given them free rein. O'Neill also uses setting as an expressionistic device to symbolize the oppressive, stifling Puritan environment. The low-ceilinged room is particularly significant, as O'Neill will use it later, along with shrinking walls, in *All God's Chillun Got Wings* to indicate the trapped existence of his characters.

30.   The First Man

The young O'Neill lacked sound critical judgment. He was too easily impressed with his early efforts and frequently failed to perceive serious flaws. After finishing the original draft for *The First Man*,* the author set it aside, as he says, "to smoulder for a while in the subconscious and perhaps gather to itself a little more flame therefrom. It looks so good now, I'm afraid of it. At this state of development, they all look fine, I've found."† Apparently, no flame ignited O'Neill's creative imagination. *The First Man* is a repetitious domestic drama that borders on melodrama.

The First Man, like its predecessor, *Diff'rent*, focuses on the man-woman relationship. The young Emma Crosby in *Diff'rent* craves an idealistic, spiritual union. Curt Jayson in *The First Man* wants a narcissistic relationship; he expects his wife, Martha, to sacrifice herself to the worship of her husband. O'Neill seems to be working out his own marital problems vicariously in the early 1920s in these plays and in *Welded*. His second wife, Agnes, was a proud woman, a successful writer in her own right, yet O'Neill seemed to desire, if Martha Jayson is any indication, a more passive wife. Like Curt Jayson, a self-portrait, the dramatist was distressed when Agnes became pregnant; he believed that the presence of a child would weaken the marital bond and shatter the quiet, harmonious working atmosphere. O'Neill conceived the

---

*The author subsequently changed the title to "The Oldest Man" for the copyrighted text of October 13, 1921. The play premiered as *The First Man* on March 4, 1922, at the Neighborhood Playhouse.

†Letter of March 18, 1921, to Kenneth Macgowan.

idea for *The First Man* soon after the birth, in 1919, of the son he nicknamed "Shane the Loud."

The play is set in Bridgetown, Connecticut, in the Jaysons' living room on an early fall afternoon. Martha is an attractive, athletic woman of thirty-eight. Curt, a year younger, is a rugged, healthy fellow with a reserved, detached manner. With the couple is Curt's former Cornell classmate, Edward Bigelow, a handsome thirty-nine-year-old widower with three children. Strangely, in a departure from his usual practice, O'Neill fails to provide a detailed description of the facial features of his characters. A reluctance to admit the autobiographical implications of the drama may explain his reticence.

Edward's attempt to prove Curt a romanticist provides the play's exposition. He traces Curt's history from his days as an engineering student to his present status as an acclaimed anthropologist. In the early years of his marriage to Martha, he had been content to remain in a small western town. After the death of their two young daughters, the couple vowed never again to have children and began a life of perpetual wandering. Now Curt is about to embark on one of the most important projects of his life, the five-year excavating expedition to China to search for man's earliest ancestor, the First Man. Martha has served as Curt's research assistant and secretary for years. Wives are barred from this trip, however, and Curt has brought his wife to Bridgetown to place her in the protective care of his family.

The plan is destined to inhibit Martha, for the family questions her liberal attitudes and her relationship with Edward. Curt's twenty-five-year-old sister Lily, a smug college student, criticizes Martha for promising to go driving that afternoon with Edward, who is reported to be a profligate. According to Lily, the only way Martha can appease Curt's father and his family, who fear scandal from her actions, is to present her husband with a son. Curt's sister Esther and his sister-in-law, Emily, have produced only daughters. Caught off-guard, Martha tells Lily confidentially that she is pregnant.

O'Neill's purpose in Act I is to demonstrate the narrow-minded provincialism of Curt's monstrous family: old Jayson, a querulous small-town New England best family banker; his seventy-five-year-old aunt, Mrs. Davidson, a rigid defender of the family honor; the snobbish Esther and her shrewd, superficial lawyer husband, Mark; John Junior, pompous, proud, self-complacent; and his malicious wife, Emily.

That afternoon when the Jaysons arrive for tea, Martha is assisting her husband in his study. The duplicitous Lily betrays Martha and informs the family that her sister-in-law is two months pregnant. The mean-spirited Jaysons, recalling that Curt had been away in New York for a month at the time the child was conceived, conclude that Martha has been unfaithful. When Curt emerges from his study, he shares a secret with his family that he has been saving until the next day, Martha's birthday, to surprise his wife: he has gotten special permission to take Martha on the expedition with him. The old aunt suggests that his wife might want to remain home to have a child. Curt responds "emphatically": "No, I tell you! It's impossible." His words fuel the family's suspicions. The scene closes with John's prediction that they will "live to regret having accepted a stranger—" and old Jayson's hope that the affair will "blow over without any open scandal."

In the second act Martha entreats her husband not to go on the expedition. Informed of her pregnancy, he accuses her of spoiling his plans to take her with him. Curt refuses to face reality and responsibility and talks of "living the old, free life together." He rejects her argument that just as she loves his work because it is part of him, he must "love the creator" in her. Accused of base treachery and told she should have an abortion, Martha at last realizes her husband's utter selfishness: "It's all my fault. I've spoiled you by giving up my life so completely to yours. You've forgotten I have one."

The third act opens the following spring. It is 3:00
A.M. Martha has been in labor for twenty-four hours. The
Jayson family has "cut her since that tea affair," but now
the members gather, in hypocritical fashion. Her suffering, they believe, is a punishment. Old Jayson hopes that
the child will not live. There has been gossip but "no real
scandal." To avoid scandal, Jayson has given the servants
orders to tell Curt that Edward is out of town. Curt
discovers the truth. He calls all of those assembled liars
and orders them out of the room.

When Edward comes in, Curt confesses he hates his
unborn child and has not been able to conceal this fact
from his wife. "There was something in each of us the
other grew to hate." Like his father, he hopes that the
child is born dead. He will give up his work, do anything
Martha wants "if only we can make a new beginning
again—together—*alone!*" The nurse enters and summons Curt: Martha has had a son. The wife lives just long
enough to recognize her husband and to beg his forgiveness. The evil-minded Jaysons interpret this request as a
justification of "all of their suspicions": they are convinced
Edward is the child's father. The curtan falls as Curt spews
forth his loathing of the child. He vows never to see it.

Three days pass. In the last act the Jaysons are shown
returning to Curt's home after Martha's funeral. Only old
Mrs. Davidson expresses genuine sorrow. Lily calls them
hypocrites for pretending to be grief stricken at the grave.
Old Jayson criticizes his son for planning to depart that
afternoon on "that infernal expedition" without acknowledging the child: "He's deliberately flaunting this scandal in everyone's face!"

When Curt arrives, his relatives accost him, one by
one, each intent on saving the family's reputation. Mark
urges Curt to show some concern for his son in the presence of servants and nurses. Emily implies that he could
not have really loved Martha if he abandons her child. He
responds scornfully, "What do you know of love—women

like you! You call your little rabbit-hutch emotions love—
your bread-and-butter passions—and you have the ef-
frontery to judge—." Unable to restrain her fury any
longer, Emily accuses Martha of infidelity. Nauseated
and outraged, Curt scans their faces and sees that all of
them, with the exception of his old aunt, harbor the same
idea.

Curt goes to see the child. Returning, he stammers:
"Well—my answer to you—your rotten world—I kissed
him—he's mine!" Still intent on leaving on the expedition
that day, he entrusts his son to the care of his aged aunt.
He announces his future plan for the child: "When he's
old enough, I'll teach him to know and love a big, free life.
Martha used to say that he would take her place in time.
Martha shall live again for me in him." The only genuine
emotion the family shows at the end of the play is relief
that Curt acknowledges the child before others.

In *The First Man*, as in the earlier *Bread and Butter*,
which is also set in Bridgetown, Connecticut, O'Neill
shows the strained relationship between two people
whose lives are further complicated by the assaults of
provincial philistines. The problem with *The First Man* is
that O'Neill fails not only to develop the two presumably
central characters but also to keep them onstage and in
focus: Martha is offstage for part of the first act and fails to
return after the second. Curt is conveniently offstage
when much of the conspiratorial action occurs; when
onstage he is frequently in some kind of scholarly cloud,
aloof and detached. For a man who has spent years studying man's early ancestors, he demonstrates a surprising
lack of awareness of his own relatives' nature, their capacity for cruelty and snobbish persecution, particularly of an
outspoken outsider like Martha.

The inclusion of the large group of relatives weakens
the play. They swarm the stage and interrupt the slight
story line with their incessant chatter. They seem to have
distracted O'Neill, taking him away from the original

marital play he was writing and leading him on to attack middle-class small-town bigots. The town is obviously New London. The big-frogs-in-a-small-pond imagery applied to the Jaysons here is used later by Mary Tyrone in *Long Day's Journey into Night* in her comment on the Chatfields.

The First Man is dull, predictable, and, worst of all, boring. Other failures in the past contained some redeeming feature: a novel twist in plot, an unusual characterization, a breakthrough in technique. In contrast, *The First Man* is merely a continuation of previously explored themes and techniques; nothing new is ventured. O'Neill apparently wanted to express the inner tensions he experienced in his own life in the early 1920s as he tried to reconcile his roles as artist and family man. He had had success in the past weaving autobiographical material into his plays, and he would again in the future. The author returned to the theme of marital relationships a year later in *Welded*, presenting a clearer picture of himself in the self-centered playwright Michael Cape than in *The First Man*'s Curt Jayson.

31.   The Fountain

O'Neill developed two historical dramas in the early 1920s: *The Fountain* and *Marco Millions*. The focus of these works would seem, ostensibly, to be the recorded adventures of the Spanish explorer Ponce de Leon in the New World (in the former play) and of the Italian merchant Marco Polo in the Orient (in the latter). The author's concern in both, however, is not history but human nature. In the program note for *The Fountain** O'Neill attributes the idea for it to his "interest in the recurrence in folklore of the beautiful legend of a healing spring of eternal youth. The play is only incidentally concerned with the Era of Discovery in America."†

Juan Ponce de Leon's pursuit of the dream, his quest for the Fountain of Youth, captured the author's imagination. All the characters, save Columbus, are fictitious. Of the central figure, O'Neill says: "Juan Ponce de Leon, in so far as I've been able to make him a human being, is wholly imaginary." The dramatist sought to capture "the truth behind his 'life-sketch' " and to present "the man it

---

*While the longhand draft is dated "(1921–'22) summer–summer," the play's copyright, like that of *The First Man*, was issued on October 13, 1921. According to Barrett Clark, *The Fountain* "was bought first by Arthur Hopkins, then by the Theatre Guild, and produced eventually in 1925 at the Greenwich Village Theater. It ran there for just two weeks and was pretty generally condemned by the press and the small part of the public that went to see it" (Clark, *Eugene O'Neill*, p. 92). In spite of his aversion for *The Fountain*, O'Neill, in response to the Theatre Guild's plan to make a musical out of *Marco Millions* in 1939, asked Theresa Helburn, "Have you ever thought of *The Fountain* as an operetta? In my opinion, it would lend itself more readily than any of my stuff to light musical adaptation."

†Ibid., pp. 93–94.

was romantically—and religiously—moving to me to believe he might have been!" He adds, "*The Fountain* is not
morbid realism."*

The dramatist resorts in *The Fountain* to a lush romanticism, a form till then never before associated with him. As
in a play of this type, there are numerous changes of time,
an overlapping of the late fifteenth and early sixteenth
centuries, and of setting, shfting from Spain to Puerto Rico,
Florida, and Cuba. The *dramatis personae* is overwhelming: twenty-three characters in addition to groups of nobles, monks, soldiers, sailors, and Indians. The play, which
is broadly divided into three parts, contains eleven scenes.

The Fountain opens in Granada in 1492 shortly after
the Spanish have decisively defeated the Moors. An elderly wealthy Moor, Ibnu Aswad, surrenders his palace
to Juan Ponce de Leon, thirty-one, a handsome Spanish
nobleman dressed in full uniform. Juan is O'Neill's first
major dual-natured hero in a full-length drama. When
The Fountain opens, the "romantic dreamer" is "gov-
erned by the ambitious thinker in him." Although his
countenance is "full of a romantic adventurousness and
courage," his actions reveal him to be a disciplined soldier
interested in the advancement of self and of Spain. There
is no place in his life for love or any emotional involvement. As he sits triumphant in the Moor's courtyard,
which is dominated, symbolically, by a large marble and
bronze fountain, Maria de Cordova, a "striking-looking
woman of thirty-eight or forty," enters. He is visibly
annoyed when she confesses her love for him. Because
she is married to his comrade in arms, he believes that her
presence taints his honor. He cruelly mocks the word
"love"; it is a weak lie of poets and minstrels. He declares
that Spain is his mistress and that he intends to sail with
Columbus and "to conquer for Spain that immense realm
of the Great Khan which Marco Polo saw." Believing that
her childlessness is God's punishment for her secret sin of

*Ibid., pp. 93–94.

loving Juan, Maria plans to retire to Cordova "to become worthy again of that pure love of God I knew as a girl." Before leaving, Maria blesses Juan: "You will go far, soldier of iron—and dreamer. God pity you if those two selves should ever clash!"

O'Neill, in his early notes in 1931 for *Days Without End*, conceived a similarly split hero whose dual good-evil natures are ascribed to his two close friends: an ascetic and a cruel cynic. The plan was subsequently abandoned, but it is used a decade earlier in *The Fountain*. Luis de Alvaredo symbolizes Juan's noble, poetic self. When first introduced, he is a dissipated soldier-nobleman; later he undergoes a seemingly miraculous transformation and becomes an ardent missionary who encourages Juan to be merciful and benevolent to captured Indians. Juan's base, ambitious self, if he allowed it to dominate him, is represented by the power-driven Franciscan monk, Diego Menendez, who becomes even more avaricious and despicable as the action progresses. Symbolically, the two men are foes. They argue in the first scene over the fate of a captive Moor, Yusef, whom Luis protects and calls "a fellow poet." Menendez wants the Moor killed. Accompanying the men are three cavaliers, Oviedo, Castillo, and Mendoza, identified as "cruel, courageous to recklessness, practically uneducated—knights of the true Cross, ignorant of and despising every first principle of real Christianity." They are so greedy, according to Luis, that they "would sack heaven and melt the moon for silver." These men are typical of the Spaniards who are sent to colonize and Christianize the New World.

Luis sings the song whose words becomes the leitmotif of the play:

> Love is a flower
> Forever blooming.
> Life is a fountain
> Forever leaping

Upward to catch the golden sunlight,
Striving to reach the azure heaven;
Failing, falling,
Ever returning
To kiss the earth that the flower may live.

Juan's nature resembles the fountain in the song. At the
outset of the play, however, it is earthbound and makes
but a feeble attempt to leap upward to lofty ideals. Only at
the end does he allow his true spiritual self to reach
heavenward. Just as the fountain in the Moor's courtyard
will be replaced by others in later scenes, so too will the
meaning of the fountain itself continually change. Here it
symbolizes romantic love against which Juan rails again.
Luis will not relinquish his "dream that life is love." The
captive Moor now sings of a sacred grove in a far country,
Cathay, where beauty resides and "is articulate." In the
center is a fountain "beautiful beyond human dreams, in
whose rainbows all of life is mirrored. In that fountain's
waters, young maidens play and sing and tend it everlast-
ingly for very joy in being one with it. This is the Fountain
of Youth." Old men drink of it and are made young; their
hearts are purified. But "it is hard to find that fountain.
Only to the chosen does it reveal itself."

The greedy soldiers scorn beauty and want only material possession. Juan, the soldier seeking only glory,
wishes the Moor had sung of "the armies and power of
The Great Khan!" Luis alone is impressed: "We'll all to
Cathay with Don Christopher." He tells Juan, "You can
burrow for dung there—but I will search for this fountain." Violence breaks out at the end of the scene: Menendez stabs the Moor. The jealousy of Maria de Cordova's
husband is aroused, and he challenges Juan to a duel. The
latter views the duel as one way of curing Maria's romantic love: "I'll prick him in the thigh and send him
home to bed. She will nurse and love him then—and hate
me for a murderer."

The flagship of Columbus provides the setting for

Scene 2. It is a year later, the last day of the voyage to the New World. Juan's duel has scandalized the court, but, as he predicted, it reconciled the couple. Maria is rumored to be pregnant. There is tension between Juan and Columbus, a "religious devotee." The latter criticizes Juan for his lack of piety and the Spanish nobles for their pursuit of easy riches rather than the glory of God. Columbus dreams of outfitting an army to regain the Holy Sepulchre of Christ. Juan boasts of being a soldier of the present rather than the ghost of a Crusader; he mocks Columbus for becoming half monk when a "world empire dawns for Spain." Juan is also dismayed by the Spanish nobles' "greedy visions of wealth." He realizes that the monks will resort to torture to make converts and says, "God pity this land until all looters perish from the earth." When land is sighted, the soldiers demonstrate their "greedy longing, the lust to loot."

Twenty years have passed when Scene 3 opens. Situated at the center of another palace courtyard is a "large, handsome fountain closely resembling that of Scene One." It represents here, as in the earlier scene, a possession of Spanish conquest. Juan, now the governor of Puerto Rico, ignores the beauty of the fountain nearby. His face is lined; his hair and beard are gray. Despite his success, he is an unhappy man. "His eyes stare straight before him blankly in a disillusioned dream." With him is his good friend Luis, who has become a Dominican monk. He too has aged, but his face is peaceful "as if he were at last in harmony with himself." Juan chides Luis for having deserted him for the enemy. Luis responds that Juan has "always had the dream of Cathay" but that his own life had been aimless until God awakened him. Juan criticizes the way the Franciscans treat the conquered Indians: "All this baptizing of Indians, this cramming the cross down their throats has proved a ruinous error. It crushes their spirits."

Three men enter: Friar Quesada, a Franciscan; the ruthless nobleman Oviedo, now a wealthy landowner;

and Nano, the chief of Juan's most recently conquered
Indian tribe. Although he is heavily chained, the middle-
aged chief "carries himself erect with an air of aloof,
stoical dignity." His refusal to be baptized infuriates
Oviedo, who seeks to enslave the Indians by leasing their
labor.* Juan tries to protect the Indians, who "die under
the lash." He asks Nano if he has heard of Cathay and
Cipango, the "great villages with high walls—much
gold." To Luis, they are located "in dreamland," along
with the fountain of youth of his drunken days. To his
surprise, Nano points to the west and relates the tale told
him by Indian priests long ago in his own native land,
before he was captured and brought to Puerto Rico. He
describes the miraculous fountain, called the "Spring of
Life," that makes the old young again. Nano's words,
"Those the Gods love can find it," remind Juan of the
Moor's statement in Spain: "Only to the chosen" is the
fountain revealed.

The evil Menendez, now a bishop, returns from
Spain bringing news of the patent Juan seeks from the
king to discover the new land known as Cathay. Menendez despises Juan's "policy of clemency" and "wants to be
dictator to introduce torture and slavery." Luis believes,
rightfully, that Menendez' efforts to obtain the patent to
explore is merely a scheme to get Juan out of Puerto Rico.
Also newly arrived from Spain is Maria's beautiful daughter, Beatriz de Cordova, eighteen, the "personification of
youthful vitality, charm and grace." She tells Juan, who is
"fascinated by her beauty," of her mother's recent death
and of her last request that Beatriz become Juan's ward.

---

*O'Neill diligently researched his material. The Spanish habitu-
ally kidnapped the chiefs of Indian tribes, which adhered to a
pyramidal form of government, and were more easily conquered
without their leaders. The Spanish instituted the *encomienda*
system, assigning groups of Indians to particular Spaniards. The
natives provided labor and were supposed to be given, in exchange, protection and instruction in Christianity.

the young people and the chant of the monks merging into a "hymn of the mystery of life."

The Fountain is a seriously flawed play. On the surface, it appears to be a melodramatic swashbuckler, full of adventure, clear-cut characters who are either admirable or wicked, and a conflict demanding the triumph of good over evil. In form the work is unlike anything O'Neill had previously attempted, a kind of throwback to the romantic extravaganzas of his father's theater. As an action adventure, it succeeds. As a serious drama, it fails. The canvas is too broad and overburdened with details to allow a single focus to emerge with clarity. The play is particularly plagued by a serious language problem. Some of the dialogue is unrealistic, even from figures of a remote sixteenth century. The poetic passages, except for the fountain song, are especially uninspired. O'Neill had the same problem with language when he wrote *Lazarus Laughed*, in which he again attempted to express lofty spiritual sentiments.

By the time O'Neill completed the 1921 drama, all other considerations seemed subordinate to the work's ultimate spiritual significance. The meaning of the fountain, the object of Juan's quest, shifts in the play as his attitude to life changes. At first it is associated with the notion of love and romance, which have eluded him until that time. When Juan believes himself to be in love with Beatriz, the fountain becomes the means of achieving youth and, therefore, love and new life through her. His own inner regeneration, occurring after he is wounded at the end of the play, transforms the lowly spring into the fountain his heart has long desired. He has a type of ecumenical mystical experience, in which the water of life he once sought becomes the now-desired Fountain of Eternity: "God is a fountain/Forever glowing."

The Fountain foreshadows, in some ways, the later historical play *Marco Millions*. In both there is a quest to a distant land called Cathay undertaken by a youthful hero, whose spiritual motives become tainted by materialistic greed, the lure of wealth, and the cruel oppression of a minority race. O'Neill uses a much more realistic approach in form and subject matter in *Marco Millions*, creating a hero who compromises in life and in love. Before this could be written, however, O'Neill apparently had to purge himself in *The Fountain* of the romantic excesses inherent in the historical drama. While Juan resembles the ambitious Marco in early scenes of *The Fountain*, he is, at the end, another regenerated ascetic like the resurrected hero of *Lazarus Laughed*.

32. The Hairy Ape

The Hairy Ape, a "direct descendant" of *The Emperor Jones*, won for O'Neill a second round of international acclaim in the early 1920s. Again using the expressionistic mode and eight-scene form, the dramatist traces the solitary struggle of another American pariah to belong, his quest for identity and place on the evolutionary/social ladder. Whereas Brutus Jones, having rejected his black heritage, was a racial misfit, Yank is a socioeconomic outcast, part of the industrial refuse of a materialistic society. O'Neill calls him a "man bewildered by the disharmony of his primitive pride and individualism at war with the mechanistic development of society."

O'Neill completed *The Hairy Ape* in less than three weeks and told Macgowan: "I was so full of it it just oozed out of every pore."* As he did in *Jones*, the author uses what he calls "extreme expressionism." When he was later charged with having been influenced by the German expressionists Toller, Hasenclever, and Kaiser, O'Neill stated that he had read the latter's *"From Morn to Midnight* before *The Hairy Ape* was written but not before the idea for it was planned. The point is that *The Hairy Ape* is a direct descendant of *Jones*, written before I ever heard of Expressionism, and its form needs no explanation but this."†

The dramatist obviously came to Expressionism by the same route used by the young Germans: the late plays

---

*The script is dated "Dec. 7–Dec. 23 1921." The play received enthusiastic reviews when it opened at The Playwrights' Theater on March 9, 1922. Acclaimed also by audiences, it moved uptown to Broadway on April 17.

†Clark, pp. 73–74.

of Strindberg, particularly *A Dream Play* and *The Ghost Sonata*. Like Strindberg, O'Neill and the Central European expressionists depicted modern man as exploited and forced to cope with social inequities. What distinguishes O'Neill from these expressionists and aligns him more closely with Strindberg is what John Gassner calls his "metaphysical mode of expressionism" in *The Hairy Ape*. Yank never becomes merely a type or pure abstraction in a social treatise. O'Neill examines not only the nature of man's role in society but also the nature of being. Using the technical devices of expressionism, he moves his hero through a series of rapidly changing scenes in his quest to belong, to find his place in the universe, yet in his highly subjective treatment the dramatist never neglects to present the effects of disharmony and dislocation on the human psyche.

What enabled O'Neill to portray Yank in human terms was the fact that he modeled his stoker on a close friend. During his days at sea, he had met a stoker named Driscoll, "one of our own furnace room gang at Jimmy the Priest's." He was a Liverpool Irishman, "the synonym for a tough customer." Driscoll committed suicide by jumping overboard in mid-ocean. The author asks "Why? It was the why of Driscoll's suicide that gave me the germ of the idea."

O'Neill wrote a short story, which he later destroyed, entitled "The Hairy Ape," after completing the *Glencairn* sea plays in 1917. Driscoll appears in these one-acters and is the prototype for Yank, a massive apelike man with a "gorilla face." The author decided not to portray Driscoll as an Irishman but as an American Yankee Everyman, "a New York tough of the toughs, a product of the waterfront turned stoker—a type of mind, if you could call it that, which I know extremely well." As an end product of a centuries-old melting pot process, Yank takes on universal dimensions. He represents the twentieth-century man who, after his faith in the machine is shattered, can find nothing in himself or in his world that can replace this lost faith. The author captures the mood of pessimism that prevailed in the 1920s following man's discovery that while the industrial world provided him with material benefits it also crushed and threatened to obliterate his humanity. The typically somber O'Neill thesis prevails in the bleak world of *The Hairy Ape*: that man has lost his place and his belief in himself and in God, that life without faith can end only in despair and death, and that man must strive to retain his humanity to give order and meaning to existence.

The dominant image in the play is of a cage that traps Yank: literally, in actual approximations, and symbolically, in the narrow framework of his limited intellect. The dark region of the stokehole on the ship reflects the underground of his mind. In Scene 1, the fireman's forecastle of an ocean liner on its New York–Southampton voyage is depicted as a cage. "The lines of bunks, the uprights supporting them, cross each other like the steel framework of a cage." The setting is expressionistic, symbolizing the trapped condition of the men, who are described as "Neanderthal" brutes, "hairy-chested, with small, fierce, resentful eyes."

Because of his superior strength and self-assurance, Yank represents to the stokers "the very last word in what they are, their most highly developed individual." Yank sits apart from the others, "tryin' to t'ink." The stokers repeat the word "t'ink," mocking him. "The chorused word has a brazen, metalic quality as if their throats were phonograph horns." The men resemble a Greek chorus in the play, speaking in unison and moving in a stylized manner. The comparison here and later between them and machines is an expressionistic device that suggests that they have been dehumanized. Yank then speaks longingly of a home and describes his unhappy childhood. Long, O'Neill's anticapitalist spokesman in the play, agrees with Yank that the ship is the only home they know and " 'ome is 'ell." The Socialist blames their unhappy state on the "lazy, bloated swine what travels first cabin." Yank calls the wealthy passengers "just baggage." "We belong and dey don't."

Yank believes that his job has worth and confers meaning on his life. Only old Paddy disagrees. If "we belong to this," he says, "God have pity on us!" Paddy remembers a time when sailors worked above deck on the old skippers and were in harmony with nature and, therefore, themselves. "Nights, when the foam of the wake would be flaming wid fire, when the sky'd be blazing and winking wid stars." Yank scornfully dismisses Paddy's "crazy tripe" as "all a dope dream." He boasts, "I'm what makes iron into steel!" The rich are nothing; "de whole ting is us!" When the bells signal the men to their watch, Yank goes out cheerfully, while Paddy remains behind "dreaming dreams."

The second scene shows the promenade deck, the world the stokers' work makes possible. Reclining on a deck chair is Mildred Douglas, daughter of the president of Nazareth Steel and chairman of the line's board of directors. She is "twenty, slender, delicate, with a pale, pretty face marred by a self-conscious expression of disdainful superiority." She appears not to be a flesh-and-blood woman but an artificial figure dressed all in white; she is described as "a waste product in the Bessemer process—like the millions." Mildred is a bored do-gooder on her way to Whitechapel to make her "slumming international." She intends to begin her social service work on board ship with a visit to the stokehole. The young woman is physically attracted to the Second Engineer, who is to be her escort; she longs to be promiscuous but fears a possible scandal and says, "would that my millions were not so anemically chaste!"

The third scene, which takes place in the stokehole, is the pivotal section of the play. The one hanging electric bulb provides little light. The Inferno is lit, instead, by the red glare of the open boiler doors, which outlines the men "in silhouette in the crouching inhuman attitudes of chained gorillas." Yank misinterprets the whistle blast announcing Mildred's impending visit, thinking it is a call for more fuel and speed. While the other stokers pause, struck dumb by Mildred's sudden appearance, Yank fails to see her and emits a stream of profanity aimed at the whistle blower. Suddenly, he sees the "white apparition."

> She has listened, paralyzed with horror, terror, her whole personality crushed, beaten in, collapsed, by the terrific impact of this unknown, abysmal brutality, naked and shameless. As she looks at his gorilla face, as his eyes bore into hers, she utters a low, choking cry and shrinks away from him, putting both hands up before her eyes to shut out the sight of his face. . . . "Take me away! Oh, the filthy beast!"

Yank feels himself insulted "in the very heart of his pride." He curses and throws his shovel after the departing visitors.

The encounter with Mildred, who emerges out of darkness like the unconscious shadowed side of Yank, rouses him from his lethargy and has a twofold effect on him: it makes him aware of his social inferiority and conscious of his inadequacies as a human being. Her rejection of his physical presence, the sum total of the self he has known until then, stuns him. He is thrown off balance when she classifies him as an animal. Until this time, Yank responded to his environment by a series of conditioned reflexes. As "part of de engines," he has adapted to his environment mechanically, bypassing conscious decision. He has worshipped the machine, becoming one with it; its power is personified in him. Proud of his animal strength and his ability to satisfy the insatiable appetite of the machine, he has never developed a social presence. Yank is not sophisticated enough to assume a mask to project a socially acceptable image. His arrogance and ignorance leave him vulnerable. In his first major contact with it, society, in the form of Mildred, crushes and rejects the raw natural state of man he represents. The woman strikes a chord of humanity within him, however, and he responds with growing sensitivity and seeks to find his place on the ladder of evolution.

Beginning in Scene 4 and continuing to the end of the play, Yank's characteristic pose will be "the exact attitude of Rodin's 'The Thinker.' " The image is appropriate for this brutish man's attempt to fathom the truth of his existence. He seeks to hurt the woman who has given him a glimpse of a higher form of life but who has neglected to sever the umbilical cord that ties him to his animalistic state. When Paddy says that Mildred looked "as if she'd seen a great hairy ape escaped from the Zoo!," he reinforces the idea in Yank's mind that he is an ape and does not belong.

Yank wants to see this ethereal being again. He longs to comprehend the world she represents and to understand the complex shuffle of the pieces in life's puzzle. He fails to see that Mildred can do nothing to help him or anyone else. Her own attempts to become fully human have failed; she remains an anemic imitation of forebears who were once vitally productive, purposeful like the country itself. Her grandfather, a rough puddler, was a self-made millionaire. Somewhere in her unconscious lies a yearning for the primitive, the animalistic, the primordial heart-of-darkness jungle, peopled by creatures like her great-grandmother "with her pipe beside her—puffing in Paradise." The horror that Yank sees but does not understand when he looks into her eyes is her realization that here in him are not only her roots, her past, but, if she would allow her sexual and emotional drives free expression, her vital self.

The first four scenes of the play are primarily realistic, although expressionistic elements—setting, sound, movement—are incorporated. The remaining four expressionistic scenes, with their disparate settings, flash by like those in Strindberg's *A Dream Play*, which also depicts a quest for the meaning of life. Yank is Strindberg's dreamer in the sense that part of him has been dormant. The distorted dreamlike sequences in the last half of the play dramatize in slow motion his search for self. Through the stylized soliloquies and monologues that proliferate in the last scenes, Yank externalizes his thoughts and feelings. Because he cannot discover by reflection who he is or where he belongs, as he does not have the mental capacity to do so, Yank turns, in vain, outward to society for guidance, understanding, and compassion.

Society in Scene 5 is represented by the stylized chorus of the wealthy on Fifth Avenue. Three weeks have elapsed since Yank's traumatic experience. It is a "fine Sunday morning," and Yank, accompanied by Long, has come to this stronghold of the rich, determined to find Mildred and to "git square wit" the "lousy tart." He is overwhelmed by the opulence of the jeweler's window, "gaudy with glittering diamonds," of a coat in a furrier's display: "Monkey fur—two t'ousand bucks!" Long remarks bitterly: "They wouldn't bloody well pay that for a 'airy ape's skin—no, nor for the 'ole livin' ape with all 'is 'ead, and body, and soul thrown in!"

When Yank asks where "*her* kind" is, his friend replies: "In church, blarst 'em! Arskin' Jesus to give 'em more money." He tells Yank that Mildred merely represents the "damned Capitalist clarss." A motif appears here for the first time in O'Neill's work: that Capitalism and Christianity are somehow linked in a mutually beneficial conspiracy to exploit the poor masses. A crowd of the wealthy enters, coming from church. Their faces wear masks of indifference; they look "neither to right nor left" and talk "in toneless, simpering voices." The women are "rouged, calcimined, dyed, overdressed to the nth degree. The men are in Prince Alberts, high hats, spats, canes, etc." These "gaudy marionettes" have "something of the relentless horror of Frankensteins in their detached, mechanical unawareness."

The churchgoers discuss ways to combat radicals (the

workers) and false doctrines (anticapitalism) and decide to "organize a hundred percent American bazaar." The passage has religious, as well as political overtones. It opens with a reference to their pastor, the sincere "Dear Doctor Caiaphas," apparently the high priest of the new temple of Moloch for wealthy traders. O'Neill alludes here to the high priest Caiaphas, who presided at the council that condemned Christ to death and declared: "It was better that one man die for all people."* (John 18:14). The other evangelists note that when Christ died "the curtain hanging in the temple was torn in two from top to bottom." The modern oppressors of man specify that proceeds from the bazaar will be used for "rehabilitating the veil of the temple." O'Neill suggests in this brief Fifth Avenue scene that the wealthy, using the pretext of religious zeal, will ruthlessly crush any movement that threatens their position and will crucify anew any presumptuous rebel. Yank falls into this category at the end of the scene.

Unable to make contact with these zombies, Yank cries out: "Yuh don't belong, get me! Look at me, why don't youse dare? I belong, dat's me!" He still smarts from Mildred's words: "I'll hairy ape yuh!" Jostled by a man rushing past him to catch a bus, Yank thinks the man wants to fight. His fist strikes the face of the fat gentleman, who calls out for the police. A platoon of policemen surrounds Yank. "He tries to fight but is clubbed to the pavement and fallen upon." The patrol wagon approaches to take him away.

---

*Certain aspects of Yank's plight—his alienation, betrayal, and rejection by all classes of society—reveal a Christ-figure quality in him. Horst Frenz, discussing a German production of the play, notes that one critic calls attention to the actor's interpretation of Yank in the union scene: "With dangling arms and dragging steps, as clumsy and artless as an animal, he opens his heart to these men of the world. When they overpower him and throw him to the ground, his simplicity takes on a savior's traits, the characteristics of a despised cross-bearer" ("Three European Productions of *The Hairy Ape*," *Eugene O'Neill Newsletter*, January 1978, p. 11).

Scene 6 takes place the following evening in the prison on Blackwells Island. Only the heavy steel bars of Yank's cell door are visible in the light from the block's one electric bulb. Sitting once again in the attitude of Rodin's *Thinker*, his face and head bruised and bandaged, Yank gropes in the dark recesses of his mind for enlightenment. At first he thinks he is in a zoo, and his cell-mates mock him with the word "ape." Sentenced to "Toity days to t'ink it over," he says, "Christ, dat's all I been doin' for weeks!" He attributes all his misfortunes to the woman who "lamped" him "like she was seein' somep'n broke loose from de menagerie." He vows to get revenge. When he mentions the name of Douglas, the prisoners tell him that Mildred's father is "filthy with dough." If Yank wants "to get back at that dame," he should join the Wobblies. One prisoner reads a newspaper article quoting a speech given in the United States Senate about the dangers posed by the Industrial Workers of the World: The "I.W.W. must be destroyed" as it represents a "dagger pointed at the heart" of this nation where all men "are born free and equal, with equal opportunities to all, where the Founding Fathers have guaranteed to each one happiness, where Truth, Honor, Liberty, Justice, and the Brotherhood of Man are a religion absorbed with one's mother's milk."

Discovering that the Wobblies "blow up tings" and determined to get out to attack the "president of de Steel Trust" who "made dis—dis cage," Yank tries to bend the bar of his cell; "his position is parallel to the floor like a monkey's." At the close of the scene an angry guard appears and, noticing the bent bar, calls for help. "Toin de hose on, Ben!—full pressure! And call de others—and a straight jacket!"

In Scene 7, which takes place a month later, Yank goes to a local I.W.W. meeting room. When the secretary questions his motives for joining, Yank responds: "Yuh wanter blow tings up, don't yuh? Well, dat's me! I belong!" He asks for dynamite to destroy the Douglas steel

factories. The secretary, calling him a "rotten agent pro-
vocator," and "a brainless ape," signals his men to evict
Yank. He lands sprawling in the street and sits there,
brooding, in the *Thinker* position. The brutality of the
treatment he has received brings him close to madness.
His search to belong has been futile. Rejected by all
segments of society—the wealthy, the imprisoned, and,
finally, the representatives of the masses, Yank sits in a
gutter, "bewildered by the confusion in his brain, pathetically impotent." In desperation, he "turns a bitter mocking face up like an ape gibbering at the moon" and says:
"Man in de Moon, yuh look so wise, gimme de answer,
huh? . . . where do I get off at, huh?"

Abandoned by humanity, Yank makes his way in the
play's last scene to the gorilla's cage in the monkey house
at the zoo. Remembering Mildred's words, he thinks he
belongs with those classified as beasts. It is twilight, that
gray-light time between day and night, suspended precariously, even as Yank is, between heaven and earth,
humanity and animality. Watching the gorilla, who sits
like the *Thinker*, a pose he has so often assumed in the
play, Yank says: "Youse can sit and dope dream in de past,
green woods, de jungle and de rest of it. But me—I ain't
got no past to tink in. . . . You belong."

Yank understands Paddy's words now about being in
harmony with nature. "I got it aw right—what Paddy said
about dat bein' de right dope—on'y I couldn't get *in* it,
see? I couldn't belong in dat. It was over my head."
Although he realizes instinctively at last what it means to
be human, he still feels locked out—he feels a greater
kinship with the gorilla. They are "members of de same
club—de Hairy Apes."

Yank confronts the beast, looking for traces of himself, and calls it "brother." He settles for brotherhood not
with man but with animals. Recklessly, he opens the door
of the cage. They will walk down Fifth Avenue together
on a pilgrimage of destruction to "git even" with society.

Something in Yank's tone of voice, perhaps his mocking desperation, enrages the gorilla, prompting it to embrace Yank "in a murderous hug." The animal then picks up the broken body and throws it into the cage. Painfully, Yank mutters: "Even him didn't tink I belonged. Christ, where do I get off at?" Grabbing the bars of the cage, he makes one final effort to rise but falls back on the floor and dies. The terrifying last line of the play, "And perhaps, the Hairy Ape at last belongs," can be interpreted two ways: either that man, as a mere brute beast, belongs in a cage, or that man, as a rootless spiritual being, can belong only in death.

O'Neill viewed Yank as a symbol of man "who has lost his old harmony with nature, the harmony which he used to have as an animal and has not yet acquired in a spiritual way." He was dismayed that audiences saw merely the stoker and not the symbol and said, "The symbol makes the play either important or just another play." The author indicates that man should at least engage in a search for the self and question the meaning of his existence. Living complacently on the animal level brings death and destruction; turning inward to discover the self can provide a degree of awareness of one's humanity.

The Hairy Ape is O'Neill's finest early work, a memorable, moving theatrical experience. In depicting Yank's increasingly desperate attempts to belong, the author successfully integrates form and subject matter. Expressionistic elements are woven more subtly into the text here than they are in *The Emperor Jones*. Unfortunately, the minor characters, particularly Mildred, come close to being pure abstractions. This weakness, however, is balanced by the sheer magnitude of the central figure and the nature of his quest. O'Neill was correct when he remarked that "Yank is really yourself, myself. He is every human being—his struggle to belong—we are all struggling to do just that." As modern technology increasingly dehumanizes and depersonalizes whomever it en-

counters, society will abound with Yank-like individuals
who seek to belong. The tragedy of today's existence lies
in the fact that the technology created to benefit mankind
will inevitably destroy it.

33. *Welded*

George Jean Nathan labeled the domestic drama *Welded**
"very third-rate Strindberg." O'Neill admits having had
the Swedish playwright in mind while working on the
preliminaries. In his letter of September 23, 1922, to
Macgowan he says that *Welded* might demand "some new
form of its own if I am to say what I want to. My conception of it as Strindberg 'Dance of Death' formula seems
hard to fit on. But have no inkling yet of the 'belonging'
method." In its finished form *Welded* is unalloyed autobiography, a recreation of its creator's marital relationship
rather than the relationship dramatized in Strindberg.

The husband, Michael Cape, thirty-five, is an early
self-portrait. His face is "a harrowed battlefield of super-
sensitiveness, the features at war with one another—the
forehead of a thinker, the eyes of a dreamer, the nose and
mouth of a sensualist." His "self-protecting, arrogant defiance of life" hides "a deep need for love as a faith in which
to relax." His wife, Eleanor, resembles O'Neill's wife,
Agnes. She has "high, prominent cheek-bones," "passionate, blue-gray eyes," and a mass of dark brown hair
combed straight back. "The first impression of her whole
personality is one of charm, partly innate, partly imposed

---

*O'Neill wrote the first half of *Welded* in fall, 1922, the remainder in winter, 1923. The copyright date is May 2, 1923. The
author called the pre-Broadway tryout in Baltimore "rotten."
The play opened in New York on March 17, 1924, but closed after
twenty-four performances. O'Neill labeled it a "flat failure," and
critics and audiences agreed. He complained that the actors
"didn't get" the silences between the speeches in the last act.
Clark states that no dramatist "has a right to leave too much to
any actor" and that "it is the author's business to give him the
necessary lines to speak or business to act" (*Eugene O'Neill*, pp.
81–82). The play was not staged again in New York until the José

by years of self-discipline." Like the O'Neills in 1923, the couple has been married for five years. Michael is a prominent playwright; Eleanor an actress who has achieved success in her husband's dramas.

In a program note for the 1981 production of *Welded*, Tennessee Williams writes, "An examination of O'Neill's life discloses the fact that the materials of his plays are transfigurations of his personal experiences." The real-life implications of the statement are unnerving. What Michael Cape asks, indeed expects, of his wife is much more than any woman, particularly an independent, creative one like Eleanor, can give. He wants nothing short of perfection in marriage. In this respect, he is a masculine version of Emma Crosby in *Diff'rent*, the person Emma would have become as a marital partner. Like Emma, Michael has an idealistic conception of the man-woman relationship, wherein the physical is subordinated and sublimated to the spiritual.

The title of the play suggests what is wrong with the Capes' marriage. To "weld" is to join inseparably. Michael wants his wife to lose herself, her being and identity, in him, making it impossible for her to be a person in her own right. He has created the roles Eleanor plays onstage and wishes to manipulate and control her offstage. Like the husbands in *The First Man* and *Servitude*, he demands his wife's complete commitment of her life to his. And, like Juan in *the Fountain*, he is a man who rejects compromise in his pursuit of the ideal.

While O'Neill continues to explore familiar subject matter in *Welded*, he does so in a novel manner, using the new experimental techniques of setting, lighting, and language typical of his work in the 1920s. The devices flaw the play, weakening the work; for in themselves they cannot communicate the meaning they are intended to convey. The medium becomes the message; the human

Quintero revival in summer, 1981. As in 1924, the production was deemed a critical and artistic failure.

factor is denigrated. The focal point of the setting, the studio floor of the Capes' apartment, is the stairway that leads to the balcony-bedroom above. Ascending the stairs symbolizes Michael's mystical concept that spiritual love is the ultimate and only worthwhile goal of any physical union. The physical act of love is to him merely the means of attaining spiritual oneness with Eleanor. She resents his stifling desire for absolute unity, feeling that his possessiveness threatens her individuality.

Because Eleanor has successfully resisted total merger with her husband, two distinct circles of light envelop the Capes on stage, reinforcing the idea the husband and wife are separate entities. The circles, "like auras of egoism, emphasize and intensify Eleanor and Michael throughout the play. There is no other lighting. The two other people and the rooms are distinguishable only by the light of Eleanor and Michael."

Michael returns from the country, where he worked on a difficult last act for his new play. He admits, to Eleanor's chagrin, that he would not compromise his art and rush to complete the scene just to return to her. The tensions in the marriage emerge almost immediately. Earlier fights and previous love affairs are cited. A new resolution, which Eleanor calls "another Grand Ideal for our marriage," is made. She recalls their first night together, her total abandonment of self: "I lost myself. I began living in you. I wanted to die and become you!" Michael reminds her of their vow "to have a true sacrament—or nothing! Our marriage must be a consummation demanding and combining the best in each of us!"

Michael traces his strong desire for unity back to Aristophanes' concept that each human was at one time a whole being until an angry Zeus split each man in two, "into you and me, leaving an eternal yearning to become one life again." He explains the oneness he seeks: "You and I—year after year—together—forms of our bodies merging into one form." He guides Eleanor, who is now "swooning in his arms," to the stairway. He ascends, but she, hearing a noise from the hall, remains below. At the top, the husband turns and stretches out his arms passionately to his wife. There is a knock at the door. He implores her to ignore it. Eleanor is "like a hypnotized person torn by two conflicting suggestions." She shakes herself free and goes to the door.

The couple's director friend, John, a gray-haired man of fifty, enters. "He is not handsome but his personality compels affection." Sensing the tension between the two, he departs hastily. Angrily, Michael clutches Eleanor's arm, asking her why she had broken the spell, ruined "a rare moment of beauty!" The two sit down.

> Their chairs are side by side, each facing front, so near that
> by a slight movement each could touch the other, but
> during the following scene they stare straight ahead and
> remain motionless. They speak, ostensibly to the other, but
> showing by their tone it is a thinking aloud to oneself, and
> neither appears to hear what the other has said.

Like the two circles of light, the chairs and the thought soliloquies reflect the self-absorbed isolation of each character. Neither is able to communicate honestly and acceptably with the other. They talk at rather than to each other. The effect of the spoken-thought device in this scene is stagy, affected. There was a natural explanation for the use of thought asides and monologues in earlier plays: fear of capture in *The Dreamy Kid* and *The Emperor Jones*, the probing of the inner self in *The Hairy Ape*.

In her speeches Eleanor reveals her inner revulsion at Michael's "grasping at some last inmost thing which makes me—my soul—demanding to have that, too! I have to rebel." She asks: "Haven't I a right to myself as you have to yourself?" She says his ideal is "too inhuman." Another quarrel erupts when the husband tells his wife that she was a failure as an actress before she appeared in his plays and that he was successful before meeting her.

He questions her former and present relationship with John and the previous lovers she has confessed she had. There were actresses, Eleanor declares, who pursued John to promote their careers, and she admits to being among them. "He loved me but he saw I didn't love him—that way—and he's a finer man than you think!" She resists Michael's possessive embrace, looks at him with hatred, and exclaims: "You can't crush—me! . . . He was—my lover—here—when you were away!" The husband turns on his wife, snarling like an animal, and attempts to choke her. Sobbing with rage, he cries: "I won't give your hatred the satisfaction of seeing our love live on in me. . . . I'll murder it—and be free!" He then rushes out the door. Her first impulse is to call him back. Then she screams: "I hate you. I'll go, too! I'm free!"

By the time Eleanor reaches John's apartment, in the first scene of Act II, she is wildly incoherent. Would he welcome her if she were to come to stay, she asks. Filled with "passionate hope," John assures her of his love and solicitously encourages her, because of her feverish condition, to go upstairs to bed. Finding herself unable, psychologically, to ascend the stairs, she laughs hysterically and says: "I swear I saw him—standing at the head of the stairs waiting for me—just as he was standing when you knocked at our door."

Eleanor describes the way she and Michael "tore each other to pieces" and confesses her lie that she had been John's mistress in Michael's absence. John criticizes her abuses of his love: "Once when you were willing to endure it as the price of a career—again tonight, when you try to give yourself to me out of hate for him!" Urged to face the truth in herself and to return home to her husband, Eleanor experiences a sudden queer, exultant pride. "My love for him is my own, not his! That he can never possess! It's *my* own. It's *my* life! I must go home now!" John encourages her to go upstairs to powder her nose. "There's no angel with a flaming sword there now, is there?" he asks. She touches her breast: "The angel was here."

Michael's way to kill love and to get his revenge is to seek out a prostitute. The second scene is set in the shabby bedroom of a "Woman." She is fairly young. Her heavily made-up face is "broad and stupid." She is "rather pretty for her bovine, stolid type—and her figure is still attractive although its movements just now are those of a tired scrubwoman." The man's eyes are wild; his face has a "feverish, mad expression." The Woman asks him if he intends to stay all night or go home "afterwards." He responds: "Hell is my home!" To her, he has been either drinking or "dopin' up on coke." Sarcastically, he inquires: "How long have you and I been united in the unholy bonds of—bedlock? . . . You were beside the cradle of love, and you'll dance dead drunk on its grave!" He takes out money contemptuously, but she ignores it.

Suddenly, his fury spent, the man begins to sob and begs her to save him and to help him gain peace. He speaks longingly of the ultimate sleep but rejects death as "the great evasion." The Woman guesses his problem and urges him to return to his wife. "It's easy to forget—when you got to!" When he insults her, she becomes resentful: "Wanter use me to pay her back? Say! Where do I come in? Guys go with me 'cause they like my looks, see?" She pushes him against the wall: "Take your lousy coin and beat it!"

Michael is surprised that love still survives in this woman. "Through separate ways love has brought us both to this room." He begs her forgiveness and calls her "Sister." As in so many of the plays, revelation, the moment of truth, and salvation come when two lonely people make contact with each other. The money he now presses on her will be given, she admits, to her pimp-lover. Her spirits revive as she talks of the game of life. "You got to laugh, ain't you? You got to loin to like it." Having learned once again to love life and vowing to join her church, Michael leaves to return home.

The third act shows the Capes' studio again. Michael
enters, finds Eleanor there, and embraces her. Some
imperceptible shadow falls, and they assume their solitary positions in their chairs as in the first act. They
become once again "like two persons of different races,
deeply in love but separated by a barrier of language."
Eleanor confesses that she went to John's apartment and
that she lied about having an affair. She still longs for
freedom, but love has brought her back. He speaks of the
"extraordinary" revelation that had changed him. Their
only solution, Eleanor suggests, is to release each other in
love. "We'll no longer stand between one another. Then I
can really give you my soul."

Eleanor goes to the foot of the stairs. "They stare into
each other's eyes. It is as if now by a sudden flash from
within they recognize themselves." Saying they will
probably still "torture and tear, and clutch for each other's
souls," Michael falls on his knees before her. He begs her
to forgive all he has done to hurt her. She responds: "No.
Forgive me—my child, you!" She ascends the stairs and
turns, her arms outstretched "to right and left, forming a
cross." He stands just below her; "as their hands touch
they form together one cross." As the curtain falls, they
embrace and kiss.

Presumably, the two circles of light would overlap in
the final scene as Michael and Eleanor embrace, indicating that they have attained not only oneness but also some
inner illumination, that they at last stand naked to each
other, "shorn of all the ideas, attitudes, cheating gestures
which constitute the vanity of personality." In the play
they have been described as masked either psychologically or actually. Michael's features are "at war with one
another." He shifts from thinker to dreamer to sensualist.
Eleanor's face "lacks harmony." Three times in Act II her
face is described as being "like a mask." Her profession as
actress demands the ability to assume various roles.

Perhaps the central problem of the play stems from
this flaw: the two main figures become the masks they

wear rather than the human beings the masks protect. Never at any time during the course of the action is either character believable. Their actions and dialogue are absurd. Actual people do not converse in real life in the kind of speeches O'Neill assigns to his characters. Only the prostitute speaks with any degree of credibility. If Michael and Eleanor Cape actually do bear a resemblance to the dramatist and his wife Agnes, the ten-year duration of the O'Neills' marriage appears miraculous.

Eleanor's reference to Michael as "my child" at the end of the play is a Strindbergian touch and reflects the mother aspect the author sought in Agnes and in his third wife, Carlotta. The Capes, however, in no way resemble Strindberg's flesh-and-blood characters, who wage their bitter battle of the sexes to its usual conclusion: final defeat, and often death, of the male. The words "auras of egoism" applied to the circles of light describe the self-absorbed Capes. They are petty figures compared to the magnificently self- and other-destructive giants of Strindberg and those similarly splendid beings O'Neill would later create: Nina in *Strange Interlude*, Christine in *Mourning Becomes Electra*, Deborah in *More Stately Mansions*.

One of the problems that continually plagued O'Neill in his writing was his inability to depict believable man–woman relationships. If he possessed spiritual expectations like those of Michael Cape, the reason would be obvious. Happiness in and through a relationship appears to be an impossibility in the canon. In the works that precede *Welded*, one or both partners commit suicide or die at the end: Emma and Caleb in *Diff'rent*, Alfred Rowland in *Before Breakfast*, John Brown in *Bread and Butter*, the wives in *The First Man* and *Gold*. The cross image at the end of *Welded* seems to indicate another possibility presented in later plays. Couples who love may live beyond the final curtain fall, but their survival exacts a terrible toll in suffering; in O'Neill's next play, *All God's Chillun Got Wings*, the price is paid in madness.

34. All God's Chillun Got Wings

The publicity preceding the premiere of *All God's Chillun Got Wings** in 1924 proved the play's premise: that racial intolerance can crucify its victims. In the play, O'Neill dared to dramatize an example of miscegenation in lily-white America, to show the crushing effects of bigotry on two innocent people, Jim and Ella Harris, whose love breaks racial barriers. The author was vilified for having the audacity to show a black man kissing the hand of a white woman. Worse, he depicted blacks not as stereotypes but as human beings; and this in 1924, at a time when twentieth-century American racism reached a new level of intensity and extremism. A second Ku Klux Klan had formed after World War I; by the mid-twenties it had spread throughout the North as well as the South. During the rehearsal period for the play, the Klan, numbering four to five million members, and other racist groups threatened the use of violence to halt production. †

O'Neill was apparently unaware of the play's poten-

---

*The play was written in late 1923 and first published in *The American Mercury* in February 1924. It premiered on May 15, 1924, at the Provincetown Playhouse, closing in June but reopening at the Greenwich Village Theatre on August 18 and running until October 10, 1924.

†O'Neill received letters threatening his life. Discussing attempts by authorities to prohibit blacks and whites from acting together, he states: "The police, on a technicality, tried to stop the play on the very evening of the opening, by not permitting the children to act in the first scene. But this was read to the audience, and the play went on smoothly" (Clark, *Eugene O'Neill*, p. 86). A comment by Clark and his use of the offensive

tial for controversy when, in 1922, he penned a two-line entry in his 1921–1931 notebook of ideas for future dramas:

> Play of Johnny T—negro who married white woman—base play on his experience *as I have seen it intimately*—but no reproduction, see it only as man's.

The brief notation suggests that the sensitivity with which O'Neill handles the problems encountered by blacks derives from first-hand observation and real-life contact with them. It also indicates the author's intention to stress the universal difficulties inherent in marriage per se rather than those peculiar to an interracial union. He did not intend *All God's Chillun Got Wings* to be, nor is it, purely a racial play; it is, rather, a study of two individuals and their struggle to attain happiness within marriage. As a domestic drama, *All God's Chillun Got Wings* continues O'Neill's penetrating analysis of man-woman relationships in the 1920s.

In the earlier 1920 work *Diff'rent*, Emma Crosby wants her fiancé Caleb to be "diff'rent" from other men. Her pride demands premarital celibacy. She rejects him because he proves not to be "diff'rent." On the other hand, the proud white Ella Downey scorns and destroys Jim Harris, who loves and is loved by her, precisely because he, being black, is different physically. Both women respond to the pressures of external forces and follow the dictates of a sexually or racially repressive society rather than their own hearts. Unlike *Diff'rent*, which ends in despair and the double suicide of the doomed lovers, *All God's Chillun Got Wings*, coming as it

---

word "nigger" illustrate the prevailing attitudes of that time: "O'Neill's error—as a practical dramatist—was in making his nigger a human being. He even forgot the susceptibilities of those good Americans who have laid down the law as to how far a negro may go in his relations with whites. . . . It is a fact that the marriage of a negro and a white—at present in the United States—arouses hatred and prejudice among all who know of it and" . . . is sure to precipitate a struggle between contracting parties (Clark, p. 85).

does immediately after *Welded*, with its imagery of marriage as an immolation on the cross, demonstrates the potential redemptive efficacy of love springing from suffering and cultivated in its ever-lengthening shadow.

Personal and social motives merged as O'Neill continued his creative efforts in the 1920s to depict the plight of black Americans made exiles in their own country. First, as the son of an Irish immigrant, he personally experienced prejudice growing up in a town dominated by snobbish Yankee New Englanders. Resentment, resulting from injustice, festers in retrospect. In addition, he observed his black friends being victimized by discrimination. The words the author emphasized in the idea for the "Play of Johnny T" show the close ties he had formed with the black community while living in Greenwich Village: "base play on his experience *as I have seen it intimately.*" Above all, the core of the author's being was innately noble. Some inner impulse springing from the well of his own suffering enabled him to strike a corresponding, responding chord in afflicted mankind; some inner force compelled him to address the problems of blacks. It was impossible for him not to respond. Using his special insights into the hearts of men, O'Neill drew his black characters with understanding and compassion. The members of the Harris family possess pride, dignity, the strength to endure all onslaughts. Their weaknesses are those common to all individuals and not peculiar to any one race.

In his first two short works, *The Dreamy Kid* and *The Emperor Jones*, O'Neill did not present the real problems blacks confront in America, the deep-seated hatred and fear that can actually coexist with love in whites. He uses a specific situation in *All God's Chillun Got Wings*, the relationship between Jim, a man who happens to be black, and Ella, a woman who happens to be white, to illustrate the prevailing sickness and intolerance of society. The author traces the physical, psychological, and emotional development of his two central characters from childhood to adolescence to adulthood, showing at each stage the powerful effect exerted by exterior social pressure.

In order to suggest the subtleties of racial segregation, O'Neill relies almost totally on expressionism to differentiate and delineate the characters and setting in the four scenes of Act I. In the first three scenes, which show a street corner in lower New York, an invisible line of demarcation separates people in ghetto-like fashion according to ethnic background. Whites inhabit the four-story tenements in the street leading to the left; blacks, those in the street leading to the right. Laughter and singing are used to distinguish racial temperament and attitudes. Laughter "expresses the difference in race": whites laugh in a constrained manner, finding it difficult to express "natural emotion." Blacks, "frankly participants in the spirit of spring," respond joyously to life.

It is spring, the season of hope. Appropriately, those appearing in the first scene, eight-year-old innocent children of both races, who play naturally together, symbolize the slim hope of improving race relations. O'Neill uses symmetry here perhaps to suggest innate equality: present are four boys and four girls; two of each sex are white, and two are black. The children, oblivious of racial differences, are free of any prejudices. What is revealed in the scene is universal human weaknesses and character flaws. Eight-year-old Ella is teasingly called "Painty Face" and the Harris boy "Jim Crow." The other children conclude that the two are "softies" about each other and taunt them, the boys calling Jim a sissy, the girls asking Ella if she has noted Jim's big feet. Alone, Jim confesses to Ella that he is drinking chalk in an attempt to look whiter. Ella asserts that she would like to be black and offers to swap colors. Each says "I like you" to the other and promises never to forget this feeling.

Nine years have passed when the second scene opens. Its setting differs from that of the first scene in two ways:

natural sound, such as the clatter of horses' hooves upon the pavements, is replaced by "rhythmically mechanical" noises, "electricity having taken the place of horse and steam." The bright sunlight of the early scene is replaced by the "sputtering flare" of an arc lamp. The changes in setting symbolize the loss of the children's innocence. Mickey, who is white, formerly a harmless marble player, is now a swaggering, arrogant prize fighter. "He has acquired a typical 'pug's' face, with the added viciousness of a natural bully." Shorty, the second white youngster, is content to be Mickey's admiring subordinate. The two sneeringly taunt Jim Harris, a "quiet-mannered Negro boy with a queerly-baffled, sensitive face," who is on his way to his high school graduation. Joe, a young street-wise black, imitates the white thugs; he is viciously jealous of Jim's education and ambition to become a lawyer.

Jim begs Mickey not to seduce Ella as he has scores of other girls. Mickey reminds Jim of Ella's hatred of "coons" and accuses him of "tryin' to buy yerself white—graduatin' and law." Ella, who is also graduating, enters and talks with Mickey. She is pretty but has "a rather bold air about her." Like Mickey, Ella has developed racial prejudices and resents the fact that Jim wants an education; they fear he will surpass them economically and socially.

At the end of the scene Joe voices the most bitter accusations against Jim. He asks him a series of questions: "Who is you, anyhow?" "What is you?" Why does Jim deny he is black? These are inquiries Jim is forced to confront throughout the play as he struggles to come to terms with his black identity. Here he assures Joe he does not want to be white, just better.

When Scene 3 begins, the five years that have passed have taken their toll on the tenement dwellers. There is no laughter from either street. The arc lamp probes the tired, cynical faces of both races with "favorless cruelty." A drunken Shorty, looking "tougher than ever, the typical gangster," waits for Ella. Her appearance has altered dramatically. She is poorly dressed and her face is "pale and hollow-eyed." Mickey had discarded Ella like "de odder dames" when she was pregnant. She refuses the money he sends for the child, saying it has died. O'Neill's life-long obsession with the friends—gangsters, pimps, prostitues—he had made at the Hell Hole in 1915 manifests itself again in this play. Shorty makes Ella an offer: "I kin start yuh right in my stable." Ella vehemently rejects him and her former way of life.

Once again Ella relies on Jim for support and protection. He confides the psychological problems he has in classes: he knows the material but finds it difficult to respond verbally with "all the white faces looking at me" or in written examinations. When Jim confesses he loves her, Ella responds by saying she "likes" him better than anyone in the world. She cannot, however, accept the fact that Jim is black and calls him the "only white man in the world! kind and white." Throughout the play Ella mentally equates whiteness with goodness. She tells Jim: "You've been white to me." After she promises to marry him, Jim tells her they will go abroad "where a man is a man" and "where people are kind and wise to see the soul under skins." He wants only to serve and protect her: "to give my life and my blood . . . to become your slave."

The first three scenes build up to the climactic last scene of Act I, set some weeks later, which contains the most vivid expressionistic images in the play: the two racially segregated groups waiting for Jim and Ella to come out of church after their marriage. The shades on the two rows of tenements are drawn, "giving an effect of staring, brutal eyes that pry callously at human beings without acknowledging them." This image is similar to the detached, mechanical unawareness of the rich marionettes on Fifth Avenue in *The Hairy Ape*. In both plays the indifference of others increases the sense of unutterable loneliness of the central characters. The existence of a nearby church implies that formal religion has failed to instill a sense of brotherhood in the hearts of men. When the church bell rings, whites and blacks pour forth from the tenements and form "two racial lines on each side of the gate, rigid and unyielding, staring across at each other with bitter hostile eyes." Jim and Ella are frightened by the hatred "concentrated on them," the two lines through which they must pass.

Earthly religious representatives offer no assistance. As though in mourning, the windows of the church are "blanked with dull green shades." As the two step outside, "the doors slam behind them like wooden lips of an idol that has spat them out." Jim, who is dressed in black, encourages Ella, dressed in white, to ignore the faces filled with animosity and to look up into the sky. God, he explains, understands and blesses them even if human beings do not. In the final lines of his long monologue, Jim enunciates the theme of the play: "We're all the same—equally just—under the sky—under the sun—under God."

When the second act begins, two years have elapsed. Awaiting Jim and Ella's return from Europe in their newly furnished apartment are Mrs. Harris, Jim's mother, a "mild-looking, gray-haired Negress of sixty-five," and his sister, Hattie, "a woman of about thirty with a high-strung, defiant face—an intelligent head showing both power and courage." Like the young couple, the furniture is mismatched. Some pieces are "cheaply ornate" and "childishly gaudy." Newer pieces are conservatively severe. On the wall hangs a picture of Jim's father dressed in an "outlandish lodge regalia," as "absurd to contemplate as one of Napolean's Marshals in full uniform." It is vaguely reminiscent of the uniform Brutus wears in *The Emperor Jones* when he imitates a white authority figure. In direct contrast to this symbol of blacks adapting to the white man's way is the visible reminder of their heritage: "a Negro primitive mask from the Congo—a grotesque face, inspiring obscure, dim connotations in one's mind, but beautifully done, conceived in a true religious spirit."

These two dominant symbols epitomize Jim's dilemma
throughout the second act. They are similar to those used
at the close of *The Dreamy Kid*. The African mask, like the
grandmother's clutching hand, reminds blacks of the past
and their true identity and destiny; the picture, like the
gun Dreamy holds, reinforces the reality of the present,
of the futile attempt of blacks to become assimilated, to be
accepted.

Jim comes in alone and gradually reveals the couple's
experiences abroad. For the first year he and Ella lived
"like a brother and sister." In the next year, after they
apparently consummated their union, Ella refused to
leave their house, fearful she would run into friends from
America. Finally, they decided that they had been cowards to run away and resolved to return home. Jim's words
of caution, to remember that Ella has "been sick," give no
hint of the seriousness of her condition. The "strange,
haunted expression in her eyes" indicates a mental rather
than a physical illness.

Hattie's description of her college years and present
teaching position elicit a boastful response from Ella; she
"hardly even looked at a book" but got through high
school easily, whereas Jim failed one year. Hattie earns
Ella's hatred for indicating that Jim could pass his law
school examinations "if you'll give him a chance." Defiantly, Ella refuses to allow Jim to take any more tests. The
Congo mask terrifies Ella, but she is strangely reluctant to
have it removed from the room. Ella begs Jim to make the
militant Hattie go away. Once this threat to her dominance over Jim is gone, she becomes her old self for a
moment, encouraging Jim to be a lawyer: "I want the
whole world to know you're the whitest of the white!"
Later, alone in the room, Ella speaks to the mask in a
mocking tone: "I'll give you the laugh. He won't pass. You
wait and see. Not in a thousand years!"

Six months have passed in Scene 2. In another departure from realism, the "walls of the room appear

shrunken in, the ceiling lowered, so that the furniture, the portrait, the mask look unnaturally large and domineering." Jim sits surrounded by books, making a heroic effort to study, but "his eyes have an uneasy, hunted look." Hattie, who has been caring for Ella, enters. The doctor has told Jim that when Ella is "out of her mind," she may "develop a violent mania." Hattie resents Ella's racial slurs, the way she curses Jim for being black, and other manifestations of mania. She begs her brother, "Send her to an asylum before you both have to be sent to one together." Jim prefers damnation to separation: "You can't scare me with hell fire if you say she and I go together. It's heaven then for me!" He sends Hattie away: "You with your fool talk of the black race and the white race! Where does the human race get a chance to come in?"

Ella enters, clutching a carving knife; her eyes glow with a "murderous mania." When Jim tries to shake her back to sanity, she becomes like a little girl reacting to bad dreams. The moment he turns to his books again, she resumes speaking in her woman's voice. "A startling transformation comes over her face. It grows mean, vicious, full of jealous hatred. She cannot contain herself but breaks out harshly with a cruel, venomous grin: 'You dirty nigger!' " The cycle of alternate schizoid moods is again played out before the scene ends.

In Scene 3 it is an early evening in spring six months later. The walls of the apartment "appear shrunken in still more, the ceiling now seems barely to clear the people's heads, the furniture and the characters appear enormously magnified." Dressed in a ragged red dressing gown, Ella, her eyes glowing "with a mad energy," approaches the Congo mask, again carrying the carving knife. To her, the African mask represents Jim's black identity: what he really is, where he came from. She addresses the mask: "What have you got against me? I married you, didn't I? . . . He's white, isn't he—the whitest man that ever lived. Where do you come in to interfere?" Like Margaret in *The Great God Brown*, Ella accepts only the external mask, that of a white man, she perceives. To her, the Congo mask, because it represents Jim's unacceptable black side, must be destroyed. In both plays the failure of the wife to acknowledge a husband's true identity precipitates his supreme agony and eventual destruction. Rejection of one's innermost being is tantamount to the ultimate betrayal.

Even in her confused state, Ella realizes that the Congo mask signifies Jim's black consciousness, the storehouse of pride in his racial heritage and past, of strength and dignity, and the belief in self-worth. Above all, it represents his potential for superiority, his ability to surpass her intellectually. When she discovers that he has not passed the bar examination, she plunges the carving knife into the mask, pinning it to the table. It is the most symbolic gesture in the play and summarizes much of its meaning. The mask is equated with black power, a strength that threatens white supremacy and white people's way of life. Ella acknowledges the existence of a mysterious living spirit in the mask: "It's dead. the devil's dead. See! It couldn't live—unless you passed. If you'd passed it would have lived in you. Then I'd have had to kill you, Jim, don't you see!—or it would have killed me." In this key speech Ella spells out the ground rules for racial coexistence. Blacks must remain suppressed and must assume inferior stereotyped roles or face the possibility of white violence to remind them of their "place."

Jim instinctively knows the racial significance of the mutilation of the mask. He exclaims, "You white devil woman!" He realizes that Ella has destroyed something in him, that inner strength that would always pose a threat to her sense of white superiority. Sadly, he resigns himself to the sacrifice of all he had ever desired for this selfish woman. In *A Touch of the Poet* Con Melody strives desperately to suppress his Irish peasant origins and to play the fine gentleman. In the last scene, with the dream of

gentility shattered, he pretends to be a lowly Irish peasant. At the end of *All God's Chillun Got Wings*, Jim
abandons his dreams to become a lawyer and to assume a
position of dignity in a white man's world and reverts to
playing the inferior stereotyped black, "Jim Crow Harris."
Once Ella sees that she has triumphed, she becomes
"happy, childlike." They will play together as they once
did as children, she announces: "Sometimes you must be
my old kind Uncle Jim who's been with us for years and
years."

All her life Ella has been conditioned by society to
associate goodness and acceptability with whites and inferiority with blacks. This indoctrination explains why
Jim's failure to get an education is crucial to her. She
recognizes Jim's goodness, pronounces him white, and
marries this image. She resents and detests his physical
presence, the blackness symbolized by the Congo mask.
Lacking self-confidence, Ella becomes totally dependent
on Jim, needing his care and protection. She deliberately
distracts Jim from his studies and makes his success impossible. She symbolizes the obstacles that beset blacks as
they attempt to advance.

The important question the play raises is, Why does
Jim allow Ella to destroy him? His emotional capacity
undoes him; he is hopelessly in love with this vain, cruel,
neurotic woman. His sacrifice of all that he is, his total
dedication to this worthless woman, redeems him. He
kneels before her and "raises his shining eyes, his transfigured face." He weeps "in an ecstasy of religious humil-
ity" and says, "Let this fire of burning suffering purify me
of selfishness and make me worthy of the child You send
me for the woman You take away!"

Crucial for the understanding of the play is Jim's
cryptic reference to God. When Ella asks her husband if
God will forgive her for destroying him, Jim replies:
"Maybe He can forgive what you've done to me; and
maybe He can forgive what I've done to you; but I don't

see how He's going to forgive—Himself." Jim seems to be asking how God can forgive Himself for creating physical racial differences and thereby making prejudice and discrimination possible. God's lack of foresight, according to this reasoning, is responsible for barriers of distinction. At the core of these words, however, is the concept that God erred when He failed to instill in the hearts of all men the capacity to accept and love all human beings. Earlier in the play, after his wedding, Jim hoped to live among those who followed the Biblical precepts encouraging universal love and brotherhood. To find people that take "count of the soul," he knew he had to leave America, to go sailing to "the side where Christ was born."

What Jim discovers ultimately is that humans are free of discrimination only as children, as the play's title implies. Adults become earthbound as their perceptions of each other become warped. For this reason, Jim agrees to enter Ella's child-world, saying in his last speech: "Honey, I'll play right up to the gates of Heaven with you!" Implicit in the last section of the play and in its title is the concept that only in another world lies true freedom and equality and only through brotherhood is this paradise attained.

O'Neill became increasingly concerned about racial attitudes in America, as his numerous attempts to dramatize them in the 1920s and 1930s indicate. Obviously, through *All God's Chillun Got Wings*, he wished to show whites how their discrimination and oppression affect and even destroy the lives of others. He also had a message for blacks. Through the portrait of the defeated Jim at the end of the play, he encouraged them not to lose their racial identity in great white Mother America. He offered blacks no answers on how to cope with bigotry. The burden, he implies, must be borne by whites. Humanity, like morality, cannot be legislated. O'Neill probably came as close as any white could to expressing with exactness the character, goals, and frustrations of blacks.

All God's Chillun Got Wings can also be interpreted as an early view of the relationship between the author's own parents, which is later given in a large-scale treatment in *Long Day's Journey into Night*. O'Neill made no attempt to disguise the identity of Jim and Ella, who are given his parents' actual names. As statements attributed to her in *Long Day's Journey* attest, Ella O'Neill always viewed herself as superior to her husband intellectually, morally, and socially. She bitterly resented being ostracized by New Londoners and attributed her alienation and loneliness to her husband's inferior social position and his profession. Just as Jim relinquished his deep-seated goal to become a lawyer for Ella, James O'Neill apparently sacrificed his dream of sustaining his reputation as a Shakespearean actor to satisfy his wife's needs.

Whereas Ella Harris escapes the responsibilities of marriage and life by retreating into alternate states of childhood and manic madness, her real life counterpart seeks release through morphine. Neither wife forgives her husband for exposing her to the harsh world of reality and, hence, suffering. Like Jim, James Tyrone adores his wife and resigns himself to caring for her, as one would a child, at the end of *Long Day's Journey*. At the close of both plays, the two women regress to the safe innocent world of the past, of their youth.

When the scope of *All God's Chillun Got Wings* is widened to reveal its autobiographical aspects, its universal dimensions become clear. It is no longer simply a study of an interracial relationship. On a broader scale, it shows the struggle of any young couple who fall in love and marry to find happiness, the conflict that can occur in any marriage when one uneducated, neurotic partner becomes jealous of the other and resolves to destroy that other's dream of success. In his later plays O'Neill reiterates the same lesson on the tragedy inherent in a marital relationship but rarely with the pathos, simplicity, and compassion evident in *All God's Chillun*.

35.   *Desire Under the Elms*

Desire Under the Elms is O'Neill's first truly American historical play. Although *The Fountain* is set, in part, in sixteenth century Florida, the author made no attempt to Americanize its idealistic Spanish hero, Juan Ponce de Leon. In *Marco Millions*, on the other hand, he purposely created in Marco Polo "The American Ideal," an "American pillar of society," but he sends his thirteenth-century Venetian on a factual journey to the East. The fictional Yankee Cabots, consumed like the Polos by desire for material possessions, are native New Englanders. Greed, in itself, is not an American phenomenon; it becomes one when justified by Puritan zealots for spiritual reasons.

Early in 1923 O'Neill recorded the first idea for "Under the Elms" in his 1921–1931 notebook, immediately after entries for *The Great God Brown* and *All God's Chillun Got Wings*. Although he made greater progress in 1923 on *Marco Millions*, having completed its outline, this play was set aside for the less difficult *Desire Under the Elms*. Because O'Neill began keeping a record of his endeavors in a Work Diary in 1924, it is possible to calculate the time spent on the play: five weeks writing it—January 15–29, February 4–11, and May 24 to June 8—and ten days in June and July revising it.* Never again would O'Neill be so admittedly careless with a major drama. In the future he spent more time and effort at every stage of composition.

The original idea contains a summary of the plot:

> Play of New England—locate on farm in 1850, time of California gold rush—make N.E. farmhouse and elm trees almost characters in play—elms overhanging house—fath-

---

*The copyright date is August 29, 1924.

> er, hard iron type, killed off wives (2) with work, 3 sons—all
> hate him—his possessive pride in farm—loves earth to be
> as hard—in old age in a moment of unusual weakness &
> longing marries young woman, brings her back to farm, her
> arrival brings on drama, youngest son falls for her.

The father, seventy-five-year-old Ephraim Cabot, is no longer between wives when the play opens but in hot pursuit of the third Mrs. Cabot, the voluptuous thirty-five-year-old Abbie Putnam. Ephraim is tall and gaunt. "His face is as hard as if it were hewn out of a boulder, yet there is a weakness in it, a petty pride in its own narrow strength." He is "extremely near-sighted," a trait that will later symbolize his blindness to Abbie's infidelity with Eben, his youngest son.

Eben, twenty-five, is the son of Ephraim and his second wife, a warm, sensitive, love-starved woman, whose marriage was clearly a mistake. Overworked and ignored, she had, according to Eben, been murdered by her husband. Eben's face is good-looking. He has black hair, mustache, and beard. "His defiant, dark eyes remind one of a wild animal's in captivity. Each day is a cage in which he finds himself trapped but inwardly unsubdued. There is a fierce repressed vitality about him." He is the child of both parents, having inherited his mother's sensitivity, desire for beauty, and hunger for love but also his father's ruthlessness, greed, and lust. His brothers, Simeon and Peter, are sons of the first wife, who must surely have come from peasant stock to have mothered such clumsy oafs. They are fleshier than Eben, "more bovine and homelier in face, shrewder and more practical."

Eben's first word, and that of the play, "Purty," a reference to the farm, is repeated by the brothers in their earliest speeches. Each has a love-hate relationship with the farm, the longing both to escape the drudgery, restrictions, and hardships of it and to possess and be possessed utterly by it. The farm assumes mythic proportions in the lives of all the Cabot men. To old Ephraim it gives meaning to his existence. In the hard rocks and menial grind he sees the hand of God, testing and strengthening him for life's battle. Simeon and Peter respond to the farm like a pair of dumb oxen, yoked to it and to each other, mechanically, routinely responding to commands, pausing only fleetingly. Eben has a mystical attachment to it. He, more than the others, appreciates the beauty of the land, the wondrous background nature provides in the everlasting daily and seasonal changes. More important, he views his own mother as the rightful owner of the farm and sees himself, not his father, as heir to it. He feels the intangible presence of the dead mother protecting him and spurring him on to avenge her wrongs against Ephraim. Her spirit is manifested in the elms that flank the house.

While *Desire Under the Elms* is undoubtedly O'Neill's most naturalistic play, it also contains strong expressionistic elements, evidenced in the lengthy monologues of characters and, more vividly, visually, in the setting. The stage directions call for a multiple setting showing both the exterior of the farmhouse and the interior of its four rooms: the two bedrooms on an upper level, and, on the lower, a kitchen and an unused parlor. The setting suggests the struggle of the play: exterior environmental societal pressures acting upon and clashing with the trapped human psyches of the Cabots. Like their lives, the walls are a "sickly gray, the shutters faded."

The two enormous elms are described in supernatural terms to signify the power of Eben's mother extending beyond the grave:

> They appear to protect and at the same time subdue. There is a sinister maternity in their aspect, a crushing, jealous absorption. They have developed from their intimate contact with the life of Man in the house an appalling humaneness. They brood oppressively over the house. They are like

> exhausted women resting their sagging breasts and hands
> and hair on its roof, and when it rains their tears trickle down
> monotonously and rot on the shingles.

The other contrasting symbols reflect the tension in the
Cabots' lives. The stone wall that encompasses part of the
land suggests all that imprisons their bodies and souls. Yet
at the center of the wall is a wooden gate and beyond it a
country road, both representing the means of emancipation. This image of external forces grinding, crushing the
inner normal desires of the human spirit becomes the
play's major motif.

The most potent force in the lives of the Cabot is
Puritanism. The setting is not merely a farm; the terrain is
specifically Puritan New England. O'Neill attacks Puritanism in the play by showing psyches shattered and lives
destroyed by it. He could describe its effects from first-
hand experience, having imbibed a tainted strain of Puritanism through his Irish Catholic heritage and witnessed
its various manifestations in his Yankee New England
environment.

In the mid-sixteenth century, the English forebears
of these Yankees believed that the heavenly city of God
could not be reached either by way of Rome or through
the Church of England. They withdrew from the state
church, set up independent congregations, and were
henceforth known as Separatists or Puritans. Rather than
face persecution, waves of Puritans emigrated to the New
World, particularly in 1620 to form the Pilgrim colony at
Plymouth, in 1630 during the reign of Charles I to form
the Massachusetts Bay Colony, and in 1660 during the
Restoration when another Stuart crushed Cromwell's Puritan Revolution.

The historian Perry Miller traces Puritan theological
concepts to the fifth century and Saint Augustine. Miller
maintains that the Puritans who settled in New England
in the 1630s "seemed to leave the impress of Augustine
upon the American character. One might demonstrate

that Augustine exerted the greatest single influence upon Puritan thought next to that of the Bible itself, and in reality a greater one than did John Calvin."* According to Miller, three fundamental conceptions, God, sin, and regeneration, are the essentials of the Augustinian and Puritan point of view.

Catholics also traced their descent from Augustine. New England Puritans, therefore, had one thing in common with many European Catholics, especially the Irish Catholics, who emigrated to America: an affinity with Saint Augustine. The young Irishmen who were sent to France to study for the priesthood in the seventeenth century were often exposed to the teachings of Jansenius, which were based on Augustinian principles. A strong Augustinian strain can thus be found in Jansenistic Irish Catholicism and in traditional Puritanism: both preached the same Augustinian doctrines on absolute predestination, original sin, and irresistible grace.

Perhaps the similarity of theological and moral outlook accounts for the bitter rivalry between nineteenth-century Puritans and Jansenistic Irish Catholics in New England. O'Neill depicts the Yankee-Irish conflict for domination in New England in two extant cycle plays, *A Touch of the Poet* and *More Stately Mansions*. Over the years the deeply spiritual Puritanism of the first English settlers of the New World underwent drastic alterations as successive generations replaced them. Seventeenth-century Puritans stressed religious and moral principles. Their eighteenth- and nineteenth-century descendants placed greater emphasis on principal and business prosperity. Wealth was viewed as a manifestation of God's blessing and an indication of a man's goodness; failure was reserved for the wicked.

O'Neill denounced the heresy of this reasoning

*Perry Miller, *The New England Mind, The Seventeenth Century* (Cambridge, Mass.: Harvard University Press, 1954), pp. 4–5.

through his grim gallery of materially blessed but morally dissolute Puritans in *Desire Under the Elms* and *Mourning Becomes Electra*. The Cabots are consumed by a powerful, obsessive greed that causes them to exploit each other and the land. Insensate greed and lust are the vices that, to O'Neill, demoralize these Puritans and ultimately cause their downfall. New England becomes a state of mind; landscape becomes mindscape. In *Desire Under the Elms* the barren coldness is contrasted with the freedom, warmth, and easy riches of California. In *Mourning Becomes Electra* the Blessed Isles in the South Seas hold the same promise of escape to an exotic, sexually liberated land.

In Part I Eben uses his brothers' desire to travel to the "fields o' gold" in the west to recover his lawful birthright. In the first scene Simeon and Peter admit that only the thought of their inheritance after Ephraim's death keeps them on the farm. Eben denounces his brothers, expending the energy he normally uses in combat with his father, for not standing "between him 'n' my Maw when he was slavin' her to her grave." He renounces his patrimony: "I hain't his'n—I hain't like him. . . . I'm Maw—every drop o' blood!"

The same lust that drove Ephraim to leave the farm two months earlier in search of a new woman is manifested in Eben's desire to visit Min, the local prostitute. All the Cabots, Simeon says, starting with their father, have visited "The Scarlet Woman": "We air his heirs in everythin'!" Repulsed at first, Eben discovers that his need for something "soft 'n' wa'm" is too powerful to deny: "I don't give a damn how many sins she's sinned afore mine or who she's sinned 'em with, my sin's as purty as any one on 'em!" Eben's words reveal his Puritan sexual inhibitions and attitudes to sin. His pathetic revolt shows his desperate need for even the semblance of love, the fleeting contact with another human.

Eben staggers into the bedroom he shares with his

brothers shortly before dawn in the third scene to tell Simeon and Peter that their father, the "devil out o' hell," has "got himself hitched to a female." When the two discuss plans to leave now that "everythin'll go t' her," Eben offers to buy their shares of the farm for the six-hundred-dollar cache Ephraim has hidden. Eben, who found out about the marriage just before reaching Min's, describes his anger and its consequences: "I begun t' beller like a calf an' cuss at the same time, I was so durn mad—an' she got scared—an' I jest grabbed holt an' tuk her!" He sees his conquest as a form of revenge on his father: "The p'int is she was his'n—an' now she b'longs t' me!" Simeon mockingly repeats his father's pious remark about riding out to learn God's message "like the prophets done." He says, "I'll bet right then an' thar he knew plum well he was goin' whorin', the stinkin' old hypocrite!"

Eben in Scene 4 goes out to do the chores and "stares around him with glowing, possessive eyes. He takes in the whole farm with his embracing glance of desire." By the time he returns to the kitchen to announce his father's approach, his brothers have drunk enough whiskey to dull their already feeble wits. He retrieves the money from under a floorboard, and the bargain is finalized. Outside, Simeon symbolically wrests the gate off its hinges, puts it under his arm, and rejoices in his new-found freedom: "The halter's broke—the harness is busted—the fence bars is down—the stone walls air crumblin'."

The newly married couple enter. The physical attributes O'Neill gives Abbie, apparently those of his ideal woman, are given later to others, such as Sara Melody in *A Touch of the Poet* and Josie Hogan in *A Moon for the Misbegotten*. Her face is pretty but "marred by its rather gross sensuality. There is strength and obstinacy in her jaw, a hard determination in her eyes." Ephraim unleashes his fury on his idle elder sons, who "do an absurd Indian war dance about the old man who is petrified

between rage and fear that they are insane." Their final
act is to toss stones at the parlor window.

Abbie's first utterance, "Hum," is spoken possessively "with lust for the word." She realizes immediately
that Eben poses a threat to her and measures his strength
against hers, "but under this her desire is dimly awakened
by his youth and good looks." She says languorously, "I'm
yer new Maw." Enraged, he orders her to "go t' the
devil." In a long monlogue Abbie narrates the story of her
tragic life. Orphaned young, she was forced to work in
other people's homes. After the deaths of her baby and
husband, "a drunken spreer," she became a house drudge
again until Ephraim's offer of marriage. Eben denounces
her as a harlot. At the end of the scene, when Ephraim
begs God to smite his "undutiful sons," Eben rebels
against his father's demanding Old Testament deity: "T'
hell with yewr God!"

Ephraim's emulation of a harsh, insensitive God vic-
timizes him. He has been conditioned by his Puritan
upbringing. His emotions have long been crushed; he
cannot respond to others' needs or voice his own. This
illustrates the most striking naturalistic element of the
play: each of the characters is a victim of his heredity and
environment. Each of the sons reveals the character traits
of both of his parents. Eben is destroyed in the end as
much by the pride, lust, and acquisitiveness that mirror
his father as by the softer need for love, the trait willed
him by his mother. Like Eben, Abbie is described as
trapped by the circumstances of her life.

Present also in the play is the Darwinian concept of
man as an animal, the end product of the process of evolution. Animal imagery is used to describe all the characters. At mealtime Peter and Simeon, "their bodies bump-
ing and rubbing together," hurry "clumsily to their food,
like two friendly oxen." Abbie is referred to as both a cow
and a sow. In the seduction scene, she and Eben pant
"like two animals," and after it, he calls himself the "prize

rooster o' this roost." Ephraim at the party dances like a "monkey on a string." In spite of the many illustrations, O'Neill himself never viewed man as a soulless animal. What he demonstrates through these examples is that man can be robbed of his human dignity by the demeaning conditions of his life; by applying the word "caged" to the characters, he implies that man has no control over these forces.

Another naturalistic element of the play is the plot, which evolves out of the family situation: the revolt of various family members against a repressive Puritan way of life—the elder brothers against their environment in Part I, the lovers against sterile moral injunctions in Part II. An additional naturalistic aspect is the language. O'Neill tries to present a faithful reproduction of the stilted, laconic speech of native nineteenth-century Yankee New Englanders. Their tone is colorless, matter-of-fact; their thought patterns are practical and unimaginative, reflecting natures schooled to discipline their emotions. The work departs from naturalism in its fluid movement to and from exterior and interior scenes, the nonrealistic qualities of setting, the monologues, and the telepathy segment of Part II.

When Part II opens, Abbie, dressed in her best clothes, sits in a rocker on the porch on a hot Sunday afternoon two months after the end of Part I. She laughs sneeringly at Eben and reminds him that he has been trying to fight against his nature since her arrival. "Their physical attraction becomes a palpable force quivering in the hot air." In one of the most sensuous passages of the play, Abbie languorously describes the effects of the hot sun "burnin' into the earth." Her speech foreshadows a later scene. The two will succumb to the burning desire that consumes them but will manage to transcend the physical and "jine" the larger spirit emanating from the elms.

Abbie mocks Eben when she discovers that he is on

his way to visit Min. When he calls her a whore, Abbie jealously retaliates: "Git along! I hate the sight o' ye!" She gets her revenge when Ephraim comes up from the barn, his face softened, his eyes strangely dreamlike, obviously the effects of his contact with her these past months. Using a passage from the Song of Solomon, he describes her as his "Rose o' Sharon." "Yer eyes air doves; yer lips air like scarlet; yer two breasts air like two fawns." Nevertheless, in spite of his feelings for her, he vows to set fire to the house in his last hour, for then he would know that everything was "a-dyin' with me an' no one else'd ever own what was mine." Goaded beyond endurance, Abbie accuses Eben of trying to make love to her. She trembles fearfully when Ephraim threatens to blow Eben's "soft brains" out, and convinces him to allow the son to remain. When she realizes that Ephraim, in his vanity, would be more favorably disposed to her if she could produce a son, she remarks: "I been prayin' it'd happen." She is scornfully triumphant when, after she promises him a son, he exclaims: "They hain't nothin' I wouldn't do fur ye then, Abbie."

In Scene 2 Abbie and Ephraim sit side-by-side on their bed that evening. Eben is in the other bedroom gazing desolately into space. Eben and Abbie's hot glances seem to meet through the wall. Unconsciously, he stretches his arms for her, and she half rises. In the longest monologue of the play, Ephraim pours out his life story to Abbie in a desperate, but futile, attempt for understanding. He concludes by saying that neither his first nor his second wife knew him. Feeling that Abbie now understands him, he turns to her expecting a response to his revelations but encounters only her blank, indifferent stare. Angered, he heads for the barn, disturbed by the "thin's pokin' about in the dark—in the corner" of the house. Abbie immediately goes to Eben's room and invites him to come to court her in the parlor, the one room that she has not yet made hers. She laughs at

him. "I on'y wanted ye fur a purpose o' my own—and I'll
hev ye fur it yet 'cause I'm strong 'a yew be!"

The seduction takes place in Scene 3 in the parlor, a
"grim repressed room like a tomb in which the family has
been interred alive." Eben's dead mother had been
waked there, and her spirit still haunts the room. Abbie
had felt the presence when she came into the parlor, but
by the time Eben arrives she finds it "growin' soft an'
kind" to her. She is motivated by her desire for a child and
lust for him; he, by his desire to possess his mother and to
punish his father: "It's her vengeance on him—so's she
kin rest quiet in her grave!" Not until Abbie demonstrates
"sincere maternal love" and promises to kiss him "pure as
a Maw" does Eben respond to her passion.

In the final scene of Part II, Abbie opens the shutters
the next morning and professes her love to Eben, who
heads for the barn, saying: "Maw's gone back t' her grave.
She kin sleep now." He feels triumphant about his conquest when he encounters his father. Having gotten his
revenge, Eben states: "Yew 'n' me is quits." His words
and antics perplex his father, who looks after his departing
son with scornful pity: "soft-headed. Like his Maw. Dead
spit 'n' image. No hope in him!"

Evident in Part II are several forces that influenced
O'Neill as a dramatist. Most apparent is his fascination
with Greek drama and mythology. He uses the Oedipal
motif in the seduction scene, where Eben is obsessed by a
strong desire for the mother figure. In O'Neill's first notes
for the play, the Oedipal impulse was even more obvious.
"Abbie adapts a very motherly attitude, not pretending
but really believing it herself. She keeps kissing him,
getting him all confused as to her identity and his." Eben
"feels through her, he gets his mother back." His motives
in this scene conform to a concept that dominates Greek
tragedy that a wrong or blood must be avenged.

The Phaedra myth is manifested in the first scene of
Part II, in which Eben repulses Abbie's advances and she

vengefully tells Ephraim that the opposite has occurred. Married to Theseus, Phaedra falls in love with her handsome but chaste stepson, Hippolytus. Rejected, she accuses him of raping her. When Theseus prays to his father, Poseidon, to punish his son, the god of the sea frightens the young man's horses, and he is dragged to death across the shoreline. In the last act Abbie bears some resemblance to Medea, who murders her offspring, but the similarity is limited to the sole act of infanticide. Medea's motive is to punish Jason, who left her for Creon's daughter; Abbie acts to please, rather than punish, her lover.

O'Neill viewed man, as did the Greeks, as a tragic figure whose downfall was the result not only of external forces but also of his tragic flaw, a weakness of his irrational self. If man were destroyed by outer forces only, he would be merely a victimized puppet. On the other hand, the exertion of free will alone is not sufficient to raise a figure to heroic heights; he must also be doomed by an external agent. Naturalism substitutes heredity and environment for the Greek concept of fate manifested through the gods. And it is precisely in the area of character as tragic figure that O'Neill goes beyond naturalism in *Desire Under the Elms*. From the outset of the play to the seduction scene, Abbie and Eben can be viewed as naturalistic characters; after it, they begin a gradual evolution and emerge at the play's end as tragic figures, having consciously chosen and contributed to their own destruction.

Nietzsche exerted a strong influence on O'Neill, who shared the philosopher's belief in the concept of Apollonian and Dionysian forces existing in man. The idea emerges later in Freud's concept of the human psyche. Man has two sides, each struggling to dominate him. One, personified by the Greek deity Apollo, the sun god, represents man's rational nature: logic, order, discipline —qualities O'Neill attributes to his materialist businessmen. Society is Apollonian in the laws it makes to legislate conduct, in its codes of morality, in its insistence on conformity. Dionysus, god of wine and fertility, signifies man's irrational and highly emotional nature, his creative power, his free-spirited, uninhibited urges, what Nietzsche labeled the "dark, tortured subterranean." O'Neill gives these traits to his idealistic poets, his rebels against society.

Nietzsche asserts that tragedy was born when the Apollonian spirit triumphed over man's Dionysian spirit. An obvious example would be Ephraim, who is totally Apollonian, although faint emotional cracks emerge briefly in Part II after his exposure to Abbie's mellowing influence. The fertile Abbie is nearly purely Dionysian, although reason dominates her at times when she schemes to possess the farm. The struggle in the play, between the drives these characters represent, pertains, in some way, to Eben. He is, as his brother Peter states, the "dead spit 'n' image" of his Paw, Apollonian in his determination to have the farm, his logic in wresting ownership of it from his brothers, and his early rejection of the sensuous Abbie. When his resistence is finally crushed in the parlor scene, his Dionysian nature, inherited from his mother, is unleashed. Totally unrestrained, his new-found passion overwhelms him. In the final scene of the play, this emotion is transformed into the highest form of love.

Part III takes place on a night in late spring of the following year. A raucous christening part is in progress in the Cabots' kitchen. Ephraim's neighbors sit on the wooden benches pushed against the room's walls. Found here is O'Neill's earliest attempt to use a Greek-like chorus of townspeople. Like the gossiping New Englanders at the outset of the three plays of *Mourning Becomes Electra*, the narrow-minded, envious neighbors pass judgment on the Cabots and express the views of the community. They share a "secret joke in common" and make crude remarks on Ephraim's ability, at seventy-six, to produce a son. The fiddler pretends to praise him: "Ye're the spryest seventy-six ever I sees, Ephraim. Now if ye'd on'y good eye-sight!"

Ephraim becomes a mythical, immortal giant. He tells his neighbors that he was fighting Indians before they were born and that he will live on to be a hundred when they will all be dead. Yet although he arouses sympathy, he never becomes a tragic figure in the Greek sense of the word. The remark about his poor eyesight, a physical weakness, suggests that he is merely a victim of external forces. He never truly sees his condition or experiences a catharsis. The only weakness that could be equated with an inner tragic flaw is his pride. But it is not this flaw that destroys him, as it would in a Greek tragedy.

The father-son animosity surfaced briefly at the end of the first and second parts of the play. Now the deep-rooted hatred erupts into violence in the next scene. When Eben boasts that the farm is his, Ephraim calls him a blind mole for not realizing that it now belongs to the new child and Abbie. He repeats Abbie's story about Eben's advances and his promise to grant her whatever she wanted should they have a son. The father recalls the price she demanded: "I wants Eben cut off so's this farm'll be mine when ye die!" Enraged by Abbie's apparent betrayal, Eben vows to murder her; only her intervention halts his "murderous struggle" with Ephraim. Alone with Abbie, whom he calls a "damn trickin' whore," Eben threatens to tell his father the truth and to leave the farm. He wishes that the child had never been born, that it will die. Devastated, Abbie asks him if he would love her again if it were "jest the same" as "afore he come." Assured he would, she promises to prove that she loves Eben "better'n everythin' else in the world!"

In the next scene, just before dawn, Eben is about to leave when Abbie enters and says: "I killed him." Throughout the play there are numerous examples of the inability of the characters to communicate. Eben misunderstands Abbie here, just as he had not realized the true meaning of her words the previous evening. He thinks she has murdered his father and promises to protect her (as does Orin later in *Mourning Becomes Electra* when he discovers that his mother has killed his father). In O'Neill, the father is expendable. When Abbie tells Eben that the baby is dead, Eben threatens to kill her: "Ye must've swapped yer soul t'hell!" Swearing to escape the spell she still casts over him and to seek vengeance, he goes for the sheriff.

Scene 4 occurs an hour later. Ephraim laments the death of the child; grief-stricken, he begins to cry. Discovering that the child was Eben's, he becomes his former self and vows to see Abbie hung. Eben returns, regretting his betrayal of Abbie to the sheriff and begging her forgiveness. Urged to escape, she responds: "I got t' take my punishment—t' pay fur my sin." He too assumes reponsibility for his "part o' the sin" and vows to share her punishment: "prison 'r death 'r hell 'r anythin'!"

Ephraim enters, having set free the cows and stock, determined to use his hidden savings to go to California. The empty hole under the floorboard mocks him, but he sees in this setback the hand of God: "his voice warnin' me agen t' be hard an' stay on my farm." In what must be one of the most desolate cries of aloneness uttered by any O'Neill character, he laments: "Waal—what d'ye want? God's lonesome, hain't He? God's hard an' lonesome!"

Eben surrenders himself to the sheriff. The lovers walk hand in hand to the gate. Like Jim, who stands at another gate with Ella after their marriage in *All God's Chillun Got Wings*, Eben urges Abbie to raise her eyes to the sky, as if God could somehow assure them of happiness and rectify their situation. They look "up raptly in attitudes strangely aloof and devout." It is their love in the end that transfixes, ennobles, and saves them. The conclusion provides the best illustration in the early plays of

O'Neill's statement: "In all my plays sin is punished and redemption takes place."

In the play's final line the sheriff expresses his admiration for the farm and his desire to possess it. In so doing, he falls victim to the greed that destroyed the Cabots. The word "desire," reduced to its lowest level, suggests lust. In Part I the focus of the lust of the Cabots is the farm. In Part II Ephraim, Eben, and Abbie are caught up in a triangular web of physical desire. A blow is struck against the Puritan ideal of chastity because of Abbie and Eben's act of adultery-incest. Part II illustrates how desire can be spiritualized when it transcends the physical and is transformed into love. As in the other plays that follow *Welded*, love is made possible only by suffering.

The drama's title lends itself to another interpretation. Throughout the play the elms represent a potent supernatural force. The dead mother's spirit pervades the trees. Ephraim feels some intangible dew "droppin' off the elums." It is apparent that the Cabots' desire can only be realized "under the elms." The many references to God in the final scene, the reconciliation of each of the Cabots to Him, demonstrates it is He they crave. One has only to recall the words from one of O'Neill's favorite poems, Francis Thompson's "The Hound of Heaven"—"I fled Him, down the nights and down the days"—to comprehend the underlying meaning of the play's last scene. What is worked out here is O'Neill's pervasive salvation cycle: temptation/sin, betrayal (usually by or of the mother figure), revenge, punishment, suffering/death, redemption.

At the close, Abbie and Eben are exultant, "devout." Just as Hickey will probably go to the electric chair for murdering his wife in *the Iceman Cometh*, they will, as Ephraim predicts, apparently hang "on the same limb." It is inconceivable to imagine these free spirits languishing in prison. The world, O'Neill seems to imply, is too small to contain them, for the lovers have found true happiness;

in O'Neill's plays, it is not possible to attain this state and live.

Two years before he wrote *Desire Under the Elms*, O'Neill was asked why he did not write about happiness; he responded that he would if he ever encountered this luxury. He identified happiness not with "a mere smirking contentment with one's lot" but with exaltation. He stated that there is more happiness "in one real tragedy than in all the happy-ending plays ever written. It's mere present-day judgment to think of tragedy as unhappy! The Greeks and the Elizabethans knew better. . . . It roused them spiritually to a deeper understanding of life."*

It should be noted that *Desire Under the Elms* is a memory play. The author told Walter Huston, who appeared as Ephraim in the work's premiere, that he dreamed the whole play in one night. The familiar characters obviously resided in O'Neill's subconscious. All he neded was a jog to his memory to raise them to the surface. The nineteenth-century Puritan Cabots were unconscious portraits of the twentieth-century Irish-Catholic Puritanical O'Neills, and through the Cabots the playwright revealed the thinly-disguised details of his personal life. Eben, who resembles both parents, the stubborn father and the sensitive mother, is a self-portrait. The vulgar older brothers, aged thirty-nine and thirty-seven, are a composite picture of Jamie, his brother (the mean of their ages represents the ten-year difference between him and the dramatist, who, as Eben, is first depicted in the early notes as twenty-eight). After his mother's death, Jamie was the sole beneficiary of property in California, where Peter and Simeon go to find gold.

James O'Neill's age, at the time his son wrote the play, approximated Ephraim's. Like Cabot, he was miserly and had a strong desire to possess land. In the original idea for the play, O'Neill noted that the father

*Clark, p. 86.

"killed off wives" and that the sons "all hate him." The father in *Long Day's Journey into Night* is continually accused of destroying his wife; his parsimony allegedly caused her drug addiction. The long-running father-son battle waged in both *Desire Under the Elms* and *Long Day's Journey into Night* is autobiographical. The elder O'Neill, like Ephraim, kept his sons dependent on him. Ephraim's two wives, the feisty, materialistic Abbie, who desires a home, and the long-suffering second wife, who is "killed by her husband," represent the two natures of Ella O'Neill.

The play opened on November 11, 1924, at the Greenwich Village Theater. It proved to be so popular that it moved uptown to Broadway on January 12, 1925. One reason for the play's success was the scandalous publicity accorded it. The District Attorney of New York, Joab Banton, tried to close *Desire Under the Elms* and several other plays that seemed morally questionable to him. All were absolved of obscenity charges. When the cast of a road company production was arrested in Los Angeles, the judge ordered the actors to stage scenes from the play in court. Again reason prevailed, and the cast was acquitted.

The charge of immorality leveled at *Desire Under the Elms* and later plays is ironic. O'Neill was, throughout his creative career, a straight-laced Puritan, in spite of his frequent attacks on Puritanism. Suggestive words such as "harlot," "whore," and "whorin' " sprinkle his dialogue, but no sexual acts are ever depicted onstage. Characters may talk about sin, but, like the murders in Greek drama, it occurs offstage. O'Neill dramatizes few scenes of passion, few deeply emotional characters in his works. Perhaps the most sensuous woman in the canon is Abbie Putnam. She is intensely passionate and one of the most fully realized characters O'Neill ever created. The love she inspires in Eben raises *Desire Under the Elms* from the level of melodrama to the realm of pure tragedy in its closing scene.

36.   *Marco Millions*

In *Marco Millions** O'Neill again retreated into history.
While the era chronicled predates the Spanish conquest
depicted in *The Fountain, Marco Millions* springs creatively from this earlier work. *The Fountain* contains several references to Cathay, described as "that immense
realm of the Great Kaan, which Marco Polo saw." A
journey to Cathay fires the imagination of both historical
figures, the Venetian Marco Polo and the Spaniard Juan
Ponce de Leon. They have different goals, however. The
Spaniard seeks the sacred grove in that far-off land and the
Fountain of Youth, the "Spring of Life." Marco undertakes his journey to the Orient to plunder its promised
wealth.

Marco Polo is the most avaricious, conscienceless
character in O'Neill's gallery of materialists. He can perhaps be traced back to an idea about a mercenary merchant that the author recorded in his 1918–1920 notebook:
"long play taking up the 'Beyond the Horizon' situation
where that play leaves off—the play of Andrew." At the
end of *Beyond the Horizon* Andrew, who had "been
almost a millionaire—on paper," plans a trip to Argentina
to become one in reality. At the start of *Marco Millions*,
the young Marco sets out from Venice dreaming of amass-
ing "millions."

Through the portraits of Robert and Andrew Mayo in
Beyond the Horizon, O'Neill presented for the first time a
full-scale study of a major motif in the canon: the clash
between the idealistic poet and the materialistic businessman. The dichotomy is suggested again by two contrast-

---

*The copyright date is January 28, 1925. The play was not
produced, however, until January 9, 1928.

ing characters in the play that follows *Marco Millions*, *The Great God Brown*: the doomed poet, Dion Anthony, and the avaricious businessman, William A. Brown. The conflicting natures merge in Marco Polo, and just as Andrew and Brown contribute to the deaths of Robert and Dion, the materialist in Marco destroys his poetic self.

O'Neill's goal in these three plays, particularly in *Marco Millions*, is to illustrate American acquisitiveness and greed. To him, the Polos—Marco; his father, Nicolo; and his uncle, Maffeo—were not simply Italian adventurers; they were envisioned, even in the period of incubation, as typical American businessmen. In the spring of 1924, the author informs Macgowan:

> Am working hard as hell on Marco. . . . It's going to be humorous as the devil if the way it makes me guffaw as I write is any criterion—and not bitter humor either although it's all satirical. I actually grow to love my American pillars of society, Polo Brothers & Son. It's going to be very long in first draft, I imagine, but I'm letting the sky be the limit and putting every fancy in.

The lengthy first scenario of 1923, which contains six parts, each having two scenes, indicates that O'Neill made no attempt to restrain his imagination. Yet he also wanted to incorporate historical facts. He describes his effort to research his material to Macgowan:

> Am reading and taking millions of notes, etc. A lot of what the actual writing must be is now clear—and a lot isn't but will, God willing! I'll soon start a lengthy scenario of the whole to find out just how and where I stand—then get right after the reading, I hope. There's a lot of reading still to be done. . . . The child will be either a surpassing satiric Beauty—or a most Gawdawful monster.

The extant collection of notes for the play contains excerpts from *The Travels of Marco Polo*, the historical hero's factual record of his journey to the East and his stay at the court of the Great Kaan. O'Neill's "millions of notes" include information about Eastern religious prac-

tices, customs, prevailing attitudes, and the existing or
potential wealth in each of the regions the Polos visit.

In the Foreword to the play, O'Neill criticizes the
travelogue, for Marco has "left the traveler out." Marco's
Venetian contemporaries would not believe his tale about
the Orient and scoffingly called him a liar. O'Neill states,
in tongue-in-cheek fashion, his intention "to render poetic justice" to the traveler. Marco, he says, was labeled an
"extravagant romancer and ever since has traveled down
the prejudiced centuries, a prophet without honor, or
even notoriety, save in false whiskers. This has moved me
to an indignant crusade . . . to whitewash the good soul of
that maligned Venetian."* The last line of the statement
illustrates why the dramatist can, with justification, call
the play "real satire."

The Marco O'Neill conceives does not have a "good
soul." In fact, he has no soul. Like the other Faustian
heroes in the canon, he sells his soul for wealth and
power. Ironically, he is sent to the East as the Pope's
response to the Great Kaan's request for one hudred wise
men. The Great Kaan wants to learn more about Christianity, but he becomes disillusioned by Marco's moral
and spiritual vacuity. Kublai Kaan sadly concludes that
Marco is an admission by the Pope of the sorry state of
Christianity. The Kaan resolves to send Marco "back to
the Pope with a soul as the symbol of the peaceful con-
quering of the West by East." The play demonstrates why
the Kaan fails to achieve his goal.

As in *The Fountain*, O'Neill pits a Christianity that
has been corrupted and reduced to opportunism, hypocrisy, and exploitation against an Eastern or primitive
non-Christian religion that retains not only its pristine
purity but also its ability to influence the lives of its
followers. There is also the clash of cultures in the two

---

*Barrett Clark, *Eugene O'Neill, The Man and His Plays* (New
York: Dover, 1947), p. 109. All future references will be to this
later edition of Clark's book.

plays: New World versus Old, East versus West. O'Neill's conception of Columbus can be used to differentiate the central figures in the two historical plays. In his spirituality, humanity, and nobility, Juan Ponce de Leon is demonstrably superior to Columbus. Marco, however, has "no transcendent superiority of character or capacity—no comparison to Columbus."

Marco Millions was three years in the making, a sporadic, rather than a sustained, effort. After completing the outline, O'Neill set it aside to write *Desire Under the Elms*, in which the greed of the New England Puritan Cabots proved to be as destructive to the human spirit as that of the Italian-Catholic Polos. He resumed work on "Mister Mark Millions," as he called the play originally, in July 1924. By mid-October the original six-part scenario was transformed into a four-part first draft so massive that it contained "two good long plays of 2½ hours each—at least!" In January 1925 O'Neill condensed the two "long plays" into the drama's final form, the present three-act work, containing eleven scenes, a Prologue, and an Epilogue.

Originally the play opened and closed with a scene showing Marco in a prison cell. After his return from the East, he was captured during the war waged between Genoa and Venice. To promote the interests of the Polo business, he has agreed to dictate his memoirs to Rusticiano of Pisa, a writer of travels. Marco's story is then told using the flashback technique. In its final form, except for the Prologue, Marco's life unfolds chronologically.

The Prologue shows three thirteenth-century merchants, a Buddhist, a Magian, and a Christian, meeting by accident near a sacred tree on a plain in Persia. Each claims a right to the tree, associating it with his religion. The Christian, sent by the firm Polo Brothers & Son to sell goods to Queen Kukachin and her husband, is dismayed to hear of the queen's death. Kukachin's funeral cortege approaches. The captain of the guard pauses to rest and informs the salesmen that the queen's grandfather, the Great Kaan, has ordered that her body be returned to Cathay. The captain pulls aside the pall of the glass coffin, revealing the face of Kukachin, a "beautiful Tartar princess of twenty-three." Her expression "seems to glow with the intense peace of a life beyond death, the eyes are shut as if she were asleep."

In this expressionistic scene, an unearthly glow lights Kukachin's face, which "becomes more and more living." She speaks: "Say this, I loved and died. Now I am love, and live. And living, have forgotten. And loving, can forgive." Laughter, "of an intoxicating, supernatural gaiety," comes from her lips. When three of his men do not stir, the captain impresses the salesmen in their place.

The play opens in Venice twenty-three years earlier. Standing in a gondola beneath a barred window, fifteen-year-old Marco serenades the twelve-year-old Donata. She promises to marry him when he returns from his journey. The union has monetary potential for their families, bringing "two firms into closer contact." Marco describes the court of the Great Kaan, "the richest king in the world." His father and uncle, who spent nine years there, have assured him that "There's millions to be made in his service." As a keepsake, Donata gives him a medallion, a painting of herself, and begs for a poem in return. The scene closes with Marco vowing to be faithful and to cherish her image.

The next scene shows the Polos six months later at the palace of Tedaldo, the Papal Legate of Syria at Acre. Marco's father is a small man with a "dry, shrewd face." His brother is stout and has "small, cunning eyes." The College of Cardinals, after two years in session, has failed to name a new Pope. The brothers ask the legate where they are to obtain the hundred wise men of the West, requested by the Great Kaan to debate religious matters with his priests. Tedaldo is bored by the brothers' continual refrain of "millions" and turns his attention to young Marco, who is writing a poem for Donata. His father calls him a heedless dreamer; his uncle grabs the poem and says scornfully that Marco's father has hatched a nightingale. The legate berates the father for mocking Marco: "Be grateful if a thistle can bring forth figs." The poem abounds with monetary images, comparing Donata's features to gold, silver, and pearls. The boy crushes the paper and stamps on it. "Poetry's all stupid," he exclaims. "You won't catch me ever being such a fool again!"

When Tedaldo is named Pope, he is asked for the hundred wise men. Saying that not even one wise man exists, he appoints Marco as his missionary. "Let him set an example of virtuous Western manhood amid all the levities of paganism . . . and I will wager a million of something or other myself that the Kaan will soon be driven to seek spiritual salvation somewhere! Mark my words, Marco will be worth a million wise men." Marco furtively retrieves the poem at the end of the scene.

The next three scenes trace the stages of Marco's mental development and his journey to the East: Persia four months later, India eight months later, Mongolia eleven months later. The grouping of characters is the same in all three scenes: in a semicircle behind the ruler's throne at center are a mother nursing a child, two children playing at being a young couple embracing, a middle-aged and an aged couple, and a coffin. In the first of these scenes Marco shows great interest in all of the Mahometan people, moving among them and talking to them, and shows no interest in the half-naked, sensual prostitute who offers herself as a gift to the youth. In the next scene, the "freshness of youth has worn off." Marco looks at the Indian figures with the "indifferent attitude of the worldly-wise." He outwits the prostitute by winning a bet but rejects her offer to make him a "real man—for 10 pieces of gold."

In the fifth scene, outside the Great Wall of China, Marco "hardly glances" at the groups of inhabitants. He rejects the prostitute's invitation to visit her again that night and orders her to return the medallion she stole from him. Scornfully, she reads the poem on the crumpled paper. When Marco denies writing it, she responds: "Don't sell your soul for nothing." She grinds the paper into the dust: "Your soul! Dead and buried!" The woman then throws the miniature at Marco's feet. A messenger from Kublai arrives, and the weary Polos struggle on to Cathay. What O'Neill does in these scenes, as in later plays such as *The Great God Brown* and *Dynamo*, is to present a character in his youth and show him later in various stages of his life after external forces have interacted, usually fatally, with his flawed inner condition.

In Scene 6 the Polos are shown in the luxurious Grand Throne Room of the Great Kaan's palace in Cambaluc, Cathay. On the elevated throne, dressed in heavy gold robes, sits Kublai, "a man of sixty but still in the full prime of his powers, his face proud and noble, his expression tinged with an ironic humor and bitterness yet full of a sympathetic humanity." With him are Chu-Yin, his Cathayan adviser, family members—wives, concubines, sons—and subjects—nobles, poets, and "hangers-on of government." Marco, carrying a salesman's sample case in each hand, gazes in stupefied awe at the wondrous splendor. When Kublai voices his dismay at the Pope's inability to send the requested wise men, Marco courageously steps forward: "He sent me in their place. He said I'd be worth a million wise men to you." Nicolo Polo boasts that his son's upright life will "illustrate, better than wise words, the flesh and blood product of our Christian civilization."

Kublai wonders if the Pope truly believes that Marco possesses "that thing called soul which the West dreams lives after death." Marco responds that he has a soul—and a body as well: "I've got to eat." The elder Polos draw Marco aside and urge him to request a job as a second-class government commission agent. He would then meet dealers who would "let him in on everything" and be able to convey secrets to the elder Polos, allowing them to prosper. In the last display of conscience in the play, Marco questions the morality of the suggestion. Using one of the numerous American clichés woven into the speeches of the Polos, he says: "Honesty's the best policy." Assured that Kublai sanctions such business tactics, Marco astutely haggles with his relatives until they agree to make him a junior partner in the firm.

Kublai tells Chu-Yin: "This Marco touches me, as a child might, but at the same time there is something warped, deformed—." The sage suggests that Marco be given "every opportunity for true growth if he so desires. And let us observe him. At least, if he cannot learn, we shall."

Act II opens fifteen years later in the Kaan's summer palace at Xanadu, the "City of Peace." The Kaan has aged; his expression has grown "mask-like, full of philosophic calm." With him is his beloved granddaughter, Kukachin, his only source of happiness since her mother died. Yet she must leave soon to marry Arghun, "Khan of the blood of Chinghiz," and become Queen of Persia. The Kaan suspects that she has fallen in love with someone else, although she agrees to marry to avoid plunging her country into war. The Kaan awaits His Honor, Marco Polo, now mayor of Yang-Chau, the city that "used to have a soul," but now has, instead, a brand-new courthouse. The Venetian no longer amuses the Kaan: "Marco's spiritual hump begins to disgust me. He has not even a mortal soul, he has only an acquisitive instinct." He "has lusted for everything and loved nothing. He is only a shrewd and crafty greed." The old man realizes that Kukachin loves Marco when she vehemently asserts that Marco possesses a soul.

The blare of two bands announces Marco's arrival outside. He moves with "mechanical dignity" through the cheering crowd like a politician seeking votes. "He has the manner and appearance of a successful movie star at a masquerade ball." His face is good looking, "carefully arranged into the grave responsible expression of a Senator from the South of the United States of America about to propose an amendment to the Constitution restricting the migration of non-Nordic birds into Texas."

Marco explains how he raised an unprecedented amount of taxes in his city. He has repealed taxes on all luxuries and written a law "that taxes everything necessary in life, a law that hits every man equally." Marco shows the Kaan his two inventions: paper money and gunpowder. Ironically the idea for the latter occurred on the last Easter Sunday as he meditated on the Prince of Peace. Marco suggests arms escalation as a way to maintain peace. Enemies would "give in and avoid wasteful bloodshed." Marco takes out a toy cannon and demonstrates its use and effectiveness. "You conquer the world with this," he remarks, indicating the cannon; and "you pay for it with this," he adds, pointing to the paper money.

Requesting permission to return to Venice, Marco is told that he must produce one witness to verify the fact that he has an immortal soul. The situation appears hopeless until Kukachin asserts that she has seen it. Arrangements are concluded: Marco is to escort the Princess to Persia and return to Italy.

O'Neill omits two scenes from the original draft for this section that showed the Kaan's attempt to enlighten the materialistic merchant. His teachers agree on Marco's three faults: "Bigotry, his gross materialism, his servile acceptance and fear of authority"; and his three virtues: "he is fearless, he is capable and energetic." They concur that he has no soul nor any faith "but only three unthinking beliefs: in the divine right of money, in the divine right of property—things as they are (business as usual), in the divine right of himself as the ruler and possessor of both."

In the following scene, the Kaan bids Kukachin farewell on a royal junk at Zayton several weeks later. The marriage seems, to her, a small price to pay in exchange for the happiness of being with Marco on the journey. Reminiscent of the expressionistic sections of *The Hairy Ape*, an endless line of slaves, each carrying a bale on his head, forms a human chain "which revolves mechanically." Chu-Yin gives Marco the Kaan's final order: once a day on the voyage he is to "look carefully and deeply into the Princess's eyes and note what you see there." Marco promises to care for Kukachin, whom he respects, he says, tremendously as she is human. The sage concludes that there may be hope for Marco after all.

Two years have elapsed when the junk reaches Hormuz in the next scene. Kukachin's face has changed; "it is the face of a woman who has known real sorrow and suffering." Told that her intended husband is dead and that she is to marry his son Ghazan, Kukachin shows no emotion. Yet she is nearly hysterical with sorrow when she contemplates her separation from Marco. She orders him to perform his duty for the last time: "See my eyes as those of a woman and not a Princess! Look deeply! I will die if you do not see what is there!" Her whole being reaches out to him; for an instant he is filled with passion; "his face moves hypnotically towards hers, their lips seem about to kiss." The spell is broken when he hears his uncle, who has been counting money, announce, "one million!" Reminded of what he stands to lose, Marco turns away; callously, he takes out Donata's locket and shows the Princess the future Mrs. Polo. She will be waiting for him, Marco says, as "her family needs an alliance with our house." Realizing at last Marco's true nature, Kukachin replies: "There is no soul even in your love, which is no better than a mating of swine!"

Ghazan, a noble, manly looking youth, comes aboard and is mesmerized by Kukachin's great beauty. She requests that an immense feast be given and Marco encouraged to gorge himself until he becomes his own ideal figure, an idol of stuffed self-satisfaction, and that a chest of gold coins be brought to her. These she throws at the Polos, saying, "Wallow for our amusement." Like her grandfather, she concludes that Marco is fit only to entertain her. Kukachin weeps bitterly at the death of love.

The following scene switches to the Grand Throne Room a year later. General Bayan tells the Kaan that the

West could easily be conquered. "Let the West devour itself," Kublai argues. "We have everything to lose by contact with its greedy hypocrisy." A courier brings a letter from Kukachin, who says that her grandfather was correct about Marco's soul: "I cannot forgive myself—nor forget." Kublai orders a servant to bring his crystal, which miraculously enables him to see what is occurring elsewhere. Through this expressionistic technique, the banquet scene in Venice is brought into focus onstage.

Donata enters with her father. She is stout but "still pretty in a bovine, good-natured way." The Polos are dressed in crimson satin robes, which, when discarded, reveal more gorgeous blue ones. These are shed, revealing the Polos garbed in their shabby Tartar traveling clothes. The three men slit their wide sleeves and "let pour from them a perfect stream of precious stones." Donata swoons and pronounces Marco her beloved prince and hero. Encouraged to share his thoughts, Marco "clears his throat with an important cough and bursts forth into a memorized speech in the grand Chamber of Commerce style." He is actually ignored by the gluttonous crowd. As his final words—"millions! . . . millions! . . . millions!"—fade, the Kaan shudders in loathing and disgust. The crystal falls and shatters.

In the second scene of Act III, which takes place two years later, the Kaan's household assembles in the Grand Throne Room, where the Kaan sits in mourning for Kukachin, his eyes fixed on the catafalque. A lengthy funeral procession enters: priests, musicians, a masked chorus. The bier of Kukachin, her face "clear and white as a statue's," is placed on the catafalque. The Kaan questions each of the priests—Confucian, Taoist, Buddhist—about the possibility of immortality and is told by each, "Death is." Bitterly, he tells Chu-Yin, "She died for love of a fool!" The sage responds: "No. She loved love. She died for beauty." At the end of the play, the Kaan, like Jim and Ella in *All God's Chillun Got Wings*, regresses to the world of pretense and the happier past of Kukachin's childhood. "You are a little girl again. You are playing hide and seek. You are pretending." Grief-stricken and confused, he talks to her "with heart-breaking playfulness" and welcomes her home.

In the Epilogue that follows, a man, sitting in the first row of the theater, rises and yawns. It is "Marco Polo himself, looking a bit sleeply, a trifle puzzled, and not a little irritated" for allowing himself to think of the play that just ended. He is dressed "as a Venetian merchant of the later Thirteenth Century." He makes his way to the lobby, "his eyes impersonally speculative," and waits for his car. A luxurious limousine drives up. He gets in "with a satisfied sigh at the sheer comfort of it all" and "resumes his life."

The first version of the Epilogue shows Marco in his Genoese prison cell. His "spiritual hump" has become even more pronounced than it was in the Kaan's court. He is as indifferent to his wife, Donata, who visits him, as he was to Kukachin. His own inner corruption leads him to believe that he can obtain his release from prison by bribing officials. Marco has not changed; he has learned nothing from reflecting on his past during the dictation of his journal. The prison walls that close in on him symbolize the trap spawned by his own flawed nature.

The published Epilogue that was substituted for the prison scene is ambiguous, an open-ended finale. O'Neill seems to incorporate here an idea for a play on reincarnation recorded before writing *Marco Millions*, contrasting "the oldest civilization of China and that of modern times —same crises offering definite choice of either material (i.e. worldly) success or a step toward higher spiritual plane." The fact that the reincarnated thirteenth-century Venetian has "disturbing" memories of what has happened onstage as he leaves the theater to enter the present world of reality suggests the hope of change. Even though Marco, with his smug self-complacency and typical gaudy display of wealth, is depicted as the apotheosis of bourgeois capitalism, the Epilogue suggests the possibility, slight though it may be, for an inner renewal, that the reenactment of the ever-ancient, ever-new dilemma will finally inspire a spiritual rather than material choice.

Although he is an object of satire, Marco is depicted, basically, as a tragic figure. When he is young, the faint manifestations of an inner beauty of soul, symbolized by his crude poetic attempt, are stifled by the mocking laughter of his father, uncle, Tedaldo, and, finally, the prostitute, each of whom seeks to use him for his or her own purpose. By the time Marco arrives at the Kaan's court, his benign "spiritual hump" had become malignant. It is this aspect of Marco, the spiritually deformed materialist, that bears the burden of meaning in the play. O'Neill's purpose in this drama is to show the tragedy incurred when man's blindness blocks out beauty and love and leaves him in a dark world grasping for objects.

Before the arrival of the Polos in Cathay, the idealistic poet-materialistic businessman conflict is centralized within Marco. After he encounters Kublai, the battle is waged between these two opposing characters. The Great Kaan, as he emerges in O'Neill's notes and drafts of the play, is one of the author's noblest and wisest creations. He is relentless in his quest for a spiritual absolute. Having examined the religions of the East and found them wanting, he turns to the West. In *The Travels of Marco Polo* Kublai expresses a desire to be baptized. The hundred wise men he requests are needed to help convert his people. He tells the Pope, "Following my example, all my nobility will then in like manner receive baptism, and this will be imitated by my subjects in general." Marco states, "If the Pope had sent out persons duly qualified to preach the gospel, the grand khan would have embraced Christianity, for which, it is certainly known, he has a strong predilection." The point O'Neill makes through his characterization of Marco the materialist is that the Kaan's contact with this living symbol of Western Christianity and civilization proves to be a painful learning experience, disillusioning him and shattering his hope for religious reassurance.

O'Neill narrows the concept of "Western" to American. He calls his self-made millionaire, who uses Chamber of Commerce rhetoric, an "American pillar of society." In his notes, the dramatist describes Marco as shrewd, prudent, and "never losing his interest in mercantile details—sparing of speech (The American Ideal!) —contempt for those whose consciences would not run in customary grooves, and on his own part a keen appreciation of the World's pomps & vanities." *Marco Millions* is the first of the trio of plays O'Neill wrote in the mid-1920s attacking American materialism. *Desire Under the Elms* shows another family, the New England Cabots, consumed by greed. In *The Great God Brown* William A. Brown, the American businessman, is corrupted, like Marco, by wealth, but unlike him, he is redeemed.

While the words assigned to Kublai and Kukachin ascend, at times, to heights of lyricism and beauty, the speeches of the Polos are often wooden, cumbersome, pedantic. *Marco Millions* is a didactic rather than a personal drama. It is one of the few works in the O'Neill canon devoid of autobiographical references. In spite of Kukachin's passion and Kublai's heartbreak at her death, the play lacks warmth and emotional intensity. The numerous scenes and characters, the panoramic passing of time and peoples, seems to preclude a sensitive treatment. *Marco Millions* remained a formidable unstaged work until the Theatre Guild production on January 9, 1928. Although the acting version, as Clark notes, was shorter than the script that was published in 1927, he still complains about the "long evening in the playhouse" and the "waits between scenes." He writes:

> Stretched out to two and a half hours Marco seemed rather thin. I believe that if it had been reduced to five or six scenes, acted on a revolving stage without intermission and turned into a dramatic ballet with dancing, music, panto-

mime and dialogue, it would have been a perfect thing of its kind.*

Just as research and work on *The Fountain* probably provided inspiration for *Marco Millions*, the latter seems to have given O'Neill the idea for a drama on the "Career of Shih Huang Ti, Emperor of China, whose rule ended in 201 B.C." This concept was recorded in 1925, the same year O'Neill condensed the two-play version of *Marco Millions*. Both plays reveal O'Neill's interest in the merits of Taoism versus Confucianism and the rule of despots, men like Marco and Shui Huang Ti, as opposed to that of enlightened, benevolent Emperors like Kublai Kaan. The playwright depicted the thirteenth century Polos as contemporary American materialists; in "Shui Huang Ti," he considers making an analogy between the avaricious leaders of ancient China and their modern counterparts.

*Clark, p. 110.

37.   *The Great God Brown*

O'Neill devises one of the most daring, complex persona schemes in dramaturgy for *The Great God Brown*.* In it, he shows through his two protagonists, Dion Anthony and William A. Brown, masked and unmasked manifestations of the continuously evolving self. The multiplicity develops as the self reacts to the interplay of its own instincts and inspiration, the pressures of society and other individuals, and the influence of a mysterious external power. To O'Neill, the latter is the most significant determinant. In explaining it, he states, "I am always conscious of the force behind fate, God, our biological past creating our present . . . and of the one eternal tragedy of man in his glorious, self-destructive struggle to make the force express him instead of being, as an animal is, an infinitesimal incident of its expression." The struggle is manifested within the context of the play in characters' face–mask dichotomy.

From the beginning, as the first recorded idea in 1922 indicates, O'Neill conceived *The Great God Brown* as a "Play of masks—removable—the man who really is and the mask he wears before the world—also abstract idea behind play the spirit of Pan that Christianity corrupts into evil—pagan flesh becomes evil." The creative spirit of this man, a failed architect, "has no outlet—becomes destructive." The other central character, "his friend and rival," is "unimaginative—success." In the outline O'Neill worked on in April 1924 and again that

---

*The copyright date is January 2, 1925. The play premiered at the Greenwich Village Theatre on January 23, 1926, and, after a successful run, moved to the Garrick Theatre on March 1 and to the Klaw Theatre on May 10.

June after completing *Desire Under the Elms*, the former, the dreamer-artist (Wint Keith), and the materialist businessman (William Brown), are depicted as complementary parts of a whole self. "They have always been exact antithesis. They needed, completed each other while at the same time subtly hated each other for the need."

At the outset of the 1924 version, Brown appears to be the central character. O'Neill was preoccupied that spring and summer with thoughts of the acquisitive Cabots and Polos. He seemed to be fashioning *The Great God Brown* into another exposé on American materialism. Brown is described as "the successful provincial American," the personification, like Marco Polo, of the American ideal, a well-rounded realization of success, "the complete attainment of an assured position—a self-made edifice made of the solid bricks of negative value. Abstractly he is the idol in which we glorify our denial of all the spiritual values which make life live." Man is no longer created in the image and likeness of God. Brown's spiritual hump is as pronounced as Marco's; God is made over into their self-assured, materialistic likeness. As Brown's self evolves in the 1925 draft, however, it is, at the end of the play, finally infused with a soul.

On February 2, 1925, O'Neill notes in his Work Diary that the play is "coming out all different from 1st scheme." At some point that month, he made the crucial decision to change his artist's name to Dion Anthony and the focus of the play to his Dionysian–Christian dichotomy. The author refers in his Work Diary to material he was reading that provided impetus for the play's new direction: Nietzsche's *Birth of Tragedy*, "Pan stuff" in Anatole France's *Revolt of Angels*, Goethe's *Faust*. On March 4, he notes: "In connection with work read in Thomas a Kempis' 'Imitation of Christ.' "

In discussing the "hidden theme," the "mystical pattern which manifests itself as an overtone in *The Great God Brown*," O'Neill states, "I had hoped the names

chosen for my people would give a strong hint of this."
Dion Anthony is a combination, he says, of "Dionysus and
St. Anthony—the creative pagan acceptance of life, fighting eternal war with the masochistic, life-denying spirit of
Christianity as represented by St. Anthony—the whole
struggle resulting in this modern day in mutual exhaus-
tion."* Margaret, the woman Dion Anthony marries, is
the "image of the modern direct descendant of the Marguerite of Faust—the eternal girl-woman with a virtuous
simplicity of instinct, properly oblivious to everything but
the means to her end of maintaining the race."* The new,
more precise, description of Brown suggests the ironic
implications of the play's title. He is the "visionless demi-
god of our new materialistic myth—a Success—building
his life of exterior things, inwardly empty and resource-
less, an uncreative creature of superficial preordained
social grooves."*

Dion, in his rebellion against the life-denying spirit
of Christianity, dons the mask of Pan, who, like Dionysus,
is a god of fertility. Beneath the mask, his face is that of an
ascetic. In addition to this inner conflict, Dion, the idealistic artist, is caught up in an outer struggle with Brown,
the materialistic businessman, the rival, complementary
Apollonian self. Brown represents the unimaginative
forces of society that jealously crush the creative spirit.
Frustrated because he himself lacked artistic talent, Billy
Brown, as a child, destroyed the picture his four-year-old
friend had drawn in the sand. He then struck him on the
head with a stick. Dion cried, as Christ wept over Jeru-
salem, because evil had apparently displaced the godlike
goodness in man. He felt betrayed, as though God had
somehow perpetrated, through Brown, this injustice.
Dion states: "Everybody called me cry-baby, so I became
silent for life and designed a mask of the Bad Boy Pan in
which to live and rebel against that other boy's God and
protect myself from His cruelty." The other boy, con-

*Clark, pp. 105–106.

sumed with secret guilt, assumed a moralistic manner,
developing a good boy-man image and becoming, in time,
the irreproachable William Brown.

In the Prologue, the two are shown years after this
incident at their high school commencement dance.
While the setting is actually the pier of the Casino, the
benches are arranged to suggest the effect of a courtroom.
Billy Brown stands before his domineering, ambitious
mother "like a prisoner at the bar, facing the judge." The
father, "a genial, successful, provincial businessman,"
wants the boy to become an architect. Like Marco, he
would be made a partner in the firm, Anthony, Brown
and Son. The mother, yearning for the realization of a
dream of affluence and social prestige, approves. Billy, a
handsome, athletic fellow, readily accepts his parents'
decision. The impassive expression on his face indicates
"a disciplined restraint."

The same scene is reenacted by Dion Anthony and
his parents. The father, whose "grim, defensive face" is
"obstinate to the point of stupid weakness," sits at center
stage in the authoritative seat of judgment. The mother
has a "gentle face that had once been beautiful," but her
manner is "perpetually nervous and distraught." Like
her, Dion is "continuously in restless nervous movement." He has worn a mask ever since the episode with
Brown: "The mask is a fixed forcing of his own face—dark,
spiritual, poetic, passionately supersensitive, helplessly
unprotected in its childlike, religious faith in life—into
the expression of a mocking, reckless, defiant, gayly scoffing and sensual young Pan."

The expressionistic devices, the masks and the asides,
through which Dion mocks his father in this scene, reveal
the son's inner state of mind. Dion is boldly antagonistic
to his querulous, miserly father. Old Anthony agrees to
send his son to college only after his wife informs him that
Brown plans to expand and control the firm by educating
his son to be an architect. The main purpose of these early
scenes of the Prologue is to show the jealousy and bitter-

ness of the fathers: each will sacrifice the future happiness of his son to defeat a hated rival.

The animosity of the fathers serves to exacerbate the insidious personal rivalry between their sons. Unfortunately, both are attracted to the same young woman, Margaret, who appears in the third section of the Prologue, followed by the "humbly worshiping" Billy Brown. She is a pretty, vivacious blond "with big romantic eyes." Her figure is "lithe and strong, her facial expression intelligent but youthfully dreamy." Like Dion's, her face is masked but "with an exact, almost transparent reproduction of her own features, but giving her the abstract quality of a Girl instead of the individual, Margaret." She rejects Billy's love and offer of marriage. In her asides, she reveals her love for Dion and her goal in life: "I'll be Mrs. Dion—Dion's wife and he'll be my Dion—my own Dion —my little boy—my baby." Two things should be noted here: first, Margaret, like Abbie in *Desire Under the Elms*, is willing to assume the role of mother in a relationship; second, she envisions herself as Mrs. *Dion*, thus rejecting the ascetic Anthony side of her lover.

Alone, Dion takes off his mask. His real face is revealed "shrinking, shy and gentler, full of deep sadness." He cries out, wanting to know why he is forced to conceal his true nature: "Why must I live in a cage like a criminal, defying and hating, I who love peace and friendship? Why was I born without a skin, O God, that I must wear armor in order to touch or to be touched?" Discovering that Margaret loves him, Dion becomes "transfigured by joy." She will protect him. Now he can unite the split self, become "one and indivisible." He looks at his mask and says: "You are outgrown! I am beyond you! O God, now I believe."

The young man's hopes are dashed when Margaret shrinks in fright from his spiritual face and asks: "Who are you?" Resignedly, Dion replaces his mask. Immediately, she professes her love for this masked self. He will dissolve now "into the Great God Pan" and "learn to pre-

tend! Cover your nakedness! Learn to lie! Learn to keep
step! Join the Procession! Great Pan is dead!" Through
these words, Dion announces the demise of his uninhibited, emotional nature; he will conform to the role
Margaret demands that he play. When the Pan spirit dies,
a Satanic mask is assumed in Act I. O'Neill writes:

> Dion's mask of Pan which he puts on as a boy is not only a
> defense against the world for the supersensitive painter-
> poet underneath it, but also an integral part of his character
> as the artist. The world is not only blind to the man beneath,
> but it also sneers at and condemns the Pan-mask it sees.
> After that Dion's inner self retrogresses along the line of
> Christian resignation until it partakes of the nature of the
> Saint while at the same time the outer Pan is slowly trans-
> formed by his struggle with reality into Mephistopheles.*

Like Pirandello, whose *Six Characters in Search of
an Author* was written at approximately the same time as
The Great God Brown, O'Neill is concerned with the
problem of identity and believes that reality resides not in
surface appearances or the masks a character wears but in
the concealed suffering face. The mask becomes the protective armor, or, in Dion's case, the skin that shields the
sensitive vulnerable soul. The face is a complete collection of instincts and emotions. At times the face breaks
through its barrier, but normally the mask succeeds in
confining it. Unfortunately, the mask makes the "knowa-
bility" of the other, and sometimes of the self, impossible.
Both playwrights use mirrors and portraits, in addition to
masks. Confused by the different views of the self, Dion
asks: "Which is the real me?"

To complicate the situation further, the mask, in
O'Neill, takes on an evolving life of its own, showing
unknown facets of the individual's personality, as in
Dion's case, in response to the roles and situations forced
on him by others and by society. Margaret refuses to
accept and love the true Dion, his suffering, spiritual

*Clark, p. 106.

nature. His parents, in forcing him to become an architect, deny his creative spirit an outlet. Trapped "in a cage," he is condemned to live behind a mask, to accept a role as his only reality.

The play opens, seven years later, in the Anthonys' sitting room. After his father died, Dion left college, married Margaret, and, like Jim Harris in *All God's Chillun Got Wings*, went abroad to live, hoping he would gain acceptance there as an artist. Discovering that he has but a meager talent, he began to drink, like that other failed artist, John Brown in *Bread and Butter*. As a consequence, his mask "has changed. It is older more defiant and mocking, its sneer more forced and bitter, its Pan quality becoming Mephistophelean. It has already begun to show the ravages of dissipation."

Throughout their years together, Margaret has never come to understand or accept Dion's true self. She continues to treat him as a child, as her fourth son. Unlike Marguerite of the Faust legend, the woman who can save a man by her love, Margaret only increases her husband's suffering by her refusal to accept him as he truly is. As a result, his real face "has aged greatly, grown more strained and tortured but at the same time, in some queer way, more selfless and ascetic, more fixed in its resolute withdrawal from life." He sits, unmasked, reading the New Testament: "Come unto me all you who are heavily laden and I will give you rest." The sorrows of his life contradict the words, and he cries out: "Where are you, Savior?" Doubt assails him, and he throws the book aside with contempt: "Fixation on old Mama Christianity." Dion tells Margaret that "they communicate in code—when neither has the other's key." They speak in asides and at cross purposes, like Michael and Eleanor Cape in *Welded*. Told of Brown's thriving firm, Dion remarks scornfully, "He's bound heaven-bent for success. It's the will of Mammon!" After Margaret leaves to ask Brown to hire Dion, "he pulls the mask from his resigned, pale, suffering face. He prays like a Saint in the desert, exorcizing a demon."

Brown, in the scene in his office, is described as a fine-looking "American businessman." Outwardly, he is rich in material possessions; inwardly, he is empty, shallow, superficial, a demigod without a soul. Still attracted to Margaret, he agrees to employ Dion as a draftsman. At the end of the scene Margaret uses the third, rather than the second, person when she replies in asides to Brown's remarks. The technique will be refined and used later when Nina and Ned conduct their negotiations in *Strange Interlude*.

Dion is befriended by the prostitute Cybel in Scene 3 when she finds him drunk outside her home. Only in her presence does he expose his real face, which is "singularly pure, spiritual and sad." An "incarnation of Cybele, the Earth Mother," she is a "strong, calm, sensual, blond girl of twenty or so, her complexion fresh and healthy." Like other idealized women in O'Neill, Abbie Putnam, Sara Melody, Josie Hogan, Cybel has a voluptuous figure, "full-breasted and wide-hipped." Her movements are "slow and solidly languourous like an animal's, her large eyes dreamy with the reflected stirring of profound instincts."

Cybel alone understands the cause and effect of Dion's suffering: "You were born with ghosts in your eyes and you were brave enough to go looking into your own dark—and you got afraid." She alone comprehends the clear distinction between spirit and body and says that life is "not sacred—only the you inside is. the rest is earth." Knowing that his own death is near, Dion kneels before Cybel and prays "with an ascetic fervor." He repeats the words the dying Christ uttered on the Cross: "Into thy hands, O Lord." When he bids Cybel farewell, she talks to him as to "her little son" and promises "after you're asleep I'll tuck you in." Asked by Brown later why Dion is popular with women—"Is it his looks" or because of his "artistic temperament?"—Cybel, who has become the businessman's mistress, responds: "He's alive."

Dion sits, unmasked in the drafting room in the next scene, reading aloud from the *Imitation of Christ*. His face is "more saintlike and ascetic than ever before." Compared to a priest "offering up prayers for the dying," he holds his desolate mask and says: "Peace, poor tortured one, brave pitiful pride of man, the hour of our deliverance comes. Tomorrow we may be with Him in Paradise!" When Margaret enters, he kneels and begs forgiveness for his "sins" and his "sickness." Terror-stricken by the unmasked stranger, she explains: "You're like a ghost! You're dead!"

In the following scene, which takes place that night in Brown's home, Dion's first speech to a servant reinforces the Faust motif of the play: "Tell him it's the devil come to conclude a bargain." Like Faust, who sold his soul to the devil in the guise of Mephistopheles, Dion will die under mysterious circumstances. Dion attributes his dissolution to Brown and resolves to destroy him in revenge. The Dion-mask has undergone a series of changes—from Bad Boy Pan-Mephistophelean to diabolical Mephistophelean. Now, in its final death throe, it has the "appearance of a real demon, tortured into torturing others."

Brown assumes a "big-brotherly tone" when he addresses Dion in this scene, which is strikingly similar to the last-act confrontation of the two brothers, Jamie and Edmund Tyrone, in the autobiographical *Long Day's Journey into Night*. Like Dion, Jamie, whose face has "a Mephistophelian cast," is drunk and has just left a piano-playing prostitute. O'Neill said of his brother, "booze got Jamie in the end." Like Jamie, Dion disregards the doctor's warning not to drink. Brown says, "It's your funeral" and adds, "Go easy. I don't want your corpse on my hands." To Edmund, Jamie says he "doesn't want to be the only corpse around the house!" O'Neill says that he finished *The Great God Brown* on March 25, 1925, "in tears! Couldn't control myself!" There is only one other recorded instance of a play being written in tears: *Long Day's Journey into Night*.

Dion utters a curse-prophecy: Brown will "devote his life to renovating the house of my Cybel into a home for my Margaret." After stealing Dion's mask, Brown will, by using the other's identity, make a prostitute out of Margaret. The dying Dion says that it is not Margaret nor Cybel whom Brown truly loves: "He loves me because I have always possessed the power he needed for love, because I am love!" When Brown angrily grabs him by the throat, Dion gasps: "Now he looks into the mirror! Now he sees his face!" Dion implies that his demonic mask-countenance is but a reflection of the other's actual face; the speech is significant because it reveals Brown as being evil *before* assuming Dion's mask. In the play's complex scheme, Dion and Brown, who are frequently called brothers, represent man's dual, good/evil natures. The face of each man is the true expression of these natures. Throughout the play, in the scenes depicting various periods of his life, the face of Dion has been ascetic. The evil of others and their rejection of his goodness led to the creation of the mask and its subsequent deterioration. On the other hand, Brown showed himself to be mean spirited and jealous as a child. These qualities grew with the boy-man. The worship of God is replaced by the worship of self as demigod and of material possessions.

Brown becomes in the play the Mephistophelean tempter of the Faust-Dion, using money to lure him into the firm. Brown covets Dion's wife and wants to steal Cybel's love, as Dion states, "as he steals my ideas—complacently—righteously. Oh, the good Brown!" That all men may behold Brown's flawed self, Dion wills his satanic mask to him and kneels before him. O'Neill states, "It is as Mephistopheles he falls stricken at Brown's feet after having condemned Brown to destruction by willing him his mask, but, this mask falling off as he dies, it is the Saint who kisses Brown's feet in abject contrition and pleads as a little boy to a big brother to tell him a prayer." Brown intones one line of a prayer. Dion repeats the first

two words, "Our Father," and then dies. Brown views
Dion's real face with contempt. He knows instinctively
that the mask he holds and covets is evil: "Say what you
like, it's strong if it is bad!" Brown then presents himself
to Margaret as Dion, wearing his mask and clothes and
imitating his voice. He kisses her, not as a son, as Dion
usually did, but as a lover. They embrace passionately,
and Brown says, "Let's go home!" This scene, with its
implied adulterous relationship, shocked theatergoers in
1926.

Act III shows both the drafting room and Brown's
private office about a month later. Each half of the play
concentrates on one side of dual-natured man and shows
the struggle of the two aspects to attain redemption and
unity. In the first two acts, the mask is used by a character
to conceal his true nature, to protect himself from the
cruelty of others, and to demonstrate how external forces,
particularly rejection and living a double life, distort the
psyche. In the last two acts, the mask serves to show the
transfer of personality from one man, Dion, to another,
Brown. The latter, however, cannot take over those inner
qualities of Dion's soul that he seeks: the power to love
and to create, which he mistakenly believed the mask
possesses. He struggles with three identitites. He wears
Dion's mask with Margaret and her chidren. Unmasked,
his real face becomes "ravaged and haggard," distorted by
the demon of Dion's mask. He cannot resume life as
William Brown without wearing a mask, which is an
"exact likeness of his face as it was in the last scene—the
self-assured success."

Brown leaves Margaret's home each morning as
Dion, who is supposedly still employed at the firm and
working on an important design for the state capitol. He
wears the mask of Brown in the office and tells his confused employees that Dion has been fired. Before Margaret, he removes the mask and begs her to love the man
revealed. Rejected, Brown now experiences the pain

Dion felt when he was not loved for his real self. Alone, the tortured man talks to himself: "You're dead, William Brown, dead beyond hope of resurrection! It's the Dion you buried in your garden who killed you, not you."

In Brown's library that night in the next scene, the businessman stares at the two masks, determined to kill off his former mask-identity immediately. He says to the Dion mask, "Then you—the I in you—I will live with Margaret happily ever after." For the first time in the play Brown consciously utters a prayer. He clutches the mask of Dion and immediately feels his strength, the "strength of love in this world" flow into him. Symbolically, Dion's clothes begin to fit him better than his own. Wearing Dion's mask, he is wounded anew slightly later in Scene 3 when Margaret complains bitterly about Brown's advances to her earlier in the office. Brown's corpselike face had frightened her. She is told to forget the man: "Mr. Brown is now safely in hell."

Act IV commences a month later in the office. Brown is seen wearing Dion's mask and displaying his sacrificial attitude. Inspired by Dion's Mephistophelean cynicism, he finishes the design for the capitol, having surreptitiously incorporated into it the ironic spirit of Pan. As himself, Brown is repulsed by the design: "Why must the demon in me pander to cheapness?" Unmasked, Brown's real face is "now sick, ghastly, tortured, hollow-cheeked and feverish." Feeling that Dion's spirit has infused him, Brown remarks, "We're getting to be twins." As Brown, he displays the design to an approving committee, but then he destroys it in disgust. As Dion, he pastes the pieces together, then informs his employees that Brown is dead. The committee members enter the adjoining room and return and file out of the office, carrying the mask of Brown as if they were actually bearing his body. The treatment of the mask as a person provides an ironic lesson on how people judge others merely by external circumstances, the masks they wear. The police are called in to track down the murderer of Brown.

Like the Emperor Brutus Jones, the now-humble Great God Brown is shown at the end of the play stripped naked except for a loincloth. His whole body writhes in agony as he kneels beside a table on which is placed Dion's mask. Brown has been purified through suffering. Now the ascetic, he begs mercy of the Savior of Man. Seemingly in answer to his prayer, Cybel enters, dressed in a mourning robe of black. In the presence of Brown's haunted face, she unmasks. Glancing from Brown's face to Dion's mask, she says, "You are Dion Brown." She urges him to flee before the police arrive. As in the scene in *The Hairy Ape* when Yank opened the door of the gorilla's cage in an apparent embrace of death, Brown puts on Dion's mask and, thus strengthened, opens the window to show himself to the police. They fire a volley of shots, and Brown falls, mortally wounded. Cybel removes his mask and lifts him onto the couch.

A captain enters, followed by Margaret, who prostrates herself weeping before the mask of Dion. Asked by the policeman the name of Anthony's wounded accomplice, Cybel replies, "Billy." Forced to lead a double life like Dion, Brown no longer is himself to anyone. O'Neill remarks that "in the end out of this anguish his soul is born, a tortured Christian soul such as the dying Dion's, begging for belief, and at last finding it on the lips of Cybel." She is the great universal mother, reciting for him the "Our Father." In an ecstatic, exultant tone, Brown exclaims, "I have found him" and dies. The pagan and Christian cycles overlap in Cybel's last speech, which predicts eternal rebirth after death: "Always spring comes again bearing life . . . bearing the intolerable chalice of life again!" Dion, buried in Brown's garden in the Dionysian rites and regenerated, becomes the "fertile earth."

In the end Brown too has worked out his salvation; having been crucified by uncaring men, he has earned the chalice of life, resurrection. Appropriately, Cybel officiates at the deaths of both men, healing the now-unified complementary halves and fusing them into Dion Brown.

Dion had remarked earlier that "Man is born broken. He
lives by mending. The grace of God is glue!" Asked at the
end of the play the name of the dead victim, Cybel
replies, "Man," symbol of Everyman. The word is significant in view of O'Neill's statement that the tragedy of
man is his self-destructive struggle to make the "behind-
life force" express him instead of being, as an animal is, an
infinitesimal incident of its expression. Both Dion and
Brown die trying to retain their dignity as "Man." Both
are portrayed at their deaths as suffering, redemptive
Christ figures.

At the end of Act IV, one cycle—birth, death, rebirth—is complete. In the Epilogue a second evolves for
Margaret and her three sons. The situation here is the
same as in the Prologue. The eldest son is eighteen; he,
like his brothers, is attracted to a young woman. Dressed
"in the height of current Prep-school togs," they have all
the characteristics of Brown and none of Dion. It is highly
improbable that they will experience their father's or
Brown's dilemma, having no trace of the artist-ascetic in
them. O'Neill seems to suggest that each generation in
this country is more materialistic and less spiritual than its
predecessor.

Margaret utters the last words of the play, a dirge for
the departed Dion. She is an early view of Mary Tyrone,
having also been uprooted from her home and family
immediately after marriage to accompany her husband on
his travels while he pursues his artistic career. Both wom-
en bear three sons. Perhaps the most striking similarity
between them is their inability to face reality. Mary
Tyrone refuses to accept the fact that her son is suffering
and may die; Margaret cannot bear to look upon Dion
unmasked and see his real, agonized face. The rejection
by the mother figure leads ultimately to despair and the
psychological or actual death of the men. The situation of
the two women in the final scenes of the two plays is
identical. Mary Tyrone drifts in a drug-induced fog, fail-

ing to recognize her husband and sons. Margaret kneels before the mask of Dion, yet ironically she never truly knew either of the two men she had lived with. In the Epilogue Margaret bids her three sons goodbye "with strange finality" and surrenders herself to the memories of the past, to a time before her marriage. Mary too regresses into the past, ignoring the three men with her, to the days preceding her marriage.

O'Neill assigns definite traits of his father and mother to the two sets of parents in the Prologue, for they strongly resemble the autobiographical Mary and James Tyrone. The mothers represent the two natures of Mary: the bitter, coarse cynic and the sensitive, suffering woman. Brown's mother is aggressive, snobbish, overdressed, clearly superior to her "always smiling" husband, who has an inferiority complex. Dion's mother is vulnerable and obviously dominated by her insensitive husband. The latter's tirade against his wastrel son, threatening to turn him out into the gutter, will be repeated almost word-for-word later by James Tyrone to Jamie: "Colleges turn out lazy loafers to sponge on their poor old fathers! Let him slave like I had to! That'll teach him the value of a dollar! Let him make a man out of himself like I made myself."

The now available early notes for *A Moon for the Misbegotten* reveal the marked similarity between its acknowledged Jamie O'Neill-like hero and Dion Anthony, The former, as Jim Tyrone, describes his opposing dreams and reveals a dual nature identical to the Mephistophelean-ascetic split in Dion Anthony. Jim's first dream is "a Lucifer dream, the cynic who believes in nothing"; the other "dates back to school—catechism— the man who loves God, who gives up self and the world to worship of God and devotes self to good works, service of others, celibacy." Josie Hogan, another Earth Mother like Cybel, tells Jim; "Well I've been trying to seduce a Saint. Or to tempt a Lucifer."

The earliest label O'Neill affixes to *The Great God Brown* is "Play of masks." While the masks are used consciously to achieve artistic and thematic goals, they also become a metaphorical device to conceal the author's personal, but perhaps unconscious, purposes. In this play he develops not only the 1922 mask idea but also a concept recorded earlier in the 1918–1920 notebook: "Long Play—Jim & self—showing influence of elder on younger brother." Although the last act of *Long Day's Journey into Night* demonstrates Jamie's destructive influence, the focus of the play is not, primarily, on the two brothers but on the parents. Dion and Brown use the word "brother" a number of times to refer to each other. Once the Dion–Jamie O'Neill connection is understood, so too is the autobiographical significance of *The Great God Brown*.

In the Foreword for the play O'Neill sounds his revolt against the realistic theater, stating that it cannot probe "the unknown within and behind ourselves." In the play itself he exposes the shattered fragments of the psyche, clothing them in masks. He shows that man possesses good and evil natures that manifest themselves in response to the interaction of outer and inner forces. The author's words, "Man is born broken," suggest that original sin is the cause of the fragmentation. The double odyssey of the two central characters illustrates the cycle of sin, forgiveness, penance, and ultimate redemption; their final merger as Dion Brown/Man demonstrates the effectiveness of the purgatorial paths they follow and of the glue, "the grace of God," that is used to mend man.

38. *Lazarus Laughed*

*Lazarus Laughed*** is an extravagant religious pageant. Inspired by the short Biblical story, O'Neill, in 1924, recorded an idea for "Play of Lazarus—the man who had been dead for three days and returned to life, knowing the secret." The key phrase, "knowing the secret," becomes the *raison d'etre* of *Lazarus Laughed.* What Lazarus discovers and proclaims to the world, upon his return, is that "There is no death"; life exists beyond the grave.

In his 1926 scenario O'Neill describes the Biblical encounter between Jesus and Lazarus (John 11:1–44) and labels the play's first scene the "Feast of Thanksgiving for his return from the dead." According to John, the deceased had actually been in the tomb for four days when Jesus arrived in Bethany, having been summoned the previous week by Martha and Mary, the two sisters of Lazarus, to restore the sick man to health. In an attempt to reconcile Martha to the death, Jesus tells her, "I am the resurrection and the life. If anyone believes in me, even though he dies he will live." Brought to the tomb of Lazarus, Jesus weeps, saddened to have to recall him from the other world. He cries out: "Lazarus, here! Come out!" and the dead man emerges from the cave. Through this event, Jesus prophesies, "the Son of God will be glorified." Not only will the miracle glorify him, he suggests, but so, too, will the plot it foments. The raising of Lazarus prompts the chief priests and Pharisees to call a meeting. "From that day they were determined to kill him."

The coming forth of Lazarus from death to life fore-

---

*The play was copyrighted June 23, 1926, and staged on April 9, 1928, at the Pasadena Community Playhouse in California.

shadows not only Christ's own resurrection but man's.
O'Neill's work in the mid-1920s reveals an obsession with
this concept. *Lazarus Laughed* seems, in fact, to take up
where *The Great God Brown* concludes. In the latter,
when Dion dies and is reborn as Brown, Margaret says of
the composite figure, "It's like a miracle." There is no
reason why she cannot behold the dead Dion, Brown
asserts: "Well, why not? It's the age of miracles. The
streets are full of Lazaruses." A miracle also occurs in the
1925 *Marco Millions* when, in the Prologue, the dead
Kukachin comes to life in her coffin and says that she now
lives. "And living, have forgotten." Her face, like that of
Lazarus, is lit by "an unearthly glow, like a halo."

Cybel, after Dion Brown dies, exults in the mysterious cycle of birth, death, and rebirth to eternal life. So too
is the cycle proclaimed in the play that follows: "then sad
old Lazarus who died of self-pity" has been reborn. "The
fields of infinite space are sown—and grass for sheep
springs up in the hills of earth! But there is no death, nor
fear, nor loneliness! There is only God's Eternal Laughter!" Always, in O'Neill, rebirth or resurrection is preceded by suffering. Billy–William Brown's acts of injustice and cruelty serve as the catalyst for Dion's gradual
purification and regeneration. In *Lazarus Laughed* the
despot Tiberius and his demonic heir, Caligula, who represent the forces of evil, persecute and eventually crucify
Lazarus. In the earlier play Dion is lured by Brown into
compromising his artistic integrity. The Roman tyrants
tempt Lazarus, but to no avail; even life itself is a dispen-
sable possession.

Immediately after the entry for the "Play of Lazarus"
in the 1921–1931 notebook, O'Neill records an idea for
"Play of Caligula—not mad but a truth-seer and driven
mad by that—the great satirist who made his horse a
consul and wished the world had but one neck—who
transferred his love from mother, to wife, to males, to a
horse." This concept is followed by a related one: "Lives

of Caesars—series of scenes each about the Emperor showing the gradual degeneration, as the Caesars became gods, of power." The author later links the three ideas with a brace and writes the words: "combine" and "Lazarus Laughed 1926–27."

O'Neill ultimately rejected the modern tendency to portray Caligula as a madman and treats him sympathet- ically, as one caught in a dilemma, desiring both the awesome power of the Caesars and the spiritual promises of Lazarus. The author scales down the third idea, "Lives of Caesars," and elects to portray the one Emperor who was actually ruling in 33 A.D., Tiberius, who professes a longing, but to a lesser degree than Caligula, to follow Lazarus. Neither despot can bring himself to relinquish power or to worship any god but the self, the mighty Caesar. In the play that preceded *Lazarus Laughed*, the middle-aged Brown, the corrupt selfish "demi-god," re- sembles "a Roman consul on an old coin."

O'Neill wrote the scenario for "The Laughter of Lazarus," as the play was originally entitled, in Septem- ber 1925. The extant first draft shows that he completed the dialogue for five of the eight scenes at this time. Incorporated into this early version are music, dancing, and a moderate amount of laughter; missing are the com- plex and innovative experimental devices found in the final text, the masks and choruses. In the later version all the characters but Lazarus wear masks; in the early one everyone is unmasked except Lazarus, who wears a black kerchief over his eyes, as the light hurts them. Originally, he is described as a "dark, olive-complected man of forty- five." His face is "gaunt, furrowed deep with lines of suffering and death." He is "illumined by a light from within—a soft phosphorescent radiance which illumines his face as if tiny invisible flames were caressing his flesh and cleansing it of sorrow and death."

In early March 1926 O'Neill began "reading for Laz- arus" and making new notes: quotations and paraphrased passages from Aristotle and Nietzsche; selections from historical works on Tiberius and on Roman history, and books on mythology, particularly Dionysus. He completed a second scenario but was dissatisfied with it. The success at that time of the production of *The Great God Brown*, in which the characters wore masks, seems to have inspired O'Neill with a new plan for *Lazarus*. He notes in his Work Diary on March 10: "Lazarus—mask-chorus conception shapes up wonderfully."

The play now assumes the proportions of a gigantic pageant that has universal dimensions. O'Neill worked out a complex age-typology scheme to show the manifold natures or periods of man. A group of forty-nine people is divided into smaller masked groups of seven to represent the periods of life: Boyhood, Youth, Young Manhood, Manhood, Middle Age, Maturity, and Old Age. Within each of these groups the general types of character are represented by seven different personality masks: the Simple Ignorant, the Happy Eager, the Self-Tortured Introspective, the Proud Self-Reliant, the Servile Hypocritical, the Revengeful Cruel, and the Sorrowful Resigned. In addition, one member of each of these types is included in a special Chorus of Seven Old Men, who wear double life-size masks.

Like *Marco Millions*, Lazarus Laughed provides a large-scale panoramic view of different cultures in a particular historical period. Like Marco, Lazarus undertakes a journey—from Bethany, Athens, and Rome to Capri—thus enabling O'Neill to depict, on a broad scale, series of groups masked to indicate their religious, ethnic, and cultural identities. The crowd masks in the first two scenes are "Semitic in racial character—in Scene Three Eastern and Greek—in the remainder of the scenes Roman."

Four central characters, Miriam, Tiberius, Caligula, and Pompeia, wear half-masks. Miriam's mask and face are, in general, in harmony with each other. The incongruous mask-mouth contrast of the Romans reflect their dual natures and desires. The mask on the upper part of the face represents what each of them appears to be or wants to be; the mouth reveals what he really is or could be if his true nature were allowed to assert itself. Only Lazarus is unmasked. He alone is a fully integrated, whole person. The unmasked Lazarus, surrounded by masked characters, becomes the focal point of the play. O'Neill states that the dramatic effect of the contrast "ought to be an arrowhead of concentration directed at the one man who is real and live in the midst of false, dead people." Unlike Dion Anthony in *The Great God Brown*, Lazarus is not in conflict; he has not only worked out his salvation but also tasted briefly the promised life beyond the grave. The veil between this world and the next is purportedly thinner for this earth's more sensitive creatures. However, in Lazarus' case, the veil is actually penetrated. He becomes, in effect, an exile on earth, longing to possess eternal ecstasy once more but resigned to sharing the vision with his fellow man.*

Lazarus Laughed, which O'Neill labeled a "Play for the Imaginative Theatre," was designed to provide a full theatrical experience. The work strays far from the realistic theater into the realm of theatricalism. In addition to the group masks, used to suggest "the presence and characteristics of mobs," and the choruses of seven, intended to emphasize and point up the action, O'Neill experimented with "other new stunts": lighting and sets. After completing the play on May 11, 1926, O'Neill drew settings for the eight scenes, designing them to conform to the massive tableau-like scheme he envisioned.

The action of the play begins in Lazarus' home in Bethany a short time after the miracle. As in *Desire Under the Elms*, an interior-exterior setting is used to reflect

---

*This idea intrigued O'Neill. In 1924 he dramatized Coleridge's "The Ancient Mariner," whose central figure shares his recent supernatural experiences with the Wedding Guest.

inner and outer action. Outside the house, on either side, is a crowd, which echoes the chant of the chorus. Also shown is the main room of the home, where Lazarus sits at a long banquet table in the midst of his family: wife, parents, and sisters, seven male guests, and, in a corner, the Chorus of Old Men. Lazarus, a tall and powerful man, is about fifty. "His face recalls that of a statue of a divinity of Ancient Greece in its general structure and particularly in its quality of detached serenity." It is calm but "furrowed deep with the marks of former suffering." He stares "straight before him as if his vision were still fixed beyond life." Miriam, his wife, is a "slender, delicate woman of thirty-five, dressed in deep black." The fixed expression of the mask on the upper part of her face is "that of a statue of Woman, of her eternal acceptance of the compulsion of motherhood." The eyes of the mask are almost closed. They dream "of the child forever in memory at her breast."

The dialogue of the Seven Guests provides the exposition. Before his death, Lazarus had been one of life's losers. Job-like, he experienced a series of misfortunes: his children died, he lost his health and the wealth inherited from his father, his farm suffered because of mismanagement. The guests describe the miracle: Lazarus' awakening, his laughter, and his "yes" to life, a response to Jesus' offer. Miriam now echoes Christ's words, "Come forth," and Lazarus rises and speaks for the first time since the miracle, repeating his affirmation: "Yes." The people cry out, desiring to know what lies beyond this world. Lazarus assures them that there is no death, "only life." "There is Eternal Life in No," he explains, "and there is the same Eternal Life in Yes! Death is the fear between!" Reborn to the love of life, he cried "Yes!" and "laughed in the laughter of God." Lazarus begins to laugh. The chorus breaks into a paean in praise of laughter and then laughs "in a rhythmic cadence." Gradually all those onstage, except Miriam, join in the laughter.

The second scene shows the exterior of Lazarus' home, now known as the House of Laughter, several months later. The occupants of the house, the close followers of Lazarus, are engrossed in a party. Outside, two groups of Jews, forty-nine in each, voice their rage at Lazarus and at each other. On the left are the Nazarenes, the adherents of Jesus; among them are Martha and Mary. On the right are the hostile Orthodox believers, a group that includes Lazarus' parents. Both groups voice a common hatred of Lazarus. The father curses his daughters for following Jesus, an imposter, who has just been arrested by the high priests. Lazarus is accused of seducing and corrupting the youth of the area, who have abandoned their families and fields to follow the risen man. Offered high wages to return to work, they ask, "What is money? Can the heart eat gold?" When Lazarus appears with Miriam on the roof among his followers, the third group of forty-nine, the unified factions below curse him and call "for a sacrificial victim." A miraculous change has occurred: Lazarus seems to be ten years younger; Miriam, to be five years older. This backward-forward movement will continue throughout the play. Lazarus faults the angry mob with deliberately forgetting "the God in you." Remembrance would impose the duty of living as a son of God.

A messenger enters and informs the crowd that Jesus has just been crucified. When the two groups draw out concealed knives and swords and fall upon each other, Roman soldiers enter and try to separate them. The newcomers are masked according to the period-personality formula, but "each face is Roman—heavy, domineering, self-complacent, the face of a confident dominant race." Lazarus exclaims "Hold," and all three groups cease the struggle.

Told that the Romans killed his parents, his sisters, and Jesus, Lazarus displays no emotion. He begins to laugh. Everyone, including the Romans, imitates him.

The Chorus longs to retain a belief in life and laughter. As Lazarus is being taken away as the prisoner of Tiberius, his followers beg him not to forsake them lest they forget. The scene ends with their hopeless wail.

The second act commences some months later in a square in Athens. The crowd of Greeks awaits the arrival of Lazarus, who is rumored to be the reincarnation of Dionysus. They call upon Lazarus to free them from Rome. Ordered to accompany Lazarus to Rome is Tiberius' twenty-one-year-old nephew, Caligula. He is a malformed, craven creature with "long arms and short skinny legs like an ape's." The discrepancy between the mask and the face is most pronounced in him. His half-mask of crimson "covers the upper part of his face to below the nose. This mask accentuates his bulging, prematurely wrinkled forehead, his hollow temples and his bulbous, sensual nose." His glazed greenish-blue eyes "glare out with a shifty feverish suspicion at everyone. Below his mask his own skin is of an anemic transparent pallor. Above it, his hair is the curly blond hair of a child of six or seven." His mouth is that of a "spoiled, petulant and self-obsessed" child.

A new Chorus of followers, each member representing a different racial group, and a larger crowd of forty-nine people, precede Lazarus. He now looks less than thirty-five and resembles the mellowed Dionysus, the figure "closest to the soil of the Grecian gods" rather than the coarse, drunken, effeminate god. Instinctively he recognizes Caligula's reliance on the people's fear of death to keep them subjected. "Death is dead," Caligula is told. "Men call life death and fear it." Implicit in Lazarus' words is the concept that death was once a gentle sleep; but man, because of his own waywardness and subsequent guilt, attaches fear and finality to it. Caligula's warped mask projects an image that terrifies not only his slave-subjects but also the despot himself. Lazarus informs him that "Life is for each man a solitary cell whose walls are mirrors." As a man withdrawn into the isolation of the self, Caligula is doomed to nothingness by death. But as a "speck of dust danced in the wind," an integral, minute part of all created nature, he is "eternal change and everlasting growth." Lazarus leads his followers to the fields for a Dionysian celebration of nature, which is symbolically repudiated by Caligula, who savagely lops off flowers from their stems.

The following scene occurs months later inside the walls of Rome. Tiberius, after fleeing in fear himself to Capri, has called the Roman Senate into session to discuss the threat posed by Lazarus and his thousands of followers encamped outside the city walls. The Senators "are all masked in the Roman mask," once refined but now "degenerated, corrupted by tyranny and debauchery to an exhausted cynicism." Before them stands Lazarus, resembling a "detached contemplative God." He has grown more youthful. "His eyes shine with an unearthly glory." When he and his supporters begin to laugh, the senators find themselves helplessly joining in. Only two persons refrain: Miriam, who fears for the safety of those assembled, and Caligula, now half-drunk, who gives the legion the signal to kill Lazarus' followers. He dances "a hopping grotesque sword dance," chanting "Kill! Kill laughter!" The followers do not wait for the soldiers' attack but joyously stab themselves. Miriam chastizes her husband for laughing while those who believed in him die. He reminds her of the promise of immortality, that men "as squirming specks" once crept "from the tides of the sea," and now they must return to it. Unworthy and unimportant, "men pass," but "the sea remains! Man remains!"

In the third act, a few days later, Lazarus is shown outside Tiberius' palace at Capri. The sound of crass music, tainted with the "joyless abandon which is vice," plays in the background. Lazarus, "looking no more than twenty-five," is "haloed in his own mystic light." Miriam, who has grown progressively older in each scene, appears "bowed and feeble." One explanation for her inability throughout the play to laugh is that she fears that Lazarus will die again. She herself suggests another reason: that Lazarus, now a spiritual rather than a physical being, has lost his human emotions: "The miracle could not revive all his old husband's life in my wife's heart." Yet it is not the man and husband Miriam fears losing but "my son, my little boy!" She perceives the Roman world as being "full of evil and shudders at the blatant manifestation of it: a full-grown male lion crucified upon a cross placed in the center of an arch." Caligula reads the inscription above the lion's head: "From the East, land of false gods and superstition, this lion was brought to Rome to amuse Caesar." Lazarus realizes that the innocent creature is being tortured because of him, and he addresses it compassionately: "Forgive me your suffering!" The "crimson-purple lights" of the palace go out as Lazarus and Miriam enter. Images of blood and poison are associated in the play with the brutal Tiberius. The laughing guards form a protective flank around the couple.

Inside the banquet hall in Scene 2, a crowd of forty-two, wearing masks of the most depraved personality types, loll about the tables on couches. The effect is "of sex corrupted and warped, of invented lusts and artificial vices." Presiding over this scene of dissipation is Pompeia, Caesar's favorite mistress. Her duality resembles that of Cybel, the prostitute–Earth Mother, in *The Great God Brown*. Her half-mask is olive-colored "with the red of blood smoldering through, with great, dark, cruel eyes —a dissipated mask of intense evil beauty, of lust and perverted passion." Her mouth is gentle, girlish beneath the mask, "set in an expression of agonized self-loathing and weariness of spirit."

Standing on the high dais in the center of the room is the corpulent but muscular Tiberius Caesar, age seventy-six. His half-mask is a "pallid purple blotched with darker color, as if the imperial blood in his veins had been

sickened by age and debauchery. The eyes are protuber-
ant, leering, cynical slits, the long nose, once finely modeled, now gross." His own mouth "looks as incongruous as
Caligula's." His stern lips are those of "an able soldier-
statesman of rigid probity. His chin is forceful and severe.
The complexion of his own skin is that of a healthy old
campaigner." When Pompeia informs Caligula of her love
for Lazarus, he tells her that Lazarus loves only his wife.
The courtesan resolves to poison Miriam. In the published text, Caligula petulantly encourages her. In the
first scenario he tries to protect Miriam, urging her not to
eat the poisoned fruit: "Do not, Jewess! Live. Marry me. I
shall need your care when I become a God." In this early
version Miriam is depicted as an attractive woman; she
does not grow older as Lazarus grows younger—a phenomenon of the later drafts, establishing the mother-son
relationship.

Lazarus kisses Miriam, telling her to "call back" from
beyond when she knows. Instinctively, he reaches out as
though to stop Miriam from eating the peach. Immediately she feels the effects of the poison, and, in a lengthy
monologue, she reminisces about the past, when Lazarus
would sit "in the evening like a black figure of Job against
the sky." When Miriam dies, Lazarus finds it impossible
at first to laugh. In the silence her body seems to rise in a
tortured last effort; she laughs and bids Lazarus farewell.
And he, his faith restored, laughs with "God's Eternal
Laughter."

The fourth act begins a short time later. Lazarus,
looking "like a young son," sits beside the still form of
Miriam. One by one, the three Romans confess their past
faults and future dreams to Lazarus. Tiberius speaks longingly of death as a means of purging "the ghosts of dreams
one has poisoned to death" by one's lusts. He wants
"youth again," he says, "because I loathe lust and long for
purity!" The Emperor blames all the unhappiness of his
life on Livia, his mother, whose ambitions prompted her

to marry that other Caesar, Augustus, and to murder his lawful heirs. At her instigation, Tiberius had divorced his beloved wife Agrippina and married Julia, Caesar's whorish daughter. Although he hated his mother and was instrumental in her death, Tiberius secretly longs to return to that time, prior to the discovery of his mother's treachery, when he loved her.

After Tiberius leaves the room Caligula expresses the revulsion he feels for "cruelty and lust and human flesh and all the imbecilities of pleasure." In one of the most important speeches of the play, Lazarus says that Caligula should not be so "proud of being evil." He should believe in the other side of his nature, "the healthy god called Man in you!" It is here that O'Neill expresses a belief in the Jungian shadow side of the self: "Laugh, Caligula, the funny clown who beats the backside of his shadow with a bladder and thinks thereby he is Evil, the Enemy of God!" In Lazarus' next words, O'Neill expresses his deep belief in personal immortality. Unworthy men pass "like rain into the sea," but Man remains and rises "from the past of the race of men that was his tomb of death! For Man death is not! Man, Son of God's Laughter, *is*!" When Caligula is sent out to observe nature, Lazarus finds himself alone with Pompeia, who kisses him passionately and demands to be loved as "a woman—not Woman." Sensing his rejection of the personal love she offers, Pompeia lashes out at him in rage and runs out to demand the death of Tiberius.

The last scene is set in the arena of an amphitheatre, just before dawn on the same night. Tiberius sits on his throne on the left and stares off to the right of the arena, where Lazarus, having been tortured and bound to a high stake, is being burned alive. The crowd jeers him, mocking his laughter. Lazarus' voice now has "the fresh, clear quality of boyhood"; he utters a triumphant assertion of life with his "Yes!" Pompeia, guilt stricken, makes her way across the arena and throws herself into the flames.

Asked what is beyond, the dying man murmurs: "Life! Eternity!" Lazarus has found the elusive secret of youth that Juan Ponce de Leon sought in *The Fountain*. Lazarus' physical regression to youth serves to illustrate the precept, "Unless you become as little children you cannot enter the kingdom of heaven."

Caligula rushes into the arena, determined to save Lazarus. He becomes upset when Tiberius professes his faith in Lazarus and laughter, in brotherhood and Man. In a jealous rage he attacks Lazarus: "You have forgotten me—my love—you make him love you." He strangles Tiberius and drives a spear into Lazarus, whose dying words mock the new emperor: "Hail, Caligula Caesar! Men forget!" Caligula kneels and begs forgiveness: "Save me from death!" The dying Lazarus assures him, "There is no death!" Overcome by remorse, Caligula in the play's last line cries "Forgive me, Lazarus! Men forget!"

The concept that "men forget" becomes the theme of "The Last Conquest," a play O'Neill started in 1940 but did not complete. In it, he depicts a Hitler-like World Dictator and a Minister of Spiritual Affairs. They torture not a mere mortal, like Lazarus, but Christ Himself in a reenactment of the Crucifixion. Both plays become, ultimately, contests of good versus evil in which the former triumphs. Strangely, although fifteen years separate the two dramas, O'Neill uses the exact words to describe the two sets of despots: the World Savior and the Minister-Magician resemble the malformed Caligula and the battle-weary Tiberius.

Perhaps O'Neill's preoccupation with "The Last Conquest" led him to consider a revival of *Lazarus Laughed* in 1943. In a letter of December 31 to Langner, he comments on the play's timeliness:

> Now give heed to this and reread it carefully in the light of what that play has to say today. "Die exultantly that life may live" etc. "There is no death." (spiritually) etc. Also think of the light thrown on different facets of the psychology of

dictators in Tiberius and Caligula. Hitler doing his little dance of triumph after the fall of France is very like my Caligula.

The emphasis in *Lazarus Laughed* is on personal immortality, the choices offered Man between good and evil, the attempt he must make to reconcile the broken split self. Herein lies the problem. Because it is preponderately philosophical and didactic, the play fails. Clark objects to the dramatist's playing the role of thinker and prophet and putting his talent "at the disposal of the propagandist." He sees no reason why O'Neill "should not try to portray characters in the throes of mental and spiritual torture, but the moment he himself tries to solve the riddle of the universe he is lost."*

The author acknowledged that *Lazarus Laughed* was a deeply flawed play, but he believed the cause to be not the content but the form: the huge cast, the complex scheme of masks and choruses, the pervasive laughter, which no leading actor could sustain and retain his character's credibility as a rational human being. When a revival was under consideration, O'Neill told Langner that "As far as the unrealistic paraphernalia of the masked mobs, chorus, etc., is concerned, forget that. We'll throw all that out. Use only a few people, the rest all offstage sound— unseen choir effect." To project the laughter, the work would become a "play with music": "it could be done by the actor starting to laugh and then have his laugh carried on and up by exultant music so that you get the feeling the music is his laugh." As for the sets, he suggests: "everything simplified to a few symbolic details—Roman Empire dominant—one enormous column—a massive wall —a distant aqueduct—temple—a throne—positions changed for each scene—and that's all."

Lazarus Laughed was never accorded a New York

*Clark, pp. 118–119.

premiere. After the success of *Strange Interlude* in 1928,
O'Neill wrote to Theresa Helburn of the Theatre Guild in
April, stating:

> I feel the same faith in "Lazarus Laughed," if you can get
> someone for the lead who can do it. You'd be amazed to see
> the letters I got from all over on that play. It seems to give
> people new faith and religion and I firmly believe, if it is
> ever done the way the script reads, it will send people out of
> the theatre with a feeling of exaltation about life that will
> send them to that theatre in droves that will make the
> success of "S.I." look paltry. I am certain that "Lazarus" fills
> a long felt spiritual want that everyone today is suffering
> from—want of faith in life.

O'Neill continued to believe in laughter as an affirmation of life, a symbol of hope, and the link that joins one
person to another and to God. Of all the possible statements in his plays that could be used to express a deeply
cherished concept, O'Neill selected one of Lazarus' lines
to Miriam to be inscribed in the wedding rings he and
Carlotta Monterey exchanged: "I am your laughter—and
you are mine!" The line concludes Lazarus' speech at the
end of Act II wherein he proclaims that "Laughing, we
give our lives for Life's sake!" While in other plays it is
used as a weapon to wound and ridicule, or as a unifying
device to evoke the spirit of camaraderie, laughter here
becomes the instrument of man's wholeness and salvation.

39.   Strange Interlude

Strange Interlude* was O'Neill's greatest achievement in
the 1920s. While he seemed to be breaking new ground
in both form and content in it, the dramatist was, to some
extent, merely recapping experiments and concepts used
previously. The play's success stems from the fact that he
used more of them and presented them in a more sensa-
tional, dramatic framework.

The first idea for *Strange Interlude*, recorded in 1923
and titled then "Godfather," seems innocuous:

> Play of the woman whose husband (married just before he
> left—affair) is killed in war—aviator—falls in final practice
> —in flames. Shock of news. She becomes ultra-neurotic,
> hysterical, desperate, goes in for many love affairs—finally
> at 20, disgusted with herself and broken down, longing for
> normality and health and, most of all, motherhood as a final
> peace, she marries a naive, young man just out of college.

This segment of the lengthy idea represents the first of the
many stages through which the heroine, Nina Leeds,
evolved.

Lazarus Laughed employs masks to indicate the sev-
en periods of human life. *Strange Interlude* uses the
nine-act form to dramatize each of the stages, from youth
to age, of its heroine's life. The mask-face dichotomy in
The Great God Brown represents the characters' public
and private images, what they pretend to be as opposed to
what they really are. *Strange Interlude* conveys the same
idea about its characters' schism, but it relies on thought
asides to do so. This technique was not new to O'Neill; he
had used it in *The Dreamy Kid* and *Welded* to indicate,

*The copyright date is July 1, 1927. The play premiered on
January 30, 1928.

through speech, the discrepancy between the character's true self, revealed in thought asides, and the persona he projects, depicted through dialogue. The mask is the inhibited, conscious, visualized self; the thought aside, the verbalized projection of the uninhibited unconscious. Because it exhibits the dark, unexplored region of the psyche, the thought aside makes O'Neill's characters multidimensional and thus intriguing to audiences.

Strange Interlude's controversial subject matter, as well as its technique, is derivative. Nina Leeds had been promiscuous before marriage, but so too had been Eleanor Cape in *Welded* and Ella Harris in *All God's Chillun Got Wings*. The plays of the early 1920s abound with prostitutes: Anna Christie, Min, Cybel, Pompeia. Both insanity and abortion had been incorporated into earlier works. The supposedly daring, novel idea of a wife purposefully selecting a man other than her husband to father her child was used in *Desire Under the Elms*. *Strange Interlude* seemed different because it clothed these borrowed taboo topics with the then new and audacious Freudian language and concepts.

Strange Interlude received widespread publicity after its publication in 1928 when a Georges Lewys, the pen name of Gladys Lewis, brought suit, which she eventually lost, accusing O'Neill of plagiarizing her book, *The Temple of Pallas-Athenae*. The dramatist's notebook, containing the 1923 idea and a collection of scenarios, including *Strange Interlude*, became Exhibit 2 in the March 13, 1931, trial. O'Neill, who was living in France at the time, stated in his deposition that he had recorded the idea in 1923 after a former aviator of the Lafayette Escadrille told him the story that was to become the basis for the plot—of a girl whose aviator fiancé had been killed in World War I.

In the 1923 idea O'Neill depicted his heroine as the flier's widow; he later reverted to the true story for purposes of characterization. Nina Leeds's father had prevented her marriage to her deceased lover, Gordon Shaw; her own inhibitions and her fiancé's timidity precluded them from having an affair. His death leaves her sexually warped. O'Neill describes Nina in the early idea as "ultra-neurotic." Her neuroticism, which springs from the non-acceptance of the dark side of her self, grows progressively worse in the play's time span. Her denial creates an inner imbalance, a vacuum of sorts, prompting her to look to men to compensate and complete her self.

Nina's problem is that she is a highly charged sexual person. In the first stage of her life cycle, youth, all the forces that affect her, the moral codes of her New England environment and her strict, Puritanical father, lead her to suppress instincts and desires that are deemed objectionable. As a result, when Nina finally breaks through the barriers of repression, she becomes promiscuous and subsequently guilt-ridden. Her conscience is further burdened by the belief that her affairs are a betrayal of her own father and God the Father, who is similarly harsh and forbidding. The journey through life that she makes in the nine acts of the play is motivated by her need for the forgiveness of the father figure, who assumes both physical and spiritual dimensions.

The first of the two scenarios for *Strange Interlude*, written in a ten-day period in September 1925, was comprised of structural divisions (six acts, the first three of which each contained scene divisions), a synopsis of the scenes, and descriptions of major characters. There is no hint in this early outline of the later stream-of-consciousness asides. The dramatist wrote the second scenario early in 1926, started the first draft on June 1, and finished the revisions a year later, on July 25. What remained constant throughout this work, which the author labeled his "woman play," is the essence of Nina, even though other characters were added, dropped, and changed. The first two acts of the play flesh out the lines of the original 1923 idea.

As he had done earlier in *Desire Under the Elms*,

O'Neill again uses a New England setting to provide a
rationale for the Puritanical, life-denying attitude and the
moral perversion of the characters. The play opens in the
library of Professor Leeds's home in a small university
town. Described as a sanctuary, the library, with its low
ceilings, cumbersome bookshelves packed with musty
classics, and oppressive, claustrophobic atmosphere, is
the professor's refuge from reality. Leeds has a strange,
paradoxical nature. While professing a liberal attitude to
the degeneracy of Greece and Rome, he has a "natural
tendency toward a prim provincialism." In his asides, he
reveals himself to be a selfish, smug snob, whose own
incestuous feelings for his daughter led him to urge Nina's
fiancé, Gordon Shaw, to refrain from marriage before
being sent into combat overseas. In his conscious speech
Leeds tells Charlie Marsden, a former pupil who visits
him, that he objected because Gordon, a popular collegiate sports hero, "came of common people and had no
money of his own."

Marsden, thirty-five, is described as being bisexual
in the early notes. Although he professes to be mildly
attracted to Nina, he is probably a homosexual, the only
one in the canon. In the 1926 notes he reminisces about
Gordon: "so like a Greek God. He was a bit coarse-
grained for a god—only flaw in Gordon too fleshy." In an
aside, Leeds thinks: "Too fleshy to him. Marsden is posi-
tively gushing about men." Marsden has a withdrawn
"indefinable feminine quality about him" and resembles
an "Anglicized New England gentleman." His thought
asides provide the play's exposition and reveal his prudish
and prurient nature. Some of the details of his life match
those of his creator. He is a successful writer, a novelist.
He was never close to his father, although the latter tried,
as James O'Neill did, to bridge the gap of misunderstand-
ing on his deathbed. At an early age, sixteen, Marsden,
like O'Neill, went to a whorehouse for his sexual initiation
and still feels revulsion when he recalls the incident.

Nina, twenty, a tall, blond, athletic girl,* is hand-some rather than pretty. Her greenish-blue eyes reflect her inner anguish: "Her whole manner, the charged atmosphere she gives off, is totally at variance with her healthy outdoor physique. It is strained, nerve-racked, hectic, a terrible tension of will alone maintaining self-possession." Her inner self, as the images of her asides reveal, is a caldron of searing emotions. She views the visitor, "nice Charlie doggy," as sexless, as one who lives vicariously through others, "watching the burning, frozen naked swimmers drown."

When Nina tells her father that she must leave the house that evening or go crazy," he puts "on his prim severe manner" and says that she has not yet recovered from a nervous breakdown. The ghost of Gordon, shot down two days before the armistice, still haunts Nina, who rightly suspects that her father's interference destroyed her happiness. Jealously, Leeds curses Gordon. He is glad that Gordon is dead and hopes he is in hell. Nina intends to become a nurse and work at a sanitarium for crippled soldiers. Like Lavinia in *Mourning Becomes Electra*, she must punish herself, "pay for my cowardly treachery to Gordon." She regrets not making him "take me" and that she is "still Gordon's silly virgin."

Marsden is revolted by Nina's latent sexuality: "All flesh now . . . lust . . . who would dream she was so sensual." He longs only to return to his mother and to get away from Nina. "With a sudden girlishness," she asks

---

*Three types of women recur in O'Neill's dramas. There is the blond, athletic woman, seemingly cool and detached but quite passionate. Anna Christie is tall, blond, and handsome "after a large Viking-daughter fashion." Margaret Anthony in *The Great God Brown* is a "pretty, vivacious blond" with a lithe, strong figure. O'Neill's idealized woman, however, has dark hair and eyes, coarse, sensual features, and a voluptuous body (Sara Melody, Josie Hogan, Abbie Putnam). Mother figures usually have copper gold or red-brown hair (Christine Mannon and the young Deborah Harford and Mary Tyrone).

Marsden to help her pack. Emerging now is Nina's innocent, submissive, childlike side, which obviously dominated her before Gordon's death. Marsden, the father
figure, responds to this quality in her throughout the
play. In this act Nina is in the process of transition,
striving to go from dependent child to independent young
woman. When her father remarks that she is not herself,
Nina responds, "No. I'm not myself yet. That's just it. Not
all myself. But I've been becoming myself. And I must
finish!"

In the next scene in the final version, which takes
place a year later, the shades are drawn in the library,
"giving the windows a suggestion of lifeless closed eyes"
and making this New England home, like those in *Desire
Under the Elms* and *Mourning Becomes Electra*, a tomb
of the dead and living dead. Leeds has just died. Marsden
awaits Nina's return and reflects on his visits to her at the
hospital, of her cynical eyes "sick with men . . . as though
I'd looked into the eyes of a prostitute." Nina arrives,
dressed in a nurse's uniform. "Her eyes try to armor her
wounded spirit with a defensive stare of disillusionment."
The abyss has widened between her inner and outer
selves. She is in a more "highly-strung, disorganized state
than ever, although she is now more capable of suppres-
sing and concealing it."

With Nina are two friends: Doctor Ned Darrell, who
goes upstairs with her, and Sam Evans, who remains with
Marsden. Evans, though twenty-five, has never grown
up. He is immature, guileless, "bashful with women."
Dressed in the latest collegiate clothes, he takes pride in
looking young. "It keeps his place in life for himself." Part
of the self is dormant in him, "a hint of some unawakened
force beneath his apparent weakness." He was in Gordon's class at college and still worships the dead sports
hero. In his asides he reveals an inferiority complex and
hatred of himself. He had been unable to pass the physical
exam to get into Gordon's military unit. Evans regards

Marsden as a father figure and awkwardly asks for permission to marry Nina. Reminded that she still loves Gordon, the young man pours out his feelings, his pure, nonsexual love: "I never think of her—that way—she's too beautiful and wonderful." Marsden thinks selfishly that Nina would not be faithful "to this simpleton" if she married him and would perhaps turn to him, Marsden.

Darrell, twenty-seven, a handsome, intelligent man, enters. From the start, it is clear that he is the type of man Nina should marry. "There is a quality about him, provoking and disturbing to women, of intense passion which he has rigidly trained himself to control." He considers himself immune to love, having scientifically explored sexuality. He knows instinctively that Marsden lives as he writes, on the surface of life, and that he is one of "those poor devils who spend their lives trying not to discover which sex they belong to!" Marsden realizes that the neurologist is analyzing him and curses "Herr Freud," saying: "pah, what an easy cure-all! . . . sex the philosopher's stone . . . O Oedipus, O my king! The world is adopting you!"

Darrell tells Marsden about Nina's promiscuity, of the numerous affairs she has had with wounded soldiers hoping to atone in her mind to Gordon. Marsden is, he says, the "last link connecting her with the girl she used to be before Gordon's death." Nina loves him—as an uncle. He must, therefore, encourage her to marry Evans, thus giving her a normal outlet for her maternal instincts and "the emotional life Gordon's death blocked up in her." Darrell regards the suggestion that he himself loves Nina as preposterous, and, commenting on her ludicrous Gordon fixation, says he could not share a woman—"even with a ghost!" He adds in an aside: "Not to mention the living who have had her!"

Later, Nina kneels before Marsden, who sits in her father's chair, and sobbingly says: "I want to believe in something! I want to believe so I can feel." She had prayed to the "modern science God." To her, God should not have been created in a male image. "But the God of Gods—the Boss—has always been a man. That makes life so perverted, and death so unnatural. We should have imagined life as created in the birth-pain of God the Mother." She creeps onto Marsden's lap "like a little girl." He admits what he really desires of her in an aside: "She is my girl . . . not woman . . . my little girl . . . and I am brave because of her little girl's pure love."

The scene foreshadows the one between Parritt and the father-confessor, Larry Slade, in *The Iceman Cometh*. Nina says that she wants to " 'fess up, tell how bad I've been, and be punished." She demands that he tell her how to punish herself "for playing the silly slut" and giving her "cool clean body to men with hot hands and greedy eyes which they call love!" Inwardly, Marsden calls her a "dirty little trollop" and wants to "hate this little whore"; outwardly, he assumes the role of father figure and confessor: her penance is to marry Evans. She falls asleep in his arms, accepting her punishment: "I must become a mother so I can give myself. I am sick of sickness."

In the next act, a year later, Nina sits writing a letter in the dining room of the Evanses' home. Images of disease, death, and ghosts are used to describe it. Cut off from sunlight, it is "cheerless and sickly." Nina decides it has "something wrong with its psyche . . . I feel it has lost its soul." Like the Mannon house in *Mourning Becomes Electra*, all its life has "long since been exhausted in keeping the dying living a little longer." As befitting her second stage, young womanhood and impending mother-hood, Nina's "whole personality seems changed . . . nothing remains of the strange fascination of her face except her unchangeably mysterious eyes." In the first month of her marriage "she was obviously playing a part," but pregnancy brings her peace and a sense of purpose.

Nina discovers the cause of the cloud that hangs

suspended over the family and house in her first private talk with Evans's mother, a small, doll-like woman, who is dangerously split. The "ghost of an old faith and trust in life's goodness hovers girlishly" about her mouth; her face "must have once been of a romantic, tender, clinging-vine beauty." Tragic external forces, however, have taken their toll on her face: "her big dark eyes are grim with the prisoner-pain of a walled-in soul." As though in retaliation for her own suffering, Mrs. Evans vengefully explains the "curse on the Evanses": hereditary insanity. Her husband had not confided his secret until after their marriage. Like Laius and Jocasta in *Oedipus Rex*, they vowed to remain childless. A son had been born; worry that he might become insane drove Evans to madness. Nina declares that she will leave her husband. Mrs. Evans persuades her to have an abortion and remain with him. To compensate for the sacrifice, the mother proposes that Nina do what she herself should have done: pick a man, "a healthy male to breed by same's we do with stock, to give the man I loved a healthy child." She herself was "too afraid of God" to do this. Nina, who has ceased to "believe in God the Father," decides to take this advice.

All of the characters seem to be unhappy in Act IV, which takes place seven months later. Evans is bitter, feeling sterile as a creative advertising copywriter and as a husband. Marsden suspects that Nina has had an abortion; the biography she is writing of Gordon does not seem to bring them "alone together" as he had hoped. Darrell finally admits in an aside that Nina "always had a strong physical attraction" for him. He has "steered clear" of her since her wedding. Nina, looking ill and nervously tense again, confides in Darrell, telling him of the Evanses' curse and the abortion. She had loved the child more than anything else in life, "even Gordon. I loved it so it seemed at times that Gordon must be its real father." Feeling guilt-ridden and responsible for her tragedy, Darrell suggests that Nina get a divorce. She proposes instead to have another child.

The two look into each other's eyes. A strange exchange, in which each speaks in the third person, follows,
one reminiscent of that between Michael and Eleanor
Cape in *Welded* in the chair scene. Outwardly, Darrell's
face assumes the mask of a doctor. His asides, however,
betray the passion he feels for Nina. He pretends to offer
himself in the interest of science as a "healthy guinea pig"
and in the hope that his sacrifice will save Evans and Nina.
The latter states: "She is ashamed. It's adultery." He asks:
"Would she rather have her husband wind up in an asylum?" Nina reaches out and turns his face toward hers
and, as herself, addresses him: "I should be so grateful,
Ned." He falls on his knees, takes her hand, and assures
her that he acts now for her happiness.

The fifth act shows the sitting room of the Evanses'
rented house in a seashore suburb near New York the
following April. Nina, for the first time in the play, shows
no trace of sickness. She is pregnant again and seems
confident and triumphant. She fell in love with Darrell
during her first afternoon with him, but after a series of
"wonderful afternoons of happiness" they remained aloof
from each other, no longer giving in to desire. Part of
Darrell hates Nina, the victimizer who destroys his peace
of mind, who jeopardizes his career; the other part is
hopelessly infatuated with her. He speaks scornfully of
marriage when Nina suggests it: "I don't admire your
character! I don't respect you! I know too much about
your past!" Nina longs for happiness with him and their
child.

Marsden enters, his face "distorted into an ugly mask
of grief." He mourns the death of his mother. Like Ephraim in *Desire Under the Elms*, he feels something menacing in the room: "Lust with a loathsome jeer taunting
my sensitive timidities!" Like Abbie, who also uses a man
who is not her husband to become pregnant, Nina gloats
over the hold she has over the father of her child. Feeling
"like a cornered fugitive" and longing to be free of Nina,
Darrell tells Evans, when they are alone, that Nina is

pregnant and that he is sailing for Europe in a few days to study. Returning, Nina becomes distraught to find Darrell gone and Evans ecstatic at the prospect of fatherhood. Longing for revenge, she tries to tell Evans the truth but finds he is not her spouse but "Sammy," her "poor little boy." Instantly, Nina becomes maternal and "seems to grow older" as she thinks first of her child and then of the afternoons with her lover, now gone forever.

In the year that now elapses between the acts, Evans has undergone a remarkable change, having "matured, found his place in the world." Determined to achieve success, he decides to ask Marsden, who has inherited half a million dollars, to back him in business. Nina looks "noticeably older" but appears to be content. She respects Evans, because he is a good father to her child, and gives herself to him "without repulsion." Whereas she is proud of this new, confident businessman-husband, Marsden prefers the old, sensitive Evans over this manipulative, brash, greedy man.

Darrell returns from Europe, looking nervous and unhealthy. Lines of desperation and "puffy shadows of dissipation" mar his face. He has failed in his efforts to fight his passion for Nina. She greets him in a "feverish state of mind." A bitter war rages within her; she is torn between her love for him and her new-found peace and contentment in her child. Nina spurns his plan for them to go away together: "I am not your old mad Nina." Young Gordon's happiness and her husband's come first. Hearing the name she gave their son, Darrell feels betrayed: "Gordon is still her lover! . . . Gordon, Sam and Nina! . . . and my son!" Selfishly, Nina muses, "I couldn't find a better husband than Sam" or "a better lover than Ned . . . I need them both to be happy." In this most memorable scene of the play, the three men, following Nina's instructions, sit down "mechanically." Triumphantly possessive, she says: "You are my three men! This is your home with me! . . . you must not wake our baby." The four seem

frozen in time and space during their asides at the end of
the scene. To Nina, the three form "one complete beautiful male desire which I absorb . . . they dissolve in me,
their life is my life . . . I am pregnant with the three." As
she goes out of the room, she kisses Evans as a brother,
Marsden as a father, Darrell as a lover. The latter reflects
on the past, the actions that must remain hidden to protect life's wounded, like Evans: "There are secrets one
must not reveal . . . memory is lined with mirrors." The
irony of the situation strikes Darrell: "the ailing ones, Sam
and the female Nina, have been restored to health," while
he "suffered deterioration." Reluctantly, he accepts the
idea of sharing Nina: "Half a loaf is better."

Act VII is set eleven years later in the sitting room of
the Evanses' apartment on Park Avenue. Nina, thirty-five
and "in the full bloom of her womanhood," reclines on a
chaise lounge. She is a woman who has been living a life
that is a lie. On the outside, "in the pink of physical
condition," she seems, "as in the first act," under a "great
mental strain." Her expression is "set and masklike."
Darrell seems no longer interested in his appearance.
Gray-haired, stout, and embittered, he lacks "definite
aim or ambition." Their eleven-year-old son sits on the
floor reading a book. Gordon's face is grave, his eyes "full
of a quick-tempered sensitiveness." Consumed with jealously, he despises Darrell. Nina regrets the suffering she
has caused her lover: "Sharing me has corrupted him."
She also reproaches herself for hurting "dear old Charlie
of her girlhood." She thinks: "I have wounded everyone . . . dear Charlie, what a perfect lover he would
make for one's old age." She then experiences great revulsion: "These men make me sick! . . . I hate all three of
them! The wife and mistress in me has been killed by
them! . . . thank God, I'm only a mother now!"

Realizing that he will never achieve anything himself
in life, Darrell is financing the work of Preston, a young
talented scientist, at his biology station in the West In-

dies. After Gordon is sent from the room because of his
antagonism to Darrell, he and Nina embrace and kiss. At
that moment, Gordon appears in the doorway and watches
them silently "in a passion of jealousy and rage." Later, he
maliciously smashes the small, delicate model yacht Darrell had given him that day as a birthday present. At the
end of the scene, Evans, exuding the image of the prosperous, confident, efficient executive, promises to give
young Gordon anything he asks for if he can "play football
or row like the Gordon who died." The boy decides to
"get back" at Darrell by being "just like Gordon was and
Mother'll love me better 'n him!"

In Act VIII, ten years later, all the characters are
assembled on the afterdeck of the Evanses' cruiser at the
finish line of a college rowing match to watch Gordon
make sports history. Nina, whose hair is now white, tries
unsuccessfully to conceal the aging process with makeup.
Only her mysterious eyes and beautiful figure remain the
same. In manner, she is the Nina of Act IV: "neurotic,
passionately embittered and torn." Her three men have
deserted her. Evans, now stout, bald, his face flushed and
apoplectic, seems his good-natured self on the surface,
but he has grown increasingly stubborn and opinionated.
He takes sides with Gordon, who wants to marry Madeline Arnold, nineteen, a pretty, athletic girl with money
and position, and resents Nina's bitter hatred of the young
woman. Nina is determined to play the role of spoiler, as
her father did in her own life long ago. Maddened by the
thought that she has lost Gordon, first to her husband and
then to Madeline, she enlists Darrell's aid, encouraging
him to talk to their son.

Darrell's appearance shows that he has freed himself, at last, of Nina's spell. Lean and tan, he is once again
the cool, detached scientist. He urges her to "give up
owning people," adding: "And you've meddled enough
with human love, old lady! Your time for that is over!" She
warns him that she is "the old Nina" again, determined

this time not to lose another Gordon. She hates her husband and is willing to tell the whole sordid story of her affair, risking Evans's sanity and life, to break her son's engagement.

Marsden too is highly critical of Nina for having, once again, "gotten into a fine neurotic state." Showing the effects of heavy drinking, Marsden, who has aged considerably, loses his inhibitions and tells Nina, "We'll only have a little longer to wait and then you and I'll be quietly married!" He encourages her to tell him her story. Addressing him as "Father," she narrates events of the past as though "in a trance." She concludes "childishly," saying she had been an "awfully wicked girl." After her confession, Marsden responds, "paternally": "I forgive you everything." She confuses him with her own father and responds: "It was all your fault in the beginning, wasn't it?" At the end of the scene Evans collapses and falls onto the deck, the victim of a stroke. Marsden makes a "motion over the body like a priest blessing." Nina vows, as her penance, to give her son to Madeline.

Several months have passed when the last act, set on the terrace of the Evanses' Long Island estate, commences. Gordon sits on a stone bench with Madeline. He resembles the sons of the widowed Margaret Anthony in the Epilogue of *The Great God Brown*. Destined to achieve the kind of success taken for granted in his circle, yet totally lacking in imagination, he will live on the surface of life, never plunging into the depths of the inner self. Now that his father has died, he assumes that his mother will marry Darrell. He realizes that she never loved her husband, despite her devotion to him during his long illness. As the young lovers embrace, Marsden, looking younger and contented, approaches. Scandalized at their display of passion, he feels that he and Nina have moved to a "passionless climate, to the moon."

The old lovers, Nina and Darrell, enter. Nina, appearing resigned, has given up the struggle to look sexu-

ally attractive. The only identity Gordon has for her now
is as Madeline's lover. In an aside, Darrell pinpoints the
flaw in his son: the Gordon Shaw ideal, which Evans
passed on to him, has made him "an insensitive clod."
Gordon lacks all the sensibilities Darrell finds in his surrogate son, Preston. The bulk of Evans's estate will be
shared by his wife and son, but a half million dollars has
been designated for Darrell's scientific work at the station. He resents the hand of the dead man, who deprived
him of wife and son, reaching beyond the grave to steal
Preston, his assistant, with the lure of money. Goaded by
years of repressed anger, Gordon slaps Darrell across the
face. Even though Gordon apologizes, Nina sees that she
has brought nothing but suffering to Darrell; she wishes
that he would go for good. In a conciliatory mood, Gordon
says that he hopes the two will be happy after their
marriage. The son assures Nina that he loves her, and she
relinquishes him forever to Madeline.

Alone with Nina, Darrell asks her to marry him and is
relieved by her rejection: "Our ghosts would torture us to
death. The Nina of those afternoons will always live in
me." He urges her to marry Marsden, whose devotion
should be rewarded. Later, with a girlish coquettishness,
she proposes to Marsden, who promises that they will
marry in a chapel "full of restful shadow, symbolic of the
peace we have found." Above them, her son flies off for
his new life, reminding Nina of the other Gordon, who
also "flew away."

Marsden encourages Nina to forget the Gordon
Shaw episode as an interlude through which their souls
were "scraped clean of impure flesh" and made worthy.
Nina responds: "Strange interlude! Yes, our lives are
merely strange dark interludes in the electric display of
God the Father! . . . I feel as if I were a girl again and you
were my father." They make plans to return to Nina's
childhood home to live, to sleep, and "to die in peace."
She puts her head on his shoulder and, like a child, falls
asleep.

This idea of Nina as a child protected by the father figure brings her full circle. Curiously, although Marsden plays a vital role in the development of the plot, he was not included in the *dramatis personae* until the second 1926 scenario. In each of the early endings, Darrell, rather than Marsden, becomes Nina's companion in old age. In one version Darrell gets married and is later divorced; in another, he is engaged twice. Either idea weakens a main premise of the plot: Nina's physical hold on him, a fascination that reduces him to abject slavery. The sequences of the play follow those cited in the lengthy original idea of 1923 except for the one that concludes it: Nina "has more children by the doctor. These children grow up instinctively hating the Doc. . . . After many years, husband dies—65 or so. They, very old, marry. This finishes estrangement of the children, grandchildren. Very old, they wait for death to let them speak the truth."

The fact that Nina is shown at the conclusion of the idea to be sixty-five indicates O'Neill's intention to take her through the seven periods of life that the mask scheme in *Lazarus Laughed* encompasses. The division of acts represents the various stages of her life: the first, set in Nina's childhood home, corresponds to youth; the second, to young womanhood; Acts III to VI, to womanhood; the seventh, to middle age; the eighth and ninth to maturity and age. The two last acts should, O'Neill points out, have "a sort of hazy quality of glowing memory—of passage of time with the events and people past, the leading characters who stand still, growing old."

The three men in Nina's life possess different personality traits and form in her disoriented mind a composite picture of her romantic ideal, Gordon Shaw. She has a man to correspond to each of her different needs and the fluctuating aspects of her personality. Unfortunately, however, Nina depends on men to provide her with a sense of identity. Exploited and in turn vengefully exploitative, she is trapped at each stage of her life: by her

abnormal father, by the child-husband, by the necessary
lover. Her only free choice is her acceptance at the end of
the father surrogate, Marsden, the selfless confidant who
smoothes her life's path. Necessity asserts itself here, in
one respect, when Nina, at the close of the play, reverts to
childhood and needs the father's protection.

The play opened on Broadway on January 30, 1928,
and ran, with great success, for six months. A second
company was equally successful on a road tour. Part of the
play's fascination, leading the Puritanical officials in Boston to ban it, was the frank, bold language used to dramatize the outrageous premise: that a woman who was, for
some reason, denied a child by her husband should commit adultery with an obliging guinea pig to conceive one.
An unusual production schedule was devised for the long,
nine-act play. The curtain rose at 5:15 P.M. At 7:45 P.M.
patrons went out to dinner and returned at 9:00 P.M. for
the two-hour conclusion.

For this play, O'Neill was awarded his third Pulitzer
Prize. While some critics deplored its melodramatic aspects and sensationalism, *Strange Interlude* did receive
favorable notices. As the numerous versions of the play
demonstrate, O'Neill spent considerable time working
out the details of the plot. Even so, the story line is weak;
the strength of the play lies in its characterizations and
what O'Neill accomplished through the use of thought
asides. These were far more comprehensible and meaningful to theatergoers than the masks in *The Great God
Brown*. Most were aware of the author's attempt to explore the depths of the inner being, the dark side of the
self. Primarily, however, they were captivated by the
character of Nina, one of O'Neill's most fascinating female
creations.

O'Neill now entered a phase in which the mother
figures in his plays become more and more identifiable
with Ella O'Neill. Some details of Nina's life correspond
to those in that of O'Neill's mother. Nina "has always

idolized" her father, as had Ella. Had he lived long enough, Ella's strict, snobbish father would have opposed the match with the socially inferior actor, James O'Neill, who, like the "common" Gordon, lacked money and background. The author's mother had an Electra complex and saw in her considerably older husband a father figure. In the notes for *Long Day's Journey into Night*, Mary Tyrone says of her husband: "14 years older—was great mistake—more like father—." Tyrone becomes the protective father to his pathetic, drug-disoriented girl-wife as does Marsden to the dualistic Nina. Described as sick throughout the plays, both women are fatally split, projecting the image of girlish-mother innocence in the outer mask while repressing an unacceptable sensual side. Mary Tyrone's dark nature manifests itself only when she is heavily drugged, as O'Neill's notes reveal: "very hipped up now, her manner strange—at the moment a vain happy, chattering girlishness—then changing to hard cynical sneering bitterness with a bitter biting cruelty and with a coarse vulgarity in it—the last as if suddenly poisoned by an alive demon." Nina also alternates between these two states. With the father figure and husband, she is girlish-maternal; with her lover, recklessly sensual. O'Neill uses the same word to describe the two women: "strange."

In the notes for *Strange Interlude* the author says of Nina, at the end of the play when her three men have deserted her: "feels cut off from everyone, bitterly lonely, and in a queer narcotic state again." It is here in the last scene that Nina most resembles Mary. The tense, nervous woman shown at the beginning of *Long Day's Journey into Night* is a duplicate of the white-haired Nina with her "still beautiful body." Just as Nina's orbit of three men drift away from her, so too the husband and two sons escape the clutches of the wife-mother in *Long Days Journey*. Striking references in *Strange Interlude* link it to the late autobiographical play. Marsden, in an aside, musing on Nina, thinks "sometimes the scent of her hair and skin . . . like a dreamy drug." Evans, who worries continually about Nina's health, boasts in an early scene, as does James Tyrone, that his wife is "getting fat." Nina prays frequently to God the Mother; Mary, to the Blessed Virgin. In the last acts both women regress to the safety of their girlhood and rely, hopelessly, on the father-husband figure.

In Act IX Nina thinks about returning to her childhood home with Marsden: "we can talk together of the old days . . . when I was a girl . . . when I was happy . . . before I fell in love with Gordon Shaw and all this tangled mess of love and hate and pain and birth began!" Mary Tyrone, reminiscing about her decision as a convent schoolgirl to become a nun, says in the last line of *Long Day's Journey into Night*: "That was in the winter of senior year. Then in the spring something happened to me. Yes, I remember. I fell in love with James Tyrone and was so happy for a time." In earlier plays of the 1920s the autobiographical mother is dead, as in *Desire Under the Elms* and most of *The Great God Brown*, or disguised as in *All God's Chillun Got Wings*. She begins to emerge gradually as the person she actually was in Nina in *Strange Interlude* and in later plays of the 1920s and 1930s until she is portrayed unequivocally as Mary Tyrone in *Long Day's Journey into Night*.

40. Dynamo

The veneration of God the Mother expressed by Nina Leeds in *Strange Interlude*, becomes the worship of the "Mother-God" by Reuben Light in *Dynamo*.* In the late 1920s, O'Neill seemed to be obsessed by a maternal image of the Deity, which may, in part, be explained by his own idealization of the mother image and the emphasis the religion of his youth, Catholicism, places on the Blessed Virgin.

O'Neill indicates in the first idea he records for *Dynamo*, in 1926, its early focus: adulation of the Mother God, when perverted, becomes worship of technology. Stated in his original concept is the equation "G:M = M:Machine." The first symbols, "G:M," or "God is to the Mother," found in *Strange Interlude*, become "M:Machine," or the Mother identified with the Machine, in *Dynamo*. The notebook entry reads:

"Mother Dynamo"

Man becomes giant, dynamo woman

Play of Dynamos—the despairing philosopher—poet who falls in love with balance equilibrium of energy—his personification of it—his final marriage with it—the consummation ending with his destruction.

The "poet who falls in love" with the machine is Reuben Light, son of a fire-and-brimstone fundamentalist minister and a domineering, possessive mother. Believing that his idolized mother has betrayed him, the despairing young man rejects her and the religion she represents and turns first to atheism and then, after a frenzied

---

*The copyright date is October 4, 1928. The play premiered on February 11, 1929.

"substitute God search," to a composite Mother-God image symbolized by a massive dynamo. Through the maternal-looking, life-sustaining machine, he "deifies and finds her again."

O'Neill asserted that he derived the concept for the play while watching a dynamo at the General Electric generating plant at Stephenson, Connecticut, near Ridgefield, his home in the mid-1920s. Barrett Clark states that "there was something in the machine that suggested a new god, just as the stone images of the past symbolized the old gods."* In the late 1920s O'Neill detected a yearning in the American character for the certainty of a former cherished absolute, which had been challenged by the new all-consuming worship of science. He viewed the play as "symbolical and factual biography of what is happening in a large section of the American soul right now." In the work, he promised to

> dig at the roots of the sickness of today as I feel it—the death of an old God and the failure of science and materialism to give any satisfying new one for the surviving primitive religious instinct to find a meaning for life in, and to comfort its fears of death with.†

Dynamo points out the dangers inherent in the worship of strange gods, which is forbidden in the first commandment. While the hero does, at the end of his search, achieve a mystical union with the Mother Dynamo, it is a "consummation ending with his destruction." The term "Neanderthal man," which appears in an introductory statement to the 1926 idea for *Dynamo*, applies also to Yank in *The Hairy Ape*. The latter's search for a substitute God leads to a reversal of *Dynamo*'s equation: Machine:G = G:gorilla. In *The Hairy Ape*, Yank equates the machine with a God force; becoming disillusioned by its inability to humanize him, he is reduced to adulation of a

---

*Clark, p. 120.

†Ibid.

primitive power. The gorilla, which embraces and destroys him at the end, can be equated with the crocodile god in *The Emperor Jones*. Yank is the apotheosis of the Neanderthal, physically and psychologically, as he attempts to scale the evolutionary ladder from machine to animal to human. In contrast, the hero of *Dynamo* is a Neanderthal spiritually. He rejects the modern-day Christian God, identified in his mind with his tyrannical father, and regresses to the most primitive religious rites, believing that the Mother God is personified in the machine idol and demands human sacrifice.

According to O'Neill, the second part of *Dynamo* (the last four scenes, which show the machine and plant), derives its structure and method, its staging and use of sounds, from *The Hairy Ape*. Sound becomes a major expressionistic device of *Dynamo*, comparable to the masks in *The Great God Brown* and the asides of *Strange Interlude*. Although the scheme is not fully realized in *Dynamo*, sounds, such as the "hypnotic, metallic purr" of the dynamo and the "overtone of rushing water from the dam," were supposed to indicate tranquil or turbulent states of mind.

Dynamo cannot be explained in any other terms than the hero's obsession with the idealized mother and her perceived betrayal, which leads him to worship the maternal machine substitute. The machine itself is described in feminine and human terms. Huge and black, it has "something of a massive female idol about it." The upper part of the "rounded torso" of the dynamo is called the "exciter." It resembles "a head with blank, oblong eyes." Reuben's substitute-God search is equated with his perception and pursuit of the continuously evolving mother figure: his own mother merges with Mrs. Fife, appropriately an immense, rotund woman, who is identified with the Mother Dynamo.

Following the theatrical failure of the play, which the author blamed on the emphasis critics gave to its religious implications, O'Neill revised *Dynamo* for publication. In this version, as he told Langner on March 25, 1929, he tries to point "up the human story of Reuben's psychological mess over his father and his mother's betrayal and how he at last deifies and finds her again (the real plot of the play which no one seems to have seen in any of its implications but which I thought was obvious)." The dramatist was disturbed because critics did not perceive the themes woven into the fabric of the play:

> No one seems to have gotten the real human relationship story, what his mother does to the boy and what that leads to in his sacrifice of the girl to a maternal deity in the end—the girl his mother hated and was jealous of—that all that was the boy's real God struggle, or prompted it. This all fits in with the general theme of American life in back of the play, America being the land of the mother complex. . . . Not a damn one mentions it. They were so damned hot on the general religious theme that they couldn't see the human psychological struggle.

O'Neill wrote two scenarios for *Dynamo*. The first is dated "Summer 1927"; the second was begun in March 1928, after he had gone to live in France with Carlotta Monterey. The area of greatest interest in the comparison of the scenarios and the final published draft of September 1928, in view of the play's autobiographical family relationships, is the evolution of the characters. In the first scenario the hero's father, Reverend Hutchins Light, fifty-five, is a short, fat Baptist minister with a "complacent, sanctimonious, holier-than-thou superiority." He is a "meek, unassuming soul, dull but kindly, preferring to be lowly and unnoticed but forced to live in prominence to carry out his duty." His wife, forty-five, completely dominates her husband with "her strength and dark good looks." The marriage, a loveless affair, was arranged by her minister-father. She is a religious fanatic who views her husband as a "minister of the Lord," not as a man, her son as "one of the Lord's anointed," and herself as "the daughter-in-law of God."

The characteristics of the parents are interchanged in the second scenario. Here the father is a "booming-voiced, over-assertive personality, autocratic and over-bearing, a stern Old Testament moralist." Inwardly, he suffers from "a sense of a sin of weakness," the temptation of sensuality, "betrayed by a large sensual mouth"; his lips "part and pout with carnal desires." Outwardly, he wears the mask of "superior complacent white-robed shepherd among black sheep." His love-starved wife, Amelia, is a "mild-looking silent woman" whose iron will is hidden "beneath her meek submissive exterior." Outwardly, she wears the mask of "passive, calm, ill-paid minister's wife." Her description approximates that of other sensual wives, Abbie Putnam and Sara Melody. She has a "youthful and active body. Her figure is extremely feminine, she is all female, her breasts are noticeably large and firm, her waist slender, her hips and thighs broad and round." Their marriage now resembles James and Mary Tyrone's in *Long Day's Journey into Night*. The two are bound by a "tie of deep love and passion" and a "strong tie of hatred." She despises his stultifying profession and the weakness of passion that led her to marry him rather than other, more suitable suitors who "have since risen in the world and could have given her its delights which she remembers with regret." Light has an "old fanatical ideal of purity" and foreshadows that other New England Puritan, Ezra Mannon. "The lust of the flesh" conquers him; "it is in bed" that his wife dominates him.

It is important to know precisely how O'Neill viewed his characters in order to understand "the real human relationship story" that he says is at the heart of the play. In the published text, he merely sketches the parents with a few lines of description. The father, in his early sixties, has a stubborn jaw, the bullying voice of a sermonizer, and reddish hair (a quality usually attributed to the autobiographical mother). His wife, fifteen years younger, is stout; her face is attractive but has "grown fleshy." While her expression is "one of virtuous resignation," her mouth is rebellious, determined, and stubborn. In the early portraits of the Lights in the scenarios, O'Neill shows unconsciously, through their opposing but complementary personalities, the duality of his own parents that he revealed later when making notes for *Long Day's Journey into Night*. In some plays, such as *Mourning Becomes Electra*, the disparate traits are integrated in one set of parents; in others, like *The Great God Brown*, in two. The parents in *Dynamo's* first scenario resemble Mr. and Mrs. Brown; those of the second, Mr. and Mrs. Anthony.

When *Dynamo* opens, Mr. and Mrs. Light, like the parents in *The Great God Brown*, are deliberating the future of their son, Reuben, seventeen, who has shy, sensitive eyes but a stubborn jaw like his father's. His dichotomy is shown in his voice: timid, hesitating, boyish, with a "feminine gentleness yet in intercourse with the world self-protectively booming." A much more comprehensive portrait of Reuben appears in the second scenario. Like the sons in *Desire Under the Elms* and *The Great God Brown*, he resembles both parents. His mouth is his father's but "exaggerated to a degree in its drooping-lipped sensuality and weakness, but with a pleasing boyish smile to redeem it." His "finely modelled nose and brow are his mother's." The general impression that Reuben gives is "of a dark deeply troubled animality beneath his surface—that positive bullish masculinity of his father curiously intensified in him by the influence of his mother's positive femininity. Yet at the same time warring with it, repeating the struggle and compelling attraction—the struggle between his parents." In the second scenario the son has already started college, where he develops a love for "erotic and sensual" poetry and, for the first time in his life, a rebellious attitude when his parents discourage him in his relationship with a fellow student, Ada Fife, whose father is Reverend Light's enemy.

The nonrealistic setting for the first half of the play shows interior and exterior views of the homes of the Lights and the Fifes. Only half sections, comprised of two rooms of the houses, are visible: the sitting room and Reuben's bedroom above in the Lights' shabby old white New England cottage, right; the sitting room and an upstairs bedroom in the Fifes' modern bungalow, left. The front walls that conceal these rooms are removed when the action requires it. The thunder and lightning of Act I, considered by Reuben as a manifestation of his Old Testament God, is replaced in later scenes by the hum of the new god, electricity. The dialogue is, as O'Neill notes, "a la *Interlude*"; asides are used, but because the author is dealing "with more simple people psychologically,"* they are far less effective.

The story presented in the first half of the play is relatively simple. Although ostensibly he is working on his next sermon, Reverend Light is hypocritically contemplating murdering his atheistic neighbor, Fife. "Is not the time ripe to smite this blasphemer who defies Thee publicly?" He is frustrated because he has failed to convert this "foul-mouthed scoundrel" who takes delight in questioning Reuben's purity in his intentions towards Ada Fife. Mrs. Light, resenting the poverty she has experienced in her twenty-three years of marriage, wants Reuben to go into business and to "marry a nice girl with money." The husband argues that it is God's will that their son become a minister. The thought of the ensuing scandal, should Reuben actually be attracted to Ada, his own humiliation, and the triumph of his nonbelieving rival maddens Light. His wife scorns the idea that her son would be attracted to a "painted flapper."

The second scene is set in the Fifes' sitting room. Ramsay Fife, fifty, has a biting tongue and a malicious sense of humor but is basically good-natured, "except when the religious bigotry of his atheism is concerned."

*Letter to Kenneth Macgowan, April 27, 1928.

His wife, May, forty, is a huge woman, weighing "well
over two hundred." Her once doll-like face, "in spite of its
fat," has kept "its girlish naïveté and fresh complexion."
Her hair is copper-colored, her eyes round and blue,
"their expression is blank and dreamy." Their daughter,
Ada, sixteen, inherits her mother's good looks and sentimentality; she also has her father's keen intelligence and
malicious sense of humor.

In earlier drafts Fife, the son of poor immigrant
parents, is forced to go to work after grammar school. He
studies electricity at night school and gets a job in a power
house. Electricity becomes his god. He loves three
things: his dynamo, his wife, and his daughter, who seems
to be a prototype of Josie Hogan in *A Moon for the
Misbegotten*: she "has a tongue that can be as scathing as
his own and a strong will of her own he cannot bully." His
wife, originally called Mary, is a good-hearted, simple
soul who is perpetually dreaming "heavily and emptily."
Like Nora Melody in *A Touch of the Poet*, the maternal
May "has been an easy victim." Seduced by Fife, she
became pregnant. She adores her husband, a "romantic
figure in her dull stupid life," for his noble offer to marry
her. Ada resembles other voluptuous O'Neill women,
such as Abbie Putnam and Sara Melody. "Her body has
soft, rounded feminine contours, full-breasted and broad-
hipped." Like Sara, "she bullies both of her parents, sees
through her father, loves her mother deeply and feels
immensely close to her—and takes up her defense whenever her father picks on her."

In the published version, Fife's plan to test Reuben
and the depth of his feeling for Ada is concocted in the
second scene and executed in the third. He sees a story in
the paper about a man who had killed another fellow in a
fight over a girl. She helped the murderer to escape, and
the two settled down, had a daughter, and became respectable citizens. Just before the daughter's marriage to
a minister, the father confessed his crime to the young

man, who then repudiated the girl and, "bound by his conscience," went to the police. Later, when Reuben expresses his desire to marry Ada, Fife confides "the secret of the family," pretending that he and his wife are the guilty couple in the story, after asking the young man to give his "word of honor, as man to man," not to repeat it. Horrified, Reuben looks at Ada: "the daughter of an adultress! . . . and a murderer!" Promising to keep the secret, the confused youth rushes from the room. Deeming the test to be unfair, Ada confounds her father by turning against him.

Mrs. Light is shown in her son's bedroom in Scene 4, dismayed by his disappearance. Just after her husband enters the room, she hears Reuben approaching and orders Light to hide in the closet. Feeling damned, but comforted by his mother's "maternal tenderness" and her oath "on the Bible" never to reveal his secret to anyone, including his father, Reuben repeats Fife's story. When the son admits his love for Ada, Mrs. Light angrily calls her a "little harlot" and summons her husband. Reuben is stunned by the betrayal of his mother, whom he had loved "better than any one in the world." All his life he had thought she loved him "better 'n any one." He denounces her now: "I'll do without a mother rather than have your kind." His father, after beating his son with a belt, goes out to report Fife to the police. The youth follows him and hears Ada explain the source of the story to Light. Reuben is overwhelmed by this second betrayal that night by a woman. Elated by the thunder, which had formerly frightened him, he rejects the God his father now evokes, saying, "There is no God! No God but Electricity!"

Fifteen months have elapsed at the start of Act II. Reverend Light, his hair nearly white, his face "a mask of stricken loneliness," is shown in his sitting room, mourning his deceased wife. Reuben stands outside the Fife home. He had left home immediatey after the row with his parents and had not returned. He has changed considerably. His face has grown callous, but not "without a desperate struggle to kill the shrinking boy in him." His eyes, chilled and frozen, "burn in their depths with a queer devouring intensity." Seeing Mrs. Fife at a window of her sitting room, he tells her of his new interest in electricity and dynamos. Dreamily, she hums in imitation of them, and he clasps her hand. When Ada appears, he boldly kisses her, becomes passionately aroused by her nearness, and invites her out to the hill where he watched the storm the night they parted: "That's the right place for us to love—on top of that hill—close to the sky—driven to love by what makes the earth go round." He asks her to encourage her father to give him a job at the electrical plant.

Reuben enters his home, still ignorant of his mother's death. Light gazes at his son, seeing him as "cruel and evil" and calling him a murderer: "You killed her as surely as if you'd given her poison, you unnatural accursed son!" Reuben believes that he converted his mother before her death to his god, electricity. This thought consoles him, and he ignores his father's comment that he has sold his soul to Satan.

In the next scene, later that evening, Reuben enters his bedroom with Ada. She regrets having slept with him and seeks the assurance that he loves her. He kisses her distractedly, informing her that "love is just sex—and there's no sin about it!" They are, he says, "married by Nature"; there is no need to have a minister pray over them. At his mother's grave that afternoon, the thought had occurred to him that "there was nothing to pray to." Like that other son who laments his sexual transgressions, Jim Tyrone in *A Moon for the Misbegotten*, Reuben longs for, but despairs of, a dead mother's forgiveness. Then he looks at the closet, remembers his mother's betrayal, and feels a surge of hatred. Yet he longs "to reach her somehow" and attributes his hunch about "praying to electricity" to her. He thinks of the mystery of "electrical wave stuff" and asks himself why "something like that" could not exist "between the dead and the living."

Scene 3 is comprised of one long soliloquy, in which Reuben venerates the dynamo. He is shown outside the hydroelectric plant a half hour later. Visible through the window of the dynamo room is the huge machine, looking like a "massive female idol." The sound of water from the dam merges with the machine's metallic purr. To Reuben, electricity, his mother, and God become one in the dynamo. It now personifies the mother figure. He uses human terms to describe the machine. Its round top forms a head, having eyes.

> Below it is like a body . . . not like a man's . . . round like a woman's . . . as if it had breasts . . . but not like a girl . . . not like Ada . . . no, like a woman . . . like her mother . . . or mine . . . a great, dark mother! . . . that's what the dynamo is! . . . that's what life is!

The song of the dynamo holds the secret of life; by knowing her, "you'd know the real God!" He addresses the "Mother of Life," begging her to seek his own mother's forgiveness. At the end of the scene he feels forgiven.

In Act III, which takes place four months later, Reuben stands outside the dynamo room with Mrs. Fife. The dynamo's singing resembles his mother's; it washes "all dirt and sin away." Reminiscent of Abbie's demeanor to Eben in *Desire Under the Elms*, Mrs. Fife puts her arms around Reuben and says: "I'll be your mother." From this point on, Reuben identifies Mrs. Fife with the dynamo and his own mother. To him, electricity is the "Great Mother of Eternal Life" and the dynamo is "her Divine Image on earth. Her power houses are the new churches!" If he remains chaste, she will give him the "secret of truth and he will become the new savior who will bring happiness and peace to men!" He becomes obsessed with the idea that he can be united with his mother through the "Great Mother into which she passed when she died."

Reuben has resisted the temptation to sleep with Ada for the past month but has not been able to kill his desire for her. He feels that he must do so. She must worship and atone with him, for "tonight the miracle will happen."

Later Reuben and Ada stand in the switch gallery above the dynamo before a network of wires, insulators, and switches. Frightened, she presses against him, but he scorns her "dirty game" and reminds her that she is in the dynamo's temple. She must pray now with arms outstretched like those of the dynamo, so that she will find him worthy. Ada must not tempt him with her protestations of love when his happiness and that of all mankind is at stake. With a moan of passion, Reuben kisses Ada "as a final test—to prove I'm purified." It is a test that he fails.

In the last scene of the play Mrs. Fife, in the dynamo room, relaxes, giving "herself up completely to the spell of its hypnotic, metallic purr." Ada stands on the platform before the kneeling, despairing Reuben, who murmurs: "Mother! . . . I've betrayed you." He attributes his new defilement to Ada, whose flesh has once again seduced him. He asks his mother for forgiveness and longs to go to her. The only thing that can free him from temptation is Ada's death. In a frenzy he runs to the switchboard room, takes a revolver from the drawer of a desk, and returns to Ada. Calling her "Harlot," he fires twice and then hastens to the dynamo room. There he climbs up the ladder rungs leading to the exciter head of his Dynamo-Mother. She need not bestow a miracle, he says: "I only want you to hide me, Mother! Never let me go from you again! Please, Mother!" When he throws his arms around the exciter, there is a flash of bluish light. All the lights in the plant dim; the noise of the dynamo is reduced to a faint hum.

> Simultaneously Reuben's voice rises in a moan that is a mingling of pain and loving consummation, and this cry dies into a sound that is like the crooning of a baby and merges and is lost in the dynamo's hum. Then his body crumples to the steel platform and from there falls heavily to the floor.

Mrs. Fife kneels beside the still body. Discovering that Reuben is dead, she pounds the dynamo resentfully, childishly and cries, "You hateful old thing, you!"

Two factors lead to Reuben's immolation; each relates to loss and a subsequent search. O'Neill stated that he wanted to stress the "unique relationship between the characters and life itself, to God." The only significant human relationship Reuben has, of any substance, is with his mother, although the rationale for this bond remains unclear. Amelia Light is a vindictive, jealous ogre; the thought that she could evoke love seems ludicrous. What O'Neill appears to be suggesting is that the mother-son relationship, irrespective of its nature—whether based on love or hate—is unique. Only the strength of this beyond-death bond explains and justifies Reuben's search for the mother after she dies and his adoration of the form she assumes for him: the dynamo. In an early draft, Reuben, like Caligula in *Lazarus Laughed*, who proposes marriage to an older woman, says to Mrs. Fife, "I wish you weren't married. I'd like to marry you." Later in the last scene of the play he "starts a queer marriage with Mrs. Fife as priestess in front of the dynamo—then suddenly realizes Dynamo should be real bride." Here he identifies Mrs. Fife with the dynamo, but the incestuous union he desires with this great earth mother is denied him. The only way left to him to attain total oneness with the Mother God figure is through immolation and death.

The first loss, of the mother, is closely associated with the second, of the mother's fanatical Calvinistic religion; in fact, the two losses are sustained simultaneously. The objects of them merge in the youth's mind, as his worship of the dynamo as both God and mother suggests. It is significant that Reuben turns to the primitive veneration of the dynamo when he perceives the failure of Calvinistic Christianity. Once again a character becomes disillusioned with religion because of man's inhumanity to man: the mother's betrayal and her cruel desire to have him beaten because he dared to love another.

The idea of betrayal by the mother, a major motif in the canon, is autobiographical in origin. When O'Neill was approximately Reuben's age, he experienced a similar sense of betrayal by his mother after he discovered that she was a morphine addict. Feeling that God had abandoned him when prayers failed to effect a cure, he subsequently confronted his father, as Reuben does, and told him of his decision to abandon the religion of his youth. Like Reuben's, his search for the lost mother merges with his quest to find a replacement for the "old God." *Dynamo* becomes a public expression of it.

The personal nature of the feelings expressed in *Dynamo* may, in part, account for its failure. O'Neill was not able to maintain an objective distance and allowed himself to be swept away on the tides of emotionalism. He tries to provide a lesson for godless America in *Dynamo* but fails when he uses a page from his own life to do so. He realized immediately after he completed the play and sent it to Langner that he released it too soon. He sensed that it was flawed. There was much he should have done: tighten up the dialogue and reduce the number of ineffective asides, shorten or eliminate the tediously long soliloquy in the second act that interrupts the action and pace of the play. The last scenes in the power plant form only a fraction of the work, but they dominate it. The intricacy of the machines cannot make up for the deficiency of conception. The feud between the fathers is melodramatic; if Reuben and Ada are the nearest approximations an American dramatist can make to those truly tragic young lovers, Romeo and Juliet, this country's theater is indeed barren.

The reviews of *Dynamo*, when it premiered in New York on February 11, 1929, castigated both the work and its author. News of the unfavorable notices reached O'Neill in France. Usually, part of his creative process was to "nurse" a play through the rehearsal period. Because he was in France and unable to assist in the staging of *Dynamo*, he assumed part of the responsibility for the play's failure, telling Langner in his letter of March 25, 1929, that had he been there he "might have been of help in clearing it up in spots." There seems to be little he could have done, however, to salvage the play.

A statement in the program note identifying *Dynamo* as the first play of a trilogy confused the critics, who were trying to comprehend and explain the work they had seen. In a letter to Robert Sisk on March 11, 1929, O'Neill states that "it was a great mistake for me to have said anything in advance about a trilogy or even to hint that it had anything to do with what was wrong with us, or to mention Gods, dead or alive, in any connection." The overall title he gives to the trilogy is "Myth Plays for the God-forsaken." Although the three plays were to be independent of each other, they were all to be "written around the general spiritual futility of the substitute-God search." He worked intermittently on the third play, "It Cannot Be Mad?" until 1937. While this play was never completed, the second work of the trilogy emerged, after many title changes, as *Days Without End*, which had, like *Dynamo*, a religious theme and was also a critical failure when it was produced in 1934.

Even after this setback, O'Neill was optimistic about *Dynamo*. In 1935 he told a friend, Leon Mirlas, an Argentine critic that "*Dynamo* I intend to rewrite someday. It has the makings of a fine play but I am by no means satisfied with it as it is." While *Dynamo* was vehemently attacked, O'Neill believed in the play, in the "human story" it told of a mother's betrayal of a son and the aftereffects: the loss of the mother and, simultaneously, the abandonment of her religion and the search for a substitute Mother God. He would continue this theme in *Days Without End*, the "Play of Catholic boyhood," and return to it a decade later, presenting the purest and most autobiographical expression of it in *Long Day's Journey into Night*.

IDEAS: 1921–1931 NOTEBOOK

Honest Honey Boy

The Homo Sapiens

The Great God Brown

All God's Chillun Got Wings

Desire Under the Elms

Silence Is Wisdom

Balaam's Ass

Marco Millions

Strange Interlude

Treason

God Goes Gaga

The Guilty One

Lazarus Laughed

Career of Shih Huang Ti

Love and Woman

Life of Saint Paul

Prester John

Squarehead Saga

Dynamo

Days Without End

Billionaire

It Cannot Be Mad?

Father and Son

Atlantis Series

The Guilty Are Guilty

Bantu Boy

Play of Astronomer

Modern Faust Play

The Sea-Mother's Son

Life of Man Play

Play of Love and Passion

Play of Divorced Wife

Play on Draft Riots

Parables of Christ

Falstaff–Prince Hal

Mourning Becomes Electra

Girl from Virginia

Uncharted Sea

The House

Life of Aeschylus

Tragedy of Man

The Mother God Death

Children's Play

Play of Psycho-therapeutist

Old Mother and Son

The Calms of Capricorn

The plays are listed in the order in which they appear in the notebook.

After two decades of writing, the playwright reassesses his life in 1933 at Casa Genotta, Sea Island, Georgia. *(Photograph courtesy of the Estate of Carl Van Vechten)*

O'Neill relaxes at Las Palmas, Canary Islands, March 1931, after completing *Mourning Becomes Electra*.

Nobel Prize recipient, 1936

Mourning Becomes Electra, New York, 1931. Christine Mannon (standing), Alla Nazimova; Lavinia, Alice Brady

Days Without End, New York, 1934. Father Baird, Richard Barbee; Elsa, Selena Royle; John, Earle Larimore; Loving, Stanley Ridges

Ah, Wilderness!, New York, 1933. Richard Miller, Elisha Cook, Jr.; Belle, Ruth Holden; Bartender, Donald McClelland

A Touch of the Poet, New York, 1957. Cornelius Melody, Eric Portman; Nora, Helen Hayes; Sara, Kim Stanley; Jamie Cregan, Curt Conway

3. Lost Horizons— Interrupted Journey

3. Lost Horizons— Interrupted Journey: "Self" Plays and the Cycle

The dramas O'Neill created in the early 1930s contain the same kind of autobiographical connotations found in work of the mid- and late 1920s. In *Mourning Becomes Electra* he follows the type of outline used earlier in *Desire Under the Elms*, *The Great God Brown*, and *Dynamo*, portraying himself as the son in conflict with the father and in love with the mother and giving all three the characteristics and/or the background of his parents and himself. He presents an even more personal portrait of the self in *Days Without End* and in *Ah, Wilderness!*, which is set in a house identical to the O'Neill family summer home. *Long Day's Journey into Night* would seem to be the logical follow-up. The sequel was deferred, however, when O'Neill was diverted in the mid-1930s by a plan to write a historical Cycle, dramatizing the lives of "five generations of a family." The purportedly imaginary family became, in time, his own.

A spate of ideas for plays conceived in the late 1920s focuses on either death or dying. Heroes commit suicide in two 1927 concepts: "Billionaire" and "Play of Catholic Boyhood" (later *Days Without End*) and in the completed dramas *Dynamo* (1928) and *Mourning Becomes Electra*

(1929–1931). The central figure in the "Modern Faust Play" (1927) finds "himself about to die"; the main character in "The Sea-Mother's Son" (1928) is "at the point of death." Most of the heroes depicted have experienced some type of loss or change in their lives; some are making a transition. The concept of betrayal, which permeates the work of these years, had its origin in O'Neill's own life.

The late 1920s were a period of tremendous introspection for O'Neill. The year 1927 was one of the most crucial in his life; he experienced a great inner personal struggle, torn between his love for Carlotta Monterey and his sense of duty to his wife, Agnes, and their two children, Shane and Oona. The decision in 1928 to abscond with Carlotta and abandon his wife and children instilled guilt feelings in him. In the 1928 idea "Play of Divorced Wife," he attempts to transfer this guilt by having the wife walk out on her husband and will "her children outright to him—she is never to see them again—the effect on her as her life goes on, and on the children as they grow up—a boy and girl—father has told them what mother has done." Even though O'Neill later railed at Agnes after she refused, at first, to give him a divorce, he felt sadness and a sense of loss when the ten-year marriage ended. More important for the effect it had on his work, the man knew that *he* had been the guilty one, the betrayer of love. Guilt came cloaked in religious raiment, as it does for his heroes. Despite the fact he was no longer a practicing Catholic, he had a deeply spiritual attitude to marriage. The sacramental nature of marriage would be stressed in *Days Without End* as it had been in the 1924 *Welded*.

In O'Neill's mind the concept of wife betrayal merges with the deeply ingrained sense of guilt for mother betrayal, although the former is always subordinate to the latter. Loss of the mother figure, usually through death, is often accompanied by some type of newly created religious vacuum. The mother is frequently responsible for the loss of faith; therefore, the hero's subsequent search

for religious certitude is associated in some way with
regaining the mother. Death becomes the usual way of
reunion.

In the late 1920s O'Neill began a trilogy, "Myth Plays
for the God-forsaken," written, as he says "around the
general spiritual futility of the substitute-God search." In
Dynamo, the first play, Reuben Light, after losing both
his mother and the religion of his youth, begins to worship
a female God figure, the "Mother Dynamo," in a power
plant, his "temple." To him, "God has become Mother
who is Electricity—his search to know Her, love Her,
adore Her." The second work, *Days Without End*, is a
Catholic version of *Dynamo*.* In his original idea for the
former, the "Play of Catholic Boyhood," dated 1927, the
hero, John Loving, was to have become a Catholic priest;
in the plan for the latter, Reuben was destined to be a
Baptist minister. John's mother betrays him by dying;
seeking a mother substitute, he marries a woman who
resembles her. He is guilt ridden when the wife becomes
ill after discovering her husband's infidelity. When he
thinks the wife-mother is dying, he decides to commit
suicide, certain that "she will be waiting" if he believes in
"his old God of Love and seeks her through Him." In the
early notes for *Days Without End*, the hero goes to a
Catholic church with a gun, determined to sacrifice himself before a female spiritual figure, a statue of the Virgin
and Child.

The trilogy "Myth Plays for the God-forsaken" is a
transition marker. The first "Myth" play, *Dynamo*, was

_____

*The third play of the trilogy, "It Cannot Be Mad?," was never
completed. Part I of the 1927 original idea traces the meteoric
rise to wealth and power of an impoverished orphan, Bessie
Wilks, who marries Howard Camp of Camp Motor. The couple,
like Sara and Simon Harford in the Cycle plays, have four
children. In March 1929, after correcting proofs for *Dynamo*,
O'Neill resumed work on "It Cannot Be Mad?," changing its title
to "On To Betelgeuse." On July 19, 1932, he again renamed the
work. At that time *Days Without End* was entitled "Without
Endings of Days." He states that the three plays were to be

the last work O'Neill finished in the 1920s; the second, *Days Without End*, is one of the first he completed in the early 1930s. The heroes of both plays can, with justification, be called "God-forsaken"; both are self-portraits. While events and characters in *Dynamo* parallel those in O'Neill's life, *Days Without End*, in its notes and seven drafts, forms the most autobiographical extant document. Whereas *Long Day's Journey into Night* focuses primarily on the author's parents and *A Moon for the Misbegotten* is a memory play about his brother, Jamie, *Days Without End* is O'Neill's account of his own spiritual odyssey. He described the feelings he experienced while writing the play to Russel Crouse: "I was sweating blood getting this opus out of my system" (letter of February 27, 1934). The words echo those O'Neill used when discussing the composition of *Long Day's Journey into Night* and *the Great God Brown*, the notes for which are more autobiographical than the published plays.

Just as O'Neill's first triology, "Myth Plays for the God-forsaken," which never completely materialized, was a transitional work in time and concept, so too was the second trilogy, *Mourning Becomes Electra*, which he did finish. The author began writing the first draft of the *Electra* trilogy on November 12, 1929, after leasing a chateau, Le Plessis, in northern France; he finished the sixth draft on March 28, 1931, six weeks before his return to the United States. It is the second work he completed after he began living with Carlotta Monterey. The first, *Dynamo*, which premiered on February 11, 1929, the day after the "1st Anniversary of our Elopement," filled him

published "in one book 'Dynamo' (rewritten), 'Without Endings of Days' and 'On to Hercules.'" The three works are linked in one of Loving's remarks in *Days Without End*. Discussing fate, he says: "We know we are all the slaves of meaningless chance— electricity or something, which whirls us on to Hercules." He refers to the constellation which shows the godlike Hercules in a kneeling position. Renamed "The Life of Bessie Bowen" in September 1932, the Bessie Wilks drama eventually became the last work of the Cycle: "Hair of the Dog."

with a sense of foreboding, as he noted in his Work Diary the next day: "This one is not right." When his fear was realized, he was disappointed, as he wanted the "first fruit" of their union to be successful. His second work, *Mourning Becomes Electra*, which opened on October 26, 1931, two years after his marriage to Carlotta on July 22, 1929, proved to be his finest play, in scope and execution, prior to the work of 1939 and one of the supreme achievements of twentieth-century drama.

The trilogy approximates in its plot and characters Aeschylus' *Oresteia*. O'Neill changes the setting from Argos to New England. The Civil War, rather than the Trojan War, becomes the "background for drama of murderous family love & hate." Even though the basic story of *Mourning Becomes Electra* parallels, in general, the Greek trilogy, the work has many autobiographical elements. These are most conspicuous in the early scenarios for the plays, as they foreshadow *Long Day's Journey into Night*. In them the setting is identified as New London; the name of New London's leading family, the Chappells, who are prototypes for the Mannons, appears. The mother figure, Christine Mannon, is clearly an early portrait of Mary Tyrone. Aspects of the Mannons' marriage are found later in the Tyrones'. For a brief time, there was to have been a second Mannon son, Hugh, who is Orin's preferred rival for the affections of the mother, foreshadowing the Jamie-Edmund relationship. The two sons merge, however, and become one, Orin, a self-portrait. *Mourning Becomes Electra* is an elaborate mosaic into which O'Neill again unconsciously embedded pieces of the "self."

Once again a motif found in the 1928 *Dynamo* and repeated in the 1932–1933 *Days Without End* emerges: the death of the mother and the desire of the son to attain union with her through death. The common theme of betrayal links the works. Christine Mannon takes a lover and deceives her son, who worships her. Orin kills the lover and thus betrays the mother, who subsequently shoots herself. Orin ceases to be a self-portrait in the fatal path he follows. At the end of the trilogy, O'Neill identifies not with this weak figure who chooses death rather than life but with the strong-minded Lavinia, the last of the Mannons, who selects a living death to atone for her crimes and those of her family and immures herself in the Mannon home.

Throughout the 1920s O'Neill and his heroes seemed obsessed with death. The most significant difference between the two completed "Myth Plays" is that *Dynamo*'s central figure, Reuben Light, kills himself, while John Loving in *Days Without End*, who also contemplates suicide, rejects death. At the end, "he walks out of the church—without love forever now—but daring to face his eternal loss and hopelessness, to accept it as his fate and go on with life." In this choice he resembles Lavinia and their creator. In the early 1920s O'Neill, like his heroine, lost parents and brother. He was, as his ideas and plays of the late 1920s reflect, consumed with a death wish and guilt for some perceived misdeeds. At some point at the start of the 1930s, he rejected death unequivocally. He suggests through Lavinia's choice that the greatest self-punishment a person can inflict is to shut himself off from mankind and to retreat behind a wall of solitude. It is a choice the author himself selected in the 1930s.

In May 1931, after returning to New York from France in May and seeing *Mourning Becomes Electra* through its rehearsal period in September, O'Neill hired a chauffeur and toured the South seeking a suitable location in which to settle. He and Carlotta found a secluded refuge in the home they subsequently built at Sea Island, Georgia. On October 4, 1936, however, four years after moving into the house, the author was packing for a trip to the West, stating in the Work Diary, "climate no good for work half of year—and feel am jinxed here." Later, in

Seattle, Washington, he received word on November 12
that he had been awarded the Nobel Prize. In December
he and Carlotta traveled to San Francisco. The following
year they moved into their second newly built home, Tao
House, in Danville, California. All the plays completed in
the 1930s, with the exception of *Mourning Becomes Electra*, were written in solitude in these isolated retreats.

Initially, O'Neill was proud and joyous about the
acquisition of the Sea Island home. Shortly before he
moved into the new house, some kind of inner transformation occurred. In his letter of May 29, 1932, to Dudley
Nichols, he discusses his positive attitude to life:

> Funny, your writing me at this particular time about affir-
> mation. I am changing inside me, as I suppose one always
> does, or ought to do if there is growth, when one has passed
> forty, and even the most affirmative Nay! of my past work no
> longer satisfies me. So I am groping after a real, true Yea! in
> the play I'm now starting [Days Without End]—a very old
> Yea, it is true, in essence, but completely forgotten in all its
> inner truth that it might pass for brand new. Whether I will
> be able to carry the writing of it up to Yea! remains to be
> seen.

The change in the dramatist is manifested in the choice
the hero makes in *Days Without End*. In the original 1927
idea, during O'Neill's death wish-despair period, the
central figure "takes a revolver and shoots himself before
a statue of Christ & Virgin." In the May 12, 1932, notes,
he rejects death and "puts his revolver at the base of the
crucifix and makes the sign of the cross." When the dramatist mentions the play in his letter of October 25, 1933,
to Macgowan, he says he "felt a need to liberate myself
from myself" and to express the "life preserving forces."

On September 1, 1932, shortly after expressing his
"real, true Yea" and while he was developing *Days Without End*, the author recorded the title "Ah, Wilderness!"
in his Work Diary and states, "awoke with idea for this
'Nostalgic Comedy' & worked out tentative outline—

seems fully formed & ready to write." As he had in *Mourning Becomes Electra* and *Days Without End*, O'Neill depicts another self-portrait: Richard Miller, a seventeen-year-old would-be writer and radical, who is trying desperately to make the transition from youth to young manhood. The comedy contains elements found eight years later in *Long Day's Journey into Night*: twenty-three-year-old Edmund Tyrone is Richard Miller grown disillusioned with life.

Ah, Wilderness!, which has always been considered so atypical of O'Neill, should be viewed as a derivation from the autobiographical material the dramatist had accumulated—both mentally and artistically—for *Days Without End*. His words attest to this statement: "I'm so close to both these plays." He called the latter a "Play of Catholic Boyhood"; he said of the former, "That's the way I would like my boyhood to have been." He cites *Days Without End* as an example of a new trend in his work: "For, after all, this play, like 'Ah, Wilderness!' but in a much deeper sense, is the pay of an old debt on my part—a gesture toward more comprehensive, unembittered understanding and inner freedom—the breaking away from an old formula" (letter to Langner, October 29, 1933). While he is announcing his movement away from his former tragic sense of life, he also seems to imply that he has come to a more "unembittered understanding" of himself, his family, and his past and has reached a stage of "inner freedom." *Ah, Wilderness!* is not only the precurser but also the prerequisite for writing *Long Day's Journey into Night*.

After completing *Ah, Wilderness!* in June 1933 and *Days Without End* the following December, O'Neill began developing a 1931 idea for a sea play, *The Calms of Capricorn*. In the next years, the drama grew from a single work to a four-play series to an eleven-play Cycle, which was eventually entitled "A Tale of Possessors Self-Dispossessed." The focus of the series was the separate lives of four brothers. O'Neill kept extending the project

backward in time, first to include the brothers' parents,
Sara and Simon Harford, and then to include their parents and forebears.

The time frame of the complete Cycle runs from 1755
to 1932. As its title suggests, one of the major themes of
the project is American greed and materialism. The author was not interested in possessiveness per se but in the
debilitating effects it has on those who came to the New
World seeking to escape the poverty of the Old World. In
a letter to Langner dated August 12, 1936, the author
states:

> I'm not giving a damn whether the dramatic event of each
> play has any significance in the growth of the country or not,
> as long as it is significant in the spiritual and psychological
> history of the American family in the plays. The Cycle is
> primarily just that, the history of a family. What larger
> significance I can give my people as extraordinary examples
> and symbols in the drama of American possessiveness and
> materialism is something else again. . . . I am not much
> interested in economic determinism—but only in the self-
> determinism of which the economic is one phase and by no
> means the most revealing—at least, not for me.

Two major conflicts emerge in the two extant plays of
the Cycle, *A Touch of the Poet*, set in 1828, and its sequel,
More Stately Mansions, set in 1832: an exterior battle
fought between the newly arrived Irish immigrants and
the firmly established Yankees and an interior struggle
waged within the soul of the central male figure in each
drama between his dual natures: the idealistic poet and
the materialistic businessman. In the first work the ambitious Irish woman, Sara Melody, the most avaricious
woman in the canon, destroys the touch of the poet in her
father, Con; in the second, she achieves a double victory:
killing her husband's poetic aspirations and transforming
him into a wealthy businessman and defeating the Yankee
Deborah Harford.

The play that inspired the Cycle, *The Calms of Cap-*

ricorn, became its fifth work. While its scenario was completed in June 1935, notes and drafts for it, along with those for the other dramas, were later destroyed. The scenario survived and was sent by O'Neill and his wife in 1951, along with the typescript for *More Stately Mansions*, to Yale University. Donald Gallup, curator of the O'Neill collection, prepared a two-volume edition of *The Calms of Capricorn* consisting of the transcribed scenario and a developed version of the play. Some O'Neill scholars have criticized the decision to release this material in its incomplete form. Such objections are unreasonable. Mr. Gallup has performed a great service to students of O'Neill's work; the new Cycle material provides valuable insights into the way the dramatist intended to develop its individual components. Mr. Gallup has done more than anyone else in this country to preserve the O'Neill legacy intact and to avoid any violation of it.

The primary focus of *The Calms of Capricorn* is the eldest son of Simon and Sara Harford, Ethan, twenty-eight, who has "the curse of the poet." Yet it also continues the story of Sara after her husband's death and of her other three sons. Seeking wealth and a new life beyond New England, the five Harfords set sail in 1857 on a clipper ship bound for California. During the voyage, three of the brothers (Ethan; Wolfe, twenty-seven; and Jonathan, twenty-five) become involved with three women who seem destined in subsequent plays to help their men "take possession of the world." Ethan, the ship's second mate, kills the malicious first mate accidentally. The ship's captain, Enoch Payne, out of necessity, promotes Ethan, who later has an affair with Payne's young wife, Nancy. The word "calms" in the play's title refers to the strange stillness of the winds after the captain's murder, thus preventing the ship, the *Dream of the West*, from beating the sailing record. As the scenario unfolds, the play becomes a dramatization of the theme of crime and punishment.

The underlying motif of *The Calms of Capricorn* and
the other plays of the Cycle is found in the Biblical quotation, "What shall it profit a man, if he shall gain the whole
world and lose his own soul." Once again, as he had done
in *Desire Under the Elms* and *Marco Millions* in the
1920s, O'Neill shows the tragic consequences of material
prosperity on the accumulators of wealth. However, the
Cycle is much more than a study of greed or a historical
project; the autobiographical characters and concepts of
the two extant plays classify it as another personal document. The Irish O'Neills, like the Melodys in *A Touch of
the Poet*, were rejected by native Yankee New Londoners. Simon Harford in *More Stately Mansions* is one of the
most accurate self-portraits in the canon—in his appearance and nature and in his relationship with his mother,
Deborah, O'Neill's closest approximation to his own
mother before Mary Tyrone. Simon is a direct descendent
of those other infatuated sons, Reuben Light, Orin Mannon, John Loving. Like them, he loses his mother—not
to death but to madness. Like them, he wants to join his
mother, and he can do so only if he relinquishes his own
sanity and follows her into the summer house.

After a brief respite in the early 1930s, O'Neill, at the
end of the decade, returned to his former "tragic sense of
life." On June 5, 1939, he notes in his Work Diary that
what he has done on the fifth play of the Cycle, *The Calms
of Capricorn*, is no good "so tear it up. Feel fed up & stale
on Cycle after 4½ years of not thinking of any other
work—will do me good lay on shelf and forget it for a
while—do a play which has nothing to do with it." The
following day he recorded his first reference to the two
great works he planned to outline: *The Iceman Cometh*
and *Long Day's Journey into Night*. After veering off
course slightly, he continued in his work his life's journey.

41. *Mourning Becomes Electra*

*Mourning Becomes Electra** had a lengthy germinal period. In the late 1920s O'Neill became fascinated with
what he called "the Electra story." In the spring of 1926
he read Arthur Symons's translation of Hugo von Hof-
mannstahl's *Electra* and recorded this entry in his Work
Diary on April 26: "Germ idea use Greek Tragedy plot in
modern setting." He did not pursue this idea until October 1928, a month after completing *Dynamo*. In his
notebook entry he reveals his intention to adapt the plot
of Aeschylus' *Oresteia*: "Use the plots from Greek tragedy
in modern surroundings—the New England play of Agamemnon, Clytemnestra, Electra & Orestes—Oedipus."

The dramatist did not begin to write the trilogy until
the spring of 1929, after his return to France from the Far
East. In addition to his regular Work Diary, he began
keeping a "Fragmentary Diary" devoted exclusively to
notations for the new Greek drama, *Mourning Becomes
Electra*. The April entries reveal his deliberate efforts to
parallel the plot and characters of the *Oresteia*. He states:
"In legend Thyestis seduces—Aerope, wife of Atreus—
hatred of Atreus for brother—revenge—banishment." In
O'Neill's version of these actions, which occurs before the
play opens, Abe and David Mannon are rivals in their love
for Marie Brantôme, who is the nurse of the former's
child. When Marie becomes pregnant with David's child,
Abe, consumed with jealousy and fearful of a scandal,
angrily expels his brother and Marie from the family

*The copyright date is May 12, 1931. The play opened in New
York on October 26, 1931, and won the unanimous praise of
critics and theatergoers.

home. He then burns down the house and builds in its place a grotesque monument to his hatred.

Maliciously, Abe gives David but a small fraction of his actual inheritance. Later, David begins to drink heavily when he fails to find employment; he is a weak man, and in his despair he commits suicide, leaving his widow and young son, Adam, destitute. After Adam goes to sea at age seventeen, his impoverished mother begs Ezra Mannon in vain for financial help. When Adam (who uses the surname Brant, a shortened form of Brantôme) comes home, he swears to avenge his mother's death.

When the play opens, Ezra Mannon, Abe's son (the Agamemnon counterpart), has married Christine (Clytemnestra) and fathered a daughter, Lavinia (Electra), and a son, Orin (Orestes). As in the Greek trilogy, the wife falls in love with the Aegisthus character, Adam Brant, and together they plot the death of her husband. At the time of the deception Ezra is serving as Brigadier General in Grant's army. O'Neill decided that the Civil War was the "only possibility" to replace the Trojan War: "fits into picture—Civil War as background for drama of murderous family love & hate." The dramatist places the House of Mannon (Atreus) in a small seaport in New England, believing this setting to be "best possible for Greek plot of crime and retribution chain of fate—Puritan connotation of man born to sin and punishment."

In his attempt to evoke the spirit of Aeschylus, O'Neill makes the exterior of the Mannon house a replica of a Greek edifice, with a white Grecian temple portico with six tall columns. These "cast black bars of shadow on the gray wall behind them." The portico is "like an incongruous white mask fixed on the house to hide its somber gray ugliness." In the earlier Puritan New England tragedy, *Desire Under the Elms*, a stone wall cut off the house, which was also a "sickly grayish" color, from the outside world. In *Mourning Becomes Electra* the property is "enclosed by a white picket fence and a tall hedge."

For the exterior scenes a special curtain, revealing the extensive grounds, "shows the house as seen from the street."

Each of O'Neill's three plays corresponds to a Greek equivalent. The first, *Homecoming,* like *Agamemnon,* shows a deceived husband returning home, grateful to have survived the war, and, ironically, being murdered in his own bed. Again, trying to emulate Greek dramatists, O'Neill uses a Chorus to provide the exposition. He writes: "Use townsfolk at the beginning of each play, outside house, as fixed chorus pattern—representing prying commenting, curious town as ever-present background for drama of Mannon family." The person who serves as the Chorus Leader is Seth Beckwith, the Mannons' gardener-caretaker. The song that he sings, the chanty "Shenandoah," the first utterance of the play, is identified by the author as a "theme song—its simple sad rhythm of hopeless sea longing peculiarly significant— even the stupid words have striking meaning when considered in relation to tragic events in play." The lines are repeated frequently in the play.

Oh, Shenandoah, I long to hear you
A-way, my rolling river
Oh, Shenandoah, I can't get near you
Way-ay, I'm bound away
Across the wide Missouri.

Implicit in the words of this "theme song" is the underlying meaning of the play. O'Neill writes that "fate from within the family is the modern psychological approximation of the Greek conception of fate from without, from the supernatural." In Greek tragedy the lives of heroes are controlled by external forces: the gods; in contrast, the Mannons are victims of their heredity and their accumulated history. The concept of family fate is epitomized in the word "bound" and its sundry interpretations. The word signifies "predetermined"; the actions of the Mannons and the circumstances that motivate them are determined by their family history and by their ancestors, whose crimes have placed a hereditary curse on them. The protective mask on the facade of the house represents their vain attempt to keep the secrets of the past hidden. Seth says, "There's been evil in that house since it first was built in hate and it's kept growin' there ever since as what's happened there has proved."

The word "bound" also means "land within certain border" and "placed under legal or moral constraint; obligation." O'Neill purposefully sets the play in New England and depicts the Mannons as being as cold, severe, and joyless as the barren landscape. They are deeply affected by the constraining Puritan codes of morality, sexually inhibited and incapable of expressing normal emotions. Significantly, the Mannons have become enforcers of legalistic Puritan morality. After accumulating a fortune from their shipping industry, they turn to civic duty. Ezra Mannon, according to Seth, "learned law on the side and got made a judge. Went in fur politics an' got 'lected mayor." Having been, as he says, "top dog around here for near on two hundred years," the Mannons are fiercely protective of their name and reputation and are devoted to duty. Lavinia's perverted sense of responsibility and justice precipitates much of the family's tragedy.

In addition, the word "bound" or "tied" describes the unnatural bonds linking the characters. One of the Greek tragedies O'Neill indicates in his original 1926 idea that he wants to explore is "Oedipus." From this, he extracts the incest motif, giving the Mannons an Oedipus or Electra complex. To illustrate visually their incestuous natures, the author gives the Mannon men and women a definite family resemblance. All of them are described as having the same type of masklike countenance. At first he intended to use half-masks, as in *Lazarus Laughed*, but he discards them for facial approximations. In describing Christine's face, for example, the author writes, "One is struck at once by the strange impression given in repose of being not living flesh but a wonderfully life-like pale mask." Amos Ames, one of the townsfolk, says, "That's the Mannon look. They all has it. They grows it on their wives. Seth's growed it on too—from bein' with 'em all his life. They don't want folks to guess their secrets."

O'Neill recorded a plan in the Fragmentary Diary to establish

> a resemblance between Ezra and Orin and Adam (and family portraits), and between Christine and Lavinia—peculiar gold-brown hair exactly alike in Lavinia and her mother—same as hair of the dead woman, Adam's mother, whom Ezra's father and uncle had loved—who started the chain of recurrent love and hatred and revenge—emphasize this motivating fate out of the past.

Christine harbors unnatural thoughts about her son and creates in him a lust for her. When Orin joins Grant's army, she finds a natural outlet for her feelings in her affair with a more sexually acceptable son substitute, Adam Brant. Orin represses his desire for his mother and transfers it, after her death, to the look-alike sister, Lavinia. She has a father fixation and asserts that she will never love any other man. She is, however, fascinated by the physically similar Adam. This unhealthy absorption with family members makes the Mannons increasingly introspective and stultifies their emotional development.

The word "bound" also has a positive connotation: "to leap forward or upward." Each of the Mannons attempts to hurdle familial and social barriers and cherishes a desire to escape to a refuge in the South Seas called the Blessed Isles. Living in a seaport town, they are continually reminded when they look out to the horizon that they are landlocked in New England by fate. O'Neill explains the significance of the Blessed Isles in his Fragmentary Diary:

> Develop South Sea Island motive—its appeal for them all (in various aspects)—release, peace, security, beauty, freedom of conscience, sinlessness, etc.—longing for the primi-

> tive and mother symbol—yearning for pre-natal, non-com-
> petitive freedom from fear—make this Island theme recur-
> rent motive—. . . .

Orin and Lavinia manage to escape to the Blessed
Isles for a short time, but on their return home they find
themselves again doomed by the Mannon curse. One way
to be free of it is through death, Orin's course of action.
The alternative, death-in-life, becomes Lavinia's choice.
She will expiate the curse and atone for the crimes of her
family and ancestors. As she remarks to the gardener at
the end of the play, after hearing him sing "Shenandoah"
a final time, "I'm not bound away—not now, Seth. I'm
bound here—to the Mannon dead!"

Homecoming

When *Homecoming* opens, Seth is shown outside the Mannon home with three of the townspeople. The gardener boasts of Ezra Mannon's brave exploits in the current war and the Mexican War. The sudden appearance of the beautiful Christine on the portico awes them. She is a "tall striking-looking woman of forty but she appears younger." Dressed in an expensive green satin dress, she has a "voluptuous figure" and "moves with a flowing animal grace." Her thick curly hair is "partly a copper brown, partly a bronze gold." Her eyes are of a dark violet blue. "Her chin is heavy, her mouth large and sensual, the lower lip full, the upper a thin bow." Lavinia, twenty-three, enters. She has a "facial resemblance to her mother. She has the same peculiar shade of copper-gold hair, the same pallor and dark violet-blue eyes . . . the same sensual mouth, the same heavy jaw." She also possesses the "same strange, life-like mask impression her face gives in repose." Her body, however, is thin, flat-breasted, and angular. She wears a plain black dress. "Her movements are stiff and she carries herself with a wooden, square-shouldered, military bearing."

Lavinia is joined by Hazel Niles, nineteen, an amiable, innocent young girl, who is in love with Orin, and Hazel's brother, Peter, twenty-two, a good-natured, straightforward fellow, who wants to marry Lavinia. When he proposes, as he had the previous year, she responds, "I can't marry anyone, Peter. I've got to stay home. Father needs me." Cynically, she says that she knows nothing about love and never wants to know anything: "I hate love!" She assures Peter that she loves him like a brother. Peter sees a rival in Adam Brant, the romantic looking, mysterious clipper captain, who has been coming to the house. Later Lavinia questions Seth about Brant's identity. The gardener performs the same role as Teiresias in *Oedipus Rex*: he knows the past crimes and intrigues of the characters. To help the unaware Lavinia piece together the puzzle of her family's history, Seth explains why Lavinia feels she has met Brant before: he resembles her father and brother and also her grandfather's brother, David.

Lavinia takes Seth's advice and tricks Brant into revealing his real identity. Tall and broad-shouldered, the captain has an aquiline nose, a swarthy complexion, and a sensual mouth. His broad forehead is framed by black hair, which he wears "pushed back carelessly from his forehead as a poet's might be." His face in repose also has the quality "of being a life-like mask rather than living flesh." He speaks passionately now and describes the islands in the South Seas where he was once shipwrecked, the Blessed Isles, where the natives "live in as near the Garden of Paradise before sin was discovered as you'll find on this earth!" Repulsed by his "cheap romantic lies," Lavinia calls him the "son of a low Canuck nurse girl!" Brant reveals the truth, curses Lavinia, and describes Abe and Ezra Mannon's cruel treatment of his parents.

The second act in Ezra Mannon's study follows immediately. The room is dominated by Ezra's portrait above the fireplace. His face is "handsome in a stern, aloof fashion. It is cold and emotionless and has the same strange semblance of a life-mask as the other Mannon faces." Having followed Christine to New York and to Brant's room, Lavinia confronts her mother, accusing her of adultery. Christine expresses her revulsion for having had to sleep with Ezra, a man she has hated, for twenty years. Lavinia was, the mother asserts, born of her husband's body, not her own, and she is a continual reminder of Christine's horrible wedding night and honeymoon. She had tried to love her daughter but failed. Orin, on the other hand, is solely hers; Ezra was in the army in Mexico when she was carrying him. The distraught woman blames her daughter for her infidelity. If Lavinia had not driven Orin away to fight in the war, the mother would never have fallen in love with Adam. Christine promises, in return for the daughter's silence, never to see Adam again. The mother accuses the jealous daughter of wanting to go away with Adam and says, "I know you, Vinnie! I've watched you ever since you were little, trying to do exactly what you're doing now! You've tried to become the wife of your father and the mother of Orin! You've always schemed to steal my place!"

When alone, the lovers conspire to kill Ezra. Adam rejects Christine's scheme at first, but she arouses his greed and his desire for revenge. As Ezra's widow, she would bring Brant that part of the Mannon estate that was stolen from his father. Brant dreams of buying his own clipper ship and sailing with Christine on their honeymoon to his Blessed Isles. Their fate together is sealed when Adam promises to send the poison she requests. Christine thinks triumphantly that Brant will never dare leave her now.

A week later, in Act III, Ezra Mannon returns from the war. The masklike look is "more pronounced in him than in the others." His voice has a "hollow repressed quality." He accepts Lavinia's joyous kisses and stares at Christine, unable to conceal the "deep undercurrent of suppressed feeling." He sits awkwardly on the stone steps, between the two women. Because of his weak heart, Ezra has been warned by doctors to avoid overexertion or excitement. When Lavinia mentions Adam Brant's name and Christine quickly implies that he is Vinnie's latest beau, Mannon remarks jealously, "I want you to remain my little girl."

After Lavinia is sent to bed, Ezra awkwardly kisses his wife and confesses his dream of returning home to her. For the first time in his life he expresses all his inner feelings and longings. Away from New England and faced continually with death during the war, Ezra began to question his previous way of life. He sees the error of the

"Mannons' way of thinking," their meditations on death on Sabbath days. "Life was a dying. Being born was starting to die. Death was being born." He wants to make up for the years lost to him because of his earlier ingrained denial of life and suggests that they go away to "some island" in the South Seas. Christine responds with indifference, as Abbie did to a similar outpouring from the love-starved Ephraim in *Desire Under the Elms*. Christine cringes at Ezra's touch. Seeing him withdraw, wounded, into his old protective armor, she realizes her mistake and forces herself to kiss him passionately.

In the last act, set at dawn the following morning, Ezra suspects that he has already been dispossessed, that the house, room, and bed are no longer his: "They are empty—waiting for someone to move in! And you are not my wife! You are waiting for something! . . . For death— to set you free!" Christine deliberately goads him "with calculating cruelty." She admits that Brant is her lover and reveals his family identity. When Ezra has a heart seizure, she substitutes a pellet from a small box for the medicine he requests. Instantly, he realizes that he has been poisoned and calls out for his daughter. Lavinia rushes to her father's side in time to hear his last words: "She's guilty—not medicine!" She accepts Christine's explanation that she had merely told him about Adam. When the distraught, guilt-ridden mother faints, however, she drops the pill box. Kneeling to determine her mother's condition, Lavinia discovers the box. Horrified, she cries out to her father for help.

O'Neill skillfully modernizes the basic plot of Aeschylus' *Agamemnon* in *Homecoming*. In an early scheme the Mannons have two other daughters, Effie and Crystal, as had Agamemnon and Clytemnestra (Iphegenia and Chrysothemis). In May 1929 the dramatist entered the "Story of the First Play" in a bound notebook. At that time he had not worked out the intricate parallels between his own trilogy and that of Aeschylus. The early concept seemed like an early version of *Long Day's Journey into Night* for a brief period. O'Neill refers in one passage to a second Mannon son, Hugh, who is Orin's preferred rival for the affections of the mother, foreshadowing again the Jamie-Edmund relationship. Here Hugh, who resembles the mother and possesses a soul too rare and delicate for war, is the self-portrait. This plan was discarded, and Orin took on all the qualities of Hugh.

The dramatist clearly identifies the setting of the trilogy as his hometown New London, stating: "Christine has always hated the town of N.L. and felt a superior disdain for its inhabitants." This sentiment will be voiced later by Mary Tyrone, who feels similarly isolated in a hostile New England environment. Similar words are used to describe these two women. Christine's hair is the same color that Mary's was before it turned white. Both women have detached, aloof, sensitive natures. Their husbands are considerably older than they, and the marriages of both are described in the notes as "a romantic mistake." As a consequence, they turn to their younger children, who resemble them, the sons Orin and Edmund, and become obsessively possessive. Christine, like the early Mary Tyrone, pays for her clothes "out of a generous yearly income left by her father," who has spoiled her.

Christine's lover was not originally related to the Mannons. Identified as Gustave de Bouville and the youngest wastrel son of a wealthy French nobleman, he was a Harvard graduate and a gentleman of leisure, "an exquisite man-about-town dabbling in the arts, his principal occupation that of a lover of women." Ezra's role in the first scheme was to have been much larger than it is in the published text. For the third act, after his homecoming, the author contemplated one of those impossible family gatherings, like those in the first scenes of *Bread and Butter* and *The First Man*. The two young couples, Effie and Crystal and their husbands, resemble those in *The*

First Man, Curt Jayson's brother and sister and their spouses. Ezra's suspicions about his wife's fidelity are aroused by an anonymous letter he receives. She quickly allays his fears at the end of Act III. O'Neill planned at first to use asides, as he had in *Strange Interlude*, to reveal secret desires and fears of the two characters: "Her heart cries out: 'O God, let him die!' He is thinking of the Doctor's warning about no sex for a while—dismissing it contemptuously."

After finishing the scenario for the first part of the trilogy on June 20, the author spent the next six days "studying Greek plays." As a result of this reading—"plots from Greek tragedy" and "Oedipus"—new elements are stressed in the second part: the Greek sense of family fate and the crime of incest. Orin's attitude to his mother becomes more like a lover's than a son's.

The Hunted

In the final draft of *The Hunted* Lavinia becomes Christine's nemesis. In its Greek counterpart, *The Libation Bearers*, the son Orestes avenges his father's wrongful death by murdering his mother. Electra plays a subordinate role. O'Neill reverses this, portraying Orin as weak and easily influenced by the dominant Lavinia, the central character. Throughout the years that he worked on the trilogy, the dramatist remained completely under the spell of his heroine; he calls Electra "the most interesting of all women in drama." In his version the mother commits suicide—she is not murdered as in the Greek trilogy. In his earliest notes on the play, O'Neill wonders why Electra escapes punishment; he asks: "Why did the chain of fated crime and retribution ignore her mother's murderess?—a weakness in what remains to us of Greek tragedy that there is no play about Electra's life after murder of Clytemnestra." In his own trilogy, he tries to compensate for the loss.

The Hunted begins two days after Ezra Mannon's murder. Five mourners come out of the house. Like the townspeople in *Homecoming*, they form a "chorus representing as those others had, but in a different stratum of society, the town as a human background for the drama of the Mannons." Christine comes out of the house, "obviously in a terrible state of strained nerves." Her eyes "burn with a feverish light." Lavinia has gone to the train station to meet Orin, and the mother anxiously awaits their return. She decides to use Hazel as a divisive weapon and warns her of Lavinia's possessive attitude to Orin. Reflecting on her own misdeeds, she is struck by Hazel's purity of heart and wonders why she herself has not remained "innocent and loving and trusting." Using words Mary Tyrone will later repeat, Christine says: "But God won't leave us alone. He twists and wrings and tortures our lives with others' lives until—we poison each other to death!"

Orin, twenty but looking thirty, resembles both his father and Brant—and his creator: "There is the same lifelike mask quality of his face in repose, the same aquiline nose, heavy eyebrows, swarthy complexion, thick straight black hair, light hazel eyes." His mouth "gives an impression of tense oversensitiveness." His face has "a gentle boyish charm which makes women immediately want to mother him." His first words to Lavinia are, "Where's Mother?" All during the war he has dreamed of Christine and of coming home, but to him the house now looks "ghostly and dead." Lavinia begs Orin not to succumb to their mother's spell, but her words are futile.

Mother and son are shown in the sitting room in the next act. "On the walls are portraits of Mannons, ancestors going back to Colonial days. All the faces in the portraits have the same mask quality of those of the living characters in the play." She says to Orin, as Deborah Harford later reminds her son Simon, "We had a secret little world of our own in the old days, didn't we?—which no one but us knew about." Like Reuben Light's mother in *Dynamo*, Christine assures her son that she loves him "better than anything in the world." They will be happy together again if Orin will only ignore the jealous Lavinia's lies and retain his belief in the mother's total innocence. Orin kneels and leans his head lovingly against his mother's knee. He describes the beautiful South Sea Islands he has read about in *Typee*; their "peace and warmth and security" reminded him of her. He wants no other woman: "You're my only girl." Dreamily, he plans their future: "We'll get Vinnie to marry Peter and there will be just you and I."

Orin stands before his father's bier in the following scene and says, "Death sits so naturally on you! Death becomes the Mannons!" The unending bloodshed of war has left this sensitive Mannon slightly deranged mentally, yet he threatens to have his sister committed when she again accuses their mother of murder. He is not concerned until she describes their mother's assignation in New York and her protestation of love to Brant. When Christine is heard approaching, Lavinia puts the pill box found at the murder scene conspicuously on her father's chest. The mother's terrified reaction on beholding it convinces Orin of her guilt. At this moment he loses his tenuous hold on sanity. Totally disillusioned by Christine's betrayal, he exclaims: "You are my lost island, aren't you, Mother?"

Lavinia and Orin avenge their father's murder in Act IV. Christine comes to Brant's clipper ship at a wharf in East Boston. A chantyman on the dock sings "Shenandoah," reinforcing once again the concept of an ominous fate. From their vantage point above the cabin skylight, Lavinia and Orin observe the reunited lovers. Christine tells Brant everything that has transpired since their last meeting and begs him to go away with her "out of Vinnie's reach." The two make plans to sail on the *Atlantis* the following Friday for China. She assures him that they will be happy "once we're safe on your Blessed Islands!" After Christine departs, Orin shoots Brant and smashes the furnishings in the stateroom to make it appear that robbery motivated the murder. Lavinia asks the dead man how he could have loved "that vile old woman." Like Josie Hogan at the end of *A Moon for the Misbegotten*, she pronounces a prayer of absolution for the dead man she secretly loves: "May God find forgiveness for your sins! May the soul of our cousin, Adam Mannon, rest in peace!"

In the last act of *The Hunted* Lavinia and Orin return home and callously taunt their mother. Vindictively, Orin describes their trip to Boston and the murder and asks her how she could have planned to go to "our island" with "that low swine." Even now, the tormented son will forgive the betrayer-mother everything; kneeling, he says: "I'll make you forget him! I'll make you happy! We'll leave Vinnie here and go away on a long voyage—to the South Seas—." He grovels before the mother, begging forgiveness. Lavinia orders her weak but obedient brother into the house and faces her mother. Christine's face "has become a tragic death mask." Told that justice has been done, the mother looks at Lavinia with a terrible look in which "savage hatred fights with horror and fear." Filled with a strange foreboding, the daughter watches her mother go into the house. She knows what the deranged woman is about to do and cries out, "You can live!" She restrains herself from following Christine: "It is justice." At that moment, Seth's mournful voice is heard singing "Shenandoah." The line "I'm bound away" is punctuated by the sound of a pistol shot. Orin rushes from the house, blaming himself for murdering his mother and seeking a way to "make her forgive me!"

In the early scenario for *The Hunted*, the meeting between the mother and her lover, here called Armand, takes place in the Mannon home, not on his ship. Armand no longer loves her and longs for freedom from her, but he

realizes that their crime binds them "indissolubly for
life." Electra (named Elena here) refuses to enter the
Mannon house after her father's murder and goes "to stay
with the Chappells* and tutor their daughter." She returns to the house secretly, however, to see Orin and to
plot their revenge. According to their plan, Orin invites
the lover to the Mannon home in a magnanimous gesture
of family reconciliation. He orders that his father's room
be aired. The lover will die in the same bed where "his
father died; as his father died—only in his case death will
be more merciful as it is morphia he has taken." Orin
prepares three glasses of wine, putting the contents of
packets his sister gave him into them: poison in the lover's
glass and what he believes to be a sleeping potion in his
mother's. Electra "has told him it is a sleeping draught
although it is a stronger dose of morphia than the one for
A." Later, in her room, the mother becomes ill, suspects
"they have been poisoned," and stumbles to her dead
lover's bedside, where she expires. This version, in which
the daughter, consciously, and the son, unconsciously,
are guilty of matricide, is closer in spirit to the second play
of the Greek trilogy than is O'Neill's final version.

---

*The dramatist depicts them as the Chatfields of New London in
Long Days Journey into Night, calling them "Big frogs in a small
puddle," and, most probably, as the Mannons in the trilogy.
Ezra Chappell, like Ezra Mannon's father, made a fortune in
trade. In 1830 Chappell purchased land on Huntington Street in
New London and built four identical Greek-structured houses,
which apparently inspired the author's idea of the Mannon home.
The dramatist states in the Fragmentary Diary in April 1930 that
"this home of New England—House of Atreus—was built in
1830, say, by Atreus character, Agamemnon's father—grotesque perversion of everything Greek temple expressed of
meaning of life." The four Chappell houses are in excellent
condition today. "There is no such important row of Greek
revival houses left standing in the United States" ("Chappell
file" in the archives of the New London Chamber of Commerce,
located in one of these historic buildings).

The Haunted

In *Homecoming* and *The Hunted*, O'Neill adheres to the basic story narrated in the first two plays of Aeschylus' trilogy, but he discards the plot of the *Eumenides* for the third work, *The Haunted*. In the Greek play the guilty son, pursued by the Furies, seeks recourse and pardon from the goddess Athena in a just trial. In its modern equivalent, the avenging furies are not an external force but an inner compunction that catapults Orin into madness and Lavinia into despair.

The play opens outside the Mannon house a year after the action of *The Hunted*. Seth and the four men who function as the chorus have been on a drinking spree. The men make crude remarks about Christine, yet they are fearful of her ghost, which supposedly haunts the house, shuttered since Lavinia and Orin departed on their trip. Hazel and Peter enter to tell Seth that they have received a telegram announcing the imminent arrival of the Mannons. Seth begs the Nileses to persuade them to live elsewhere and asserts that an evil spirit haunts the house: "I've felt it, goin' in there daytimes to see to things—like somethin' rottin' in the walls!"

Orin and Lavinia arrive. Both have changed considerably; they have become their dead parents. "She now bears a striking resemblance to her mother in every respect, even to being dressed in the green her mother had affected." Orin carries himself like a soldier; he has the "statue-like quality that was so marked in his father." The Mannon semblance of his face in repose to a mask is more pronounced than ever." His face is set "in a blank lifeless expression." Guilt-ridden, Orin refuses at first to look at the house, but Lavinia coaxes him to do so in a "motherly tone."

The next scene in the sitting room follows immediately. Lavinia, "sure now of her feminine attractiveness," her hair arranged like her mother's, urges Orin, who has searched the study in vain for his mother's spirit, to compose himself. Lavinia's transformation is not limited to her appearance. Orin comments on the change in her soul: "I've watched it ever since we sailed for the East. Little by little it grew like Mother's soul—as if you were stealing hers—as if her death had set you free—to become her!" Lavinia reminds him of his earlier belief: that by returning home to "face your ghosts, you knew you could rid yourself forever of your silly guilt about the past." She has failed to convince him that he is not responsible for their mother's death: "It was an act of justice."

In addition to her mother's way of dress and manner, Lavinia has assumed her teasing sexual nature. When Peter enters, she "takes him in with a smiling appreciative possessiveness." He is overwhelmed by feelings of love and desire but disturbed by Orin's description of Lavinia's behavior on the islands with the handsome men, particularly with Avahanni. "If we'd stayed another month, I know I'd have found her moonlight dancing under the palm trees—as naked as the rest!" Alone with Peter, Lavinia calls Orin a "regular bigoted Mannon" and remarks, "I'm only half Mannon." The islands have freed her from the Mannons' obsession with sin and death. She throws her arms around Peter in total abandon and kisses him passionately. Her brother sees the couple kiss and and reacts as Gordon Evans did in *Strange Interlude* when he observed his mother kissing Darrell. Orin glares at them with jealous rage and clenches his fists as if he were going to attack them.

In Act II, which takes place a month later, Orin is working in his father's study on a manuscript. He hides it when Lavinia comes in and tells her that their only hope of washing "the guilt of our mother's blood from our souls" is to "confess and atone to the full extent of the law." The brother finally informs Lavinia that he is writing a true history of the Mannons, of "all the family crimes, beginning with Grandfather Abe's." He has found Lavinia to be "the most interesting criminal of all." Jealously, Orin accuses her of having desired Brant and the native Av-ahanni. The brother and sister act out the roles of their parents. She deliberately taunts him; he reacts "as his father had," calling her a whore. He begs Lavinia to murder him, free him. "Can't you see I'm now in Father's place and you're Mother? That's the evil destiny out of the past I haven't dared predict! I'm the Mannon you're chained to!" She cannot escape him, either, for he is putting the confession in safe hands; it is to be made public if she attempts to marry or he dies. When she begins to sob, he remarks, "The damned don't cry."

Orin, in Act III, gives Hazel a sealed envelope with instructions that it should be opened only in the event of his death, if Lavinia "tries to marry Peter—the day before the wedding. . . . She can't have happiness. She's got to be punished!" Lavinia enters. Part of her secretly wants to be rid of Orin; she thinks: "Why hasn't he the courage—?" The sister sees the envelope and entreats Orin, "Make Hazel give that up and I'll do anything—anything you want me to!" She shrinks back from her brother, who laughs crazily and reclaims the envelope.

Later, when alone with Lavinia, Orin explains that her promise involves more than giving up Peter forever. Only an incestuous union, he suggests, will keep his sister bound to him always. "He stares at her and slowly a distorted look of desire comes over his face." No longer does Orin consider her as his sister or mother "but some beautiful stranger with the same beautiful hair—Perhaps you're Marie Brantôme, eh? . . . You would be as damned as I am!" Seeing her look of "horrified repulsion," Orin says that the only alternative is to go to the police to confess, pay the penalty, and "find peace together!" The two resemble, on the surface, Abbie and Eben after the child's murder in the earlier Puritan play, *Desire Under the Elms*, but hatred, rather than love, joins them. The two Mannons are more complex, however, than the Cab-ots, more driven and tormented by guilt, not merely for their own offenses but for the aggregated onslaught of family crimes. In an uncontrollable burst of rage, Lavinia, now bordering on madness herself, lashes out, "I hate you! I wish you were dead! You're too vile to live! You'd kill yourself if you weren't a coward!" The suggestion wars with the remaining shreds of Orin's sanity, which now fails him: "That would be justice—now you are Mother! She is speaking through you!"

As she did before Christine's suicide, Lavinia struggles with the dark forces within her. She knows what Orin intends to do, yet her selfish desire for survival triumphs. She tries to drown her conscience in the passion of Peter's embrace. He offers to make certain that Orin does nothing rash, but Lavinia ignores him, talking wildly about peace and their future happiness. When the expected shot is heard, she whispers: "Orin! Forgive me!" All traces of the crime have been destroyed. The fateful envelope is locked in a drawer. Feeling a sense of total freedom, she looks defiantly at the Mannon portraits: "Wasn't it the only way to keep your secret, too? But I'm through with you forever now, do you hear? I'm Mother's daughter—not one of you! I'll live in spite of you!"

The trilogy comes full circle in its final act, which takes place three days later. As at the start, Seth sings "Shenandoah." A "remarkable change" has taken place in Lavinia. Dressed in mourning, she looks like her former repressed prim self. "The Mannon mask-semblance of her face appears intensified now." She has refused to enter the house since Orin's death and has spent the nights sitting on the steps. Desperately, she clings to her plan of marrying Peter and leaving the house. She rejects Hazel's plea that she give up Peter. For the first time in her life Hazel confronts evil and tries to protect her brother from it: "Living alone with you, married, you couldn't hide it, he'd get to feel what I feel. You could never be happy because it would come between you." Lavinia orders Hazel to leave and threatens to kill her.

Later, when she observes Peter's haggard, tormented face, Lavinia realizes the toll his love and loyalty are taking on him. Desperately, she begs him to marry her that day; after Peter rejects this idea as unseemly on the day of Orin's funeral, she asks him, passionately, "to make up for what's coming," to forget sin and "take me in this house of the dead and love me!" In her confusion, she speaks another's name: "Want me! Take me, Adam!" Lavinia can no longer shut out the truth from her mind. It is the dead Adam she truly wants. Sadly, regretfully, she sends Peter away, because their marriage is impossible: "The dead are too strong!"

Hearing Seth intone again the song "Shenandoah," Lavinia repeats the word "bound": "I'm bound here—to the Mannon dead!" Seth tries, unsuccessfully, to stop her from entering the house. She rejects her mother's and brother's way as "escaping punishment—or prison!" She vows never to go out again or to see anyone. "I'll live alone with the dead, and keep their secrets, and let them hound me, until the curse is paid out and the last Mannon is let die!" As Seth nails the first shutter closed, she turns and "marches woodenly into the house, closing the door behind her."

The last line O'Neill recorded in the notebook containing the scenario for the first two parts of *Mourning Becomes Electra* was "Electra Trilogy—Story of the Third Play—Act One." Nowhere does he explain why he did not write the scenario for the third play in the notebook. On July 15, 1929, four days after he finished the scenario for the second play, he states in his Work Diary, "feel off of Electra for the moment." The dramatist must have inadvertently destroyed the earliest notes made for this play. In the only entry for August 1929 in the Fragmentary Diary, he noted, "have given Yankee Electra tragic end worthy of her—and Orestes, too."

Lavinia's entrance into the Mannon house of the dead, "closing the door behind her," is one of the most dramatic images in modern drama. How inconsequential that other closing of the door seems, in Ibsen's *A Doll's House*, which ushered in the era of modern drama. Ibsen's slamming door heralds a woman's emancipation from the past, her entrance into the outside world. The closing of the door in O'Neill signals a woman's enslavement to the past, her immuring in a tomb of living death.

Through this scene O'Neill achieves his goal, to show that "fate from within the family is the modern psychological approximation of the Greek conception of fate from without, from the supernatural." In the *Oresteia* Athena and the court render justice for crimes committed; in *Mourning Becomes Electra* Lavinia's conscience decrees her punishment, the fate ordained by the Mannons' perverted sense of justice. The family history that Orin writes is the visible representation of all the felt but unseen forces that link Lavinia irrevocably to the dead Mannons and seal her fate. For good reason, O'Neill specifies that his male and female characters closely resemble one another. The transfer of outward physical qualities signifies a transmission of an inner family legacy. The Mannon portraits in the house are a continual reminder to Lavinia of her fate. She is doomed to join them, a still-life tragic figure. Just before Orin's suicide, Lavinia looks at those dead Mannons on the walls "as if they were the visible symbol of her God." At the end of the play the dead wait to reclaim her, but she refuses to go into the house after Orin's death. Her entrance at the end signifies her surrender to the Mannons and, through them, to her fate.

Orin plays a more vital role in the 1929 scenario than he plays in the final text. He bears a greater resemblance to Reuben Light in *Dynamo*, the author's last completed work before the trilogy. Like Reuben and John Loving in *Days Without End*, the play that follows *Mourning Becomes Electra*, Orin feels betrayed by his mother, by her affair with Adam; similarly, he betrays her by killing her

•

lover. After losing his mother to death, Orin concludes, as do the other two heroes, that he must die in order to be united with her: "It's the way to Peace—to find her again—my lost island—Death is an Island of Peace." Of the many guilt-ridden sons who have sinned against the mother, including Jim Tyrone in *A Moon for the Misbegotten* and Don Parritt in *The Iceman Cometh*, Orin is perhaps the most pathetic. In Act III of *The Haunted*, when he urges Hazel not to love him, he says: "The only love I can know now is the love of guilt for guilt which breeds more guilt—until you get so deep at the bottom of hell there is no lower you can sink and you rest there in peace!"

Because of his weakness, Orin can find release from guilt only through death. When he views his dead father's body, he says, "Death becomes the Mannons." The title of the play, however, refers to Lavinia. Because of her strength, mourning, or a living death, not actual death, becomes her. In the fate she chooses, Lavinia reveals her awareness of the enormity of the evil acts she has committed and a glimpse of her own tortured being. Hers is, undoubtedly, the supreme gesture of atonement in the canon, more dramatic even than Parritt's leap to his death in *The Iceman Cometh* or any of the other suicides.

As he did in the two earlier New England plays, *Diff'rent* and *Desire Under the Elms*, O'Neill shows in *Mourning Becomes Electra* the deadly consequences of living in a repressive Puritan society. In each drama man's true nature becomes distorted. In the two family plays normal love and emotional channels are blocked, and denied love finds an abnormal expression in sexual perversion: lust and incest. The once purely Apollonian Ezra Mannon, after his return from the war, rages against the "white meeting-house on Sabbaths," that "temple of death" where he was taught how to die but not how to live. Never, until that moment, had he allowed his Dionysian side to emerge. He is rejected by his purely Diony-

sian wife. Lavinia, in her ability to reverse her two natures is the best example in the canon of the Apollonian–
Dionysian split. After she allows her Dionysian side expression in her Christine-like transformation, Lavinia
says to Peter, "I'm only half Mannon." The manifestation
of this repressed side of Lavinia illustrates Jung's conception of the shadow side of the self that one deliberately
suppresses. Speaking of what she once was and looking
forward to a future with Peter when everything will be
"straight and strong," Lavinia says, "I hate what's warped
and twisted and eats into itself and dies for a lifetime in
shadow." Lavinia knows what she once did to herself by
crushing her true self, and this awareness is her tragedy
when she deliberately allows the warped nature to dominate at the end of the play and entombs herself.

O'Neill wrote six drafts of *Mourning Becomes Electra*,
working on them from August 15, 1929, to March 27,
1931. In them he had tried and discarded a number of
experimental devices: masks, soliloquies, and asides.*
Rehearsals began on September 7, 1931, and the author,
who had returned from France, attended them and made
the necessary revisions. When the play opened on October 26, it was highly acclaimed by critics and theatergoers. *Mourning Becomes Electra* ranks third in the canon, after *Long Day's Journey into Night* and *The Iceman
Cometh*, in overall importance, but in its conception and
execution the trilogy is one of the great achievements in
twentieth-century drama.

---

*Enclosed with the sixth draft was a letter to Lawrence Langner
in which the author states, "As you will see, no departures in
technique are involved. 'Interlude' soliloquies and asides only
got in my way in these plays of intense passions and little
cerebration. The mask idea has also gone by the board. It simply
refused to justify itself in the final accounting. . . . All that is left
of it is the masklike quality of the Mannon faces in repose, an
effect that can be gained by acting & make-up. The dialogue is
colloquial of today. The house, the period costumes, the Civil
War surface stuff, these are the masks for what is really a modern

As a young playwright O'Neill always had a problem depicting women. The women characters in the early one-acters are spineless creatures. After a decade of living and growing, he brought forth Lavinia, the strongest, most fully developed woman in the canon. Although his appearance is brief, Ezra Mannon is another monumental figure, a pathetic, helpless victim of fate, like Ephraim Cabot. *Mourning Becomes Electra* has been produced in theaters throughout the world and is particulary popular in countries having a strong Greek classical theatrical tradition. The universal appeal of the trilogy lies not in its technical brilliance but in its majestic ability to show, in a moving dramatic story, characters driven inexplicably to their unavoidable tragic destinies by uncontrollable forces—family fate acting upon human passions.

---

psychological drama with no true connection with that period at all. I think I have caught enough Greek sense of fate—a modern approximation to it, I mean—out of the Mannons themselves to do without any Greek theatrical effects."

42. *Days Without End*

Days Without End* is a Catholic version of *Dynamo*.
O'Neill conceived the two as complementary parts of a
whole, a trilogy entitled "Myth Plays for the God-forsak-
en," whose theme was "the spiritual futility of the substitute-God search." The quest in both dramas is linked to
losing and regaining the mother figure. Like *Dynamo's*
Reuben Light, John Loving in *Days Without End* rebels
against the religion of his youth and struggles with his
unbelieving self to attain unity with the Deity. Mother
and God merge in Reuben's mind as the "Mother Dynamo" in his temple, the power plant. The visible manifestation of both to John Loving in the early notes is the
statue of the Virgin and Child in a Catholic church. In the
final version this object of worship is replaced by the
Christ figure on a cross.

O'Neill's first working title for the play is "Without
Endings of Days"; the earliest concept for it is labeled
"Play of Catholic Boyhood." The first few lines of the
lengthy original idea for the drama, recorded in his notebook in 1927, reveal that his new hero, like Reuben Light,
turns initially to science in his search for the substitute
God:

> Play of Catholic boyhood—revolt—free-thinking scien-
> tist whose pride in man becomes the human reason—the
> rational world of fact—but always fighting against his deep-
> ly religious pull—his deadly fear that he will, as age enfee-
> bles his reason or when the death of loved ones, etc. over-
> comes him emotionally with sorrow & despair, return to
> Church—this becomes his obsession.

*The copyright date is July 20, 1933. The play was first staged on
December 27, 1933.

The author experimented with different methods of dramatizing the conflict between religious certainty and human reason, faith versus science, that in *Days Without End* ultimately becomes the struggle between good and evil. In the earliest notes the good-evil conflict is not centered within John Loving; the two forces are external-ized and appear in two close friends: a Catholic convert and a sneering Mephistophelian cynic. Loving merely reacts, alternately, to the good and bad influences these characters exert over him. In the second set of notes, the hero, like Dion Anthony in *The Great God Brown*, has a "duality in his character," symbolized by a face and a Lucifer mask: "the scoffing unbelieving devil-self—mask one's own face but twisted into an eternal ironical leer." Not until the fifth draft did O'Neill incorporate the "Mask Scheme," in which two separate entities (and actors) are used to depict the hero's dual natures: John, representing his nobler side, and Loving, wearing the "dead Mask" of John's sneering cynicism. Loving can be seen only by John and the audience, but his scornful remarks can, at times, be heard by other characters, and these they at-tribute to John.

The heading at the beginning of each of the three acts is "Plot for a Novel." The title refers to the novel John is writing, an autobiographical work, although he denies that it is so. Ironically, *Days Without End* itself has auto-biographical elements, which are particularly evident in the notes, yet O'Neill, like his hero, rejected the charge. The author conceived the original idea for the play during a period of tremendous introspection, as the autobio-graphical ideas recorded in his notebook and the com-pleted dramas of the late 1920s reveal. Both the "Modern Faust Play" and "The Sea-Mother's Son" (1927) show a dying man in his forties reflecting on his life. The latter was to include a "series of plays based on autobiographical material." The last notations for the series were made on July 1931, the same month O'Neill wrote the first set of

notes for *Days Without End*, which, with its autobiographical plan and purpose, replaces "The Sea-Mother's
Son." The hero for the former encounters "his dead selves
—masked—7, 14, 21, 28, 35, 42"; in the latter, after
witnessing scenes from his childhood and youth, "the
character of himself is taken by himself while a man
wearing his mask takes his place in bed."

Days Without End opens in an office at Eliot and
Company in New York City in the early spring of 1932.
Seated at a table are John and Loving, each of whom represents one side of the central character, John Loving. John is
handsome and has the "rather heavy, conventional American type of good looks—a straight nose and a square jaw,
a wide mouth that has an incongruous feminine sensitiveness, a broad forehead, blue eyes." Loving is the same
height and build. He is dressed in an identical dark business suit. Yet, there is a strange dissimilarity, "for Loving's face is a mask whose features reproduce exactly the
features of John's face—the death mask of a John who has
died with a sneer of scornful mockery on his lips. And this
mocking socrn is repeated in the expression of the eyes
which stare bleakly from behind the mask."

It is clear that from the start O'Neill was unconsciously writing another version of the 1918 idea: "long
play—Jim & self—showing influence of elder on younger
brother." The alter ego of the hero is described in all the
notes for the drama as being Mephistophelian and as
having considerable influence over the weaker self. In the
outline, the author considered making the Mephistophelian counterpart the hero's brother but discards this idea,
possibly because the character would be identified as
Jamie, who is later described as Mephistophelian in
Long Day's Journey into Night and *A Moon for the Misbegotten*. He also contemplated making him "a man of the
same age who has been his friend since boyhood—(who is
a living reminder and participator in all his past—in all his
struggles, dissipations, despair, love affairs, former mar-

riage—a former Catholic like himself—a sneering skeptic now about religion and everything else—a philosophical Nihilist)."

Because of the Depression, business for John's firm is slack. He occupies himself with outlining his novel, focusing on the central character's marital infidelity. The cynical Loving suggests repulsive ideas, such as allowing the hero's wife to die at the end. Remembering his own betrayal of his wife, Elsa, John determines that the novel's purpose is "to try to explain to myself, as well as to her . . . to get at the real truth and understand what was behind—what evil spirit possessed me." He had been a writer before settling down with Elsa, but, Faust-like, he had sacrificed his ideals, becoming a businessman in order to make money. He resembles the failed artist Dion Anthony in *The Great God Brown*, who joins the businessman Brown's firm. A renegade Catholic, John had, in his youth, written articles denouncing religion and capitalism.

An unexpected visitor is announced: Father Baird, John's uncle, whom he has not seen since his childhood days. Instantly, Loving feels threatened by the priest; his eyes are "fixed before him in a hostile stare, his body tensed defensively." The uncle, a ruddy-faced, white-haired man, radiates good health and kindliness; "one gets immediately from him the sense of an unshakable inner calm and certainty, the peace of one whose goal in life is fixed by an end beyond life."

John's partner, Bill Eliot, ushers the priest into the room. The uncle's reminiscences about his nephew's youth to Eliot provide the exposition. Father Baird had been made the orphaned John's guardian, but, receiving an assignment in the west, had been forced "to leave him to his own devices." The word should have been shortened to "vices," as John, after many years of repressive supervision, became totally uninhibited. At eighteen John went to college, where he assumed the pose of rebellious "devil's advocate." In his letters he tried to convert his uncle to some new radical belief:

> First it was Atheism unadorned. Then it was Atheism wedded to Socialism. But Socialism proved too weak-kneed a mate, and the next I heard Atheism was living in free love with Anarchism, with a curse by Nietzsche to bless the union. And then came the Bolshevik dawn. . . . And what do you think was his next hiding place? Religion, no less— but as far away as he could run from home—in the defeatist mysticism of the East. First it was China and Lao Tze that fascinated him, but afterwards he ran on to Buddha. But the next I knew, he was through with the East. It was not for the Western soul, he decided, and he was running through Greek philosophy and found a brief shelter in Pythagoras and numerology.*

Since John's marriage to Elsa, "his last religion" seems to be love. The uncle asserts that John is "running from the truth"—that is, Catholicism—in order to find it where "the road finally turns back toward home." He quotes lines from Francis Thompson's poem "The Hound of Heaven": "I am He Whom thou seekest!/Thou dravest love from thee, who dravest Me."

Prodded by his uncle, John describes his novel, disclaiming it as autobiography. The first part, which deals with the hero's boyhood to the age of fifteen, seems like a page taken from O'Neill's own life. John had admired his father and adored his mother. Both were devout Catholics, but the mother had "an absurd obsession with religion." Their God was human, lovable, compassionate, the "God Who became man for the love of men and gave His life that they might be saved from themselves" and not a "stern, self-righteous Being Who condemned sinners to torment." The boy grew up believing ardently in this loving God. At school, however, "he learned of the

---

*These are the stages through which O'Neill himself passed in his attempt to find some meaningful belief to replace his abandoned Catholicism. It is doubtful, however, that he was ever as strident an atheist as his hero.

God of Punishment" and could not "reconcile Him with
his parents' faith." When he was fifteen, all of his "pious
illusions" were destroyed when, during a flu epidemic,
his parents contracted penumonia and died. His father
died first. After his mother became ill, the young man
"vowed his life to piety and good work . . . *if* his mother
were spared to him!" He prayed in vain.

John.   Something snapped in him then.

Loving.   He saw his God as deaf and blind and merci-
               less—a Deity Who returned hate for love
               and revenged Himself upon those who trust-
               ed Him!

John.   His mother died. And, in a frenzy of insane
               grief—

Loving.   No! In his awakened pride he cursed his God
               and denied Him, and, in revenge, promised
               his soul to the Devil—on his knees, when
               every one thought he was praying!

It was at this precise time in the hero's life, which duplicates John's, that the doubting, diabolical Loving was
born.

   In the next act, later that afternoon in the Lovings'
apartment, John's beautiful wife, Elsa, thirty-five, converses with her friend Lucy Hillman. The two have not
seen each other in months, not since Elsa went to Boston
in February. Lucy wonders how Elsa manages to live
consistently "in some lost world where human beings are
still decent and honorable." Elsa's first miserable marriage should have disillusioned her, yet she sits "calm and
beautiful and unscarred." Elsa maintains that John's love
has healed her; he is everything to her: child and father as
well as husband. Crudely, Lucy adds "lover" to the list
and speaks of experimenting with lovers.

   Eventually, Lucy reveals the reason for her bitterness. She is "sick of marriage and motherhood," having

been humiliated by her husband's "open affairs with every damned floosie he meets." She refuses to leave him, as Elsa left her first husband when he deceived her, because she still loves him. At a party, after he went off with another woman, she singled out a happily-married guest to seduce. Reluctant at first, he later seemed possessed by "another man, a stranger whose eyes were hateful and frightening. . . . I seemed for a moment to be watching some hidden place in his mind where there was something as evil and revengeful as I was." Elsa boasts that John would never be unfaithful to her because he knows the effect it would have on her: "It would kill forever all my faith in life—all truth, all beauty, all love! I wouldn't want to live!" She had been the liberal one before their marriage and had suggested that they merely live together. In his defense of marriage, John, an idealist, repeated words uttered earlier by Michael Cape in *Welded*, who stresses the spiritual side of a relationship: "He said no matter if every other marriage on earth were rotten and a lie, our love could make ours into a true sacrament." As he did through asides in *Welded*, O'Neill in an early draft of *Days Without End* considered "using 'interlude' technique bringing out John's infidelity with Lucy—and implanting of doubt in Elsa's mind."

In the third act, that evening in the Lovings' living room, John hovers solicitously over Elsa to make certain that she is warm. Her recovery from the flu has been slow, and it is a "rotten, chilly, rainy" night. She and Father Baird encourage John to continue narrating his novel. He assures them that the plot is totally imaginary: "It's the story of a man I once knew." After his parents' death the hero, in his despair, "had given his soul to some evil power." He wanted to pray and to be forgiven; feeling cursed, he had contemplated suicide. "Cursed with the inability ever to reach a lasting belief in any faith," he became an atheist and, as Loving adds, "a damned soul." He sought, unsuccessfully, to replace his lost faith, experimenting with "one social philosophical Ism after another." Finally, after finding the "Truth" in love, he felt something threatening in this new emotion; recalling the death of his beloved parents, he feared that the woman he loved might die too.

John describes the hero's act of infidelity, unaware of Lucy's earlier revelation. He cites the same details she had included in her narration that afternoon: the unfaithful, drunken husband, the jealous wife, the seduction. Some "hidden spirit of evil" had taken possession of the hero; he wanted only to kill his love for his wife. Elsa conceals her knowledge of the facts but becomes terribly upset when she learns that the "fictitious" wife dies: "flu, which turns into pneumonia." Loving says insinuatingly, "You must be very careful, Elsa. Remember it's cold and raining out." "As if in obedience to his will," she walks to the hall and out into the night.

Scene 2 is set in John's study later that night. After his lengthy discourse on the "blind greed" of his fellow man and the need for a "new savior," John continues his story. The hero believes that his wife lives on after death and will forgive him his sin if he believes in "his old God of Love." At his death, she "will be waiting." He rushes out one night and returns to the church of his youth. Loving remarks, "Now we come to the great temptation scene, in which he finally confronts his ghosts." Kneeling at the foot of the cross, the hero feels forgiven. He walks out of the church, accepting his wife's loss "as his fate."

Later Elsa returns. Her clothes are wet, her face flushed with fever. Bitterly, she informs John she went to one of Lucy's parties to seek revenge, but was disappointed: "Hardly any adultery going on." Humiliated, she accuses her husband of making a "smutty joke" of their love and of "hating the ideal of our marriage."* She

---

*There is much in *Days Without End* reminiscent of *Welded*: the husband who tries to attain the ideal in marriage but who is driven by some inner compulsion to kill love. Michael Cape goes to a prostitute; John turns to Lucy. Both are hopelessly guilt-ridden and shattered by their temporary lapse into infidelity.

will not forgive him: "I want my dream back—or I want to be dead with it!" Seeing Elsa's chilled condition, the priest urges John to summon the doctor. After Elsa goes to her bedroom, insisting mockingly, that she does not want to get well as "that would spoil John's story," Father Baird begins to pray. As he did in the early one-acters *The Web, Thirst*, and *Fog*, O'Neill injects a supernatural element. John senses the presence to whom the priest is praying. Haltingly, he begs God not "to take love from me again." Loving contemptuously mocks him: "There is nothing—nothing!"

The first scene of Act IV, entitled "The End of the End," shows two rooms a week later: the study and Elsa's bedroom. John, who is on the verge of a mental and physical collapse, sits beside Elsa's bed. Loving stands behind him, "the sinister mocking character of his mask is accentuated now, evilly intensified." John's irrational outbursts in response to Loving's snide remarks alarm the doctor, who is, incredibly, named "Stillwell." He banishes John from the room and tells the priest that Elsa refuses to fight for life; he believes that John secretly wants her to die. While her problem stems from her refusal to forgive John, the physician senses the mystical undercurrents of the sickness, which, he tells the priest, is "more in your line. A little casting out of devils would have been of benefit—might still be."

Loving taunts John with visions of "Elsa rotting in her grave" and urges him to end his life. Death is "the dream in which you and Elsa may sleep as one forever." John, moved by the sense of fate in his story, "a fate in the church," desires to "see the Cross again." Loving tries to prevent him from leaving, but a hidden power within John manifests itself, enabling him to defeat his formerly stronger self. After John goes, Elsa regains consciousness and cries out that she forgives John. The crisis has passed; she wants to live.

In the play's final scene, which takes place a few minutes later, John stands in the doorway of a church and

pushes Loving aside when he tries to bar him from entering. Inside, on one wall, is a large cross about five feet
from the floor "with a life-size figure of Christ, an exceptionally fine piece of wood carving." John kneels before
the cross, begging for mercy and forgiveness. Through
the penitent's words O'Neill seems to profess his own
belief in the doctrine of the Mystical Body: that the
Church, with Christ as its head, is the aggregate of mankind. John says, "I am Thou and Thou art I! Why hast
Thou forsaken me? O Brother Who lived and loved and
suffered and died with us." Throughout the scene John
and Loving wage a bitter battle. After the evil self shouts:
"I hate Thee! I curse Thee!" and John responds: "No! I
bless! I love," Loving seems to have been struck a mortal
blow. He falls to his knees beside John "as if some invisible force crushed him down" and says, "Thou hast conquered, Lord. Thou art—the End. Forgive—the
damned soul—of John Loving!" He slumps to the floor
dead, his arms outflung "so that his body forms another
cross. John rises from his knees and stands with arms
stretched up and out, so that he, too, is like a cross." At
that moment, in an ending that might be found in a
medieval morality play, the hero's two selves merge:

> John Loving—he, who had been only John—remains
> standing with his arms stretched up to the Cross, an expres-
> sion of mystic exaltation on his face. The corpse of Loving
> lies at the foot of the Cross, like a cured cripple's testimonial
> offering in a shrine.

Day's Without End is the weakest and least successful play of O'Neill's mature period. Oddly enough, he
spent more time and effort on it (over two years, writing
seven drafts) than on the three-play *Mourning Becomes
Electra*. Material in the notes for it suggests that a better
play could have been devised. Originally, *Days Without
End* took up the theme of the first trilogy, "Myth Plays for
the God-forsaken": the spiritual futility of "the substitute-
God search" and the theme of *Dynamo* by linking the

hero's quest to the mother. His rejection of faith is always associated with guilt for some wrong done to the mother. In one early draft the hero's rebellion predates his mother's death. His jealousy of her obsessive dedication to the Church leads him in revenge to identify with Lucifer and "with knowledge, science—rebellion—break with church which he hides for mother's sake." She purchases a medical practice after he becomes a doctor, and he experiences "freedom from her—scientific freedom from church." As in *Dynamo*, the mother is responsible for the son's substitution of science for religious belief. But even more significant is the fact that the son is shown once again in rebellion against *both* the mother and the Church.

John Loving resents his mother's total "absorption in Catholicism." Her loving, forgiving Christ replaces the harsh, demanding Old Testament God of Reuben Light's mother in *Dynamo*. Both young men suffer two crucial losses simultaneously: loss of faith and loss of the mother, leaving them with a deep sense of guilt and a desire for an incestuous spiritual union through a substitute mother figure. Reuben's search for a mother figure prompts him to propose, in an early version, to the earthy, maternal Mrs. Fife, who merges with the "Mother Dynamo" that he "deifies" and in which he finds his mother. John marries a woman who resembles his own mother, Erda, the "primitive poetic Mayan earth spirit." O'Neill inserts the statement here that "mother worship, repressed and turned morbid, ends by becoming death love and longing." Reuben, having sinned against the celibate priesthood, builds an altar in the "temple" and immolates himself as a sacrifice to his idol, the Mother Dynamo. John, having broken his marriage vows, goes to a Catholic church and kneels before the altar of the Virgin and Child: "identification of mother and Elsa with Her, himself with child, longing for reunion with them through Mother Goddess that really lures him to point of suicide before statue of Virgin." The betrayal of both heroes of their

deities relates to a violation of chastity: the affair of the
Reuben with Ada, of John with Lucy.

O'Neill eliminates the statue of the Virgin and Child
in the last scene and the mother-son conflict of the early
notes in the final play, but the fact that he again intended
to depict the same struggle found in *Dynamo* indicates
that he himself was a victim of "Mother worship." A
decade had passed since the death of his own mother, yet
he was again reliving the experiences of his youth. He still
bore the scars of the past and kept dramatizing ancient
battles as though reenacting them would exorcise his
ghosts. Perhaps if the author had continued the mother-
oriented scheme of the early notes, he might have produced the play he wanted to write in *Dynamo*. Instead of
substance, O'Neill concentrated on deceptive gimmicks
in *Days Without End*: the hero's autobiographic novel,
his dual presence as John and Loving. However, even the
motive for the creation of the duality is weak.

A perceived betrayal of his mother leads to the emergence in John, when he is a youth, of a suppressed evil
self. In *The Great God Brown* Dion's evil nature manifests itself in the Mephistophelian mask he wears.
O'Neill goes one step further in *Days Without End* by
having the base self assume a separate shape. It is important to note that just as in the earlier play the two
complementary selves merge into one form, Dion Brown,
Man, at the end, the "good" John and the "evil" Loving
become one: John Loving. O'Neill explains the rationale:

> Consider Goethe's *Faust*, which, psychologically speaking,
> should be the closest to us of all the Classics. In producing
> the play I would have Mephistopheles wearing the Mephis-
> tophelean mask of the face of Faust. For is not the whole of
> Goethe's truth *for our time* just that Mephistopheles and
> Faust are one and the same—*are* Faust?*

In this statement O'Neill verbalizes for the first time
an idea he had visualized through his use of masks in

*Eugene O'Neill, "Memoranda on Masks," *American Spectator*
(November 1932), p. 3.

previous plays: that good and evil do not exist in isolation —are not mutually exclusive—when applied to man. Caligula and Tiberius in *Lazarus Laughed* illustrate this point. Their half-masks are caricatures of all that is evil and base in them and in man; their mouths, however, reveal an inclination, a longing to manifest their suppressed nobler side. The Dion-masked Brown of the second part of *The Great God Brown* is an early variant of the John-masked Loving. Like Hawthorne, O'Neill uses a visible symbol—the Mephistophelian mask of the face of Faust, of the face of John—to remind us of the vestiges of original sin, the potential for evil within us.

O'Neill agonized over the ending of *Days Without End*, reluctant to have his lapsed-Catholic hero return to his faith. He feared that the gesture would be misconstrued as an expression of his own desire to return to Catholicism. He cautions Macgowan that the ending will "trouble you a bit, coming from me. It was an end I resisted (on personal ground) but which finally forced itself on me as the inevitable one" (letter of October 25, 1933). The ending seems hopelessly contrived and outrageously dramatic, considering the actions that preceded it. As he did in *Welded*, O'Neill takes a simple domestic drama and attempts to make a profound philosophical commentary on spiritualized love, the sanctity of marriage, and, in *Days Without End*, the duality of man. The only conflict in the play is the hero's good-evil struggle. Neither he nor any of the other characters is appealing or interesting. The plot is contrived: a hero writing an autobiographical novel containing events that are currently unfolding in his own life. *Days Without End* is an autobiographical play about a hero who writes an autobiographical novel. The ruse does not produce credible drama.

In spite of the difficulties encountered, O'Neill was determined to complete this "Play of Catholic Boyhood." The reason is obvious: the drama contains a personal statement that he wished to make during this particular

period in his life. The notes for this play have more
autobiographical references and revelations than those of
any other, with the exception of *Long Day's Journey into
Night*. *Long Day's Journey* focuses on O'Neill's parents; *A
Moon for the Misbegotten* is his brother Jamie's play;
Days Without End is the dramatist's account of his own
spiritual odyssey. The notes for the latter, in their totality,
reflect the personal struggle the author waged within his
own soul. Despite his denials, he *was* expressing his own
dilemma through his hero and seeking a similar return to
his faith. There is specific proof of this in a personal and
artistic record he kept—a journal listing significant events
in his life, arranged in a seven-year cycle. This is reminiscent of the outline found in "The Sea-Mother's Son" and of
the very first line in the earliest notes for *Days Without End*:
"His dead selves—masked—7, 14, 21, 28, 35, 42,—." For
the year 1932–1933, O'Neill writes:

> "Ah, W" (Writing D.W.E.) (return toward Cathol[icism].)
> away from tragic sense of life

The entry for 1933–1934 states:

> Days W.E. (Finish D.W.E.) (return toward Cathol.)

O'Neill tried in November 1931 to make the religion
of the play "less definitely Catholic—more general—
Christian religion." Yet in the end he reverted to Catholicism. He explains why he did so in a letter written in 1935
to Leon Mirlas. In the rough draft of this letter he states,
"I chose Catholicism because it is the only Western religion which has the stature of a real Faith, because it *is* the
religion of the old miracle plays and the Faustian legend
which were the sources of my theme—and last and most
simply because it happens to be the religion of my [de-
leted words: Irish background, tradition and] early training and therefore the one I know most about."

Days Without End was assailed by critics when it
opened on December 27, 1933. It ran for only fifty-seven
performances. Explaining why the work was a "flat fail-

ure," O'Neill states in his letter to Mirlas that "a play that
even mentions any religion these days is doomed in advance—especially doomed if the religion happens to be
Catholicism. They took the easy line of attack that I must
have gone back to Catholicism."* If O'Neill had any intention of making a formal public "return toward Catholicism" in 1932–1934, the unfavorable critical reception of
the play and the antireligious attitudes in the country at
the time might have made him reconsider. The phrase
that is used repeatedly throughout the notes in reference
to the hero of *Days Without End*—"once a Catholic always a Catholic"—seems to apply to the playwright, if
only in the deep, secret recesses of his heart. One thing is
certain: he never lost his faith, his belief in God. Inserted
in a first-edition copy of *Days Without End* is a letter
O'Neill wrote to its original owner in gratitude for that
person's "sensitive appreciation in view of the narrow-
minded hostility and antireligious prejudice which recently greeted this play." He remarks:

> I do believe absolutely that Faith must come to us if we are
> ever again to have an End for our days and know that our
> lives have meaning. All of my plays, even when most mate-
> rialistic, are—at any rate, for me—in their spiritual impli-
> cations a search and a cry in the Wilderness protesting
> against the fate of their own faithlessness.

---

*On February 14, 1934, ten days before the play closed, O'Neill
told Macgowan, "I've had more letters from people about this
play than any play I've ever written—which must prove something." He is dismayed that no one "saw its larger—and obvious
—aspect as a play which beyond its particular Catholic fore-
ground is a drama of spiritual faith and love in general. . . . it
holds audiences tensely and silently all thro' to six to ten curtain
calls nightly. . . . And yet the critical jackasses have the nerve to
say the technique doesn't come off! If we could get people in the
theater, I really believe now this play could be a success—but
the reviewers keep too many away, that's the trouble. It's alive
for those who go."

43. Ah, Wilderness!

Ah, Wilderness!* is a sunny, warm, sentimental comedy, an unexpected anomaly from the pen of Eugene O'Neill, a luminous, cheerful drama nestled among the late cluster of dark tragedies. The idea for the play came to O'Neill while he was writing the first draft of the bleak *Days Without End*. On September 1, 1932, he awoke, as he states in the Work Diary, "with idea for this 'Nostalgic Comedy' & worked out tentative outline—seems fully formed & ready to write." He indicates his decision the following day to put *Days Without End* "aside for time being and write this Comedy of ye old Sentimental Days —'Ah, W!'—seems crying to be written!"

A close study of *Ah, Wilderness!* and its autobiographical hero, Richard Miller, explains why the play was so "fully formed" in the author's mind. Actually, the idea was not a spontaneous overnight inspiration as it would appear. Almost a decade earlier the dramatist indicated that he had dreamed in one night the entire plot for *Desire Under the Elms*, which is actually his unconscious autobiography. He called *Ah, Wilderness!* "a dream walking" and "a comedy of recollection." The key word, of course, is "recollection." The previous year, on July 1, 1931, O'Neill went to his hometown, New London, stating in the Work Diary, "revisit Pequot Ave. old time haunts." Later that month he made the first set of notes for *Days Without End* and continued work on the autobiographical "The Sea-Mother's Son," labeling this latter effort " 'Nostalgia' notes."

---

*The copyright date is August 8, 1933. *Ah, Wilderness!* was completed and produced before *Days Without End*. It is discussed here after *Days Without End*, however, so that its derivative elements can be readily perceived.

As O'Neill sketched the family background for the hero of *Days Without End*, the "Play of Catholic Boyhood," he reflected on his own youth. The autobiographical data he accumulated for *Days Without End*, particularly the material relating to the hero's life at ages "7–14–21," led him apparently to do some wishful thinking and to conceive Richard Miller and *Ah, Wilderness!* He told Lawrence Langner, "I'm so close to both these plays," citing *Days Without End* as an example of a new trend in his work. "For after all, this play, like 'Ah, Wilderness!' but in a much deeper sense, is the pay of an old debt on my part—a gesture toward more comprehensive, unembittered understanding and inner freedom" (letter of October 29, 1933). In many of his earlier autobiographical dramas, the author had presented bleak portraits of the four O'Neills and a tragic view of their relationships and lives. He seems to imply in his letter that he reached an "unembittered understanding" of himself, his family, and his past in the early 1930s. In *Ah, Wilderness!* he uses the Millers to depict the O'Neills; later in *Long Day's Journey into Night* he did so through the Tyrones. Together the Miller-Tyrone families represent the ideal and the real, the light and the dark aspects of the O'Neills. These two plays and *Days Without End* are interconnected.

At the end of the first part of John Loving's autobiographical novel in *Days Without End*, the central character, at the age of fifteen and after a happy childhood, suffers a traumatic loss of his beloved parents; he attributes the loss to an uncaring God and rebels against Him. At eighteen, he goes to college, where he dabbles in socialism, anarchism, and antigovernment activities. John is actually recording events in his own life; the play itself depicts his struggle to regain his faith and come to terms with the feeling of loss as an adolescent. Richard Miller in *Ah, Wilderness!* is an early view of John before he suffers the loss of his parents and became a full-fledged radical. Richard is seventeen and preparing to enter Yale.

The play is set on the Fourth of July in 1906, the same year O'Neill entered Princeton. The young O'Neill must sure have experienced some of the emotions he attributes to Richard: his anguish and apprehensions about change and partings, but also his sense of adventure and hope regarding his new way of life. Perhaps the summer of 1906 represented the last time that O'Neill retained some of the optimism of youth, a last oasis before the later gnawing cynicism.

The title of the play and its central motif derive from a stanza in *The Rubaiyat of Omar Khayyam*:

A Book of Verses underneath the Bough,
A Jug of Wine, A Loaf of Bread—and Thou
Beside me singing in the Wilderness—
And Wilderness is Paradise enow.

The lines express Richard Miller's optimism about life as the play begins, his belief that all he needs to make his world a paradise are his favorite Swinburne poems, his lofty ideals, and the companionship of his first love, Muriel McComber. He finds, as the drama unfolds and he attempts to make the transition from adolescence to young manhood, that the path to paradise is beset with thorns. He experiences opposition from unexpected quarters: first from his mother, Essie, who objects to his taste in literature; second from his father, Nat, who questions his radical anticapitalist views; and finally from his beloved Muriel, who terminates their relationship at her father's command. As a consequence, Richard finds himself in a veritable wilderness of alienation and loneliness. The play describes his long journey back to reconciliation and unity with those he loves. There is a price to be paid, however. Initially he is naive, trustful of others, uncontaminated. At the conclusion of the play, after his pilgrim's progress from innocence to experience, he has gained wisdom and an understanding of life, but he has also attained a knowledge of deception, corruption, and vice.

Richard is an average-looking youth; his features are neither handsome nor homely. He is a "blend of father and mother," like other self-portraits, such as Eben in *Desire Under the Elms* and Edmund in *Long Day's Journey into Night*. They also share his other characteristics: "extreme sensitiveness," "a restless apprehensive, defiant, shy, dreamy" poetic nature. Richard's father, who is in his late fifties, is "more than a little bald" and has "large, irregular, undistinguished features." He attempts to project a "sober respectability" in dress but has "an innate heedlessness of clothes." In *Long Day's Journey into Night*, set six years later, in 1912, James Tyrone is sixty-five; his hair is "thin with a bald spot like a monk's tonsure." He wears a commonplace, "threadbare, ready-made, grey sack suit." Nat Miller, editor of the local newspaper, is a wise, warm-hearted husband and father. He is, however, a man of definite opinions, and he rules his domain, and all therein, with an iron hand.

The only member of the Miller circle over whom Nat has little influence, but for whom he has great affection, is his wife's brother, Sid Davis, who is "forty-five, short and fat, bald-headed." When the play opens, the family believes that Sid is still employed as a reporter in Waterbury, but he has lost his job because of his frequent drinking sprees. His counterpart in *Long Day's Journey into Night* is Jamie O'Neill, the wastrel alcoholic son, who is "shorter and stouter than his father and whose thinning hair already indicates a bald spot." Sid's "puckish face of a Peck's Bad Boy," like Dion Anthony's first-stage bad-boy Pan face in *The Great God Brown*, has not yet acquired the "Mephistophelian cast" of Jamie's countenance. Like Jamie, Sid, a bachelor, possesses a gregarious, fun-loving nature; he is, in reality, a failure.

Through the aggressive, destructive Mrs. Brown and the gentle, detached Mrs. Anthony in *The Great God Brown*, and the religiously fanatic, equally destructive Mrs. Light and the placid, immense, maternal Mrs. Fife in *Dynamo*, O'Neill uses a composite picture to portray his mother. He does so again through the mother and the aunt in *Ah, Wilderness!*, although Essie Miller is more idealized than either of the latter mothers cited above. She is "around fifty, a short, stout woman with fading light-brown hair sprinkled with grey, who must have been decidedly pretty as a girl." She has "big brown eyes, soft and maternal—a bustling, mother-of-a-family manner." A good wife and a concerned, loving parent, she is both aggressive when she perceives her son's reading habits to be reprehensible and defensive when her husband wants to punish Richard by not allowing him to go to Yale. Nat's unmarried sister, Lily, forty-two, who lives with the Millers, is tall and thin and "conforms outwardly to the conventional type of old-maid school teacher, even to wearing glasses." In contrast to her authoritative appearance, she is pensive and shy and miserably unhappy. Sid's alcoholism and "taking up with bad women" had compelled her sixteen years earlier to break their engagement. Ever since, they have been locked into a love-hate relationship, hopelessly trapped because neither will ever change. Even so, she is maternally solicitous about his health and well-being, representing to him the caring mother figure Jamie Tyrone always sought.

The Millers have three other children residing at home: a daughter, Mildred, fifteen, a vivacious flirt, whose personality compensates for her lack of beauty; Tommy, eleven, a normal, energetic youngster with "a shiny, good-natured face"; and Arthur, nineteen, "tall, heavy, barrel-chested and muscular, the type of football linesman of that period." An indifferent student, he dresses "in the latest college fashion" and ostentatiously flourishes "the big Y" stamped on his pipe and tobacco pouch. Like John Brown's older brother, Edward, in *Bread and Butter*, he is annoyingly virtuous and conservative. The brief glimpse of the Brown family in their Connecticut home in the early play foreshadows the later, more comprehensive, view of the Millers.

Much of *Ah, Wilderness!* is set in the sitting room of

the Miller home, located in a "large small-town in Connecticut—about 7:30 in the morning of July 4th, 1906."
The room is a replica of the living room in the O'Neill
family's summer home; it is also reproduced intact in
Long Day's Journey into Night. The furnishings of the
rooms in both plays are identical, the only differences
being the types of books in bookcases and the number of
chairs—five, rather than four, in the Miller home—arranged around the table.

The specific date of the setting is appropriate, in view
of Richard's tirade against greedy, wealthy capitalist industrialists. He expresses the author's personal sentiments about the discrepancy between the noble principles upon which the country was founded and their subsequent deterioration. In the Wilderness Edition of Ah,
Wilderness! O'Neill explains one of his goals for undertak-
ing it:

> My purpose was to write a play true to the spirit of the
> American large small-town at the turn of the century. Its
> quality depended upon atmosphere, sentiment, an exact
> evocation of the mood of a dead past. To me, the America
> which was (and is) the real America found its unique expres-
> sion in such middle-class families as the Millers, among
> whom many of my own generation passed from adolescence
> into manhood.

Ah, Wilderness! is O'Neill's first totally nonexpres-
sionistic play since the early 1920s. It does what it sets out
to do: tell a simple story in a realistic, straightforward
manner. When it opens, the family is bickering good-
naturedly and making plans to celebrate the holiday.
Tommy is warned to set off his firecrackers away from the
house. The admonition is unheeded, and the sound of
small explosions punctuates the dialogue of the first
scene. Arthur and Mildred intend to spend the day with
friends. Sid is to accompany Nat to the Sachem Club
picnic. Sid has assured Lily that he has reformed and will
not use the occasion to get drunk as he has done in the
past.

Richard refuses to observe the Fourth of July, decrying "all this lying talk about liberty—when there is no liberty!" He lashes out at wealthy capitalists and states that he looks forward to celebrating "the day people bring out the guillotine again and I see Pierpont Morgan being driven by in a tumbril!" The father tries to reconcile his son to the realities of life, pointing out that he himself has had "to listen to at least one stump speech every Fourth."* Richard calls on workers of the world to unite, rise, and cast off their chains; he uses the quotation the anarchist Hugo Kalmer repeats continuously in *The Iceman Cometh*: "The days grow hot, O Babylon! 'Tis cool beneath thy willow trees!" He is surprised to discover that his father has also read Carlyle's *French Revolution* and asks, "Isn't it a great book though—that part about Mirabeau—and about Marat and Robespierre."†

Essie indignantly lists the authors of the books she has found in Richard's room: Oscar Wilde, Shaw, Ibsen, Swinburne. When Richard announces that his favorite work is *The Rubaiyat of Omar Khayyam*, Lily quotes "with a sad pathos" her favorite stanza:

> The Moving Finger writes, and having writ,
> Moves on: nor all your Piety nor Wit
> Shall lure it back to cancel half a Line
> Nor all your Tears wash out a Word of it.

Her words indicate an awareness of the impossibility of altering the sorrows of the past. Later Mary Tyrone will

---

*On October 6, 1932, a week after completing the first draft of the drama, O'Neill made an entry in his Work Diary for a "Thomas Jefferson Play." In it he contrasted "President of To-day" presenting a political speech on the "4th of July—evasive, opportunistic, cowardly" to an apathetic crowd, and, in a flash-back, President Jefferson rousing his listeners and inspiring them to feel "their rights and responsibilities as voters. End of Induction—End of President's speech—same spirit—again taking the name of Jefferson in vain."

†O'Neill admired the courage and moral integrity of Robespierre, thought by some to be the "savior of democracy" and "protector of the rights of man." On January 13, 1938, he began a

voice similar sentiments when she says, "None of us can help the things life has done to us."

Nat is alone when his newspaper's most valued advertiser, David McComber, arrives and accuses Richard of corrupting his daughter Muriel by sending her immoral letters. When Nat defends his son, McComber threatens to have Richard arrested if he tries to see Muriel again; in addition, he vows to cancel his regular advertisement in the newspaper. Infuriated, Nat refuses henceforth to print the "damned ad." Actually, he is shocked when he reads the passionate letters, but the "young anarchist" assures his father that his motives are pure and that he wants to marry Muriel. He feels betrayed, however, because she has showed his letters to her father; heartbroken, he plans to spend the day in solitude.

In the second act, set in the Miller dining room that evening, Richard assures Wint Selby, a classmate of Arthur's, that he is old enough to replace his absent brother for a date that evening with "a couple of swift babies from New Haven," Edith and Belle. Later, the sound of drunken singing announces the return of Nat, now "mellow and benignly ripened," and the inebriated Sid. Sid's antics and jokes during dinner provoke uproarious laughter from all members of the family except Nat, whose avowal that bluefish poisons him and his "oft-told tale" of his rescue of his drowning childhood friend, Red Sisk, are mocked. After Sid is sent to bed, Nat informs the family that his brother-in-law has lost his job in Waterbury and that he intends to take him back on the paper. The act closes with Nat reproaching his son, the "Melancholy Dane," for his cynicism and Richard, feeling misunderstood and wronged by his family, promising to "show them."

Richard is shown in the following act in the back

"Robespierre play," spending a week the following March outlining the various stages of the revolutionary leader's life, from his unhappy childhood to his death on the guillotine.

room of a bar in a small hotel later that evening. Wint has
gone upstairs with Edith, leaving his friend seated at a
table with Belle, twenty, a "rather pretty peroxide blond,
a typical college 'tart' of the period." Impressed by the
young man's generosity when he tips the bartender, she
sits on Richard's lap and encourages him to go upstairs
with her for five dollars. Richard's shocked modesty
struggles "with the growing tipsiness that makes him
want to be a hell of a fellow and go in for all forbidden fruit,
and makes this tart a romantic, evil vampire in his eyes."
Hurt when Belle calls him a "piker" for not going up with
her, Richard takes out a five-dollar bill and gives it to her.
After she abandons him for a newly arrived salesman,
Richard sadly recites poetry about lost love. The salesman
gazes wonderingly at him and asks Belle, "What is it—a
child poet or a child actor?" The drunken Richard vows to
protect Belle's honor and threatens to punch the salesman. The bartender rushes in, grabs Richard, and throws
him out of the bar.

In the act's second scene, set in the Miller home at
about eleven that evening, Essie expresses her fears that
Richard might have been run over by an automobile or
have gone down to the beach dock and fallen overboard.
Nat is just about to go out to look for his son when Richard
enters, pale and glassy-eyed. Sid, who is "suffering from a
bad case of hangover," is the first to realize that his
nephew is drunk. Richard parodies Hedda Gabler's remark to Eilert Lovborg in Ibsen's play wherein she urges
him to return from the male stag party triumphant and
sober. Suddenly, Richard loses his cynical bravado and
becomes violently ill. Sid, saying he knows "this game
backwards," takes Richard upstairs to sober him up, leaving Essie fearful that the Hedda he mentioned is a fancy
woman who has seduced her son.

In the first of the three scenes in the last act, Richard
promises his mother the next day that he will never
consume alcohol again, not for moral reasons but because

drinking didn't make him "happy and funny like it does Uncle Sid—It only made me sadder—and sick." He startles his mother with a reference to General Gabler's pistols but assures her, "You need not worry, Ma. It was only my despair talking. But I'm not a coward. I'll face— my fate." After receiving a letter from Muriel in which she begs him to meet her that evening, Richard manifests a new-found courage; he is determined to see Muriel "if it's the last thing I ever do! I don't care how I'm punished after!"

Later that evening the young lovers meet at the beach. Muriel is "a pretty girl with a plump, graceful, little figure, fluffy, light-brown hair, big naive wondering dark eyes, a round dimpled face, a melting drawly voice." Each speaks of the suffering endured for the other. Dramatically, Richard narrates his adventures the previous night, distorting the actual facts. He tells her that he went to a "secret house of shame, met a Princeton Senior he knew who had two chorus girls from New York with him, and drank champagne with them." Muriel becomes jealous, and the two argue. After they reconcile, she allows him to kiss her and expresses the hope that his punishment will not be severe. Richard professes not to care: "Nothing would have kept me from seeing you tonight— not if I'd had to crawl over red-hot coals!" Asked where they should go on their honeymoon, Richard responds dreamily that they will go to Mandalay and "watch the dawn come up like thunder out of China."

In the final scene, that evening in the Miller sitting-room, Nat confronts his son, who returns home "like one in a trance, his eyes shining with a dreamy happiness." Having discovered some of the details about the previous evening, the father asks, "How about that tart you went to bed with at the Pleasant Beach House?" Richard shows his revulsion: "She made everything seem rotten and dirty." Nat warns him about "girls there's something doing with" and announces his son's punishment: he is not to go to Yale that fall. Richard is overjoyed; now he can marry Muriel. Frustrated, the father announces: "Then you'll go to Yale and you'll stay there till you graduate."

Essie comes in from the piazza, speaking enthusiastically about the beautiful night and moon. Her husband recollects the period when they were young and planning to marry. For the first time in his life, Richard looks at them not as his parents but as they once were, eager lovers like Muriel and him. His face "is transfigured by a smile of shy understanding and sympathy," and he says: "I'll bet those must have been wonderful nights, too!" He kisses his mother and, awkwardly and impulsively, kisses his father. After the son goes out to look at the moon, Nat remarks, "I don't think we'll ever have to worry about his being safe—from himself—again. And I guess no matter what life will do to him, he can take care of it now." They pause on their way to bed. Nat embraces his wife and looks out at his son: "There he is—like a statue of Love's Young Dream." He recites a passage from *The Rubaiyat*:

> Yet Ah, that Spring should vanish with the Rose!
> That Youth's sweet-scented manuscript should close!

Then he turns from his son to his wife and smiles lovingly: "Spring isn't everything, is it, Essie? There's a lot to be said for Autumn."

The father's words signal the end of an era: his son's coming out of the wilderness of adolescence and making the transition to young manhood. Although O'Neill claimed never to have had a youth, he must have experienced some of Richard's adolescent uncertainty about life, his sense of separateness from his family. The play does have autobiographical aspects. The works of the authors Richard admires are found in the bookcase of Edmund, a self-portrait in *Long Day's Journey into Night*. The dramatist was attracted to a neighborhood girl, Maibelle Scott, whose father frowned on the relationship. The young couple had a go-between, Mildred Culver, who delivered their love letters as Richard's sister Mildred does in the play (the sister has a friend named Anne Culver). In addition to the identical houses, other elements in the setting for *Ah, Wilderness!* are later incorporated in *Long Day's Journey into Night* from the O'Neill family's Pequot Avenue locale: the lighthouse, the ocean avenue drive, the dock, the trolley.

On a more important level, the family life in the actual O'Neill home could not always have been as gloomy and tragic as it is depicted in *Long Day's Journey into Night*. Perhaps Jamie, like Sid, livened the conversations at meals with his genuine humor. At the end of *Ah, Wilderness!*, when Nat discovers that Lily has gone to a concert with Sid, that Arthur is with Elsie, Mildred with "her latest," and Richard with Muriel, he tells Essie, "Then, from all reports, we seem to be completely surrounded by love!" It is this feeling of warmth and love permeating the entire family and its interactions with others that O'Neill lacked and craved. There was love in the O'Neill home, but it was so intermingled with hate, guilt, and recrimination that relationships both within the family and without became distorted.

When O'Neill finished the first draft of *Ah, Wilderness!* in September 1932, he was hesitant about staging it. In a Work Diary entry on September 29, after noting that he had finished the play and put it "aside for while," he writes, "great affection for this one even if never produce it!" Nearly a year later, however, he halted work on the fifth draft of *Days Without End* and spent a week in June on a second draft of *Ah, Wilderness!* On August 1, he submitted the play to the Theatre Guild, and Lawrence Langner decided to produce it immediately. O'Neill attended rehearsals for the first three weeks of September 1933 and went to Pittsburgh for the pre-Broadway tryout, where he made necessary cuts. The play opened in New York on October 2 and was welcomed enthusiastically by critics and audiences. O'Neill was pleased by the praise

lavished on it. On October 16, two weeks after the opening, he wrote to Macgowan:

> I hoped you liked my nostalgic adventure into comedy in
> 'Ah, Wilderness.' I think it should hand you many reminis-
> cent grins. You will remember those good old days as well as
> I, and you must have known many Miller families. I had a
> grand time writing it—also a grand time rehearsing, for the
> cast, taking it all in all from bits to leads, is the best I have
> ever had in a play . . . and how the damn thing moves
> young, middle-aged and old! It's astonishing. And a proof to
> me, at least, that emotionally we still hanker after the old
> solidarity of the family unit.

O'Neill did not forget the Miller family after creating
it. On September 5 and 6, 1934, he made notes for a
sequel to *Ah, Wilderness!*, which would have presented a
tragic view of family life in the post–World War I period,
life as it "exists today," in contrast to the earlier sentimental picture of the Millers at the turn of the century. He
notes that the sequel is set "15 years after 'Ah, W[ilder-
ness!].'—or 1919?" Numerous tragedies have beset the
Miller family; its moral fiber has degenerated. Essie dies
in 1919—"worry over sons in war brought on illness—
cancer," and Lily manages the house after her death. Nat
collapses after his wife's death, "lost, bewildered in
changed times—waiting for death—feels children alien,
can't understand their view—same about everything."
After being told that he would die if he continued drinking, Sid has reformed. Even though he outwardly disapproves of drink, he has "attacks of unregenerate longings
for good old days." Tommy is in the Air Corps; Arthur
"has developed into smug, social-climbing, country club,
golfing success—made 'good' marriage to merchant's
daughter—three children—but is loose on side—affair."
Mildred is "getting divorce—lover—feels no responsibility toward two children." After graduating from Yale,
Richard "goes into newspaper game with father—makes
good—city editor—then war and he goes (27)—engaged

before he goes—but on return breaks engagement—
maimed, embittered, idealism murdered—lost leg?"

Lacking the joyous enthusiasm he felt for the original
"Nostalgic Comedy," the author decided on September
7, while vacationing in Maine, to "give up idea working up
here—no impulse" (Work Diary). He took up the story of
the Miller family, interrupting his work on *A Touch of the
Poet*, on January 9, 1936: " 'Ah, Wilderness!' sequel (for a
change—notes—but don't make much of it" (Work Diary). O'Neill's goal, obviously, in the sequel was to give
tragic dimensions to the lives of the Millers, who were
loosely modeled on his own family. In the next years he
continued to avoid his actual family as a unit, but he
continued to portray versions of individual members in
the Cycle plays, *A Touch of the Poet*, and *More Stately
Mansions*. Not until 1939 did O'Neill, as he states in the
dedication to *Long Day's Journey into Night*, have the
courage to "face my dead at last."

The comic mode of *Ah, Wilderness!* suggests that it
should have been created during O'Neill's first decade as
a playwright, before he entered the period characterized,
in its entirety, by the "tragic sense of life." Its style,
however, justifies its place among the mature work of the
1930s; it is a superbly crafted play. Content classifies it as
one of the dramas of the final decade marked by a heavily
autobiographical cast. *Ah, Wilderness!* is not pure comedy; there are dark shadows as well as light-hearted
humor. Sid is a pathetic casualty of life; behind the jovial
banter lies the despair of a man too weak to cope with
reality. The sensitive, tragic Lily is another one of life's
lost wounded. Nat Miller calls his son the "Melancholy
Dane." Richard is, like his creator, moody and introspective. He has been sheltered all his life by his parents but is
about to leave his refuge to face the outside world. He has
survived the first step of maturation in the play, but he
seems destined to become another Edmund Tyrone
somewhere along the way of life's journey.

44.   A Touch of the Poet and the Cycle

A TALE OF POSSESSORS, SELF-DISPOSSESSED

"I am at present working on the most important and ambitious project I have ever attempted. This is a Cycle of seven plays—the material, psychological, and spiritual history of a family over a period of one hundred years." The Cycle O'Neill refers to in his letter to Leon Mirlas in 1935 is "A Tale of Possessors, Self-Dispossessed," which began as a series of "4 or 5 plays" in 1934 and mushroomed in subsequent years to a seven-, nine-, and, finally, an eleven-part work. The Cycle concept seemed inevitable after the increasingly longer plays of the 1920s, culminating in the nine-act *Strange Interlude* and the *Mourning Becomes Electra* trilogy.

In addition to these lengthy completed dramas, O'Neill conceived a second trilogy in 1927, "Myth Plays for the God-forsaken," finishing its first two works, *Dynamo* and *Days Without End*, but not its third, "It Cannot Be Mad?" The original purpose of the trilogy was to show the "spiritual futility of the substitute-God search." He was also planning "The Sea-Mother's Son," which would have, as he told Benjamin De Casseres in September 1929, "ten or more *Interludes* in it." The author described the latter work, a "series of plays based on autobiographical material," as the "grand opus of my life."

This "opus" is probably the same autobiographical project O'Neill cites in a letter to Barrett Clark in the early 1930s:

All the most dramatic episodes of my life I have so far kept out of my plays, and most of the things I have seen happen to other people. I've hardly begun to work up all this material, but I'm saving up a lot of it for one thing in particular, a cycle of plays I hope to do some day. There'll be nine separated plays, to be acted on nine successive nights; together they will form a sort of dramatic autobiography, something in the style of *War and Peace* or *Jean-Christophe*.*

The dramatic episodes of O'Neill's life and those of the lives of his friends would not find conscious expression until 1939 and the early 1940s, when he wrote three of these autobiographical plays: *Long Day's Journey into Night*, *A Moon for the Misbegotten*, and *The Iceman Cometh*. In the historical Cycle he developed, the author unconsciously incorporated portraits of himself and his parents. The scope of the substitute-God search of the individual, of the central figures of the three "Myth Plays for the God-forsaken," was broadened in the Cycle to show the spiritual quest of a family that spanned nearly two hundred years of American history.

"A Tale of Possessors Self-Dispossessed" actually began as an idea for a single clipper-ship play, which was recorded in the Work Diary on June 20, 1931.† The following year, on March 8, O'Neill found the "right title" for the new concept: *The Calms of Capricorn*. The word "cycle" first occurs on January 1, 1935: "Calms of Capricorn cycle (Notes) (grand idea for this Opus Magnus if can ever do it—wonderful characters!)." As originally conceived, the Cycle comprised four plays, depicting the interconnected but separate adult lives and careers of four brothers. On January 27, 1935, O'Neill decided to assign a more prominent role to the brothers' parents: "story of [Simon] Harford and Sara before 1st play opens—this may develop into additional 1st play, making five in all."

*Clark, p. 162.

†All quotations, unless otherwise indicated, in this discussion of the development of O'Neill's Cycle are from the Work Diary, a two-volume record of the author's daily creative efforts for 1924–1943, transcribed by Donald Gallup (New Haven: Yale University Library, 1981).

The next day he outlines the "spiritual under-theme of Cycle" and gives the work its first name on February 3: " 'A Touch of the Poet' Cycle (get this title for Cycle & like it—'Calms of Capricorn' having always been title for particular 1st play–clipper ship. Also decide new first play of Sara Harford—marriage—parents, etc.)" At one stroke O'Neill has both the title and the germ of the story for the only surviving Cycle play that he labels "finished": *A Touch of the Poet*, which at this time is named "The Hair of the Dog." On February 25 he made an outline and notes for its sequel, "Oh, Sour-apple Tree," later entitled *More Stately Mansions*. While writing the scenario for the sequel on March 9, O'Neill stated, "seems to be working out as built around Abigail [Deborah Harford, Sara's mother-in-law], new conception of her character." A new tentative title was given to the Cycle on April 25, "Threnody for Possessors Dispossessed," and notes were made on May 3 for the scenario for *The Calms of Capricorn*, now the third play.

Striving for continuity in the Cycle plays, O'Neill inserted a passage in the second drama, *More Stately Mansions*, in which Simon Harford envisions the future of his four young sons: "We want them trained to live with reality so when the time comes they will be capable of serving our Company—Ethan as manager of our marine division, Wolfe to direct the banking branch which we will own before long, Jonathan as our railroad executive, and Honey our representative in politics." *The Calms of Capricorn* shows Sara Harford and her four sons, after Simon's death, leaving the farm that she had salvaged when the family business went bankrupt and sailing to California on a clipper ship.

Ethan, born in 1828 and the eldest son of Sara and Simon Harford, is the central character in *The Calms of Capricorn*, the third Cycle play. In "The Earth Is the Limit," the fourth play, Wolfe, born in 1829, the aristocratic second Harford son, becomes a successful banker.

Honey, who is three and a half years younger than Wolfe, is the main character in the fifth play, "Nothing Is Lost But Honor." "The Man on Iron Horseback," the sixth play, focuses on the third son, Jonathan, born in 1831, who becomes a railroad magnate. According to O'Neill's original plan, the four brothers would appear in all of the dramas. Each play was to be "complete in itself," yet each was to concentrate "around the final fate of one member of the family" and to "carry on the story of the family as a whole."

The seventh Cycle play at that time, "Twilight of Possessors Self-Dispossessed," follows "the old 'Bessie Bowen' theme," which was an expansion of the story of Bessie Wilks in the discarded 1927 "It Cannot Be Mad?" On September 7, 1935, O'Neill expanded the design of the Cycle to include an eighth work: "Playing around with idea new first play to precede 'Hair Of The Dog' [later *A Touch of the Poet*], to go back to 1806 and show Abigail as girl—marriage to Henry H.—and their house & parents —Henry's father [Evan] big character—title, 'Greed Of The Meek.' " On September 16, the author said that he was trying to put this play, which started "at revolution," out of his mind—"God knows don't want extra play tacked on to this damned trilogy unless it absolutely must be written." On June 7, 1936, he "decides a 9th play may be necessary to tell the story of the three sisters of Evan Harford, Simon's grandfather."

After his move from Georgia to California, O'Neill became ill and was ordered by the doctor, after a lengthy stay in the hospital in early 1937, to rest for six months. In early 1938 he again had health problems; the neuritis in his arm made writing "too painful." On March 26 he took up *More Stately Mansions*, working on it continuously until January 20, 1939. The next two days he wrote general notes "on all 9 plays, interrelationship." On January 23 he returned to *A Touch of the Poet*, completing its third draft on May 19. He concluded this particular period devoted to the Cycle as he began it, with *The Calms of Capricorn*, now the fifth play. On June 5 he felt "fed up and stale on Cycle after 4½ years of not thinking of any other work" and decided to take up something new. The following day O'Neill recorded the first ideas for *The Iceman Cometh* and *Long Day's Journey into Night*.

After finishing these two dramas, the author resumed work on the Cycle in October 1940 but found its first two plays "too complicated—tried to get too much into them, too many interwoven themes & motives, psychological & spiritual." The next day he asked himself if he should abandon these dramas and "go back old 7 play Cycle, starting with what is now 3rd play—material too valuable for that." His entry the following day reads, "Having slept on it, awake with idea for four plays to take place of 1st & 2nd, expanding Cycle to eleven!— 1st to go back to 1755 when the Three Sisters were young girls." On October 23 he decided to "go ahead & make notes & outlines for the four plays of new idea which would replace 1st and 2nd plays—very interested, as it is worth the time & trouble." During the next month he made notes for these four "new" plays and for rewriting *A Touch of the Poet* and *More Stately Mansions* "into new scheme by carrying on the Three Sisters into these plays."

O'Neill spent only thirteen days on the Cycle in 1941. Determined to complete "at least one play of Cycle," he resumed work on *A Touch of the Poet* the following year, noting on November 15, 1942, that he had finished the new version of it and "made it much better play, both as itself & as part of Cycle—a triumph, I feel, considering sickness & war strain—still has minor faults —needs some cutting and condensing, but that can wait a while." His last comment on the Cycle, dated February 21, 1943, reads, "tore up the part of Act One, 'The Life of Bessie Bowen,' I had written—n[o]. g[ood].—and this play is basis for last play of Cycle now (with many changes)." On this day he also destroyed the completed first longhand drafts of the Cycle's first two plays, "The Greed of the Meek" and "And Give Me Death." Sixteen years had elapsed between the time he recorded his first idea for the Bessie Bowen concept, "It Cannot Be Mad?," and this date of destruction, twelve years since he entered his initial idea in the notebook for *The Calms of Capricorn* in 1931. O'Neill's despair, the result of many factors—the war, ill health, human materialism—is reflected in his letter of July 17, 1940, to Langner: "The Cycle is on the shelf, and God knows if I can ever take it up again because I cannot foresee any future in this country or anywhere else to which it could spiritually belong." On two occasions, in 1943 and in 1953, O'Neill destroyed unfinished Cycle plays; only *A Touch of the Poet* and a typescript of *More Stately Mansions* were spared.

A TOUCH OF THE POET

In September 1937, while thinking "in terms of nine plays and a continuity of family lives over a space of 150 years," O'Neill described the mode of the Cycle to Barrett Clark, saying it "goes back to my old vein of ironic tragedy— with, I hope, added psychological depth and insight." There was to be "nothing of *Ah, Wilderness!* or *Days Without End* in this Cycle. They were an interlude." As the overall title, "A Tale of Possessors Self-Dispossessed," suggests, the Cycle shows the disastrous effects that greed and material prosperity have on the accumulators of wealth.

The central character of the Cycle's first play, which is set during the French and Indian War, is an Irishman who had enlisted in the British Army to escape the poverty of his native Ireland. After being sent to America, he deserts and eventually makes his way to a prosperous farm owned by an attractive young widow. There he sacrifices his dream of freedom and succumbs to the two vices, greed and lust, that destroy the characters of

O'Neill's other historical New England plays, *Desire Under the Elms* and *Mourning Becomes Electra*. Hamilton Basso states that "according to O'Neill's scheme, the seed of greed that had thus been planted was to grow and flower throughout the cycle. The cycle, although primarily the story of an American family, was also intended to be the story of America."* The dramatist prophesied the coming of the retribution Americans deserved for their materialism. He comments:

> We've followed the same selfish, greedy path as every other country in the world. We talk about the American Dream, and want to tell the world about the American Dream, but what is that dream, in most cases, but the dream of material things? I sometimes think that the United States, for this reason, is the greatest failure the world has ever seen. We've been able to get a very good price for our souls in this country—the greatest price perhaps that has ever been paid—but you'd think that after all these years, and all that man has been through, we'd have sense enough—*all* of us—to understand that the whole secret of human happiness is summed up in a sentence that even a child can understand. The sentence? "For what shall it profit a man if he shall gain the whole world and lose his own soul?"*

O'Neill's final sentence was to become the central motif of the Cycle.

By the time O'Neill started *A Touch of the Poet*, the only extant, completed Cycle play, he seems to have abandoned his plan to tell the story of a single Irish Anglo-American family. Instead, he shows two ethnically different families in conflict: the immigrant Irish Melodys and the aristocratic Yankee Harfords, drawing, undoubtedly, on his own experiences: the rejection of his Irish family by wealthy, socially prominent New Londoners. Yet the play's central character, Con Melody, seems to be an authentic descendant of the Irishman who, after join-

---

*Hamilton Basso, "The Tragic Sense—III," *The New Yorker*, March 13, 1948, p. 40.

ing the British army and coming to America, had to choose between his dream and his lust for women and wealth.

The son of a "thievin' shebeen keeper" in Ireland, Con enlists in the British army and rises to the rank of major. While serving gloriously in Spain, he allows his weakness for women to destroy him. Caught by a Spanish noble making love to the nobleman's wife, Con kills the husband and is subsequently forced to resign his commission in disgrace. In spite of his lowly origins, he has always considered himself a "gentleman's son," a pretense he maintains even after immigrating to America and encountering the rejection of "the damned Yankee gentry." To maintain his illusion of being a true aristocrat, Con dresses in "old, expensive, finely tailored clothes of the style worn by English aristocracy." He overplays his role of polished gentleman, "which has become more real than his real self to him." He is a tall, powerful man and has the haughty, erect stance becoming an officer. Beyond shaky nerves, his body

> shows no effects of hard drinking. It has a bull-like, impervious strength, a tough peasant vitality. It is his face that reveals the ravages of dissipation—a ruined face, which was once extraordinarily handsome in a reckless, arrogant fashion. It is still handsome—the face of an embittered Byronic hero, with a finely chiseled nose over a domineering, sensual mouth set in disdain, pale, hollow-cheeked, framed by thick, curly iron-gray hair.

Con's affair in Spain was only one of his betrayals of his young wife, Nora. After marrying her, he had left her alone "to have her child and nivir saw her again till he was sent home from Spain." Although he was in love with her, he was "ashamed of her in his pride at the same time because her folks were only ignorant peasants on the Melody estate." Years of sacrifice, overwork, and abuse have taken their toll on her. Once pretty, at forty Nora looks "much older" and "has become too worn out to take care of her appearance." She has beautiful blue eyes, but her black hair is streaked with gray and her red hands are knotted by rheumatism. "Her body is dumpy, with sagging breasts." She possesses spirit, however, "which shines through and makes her lovable, a simple sweetness and charm, something gentle and sad and, somehow, dauntless."

Sara Melody, twenty, is a pretty girl with black hair, rosy cheeks, and beautiful deep-blue eyes. Like the offspring in many O'Neill plays, she resembles both parents: "There is a curious blending in her of what are commonly considered aristocratic and peasant characteristics." She has a fine forehead, a slender neck, and a thin, straight nose. On the other hand, she has "large feet and broad, ugly hands with stubby fingers." Sara, like Abbie in *Desire Under the Elms* and Josie in *A Moon for the Misbegotten*, is the typical idealized O'Neill woman. Her mouth "has a touch of coarseness and sensuality and her jaw is too heavy. Her figure is strong and graceful, with full, firm breasts and hips, and a slender waist." While her voice is soft and musical, her speech has a "stilted quality about it, due to her restraining a tendency to lapse into brogue."

Con reportedly was born in a castle in Ireland, but because of his disgrace, which drove him out of Ireland, and his extravagant way of life in imitation of European gentility, he has been reduced to running a small tavern in a village a few miles from Boston. Considering it beneath his dignity to work, he has forced his wife and daughter to assume responsibility for supporting the family. Significantly, the play is set in July 1828, the year President John Quincy Adams, the New England Yankee aristocrat whom Con initially supports, is defeated by Andrew Jackson, son of a poor Irish immigrant, who is championed by the lowly Irish laborers who patronize the barroom. Preferring to disassociate himself from his crude fellow countrymen, Con rarely enters the barroom, which is separated from the tavern's dining room, the scene of the play's action, by a thin partition.

Con is hopelessly split. He wears the mask of gentleman and maintains, on the surface, an aura of aristocratic respectability. The facade nearly extinguishes his peasant identity. The reality of the latter self lies beyond the doorway to the barroom in the rough Irishmen he shuns. Beside this door hangs a large mirror, a through-the-looking-glass escape, facilitating Con's flights of fancy about his idealized identity. Con, the consummate actor, preens himself before the mirror, reciting lines from Byron in a manner worthy of James O'Neill.

There is much about Con and the other characters that is autobiographical. He, like James O'Neill, is an Irish immigrant with unpleasant memories of his father. Each, in an effort to be accepted as a gentleman, worked hard to eliminate his Irish brogue and to lose his peasant manners. Each, lacking sound business judgment, has been swindled in land speculation deals. Each was notorious in his youth as a womanizer, Con with whores and ladies he met while serving on the continent, James with actresses met on company road tours. Both are heavy drinkers and indulge for the same reasons: to forget the tragedies of their wasted lives and to blot out the vision of what their wives have become. Both made a tragic error. Con forfeited a brilliant future as an officer because of his affair in Spain; James sacrificed his career as a leading Shakespearean actor because of the lure of easy money. The two men are criticized by their offspring, with whom they are usually in conflict, for their shoddy treatment of their wives and for not providing adequately for their families.

While the peasant side of Con resembles James O'Neill, the dreamer side bears a likeness to the dramatist. Both have the same physical qualities: the sensual mouth and aquiline nose, the tall, muscular body, the shaky hands and nerves. Both have a touch of the poet and frequently quote Byron. Both were forced into ill-advised marriages with pregnant young women whom they later abandoned. The author's true self-portrait in the play, however, is the offstage character Simon Harford, the aristocratic Yankee gentleman Sara hopes to marry. Simon's description, which appears in *More Stately Mansions*, the sequel to *A Touch of the Poet*, matches that of the playwright: both have a tall, wiry build, a wide, sensitive mouth, a fine forehead, a long face, and brown hair and eyes. Simon, like O'Neill, has a touch of the poet; he also has a similar political philosophy.

The two mothers in *A Touch of the Poet*, Nora Melody and Deborah Harford, are the two sides of Ella O'Neill. Nora, the victimized wife-mother side, married a man who uprooted her from home and family and took her to live in hostile Yankee New England. Nora and Ella are forced to cope with alcoholic husbands and guilt feelings for having abandoned Catholicism; both attempt to escape into the past to a happier time. The two women have little in common physically except their beautiful eyes, sweet charm, and sad gentleness. Each is described as having been pretty as a girl.

Deborah Harford is Ella O'Neill/Mary Tyrone in her victimizer role. Both have nearly identical physical attributes: the youthful figure, the pale face with its high cheekbones, thin nose, and full lips, brown eyes, and long lashes. Deborah's face is framed by thick red-brown hair; Ella/Mary's by thick white hair that was once a "rare shade of reddish brown." About Deborah's "whole personality is a curious atmosphere of deliberate detachment," a "studied aloofness"; there is "something perversely assertive about it too." These qualities are found in Ella/Mary, the morphine addict, who retreats from reality and family, becoming increasingly detached and defensive.

There are a number of themes in *A Touch of the Poet*. Most evident is the external Irish-Yankee conflict, which concludes with the ultimate emergence and triumph of the Irish immigrant Melodys over the native New England Harfords. The chief adversaries in this conflict are

Sara and Deborah, each of whom wants to possess Simon, the lover/son. In this play two women vie for the affections of a man; in *Desire Under the Elms* the triangular situation was reversed. The objective in both plays is the same: greed for the land, for material possessions, and security, and lust. Sara possesses the same promiscuous spirit that caused her father's downfall, only in her it facilitates her rise in the world. Her willingness to seduce a man to force him to marry her brings her victory.

A secondary theme of the play is the usual internal family clash between parent and offspring. The traits Sara resents in her father are the very ones that are dominant in her. Both want to "belong" to respectable Yankee society and will use ruthless, selfish means to achieve their goal. After Con, a former officer in Wellington's army, emigrates to New England, he resumes his title of "Major" and buys a thoroughbred mare to project the image of a gentleman. Because of his extravagances, his wife, Nora, becomes a drudge as she tries to pay creditors and keep the inn operating. In addition, Con scorns and mistreats his worn, unkempt wife because of her peasant manners and Irish brogue. Sara, in turn, despises her father for his cruelty to her mother and for his drinking. Having been sent to a good school, Sara left, unable to bear the thought of her mother "slaving her heart out."

Con is in conflict with "the faith" and the Catholic clergy, as well as with his daughter and his Yankee neighbors and Irish patrons. Scornful of his Catholic heritage, he says he "hates priests," believing they "tricked him" into marrying the pregnant Nora. When the drunken Irish sing a disrespectful song about the Catholic clergy, Con is pleased by their irreverence and urges them to repeat it for his wife, who "still has a secret fondness for priests." All three Melodys are apostates, but only Nora longs for the old peasant faith and cherishes its dogmas. Con's most important conflict is with himself, for he rejects the reality of who he is and what he is and clings to the pretentions and illusions he has created for himself.

The play opens in the dining room of Melody's tavern on the morning of July 27, 1828. Appearing briefly are Mickey Maloy, twenty-six, the amiable but cunning bar-keep, and Con's cousin, Jamie Cregan, a tall middle-aged Irishman whose face is marred by a saber cut inflicted at the battle of Talavera, where, as a corporal, he served under Con. Sara's entrance ends their conversation, which provides the exposition. Later, when alone with her mother, Sara urges her to leave the profligate Con. Nora boasts of her pride in the love she has for her husband and warns Sara, "It's little you know of love and you never will, for there's the same divil of pride in you that's in him, and it'll kape you from ivir givin' all of yourself." Nora would walk through the "fires of hell" to be with Con and "sing with joy" at the pain "if only his kiss was on" her mouth. To Sara, love is a token to barter: "I'll love where it'll gain me freedom and not put me in slavery for life." She has this type of utilitarian love for Simon.

Sara describes Simon as a "born dreamer." After graduating from Harvard, he declared his independence from his father, owner of one of the largest shipping companies in the country, left home, and built his own cabin by a nearby lake. He aspires to live a simple life, like that of Thoreau, and to write a book denouncing material-ism. Sara discovered him in his rustic dwelling and quickly won the love of this lonely hermit. Simon failed to see that Sara, in her own person, contains all the seeds of the greed he abhores. When the young man became ill, she brought him home to the inn to care for him. She says: "I want to love Simon just enough so I can marry him without cheating him, or myself. For I'm going to marry him, Mother. It's my chance to rise in the world and nothing will keep me from it."

Con, suffering from a hangover, appears. He informs Sara that he has made inquiries about the Harford family and has discovered that the father is a gentleman "by

Yankee standards" and that the mother "springs from generations of well-bred gentlefolk." Con is totally deluded about his own situation and worth, being fully convinced Simon's father will formalize a marriage contract with him. Sara tells him, sneeringly, that he lives in "a fairy tale where only dreams are real . . . you can't tell any more what's dead and a lie and what's the living truth." When alone, after his third drink, the "hair av the dog," Con, now "arrogantly self-assured," swaggers to the mirror and praises the image it reflects. He stares into his eyes in the glass and recites from Byron's *Childe Harold*, as if it were an incantation by which he summons pride to justify his life to himself:

> I have not loved the World, nor the World me,
> I have not flattered its rank breath, nor bowed
> To its idolatries a patient knee,
> Nor coined my cheek to smiles,—nor cried aloud
> In worship of an echo: in the crowd
> They could not deem me one of such—I stood
> Among them, but not of them. . . .

In the next act, which takes place later that morning, Sara complains about the additional work involved in preparing for the dinner with which her father plans to celebrate the anniversary of Talavera. Only Cregan is deemed worthy to sit with Con. The Irish rabble are to sit at a separate table. Father and daughter argue. He calls her a "scheming Peasant" who is "laying snares" to trap Simon. "And if all other tricks fail, there's always one last trick to get him through his honor!" Nora defends Sara and prophesies "her rise in the world. We'll see the day when she'll live in a grand mansion, dressed in silks and satins, riding in a carriage with coachman and footman."

Alone, Con again stands before the mirror and recites favorite lines from Byron. This time he is observed by Deborah Harford, who enters and "stares incredulously" at him. She is impressed in spite of herself by his bearing and handsome face. Con bows gallantly, appraising this delicate, aristocratic woman with the sensual pleasure "a lover of horseflesh would have in the appearance of a thoroughbred horse." She falls under the spell of "the successful seducer of old"; "their eyes meet and at the nakedly physical appraisement she sees in his, a fascinated fear suddenly seizes her." He is just about to kiss her when she smells the whisky on his breath. Con is humiliated when he discovers Deborah's identity, and he flees to his room, where he plans to don his British uniform and redeem himself in her eyes.

When they meet, Sara knows instinctively that Deborah hates her, but she is determined to fight for Simon. After the mother returns from a visit with her son, she warns Sara that Simon, "an inveterate dreamer" like herself, is about to be disinherited by his father, who also "has a dream—a conservative, material dream." She relates details of the Harford history, the unhappy end of the Harford men who instilled their avarice into their women, who would have approved of Sara. The Harford men cannot part with their dreams: "that is the family curse."* Simon's book, she assures Sara, will never be completed, but it is "written on his conscience." Frightened by her contact with the Melodys and the threat they represent, Deborah longs to return to her enclosed garden, which symbolizes her repressed, joyless Yankee society, and to "listen indifferently again while the footsteps of life pass and recede along the street beyond the high wall." Con is furious when he enters later and discovers that Deborah has gone. He looks "extraordinarily hand-

---

*Information about Simon's grandfather, Evan, that appears here is taken from plays of the Cycle that precede *A Touch of the Poet*. Evan, scornful of the Revolution, went to France and became a "Jacobin, a worshiper of Robespierre." Evan's half-sisters and wife were drawn into a greedy scheme to make a fortune out of privateering. Deborah herself had been caught up in the sisters' worship of Napoleon and dreamed at one time of being Josephine. Her husband took her to Paris on their honeymoon to witness Napoleon's coronation.

some and distinguished" in his brilliant scarlet full-dress
major's uniform. Sara pleads with him: "Oh, Father, why
can't you ever be the thing you seem to be? The man you
were. I'm sorry I never knew that soldier. I think he was
the only man who wasn't just a dream."

By eight that evening, in Act III, Con and his dinner
guests are all drunk. Yet the host holds "his liquor like a
gentleman." The men return to the barroom, and Sara
appears. She cannot conceal her disgust at her father's
vanity: "All I pray to God is that someday when you're
admiring yourself in the mirror something will make you
see at last what you really are! That will be revenge in full
for all you've done to Mother and me!" The father retaliates by ridiculing her peasant qualities, her "thick
wrists and ugly, peasant paws." Sara's curiosity quells her
anger when Con speaks of his visit that afternoon with
Simon. He discovered that Deborah had warned her son
that a hasty marriage would "start a lot of evil-minded
gossip." In his best grand-gentleman manner, Con announced earlier that he plans to work out a "settlement"
with Simon's father. Henry Harford must be made to
provide an allowance for Simon that befits Sara's position.
Sara laughs, remarking that "Old Harford might not
think it an honor to have his son marry your daughter."

Con tells Sara, confidentially, that Simon is too good
for her. "To be brutally frank, my dear, all I can see in you
is a common, greedy, scheming, cunning peasant girl,
whose only thought is money and who has shamelessly
thrown herself at a young man's head because his family
happens to possess a little wealth and position." Remembering his own marital mistake, Con says, "Such a marriage would be a tragic misalliance for him—and God
knows I know the sordid tragedy of such a union." He will
not refuse his consent to the marriage, however, if she
tricks Harford into getting her pregnant. Looking at him
with hatred and contempt, Sara thanks him for his "fatherly advice": "If the worst comes to the worst, I promise

you I'll remember." Overwhelmed with sorrow for his cruel words, Con apologizes, but Sara has left the room.

When Nicholas Gadsby, the Harford family's pompous lawyer, enters, Con again makes a terrible blunder and asks him if he has come to arrange a settlement. Gadsby, who has been sent to "buy off" the Melodys, misunderstands Con and interprets his speeches as a ploy to get a larger sum of money. Their conversation degenerates into a kind of comic exchange that foreshadows that of the Yankee Harker and the Irishman Phil Hogan in *A Moon for the Misbegotten*. Gadsby asks if Melody is trying to "make a fool of me." The Irishman responds: "As for making a fool of you, Sir, I would be the fool if I attempted to improve on God's handiwork." Gadsby finally explains Harford's offer: the payment of $3,000 if the Melody family will leave the area and move, preferably to the "West—to Ohio, say." The idea of marriage with "such a difference in station" is "preposterous."

Humiliated and enraged, Con raises "his fist to smash Gadsby in the face," but Sara rushes in to stop him. Having overheard the conversation, she too is humiliated. Con orders two of the Irishmen who burst into the room, drawn instinctively by a good fight, to "throw this thing out! Kick it down to the crossroads!" His pride wounded, his mind still clouded by drink, Con asks Cregan to accompany him on a visit to old Harford, who must either apologize or face him in a duel. "I'll put a bullet through him, so help me, Christ!" Desperately, Sara begs her father to reconsider and promises to avenge the family by marrying Simon. When he forbids the marriage and Sara threatens to defy him, Con exclaims: "You filthy peasant slut! You whore! I'll see you dead first!" Sara vows not to let her father destroy her dreams: "I'll show him I can play at the game of gentleman's honor, too!" She goes upstairs, leaving her mother to her lonely vigil.

Act IV opens at around midnight that night. Maloy appears briefly, trying to get Nora to take a drink. All the

Irish in the area have congregated in the barroom, waiting to hear of the great Irish victory. Maloy says, "If they do hate Con Melody, he's Irish, and they hate the Yanks worse. They're all hopin' he's bate the livin' lights out of Harford." Nora sits huddled in a shawl. Sara enters, wearing nightclothes. "There is a change in her. All the bitterness and defiance have disappeared from her face. It looks gentle and calm and at the same time dreamily happy and exultant." In a long monologue, Nora at last expresses her resentment toward her husband. In many of O'Neill's plays, particularly the later ones, a character confesses past misdeeds. Here Nora says, "I have the black tormint in my mind that it's the fault of the mortal sin I did with him unmarried, and the promise he made me make to leave the Church that's kept me from ever confessin' to a priest." She yearns for the courage to wake a priest to hear her confession "and give me God's forgiveness that'd bring my soul peace and comfort so I wouldn't feel the three of us were damned." She goes toward the door, as if to go out, but shrinks back, fearing that her confession would be a betrayal of Con.

Nora wonders why Sara talks as if "still half in a dream" and is shocked to hear that she went to Simon's room in her nightclothes. He proposed and warned her that they would be poor at first. Although he hates trade, he will accept a friend's offer of a partnership in a small mill. He will, however, write his book and "never let himself become a slave to the greed for more than enough." Like Abbie in *Desire Under the Elms*, Sara set out deliberately to seduce a man for materialistic purposes but afterwards found herself trapped by her own emotions. She laughs now at her "crazy dreams of riches and a grand estate." Told that God will punish her for her mortal sin, Sara repeats her mother's earlier reckless words: "Let Him! If He'd say to me, for every time you kiss Simon you'll have a thousand years in hell, I wouldn't care, I'd wear out my lips kissing him!"

Cregan comes in, supporting the dazed Con Melody. His halting movements are not "those of drunkenness. It is more as if a sudden shock or stroke had altered his coordination and left him in a stupor." His uniform is torn, his face bruised and bleeding. "His eyes are empty and lifeless. He stares at his wife and daughter as if he did not recognize them." Throughout Cregan's narration, Con sits lifeless and speechless. Arriving at the Harford home, the two men had been called "drunken Micks" by a servant. When Con tried to enter the house, the butler and two other servants attempted to push him back. A brawl ensued. The Irish victory was short-lived; four policemen, carrying clubs, pulled Con and Cregan out to the street, where they were beaten and subdued. Con mumbles to himself, jeeringly, "that pale Yankee bitch watching from a window, sneering with disgust." When Cregan tells Sara that she is to blame for her father's condition, Sara responds, "I can revenge my own insults, and I have! I've beaten the Harfords—and he's only made a fool of himself for her to sneer at. But I've beaten her and I'll sneer last!"

Later, after Con rushes out of the house carrying his dueling pistols, Sara reacts as Lavinia Mannon did just before her brother shot himself; she says, "I wish he was—." At that moment the sound of a shot is heard, and she becomes genuinely concerned and repentant, fearing that her father has killed himself. He has, however, shot the mare, not himself. When he returns, he "appears completely possessed by a paralyzing stupor." Sara laughs hysterically, and her father, "in the broadest brogue, his voice coarse and harsh," says that he is roaring with laughter himself. "It's the damnedest joke a man ivir played on himself since time began."

From this point to the end of the play, Con is referred to as having died. Deborah Harford symbolized all that the pretentious gentleman side of Con admired. Her witnessing his disgrace destroyed the illusions he had of being a gentleman. After the beating, he identified the "pale Yankee bitch" with his beautiful thoroughbred mare. He had intended to kill himself after shooting the mare, the living reminder "av all his lyin' boasts and dreams," but, as he says, her death finished him. So he didn't bother to shoot himself "because it'd be a mad thing to waste a good bullet on a corpse!" He puts to rest "the late lamented auld liar and lunatic, Major Cornelius Melody."

For one brief moment Con recalls the loving look the mare gave him before she died: "proud, understanding pride—loving me—she saw I was dying with her. She understood! She forgave me!" Just as Margaret in *The Great God Brown* promises to bury the mask of Dion, symbol of his assumed self, Con says in brogue, "I'll bury his Major's damned red livery av bloody England." Honor should also be buried, he advises Sara, if she would "rise in this world. Remember the blood in your veins and be your grandfather's true descendent." She can easily seduce Simon, who is "full av dacency and dreams, and looney, too, wid a touch av the poet in him." Told she has already done so, Con prophesies that she will have a difficult time "rootin' out" Simon's dreams but that eventually she will "live in a Yankee mansion as big as a castle." He then makes her a wedding present of the "Major's place" where Simon built his cabin in the woods, the land the "Yankees swindled him into buyin' for his American estate."

Con kisses Nora, promises to be a "real husband," and heads for the bar. Desperately, Sara pleads: "Won't you be yourself again?" Con warns her not "to raise the dead." He passes the mirror and mocks his old self, the "loon" that pretended he was a "lord wid a touch av the poet." Of the Major, he says, "God rest his soul in the flames av tormint!" Sara makes a final desperate attempt to hold him back. She even promises to tell Simon she cannot marry him. Con crumbles visibly, having "no character left in which to hide to defend himself." He gives her a slight blow and says he will force her to make an honest gentleman of Simon. He then goes into the bar where, after a roar of shouts, his voice is heard proposing a toast to Andy Jackson. Nora is reconciled to Con's new self, saying, "God pity him, he's had to live all his life alone in the hell av pride." Like Jim Harris, who promises at the conclusion of *All God's Chillun Got Wings* to play right up to the gates of heaven with the demented Ella, Nora says: "And I'll play any game he likes and give him love in it." When the music resumes in the bar, Sara calls it "a requiem for the dead. May the hero of Talavera rest in peace."

Nowhere in plays depicting the Irish-Yankee conflict does O'Neill surpass the comprehensive dramatization of it presented in *A Touch of the Poet*, which probes the inner frustrations and tragedies facing the immigrant Irish in a new country. The battle Con wages within his poet-peasant soul was fought by every Irish immigrant in the early nineteenth century who sought to preserve his dignity and identity in an alien land. Con is a man with a dream; because he desires more from life than an ordinary existence and bare necessities, he is beaten and humiliated. The dream is shattered, the poet destroyed, and only the Irish peasant remains.

It is Sara who triumphs over the Yankees in the end, but she pays a tragic price. She, more than anyone else, is responsible for her father's defeat. Profiting from the errors of her father, who had been swindled by the Yankees, Sara fights back with the weapons of deceit the Yankees themselves use. Like Abbie in *Desire Under the Elms*, Sara is redeemed by love. *A Touch of the Poet* concludes with Sara's vow to sacrifice all her dreams of wealth for Simon's love; there is, however, still a latent wellspring of greed in her nature, and the consuming passion of it will be revealed in *More Stately Mansions*. Sara's avarice destroys the touch of the poet in her father in this play; in *More Stately Mansions* her greed merges with lust and corrupts Simon and the poet in him.

The world premiere of *A Touch of the Poet* was presented at the Royal Dramatic Theatre in Stockholm on March 29, 1957. The following year, on October 2, it opened in New York. While the play received favorable reviews, some critics failed to comprehend Con's multi-faceted nature; yet it is the complexity of this character that raises the play from the level of melodrama to pure tragedy. His dreamer-poet aspirations, while at times vain and ridiculous, represent a man's highest hope to assert his humanity, the weapon this Irishman brings to America to ward off crass Yankee materialism. His defeat can be viewed as a blow dealt to every man who resists selling his soul for wealth and power. *A Touch of the Poet* clearly shows how O'Neill intended to attack American materialism in the Cycle, "A Tale of Possessors Self-Dispossessed." In this play, Sara, riding roughshod over her father, is on her way to becoming a possessor. In *More Stately Mansions* and subsequent Cycle plays she becomes one of the "self-dispossessed." For its vivid, believable characters and the strength of its message and story, *A Touch of the Poet* deserves a reputable place in American drama. While it does not rank with the two masterpieces, *Long Day's Journey into Night* and *The Iceman Cometh*, *A Touch of the Poet* is one of O'Neill's great plays.

45. *More Stately Mansions*

More Stately Mansions continues the chronicle of the immigrant Irish Melody family in America. In the final scene of *A Touch of the Poet*, Con Melody envisions his daughter Sara's future after her marriage to the wealthy, aristocratic Simon Harford: "She'll live in a Yankee mansion, as big as a castle, on a grand estate." His prediction is realized in the sequel, although Sara's ascent to grandeur is not without tragic consequences. Her ruthless scheming destroys her husband's touch of the poet as it did her father's in the earlier play. While she was at odds with only her father in *A Touch of the Poet*, she is in conflict with two characters in *More Stately Mansions*: her husband, Simon, and her mother-in-law, Deborah Harford. At the close of the first play, Con is "completely possessed by a paralyzing stupor" and left "empty and lifeless" after his defeat by the Yankees. The sequel could be called "Sara's Revenge," for both Simon and Deborah are plunged into madness at its conclusion. Not until that final tragic scene does Sara realize the role she has played as destroyer of the lives of others. In the Cycle play that follows *More Stately Mansions*, *The Calms of Capricorn*, she repents her former misdeeds and lives selflessly, in atonement, for her demented husband and their four sons.

The four Harford brothers were the central figures in O'Neill's original scheme for the Cycle in 1935. Each brother was to be the focus of one of the four plays in *The Calms of Capricorn* series. On January 27, however, he conceived the idea for *A Touch of the Poet*, deciding to continue the "story of Harford and Sara before 1st play opens—this may develop into additional 1st play, making five in all" (Work Diary). The following month, on February 25, he began an outline for the fifth drama, *More Stately Mansions*, finishing it two months later. He completed the four acts and Epilogue of the first draft of *More Stately Mansions* on September 8, 1939, noting in his Work Diary that it "needs lot of revision & rewriting—is as long as Strange Interlude!*—but don't think will be able to cut length much." In January 1939 he finished a second longhand script and a typed third draft. The following year, in November, he revised and pruned *More Stately Mansions*, but he never wrote a final draft of it.

On February 21, 1943, O'Neill made the decision to destroy the Cycle's first two plays, "Greed of the Meek" and "And Give Me Death," and the two longhand drafts of *More Stately Mansions*. The typescript of the latter draft, however, was spared, but the author inserted a note into it, stating: "Unfinished Work. This script to be destroyed in case of my death! Eugene O'Neill."† The typescript was included, accidentally, in a box of material sent to the O'Neill collection at Yale University in 1951 when O'Neill and his wife, Carlotta, moved from Marblehead to Boston. In 1957, four years after the dramatist's death, Mrs. O'Neill gave Karl Ragnar Gierow, then Director of the Royal Dramatic Theatre in Stockholm, permission to shorten the script for a Swedish production. Gierow worked for the next five years translating the script into Swedish and reducing it by half. He eliminated the first scene of Act I and the Epilogue, which link *More Stately*

---

*On October 20, 1940, after the project had become a nine-play Cycle, O'Neill expressed his concern in the Work Diary about the length of its first two plays, "Greed of the Meek" and "And Give Me Death": "both as long as 'S[trange] I[nterlude].' . . . too many interwoven themes & motives, psychological & spiritual." Two days later he states: "Awake with idea for four plays to take place of 1st & 2nd, expanding Cycle to eleven!"

†Eugene O'Neill, *More Stately Mansions*, edited by Donald Gallup (New Haven: Yale University Press, 1964). This and the following statements about the Swedish acting version appear in Mr. Gallup's Prefatory Note, p. x.

Mansions with the Cycle play that precedes it, *A Touch of the Poet*, and the one that follows it, *The Calms of Capricorn*. The world premiere of this four-hour version was presented in Stockholm on November 9, 1962, and was well-received. A program note informed the audience that "there is not a scene, not a passage, not a line in the drama which is presented tonight that is not by O'Neill himself."

Using the Swedish script, Donald Gallup prepared an English version for publication, restoring some of the passages originally omitted but retaining "the words as O'Neill wrote them." In his Prefatory Note for the play, he makes a cautionary statement that must be remembered by all those who either see or read *More Stately Mansions*: "It is, of necessity, far from the finished work that the dramatist envisioned. Had he lived to see the play published and staged, O'Neill would certainly have revised and rewritten extensively, as he always did, in galley and page proofs, and even in the course of production." It is Mr. Gallup's belief that the play "provides, even in its incompletely revised state, a *better* indication than does *A Touch of the Poet* of what he had intended in the Cycle."

Carlotta O'Neill gave director José Quintero permission to prepare an American acting script for *More Stately Mansions*. He made his own cutting, restoring the first scene of Act I and other segments but reducing the script to a three-hour version. The play opened on September 12, 1967, in Los Angeles and on November 11 in New York. Critics disagreed on the feasibility of producing a play O'Neill had not pronounced to be finished. They were unanimous, however, in their castigation of Quintero's efforts. Clive Barnes wrote, "In its unfinished, raw and tortured state it does, in my view, O'Neill's memory a disservice. With friends like Mr. Quintero, the shade of O'Neill might think he needs no enemies." Barnes lamented the fact that "at the end, disregarded and underestimated," O'Neill "was reduced to tearing up plays in a dead hotel room. Yet it was toward the end that he found his real greatness, and there are passages in *More Stately Mansions* that make you wonder what kind of play he might have written had he written it." He concludes by saying he left the theater in "sadness for what had been done, what could have been done, and what might thought to have been done.*" Walter Kerr praised Ingrid Bergman's performance as Deborah Harford and Colleen Dewhurst's as Sara but criticized Arthur Hill's interpretation of Simon. Citing Hill as a "first-rate actor," Kerr stated: "Blame must be passed on to director José Quintero, who has here really helped no one. . . . Mr. Quintero seems determined to reinforce what is already wrong." Kerr called the play "a ruin: a great architectural emptiness derived from slaved-over blueprints," yet he believed that it should have been produced. "Because it was a project for the stage, our information about it can only be increased by seeing it on the stage." Kerr closes by saying he will remember the play "with regret and a kind of longing."†

In his explanation of the overall scheme for the Cycle, O'Neill told Ingrid Bergman when they met in 1941: "I am writing one hundred and fifty years of American history. It is the same family, and they go from young to middle-age, to old and dying, and then on to the next generation. It is going to be about American history and a family that we follow through the ups and downs of this country."** He had depicted nineteenth-century Yankee

*Clive Barnes, "Quintero's Completion of Play at Broadhurst," *The New York Times*, November, 1, 1967, p. 45.

†Walter Kerr, "No One Will Ever Live in It," *The New York Times*, November 12, 1967, Section 2, pp. 1, 5.

**Ironically, O'Neill himself had asked Ingrid Bergman to appear in all of the nine plays of the Cycle on August 14, 1941, when she visited him while she was starring in a revival of *Anna Christie* in San Francisco. He told her that he wanted to engage a repertory company "that stays with me. After all it is the same family that goes through many generations, and I want the same

families in earlier plays: the Cabots in *Desire Under the Elms* and the Mannons in *Mourning Becomes Electra*. Like these two New England plays, *More Stately Mansions* dramatizes the degeneration of a family obsessed by greed, lust, and incest. Deborah Harford resembles those other two sex-starved Yankee wives, Christine Mannon and Abbie Cabot, abhoring her husband and desiring her son, who, like Orin and Eben, detests his father. These are the same people who inhabit numerous plays in the canon. They are all drawn from the same source: O'Neill and his family. *More Stately Mansions* is the last thinly disguised biography before the searing *Long Day's Journey into Night*. There is, however, one significant difference: the portraits of Deborah and Simon Harford are perhaps closer approximations of O'Neill and his mother than are Edmund and Mary Tyrone. In *Long Day's Journey into Night* the author is still partially protective and guarded in depicting his actual family, although the details of the story duplicate actual events.

The older Deborah Harford in *More Stately Mansions* is a more accurate prototype of Mary Tyrone than the younger view of her in *A Touch of the Poet*. The once red-brown hair is now white. Like Mary Tyrone, Deborah Harford has a youthful figure, a high forehead, and a full-lipped mouth. Deborah's eyes are "so large they look enormous, black, deep-set beneath pronounced brows." Mary's "dark brown eyes appear black. They are unusu-

---

faces. In one play you will have a big part, and in another one you will have a small part. You will play a sister, an aunt, a young daughter." Having recently launched her career in Hollywood, the actress refused the offer. Later, when asked to appear in *More Stately Mansions*, she remembered O'Neill's question: "Are you abandoning me?" and accepted the role—"never mind what the play is like." She notes that while "the play was not really praised by the critics," it was important and should be produced. "After all O'Neill is one of America's greatest playwrights. Even if *More Stately Mansions* is not his best play, it was written by a playwright who will go down in history as the greatest of America." "A Meeting with O'Neill," in *Eugene O'Neill: A World View*, pp. 293–295.

ally large and beautiful, with black brows." Neither woman has found happiness within marriage. In Deborah's recurring daydreams, she envisions herself "a noble adventuress of Louis' Court." Her walled garden becomes "the garden of Versailles," its "summer-house a Temple of Love the King has built as an assignation place where he keeps passionate trysts with you, his mistress, greedy for lust and power." While there is no suggestion in *Long Day's Journey into Night* that Mary Tyrone was ever unfaithful to her husband, either mentally or factually, other mother figures who resemble her, Christine Mannon in *Mourning Becomes Electra* and Nina Leeds in *Strange Interlude*, do indeed have lovers, to the consternation of the O'Neill-like sons, Orin and Gordon. Like Mary in her love-hate attitudes to Edmund and Jamie, Deborah idolizes and overprotects one son, Simon, and rejects the other, Joel. The two women are given the same dual personalities: the vain, chattering, girlish, harmless nature and the cynical, withdrawn, cruel, destructive self that morbidly rakes over the tragic embers of the past, the wrongs, imagined and actual, she has endured.

Like Mary Tyrone, Deborah is desperately lonely in her self-imposed isolation; she too scorns Yankee New Englanders and retreats to an illusionary world. Deborah escapes through hallucinations and near-madness; Mary, through morphine injections. The former's secret place of indulgence is the summerhouse; the latter's, the spare room upstairs. By the end of the two plays, both are in a state of oblivion; neither responds to anguished cries of family members, particularly those of the adored sons, to return to reality. The women have relinquished all hold on the present and regress to a past that held some degree of happiness for them.

Simon, twenty-six, has the same physical attributes as Edmund, twenty-three, the author's self-portrait in *Long Day's Journey into Night*. He is tall and wiry and has a long face with a sensitive mouth and brown eyes and hair. Simon is ill when he is first introduced, as an offstage character in *A Touch of the Poet*. Edmund is waiting for a doctor's diagnosis of his sickness in the first act of *Long Day's Journey into Night*. Like Edmund, Simon has a love-hate relationship with his mother. Infatuated with her, he is willing to follow her into her house of madness, yet at the same time he abhors her efforts to seduce his mind with her illusions. Like many sons in the canon, Simon is the child of both parents: he has his mother's erotic nature, her idealism, and her tendency to escape the real for the illusionary world; he also possesses his father's greed, his business instinct, his inherited love of "perfect freedom." He is the most fully realized example in the canon of the idealistic poet-materialistic business-man dichotomy. In previous plays the dual natures had been found in complementary characters: Dion Anthony and William Brown in *The Great God Brown*, Robert and Andrew Mayo in *Beyond the Horizon*, John and Edward Brown in *Bread and Butter*. Simon is also obsessed by the Madonna-whore complex, identifying his mother in her garden with the former and his wife, Sara, in their afternoon assignations in his office with the latter. Sara demoralizes him by playing the prostitute and destroys his company by her demands that she be paid with pieces of it.

Sara has the same physical attributes as Abbie Cabot in *Desire Under the Elms* and Josie Hogan in *A Moon for the Misbegotten*: the full, firm breasts, slender waist, and wide hips, the sensuous mouth, heavy jaw, black hair, and blue eyes. In *A Touch of the Poet* Sara demonstrates that she is, like them, willing to use her sexuality for precisely the same reasons: to win over the men they desire or love and to gain a home or security. In her greed and ruthlessness, Sara bears a close resemblance to Abbie. The two identify themselves with the lover/sons' mothers; both are undone in the end by their greed and lust.

The unpublished first scene of Act I, which was

retained in the American production of *More Stately
Mansions*, opens in the Melody Tavern in October 1832,
four years after the last scene of *A Touch of the Poet*. It is
the day before Con's funeral, and the wailing keen of
mourning women can be heard from upstairs. According
to Jamie Cregan, a cousin, Con Melody remained a
"walkin' corpse" ever since his humiliation at the Harford
home four years earlier. Con's widow, Nora, plans to pay
her husband's debts and to enter a convent to atone for
the past. Con, she asserts, died from "the broken heart of
his pride," not from drink.

Sara, who has not seen her father in the years since
her marriage, arrives with Simon and their three sons.
Nora coddles the youngest, Jonathan, calling him the
image of his grandfather. She ruminates about her grand-
sons' names: the Yankee name, Ethan, given to the oldest;
the Irish name, Wolfe Tom, to the next son; and Owen
Roe, selected for Sara's expected child should it be another boy. Like Orin in *Mourning Becomes Electra*, who
returns home when Ezra Mannon is being waked, Sara is
reluctant to view her father's body. After doing so, she is
shaken to see him lying in his major's uniform with the
"old sneer" on his face. Nora asserts, "It's the smile av his
soul at peace." Con had, at her request, "died with the
rites av the Church." Sara admits that the thing she
admired most about her father was "his defense of a God
he denied but really believed in!"

Nora wants only to see Sara's rise in the world and
promises, "I'll be praying to the Blessed Virgin to help
you! Ah, I know Almighty God will find it enough if I give
up all worldly thoughts for myself an' He'll forgive my
pride in you!" Sara boasts of Simon's progress in business
and of her own contributions. His only transaction undertaken without her advice was the purchase of the old farm
and cabin by the lake where they had first loved each
other.* Sara is determined to build her mansion on the

*There is a discrepancy here. In *A Touch of the Poet* Con gives
Sara this cabin, the "Major's place," and the land the "Yankees

hill by the lake and to be successful, "for this is America. Not poverty-stricken Ireland where you're a slave. Here you're free to take what you want if you've the power in yourself." To her mother, she confides her concern about Simon's "queer lonely spells" when "he's in a dream world far away." Were it not for her and the children he would be back in his cabin living alone and "writing poetry like he used to, or else writing a book he was planning to show people how to change the Government and all the laws so there'd be no more poor people." She has laughed such talk "out of him."

Simon assures Sara that he will be able to pay off her father's debts and still have enough money to buy out his partner. When he receives a request from his mother to meet her at the cabin, Sara begs him not to go. Instinctively, she feels that the mother "would like nothing better than a chance to come between us." She becomes "suspicious and calculating" and plans to filch Simon's key to the cabin and eavesdrop. "Ah, the divil take honor. It's something men made up for themselves."

When the four-act version of *More Stately Mansions* was shortened to a three-act text for publication, the first scene of Act I was eliminated and the second scene was combined with the two scenes of the original second act to form a new first act. In the published text, the play opens at Simon's cabin "on a small lake near a Massachusetts village, an afternoon in October 1832."* Sara enters first,

---

swindled him into buyin' for his American estate" as a wedding present.

*In the Epilogue Sara takes her sons and her husband, who has amnesia, to live here. This cabin, "ten feet by fifteen," with its "garden near it—beans, potatoes, corn, peas & turnips," is an exact replica of Thoreau's hut at Walden, described in *The Flowering of New England 1815–1865* by Van Wyck Brooks (New York: E. P. Dutton, 1936): "ten by fifteen . . . a door facing the cove . . . a bean-field close by, with a patch of potatoes, corn, peas, and turnips" (p. 359). O'Neill's notes from this book includes a reference to a "China summer house" (p. 21), which is used later to depict Deborah Harford's summerhouse, "with

looks furtively about her, and then enters the cabin, locking the door from the inside. Deborah arrives and allows herself to dream of "romantic evil," of an assignation with her lover-king. She knows that what she is doing to her mind is dangerous and longs to end the "insane interminable dialogues with self." Simon arrives and kisses his mother. She warns him that he is getting his father's "successful-merchant look." Revealing that the dreamer still exists in him, he discusses the book he is planning to write on the perfect society "where there would be no rich nor poor."

Simon questions Deborah's apparent loneliness and is told that his father is wrapped up in politics, fearing Jackson's reelection, and that his brother Joel has become a "confirmed ledger-worm." Asked to visit his mother in her garden, Joel "looked as astounded as if a nun had asked him to her bedroom." It is life that is eluding her, the world beyond her garden wall. All that remains is "the soul, staring into the mirror of itself, seeing the skull of Death leer over its shoulder in the glass!" Simon recalls the roles she played for him as a child, switching from the good queen to the evil queen or wicked witch and wonders what part she is currently enacting. For a moment Deborah allows him to enter her crazed world and reveals a ruthless side as deadly as Sara's. She is the "secret power

---

arched door, painted a Chinese lacquer red." Another passage seems to apply to Deborah Harford. Brooks compares the women who "peered from behind the curtains" to "pixilated creatures . . . half dead and buried in their houses, or buried in the morbid family pride that flourishes where life runs low." Sara and Simon's early home in *More Stately Mansions* is in "a textile-mill town about forty miles from the city" (of Boston). The references to Lowell, Massachusetts, in O'Neill's notes suggest that it is the site of Simon's five mills. He discusses his research for the Cycle in a 1935 letter to Leon Mirlas: "As you can imagine it involves a trememdous amount of reading and note-taking— for even if I find it beside my point to use much historical fact background, still I wish to live in the time of each play when writing it."

behind the throne" who "lets nothing stand in the way of the final goal of power": to make the king her slave. She looks at Simon with "bitter hatred in her eyes" when he ridicules her and contrasts the sedate image she projects with her sordid fantasies. Deborah calls him his "father's son" and warns him that his discontent about his "lost poet's dream" will grow with his success.

As Simon departs, Deborah urges him to be happy: "Love is worth everything!" Alone, she dismisses "that Irish biddy's husband" from her life. Sara angrily confronts her, at first speaking carefully, in "articulate English." She lapses into a brogue, however, when she expresses her willingness to take what she wants from life and mocks Deborah for being a "greedy, contrivin' whore" in her dream. The battle line is drawn: Sara is determined to possess Simon totally.

The following scene takes place in Deborah Harford's garden four years later. The garden is enclosed by an eight-foot-high wall. In the center of the garden is Deborah's octagonal summer-house, which has three steps leading up to its door. Awaiting Deborah are the Harford family's pretentious lawyer, Nicholas Gadsby, fifty-six, and Joel Harford, twenty-nine. His face, while pale and handsome, is "the face of a methodical mediocrity." He appears to possess "a rigid integrity" but lacks self-confidence and ambition. "His whole character has something aridly prim and puritanical about it." Gadsby cannot believe that Deborah is in the summer-house, where she has been hiding since her husband's funeral that morning. Called, she reluctantly comes forth, looking "much older than her forty-nine years." Her eyes are sunk in deep hollows and "have an unhealthy feverish glitter. . . . There is the quality of a death's head about her face, of a skull beginning to emerge from its mask of death." She tells Gadsby that she has only to push open a door in her mind to be free of reality.

The family business, Gadsby states, "stands on the

brink of bankruptcy" because her husband lost his money speculating in western lands. The company can only be saved from ruin, Harford believed, if Simon takes control of it. Deborah loathes the thought of humiliating herself before Sara, who is to be offered the Harford mansion, but she agrees to urge Simon to accept the proposal. She tells Gadsby, "I will cast out my devil"; the old Deborah will be pushed "back where she belongs—in there—in perpetual darkness." She locks the door of the summer house, cursing her mad self and condemning it to "die of starvation."

In the next scene Simon and Sara are shown the following night in the sitting room of their home in a textile-mill town about forty miles from the city. He is nervous and tense from overwork. He has burned his book because of the discrepancy between his idealized "greedless Utopia" and the reality of his life, the pride he takes in "beating competitors in the race for power and wealth and possessions." When Deborah and Joel arrive, Simon goes to the study with his brother to discuss Harford's proposal while their mother explains it to Sara. She is told that a one-half interest in the Harford home and garden is to be hers if she agrees to Simon's taking over the business. Deborah asserts that she has changed and begs for the chance "to find a new life." Simon returns, gloating; he will accept the proposal if he is allowed to absorb the Harford Company into his own. Joel objects, but he is dismissed by his mother as "God's most successful effort in taxidermy." Simon and Deborah establish a truce and resume "their old affectionate intimacy." He objects, however, to living with her. He warns his mother and wife of the difficulty two such opposite characters will have living in the same house, but the women assure him that they have reconciled.

Simon sits alone in his private office at the company, four years later, in Act II. He has aged dramatically. His manner is tense and "curtly dictatorial." He has acquired five profitable mills and has transformed his father's failed business into a successful marine division. Yet he despises being "a Napoleon among traders" and feels that he has been separated into two selves, which must, by necessity, wage "a duel to the death." Joel vainly urges his brother to cease borrowing recklessly and to avoid making the company hated for his unscrupulousness. One thought continually plagues Simon: the idea of the loving friendship his wife and mother have established. Jealously, he feels "entirely left out of it now" and vows to punish his mother for taking possession of Sara. The two women seem to have lost their separate identities and become one woman. Simon no longer sleeps in the same room with Sara, as he feels his mother's living presence near him in the house, just as Eben senses the spirit of his dead mother near him in *Desire Under the Elms*. If he can get his wife out of the staid Yankee atmosphere, Simon decides, she will become the former reckless, lustful Sara. He will test the extent of his wife's greed, aware now that she used her body when they first met to get what she wanted.

Sara arrives looking matronly but still attractive. Just as her father had imitated the refined ways of Yankee gentlemen, Sara, too, having come in close contact with an aristocratic woman, has "taken on a lot of Deborah's well-bred, self-assured pose, and her way of speaking copies Deborah." Simon is determined to repossess what is his: he will inform his mother that evening that the children will not be permitted to see her in the garden or in her rooms in the future; he then tells his wife that he wants the old lustful Sara "to come back to me here" willing "to gamble with the highest possible stake, all she has, to sell her dearly." He asks her to work with him at the office "as my secretary and secret partner." The price to be paid if she agrees to become his mistress is all his worldly goods. "You can get the whole Company from me—that is, of course, piece by piece, as you earn it!" She responds greedily: "The whole Company to be mine! . . . I'll play any game with you you like, and it will be fun playing I'm a wicked, lustful, wanton creature!" Sara does not realize that the plan she accepts will eventually destroy her husband financially and morally. She learns two things from the arrangement: how to run his business and how to play the whore.

That evening, when he visits his mother in her summer-house, Simon forms a partnership with her: a "company of the pure spirit." He now resembles Nina Leeds in *Strange Interlude*, who has different mates to accommodate her different desires. Sara is to be Simon's body's mistress in the afternoon; his mother will be used to "restore his soul" in their late afternoon trysts. The garden now casts a spell on him; it becomes the paradise he knew as a child. He asks Deborah why only she is allowed in the summer-house, "as if it were some secret temple" and she the high priestess. She explains that it is the one place in the world that is totally hers. He recalls the story she used to tell him of the young king of a happy land who was dispossessed by an evil enchantress and forced to wander the world, a homeless outcast. His only salvation was to find a magic door. Finding it at last, he was just about to enter when, from the other side, the enchantress warned him that the door led to night, ruled by ghosts and a wicked witch set to devour him. A spell forced the king to remain for life a beggar before the door. Simon had wanted a new ending in which a good fairy "opened the door and welcomed him home and they were both happy ever after." Now Simon moves as if to enter the summer-house, but Deborah restrains him. He draws back, content for the time being that he has successfully reclaimed his women.

In the third scene, set later that night in the Harford parlor, O'Neill uses thought asides, as in *Strange Interlude*. Simon gloats because his wife and mother sit apart, rather than beside each other on the couch as they always had on previous evenings, chatting about the children

and ignoring him. Old jealousies and suspicions nag the
two women. In an aside, Deborah recalls that she had
never wanted Simon to be conceived. She deplored her
grotesque body made "ugly by his presence." Sara, in
retrospect, secretly resents Simon's treatment of her that
day as a common whore with a price. The two women get
their revenge and resume their old places on the couch.
Deborah whispers that they must never allow Simon to
come between them again. He now feels as though his
wife and his mother have become one woman, the "canni-
bal witch whose greed will devour!" They lock arms and
approach him with the "calculating coquetry of two prostitutes trying to entice a man." Simon tries to ward them
off, saying: "I will be compelled to force either one or the
other of you to leave my home—and my life!—forever!"
The act concludes with thought asides in which each
woman admits that she hates the other and vows in the
end to make Simon entirely hers.

A year has passed when the third act begins. Simon's
office resembles a best room in a bordello. A large garish
sofa has been installed. An ornate, gilt-framed mirror
hangs over Sara's desk. After a year of playing the whore,
she looks frightfully dissipated, her body grown "strikingly voluptuous, her face bloated." Her mouth has become "repellently sensual, ruthlessly cruel and greedy.
Her eyes have hardened, grown cunning and unscrupulous." Sara has corrupted not only Simon but also his
puritanical brother, Joel, who offers her his interest in the
company and everything he has to possess her. It is one of
Sara's great moments of triumph as she stares at herself
admiringly in the mirror, striking a pose similar to the one
her father had assumed in *A Touch of the Poet*, and says:
"Who'd have dreamed it, Sara Melody—you in your
beauty to have such power! By the Eternal, as my father
used to swear, I think you could take what you wanted
from any one of them!"

Simon, who has added an extra morning visit to

Deborah to his daily schedule, comes in late. He looks pale and haggard and behaves like someone in a trance. His mother's power over him is now stronger than Sara's. Simon watches Sara gaze longingly at her design for their new mansion; he quotes lines from Holmes's "The Chambered Nautilus": "Build thee more stately mansions, O my soul." He tells Sara to sit at his desk for an interview with Benjamin Tenard, who has just lost his bank to Simon. Though he is ruined, the banker can still be useful to them. The banker is unaware of Simon's reckless borrowing; a mere rumor of overextension could destroy the firm. Ruthlessly, Sara taunts the broken man. He refuses the job she offers, as to accept it he would have to forget all scruples and "become a conscious thief and swindler." Angrily, he rises to leave, but reminded of his duty to his family, he sinks back into his seat, acquiescing to her demands. Later, Simon resolves to end the conspiracy between his wife and mother, even if it means driving the latter, through loneliness, back to the madness of the summer-house. In *Desire Under the Elms* Eben plants the idea of murder in Abbie's mind. Here Simon, in a desperate effort to rid himself of his mother, says to Sara, "Can't you rid our life of that damned greedy evil witch?" Sara responds "with a fascinated eagerness," knowing what Simon wants of her and secretly longing to destroy the demanding, possessive mother once and for all.

In the play's final scene Deborah is shown waiting for Simon to return that night from the office. Like Sara, she too has become a grotesque; the secret hatred these two women have for each other poisons and shrivels their souls. Emaciated, witchlike, Deborah now looks like "an evil godmother conjured to life from the pages of a fairy tale." Her face is haggard, pale, and wrinkled; "it seems bloodless and corpse-like, a mask of death." She is dressed and made up to look like an eighteenth-century coquette. She senses that Sara seeks to drive her mad, but she vows to take Simon with her.

Later, when the mother and son are together, Simon
makes the same type of proposal to his mother that he had
made to his wife. He tells Deborah that he wishes only to
remain with her and to be free of Sara forever. To convince her that he is sincere, Simon discusses ways of
murdering Sara: an accidental fall, poison. It is the son
who now becomes deranged as he talks of the old fairy
tale, the search for the "magic door and a lost kingdom of
peace." They must escape Sara and reality, he says, and
enter the summer-house together. Either that or the
mother must go into it alone. She must choose as he has
done. He will be "free of one of my two selves, of one of
the enemies within my mind, before their duel for possession destroys it."

Mother and son are just about to enter the summer-
house when Sara enters and begs her husband to come to
his senses. Simon's detached, dreamlike state resembles
that of Con Melody and Mary Tyrone in the last scenes of
A Touch of the Poet and *Long Day's Journey into Night*.
He stares at Sara "without recognition. His face has a
strange, mad, trance-like look." He has abandoned reality
and accepted the illusionary world of his mother. Deborah opens the door, and Sara falls on her knees, begging
for pity. To save Simon, she promises to go away with the
children and to sign everything over to Deborah except
the farm, where she will raise them. In a parting speech
very much like Josie Hogan's final benediction on Jim
Tyrone in *A Moon for the Misbegotten*, Sara says, "God
bless you, Simon, Darling, for all the joy and love you
gave me, and give you peace and happiness!" Many of the
same elements are found in the last scenes of both plays:
the heady moonlight; stairs symbolizing the steps Simon
and Jim wish to climb to forbidden worlds; the dazed,
senseless states these men reach through illusion or
drink; the betrayal of the sons by their mothers. Deborah
cannot bear to be deemed the destroyer of her son; she
longs to prove that she is the "one who loves him most."

Summoning all her strength, she pushes Simon away, sending him "spinning down the steps to fall heavily and lie by the stone bench."

Sara rushes to Simon's side and determines that he has only fainted. Glancing up, she sees that Deborah has entered the summer-house. Sorrowfully, she laments, "I see now the part my greed and my father's crazy dreams in me had in leading Simon away from himself until he lost his way and began destroying all that was best in him!" She vows to give her life to setting free the man she loves best, "the dreamer with a touch of the poet in his soul, and the heart of a boy!" She herself will provide the banker Tenard with information to "smash the Company into smithereens." Before doing so, however, she will put all the company money and the Harford estate in Deborah's name to provide the "luxury that's due the great Princess on her grand estate." Then she will take Simon and the boys to live at the old farm.

Deborah comes out of the summer-house and addresses Sara as an "Irish kitchen maid," asking her what she is doing on the palace grounds. Seemingly, she fails to recognize Simon. Sara, playing the dutiful servant, finds it impossible to determine if Deborah is merely pretending or truly mad. Asked if she is happy, Deborah replies that she is and goes into the darkness again. Simon regains consciousness but fails to recognize Sara, calling her "Mother." Sara assures him in the final line of the play that she will be his Mother and his "peace and happiness and all you'll ever need in life!"

The play's unpublished Epilogue is set one year later, in June 1842, outside Simon's old cabin by the lake on the farm. The two younger Harford sons, Owen Roe, or "Honey," as he is called, and Jonathan, eleven, discuss their father's condition. The former is a good-natured, charming child with a droll sense of humor. The latter is more serious and full of a tense, nervous vitality. He bullies the easy-going Honey, who is content to be Jonathan's admiring satellite. The boys are elated by the fact their father seems to have recovered suddenly from brain fever that morning. Sara, who has just returned from Deborah's funeral, rejoices to have her husband sane again. Tanned and healthy looking from working on the farm, she wears a cheap calico working dress. She urges her sons to pray for their grandmother, telling them that she had been the only person that day to mourn Deborah. "Ah, if she ever knew in her dreams what I've suffered with him all mixed up and lost in his mind, calling me Mother, as if I was her, and forgetting he'd ever had a wife, she'd feel she was the one who'd won in the end after all."

The door of the cabin opens and Simon appears, looking "emaciated, pale, and hollow-eyed, as though he had passed through a long and devouring fever." He walks falteringly toward Sara, who embraces him. He feels as if part of him "were lost—or had died" and wonders what has happened to him. The last thing he remembers is the day he signed the agreement to take over a bankrupt railroad. He accuses himself of being a "damned hog." Sara tells him that she was the greedy fool "with my dream I got from my father's boasting lies that I ought to rise above myself and own a great estate." She assures him that he need not go back to the company, which has gone bankrupt. They have the farm and their love. Simon admits that he always desired release "from the soul-destroying compulsion to keep on enslaving myself with more and more power and possessions." Sara confesses to having smashed the company deliberately. She had learned a great deal while working for Simon, "watching the fools come in and try to hide their greed and fear and the price tag of their souls hanging in their eyes."

It was a mistake to leave the cabin and go into business, Simon concludes. Sara encourages him to write the book he planned in the old days. He recalls having engaged in the study of the duality of man's nature, but he says, "There's no duality in me I know. At least, not now." Feeling sleepy, Simon rests his head on Sara's breast and falls asleep. The scene foreshadows that in *A Moon for the Misbegotten* when the Irish Josie holds the sleeping and seemingly dead Jim Tyrone in her arms. Sara says, "Rest in peace. You're home at last where you've always wanted to be." A thought occurs, and she laughs bitterly: "But ain't you the craftiest, greediest man that ever walked the earth, God forgive you, to keep on and never let anybody beat you, not even yourself, but make life give you your own stubborn way in the end!"

The four boys enter on their way to the lake. The eldest, Ethan, fourteen, has his grandmother's forehead and deep-set eyes, his mother's black hair and passionate mouth, his father's nose and swarthy complexion. Wolfe Tom, a year younger, has a handsome, aristocratic face and resembles both his mother's father and Deborah Harford. While his manner is always politely pleasant, it is the "distant amiability of indifference." Sara's eyes follow her sons with pride. She knows that the farm will not hold them long. "Ethan, now, he'll own his fleet of ships! And Wolfe will have his banks! And Johnny his railroads! And Honey be in the White House before he stops maybe! And each of them will have wealth and power and a grand estate." Guiltily, she stops herself, resolving not to interfere and to let the sons be what they want to be, "if it's a tramp in rags without a penny." She kisses Simon lovingly as the scene closes.

More Stately Mansions is more successful than *A Touch of the Poet* in illustrating the underlying theme of the Cycle, the destructive greed that leads man to sell his soul for material possessions. O'Neill's favorite quotation to illustrate the meaning of the Cycle's title, "A Tale of Possessors Self-Dispossessed," was inserted in an early draft of *More Stately Mansions* in the first scene between Deborah and Simon. In that version the mother was called Abigail, and like Reuben Light's mother in *Dynamo*, she is the daughter of a minister. She describes her inability to adjust in her husband's household: "Something in me never did grow reconciled to the complete change of atmosphere from my Father's house. There the grinding maxim was 'what shall it profit if you gain the whole world and lose your soul.' " In her husband's home, "the guiding maxim is 'what shall it profit if you gain your soul and lose the world.' "

More Stately Mansions is not a great or even a good play. The incidents of plot, the characters' shifting loyalties and attitudes to one another, are tediously repetitious. The bitter verbal battle waged by Deborah and Sara lacks the brittle tone, the fire that characterize the arguments of Con and Sara in *A Touch of the Poet*. No single central figure emerges in the sequel as the focus of audience interest and concern. It is difficult to feel sympathy for any one of the wounded persons in the troika O'Neill devises. What should be stressed is the fact that these characters are stillborn. O'Neill had not completed the process of giving either them or their story life. While he made a serious effort to develop a credible plot for the characters he created, he had another story on his mind. On March 28, 1938, O'Neill read the scenario for *More Stately Mansions* and wrote in the Work Diary, "like it & will go ahead on it." He labored almost a year on this one play, finishing the third draft on January 20, 1939. The following June he completed an outline for *Long Day's Journey into Night*. His Work Diary entry for June 6 indicates that he had made notes earlier for this play. Deborah and Simon Harford do not really belong in the Cycle play but in the Tyrone household in *Long Day's Journey into Night*.

More Stately Mansions is a valuable play for what it reveals not only about the nature of the Cycle but also about the nature of its author and aspects of his relationship with his mother that simply do not appear in *Long Day's Journey into Night*. The scenes in which Deborah

tries to escape reality and her son by entering the summer-house are harrowing and illuminating. Reportedly,
there was a gazebo a short distance from the O'Neill home
to which Ella retreated when her son was young. The
kingdom of happiness from which the young king is dispossessed in Deborah's story symbolizes either this gazebo or the spare room in the O'Neill home where Ella gave
herself morphine injections. O'Neill never forgot the day
he discovered that his mother was a drug addict, never
truly forgave her for betraying him every time she escaped to her pleasurable world of oblivion. Simon never
forgets the way he felt when he was told the story of the
young king's banishment, the anguish of "being suddenly
betrayed, of being wounded and deserted and left alone
in a life in which there was no security or faith or love." He
tells his mother, "By God, I hated you then! I wished you
dead! I wished I had never been born!"

O'Neill spoke, in the early 1930s, of writing an autobiographical opus, saying that he had saved up a lot of
material for a "cycle of plays I hope to do some day.
There'll be nine separate plays." *Long Day's Journey into
Night* and *A Moon for the Misbegotten* would certainly be
included in this opus, but so too would the two extant
Cycle plays. A James O'Neill-like figure, the poet-peasant Con Melody, dominates *A Touch of the Poet*, which
dramatizes the struggle of the immigrant Irish to survive
in Yankee New England, a struggle the O'Neill family
experienced. *More Stately Mansions* depicts two other
O'Neills and sheds light on situations that precipitate the
action of *Long Day's Journey into Night* and the emotions
the young Eugene experienced when his mother abandoned him for her fantasy world, his fears of being left
alone, the sense of mother betrayal that haunted him and
emerges in most self-portraits of the canon. Simon says to
his mother, "You dispossessed yourself when you dispossessed me." As a consequence each has been cursed with
"an insatiable greed for substitutes." The theme of the

two trilogy plays, *Dynamo* and *Days Without End,* whose heroes are self-portraits, is the futility of the search for the substitute Mother God figure. The simple gesture of her opening the door, Simon assures his mother, will symbolize the "act by which your mind wills to take me back into your love, and become again the mother who loved me alone, whom alone I love." Simon is a pathetic creature in *More Stately Mansions,* longing desperately for the love of an indifferent mother who recklessly wills her own destruction. *Long Day's Journey into Night* continues the story of the dispossessed young king, grown older and wiser and more impatient as he waits for the enchantress mother to open the "magic door."

46.   The Calms of Capricorn

On June 20, 1931, O'Neill recorded an "idea for Clipper Ship-around-Horn play" in his Work Diary. That same year he made an entry in his notebook for *The Calms of Capricorn*:

> Play whole action of which takes place on clipper ship bound round the horn and winds up in Shanghai Brown's boarding house in Frisco—what year best (?) look up data on Shanghai Brown, if any.

He made notes for this sea play in 1932. In December 1934 the author broadened the concept to the " 'Calms of Capricorn series' 4 or 5 plays," having as central characters "4 sons," but he restricted the title of the series the following February to its "1st play—clipper ship." These four characters are the sons of Sara and Simon Harford. Each was to be the main figure in one of the four Cycle plays that chronologically followed *A Touch of the Poet* and *More Stately Mansions*: Ethan, first mate of the clipper *Dream of the West*, in *The Calms of Capricorn*; Wolfe, a gambler/banker in "The Earth Is the Limit"; Owen Roe, or "Honey," a politician in "Nothing Is Lost but Honor"; and Jonathan, the railroad magnate, in "The Man on Iron Horseback."

O'Neill began the scenario for *The Calms of Capricorn* on April 29, 1935, and finished it on June 9. Four years later, on May 23, he started the Prologue for the drama, which was, at that time, the fifth play of the Cycle, "A Tale of Possessors Self-Dispossessed." On June 5, 1939, after deciding that the work was "no good" and destroying much of it, the author put aside the Cycle and wrote outlines for *The Iceman Cometh* and *Long Day's Journey into Night*. In 1951 the scenario for *The Calms of*

Capricorn, along with the salvaged typescript for *More
Stately Mansions*, was sent by the dramatist and his wife
to Yale University to be added to the O'Neill collection.
Donald Gallup, curator of this collection, prepared a
two-volume edition of *The Calms of Capricorn* for publication, the first volume containing the transcribed scenario and the second, the play Gallup developed from it. In
his Introductory Note, Mr. Gallup states:

> Although it is not even a first draft of the play as O'Neill
> would eventually have written it (notes for its reconstruc-
> tion exist, made from time to time, especially in 1939 and
> 1941, while O'Neill was working on other plays), the scenar-
> io is sufficiently detailed and incorporates enough dialogue
> either directly or indirectly quoted so that the nucleus of
> the play O'Neill had in mind can be substantially recov-
> ered. . . . The scenario is, at least in some respects, both
> more and less satisfactory than a first draft. Its conclusion
> generally avoids the charges of excessive wordiness and the
> "too many interwoven themes & motives," which O'Neill
> acknowledged as faults of the first drafts of the first two plays
> of the nine-play Cycle. But, especially in scenes where the
> dialogue is only sketched, the speeches in their revelation
> of character and motive are the merest notes for what
> O'Neill would have made them. The scenario is, even so, of
> great documentary interest as the most nearly complete
> indication we have of O'Neill's plays for any of the unwritten
> Cycle plays.*

Some scholars may object to the publication of a work
O'Neill did not complete himself. However, as Mr. Gallup
points out, the scenario's "importance is so great" that
students of O'Neill's work should have access to it. "Its
'development' into a more accessible form is designed
merely to increase its readability, while adhering as closely as possible and with a minimum of elaboration to
O'Neill's original text."†

*The Calms of Capricorn, Developed from O'Neill's Scenario by
Donald Gallup (New Haven: Ticknor & Fields, 1981), pp. ix–xi.

†Gallup, p. xi.

The Calms of Capricorn is linked to the Cycle play
that precedes it, *More Stately Mansions*, by setting; the
first line of the scenario for the former states, "The same
as the Epilogue of 'More Stately Mansions,' the potato
field on Sara's farm. It is now the spring of 1857, a fine
morning." Sara Harford, her husband Simon, and their
four sons have been living on the farm for fifteen years.
Although she is forty-seven, Sara still retains the attractive qualities she possessed in *A Touch of the Poet*, except
that her eyes have "a look of resigned sadness" and her
black hair has "streaks of white." With her are Captain
Enoch Payne, sixty, a solid and imposing figure, and his
pretty, younger wife, Nancy, thirty-eight, who has brown
hair and eyes and a shy, reserved nature. "Her deep
respect for her husband is apparent as is his love for her."
They have just returned from a voyage on his ship, *Dream
of the West*. Alone with Sara, Nancy entreats her to
persuade Ethan, Payne's second mate, to change to another ship, as he and her husband are engaged in a subtle
struggle. Nancy describes Ethan as being reserved and
sensitive, "isolated and lonely in his freedom." Sara remarks, "He's a touch of the poet in him, God pity him,
like his father."

Ethan arrives. Now twenty-eight, he has brown hair,
a visionary's intense blue eyes, and "a powerful, muscular
body, full of intense, nervous vitality." Later he discusses
his father's health and the book Simon has been working
on for years, "The Meaning of Life." Discouraged, Simon
had destroyed it. Subsequently he became a changed
man and began accompanying his youngest son, Honey, a
tin peddler, on his wagon trips, which were "full of gossip
and the news of the world and politics." Sara urges her
discontented son to change ships, but he believes that his
fate is linked to his present berth. Sara, the materialist,
urges him to strive to become captain and a partner; then
will come "ownership and freedom." Ethan admonishes
his mother for being "earthbound by possessions" and
uses the quotation that provides the underlying theme of

the Cycle: "What can it profit a man if he own the world and pay his soul for it?" What Ethan truly desires is "victory over the sea"; he wants to "make a faster voyage around the Horn to the Golden Gate than ever man has made." He has "the curse of the Poet," his mother tells him. "For it's the moon you want and you hunt her in the skies of the broad day when the rest of us don't see her there at all."

The only physical change in Simon, who is now fifty, is that he is slightly emaciated and bears "the marks of having passed through a long and devouring fever." His eyes have "a groping and bewildered stare." With him is Honey, twenty-four, who resembles his mother and is "all peasant Irish." He is tall and heavily built and has "curly black hair and inquisitive blue eyes, with a sparkle of sly, droll humor. His habitual expression is happy and good-natured." Left alone with his oldest son, Simon says, "You and I, Ethan, have always been strangers to each other, such strangers that I know there is a soul so identical in each that we have never felt the need to be anything but strangers." In *More Stately Mansions* the young Simon's soul was a battleground wherein his two contradictory natures struggled: the idealistic poet and the materialistic businessman. By the last act of the play, the latter had, with the help of Sara, soundly defeated the former. At the end each self destroyed the other; Simon's mind was a blank slate. In the Epilogue, when he suddenly regained his memory, Simon said, "There's no duality in me I know. At least, not now." To Ethan, he explains that he has just awakened from a dream in which "the opposites at last blended and were one, and even now as the dream recedes, I am still in a place where the edges of the opposites still merge, and I can see and guess so much that is behind the senses." Simon sees that Ethan is now engaged in the battle he himself waged as a young Thoreau-like idealist living in his cabin by the lake. He warns his son of what lies ahead: "And I speak to the part of me which is three parts of you, and therefore is the dominant

you, the you which is a fierce contempt for me and for
yourself, a fierce pride and a lust for power and possession
—but in the spirit, not the flesh." He prophesies Ethan's
defeat by the sea, but "your losing will be your final
victory and release." The son is doing the one thing a
lonely exiled man should do: "to choose his dream and
then to follow that dream to the end." At the end of the
scene, Simon, who perhaps senses that he will die shortly,
explains to Sara the value of life: "Life is worth one's life,
one must pay for life with life. Oh to be able to give oneself
to life and love and beauty—to belong—to let oneself be
possessed in order to possess—to live and be free, to be
freed by love."

In the next scene, which takes place two weeks later,
Sara and her sons have assembled in their sitting room for
Simon's funeral. Jonathan, twenty-five, who is a clerk in a
railroad office, resembles his father and has "a long New
England bony face," brown hair, intelligent hazel eyes,
and a large nose. He is "full of tense nervous vitality, but
remarkably self-disciplined and sure of his own capabili-
ties." As he will demonstrate through his actions in the
play, he has inherited his father's calculating businessman's nature. Wolfe, twenty-seven and a clerk in a bank,
is tall, handsome, and distinguished, "a mixture of his
father and his mother—with a pale aristocratic face. He
suppresses all emotional reaction under a mask of smiling
indifference. A man's man." Like Ethan, he too has his
father's touch of the poet. Later Sara says of him, "his
head's full of queer dreams." Jonathan suggests that the
family sell the farm and go to California, where money is
to be made in the mines. While Sara truly laments the loss
of Simon, one part of her rejoices to be free: "I've a new
life starting and I'll do as I please now and as I've always
wanted and I've four strong sons to work with me and to
help me to the wealth and power of this world and all I've
dreamed." She then curses herself for being "a greedy
sow."

The Harfords are shown in Act II, six weeks later, on the clipper ship *Dream of the West* at dock in New York. Ethan has just been made first mate because the ailing Hull has been ordered to rest. On board is a motley assortment of humanity: the owner of the ship, Theodore Warren, forty-eight, a robust, good-looking widower, and his daughter, Elizabeth, eighteen. She is tall, dark, slender, with a boyish figure, a wiry body, full of intense nervous energy beneath a coldly beautiful, calm, disciplined exterior. She snobbishly disdains, at first sight, the beautiful, opulent Leda Cade, twenty-five, who has a handsome, frankly sensual face and is "all emotion, intuitive female instinct." With her is Ben Graber, fifty-three, a banker and a furtive, unkempt, broken man. Also making the trip is a Protestant minister, the Reverend Samuel Dickey, thirty-four, a crass sensualist and materialist.

The petulant Hull is allowed to resume his former position after asserting that there is nothing wrong with him. When he gloats before Ethan, Leda suggests that they could "give him a push" overboard, and Nancy threatens to report him to the captain. Hull says that he might submit his own report: "I'm older than him but not as blind." The second time Hull insults Ethan, the younger man strikes him on the jaw. Hull falls and hits his head on the stairs. Leda kneels and pronounces him dead. She immediately takes command of the situation, sending Ethan away from the scene and telling Nancy that they must lie to the captain and say that Hull slipped accidentally. Leda adds, "And now you're looking at this dead old man and thinking of another old man and that if only he were—." Nancy's cry of horror in response to Leda's words brings others to the scene.

There is a time lapse of a few minutes between scenes. The captain and the ship's owner are shown examining Hull's body. Warren gives orders barring his inquisitive daughter from coming below. "She mustn't see death—never has—a terrible shock to one so delicate and

high-strung." When the practical Leda suggests that the
sight of death might wake her up and encourage her to
start living, Warren stares at her, fascinated and spell-
bound. The only man on board who attracts Leda is the
indifferent, blasé Wolfe, who ignores her and the other
passengers and plays endless games of solitaire. She
offers to bet herself against himself that she will make him
want her "before we're through." Honey and Graber
enter, singing drunkenly; seeing the dead man, they
become superstitious. The minister comes in to offer
prayers. Leda volunteers to "join in the hymns." She
says, "You may not believe it but I had the strictest kind of
religious bringing up. I owe all my success to that—."
Ignored by Dickey but applauded by Honey and Graber,
she sings "Fields of Eden." The captain becomes suspicious when, after he summons Ethan, his own wife begins
to defend Ethan. Nevertheless, Ethan is again appointed
first mate but is warned not to attempt to break records for
speed on his watch or he will find himself an ordinary
seaman again. After noting that the man Ethan replaced
as second mate had also fractured his skull, as had Hull,
the captain implies that the younger man is hoping that
his superior too will die in such a fall, thus enabling him to
take command of the ship.

When the third act opens, in late November, the
Dream of the West is "becalmed in the South Atlantic."
The clipper has beaten the record of the *Flying Cloud* to
the equator. Had the Captain "cracked on," Warren as-
serts, "we'd have crossed the Tropic days ahead of the
*Flying Cloud** and we could have afforded this calm." The

---

*There seems to be a discrepancy in time here. The *Flying
Cloud*, launched on April 15, 1851, set a new record—89 days—
in a trip around Cape Horn to California. *The Calms of Capricorn*
opens in spring 1857. The Harfords and other passengers are
shown boarding the clipper eight weeks later. Approximately
five months would have elapsed by the date given, late November, at the beginning of Act II. O'Neill made notes for the
"measurements, etc., plans for ship scenes" on May 3, 1935. In
order to determine the exact measurements for the settings on

ship's owner tacitly approves Ethan's secret efforts to "set on more sail in his watch." Warren worries about his daughter and the influence Leda Cade has on her. Told by her father to ignore this woman she feels is evil, Elizabeth says: "I—I can't—there's something—I mean, look at her, you can't help seeing her." Both Elizabeth and the captain's repressed wife, Nancy, instinctively feel and subsequently crave Leda's reckless eagerness to wrest what she wants from life, her willingness to indulge her sensual desires regardless of society's restrictions.

Leda describes her past to Nancy in an attempt to explain her present ruthless attitude. Orphaned at seventeen, she married the man who ran her father's prosperous mills. He was thirty years older than she and interested only in her money and her body. She grew to hate him and finally left him, determined, if she had to be a whore, to get pleasure out of it. Since that time, she has selected the men she wanted. Graber is an exception; she sleeps with him only because she pities him. Aghast, Nancy says, "You make love into nothing but—bodies." Leda assures her that bodies are healthy, natural: "Can you go to bed with a soul? Poetic drivel aside, love may start in heaven but it goes on—or it dies—in bed." She then explains what Nancy must do to get Ethan "down to earth" and aware of her. She must be more aloof and "stop playing the family friend." Leda devises a plan in which she talks with Ethan alone. She accuses him of wanting to sleep with Nancy and kisses him, arousing his anger, before leaving. Later, when Ethan meets Nancy in the passageway, he embraces and kisses her. In a thought aside, Nancy is repelled by the idea of going to bed with her husband, "the disgusting old fool," and longs only for her lover. The situation is foreshadowed in *Mourning*

Dream of the West, O'Neill consulted *Some Famous Sailing Ships and Their Builder Donald McKay* by Richard McKay (New York: G.P. Putnam's Sons, 1931). On one page of his computations the dramatist gives the dimensions of the *Flying Cloud*: "Her length on the keel in 208 feet, on deck, 225, and over all from knight head to the taffrail, 235" (p. 142).

Becomes Electra, wherein Christine Mannon is repulsed
by the thought of sleeping with her older husband and
plots his death with her younger lover.*

It is the tenth day of the calm in the next scene,
which is the weakest section, structurally, of the scenario.
In a series of short scenes, O'Neill switches the setting
back and forth between Leda's stateroom and the wheelhouse, the poop deck, and Nancy's cabin. The action and
dialogue are consolidated in the following discussion. In
the first scene Leda converses with Honey after sleeping
with him, not for money but for the fun of it. He is the only
one on the ship, she asserts, "who doesn't want everything to be more than it is and doesn't blame himself
because it isn't." The cheerful, likable Honey assures her
that he will find "slews of gold in California" and will give
her a hatful of nuggets. She had received "a good price"
from Warren the previous evening and had encouraged
Ben Graber, who bestows his gambling winnings on her,
to play cards with the ship's owner.

Later, Leda tells Jonathan that the only way to win
Elizabeth is to seduce her: "You've got to show her you
want her, not her father's influence or money." Jonathan
is attracted to Elizabeth for mercenary reasons; he is
O'Neill's consummate materialistic businessman. Earlier,
when Nancy spoke of the importance of love and happiness and the minister had given the highest priority to
saving one's soul, Jonathan had stated: "I know nothing of
the soul—what shall it profit—?" To his mother, who
favors a match between her son and Elizabeth, he admits
he is "not looking for love. She has money, brains. This
would be strictly a business proposition." Elizabeth also
denounces love and seeks marriage with a man of "brains

*O'Neill probably conceived the idea for *The Calms of Capricorn*
while writing *Mourning Becomes Electra* after he had changed
the setting of Act IV of *The Hunted* to Adam Brant's ship, the
Flying Trades. Like Captain Payne, Brant is murdered on his
ship. O'Neill finished *Mourning Becomes Electra* on March 27,
1931, and recorded the "clipper ship idea" three months later.

and ability who will be rich." Leda has, however, aroused
the sensual urges of Elizabeth, who tells the minister she
feels "as if there was a fire inside me." The hypocrite strokes
her arm amorously and urges her to pray. She rejects his
advice and accuses him of desiring "that harlot," who will
"end up by committing fornication with every man on
board, perhaps even including—." The minister protests,
but talking about Leda emboldens him to profess his love
for Elizabeth, who scorns him.

Leda has an effect even on the sedate Captain Payne,
who still smarts from Warren's humiliating accusation
that he is too old to run a ship and to function as a
husband. Urged by the minister, the captain warns Leda
not to carry on while on his ship. She flatters him by
saying that he is not an old man, as he believes, and
inviting him to her stateroom. Leda is labeled a whore by
Elizabeth, who accuses her of corrupting Honey. Sara
defends Leda, pointing out that she "can't corrupt anyone
who doesn't want to be corrupted." The older woman
recognizes something of herself in Leda and tells her
confidentially that she disapproves of Elizabeth, who "has
no more blood than a fish," but wants Jonathan to marry
her because of her wealth. When Sara apologizes for these
thoughts, Leda responds, "Don't you get a guilty conscience, too. You can't fool me. You're a real woman. You
want to get what you want."

In a final passage Ethan converses with Wolfe, telling
him that they had something in common at one time,
"something of our father." Now, however, Ethan feels
that he is lost. He disavows love: "Possessions, power—
those are the things that count." Thinking he can substitute one woman for another, "to escape in phantoms,"
Ethan goes to Leda's room but finds Nancy there. The
captain is heard descending the stairs. Denying that she
wishes him dead, Nancy calls out, "Be careful on the
stairs!" Her husband, himself longing for death and fearing it, falls. Ethan drags him into Nancy's cabin. The

young couple embraces, believing the man is dead. When he groans, the same thought occurs to each of them but is banished as Nancy vows to take care of her husband and to make him well.

The next scene takes place on the twentieth day of the calm. O'Neill uses the same pattern of rapidly changing scenes here. In the wheelhouse Warren faults Ethan for being fifty miles behind the ship's position two weeks earlier. Reminded that the captain still gives the orders, Warren calls Payne a Jonah and attributes his miraculous recovery to Nancy's selfless care. The ship owner expresses his concern about his inability to arrange a marriage for Elizabeth, who has always repelled men, even those desirous of her money. She is beautiful but "as cold as dead fish," like her mother. Standing outside the wheelhouse, Elizabeth overhears her father's denunciation and begins to cry. Leda approaches and asks Elizabeth if she wants "professional advice—secrets of the trade. You have wished to sell yourself, but before you can sell, you must make men want." Elizabeth admits that she is "a little in love with Jonathan" but that he is aloof. She appreciates the logic of Leda's advice to allow Jonathan to seduce her: "he seems like a man of honor—I would have him then." Elizabeth's suspicions about the minister's proclivities are correct. He accosts Leda and asks her if he can visit her again that night, saying, "What shall it profit a man if he give you up for a supposition like his soul?" She laughs at the hypocrite and walks over to Ethan, who, in a thought aside, expresses his regret that he had not killed the captain when he had the opportunity. Leda reads his mind and urges him to banish his guilt feelings. She confesses that she herself has fallen in love with his elusive brother Wolfe and has been trying to lull her guilty conscience for the past by drowning herself in lust. She detests herself for having built her life on men's desire for her body. Leda informs Ethan that if Wolfe loved her and were married to "an old fool he didn't love," she would not hesitate "to murder for love." This woman, whom Ethan from the first likened to the sea, suggests that only the captain's murder will release the ship from the calm.

Leda meets Elizabeth returning from Jonathan's room after a fruitless search for him. Praised for coming alive, Elizabeth confides: "You are the only one on board who knows what life is about. You—you will teach me, won't you?" Leda agrees. Nancy joins the two women, and the three, while taking a walk, meet Honey, who, although drunk, has been delegated by the gold seekers on board and the crew to demand that the captain "resign all power to Ethan." Proud of his skill in manipulating men, Honey exclaims, "I ought to be a politician!" Ethan earns Payne's gratitude when he warns Honey that he will shoot anyone who goes against the captain. Assured by Ethan that he has not slept with Nancy, Payne falls asleep. Just as Ethan approaches the captain with a pillow in his hands, Nancy enters, saying: "Give me what is mine!" Like Abbie in *Desire Under the Elms*, she suffocates the person who threatens her happiness with her lover. At that precise moment, the third mate shouts down to Ethan: "There's a squall coming. Maybe it means wind."

In Act IV the *Dream of the West* is shown approaching the Golden Gate. It is late January, and the clipper seems destined to set a new record. Ethan has beaten the *Flying Cloud* and the sea in spite of treacherous storms. Ethan and Nancy were married by the minister immediately after the captain's burial service. Warren takes great satisfaction in the new sailing record. Even though the ship has been wracked to bits, it can be sold to England for a good price. He suspects that Payne had an untimely death, but he decides to help "the happy lovers keep their little secret."

Sara brags about Ethan's feat, saying that the touch of the poet he inherited from both sides of the family makes his dreams possible. She hopes that he will now abandon the sea and "dream of wealth and power on land and get that, too." Elizabeth states, "That's Jonathan's dream. Ethan and he will work together." Nancy and she will be like sisters and help their men "take possession of the world." Elizabeth attributes her awakening, "soul and body," to Leda and blesses the day they met. Even the indifferent Wolfe, Elizabeth reasons, will be humanized by Leda. When Sara seemingly shrinks from Nancy's touch, the young woman tells her that she feels guilty in Ethan's arms. Sara responds: "Why in the world would you feel guilty? You are lovers and love is worth all it costs!"

The clipper again becomes ensnared in a deadly calm, which persists into the next scene, some hours later. Ordered by Warren to pray for wind, the minister tells him that God is punishing them for the crimes of lust and gambling on board. All except Jonathan exclaim, "Yes, we've sinned." Sara assumes part of the blame "for not remembering the religion of my sainted mother." The close bonds the characters have formed are now shattered. Waren calls his daughter "a dirty little slut"; she labels him an "old whoremonger." Elizabeth informs Jonathan that she had been "a pure girl" after he tells her that the lessons she has learned will inspire her "to be a helping brain instead of a sexual organ," a wife who will be a partner, not an animal. Elizabeth, in turn, berates Nancy, calling her a murderer. Nancy allows no one to blame Ethan; she alone is guilty. The minister announces that the only way to set a sailing record is to "cleanse the ship of sin by sacrificing the sinners to the sea—to God. Throw them overboard!" Ethan takes out a pistol to defend Nancy from the unruly crew and the gold seekers, who rush forward to follow Dickey's bidding. Honey pacifies the men, telling them that the hills are full of riches and urging them to celebrate the end of the voyage. Warren fires Ethan for his negligence and failure to win the record and praises Honey for calming the crowd: "He'll wind up in the Senate, if he doesn't look out!"

It is midnight in the last scene. A gentle breeze comes from astern. To his brothers, Ethan confesses that he murdered the first mate and the captain. Jonathan accuses him of "playing the romantic Harford—covering up for Nancy." Selfishly, he urges him to consider the family name and not to confess his crimes to others. "It's going to be hard enough to get started out here on a shoestring without—." Honey is shocked but promises to "stick by" Ethan, who asks his youngest brother to console their grieving mother. Had he only himself to consider, Ethan would "let the sea possess what it has won." Only to himself does he admit that he does not love Nancy: "It was only the lust to possess." Yet he lies to her and assures her that he loves her. She senses the truth and tells him that she will confess, take the blame, and set him free. Ethan's pride and sense of honor force him to refuse: "We will go together." He stops to bid farewell to his mother, who will not sanction his decision to sacrifice himself to the sea. Then she tells him that he is right: "Now go, and God damn the honor of the Harfords." Ethan and Nancy interrupt Graber and Wolfe's card game and bid those in the wheelhouse goodbye. Leda's first impulse is to stop them; then she says: "Go on! Get out of here! God bless you!" The couple goes out hand in hand. Ethan states: "We'll swim out together—until the fog lifts. And the sea will be alight with beauty forevermore—because you are you." When Nancy says that hell with him will be heaven, Ethan tells her there is no hell—only the sea where they will sleep in each other's arms. The final scene of the scenario shows Sara alone in her cabin. "She senses the moment Ethan and Nancy go overboard from the bow and leaps to her feet. 'Ethan! My firstborn!' "

Ethan's ultimate fate is never stated. O'Neill omitted the final scene from the scenario. He stated on June 9, 1935, "Finish Scenario (IV—3—decide leave out IV—4 as outlined)" (Work Diary). Presumably, Ethan somehow survived his plunge into the Pacific and emerged as

O'Neill had envisioned, as a subordinate character in the next three Cycle plays, in which his brothers would in turn be the central figures. On June 16, 1935, three days after he finished the scenario for *The Calms of Capricorn*, O'Neill began the outline for "The Earth Is the Limit," set in the 1860s, in which Wolfe, the detached gambler, becomes a successful banker. In the last act of *The Calms of Capricorn*, he wins all that Ben Graber possesses. Graber, who had been connected with a bank that failed, rejoices at his loss: "every cent I stole for you, Leda. I've lost it all! I'm free!" When Graber refuses to gamble with Wolfe for her, Leda offers to do so. She cuts the cards. A ten surfaces. Wolfe wins her with the Queen of Hearts. He refuses to accept her, but Leda assures him that he will never get rid of her because she loves him.

Honey, the charming, easy-going youngest Harford brother, demonstrates his oratorical skill and his ability to manipulate a volatile mob in *The Calms of Capricorn*. He will become, as Warren predicts, a senator in "Nothing Is Lost but Honor," which O'Neill outlined from July 2–28, 1935. Jonathan's destiny as a railroad magnate in the following Cycle play, "The Man on Iron Horseback," is also suggested in *The Calms of Capricorn*. He warns Warren, the ship owner, that sail is dead and that steam is the future. Elizabeth's accusation that Jonathan intends to use her is valid. He admits that he has studied her and found her to be intelligent enough for the kind of partnership he desires. She dismisses her father's maudlin sentiment about losing her in marriage and agrees with him that she can always divorce Jonathan "if he doesn't make good."

O'Neill's notes suggest that he got the play's title and model (railroad tycoon Jay Gould) for its hero Jonathan from *The Robber Barons*, one of the many books he used to research nineteenth-century American history.* One

*Matthew Josephson, *The Robber Barons—The Great American Capitalists 1861–1901* (New York: Harcourt Brace & Co., 1934). Josephson discusses what "the coming of the Iron Horse

page of notes that is taken directly from various sections of this book contains biographical data on Gould, whose father, like Jonathan's, came from old "Yankee stock." Gould is described as "undersized," a term O'Neill applies to Jonathan. Like Jonathan, Gould at age twenty-five worked as a railroad operator. He developed "a technique of seizure and 'conversion' which was as magical as that of the alchemist who turned dross into gold" (p. 64). Determined to acquire a transcontinental line, this "Mephistopheles of Wall Street" began buying and consolidating railroads and was challenged only by Collis Huntington, leader of a ring known as the Pacific Associates. Honey Harford, the politician—who as a boy had been his bullying brother Jonathan's "admiring satellite"—would probably be used by this Gould-like character to obtain railroad subsidies in Washington. Huntington's letter of December 17, 1877, states that "Jay Gould went to Washington about two weeks since, and I know, saw Mitchell, Senator from Oregon. Since which time money has been used very freely in Washington. . . . Gould has large amounts of cash and he pays it without stint to carry his points" (p. 204). O'Neill's original plan was to begin the action for "The Man on Iron Horseback" in 1876 in New York City in the midst of the 1874–1878 railroad war and close it in 1893, just before the three-year depression in which 156 lines collapsed. Wolfe is probably based on the flamboyant banker Pierpont Morgan, who eventually gained control of twelve railroad systems and who, like Deborah Harford, was a Bourbon to the end of his life.

O'Neill's final Cycle drama, "Hair of the Dog," is a revised version of a 1927 play, "It Cannot Be Mad?," originally conceived as the third work of the trilogy "Myth Plays for the God-forsaken." Its title was changed to "The

meant" to those living in California (p. 81). All further references to this book are from this edition and are followed by an Arabic numeral to indicate the page.

Life of Bessie Bowen" in 1932, to "Career of Bessie Bowen" in 1934, and to "Twilight of Possessors Self-Dispossessed" in 1935. Bessie is probably the daughter of Honey
Harford, the youngest of Sara and Simon's four sons. In
"It Cannot Be Mad?," which opens in Indiana in 1894, she
was depicted as Bessie Wilks, an orphan. After leaving
the orphanage, she marries Howard Camp, an automobile executive, has four children, and, like Sara Harford,
assumes a major role in running the family business,
Camp Motor. The play would take the "five generations of
a family" up to 1932. After a lengthy illness in early 1937,
O'Neill resumed work on the Cycle, noting on July 26 in
the Work Diary while he was working on the ninth play,
"will require extra generation in new scheme—'Honey'
to live till end?" Unless the author changed this character's age, Honey Harford would be nearly a hundred
years old in 1932 at the close of the Cycle.

In the scenario for *The Calms of Capricorn*, Ethan
does not become the focal point until the last act, when he
assumes responsibility for his earlier misdeeds. O'Neill
was forced to introduce and develop all four Harford
brothers in this work and to set the course of action for
subsequent Cycle dramas. Sara plays an insignificant role
in the scenario, considering her position as matriarch of
the family and the primary link connecting the Cycle
dramas. She is eclipsed by the vital, earthy, riveting
Leda. She, rather than Ethan, is the dominant character. Although the scenario does not suggest it, Ethan
would certainly have risen to heroic stature in the completed draft of the play.

Throughout his writing career, O'Neill adhered to
the principles he learned in 1914 in George Pierce Baker's
47 Workshop at Harvard: recording the original idea,
writing a scenario, and, to add "meat," as he says, to this
skeleton, setting down dialogue for a first draft. While this
draft usually evolved from the scenario, initial ideas about
characters and themes often changed. For example,

O'Neill remarked that he thought he had *The Great God Brown* "doped out" in the scenario, but when he started to write it, he found it was "coming out all different."

Donald Gallup has done an admirable job in his development of the scenario of *The Calms of Capricorn*, presenting a lucid, intelligent, readable text and making valuable insertions of the author's "second thoughts." The original script itself, however, is seriously flawed. It lacks continuity. Often a situation is presented, but before it is developed substantially, a new action involving other characters is introduced. The scenes shift too rapidly from one section of the boat to another and then back again, interrupting the flow of dialogue. The work could never be staged effectively unless the scenes were rearranged logically in proper sequence. It would make an interesting project, however, for an experimental theater group. Even though the scenario for *The Calms of Capricorn* is faulty, it is a valuable document, for it provides new insights into O'Neill's monumental project of the late 1930s and a better understanding of the characters and of how they were to function in the Cycle.

O'Neill had in the Cycle attempted to go beyond the narrow range of his own experiences to dramatize the historical saga of an American family. In *A Touch of the Poet* and *More Stately Mansions*, members of the Melody –Harford family closely resembled the O'Neills. Missing from the scenario for *The Calms of Capricorn* and the outlines for subsequent Cycle plays are the usual familial figures. Perhaps, unconsciously, O'Neill realized that he never could successfully develop totally imaginative characters in the Cycle and make them live. It may be he knew in the late 1930s that there were but a few years left to him to write the plays that really mattered. Whatever the reason, the author put the Cycle aside in 1939 and resumed his interrupted journey into his own personal historical past.

IDEAS: 1931–1938 NOTEBOOKS

Rabelais Play

Lazarus–Combination Talky

House with the Masked Dead

Man and His Soul

Romanticist

Gnosticism

Symphony Form Play

Philip II-Don Juan of Austria Play

Testament for Tomorrow

On To Betelgeuse

Thomas Jefferson Play

Rolling River

Love Play

Pyramid Form Play

The Reward of Dream

Reverse "Interlude"

Sequel to *Ah, Wilderness!*

Life of Sturgo Nacimbin

Romance of Aged Play

The Germinating (dramatization of Zola's *Germinal*)

Runaway Slave Play ("Germ for this idea in Thoreau's Journal")

Day

Robespierre

Astronomer

Play Idea

Time Grandfather Was Dead

O'Neill and his beloved Blemie, Tao House, 1938

O'Neill conceives his two masterpieces at Tao House in 1939.

Oona O'Neill visits her father at Tao House. July 16, 1941

The Sea-Mother's Son returns to New England. O'Neill at his Marblehead home, 1948/9

The Iceman Cometh, Royal Dramatic Theatre, Stockholm, 1947. Hickey is hailed as a hero by his friends at Harry Hope's Saloon.

The Iceman Cometh, Dublin, 1948. "Come to look at you Hickey, old chap. You've sprouted horns like a bloody antelope."

Long Day's Journey into Night, Royal Dramatic Theatre, Stockholm, February 10, 1956. Mary Tyrone (Inga Tidblad) ignores the pleas of sons Edmund (Jarl Kulle) and Jamie (Ulf Palme).

Long Day's Journey into Night, New York, November 7, 1956. Mary Tyrone (Florence Eldridge) is oblivious to the despair of her sons Edmund (Bradford Dillman) and Jamie (Jason Robards, Jr.) and husband James (Frederic March).

4. Homecoming— The Last Harbor

4. Homecoming— The Last Harbor: The Late Great Plays

In the years of young manhood, Eugene O'Neill, the "Sea-Mother's Son," felt dispossessed on land. In *Long Day's Journey into Night*, Edmund Tyrone, a self-portrait at age twenty-three, recalls the sense of oneness and well-being he experienced while at sea: "The peace, the end of the quest, the last harbor, the joy of belonging to a fulfillment beyond men's lousy, pitiful, greedy fears and hopes and dreams." The single place on land capable of evoking the same "beautiful calm" of the sea is Harry Hope's saloon. In *The Iceman Cometh* Larry Slade, another alter ego of the author, uses sea imagery to describe this sanctuary: "it's the last harbor," the "Bottom of the Sea Rathskeller," where men "keep up the appearances of life with a few harmless pipe dreams about their yesterdays and tomorrows." The O'Neill-like characters in these two plays drown themselves either in the vastness of the sea or in alcohol in an attempt to forget the past. Both cry out for a port of refuge, "the last harbor." Like his heroes, the dramatist also sought a safe haven, but, as both man and artist, he continuously skirted his last harbor, the guarded, locked storehouse of memories. In the period 1939–1940 O'Neill made his "Journey into Light— into love," as he notes in the dedication to *Long Day's Journey into Night*. This play and its sequel, *A Moon for the Misbegotten*, were a familial homecoming for him; in them he was able "to face my dead at last" after shunning the ghosts of "all the four haunted Tyrones" (O'Neills) for nearly two decades.

The dramatist began writing *Desire Under the Elms*, his unconscious autobiography, in early January 1924, shortly after the death of the third O'Neill, his brother Jamie. Later, when he was interviewed during the rehearsal period, he denied the report that the play was a personal document: "It isn't really true. It isn't I. And the truth would make a much more interesting and incredible legend. I see no hope for this except some day to shame the devil and myself if I can ever muster the requisite interest and nerve simultaneously."* On March 8, 1927, the author made his first conscious effort to outline "The Sea-Mother's Son," a "series of plays based on autobiographical material." The final entry in the Work Diary for this project, which he called the "grand opus of my life," is dated July 23, 1931. During this same month he started the first set of notes for *Days Without End*, which, with its autobiographical plan and purpose, could serve as the play in the series focusing solely on the author himself. In the early 1930s the dramatist described a project for a "dramatic autobiography," a Cycle of nine plays, to Barrett Clark. He stated, "All the most dramatic episodes of my life I have so far kept out of my plays, and most of the things I have seen happen to other people." He was "saving up" this material "to do some day." That day came on June 6, 1939, when the author announced his decision to outline two plays "that seem [to] appeal most": the Jimmy the Priest–Hell Hole–Garden idea and the New London family one.

In one stroke, in a single Work Diary entry, O'Neill envisioned his two greatest plays: *The Iceman Cometh*

---

*Philip Weissman, "Conscious and Unconscious Autobiographical Dramas of Eugene O'Neill," *Journal of the American Psychoanalytic Association*, 5 (1957), p. 432.

and *Long Day's Journey into Night*. Both plays are set in 1912, the most portentous year, personally and artistically, in the author's early life. Many of the "dramatic episodes" he mentioned to Clark occurred during this year. In early 1912 O'Neill made an unsuccessful attempt to commit suicide at Jimmy the Priest's, a seedy New York waterfront barroom-hotel. He recreated this incident in a 1918 one-acter, "Exorcism." In "Exorcism," after he is rescued by two drinking companions, Ned Malloy, a self-portrait, utters his "yes" to life. The two friends who save Malloy are depicted in *The Iceman Cometh* as Captain Lewis (Major Adams) and "Jimmy Tomorrow" (James Byth). Later that year, when O'Neill was working as a reporter in New London, a local doctor diagnosed a chronic cold as tuberculosis. The subsequent stay in a sanatorium had a profound effect on the young O'Neill, for it was there that he read the plays of Strindberg and decided to become a dramatist. He dramatized the day he was told he had tuberculosis in *Long Day's Journey into Night* and the period of recuperation in *The Straw*. The latter can be labeled a "self" play; the former focuses on all four O'Neills, particularly the mother, Ella, who is portrayed as Mary Tyrone.

Ella O'Neill exerted the greatest single influence on her playwright son. Her restless desire to belong became his lifelong aspiration. She, more than anyone else, was responsible for the fragmentation of the O'Neill family unit. She succumbed to morphine addiction for a lengthy period, extending from the time of Eugene's birth in 1888 to 1913, the year after the action of *Long Day's Journey into Night*. During this period Ella was lost to her husband, her sons, and herself. Her younger son's dramaturgic search to belong in the autobiographic plays occurs within a familial context and is always associated with the quest for the lost mother. Frequently, the mother has in some way betrayed the son, whose search for the substitute mother figure is usually fruitless.

In the completed works of the late 1920s and early 1930s, such as *Dynamo* and *Mourning Becomes Electra*, and in the ideas for plays of this period, the sons commit suicide to achieve union with their deceased mothers. In *Days Without End* and subsequent dramas, the sons reject physical death but they are usually maimed psychologically by their destructive mothers, as, for example, Simon Harford by Deborah in *More Stately Mansions* and Jamie and Edmund Tyrone by Mary in *Long Day's Journey into Night*. Invariably, all the sons—from Reuben Light in *Dynamo* to Edmund Tyrone in *Long Day's Journey into Night*—are self-portraits. All the mothers are variations of Ella O'Neill. She does not completely emerge until depicted as the dazed, detached Mary Tyrone at the conclusion of the latter play. Thinly disguised views of the deranged Ella appear in the final scenes of earlier plays, however, in a gallery of neurotic, childlike wives or mothers: Annie Keeney in *Ile*, Ella Harris in *All God's Chillun Got Wings*, Nina Leeds in *Strange Interlude*, Deborah Harford in *More Stately Mansions*.

The husbands of these dependent women, who are usually modeled on James O'Neill, are always depicted as parsimonious and partially responsible for the degeneration of their wives. In the 1929 "Scheme for a Life of Man play," the dramatist planned to use "life-sized puppets" to reenact the life of the hero: "his father or his mother for example—while in his memory they remain alive as they were." The memory of a father and mother depicted "alive *as they were*"—in this statement lies the key to an understanding of the many autobiographical plays, haunted as they are by the ghosts of James and Ella O'Neill. The author had one major story to communicate in his work: the tragic tale of the four O'Neills. Variations of them appear throughout the canon: the Mayos in *Beyond the Horizon*, the Cabots in *Desire Under the Elms*, the Browns and Anthonys in *The Great God Brown*, the Mannons in *Mourning Becomes Electra*, the Millers in *Ah, Wilder-*

ness!, the Melodys and Harfords in *A Touch of the Poet* and *More Stately Mansions*—all climaxing in the apotheoses, the closest approximations, the four Tyrones in *Long Day's Journey into Night*. All of O'Neill's major full-length plays are set within the context of the family.

The primary goal of the typical O'Neill hero is his attempt to give his life meaning. Whether the author realized it or not, he apparently reached a significant conclusion as he entered his final creative phase in 1939: life is made meaningful by other people, by familial relationships, illustrated by *Long Day's Journey into Night* and *A Moon for the Misbegotten*, or by close bonds of friendship, demonstrated by *The Iceman Cometh* and *Hughie*. As his health deteriorated, O'Neill became more and more obsessed by the desire to complete the plays that were most meaningful to him: those that related to his immediate family and his friends. He had to make a choice in 1940 between completing autobiographical plays and continuing the Cycle. On August 3, in a letter to Robert Sisk, he wrote: "The Cycle is definitely on the shelf. Pending the duration! It's simply impossible to go on with a long job like that now. For me, at any rate, There isn't enough future visible."

It is lamentable that the Cycle was not completed. Yet even that project should be willingly surrendered in exchange for the final masterpieces O'Neill produced: *Long Day's Journey into Night* and *The Iceman Cometh*, the crown jewels of the American theater. Strangely, O'Neill did not achieve true greatness until he immersed himself totally in the reality of his own early life, his family and friends. *Long Day's Journey into Night*, illustrating the complex relationship of the four O'Neills, provides the key to understanding many of the preceding plays. It alone reveals the precarious state of Ella O'Neill's mind, destroyed as it was by drug addiction, and the reactions of her husband and sons to her condition. Her younger son was devastated by the thought that throughout his early years she had preferred the pleasure of the release from reality to his well-being. Ella's addiction haunted him. In numerous plays, the hero, who is always a self-portrait, is betrayed by his mother. Whatever emotions forged the bond between Ella and her son—love, pity, hatred, fascination—it was the most meaningful relationship in his life.

Jamie O'Neill exerted an influence on his brother that was second only to that of Ella. The playwright told Hamilton Basso, "We were very close, my brother and I. We were a very close family—perhaps *too* close."[*] In numerous completed and contemplated works, the dramatist continuously develops an early idea recorded in the 1918–1920 notebook: "play of Jim & self—showing influence of elder on younger brother." Psychologists have noted that a child who is neglected by his parents will frequently turn to a sibling for guidance and consolation. The young Eugene seems to have turned to Jamie in their parents' absence. As the less-loved son, Jamie jealously tried to destroy his brother. The causes and effects of the love-hate relationship of the two brothers are revealed in the last act of *Long Day's Journey into Night*. The author had to write this crucial scene in order to purge himself of the bitterness and resentment he felt for Jamie. In the sequel to this play, *A Moon for the Misbegotten*, he manifests his deep pity and affection for Jamie and an awareness of his desperate loneliness. In the early notes for the play Josie describes the deep love that unites her and Jim Tyrone. Her words apply aptly to the bond that links Eugene and Jamie: "It's the two of us in the world alone, two that do be dreaming, two born of the sadness of beauty, two in the dark night, two waiting in the dawn homesick for the land of heart's desire where only dreams come true."

In the first idea recorded for *A Moon for the Misbegotten*, the author remarks that the work is "based on story" (the Shaughnessey pigs-in-the-pond episode) told

---

*Basso, p. 47.

by Edmund in the first act of *Long Day's Journey into Night* "except here Jamie principal character and story of play otherwise entirely imaginary except for J.'s revelation of self." Set in 1923, the year Jamie died, *A Moon for the Misbegotten* is a eulogy for him. While the major focus of the play is Jim Tyrone's attempt to transcend the degeneracy of the past and to find forgiveness for this transgression against his mother, several other significant themes coalesce. The Irish-Yankee conflict rages again in New England; the participants in *A Moon for the Misbegotten* are the Irish tenant farmer Phil Hogan and his pro-English neighbor, T. Stedman Harder, through whom the author again attacks materialism and his favorite capitalist target, Standard Oil. Autobiographical elements are woven into the play: incidents from Jamie O'Neill's life and his relationship with his mother and father, the father-son conflict between Phil Hogan and his son, Mike, whose mother died when he was born.

Jamie is described as having a "Mephistophelian cast" in both *Long Day's Journey into Night* and *A Moon for the Misbegotten*. He is depicted in a similar manner in earlier plays—as the Mephistophelian Dion Anthony in *The Great God Brown*, whom William Brown addresses several times as "brother," and as the Mephistophelian Loving in *Days Without End*. In the early notes for the latter play, the "evil" Loving was depicted as the brother of the "good" John. Hickey in *The Iceman Cometh* uses the word "brother" when he addresses Parritt, who, in the notes, seems to be yet another thinly veiled portrait of Jamie O'Neill. Parritt has just traveled east from California, where he betrayed his mother, as had Jamie. Erie uses the word "brother" when addressing the Night Clerk in *Hughie*, which, like *A Moon for the Misbegotten*, is an obituary for Jamie. In a scene similar to the one between Jim Tyrone and Josie, Erie narrates the story of his wasted life to the Night Clerk in an effort to form a friendship with him. Erie's account of his gambling adventures captures the imagination of the clerk, who, at the close of the one-acter, "resembles a holy saint, recently elected to Paradise." Erie produces a pair of dice for "a little crap," his soul "purged of grief."

The Iceman Cometh is O'Neill's loving tribute to the close friends he had made at Jimmy the Priest's in 1911– 1912 and at the Hell Hole in 1915–1916. In his early character sketches, first set designs, and notes, the playwright used the real names of these people. To the consternation of his wife, Carlotta, O'Neill retained the friendship of many of them—outcasts, alcoholics, losers all—throughout his life. Six months after her husband's death, Carlotta wrote disparagingly of the "so-called 'Bohemian' existence of those few early years. The parasites, the spongers, the hangers-on, dogged this poor man's steps until Death stepped in. He never had a day's respite from someone writing for money—it was hideous!" (letter to Dale Fern, May 7, 1954). Ironically, O'Neill was perhaps happier during the years with these close friends than he was during any comparable period with Carlotta.

The Iceman Cometh focuses on the value of friendship and the necessity of the pipe dream. Larry Slade calls Harry Hope's saloon the "Palace of Dreams." The only way its habitués can cope with the present is to escape into an illusionary world in which the past merges with and becomes the future. One of the earliest titles O'Neill assigned the play was "Tomorrow," the time when all pipe dreams are realized. Only Larry realizes both the futility of and the need for the dream: "The lie of a pipe dream is what gives life to the whole misbegotten mad lot of us, drunk or sober." To this "last harbor" comes Hickey, who brings a message of salvation: temperance and the abolition of pipe dreams. He destroys not only the characters' precious illusions but also their bonds of friendship by sowing the seeds of dissension. Harry Hope's can justly be called "The End of the Line Cafe," yet the play's tone is not one of despair but of hope. O'Neill's ultimate message is one of life rather than death. After Hickey, the spoiler who brings death, is declared mad and taken away, the misfits resume their former friendships and dreams. Shortly after the premiere of *The Iceman Cometh* in 1946, O'Neill explained his aspirations for the American theater to Lawrence Langner and added, "We must live in that pipe dream—or die—(as I believe I've said in this play). Love remains (once in a while); friendship remains (and that is rare, too). The rest is ashes in the Wind! We have friendship, so what the hell."

Hughie, which also stresses the need for friendship, is O'Neill's finest one-acter. It is the only completed play in the "By Way of Obit" series he intended to write. Like *The Iceman Cometh*, the series had been on his mind for decades. In the 1918–1920 notebook he made entries for a "Jimmy the Priest series" and a "Gunman Series," which would include a play entitled "The Pig of the Hell Hole." Two decades later, on November 29, 1940, he began the "By Way of Obit" series, which included "Pig of the Hell Hole play" and "Jimmy the Priest idea of guy who recited Homer." He developed the former one-acter on February 3, 1941, and the latter three days later. Seven of the eight one-acters are obituaries for people O'Neill had known. In the eighth he planned to eulogize his deceased Dalmatian, Blemie.

All four of O'Neill's last plays, which represent the greatest achievement of his career, are obituaries—for his family and his friends. Only one, *Long Day's Journey into Night*, ends in the midst of night's dark despair. The characters in the other three survive the long night and find with the coming of dawn some semblance of hope. At the conclusion of *A Moon for the Misbegotten*, Josie Hogan, the priestess-mother figure, absolves the penitent son, Jim Tyrone, and holds out the promise of salvation. O'Neill maintained that he wrote *Long Day's Journey into Night* "with deep pity and understanding and forgiveness for all the four haunted Tyrones." What he sought, personally and reciprocally, as he concluded *A Moon for the Misbegotten*, was the forgiveness he extended to his brother Jamie, through Josie, in the last line of the play: "May you rest forever in forgiveness and peace."

In 1913 O'Neill started writing plays at "Our house," the family summer home in New London. Forty years later he tried valiantly to surmount the pain he was experiencing to complete his final play, *A Moon for the Misbegotten*, which was set a short distance from the house on Pequot Avenue. To read the entries of the Work Diary for the first four months of 1943 is a sorrowful experience; the man, as dramatist, was dying. On January 31 he wrote, "what I am up against now—fade out physically each day after about 3 hours—page a day because work slowly even when as eager about play as I am about this—Park[inson's] main cause—constant strain to write." The March 10 entry reads: "eager but little done because nerves jumping out of hands, arms—can't control." As she had for other plays for years, Carlotta was typing the manuscript of *A Moon for the Misbegotten*. She alone knew the effort involved in completing this play and stated later: "Moon I loathe that play—for personal reasons! . . . The whole thing was a ghastly business—it was at that time his real illness took hold of him! He was not at his writing best" (letter to Dale Fern, August 15, 1953).

O'Neill's method of composition was unusual. He could only create—in his final days as throughout his career—by writing down his ideas himself in that peculiarly small scrawl of his. Dudley Nichols offered to complete an unfinished play, "The Last Conquest," following the author's directives. Nichols states: "He could no more do this than he could dictate his work. His handwriting was a part of his mind, almost a part of his imagination, which is what makes his MSS so fascinating. His hand stopped, his work was stopped, and he knew it." In 1944 Lawrence Langner sent the dramatist a Sound Scriber, hoping that he could dictate his plays. O'Neill experimented with the machine but was unable to compose in this manner.

Throughout his creative life O'Neill lived for some part, if not all, of each year by the sea, except for the last years spent at Tao House, his home in California. In 1943, when he could no longer write, he must have viewed the house, set in the midst of hills, as a prison. Possibly he felt then like his sensitive hero, Robert Mayo, in *Beyond the Horizon*, who in the last scene looks for the secret of life that lies beyond the rim of the hills and the horizon. In 1944, after selling Tao House, the O'Neills moved into an even more confining environment: an apartment in a San Francisco hotel. In 1946 they moved to New York, where the dramatist became involved in preparations for the Broadway premiere of *The Iceman Cometh* and the road company production of *A Moon for the Misbegotten*. The couple purchased a house in 1948 in Marblehead, which resembles New London in its proximity to the sea. The O'Neills were both hospitalized in February 1951 and later moved to a suite at the Hotel Shelton in Boston, where they lived until the dramatist's death on November 27, 1953.

The final decade, particularly its last two years, was, undoubtedly, the unhappiest period of O'Neill's life. The love he and Carlotta had once shared had disintegrated. Their last years together were marred by bitter scenes, recriminations, and periods of gloomy silence. With his creative outlet blocked, he seemed to take out his frustrations on her. Jealously, she deliberately isolated him from his children and friends. In the reality of his life, he became a far more tragic, haunted figure than any he had created in his plays. In each of the dramas, there was at least one family member or friend whose compassion served as a buffer for the soul in agony. For him in his final years, there was no one.

All creative inspirations withered within the confines of his mind. If he had yearned in his youth for the release of death to ease his mental anguish and to reunite him with his loved ones, the longing of his tortured spirit in the final months must have known no bounds. During his forty-year career, O'Neill made a concerted effort to exorcise the tragic familial memories of his youth and to memorialize the friends he cherished. Friends and family members died, but not to him; they forever haunted him. His plays are dramaturgic and autobiographic milestones—reminiscences for his dead, the mainspring of his tragedy and his greatness—on his long day's journey through life.

47. *The Iceman Cometh*

The Iceman Cometh is a memory play. In it, O'Neill assembles a group of homeless, hope-foresaken outcasts who, as he states, "all derive from actual people I have known," in a dump called Harry Hope's saloon, "a combination of three in which I hung out." He first recorded the original idea for *The Iceman Cometh* and his other great play of reminiscence, *Long Day's Journey into Night*, on the same day, June 6, 1939, noting later that they had been on his mind for years (letter of October 13, 1940, to Dudley Nichols). In the latter he attempted to still the ghosts of the family that forever haunted him. In the former he paid tribute to those he cherished most dearly after his family: the close friends he made during his "down and out" period at Jimmy the Priest's, a waterfront dive, in 1911–1912; the Hell Hole, a Greenwich Village barroom-hotel, in 1915–1916; and the taproom of the Garden Hotel, located across the street from Madison Square Garden.

O'Neill told Kenneth Macgowan that "*The Iceman Cometh* is something I want to make life reveal about itself, fully and deeply and roundly—that it takes place for me in life not in a theatre" (letter of December 30, 1940). As he entered the final phase of his productive career, the dramatist had a vital twofold message to impart. His most important revelation was not a new notion but a concept that appears throughout the canon: humanity's desperate need for a life-sustaining illusion to lessen the naked despair of soul-destroying reality. In early plays, such as *The Straw* (1918) and *Beyond the Horizon* (1918), characters are given a "hopeless hope"; two decades later they cling forlornly to an equally elusive illusion, the pipe dream. Ironically, the author himself in the last years of his life was stripped of all illusions that remained to him relating to love, fame, health and well-being. Yet he stridently defended the need of the pipe dream in the last plays, particularly in *The Iceman Cometh*, through his spokesman, Larry Slade. The author was also deprived of what he considered the second essential requisite in life, the companionship of cherished friends, because of geographical distance, his wife Carlotta's decrees, or their deaths. No one, however, could take from him the precious memories he had of these people and their tragic lives.

O'Neill described an idea in his Work Diary in early 1940 using an "orchestral technique for a play—playwright as leader symphony, characters, chorus an orchestra." He actually composed this drama when he wrote *The Iceman Cometh*. The four acts serve as the four related movements of the symphony; the repetitious injections of the personal stories of the characters are variations of the work's major interconnected themes. At given signals from the maestro-conductor, the sodden misfits at Harry Hope's raise their heads from the saloon tables and narrate their individual tales.

O'Neill identified his friends in the earliest set design he drew for the first act, giving the characters grouped around the tables their real-life rather than fictitious names.* The prototype for Harry Hope was Tom Wallace, the proprietor of the Hell Hole when O'Neill frequented it. Harry, sixty, is a likable "softhearted slob, without malice, feeling superior to no one, a sinner among sinners, a born easy mark for every appeal." His sight and hearing are failing, and he has rheumatism. He has built up a myth about his wife, Bessie, as being a "loving

---

*The design appears in my *Eugene O'Neill at Work* (New York: Ungar, 1981), p. 264. The complete list of actual names is also given in the section discussing the first notes and scenario for *The Iceman Cometh*, (pp. 262–263).

helpmate—fact is she nagged him to death and he was relieved when she died." His brother-in-law, Ed Mosher, a one-time circus man, was modeled on another friend, Jack Croak. A habitual drunkard, Mosher is "congenitally indolent, a practical joker, a born grafter and con merchant." He and his friend Pat McGloin are parasitic "lifetime guests" at Harry Hope's. McGloin, a bullet-headed, jowly man in his fifties, has "his old occupation of policeman stamped all over him." He was once brutal and greedy, but his face has been melted down by time and whiskey "into a good-humored parasite's characterlessness."

Two close drinking companions from the 1915–1916 period who remained the author's lifelong friends are depicted in the play. Larry Slade, the play's central figure, is an accurate portrait of Terry Carlin, a former Syndicalist-Anarchist. Larry, sixty, has straight white hair, a gaunt Irish face, and "a mystic's meditative pale-blue eyes with a gleam of sharp sardonic humor in them." His expresion, that of tired tolerance, gives his face "the quality of a pitying but weary old priest." Joe Smith was the real-life prototype for Joe Mott, a one-time proprietor of a black gambling house. He is a good-looking brown-skinned man who still "manages to preserve an atmosphere of nattiness" in spite of a run of bad luck.

James Cameron, "Jimmy Tomorrow," and Cecil Lewis, "The Captain," are portraits of James Byth and Major Adams, former habitués of Jimmy the Priest's. They had been portrayed two decades earlier in "Exorcism" as the friends who save Ned Malloy (O'Neill) when he attempts to commit suicide. Jimmy, a former Boer War correspondent in his late fifties, is an intelligent, well-bred gentleman who blames his alcoholism and inability to retain a job on his wife's infidelity. Lewis, sixty, a one-time Captain in the British army, is engaged in a long-running but harmless quarrel with Piet Wetjoen, called "The General," a former leader of a Boer com-

mando. The prototype for General Wetjoen is the famous
General Christian De Wet; he and his brother Piet waged
numerous campaigns against the British. The actual De
Wet and his fictitious counterpart have numerous similarities: appearance, their physical strength and pride in
it, nobility of character, the battles in which they fought.
O'Neill did extensive research on the Boer War, recording information on signficant dates and battles, to present
an accurate account of it in the now-friendly conflict between the former foes.

Hugo Kalmar is a close approximation of Hippolyte
Havel, a colorful Czech anarchist friend whose physical
description, mannerisms, and political background are
attributed to his fictional counterpart. After years of im-
prisonment, suffering, and persecution, Havel found refuge in London and became Emma Goldman's lover in
1899. The dramatist portrays these two anarchists as
Hartmann and the Russian Olga Tarnoff in his 1915 play
"The Personal Equation." Hugo, a small man in his late
fifties, has long, gray-streaked black hair, a walrus mustache, and "black eyes which peer near-sightedly from
behind thick-lensed spectacles." There is a "foreign atmosphere about him, the stamp of an alien radical, a
strong resemblance to the type Anarchist as portrayed,
bomb in hand, in newspaper cartoons."

Also included in the group of outcasts, most of whom
are in their late fifties or early sixties, are two lost younger
men, who blame their current state of dissolution and
despair on an erring parent. Willie Oban, son of the late
world-famous Bill Oban, King of the Bucket Shops, is
identified in O'Neill's early notes for the play as the
real-life Morris Adams, son of "Al" Adams, who was a
notorious policy king. The latter was a friend of Deputy
Commissioner of Police William S. Devery,* whose

*When Joe Mott, as a young man, wanted to open a gambling
house, Harry Hope had sent him to his "good friend," a police
chief called "big Bill."

brother-in-law, Michael J. Brennan, was indicted with
Adams in 1902. Adams was sent to Sing Sing for his illegal
policy activities in 1903; when released the next year, he
tried to establish a chain of bucket shops. Two of his sons
were educated at Harvard and Heidelberg and became
lawyers. A third, Louis, was arrested and sentenced to six
months on Blackwells Island for attempting to shoot his
father. This rebellious, vengeful son, Louis, seems to be
the prototype for Willie Oban, whose father, hoping to
keep one step ahead of the law, sent him to Harvard Law
School. Mocked by his fellow students for his father's
unsavory reputation, Willie "discovered the loophole of
whiskey and escaped his jurisdiction." Now in his late
thirties, Willie is clearly in the final stages of alcoholism,
wherein he perceives "de Brooklyn boys is after him." His
face is haggard and dissipated; his tattered and dirty
clothes give him the appearance of a "skid row" derelict.

The eighteen-year-old former anarchist, Don Parritt, is actually Donald Vose, whose anarchist mother,
Gertie Vose, and Emma Goldman became friends in
1897. Like Parritt, Vose betrayed his anarchist friends
and came to New York from the west after the *Times*
building explosion in Los Angeles. Employed by Detec-
tive William J. Burns, Vose used Goldman to track down
two associates who were later arrested and charged with
the crime. While he did not actually betray his mother, as
does Parritt, Vose behaved treacherously to Goldman,
who resembles the fictitious anarchist mother Rosa Parritt. Although he is good-looking, Parritt has an unpleasant personality. "There is a shifting defiance and ingratia-
tion in his light-blue eyes and an irritating aggressiveness
in his manner."

The three tarts, Pearl, Margie, and Cora, are composite portraits of prostitutes O'Neill had met during his
years of dissolution in New York. Harry Hope's two bar-
tenders, Rocky Pioggi and Chuck Morello, had their real-
life counterparts at the Hell Hole: Lefty Louis and John

Bull. In O'Neill's first notes for the play, in which he frequently interchanged his characters' real and fictitious names, Bull plays the role Hickey later assumes, as the long passage describing him indicates: "It is Bull who encourages Jimmy in 'tomorrow' [to make his pipe dream a reality today] and Tom [Harry Hope] to get out of house." These efforts arouse Terry-Larry's "growing irritation & hostility to Bull." The specific purpose of the Bull-Hickey character is to shatter not only the characters' pipe dreams but also their close friendships.

There is one fictitious figure in *The Iceman Cometh*. In response to Macgowan's inquiry about the identity of the hardware salesman, O'Neill wrote, "What you wonder about Hickey: No, I never knew him. He's the most imaginary character in the play. Of course, I knew many salesmen in my time who were periodical drunks, but Hickey is not any of them" (letter of December 30, 1940). The fact that O'Neill never knew Hickey—that he was not, like the other characters, one of his friends at Jimmy the Priest's or the Hell Hole—explains the most significant revelation in the early notes for *The Iceman Cometh*: Hickey was not originally an integral part of the scheme; he was, rather, an afterthought.

Hickey is the outsider, the spoiler. At the outset of the play, before his arrival, harmony reigns at Harry Hope's. Bonds of deep friendship link all the characters. While these misfits might have been forced by fate to seek refuge at Hope's, the End of the Line Cafe, each is consoled in his misery by the other. When Macgowan urged the dramatist to condense Act I, O'Neill explained the need to build "up the complete picture of the group as it now is in the first part—the atmosphere of the place, the humour and friendship and human warmth and *deep inner contentment* at the bottom." If he failed to so so, he cautioned, "You wouldn't feel the same sympathy and understanding for them, or be so moved by what Hickey does to them."

Larry Slade calls the saloon the "Palace of Dreams"
and encourages his friends in the pursuit of their illusions,
knowing full well from his own situation the despair of
cold, comfortless reality. One of the first titles O'Neill
assigned the play was "Tomorrow," the time when all
pipe dreams are realized. Harry Hope, who has not gone
outside the saloon in the twenty years since his wife's
death, plans to do so "tomorrow." On that dream day
Jimmy will be offered his old job on the newspaper; Joe
will start a new gambling house; the Boer War foes will
have enough money to go back to their native countries;
Pat, who was dismissed from the police force for taking
bribes, will be vindicated and reinstated; Willie will work
for the district attorney; and Cora and Chuck will marry
and settle down on a farm in "Joisey." Margie and Pearl's
pipe dream is that they are "tarts," not whores; Rocky's
protective lie is that he is their manager, not a pimp.
Hugo's dream is to lead a revolutionary anarchist "mob to
the sack of Babylon"—modern capitalist society. Larry,
the "old Foolosopher," who sits "in the grandstand of
philosophical detachment," deludes himself by believing
that he welcomes the "fine long sleep" of death. He alone
realizes both the futility and the need of the dream: "The
lie of a pipe dream is what gives life to the whole misbegotten mad lot of us, drunk or sober." This quotation
contains the central message of the play: man must have
his illusions to sustain him; however inconsequential or
foolish, the lie of the pipe dream gives meaning to life.

Ibsen makes the same point in *The Wild Duck*. Some
scholars view *The Iceman Cometh* as the American counterpart of Gorki's *The Lower Depths*. It has, however, a
greater affinity with the Ibsen drama. Like Hickey,
Gregers Werle has a savior complex and attempts to shatter the illusions of a group of inveterate dreamers, primarily the Ekdal family. Both men are guilt-ridden destroy-
ers who refer to illusions as the things that "poison a guy's
life." Doctor Relling, a drunkard who is described as a

"man who has thrown away what is best in himself," resembles Larry Slade in his defense of the pipe dream. Relling says, "Rob a man of his life-lie and you rob him of happiness." Sea imagery is used in both plays to depict the depths to which the shipwrecked outcasts have sunk in life. The regulars at Hope's reside in a "Bottom of the Sea Rathskeller"; each of the Ekdals is compared to a wounded wild duck, which dives straight to the bottom of the sea and hooks itself "into the weeds and muck." Gregers and Hickey are responsible for the deaths of two innocent victims, Hedvig Ekdal and Evelyn, the salesman's wife, and for the destruction of the dreams and the lives of other characters. Not until the final scenes do the wretched men realize the consequences of their meddlesome actions.

O'Neill could be accused of plagiarism were it not for the fact that his characters were ready-made in his memory. Each came forth fully formed, like Athena from Zeus' forehead, equipped with his own real-life pipe dream and peculiarities. The only imaginary figure in *The Iceman Cometh* is Hickey. O'Neill may or may not be indebted to Ibsen for inspiring this character. In the complexity of his overall scheme and characterization, the American surpasses the Norwegian dramatist. The latter's central figure, Hjalmar Ekdal, is a buffoon. Because of his simpleminded buoyancy, he will, as Relling predicts, rise from the depths of his sorrow and use his daughter's death to create another sentimental pose. The entire circle of characters in *The Iceman Cometh* is forever caught in the tragic quagmire of the past. Their minds allow them the luxury of the pipe dream but deny them total obliviousness to the reality of their lives.

The American playwright makes a political as well as a psychological statement in *The Iceman Cometh*, using two groups of characters—disgraced grafters and former anarchists—to recreate the radical atmosphere of the Hell Hole. The author attacks American greed and the

corruption of the early twentieth centry, the byproducts
of capitalism, through his portraits of Harry Hope, Pat
McGloin, Joe Mott, Rocky Pioggi, and Willie Oban. A
former "jitney Tammany politician," Hope has the connections that enable Joe to open his gambling house, but
Joe has to bribe McGloin so that it can stay open. Because
the policeman got greedy and forgot to pass on part of the
money Joe gave him, the gambler had to close his house.
From the district attorney and police commissioner to the
lowliest cop on the beat, all are said to be "on the take."
Once the massive scale of corruption is perceived, Harry's statement about the snakes of Ireland finding their
way onto the New York police force becomes more meaningful.

The success of the greedy pimp-bartender Rocky,
who would, Hope states, steal pennies off his dead mother's eyes, demonstrates the way law officials and criminals
act in collusion. Margie and Pearl actually need protection from Rocky, not by him. In the first notes for the play,
when the two women refuse to work for Rocky, he goes to
the nearby police station and tells his friends on the force
to arrest the prostitutes if they try to solicit customers.
Willie's father is also aided by elected officials. The bucket
shops he operates are actually bogus stock brokerages.
He lined his own pockets and those of favored customers
by bilking hordes of average clients. The son knows
that his father is taking hard-earned money from poor
people who cherish the pipe dream of "striking it rich."
Willie, when first shown in the play, wakes up from a bad
dream crying "Papa, Papa." Forced to live with guilt for
his father's crimes against the poor, Willie turns to alcohol
to escape.

A second group of characters, designed originally to
illustrate the corruption of the capitalist system, is the
renegade remnant of the Anarchist Movement: Hugo,
Larry, and Parritt. O'Neill was a lifelong believer in anarchism, the nonviolent type advocated by Proudhon. The

playwright viewed the Movement as a means of attaining economic, social, and political equality. When Rocky refuses to loan Hugo a dollar, the latter, in his first speech, calls the bartender a "damned bourgeois wop" and says, "The great Malatesta is my good friend." Hippolyte Havel, the model for Hugo, was a friend of the famous Italian anarchist Enrico Malatesta. At the same time that O'Neill was writing *The Iceman Cometh*, he was also planning a comedy, "The Visit of Malatesta," whose central character is Cesare Malatesta. Pat McGloin, the corrupt Irish policeman in *The Iceman Cometh*, emerges in the comedy as Big Jim Delehanty. The conclusion reached at the end of *The Iceman Cometh* is that neither "ism," capitalism or anarchism, is able to provide its followers with sufficient hope for the present; as a consequence, the believers retreat into a world of "tomorrow" pipe dreams.

O'Neill also injects a social message into *The Iceman Cometh*. He apparently never forgave the Yankee New Londoners who rejected his Irish family. Having roomed at the Hell Hole with Joe Smith, the model for Joe Mott, and been befriended by numerous blacks in Greenwich Village, the dramatist was particularly aware of and sympathetic to the problems of blacks. As a result of his own experiences and those of his friends, he became a champion of victims of discrimination, the outcasts of society. *The Iceman Cometh* depicts a wide social spectrum: people from various walks of life and of different nationalities—British, Czechoslovakian, South African, Italian, Irish. Hope's saloon symbolizes the American melting pot where all men are equal (the word "brother" is frequently used). Alcohol is the great leveler of social distinctions. When Hickey arrives, he sows the seeds of dissension and temporarily destroys the close bonds of friendship. He could, therefore, symbolize any form of racism or bigotry abhorrent to the author.

The play opens in the back room of Harry Hope's saloon on an early morning in the summer of 1912. The characters await the arrival of Hickey, who is certain to join them to celebrate Harry's birthday the next day. Seated at the tables, where they have been sleeping since the previous evening, are all the regulars of the saloon. Only Larry is awake when Rocky, the night bartender, enters. Told that Hope is determined to demand room rent "beginnin' tomorrow," Larry, in his first speech, describes his friends' "touching credulity concerning tomorrows. It'll be a great day for them, tomorrow—the Feast of All Fools, with brass bands playing! Their ships will come in, loaded to the gunwales with cancelled regrets and promises fulfilled and clean slates and new leases!"

The appearance of Don Parritt, the outsider, provides the motivation for much of the first act's exposition. The young man views Larry, one of his mother's former lovers, as a surrogate father. Rosa was arrested and imprisoned after a bombing on the West Coast, in which several people were killed. Larry wonders who betrayed Rosa and the Movement and tipped off the "Burns dicks." After thirty years of radicalism, Larry quit the Movement eleven years ago, as he failed to detect any appreciable improvement in himself and others. He tells Parritt, "The material the ideal society must be constructed from is men themselves and you can't build a marble temple out of a mixture of mud and manure. When man's soul isn't a sow's ear, it will be time enough to dream of silk purses." Parritt also spurns the movement now, declaring it to be "a crazy pipe dream."

Larry suspects that Parritt betrayed Rosa, but he banishes this thought and begins to describe the denizens of the saloon and their backgrounds. Occasionally, the sleepers stir and become conscious briefly. Willie sings a risqué song he claims to have learned at Harvard; the two Boer War opponents exchange harsh words and are pacified by Jimmy, the peacemaker: "We are all brothers within the Empire united beneath the flag on which the sun never sets." Jimmy's resolution to take hold of himself "first thing tomorrow morning" evokes a similar response from the others, prompting Larry to remark, "The tomorrow movement is a sad and beautiful thing." Margie and Pearl, described as plump, pretty "typical dollar street walkers," return from their night's work and good-naturedly turn over their earnings to Rocky, their "manager." Cora, a thin peroxide blond, and Chuck, a tough but amiable Italian-American with the strength and build of a prize fighter, come in. His weakness, ostensibly Cora's reason for not marrying him, is his occasional periodicals or "drunks."

Throughout the act the characters speak longingly of Hickey, whose coming in the past meant free alcohol and good times. In the last scene he arrives. About fifty, Hickey is a stout, roly-poly man with a round face and a jovial, friendly personality. "He has the salesman's mannerisms of speech, an easy flow of glib, persuasive convincingness." What he sells during this visit is salvation: temperance and the destruction of the pipe dream. He himself no longer needs "booze" as he has finally faced himself and thrown "overboard the damned lying pipe dream that'd been making me miserable." As self-appointed Messiah, he points out the dishonesty of the characters' dreams, asserting that they poison people's lives. It is Hickey himself who carries the poison of reality that brings death to their dreams. Earlier Willie had said, "Would that Hickey or Death would come!" The two are synonymous, for Hickey brings psychological death to the characters.

In the following act, the characters gradually assemble in the back room toward midnight for Harry's birthday party. Hickey's coming has affected all of them adversely. To avoid the salesman, the regulars hide in their rooms. Those preparing for the party quarrel bitterly: Cora with Pearl and Margie; the three women with Rocky; Chuck with Joe. They call a truce for Harry's sake. Later Hickey mocks Hugo, stating that his words about drinking, "vine

beneath the villow trees," reveal that his dream is to
become a bourgeois capitalist. Larry immediately attacks
Hickey and tells him that Hugo has earned his dream
because of his years of suffering in prison. The salesman
then attacks Larry, remarking that his "big Sleep stuff is a
pipe dream." If he really wanted to die, he would take a
hop off his fire escape. Hickey then urges the older man to
help Parritt punish himself. "I've had hell inside me. I can
spot it in others." Larry ridicules Hickey's stance as
prophet: "Be God, it's a second feast of Belshazzar, with
Hickey to do the writing on the wall."*

Taunted by Hickey to face the truth, Parritt makes
several attempts to confess his crime to Larry. At first he
tries to arouse the older man's sympathy, saying that
Larry was justified in leaving Rosa because of her blatant
promiscuity. The young man reveals his bitter resentment toward his mother for his early home life: "It was
like living in a whorehouse—only worse, because she
didn't have to make her living—." Parritt next attributes
his betrayal of his mother to patriotism, his duty to his
country. "I never thought Mother would be caught." He
later claims that he needed money; he "got stuck on a
whore and wanted dough to blow in on her." Larry refuses to listen to Parritt and warns him about "the thing
they call justice."

Hickey has sown the seeds of dissension in all those
around him. No sooner are the captain and the general
reconciled in this scene when two other good friends,
McGloin and Mosher, begin to quarrel. Hope too is in a
vile, pugnacious mood and complains about the "bums"
and "hookers" who take advantage of him. He will show
them all he is not a coward and will take a "walk around
the ward." His anger subsides and his voice catches as he

*At the Biblical feast of Belshazzar, the last king of Babylon,
mysterious handwriting appeared on the wall. The prophet
Daniel interpreted it as a prophecy of doom. That night Babylon
fell to Cyrus. Larry, a prophet like Daniel, is the only one
capable of understanding the latter-day prophet's words.

gazes at his bewildered friends: "Bejees, you know you're
all as welcome here as the flowers in May!" Hickey apologizes for "sicking some of you on to nag at each other," but
he insists that he only wants to free them from the guilt
and remorse that make them "hide behind lousy pipe
dreams about tomorrow. . . . And I promise you, by the
time this day is over, I'll have every one of you feeling the
same way!"

Larry demands that Hickey tell "us poor pipe-
dreaming sinners along the sawdust trail to salvation"
what inspired his conversion. "Did this great revelation of
the evil habit of dreaming about tomorrow come to you
after you found your wife was sick of you?" In previous
years Hickey had entertained the regulars with a humorous story about his wife's affair with the iceman. Now they
turn on Hickey and jeeringly taunt him about Evelyn's
presumed infidelity. The salesman startles them by saying that his "dearly beloved wife is dead." Larry exclaims,
"Be God, I felt he'd brought the touch of death upon
him!" Then he grows ashamed, as do the others, and they
beg forgiveness. Hickey assures them that he does not
feel any grief: "Evelyn was now at peace as she always
longed to be."

Act III depicts the barroom of Harry Hope's on the
dreaded "tomorrow," that day all pipe dreams are supposedly fulfilled. The denizens of Hope's turn in their
keys to their rooms, resolving never to return. Hickey has
spent the night tormenting them and has changed them
into aggressive, preying animals, snarling at each other
and opening old wounds. Chuck and Cora have been
arguing for hours, but they are still determined to get
married that day to spite Hickey. Chuck and Rocky quarrel, and the latter takes out a gun from his pocket. Joe
steps between them to stop the fight, and the two bar-
tenders join forces and attack him, uttering racial slurs.
Larry blames Hickey for their edginess. "Didn't I tell you
he'd brought death with him?" Joe agrees. "Bad luck
come in de door when Hickey come." Vowing to open his

old gambling house and to show them he can succeed in life, he swaggers out through the swinging doors.

Willie enters, dressed in an expensive suit Hickey has provided. While sober and badly in need of a drink, he rejects it, saying: "I'd have no chance if I went to the D.A.'s office smelling of booze." Ludicrously, he offers to defend Parritt if he will entrust him with his case. The Captain appears, attired in his good suit and determined to get a post with the Cunard line. The General, feebly holding his booze-sodden body together, follows Lewis into the room and starts to argue with him. Another pair of former friends, now turned foes, arrives: Mosher, who seems sick, nervous, and apprehensive; and McGloin, looking as bedraggled as the others.

All those assembled strive to force themselves to go out the swinging doors; but filled with dread, they hang back, avowedly to say goodbye to Harry yet actually to cling a little longer to their pipe dreams. The Finnish poet Uno Kailas wrote: "I have but two doors, but two: to the dream and to death." The key symbol in the play is the swinging doors in the barroom setting of Act III. Swinging in, they lead to the dream, to the world of illusion, safety, companionship. Swinging out, they lead to death, to the world of reality, danger, alienation.

Finally Harry and Jimmy walk in, wearing their best attire; their desperate bravado suggests "the last march of the condemned." Hickey follows triumphantly, promising the men peace if they will kill their dreams. The sullen, resentful men look at him with hatred. One by one, they bid farewell to Harry and go out, fearfully, reluctantly. Harry complains about his bad eyesight and hearing, his rheumatism, and the "damned automobiles." Goaded beyond endurance, he curses Hickey and strides blindly out into the street. When Rocky predicts that he will turn back, Hickey agrees and says, "by tonight they'll all be here again. You dumbbell, that's the whole point."

Harry gets no farther than the middle of the street; he comes back "lurching blindly through the swinging

doors" and says, "Feel all in. Like a corpse, bejees."
Larry tells Hickey, "It's the peace of death you've brought
him." He then asks the salesman how his wife died. The
reply shocks and terrifies all of them: Evelyn was murdered. At the end of the act Hugo admits that he does not
have the courage to become a revolutionary; Harry reveals his deep-seated hatred for his wife, Bessie. He
seeks, unsuccessfully, to find escape in alcohol and asks,
"What did you do to the booze, Hickey? There's no
damned life left in it." Hickey experiences his first doubts
about his experiment; he hovers anxiously over Harry:
"It's time you began to feel happy—." All of the outcasts
are dead psychologically; neither liquor nor the pipe
dream can drown their reality.

The last act is set in the back room at around half past
one in the morning of the following day. All the regulars
have returned, their hopes shattered, their condition
similar to Harry's. They sit in silence "in a numb stupor
which is impervious to stimulation." Hickey comes back
from making a telephone call and overhears Larry's accusation against him: "He's lost his confidence that the
peace he's sold us is the real McCoy and it's made him
uneasy about his own. He'll have to prove to us—." In the
longest monologue O'Neill ever wrote, Hickey describes
how and why he murdered his wife and what pipe dreams
did to him and Evelyn. He reminisces about his early life
in a small town: the strictness of his father, a minister; his
love, even as a youth, for Evelyn; their marriage after he
settled in the Big Town and got a job. Two detectives,
Lieb and Moran, arrive, looking for Hickey. They stand
near the doorway listening to his outburst. From time to
time others in the room interrupt Hickey and try to
silence him. Undaunted, he continues his story, describing his numerous acts of infidelity with tarts, the venereal
disease he transmitted to his wife, the countless times he
returned home hopelessly inebriated. And Evelyn had
borne every indignity and had always forgiven him, cling-
ing to the pipe dream that he would reform. Guilt-strick-

en, he began to hate the pipe dream and to hate Evelyn. Realizing that he could never again bear to be forgiven by her, he took out the gun he had given his wife to protect herself and shot her while she slept.

Hickey's confession evokes a similar unburdening by Parritt, who confesses at last the real motive for his betrayal of his mother: "It was because I hated her." Hickey expresses the same kind of bitterness: "Well, you know what you can do with your pipe dream now, you damned bitch!" He is horrified by his revelation that he himself still nourishes a pipe dream, that he loved his wife, when in reality he hated her. Frantically, he denies his statement: "Good God, I couldn't have said that! If I did, I'd gone insane!" The only way he can retain his dream that he did love Evelyn is to plead insanity. Harry and the others seize the word "insanity," using it to justify the retention of their dreams. Hickey is momentarily amused and says to Harry, "Up to your old tricks, eh?" Then, seeing the resentful expressions of the others, he states, "Yes, Harry, of course, I've been out of my mind." Moran thinks he is merely trying to avoid going to the chair, but Hickey asks, "Do you suppose I give a damn about life now? Why you bonehead, I haven't got a single damned lying hope or pipe dream left!"

As Hickey is led off, Larry pronounces absolution for the penitent: "May the Chair bring him peace at last." Longing for the same peace and believing his crime to be worse than murder, Parritt begs Larry to tell him what to do. The penance Larry exacts is suicide: "Go! Get the hell out of life, God damn you, before I choke it out of you! Go up—!"* At once Parritt seems transformed and at peace.

---

*The value of Parritt's private and Hickey's public auricular confessions is dubious. While confession to a layman is effective if it is reported subsequently to a priest, given the circumstances of possibility, a major heresy is involved here: a layman cannot impose penance; he can only urge a "Perfect Contrition." Larry's imposition of suicide on Parritt for what he had done is totally outside the Catholic Church's acceptance.

He thanks the older man and leaves. Larry braces himself and listens. At the sound of "something hurtling down" off the roof, he shudders. "'Poor devil!' (A long-forgotten faith returns to him for a moment and he mumbles) 'God rest his soul in peace!'" Larry sits in silence, apart from the others, and concludes: "Be God, I'm the only real convert to death Hickey made here."

While Larry is seemingly brought closer to death by the coming of Hickey and Parritt, the other characters reassert the validity of their pipe dreams and return to their earlier state of drunken oblivion. Yet they are the survivors of life's shipwreck. Having touched bottom in the last harbor, they choose life over death. Their life lies give them the illusion of having a meaning in life; shadow suffices for substance in the Palace of Dreams.

In contrast, the two who deny the dream deny life. Parritt asserts that his dream had been the Movement, but the focus of his life had actually been his mother. He was devastated by her promiscuity, the endless parade of men who robbed him of her. Betrayal of the Movement was his way of punishing her; his own death was his means of punishing himself for hating her. The same can be said of Hickey, the wife, rather than the mother, hater. He paid dearly to destroy the pipe dream; to free himself he had to kill his wife. Yet in the end he sinks farther into self-deceit, maintaining that he murdered her out of love when he did so out of hatred. He claims to be insane to protect this final illusion, realizing too late the necessity of the dream both for himself and others.

Betrayal becomes a major motif in the play, not merely of women by men but vice versa. The four offstage women are partially responsible for destroying the four onstage male characters; they form a composite picture of O'Neill's mother: Evelyn is Ella, the long-suffering but forgiving wife, frequently left alone by a traveling, alcoholic husband; Rosa is the detached mother, caught up in the Movement as Ella was in drugs and hopelessly lost to her son; Bessie is the pious, nagging, intolerant shrew;

Marjorie, the attractive but unfaithful spouse. Hickey and Parritt avenge themselves for perceived betrayal by committing actual or psychological murder; Harry and Jimmy find a symbolic revenge in their refusal to go out of the saloon and their indulgence in the vice their wives resented most: alcohol.

The circle of betrayal broadens to include not only one's wife/mother and husband/son but also one's friends: Hickey of his companions at the saloon, Parritt of his associates in the Movement. Both men are outsiders, pariahs at Harry Hope's, symbolically man's last refuge. Frequently it is stated that neither belongs there. O'Neill told Langner that people must live in the "pipe dream— or die. . . . Love remains (once in a while); friendship remains (and that is rare, too). The rest is ashes in the wind!" (letter of October 9, 1946). Friendship and the pipe dream or death: these seem to be the only alternatives in the play. Larry observes that death comes with Hickey; he *is* the Iceman, for he kills what man needs most for life, according to the author: his illusions and his ties to his fellow man, the only visible proof that he belongs. The reluctance of the characters to face the outside world to pursue their pipe dreams stems not only from their awareness of the impossibility of realizing them but also from the fear of losing their only realities, the consolation of friendship and the security of their "home" at Harry Hope's.

In December 1942, when Theresa Helburn of the Theatre Guild asked O'Neill for permission to produce *The Iceman Cometh*, he urged her to wait until the war had been won and the "reaction to the realities behind the surface of the peace sets in." Then "there will again be an audience able to feel the inner meanings of plays dealing with the everlasting mystery and irony and tragedy of men's lies and dreams." The dramatist was mistaken about his countrymen's ability to comprehend the message of the play once the victory was won. When the drama opened on October 9, 1946, audiences and most critics failed to understand it. Americans at that time were euphoric, optimistic about their lives and future, their country's strength and power. In the past two decades, the United States has suffered innumerable tragedies. Perhaps *now* Americans can not only understand *The Iceman Cometh* but also identify with its characters.

The play's tone is not one of despair but of hope. O'Neill's ultimate message is life rather than death, as his letter of December 1940 to Macgowan indicates. He explains the last scene, in which each character narrates his "face-saving version of his experience when he went out to confront his pipe dream." He states: "I don't write this as a piece of playwrighting. *They do it. They have to.* Each of them! In just that way! It is tragically, pitifully important to them to do this! They *must* tell these lies as a first step in taking up life again." It was vitally important to the author that the characters react as their real-life counterparts would, for, as he states, *The Iceman Cometh* "takes place for me in life not in a theatre." In this memory play he salutes the ghosts of his friends; in the next one, *A Long Day's Journey in Night*, he exorcises those of his family.

48.   *Long Day's Journey into Night*

Long Day's Journey into Night is the supreme achievement of both O'Neill and the American theater. The
dramatist instinctively knew its value and that of the work
that preceded it, *The Iceman Cometh*. He told Barrett
Clark in September 1943, at the conclusion of his writing
career: "These two plays give me greater satisfaction than
any other two I've ever done." While both dramas are
autobiographical documents, they transcend personal
concerns and express the universal longings of man to
assuage his loneliness and to instill his life with meaning.
The plays stress the author's steadfast belief that familial
love and friendship are the mainstays of the individual in
his journey through life.

The *Iceman Cometh* and *Long Day's Journey into
Night* are linked not only autobiographically but also creatively, as O'Neill recorded the first idea for both on the
same day, June 6, 1939, in a one-line statement in his
Work Diary. Just as the significant events presented
chronologically in these plays—his stay at Jimmy the
Priests's saloon-hotel and the discovery that he had tuberculosis—occurred in the author's life in a one-year period,
1911–1912, he recreated them in a similar time frame,
1939–1940. The focus of *The Iceman Cometh* is the
unique group of former drinking companions, cherished
friends he lovingly immortalized; that of *Long Day's Journey into Night* is the author's family: his parents, Ella and
James, his brother, Jamie, and himself. In earlier family
plays—*Desire Under the Elms, Dynamo, Mourning Be-*

comes Electra, A Touch of the Poet, and *More Stately Mansions*—he had presented thinly disguised portraits of the four O'Neill's. *Long Day's Journey into Night* is the drama he skirted when he wrote these plays, the story that haunted him throughout his creative years. In it he depicts not only exact replicas of the four O'Neills but their actual story and the home that witnessed their tragedy.

In the dedication to his wife, Carlotta, O'Neill calls *Long Day's Journey into Night* a "play of old sorrow" and states that it was "written in tears and blood." Her love, he asserts, gave him "the faith in love" that enabled him to face his "dead at last" and to write the play "with deep pity and understanding and forgiveness for all the four haunted Tyrones." *The Iceman Cometh* seems to have been a prerequisite for *Long Day's Journey into Night*. In the former, Hickey could not accept the "understanding and forgiveness" that were integral components of Evelyn's love for him. His inability to forgive her for forgiving him filled him with murderous feelings of rage and guilt. "I caught myself hating her for making me hate myself so much." While the author professes in his dedication to have forgiven his parents and brother for old wrongs, he had not done so in 1939 when he started the play. He could not forget the pain and guilt evoked by memories of their love-hate relationships. There is a vast difference between the early, more disparaging portraits of the O'Neills in the scenario and the final conception of them in the published text. *Long Day's Journey into Night* is a cathartic absolution the author accords the four O'Neills.

The play telescopes time and story in a morning-to-night context, supposedly a single day in August 1912. The actual time is fragmentary, surreal, for as the title implies, the play is a journey into the "long day" of the past, recreating the crucifying events that comprise the present reality of the Tyrone-O'Neills. When the night is at last reached in the final scene, the mother, Mary Tyrone, has regressed so completely in time that she remains lost in the past; her husband, James, and elder son, Jamie, are mired in a sodden, guilt-laden present; her younger son, Edmund, O'Neill's self-portrait, because of his serious illness, copes with an uncertain future.

All the Tyrones, with one exception, wear masks—not actual ones, like those in *The Great God Brown*, or the symbolic grim visages of the Mannons in *Mourning Becomes Electra*, but mercurial facades designed to control their dual personalities. Mary Tyrone is O'Neill's most complex character, the full-blown apotheosis of all the mothers he ever created. Into this character he poured his own mother's being, her tormented soul. Some of Ella O'Neill's traits had been given to other wives and mothers in the past: neuroticism and detached, near madness (Nina Leeds, Deborah Harford), ruthless destructiveness (Christine Mannon, Ella Harris), long-suffering endurance (Nora Melody, Eben Cabot's deceased mother). All attributes converge in the victimizer-victim of *Long Day's Journey into Night*. For the first time O'Neill presents the underlying problem that stigmatized his own mother: her twenty-five-year-long morphine addiction that motivated, in part, her duplicity.

Mary, fifty-four, has a slightly plump but young and graceful figure, a striking, "distinctly Irish face," full, sensitive lips, a high forehead "framed by thick, pure white hair," dark brown eyes that are "unusually large and beautiful," "black brows and long curling lashes." On the surface, she seems girlish, naive. "Her most appealing quality is the simple, unaffected charm of a shy convent-girl youthfulness she has never lost—an innate unworldly innocence." Yet a careful perusal contradicts this initial impression. Her face "does not match her healthy figure but is thin and pale. . . . What strikes one immediately is her extreme nervousness. Her hands are never still." Her hands bespeak her duality. They were "once beautiful," healthy, 'but rheumatism has knotted the joints and warped the fingers, so that now they have an ugly cripped look. . . . She is sensitive about their appearance and humiliated by her inability to control the nervousness which draws attention to them." The word "beautiful" and its opposites, "warped," "ugly," and "crippled," represent Ella O'Neill's duality, the linchpin for her son's love-hate attitude to her. In his earliest notes for the play, the dramatist described his mother's disturbing dichotomy in vivid terms that are omitted in the final text. For example, in Act III, when morphine frees her of inhibitions, she is depicted as "very hipped up now, her manner strange . . . at the moment a vain happy chattering girlishness—then changing to a hard cynical sneering bitterness with a bitter biting cruelty and with a coarse vulgarity in it—the last as if suddenly poisoned by an alive demon."

In the play, as in real life, much of the blame for the mother's condition is attributed to her husband's miserliness. James Tyrone, sixty-five, has a solid, healthy-looking physique, a stately, soldierly bearing. His face is "still remarkably good looking." He has a handsome profile and deep-set light-brown eyes. "His grey hair is thin with a bald spot like a monk's tonsure." As a matinee idol, he is accustomed to projecting a carefully studied image. "The stamp of his profession is unmistakably on him." All his "unconscious habits of speech, movement and gesture" bespeak the actor. "His voice is remarkably fine, resonant and flexible, and he takes great pride in it." He cannot, however, completely conceal the man beneath the polished veneer. His inclinations are "still close to his humble beginnings and his Irish farmer forebears. . . . there is a lot of stolid, earthy peasant in him, mixed with streaks of sentimental melancholy and rare flashes of intuitive sensibility." The paucity of these flashes prevents him from fully understanding the complex natures and weaknesses of his wife and sons and from accepting and correcting their grievances. Nerveless and healthy, he is perhaps the most balanced and normal member of the family.

The elder son, Jamie, thirty-three, is broad-shouldered and deep-chested and resembles his father physically. He is, however, a flawed copy, lacking the older man's stamina and rectitude. "The signs of premature disintegration are on him. His face is still good looking, despite marks of dissipation." He masks his vulnerability with a "habitual expression of cynicism" that gives his countenance a "Mephistophelian cast." Yet "on the rare occasions when he smiles without sneering, his personality possesses the remnant of a humorous, romantic, irresponsible Irish charm—that of the beguiling ne'er-do-well, with a strain of the sentimentally poetic, attractive to women and popular with men."

The younger son, Edmund, twenty-three, is "more like his mother." Tall, thin, and wiry, he has big dark eyes, the "dominant feature in his long, narrow Irish face. His mouth has the same quality of hypersensitiveness hers possesses. His high forehead is hers accentuated, with dark brown hair, sunbleached to red at the ends." Even his hands are like hers and have the "same nervousness. It is in the quality of extreme nervous sensibility that the likeness of Edmund to his mother is most marked." Similarly, he is "plainly in bad health. Much thinner than he should be, his eyes appear feverish and his cheeks are sunken." As a self-portrait, Edmund wears no mask, presumably because the author sees himself as a fully integrated person, more acted upon than acting. He provides precious few insights into his own nature. He alone is not stripped naked to the core of his soul.

These four tormented beings have come together, as is their usual custom during the father's off-season, in the family's summer home, which is, both in the written description and the set designs the author drew, an exact replica of the O'Neill cottage in New London. As in *Ah, Wilderness!*, the nontragic counterpart of *Long Day's*

Journey into Night, O'Neill makes references to actual landmarks and people in his home town: the lighthouse on Pequot Avenue, the dock across the street from the family's house; the Chatfields (Chappells), the town's most prominent Yankee family; and, at the other end of the social spectrum, Mamie (Addie) Burns, madam of the area's most popular bordello. While the house was on the Sound in the midst of lavish summer homes of wealthy New Londoners, it was a makeshift affair, two ill-matched structures seamed together. In the actual O'Neill home, the three upstairs bedrooms and the spare room where the mother retreated to give herself morphine injections were so oppressively small and clustered that no member of the family was assured of privacy. The porch, which circled the front of the house in 1912, and the stained glass windows in the front parlor cut off the light. The furnishings bear testimony to the father's parsimony. The wife and sons are justified when they accuse him of not having provided the family with a decent home.

Here in this house the annual charade of togetherness was staged each summer; here some of the most crucial events of the dramatist's life occurred: the mother's suicide attempt, his discovery of her addiction and his subsequent break with Catholicism, the family's ostracism by wealthy Yankee New Londoners. Two forces formed O'Neill, the man and the playwright: his Irish Catholic heritage and his New England environment. Two of the author's comments support this statement: first, "the one thing that explains more than anything about me is the fact that I'm Irish"; second, "the battle of moral forces in the New England scene is what I feel closest to as an artist."

All of the dramatist's late autobiographical family plays, from *A Touch of the Poet* to *A Moon for the Misbegotten,* deal, in some way, with the Irish-Yankee conflict in New England. In every instance the Celts triumph over the Puritans, who are invariably portrayed as rapacious and materialistic. The only two Irish characters who do not experience some type of victory are Mary Tyrone and Con Melody; both desperately want the acceptance and approval of native New Englanders but receive only cruel rebuffs. To them, the Chatfields and Harfords, the descendants of Puritans past, "stand for something." They belong. The Irish never had and never would. Mary's constant lamentation for a home and social acceptance demonstrates the essential rootlessness of the Irish.

In the late dramas all of the Irish families—the Melodys, Tyrones, and Hogans—are renegade Catholics. Mary Tyrone's cry, in her dazed, drugged state at the end of the play, for "something" she has lost is a sorrowful lament for her religious faith, the inner core of her existence. No other character in the canon portrays more effectively than Mary Tyrone the cruel consequences of the migration of the Irish to America and the price they often paid for assimilation. In their centuries-long struggle with the British, the Irish were forced to relinquish their possessions and their rights; they surrendered everything but their faith. The loss of faith to religiously indoctrinated first- and second-generation Irish immigrants was a traumatic experience. Interpreted in religious terms, Mary Tyrone's long day's journey ends in spiritual despair, in what John of the Cross called the dark night of the soul.

The rejection of Catholicism by the Tyrones and, by autobiographical implication, by the O'Neills, and their Yankee neighbors' repulsion of them alienate these Irish from God, New Londoners, and, in the end, from each other. The inner conflict of the Tyrone-O'Neill family—spiritual vacuity and blind attempts to fill the void with drugs, drink, and sex—reveals the important role Catholicism plays in the lives of the Irish. The Tyrones are haunted not only by what was lost but by what replaced it: the subconscious layers of guilt. One of the major motifs in *Long Day's Journey into Night* is physical illness, which obviously signifies the inner sickness of soul. Edmund, who is described at the start of the play as "sick right now," and "plainly in bad health," is diagnosed as having tuberculosis. His father, at the outset, has "never been really sick in his life," yet at the end even he has become "sick and sober," for him a crucifying combination. Mary Tyrone is, of course, most afflicted. Disoriented by excessive morphine injections, she manifests visible signs of illness in her face and body. Even the New England environment shows signs of being infected; the foghorn is described as a sick whale in the back yard.

The deepening fog, like the night, symbolizes the family's hazy spiritual perceptions, but more specifically, it signifies Mary's mental state. In the notes of February–March 1940, labeled "weather progression," O'Neill parallels the worsening condition of the weather, the increasing density of fog, and the deteriorating state of the mother's mind. It is at this time that the mother's condition becomes the focal point of the play. In the first notations of June 1939, the second familial concern, Edmund's illness, not only vied in importance with the addiction but had, according to the mother, "started her off again." The truth is, however, that if she did not have this excuse to indulge in morphine she would have found another pretext, as she had innumerable times over the previous twenty-four years.

It is clear, too, that, being the person she is, had she not discovered morphine, Mary Tyrone would have resorted to some other means of escape—not from reality, but from herself. Geraldine Fitzgerald, having analyzed Mary Tyrone before playing her—and providing one of the most moving experiences in the history of American theater—states:

> If Mary Tyrone had never had a drug in her life, she would have been more or less the same! She is what she is because of her sense of guilt. She feels deeply guilty about her relationship with her mother, whom she didn't like, and

about her father, whom she adored but who died young. Many of O'Neill's characters are based on ancient prototypes, and Mary Tyrone was a kind of Electra. Her behavior is based on the fact that she was a person who felt she was going to be given the worst of punishments for her own crime of cutting out her mother with her father.*

In the early outline for the play's last act, James Tyrone objects to his wife's "digging up old grievances" and tells Edmund, "You'd think before she married she'd lived in heaven—her father spoiled her—you'd think he was an angel—a nice enough man—her father spoiled her sending her to most expensive convent—never forgets it—you'd think her days there happiest of her life." Earlier in this set of notes the mother reveals that she, like Christine Mannon in *Mourning Becomes Electra*, had been left independently wealthy by her father; both women use the money for clothes, even though their husbands resent this act of independence. Mary Tyrone must have depleted her capital, perhaps to support her habit.† The maid who had accompanied her to town speaks "about hocking ring that p.m." to get money to pay for the "medicine" at the drugstore. Miss Fitzgerald's belief that the mother had an Electra complex seems well-founded. Presumably, Mary Tyrone, like Ella O'Neill, married her husband shortly after her father died and identified the former with the latter. At the close of the scene with the maid, the mother says that her husband "doesn't like anniversaries—cost money—and remind him getting

---

*"Another Neurotic Electra: A New Look at Mary Tyrone," in my *Eugene O'Neill: A World View* (New York: Ungar, 1979), pp. 291–292. The actress reports that she went to three doctors to try to determine why Mary was aggressive rather than passive after taking morphine. She was told that Mary suffered what is called in medical slang a "cat" reaction to morphine, which made her overactive and excitable rather than drowsy (the so-called "dog" reaction).

†Ella O'Neill lost her money in 1909 when the Brittain Company went bankrupt.

old—14 y[ears]. older—was great mistake—more like father—."

In each play that has a couple clearly modeled on O'Neill's parents, the husband is at least ten years older than the wife, and the marriage is always described, either in the final text or in the early notes or scenario, as a "mistake." The woman frequently seeks, usually unsuccessfully, security and fatherly protection in marriage. Mary Tyrone, for example, is denied the lavish home and the minor social triumphs she experienced as a young girl at home and at exclusive schools, the munificence that her father provided. He not only spoiled her, he made her a snob. Obviously, she would have difficulty adjusting to her actor-husband's life—the continual stream of small-town hotels, one-night engagements, endless train travels—and his friends, whom she considered socially inferior. She was hopelessly inefficient at running a household and raising children. Her failure as a wife and mother and her subsequent retreat into an illusionary world may have been forms of revenge. Detesting alcohol, which brought her beloved father to an untimely end, she takes the morphine route, wallowing in self-pity for the failures of her life.

Mary Tyrone blames her husband, primarily, and at times her sons for what she has become, a "dope fiend," and argues that "None of us can help the things life has done to us. They're done before you realize it, and once they're done they make you do other things until at last everything comes between you and what you'd like to be, and you've lost your true self forever." This statement explains why O'Neill, in describing his parents and brother, offers a twofold view of them, the selves they might have been and the selves they became. Inherent in each character's physical duality is the additional dichotomy within the self: the innocent victim versus the guilty victimizer.

As victim, Mary Tyrone was spoiled by her father

and, when only eighteen, faced a difficult transition: having to go from a romantic schoolgirl to wife of a touring actor. After her younger son's birth, she became addicted to morphine prescribed by the cheap doctor her husband, in his miserliness, supposedly hired. Denied a normal, regulated home and life, she felt alienated in New London. Yet, on the other hand, Mary is a victimizer and is partly responsible for her condition. She had been infatuated with her father and cruel to her mother. Similarly, she makes no attempt to conceal her all-absorbing love for her younger son and her contempt, at times, for her older son and her husband. Although the latter has spent thousands of dollars to cure her, Mary will not help herself; she is reluctant to forgo the precious euphoria morphine provides. She is selfish, vindictive, vengeful, and irresponsible.

James Tyrone's greed and his obsession to buy land, which frequently proves to be worthless, have destroyed his family, his home life, and his career. Just as he took a cheap way out when his wife was ill after Edmund's birth, he intends now to send his tubercular son to an inexpensive state farm for treatment. In his youth, James was hailed as a remarkable Shakespearean actor, but he sacrificed artistry for money, wasting himself by appearing endlessly in the melodramatic *Count of Monte Cristo*. Yet as his wife remarks, "life has made him like that, and he can't help it." As a child, he knew poverty and was forced to go to work to help support his fatherless family. He overcame his brogue and awkward manners but failed to stamp out his peasant mentality, which values concrete investments such as land. Tyrone professes to have discovered the dangers of morphine too late and to have tried to help his wife, yet she "always start[s] again." He supports two wastrel, alcoholic sons, whose pranks resulted in the expulsion of both from college.

Jamie has been lazy, irresponsible, and self-destructive. He has frittered his life away on whiskey and whores and, because of spite and jealousy, has been a bad influence on Edmund. Yet he did lose his mother, whom he loves more than anything else in life, when Edmund was born. The latter, who is adored by the mother, became the enemy. Supposedly, when he was seven, Jamie deliberately gave his younger brother Eugene* a case of the measles. The child died, and Mary, who was away on a tour with her husband at the time, never forgave Jamie. He is, more or less, the scapegoat of the family; upon him the others vent their anger and frustrations. Years of shabby treatment have made him cynical and bitter. He has, in his dissolute life-style, fulfilled his father's worst expectations.

The main accusation leveled against Edmund by his parents and brother is that his birth precipitated his mother's drug addiction. He is, obviously, blameless. Edmund, a self-portrait, is depicted as relatively flawless. At one point Jamie denies that he has ever exerted any influence over Edmund and says, "he's stubborn as hell inside and what he does is what he wants to do, and to hell with anyone else!" Before his recent illness, Edmund had been trying to become independent of his father by working as a reporter. However, there is sufficient evidence to support Jamie's accusation that Edmund is "Mama's baby, Pappa's pet."

The entire play is set in the living room of the Tyrones' summer home. In the first act it is 8:30 A.M. of a day in August 1912. Mary and James come in from the dining room. The recurring motifs are introduced immediately. James compliments his wife on her healthy appearance and mentions his latest "real estate bargains." She frets over Edmund's poor health. The sons enter, laughing over a story Edmund has just told about the great Irish victory of Shaughnessy, the father's tenant farmer, over his aristocratic Yankee neighbor, Harker,

---

*O'Neill interchanges his own name and that of his deceased brother, Edmund, in the play.

the Standard Oil millionaire. A break in the fence between the two properties enabled the Irishman's pigs to go
bathing in Harker's ice pond. When the Yankee went over
to complain, the wily Irishman accused him of enticing
the pigs to wade in the pond, an act that resulted in "some
dying of pneumonia" and others coming down "with chol-
era from drinking the poisoned water." He threatens to
sue for funeral expenses and damages. When Edmund
shows his disdain for the wealthy Harker, the father warns
him, "Keep your damned socialist sentiments out of my
affairs!"

Although the father enjoys the story, he fears that he
may be sued by Harker for his tenant's actions. He finds
fault with Jamie, rather than with Edmund, when the
latter is clearly to blame for encouraging Shaughnessy to
get his revenge. Likewise, the sons attack the father or
each other rather than the mother, who is the most vulnerable member of the family, when she is clearly responsible for something. It is Jamie, who has had experience with drug-addicted whores, who first suspects that
the mother has begun taking morphine again. The father
rejects the suggestion. The two quarrel and go out to trim
the front hedge.

Later, Mary calls Edmund's attention to the prosperous Yankee Chatfields, who pass by the house in their
new Mercedes. She complains about her husband's "sec-
ondhand Packard" and the shabby clothes he is wearing.
She cannot conceal her envy of the Chatfields: "They have
decent, presentable homes" and are "not cut off from
everyone." She blames her husband for the family's isolation. Edmund defends his father and says, "even if he'd
wanted to, we couldn't have had people here—." His
words and suspicions enrage her. "Suddenly a strange
undercurrent of revengefulness comes into her voice. 'It
would serve all of you right if it were true!'" Yet, even as
she gives her "sacred word of honor" to abstain from
drugs, she is making plans mentally to escape from him
and the world of reality. She looks at him in a calculating,

sly manner and says she is going upstairs for a nap before lunch. Edmund goes outside, suspecting her deception but pretending to believe her. At the close of Act I, she "begins a desperate battle with herself," a battle she is doomed to lose.

The next act opens at around 12:45. Like the mother, the men try to escape reality—through alcohol. Cathleen, the maid, a "buxom Irish peasant," ritualistically brings in a bottle of bourbon and glasses. The brothers drink, and Jamie cynically scoffs at his mother's promise. Both recall earlier vows and the night, when Edmund was in prep school, that she ran out of morphine and tried to commit suicide by jumping off a nearby dock. When his mother enters, Jamie knows at once that his fears are justified. She is "less nervous," her eyes are brighter, and there is "a peculiar detachment in her voice and manner, as if she were a little withdrawn from her words and actions." The three men feel betrayed. Their hopes of the past two months, when they believed she was cured, are shattered, Angrily, Tyrone says, "I've been a Goddamned fool to believe in you!" Then, "in spite of himself," he asks "grief-strickenly": "For the love of God why couldn't you have the strength to keep on?" In the early notes the scene concludes with the parents looking "at each other as a man and woman who have lived together many years and known each other but who do not truly know each other."

The following scene takes place a half hour later. An insufferable air of gloom hangs over the room. When they entered it after breakfast, the parents were jovial, lighthearted. Tyrone had his arm around Mary's waist. Now, after lunch, "he avoids touching her or looking at her. There is condemnation, helpless resignation in his face." Jamie's face is "hard with defensive cynicism." Edmund "plainly shows he is heartsick as well as physically ill." All three have finally relinquished the pipe dream that the mother is cured.

Doctor Hardy's telephone call to arrange an appointment for Edmund that afternoon reminds the mother of Edmund's illness, and she again retreats to the spare room upstairs. Tyrone chastises his sons for their cynical behavior, attributing it to their loss of faith in Catholicism. Reminded of his own indifference to Mass, the father replies, "It's true I'm a bad Catholic in the observance, God forgive me. But I believe!" According to him, his wife has forgotten her faith, and "there's no strength of the spirit left in her to fight against her curse."

Later, Tyrone begs his wife, who is "more detached" than before, to "stop now." Nostalgically, she drifts into the past, regressing to the period after their marraige when he fought a paternity suit his former mistress brought against him and, as a result, her friends "cut me dead." Tyrone says despondently, "If you're that far gone in the past already, when it's only the beginning of the afternoon, what will you be tonight?" She relives the trauma of the death of her second son and of Edmund's birth. She felt that God would punish her if she had this child. "I never should have borne Edmund." Urged to forget the past, Mary asks, "How can I? The past is the present, isn't it? It's the future, too." Here O'Neill enunciates his belief in the significance of family fate, in which the past shapes the present and controls one's future destiny.

With Edmund, Mary finally assumes full responsibility for her addiction and laments the day long ago when, as she says, "I could no longer call my soul my own. But some day, dear, I will find it again. . . . Some day when the Blessed Virgin Mary forgives me and gives me back the faith in Her love and pity I used to have in my convent days." She knows instinctively that she must believe in herself before anyone else can do so, but it is impossible for her to do so when she lacks religious faith. After the three men leave to go to town, Mary pretends at first to be glad to be alone; then she laughs despairingly, "Then Mother of God why do I feel so lonely?"

It is 6:30 that evening in Act III. The day, at the outset of the play, was clear, like the mother's mind. Now

the fog-laden dusk rolls in from the Sound and descends
"like a white curtain drawn down outside the windows."
From the nearby lighthouse a foghorn moans "like a
mournful whale in labor." Mary's mind is a disembodied
haze, alternating between states of hard cynicism and
naive chattering girlishness. As a result of the drugs she
has taken, she "has hidden deeper within herself and
found refuge and release in a dream where present reality
is but an appearance to be accepted and dismissed unfeel-
ingly." Lonely and desperate for companionship, she has
been entertaining Cathleen with stories from the past and
plying her with Tyrone's whiskey. The two make an incongruous couple: a tipsy maid and a drugged mistress.
Mary ruminates over the past: her health, her views on
the theater and theatrical professionals, and her two early
dreams in life, to become either a concert pianist or a nun.

Like those of other characters, Mary's long monologues reveal inner contradictions and shed light on the
complex family love-hate relationships. After the maid
leaves, Mary "loses all the girlish quality and is an aging,
cynically sad, embittered woman." She exclaims longingly, "If I could only find the faith I lost, so I could pray
again!" Then, derisively, she reasons that the Blessed
Virgin would not be "fooled by a lying dope fiend reciting
words." Her protective glow is diminishing slightly: "I
must go upstairs. I haven't taken enough. When you start
again you never know exactly how much you need."

Tyrone and Edmund return; both have been drinking heavily, but neither is drunk. "What they see fulfills
their worst expectations." Mary raves on hopelessly about
the past, belittling her husband for having given whiskey
as medicine to his sons when they were young: "He didn't
know any better. He never went to school after he was
ten. His people were the most ignorant kind of poverty-
stricken Irish."* She continues to dredge up ghosts of the

---

*Mary's speeches, in which she reveals her smug sense of social
superiority to Tyrone, echo those of Ella Harris to the husband
she considers racially inferior in *All God's Chillun Got Wings*.

past, the nights in dirty hotel rooms when her husband's
actor friends brought him home drunk from local bar-
rooms. She regresses to the early days of her marriage and
finally to the wedding itself. Her dress is described lovingly. Significantly, she has misplaced the dress, an act
that seems to symbolize the loss of her young hopes and
dreams.

In a scene with Edmund, the mother reacts violently
when he informs her that he must go to a sanatorium; she
attacks her husband for being jealous of her "babies,"
particularly Edmund because he "knew I loved you
most." Hurt deeply by her apparent indifference to his
illness, the son strikes back at her ruthlessly: "It's pretty
hard to take at times, having a dope fiend for a mother."
The life drains from her face, "leaving it with the appearance of a plaster cast." In despair, Edmund rushes out of
the house. Mary resolves to go upstairs; she has not
"taken enough." Only the vestiges of her religious faith
prevent her from committing suicide: "I hope, sometime,
without meaning it, I will take an overdose. I never could
do it deliberately. The Blessed Virgin would never forgive me, then." The act closes with her husband's hopeless
statement to his departing wife: " Up to take more of that
God-damned poison, is that it? You'll be like a mad ghost
before the night's over!"

In the last act, which takes place around midnight,
James Tyrone sits alone playing solitaire. Despite all the
whiskey he has consumed, he "has not escaped." He looks
like a "sad, defeated old man, possessed by hopeless
resignation." In his usual miserly fashion, he has put out
the hall lamp and the chandelier lights and uses a small
reading lamp. The darkness of the room and the father's
continual efforts to extinguish the lights Edmund recklessly flings on when he returns reflect his blind refusal to
accept his share of blame for the family's tragedy and to
remedy his ways.

Edmund is a cantankerous drunk and is as determined as his father to find the kind of oblivion needed to obliterate hopelessness. His reaction to the fog resembles Mary's. One can hide in it and be "nothing more than a ghost within a ghost." He resents her deliberate attempt to lose herself in the fog, "to get beyond our reach, to be rid of us, to forget we're alive! It's as if, in spite of loving us, she hated us!" In one of the few speeches in which he reveals himself, Edmund-O'Neill speaks of his affinity with the sea, the one place where he felt he belonged, "without past or future, within peace and unity and a wild joy, within something greater than my own life, or the life of Man, to Life itself! To God, if you want to put it that way." Traveling on a square rigger to Buenos Aires had provided him with a "saint's vision of beatitude." He concludes that he should have been born a fish; as a man he will "always be a stranger who never feels at home, who does not really want and is not really wanted, who can never belong, who must always be a little in love with death!"

The act, like the play itself, becomes a round-robin battle.* The characters take turns delivering lengthy monologues filled with self-defensive explanations, bitter accusations, and vicious recriminations. In his own agony, each strikes out, attempting to wound the others. Each ponders his own and the collective family fate: what life, the unseen forces of heredity and environment, has done to them. Edmund berates his father for his poorhouse cries, blaming him for the mother's addiction and homelessness; he attributes Tyrone's refusal to send him to a

---

*In his notes for the play the dramatist worked out a systematic series of confrontations to show the love-hate relationships within the family. The section is entitled "Shifting alliances in battle—(direct movements to correspond)" and includes the following: "Father, two sons versus Mother; Mother, two sons versus Father; Father, younger son versus Mother, older son; Mother, younger son versus Father, older son; Father and Mother versus two sons; Brother versus brother; Father versus Mother."

good hospital to his belief that the son will die. The father responds pathetically, in a monologue, recounting the hardships of his youth and the hapless factors that led to his miserliness. Edmund, he says magnanimously, can choose any hospital he desires, any place "within reason." At some point in the play, each member of the family confesses what he or she has contributed to the family tragedy. In the last act the father admits that he prostituted his acting talents to become rich; he ruined his career with a big money maker. He asks himself, "What the hell was it I wanted to buy, I wonder, that was worth—. Well, no matter. It's a late day for regrets." The father, after his confession, is forgiven by Edmund; the two seem to form, at last, an enduring bond of mutual love and understanding.

Later, Tyrone goes out to the porch to avoid seeing Jamie, who returns "very drunk and woozy." His speech is "blurred, his mouth slack like his father's, a leer on his lips." He regales his brother with a tale of his adventures at Mamie Burns's establishment.* Jamie's account of his evening with Fat Violet and the description of the pigs-in-the-pond incident in Act I provide the play's only genuine comic relief. Jamie had taken pity on the prostitute, who was demoted to pianist† because of her ever-increasing bulk. He had only wanted to unburden his soul when he selected her to go upstairs with him, but, seeing

---

*Jamie is referring to Addie Burns's place on Bradley Street, part of the Barbary Coast area in New London at the turn of the century. Respectable New Londoners frequented her house. In 1915, Addie was arrested for murder and defended by a prominent criminal lawyer. After the prosecuting attorney, a pompous Yankee, vividly described Addie's place as a house of degradation, the defense lawyer rose dramatically and said: "You should know. We've spent many a happy night there together" (interview with Dennis Murphy, a former New London friend of Jamie O'Neill, July 1969).

†When he portrays musically inclined mistresses or prostitutes, O'Neill is unconsciously motivated either by revenge or by a desire to provide his heroes with sympathetic mother figures. Jamie, who is ignored by his own mother, wants compassion, not

her grief and humiliation, he "stayed with her." He concludes dramatically, "By applying my natural God-given
talents in their proper sphere, I shall attain the pinnacle of
success! I'll be the lover of the fat woman in Barnum and
Bailey's circus!"

In one of the most brutal scenes of the play, Jamie
reveals his Mephistophelian self. He boasts of his destructive influence on Edmund: "Hell, you're more than my
brother. I made you! You're my Frankenstein!" He describes how he deliberately tried to destroy him:

> Made getting drunk romantic. Made whores fascinating
> vampires instead of poor, stupid, diseased slobs they really
> are. Made fun of work as sucker's game. Never wanted you
> succeed and make me look even worse by comparison. . . .
> And it was your being born that started Mama on dope. . . .
> I can't help hating your guts! . . . The dead part of me
> hopes you won't get well. Maybe he's even glad the game
> has got Mama again! He wants company, he doesn't want to
> be the only corpse around the house!*

Tyrone comes in and tries to quiet Jamie. None of
them wants to see what the long day and the numerous
morphine injections have done to the mother. They are
startled when the parlor light is turned on; they "listen
frozenly" to an awkwardly played Chopin waltz. Suddenly, Mary appears, carelessly carrying her white wedding
gown; her face is pale and her eyes glisten "like polished

sex, from Fat Violet. Similarly, in *The Great God Brown*, Dion
Anthony, another portrait of Jamie, seeks only companionship
and solace from the prostitute Cybel, who has a player-piano. In
the notes for *Days Without End*, the hero, a self-portrait, recalls
that "in his childhood his mother had played and sung sad,
sentimental songs of lost love." Perhaps Ella O'Neill, like this
mother, sang as well as played similar songs. Notes for unfinished plays demonstrate the dramatist's obsession with mothers
with musical ability. Barbara Blomberg, mistress of Emperor
Charles V and mother of Don Juan of Austria, a self-portrait, had
"played and sung for Charles." The beautiful concubine-mother
of Shih Huang Ti was a "singing girl."

*Compare this scene between Jamie and Edmund and a similar
one, the third scene of Act II of *The Great God Brown*, in which

black jewels." Her face "appears so youthful"; she wears a "marble mask of girlish innocence." A complete captive now of the past, she is unaware of the presence of others. Her mind has receded to the time prior to her marriage. Three times she refers to "something I lost," "something I miss terribly." Each man tries, unsuccessfully, to rouse the "sleepwalker." The play concludes with the three men, in despair, lifting their glasses as the mother recalls her senior year at school. "Then in the spring something happened to me. Yes, I remember. I fell in love with James Tyrone and was so happy for a time."

The ending seems singularly appropriate, as the mother identifies the tragic mistake that had changed and, some might say, ruined her life. She sees herself as an innocent schoolgirl praying at the shrine of the Blessed Virgin, long before the loss of faith, which she laments bitterly in this scene. O'Neill's conception of the mother in the scenario's last act differs substantially from the view of her in the published text. Mary was not originally depicted as a detached, ghostlike spirit; she converses, at times quite rationally, with her sons and husband. In her manner and movement she is "vague and aimless yet intent and concentrated—she seems to see them and yet not to see them." When Edmund says bitterly, "You ought to read Heine's poem on morphine," she replies vaguely, "Morphine! I have enough now to last for while—when that's gone, pawn another piece of jewelry—Doctor said I was taking enough drugs to kill [a] herd of elephants (She smiles with a precocious childish pride—they shudder). First week at cure so horrible—it's so suspicious later on—have to pawn all jewelry—and the times when you can't get—oh, so horrible!" She tells them scornfully, "You can't touch me now—I'm safe beyond your reach. You can't make me remember." The

Dion Anthony states that William Brown has "always been the Big Brother." Cybel also comments on the strange bond linking the two and says, "You're brothers."

only religious reference in the scenario is contained in the mother's final speech, in which she mentions praying "without shame" to the Blessed Virgin. In the margin, beside the last passage, O'Neill wrote: "Mother (quote at end—quotes strongly) 'Forgive us our trespasses as we forgive those who trespass against us.'"

One page of computations in the early notes reveals the dramatist's attempt to depict exact representations of the four O'Neills in the play. He added and subtracted ages and dates in an effort to verify the date of birth of each of them. Originally, the drama was set in 1907 on the parents' "30th Wedding Anniversary." One of the early titles, "Anniversary," suggests that he intended to make the parents the play's central characters. Perhaps the emphasis on the small but precise autobiographical details is the most startling point about the notes, for it reinforces the idea that O'Neill and his family actually endured and survived the torturous, soul-shattering events depicted. Actually, the portraits, with one exception, are drawn with greater restraint in the final version than in the original one. O'Neill presents a far more compassionate picture of his father in the scenario; the early softness of the elder Tyrone's nature and his tremendous vulnerability seem muted in the published text.

Because of the play's deeply personal nature, O'Neill refused to allow it to be produced in his lifetime. In an interview given in 1946 during rehearsals for *The Iceman Cometh*, he specified that it was not to be offered until twenty-five years after his death. "It is a real story" that was, like *The Iceman Cometh*, "also laid in 1912. There's only one person in it who is still alive."* He was referring to his son, Eugene, Jr., who, while not an actual character in the play, objected to the searing, autobiographical revelations about his family. O'Neill entrusted the manuscript of the play to his editor, Bennett Cerf at Random House, for safekeeping. The author's widow, Carlotta,

*Clark, p. 154.

however, gave permission to the Yale University Press to publish it in 1956, three years after his death, and to the Royal Dramatic Theatre in Stockholm to present its world premiere on February 10, 1956. The play opened in New York later that year on November 7.* Theaters throughout the world have produced *Long Day's Journey into Night*. It has received international acclaim because of its universal applications.

Long Day's Journey into Night is an Everyman play. Each person can make a similar journey into the night of his past to determine the facts that shaped his individual destiny. Each family harbors its own love-hate relationships and secrets. They may not be as riveting as those dramatized in the play, but they can be as painful and memorable. Eligio Possenti, in reviewing the Italian premiere of *Long Day's Journey into Night* in Milan on October 16, 1956, states: "O'Neill's drama is a re-creation of a past punctuated by sobs as if the author had told his own life weeping. The moans of a soul are heard in this work." The last glimpse of the four shattered Tyrones in the catastrophic final scene of the play is probably the most memorable moment in American theater. Reliving the tragedy left O'Neill "in tears"; living it left him a lifelong casualty, a figure forever obsessed by "all the four haunted" O'Neills.

---

*The American premiere was offered on October 15, 1956, the eve of the sixty-eighth anniversary of the playwright's birth, in Boston, where he had begun his career, at Harvard's 47 Workshop, and had died.

49. *Hughie* and "By Way of Obit"

Hughie is the finest American one-act play, a small, price-less gem that enhances the O'Neill canon dramatically, thematically, and autobiographically. It was orginally conceived as one of eight plays in a series entitled "By Way of Obit." O'Neill's first reference to the project appears in the Work Diary entry for November 29, 1940: "new idea for series [of] monologue plays—short—'By Way of Obit.'—for book more than stage, perhaps—scene, one character, one marionette (life-size) The Good Listener— I do brief outlines for five of them." He identifies the one-acters he worked on that day as "Pig [of the] Hell Hole play, R.R. man play, Jimmy the Priest idea of guy who recited Homer, Hughie, Minstrel man idea." On December 1 and 2 he made notes for the three other one-acters: Miser one, Rudie (the chambermaid play), Blemie one.* Unfortunately, the author destroyed the original outlines and notes for all of these plays. The only extant remnants are the two early drafts, one handwritten, the other typed, for the only completed drama, *Hughie*.

In a letter to George Jean Nathan on June 19, 1942, the dramatist explained the method he intended to use in the plays and the significance of the series' title. Each

*On May 23, 1941, when he drew "sets for several of [the] plays," O'Neill states "will be 8 in all, I think." The next year, however, on February 9, 1942, he refers to what might have been a ninth play for the series: "Thompson—rat idea—outline." He makes notes at this time for all the one-acters, specifically identifying each of them with the exception of the "Miser one" and "Blemie one," either of which he may have developed as the Thompson idea.

one-acter was to be an expanded obituary. The author describes the character to whom each story is told as "a person" who does "little but listen. Via this monlogue you get a complete picture of the person who has died—his or her whole life story—but just as complete a picture of the life and character of the narrator. And you also get by another means—a use of stage directions, mostly—an insight into the whole life of the person who does little but listen." The "stories," had they been complete, would have provided new insights into the early life of the dramatist. Through them he retreats autobiographically into the past; creatively he comes full circle. The characters were to be modeled primarily on people he knew or befriended at Jimmy the Priests's (1911–1912) and the Hell Hole (1915–1916). His first notebook, for 1918–1920, shows that twenty years earlier he had contemplated two series of plays resembling the one-acter planned for "By Way of Obit":

> Stories—Jimmy the Priest series;
>
> Gunman Series—"The Pig of the Hell Hole," "Exit Baby Doll," "The Dirty Half-Dozen."

A common motif links O'Neill's early projected one-acters and series and the late play, *Hughie*, and the "By Way of Obit" series: the "gunman" concept. In two distinct periods of his career, in 1918–1920 and two decades later in his final creative years, O'Neill seemed to be obsessed with guns and figures who either live outside the law or who are recklessly, violently a law unto themselves. The author was befriended by an all-Irish group of "small-time" gangsters, the Hudson Dusters, when he frequented the Hell Hole in 1915. His fascination with guns and gunmen predated this period, however, and probably derived from his association with the colorful characters he met at Jimmy the Priest's or from the stories his brother, Jamie, narrated about underworld figures in New York. If this is the case, O'Neill could be identified as

"The Good Listener" in the series, or more specifically, as the Night Clerk in *Hughie*.

Hughie's central character, Erie Smith, the "small-fry gambler" who boasts of his association with gangland "Big shots," resembles Tim Moran, the gangster in O'Neill's first one-acter, *The Web* (1913). Moran tries to rescue the prostitute-heroine Rose from the brutal pimp-gunman, Steve, an early version of Rocky Pioggi, the gun-toting pimp-bartender of *The Iceman Cometh*. Tim uses his gun to dislodge the pimp from Rose's room, but he is later shot by Steve, who frames the unfortunate woman for the murder. Guns and either attempted or actual violent shooting deaths abound in other early plays: the betrayed husband in O'Neill's first effort, *A Wife for a Life*, fingers his gun, contemplating his revenge on his wife's lover; four characters in subsequent 1913–1914 one-acters shoot themselves: Mildred Baldwin in *Recklessness*, James Knapp in *Warnings*, John Brown in *Bread and Butter*, and Jack Sloan in *Abortion*. Sons are shot in two 1915 plays: *The Sniper* and "The Personal Equation." A suicide attempt literally "backfires" in the 1916 farce, *Now I Ask You*. The central character in the 1918 *The Dreamy Kid*, a black gunman, is modeled on an actual person in one of the stories told O'Neill by his former roommate at the Hell Hole, the black gambler Joe Smith, the prototype for Joe Mott in *The Iceman Cometh*.

The Iceman Cometh is the first of the late completed or contemplated plays using the gangster-gunman motif. Chronologically, it is followed by the unfinished 1940–1941 "The Visit of Malatesta," which depicts a gangster, Angelo Daniello, who operates a speakeasy and plans to use hired assassins and violence to become Artichoke King of the state. The abandoned "By Way Of Obit" series presumably would have contained figures like Erie Smith, a "Broadway sport and a Wise Guy," who lives "hand to mouth on the fringe of the rackets" during the days of Prohibition. The most striking example of the gunman motif is found in a play O'Neill worked on intermittently from 1940 to 1943, "Blind Alley Guy," which as originally conceived told the story of a Mephistophelian gangster hero, Walter White/Black.

More emphasis is placed on Erie's gangster connections and his subservient role "on the fringe of the rackets" in the earliest draft of *Hughie* than in the final text. He is "used as the errand boy and contemptuously tolerated as the butt of jokes by the Big Shots, too insignificant for the police"; he "never knew enough to lead them to anyone important to bother about, too timid ever to commit any serious infraction of the Law." He and his kind believe that they are "oracles of the One True Grapevine," when actually "they are used to pass along and give publicity to the misleading lie, because it is well-known stunt. It is difficult to see anything in him one shouldn't despise."

Thematically, *Hughie* resembles the other late plays in its focus on the dead and the past. O'Neill depicts his former friends in *The Iceman Cometh* and deceased members of his own family in *Long Day's Journey into Night* and *A Moon for the Misbegotten*. In *Hughie* the author writes an expanded obituary for one Charles Hughes, the recently-departed Night Clerk of a small, sleazy hotel in midtown New York, a "third class dump, catering to the catch-as-catch-can trade." The narrator who provides the "complete picture" of the departed Hughie is Erie Smith, a desperately lonely failure and a frequent guest at the hotel. Erie mourns a part of himself that died with Hughie, the image he had projected of being an important intimate of underworld figures. Hughie had been a good luck charm for Erie in his gambling exploits. Since the clerk's death, Erie has not won a single bet. He seeks to reverse his fortunes now by cultivating the friendship of the recently hired replacement, whose surname is also Hughes. The new Night Clerk steadfastly resists Erie's friendly advances and erects an invisible wall of indifference. The play dramatizes Erie's efforts to break this barrier and to establish a relationship with him.

Like *A Moon for the Misbegotten*, *Hughie* could be considered an epitaph for the author's brother. In many respects Erie resembles Jamie, whose lifelong loneliness made him the most tragic member of the O'Neill family. He never found any place where he felt he belonged, and he spent most of his nights, as Erie does, in cheap New York hotels drinking heavily and buying the company of prostitutes. Like many of the portraits of Jamie O'Neill, Erie wears a mask: on the surface, he is the sophisticated, happy-go-lucky charmer, boasting endlessly of his success with horses and women. Inwardly, he is a tragic figure, a lost loner, wanting only to be accepted and loved by others.

Conceived during the late autobiographical period, *Hughie* is sandwiched between two plays that include acknowledged portraits of Jamie, *Long Day's Journey into Night* and *A Moon for the Misbegotten*. Erie is given the same physical traits found in Jim Tyrone in the latter play. Both are in their early forties and are stout, of medium height, and beefy or broad-shouldered. Jim's physique has become "soft and soggy from dissipation"; his face is marred by an "unhealthy puffiness and the bags under the eyes. He has thinning brown hair, parted and brushed back to cover a bald spot." Erie has a pasty, perspiry, night-life complexion, "puffy pouches" under his eyes, thinning sandy hair, and a bald spot on the top of his head. Jim's face has a habitual "cynical expression," but when he smiles he reveals "the ghost of a former youthful, irresponsible Irish charm," sentimental and romantic. Erie's mouth is "always crooked" in a "cynical leer"; there is "some sentimental softness" behind his "phoney" characterization, "which doesn't belong in the hard-boiled picture." Jim "follows a style set by well-groomed Broadway gamblers": he wears a brown suit, "tight-fitting and drawn in at the waist" and a white silk shirt. Erie wears a grey suit "cut in the extreme, tight-waisted Broadway mode" and a garish blue silk shirt. Both men are pathetic alcoholics. When first seen, the two have been on prolonged drunken binges—Jim since the death of his mother and Erie since the death of his friend Hughie.

Chronologically, the events in *A Moon for the Misbegotten*, set in 1923, precede those of *Hughie*, set in 1928. At the end of the former play, Jim abandons Josie and returns to his old way of life in New York and to his Broadway tarts. Erie describes his successful attempts to sneak Broadway prostitutes into his hotel room. Like Jim, he is unable to have a normal relationship with a woman. Both men have traveled in the past in the drawing room of a train with a "blonde doll"; both prefer horses to women. Jim wants to "follow the horses South in the winter and come back North with them in the spring and beat the track every day. It seemed that would be the ideal life for me." Erie's enthusiasm for horses is waning. While he would still "rather sleep in the same stall with old Man o' War than make the whole damn Follies," he says that while he "used to follow the horses South every winter, I don't no more. Sick of traveling." At the end of *A Moon for the Misbegotten*, Jim admits, "I found that every day I was glad when the last race was over, and I could go back to the hotel—and the bottle in my room." When *Hughie* opens, this is exactly where Erie is discovered—back at his hotel.

There is one essential difference, however, as Erie, like the denizens of Harry Hope's in *The Iceman Cometh*, is trying desperately to avoid returning to the loneliness of his room. Erie, like Harry's patrons, spurns the key to his room, which he considers a prisoner's "cell." Except for prostitutes, Erie and the male characters in *The Iceman Cometh* live in a world devoid of women. Hickey is given the same physical attributes as Erie's external extrovert self and some of his biographical data: each ran away from unhappy homes in a small "hick town" to make his fortune in the "Big Town"; each tried to escape a woman (Evelyn and Daisy) who loved and wanted to marry him. While they pretend to be sophisticated and practical, the two men's long confessional monologues reveal a deep need for a cherished pipe dream. Only when they allow others to pursue their pipe dreams in the last scenes of the plays do they finally achieve acceptance and a kind of salvation.

The Night Clerk is identified in the *dramatis personae* of the first version of *Hughie* as "the listener." He is, however, totally indifferent to Erie at the outset of the play. The same age as Erie, the Clerk is tall and thin. He has "a scrawny neck and jutting Adam's apple" and a long, narrow face. His features are "without character." Everything about him is dead; he speaks in the "vague tone of a corpse." His eyes are "blank" and "empty"; his face, an inscrutable mask. He is professionally submissive externally; inwardly he is seethingly aggressive and desirous of striking out violently at the world. It has been years since he has felt any emotion, either hope or despair, interest or boredom. He seems totally unaware of his shabby surroundings. The Night Clerk's desk faces left and extends into the dreary lobby. At the right are tiers of mailboxes; above them is a clock. It is between 3:00 and 4:00 A.M. of a day in the summer of 1928. The telephone switchboard seems to be an ironic, superfluous fixture; the Clerk, wrapped in mute isolation, is incapable of properly communicating with anyone.

Whereas the Night Clerk inhabits a world of total negation, Erie lives mindlessly in a land of illusion. Mentally, he has become the image he projected to Hughie: the daring popular gambler and confidant of chieftain mobsters. He states, "I'd get to seein' myself like he seen me." Because of Hughie's belief in him, Erie became confident of his own worth and ability. "Some nights I'd come back here without a buck, feeling lower than a snake's belly, and first thing you know I'd be lousy with jack, bettin' a grand a race." He strives continually to see similarities between the two Night Clerks. It is vitally important to Erie that he establish the same spirit of

camaraderie with the new clerk he had with Hughie.
Replacing Hughie becomes a matter of life or death,
literally and symbolically. He needs another Hughie, first
of all, to regain his "good luck streak." One of the central
symbols of the play is the huge good-luck horseshoe floral
piece Erie bought for Hughie's funeral. He had to borrow
a hundred dollars from mobsters and has no other means
except gambling winnings to pay back the loan. He is "on
a spot" at present and fearful of the consequences of
welshing. Second, and perhaps more important, Hughie's belief in the projected gambler image enabled Erie to
believe in the pipe dream himself.

Erie's friendship with Hughie was an enduring,
mutually beneficial affair, spanning the past fifteen years.
The clerk had lived vicariously the life Erie projected.
Hughie was so naive in his youth that he believed, after
leaving his small town, that instant success, "the key to
the city," would be waiting for him when he arrived at
Grand Central Station. The position of Night Clerk was
the only one he could find. He apparently fell in love with
and married a "salesgirl in some punk department store,"
whom Erie describes as "a bum—in spades." The gambler had encouraged the tarts he brought back to the hotel
to flirt with Hughie. Erie supplied the real "jack" used in
games the two men played. Hughie proved to be a "suck-
er" and was easily taken "to the cleaners." He was so
trusting that he never checked the dice before playing;
but Erie had his own code of ethics and never cheated on a
friend. The clerk "lapped up" Erie's stories "like they was
duck soup, or a beakful of heroin." He wanted to think
Erie and "Legs Diamond was old pals."

The new clerk's senses are suspended; he is lost in a
wasteland of nothingness and longs for death, identifying
it with the night, which is destined to recede and "die and
join all the other long nights in Nirvana, the Big Night of
Nights." Throughout Erie's monologue, the clerk's "mind
escapes to the street"; his aggression finds an outlet in the

clashing sounds of the night. Sound becomes a thematic device in the play, as it did in *The Emperor Jones* and *Dynamo*, again representing a state of mind. Any director staging *Hughie* must incorporate the noises of the night, for they reflect the inner rage and frustration of the clerk. Verbally speechless, he shrieks mentally. Thoreau's words, "Most men live lives of quiet desperation," aptly apply to him.

Oblivious to Erie, the clerk dreams desperate deeds. "Counting the footfalls of the cop on the beat," he thinks, "If he'd only shoot it out with a gunman some night! Nothing exciting has happened in any night I've ever lived through!" In his mind he follows the siren wail of a fire engine. He wonders if it is "a real good one this time." Wanting to see the whole city engulfed, he asks an imaginary fireman, "Will it be big enough, do you think?" Hearing the clanging clash when garbage cans are tossed onto the street, he thinks viciously, "A job I'd like. I'd bang those cans louder than they do! I'd wake up the whole damned city!" He greets the noise of a far-off el train "like a memory of hope." He can tell the precise time of night by the sound of the surface car. Finally, his mind hops "an ambulance clanging down Sixth," and he asks, "Will he die, Doctor, or isn't he lucky?"

At this precise moment, Erie is describing his one visit to Hughie's home in Brooklyn and the thrilling stories he had told the children after dinner. Evidently, either Erie or the tales displeased Hughie's wife, for she hustled the children "off like I was giving 'em measles." Clearly, Erie had seen, even in this bleak home, a semblance of family life that his own life lacked. Erie's forced chuckle evokes a mechanical hearty laugh from the night clerk, as he attempts to respond on cue. Erie is "so hurt and depressed he hasn't the spirit to make a sarcastic crack." He twirls the key, speaks vaguely of beating it "up to my cell," but doggedly pursues his monologue.

A frightening thing occurs; the noises of the city

cease. The clerk's face is "taut with vacancy." His mind
tries "to fasten itself to some noise in the night." It "cannot make a getaway." The night again reminds "him of
death, and he is vaguely frightened." Now when he needs
company, the clerk wonders, why can't he remember one
thing Erie discussed? He recalls one word, gambling, and
inquires: "Do you, by any chance, know the Big Shot,
Arnold Rothstein?"

For the first time that evening, the Night Clerk's face
comes alive; he "dreams, a rapt hero worship transfigur-
ing his pimply face." He holds an imaginary conversation,
as he gambles mentally, with the man who "fixed" the
1919 World Series. "Beatific vision swoons on the empty
pools of the Night Clerk's eyes. He resembles a holy saint,
recently elected to Paradise." Impressed that Erie knows
the gambler, he asks if a white chip is actually worth a
hundred dollars when Rothstein plays poker. Erie stares
"probingly at the Clerk," and "suddenly his face lights up
with a saving revelation." At that moment human contact
is made, mentally and physically; the two men shake
hands. Erie's demeanor changes, his old confidence returns, and he speaks "with a magnificent carelessness" of
lighting a cigar "with a C note" when he was " in the
bucks." To the clerk "nothing is incredible"; he sees Erie
now as "the Gambler in 492, the Friend of Arnold Rothstein." The two conspire to break the house rules if Erie
wins money in a race the next day and rolls "in here with a
blonde." Erie asks, "carelessly," if the Night Clerk wants to
check the dice before their crap game. The clerk's words
of trust prompt Erie to say, "You remind me a lot of
Hughie, Pal." Then he adds, "It's time I quit carryin' the
torch for Hughie." He completes the obituary; "his soul is
purged of grief, his confidence restored."

Hughie focuses on the two things O'Neill thinks a
man needs to survive and to give his life meaning: the
pipe dream and some type of human relationship. When
the Night Clerk enters Erie's world of illusion at the end

of the play, he instantly creates a dream life for himself
and revives the badly needed dream of the gambler. The
clerk assumes the dead Hughie's role in Erie's life and
instills in him a sense of worth as a human being. Erie's
life-style and temperament preclude close family ties; the
clerk obviously finds no satisfaction or joy in his family and
home. The two are loners and losers. Both are described
as being transfigured and saved after establishing their
relationship. In discussing *The Iceman Cometh* with
Lawrence Langner in 1946, O'Neill stressed the importance of both the pipe dream and friendship. "Love remains (once in a while); friendship remains (and that is
rare, too). The rest is ashes in the wind! We have friendship, so what the hell!"

The scheme for "By Way of Obit" shows that the
series could have become a sequel to *The Iceman Cometh*. The titles of the unfinished series plays suggest that
the characters would be homeless like Erie Smith and the
outcasts of Harry Hope's saloon. Unconsciously, perhaps,
the author depicted in the late plays, through characters
such as the Jamie O'Neill-like Erie, the bitter loneliness
and aimlessness of his brother's last years. *Hughie* presents a loving, gentle remembrance of him, a far different
picture than the vindictive, hateful Jamie in the last act of
Long Day's Journey into Night. The dramatist did not
entirely lay his brother's ghost to rest; he did not do so
until the last scene of *A Moon for the Misbegotten*.

Hughie is one of O'Neill's more optimistic plays; its
message is that a man can, by a word or slight gesture
bespeaking human compassion, be a means of salvation to
his fellow creature. *Hughie* was given its world premiere
on September 18, 1958, at the Royal Dramatic Theatre in
Stockholm. It was not produced in this country until
December 22, 1964. Wherever *Hughie* is staged, it is
greeted enthusiastically by theatergoers and critics.

50. A Moon for the Misbegotten

A *Moon for the Misbegotten*, O'Neill's brutally honest but loving remembrance of his brother, Jamie, is a continuation of the memory play *Long Day's Journey into Night*. Set over a decade later, in September 1923, two months before the brother's actual death, the play is a requiem for Jamie, called here Jim Tyrone. In the last years of his creative life, 1939–1943, when he completed his most autobiographical works, O'Neill told the tale of his tragic family in two stages. *Long Day's Journey into Night* explains the early fatal familial events leading up to the actual long day in 1912 and focuses primarily on the author's parents; *A Moon for the Misbegotten* takes place eleven years later after their deaths and concentrates on Jamie O'Neill. It shows what happened to Jamie in the years following the final heart-rending view of him at the end of *Long Day's Journey into Night*. This was a play of "old sorrow, written in tears and blood." *A Moon for the Misbegotten* is a joyous tribute to the regenerative power of love, a drama conceived and created in deep affection.

A single, simple idea from *Long Day's Journey into Night* seems to have inspired the original idea for its sequel. In his Work Diary entry for October 28, 1941, O'Neill states:

> S[haughnessy]. play idea, based on story told by E[dmund]. in 1st Act of "L[ong]. D[ay's]. J[ourney]. I[nto]. N[ight]."—except here Jamie principal character & story of play otherwise entirely imaginary, except for J[amie].'s revelation of self.

In the early notes for the play, the author subordinates the "Shaughnessy idea," developing it as a minor theme, the

Irish-Yankee conflict, and focuses on dramatizing an idealized, imaginative account of the period immediately preceding his brother's death. The decision to eulogize Jamie in the last play of the canon can be viewed as both a personal and a creative act of retribution. In previously completed and contemplated works depicting Jamie, the dramatist developed an idea contained in the 1918–1920 notebook for "a play of Jim and self—showing influence of elder on younger brother."* The struggle of the brothers for dominance is depicted in earlier plays in two ways: as the battle waged by one dual-natured ascetic/Mephistophelian figure (John versus his shadow self, Loving, in *Days without End*) and as a long-running rivalry between two separate antithetical characters (Dion Anthony and William Brown in *The Great God Brown*). Only after he revealed his brother's destructive attitude to him in the last act of *Long Day's Journey into Night* was the author purged of the bitterness, resentment, and hatred he felt for Jamie. In the sequel to this play, *A Moon for the Misbegotten*, he manifests his deep compassion and love for Jamie and an awareness of Jamie's desperate loneliness.

The two late autobiographical plays are linked thematically by the "S." (Shaughnessy) story of an Irish tenant farmer whose land is owned by James Tyrone Sr., which Edmund relates in *Long Day's Journey into Night*. Edmund outwardly and his father inwardly gloat that the "wily shanty Mick" wins a "great Irish victory" over Harker, his Standard Oil millionaire neighbor, by defending and exonerating his adventurous pigs in a trespas-

---

*Psychiatrists find that a child turns to a sibling when parents are absent or indifferent. The young Eugene formed a close bond with Jamie, who was ten years older. By age fifteen Eugene has been taught important lessons in life: how to consume vast quantities of alcohol, how to romanticize sordid encounters with prostitutes, how to get the better of a tight-fisted father. Jamie was a disastrous role model; he was a hopeless alcoholic, a failed writer, a pathetic cynic, dependent on his father for financial sustenance and on his mother for emotional support.

sing dispute. The protoype for Shaughnessy is James O'Neill's tenant, John Dolan, whose name appears in the early notes for *Long Day's Journey into Night*. In Act IV, after Edmund returns from his walk, he tells his father that he went over to see Dolan. The pigs-in-the-pond incident mentioned briefly in this work is recreated in *A Moon for the Misbegotten*, labeled the "Dolan play," in the first 1941–1942 notes. Shaughnessy is now called Phil Hogan; his wealthy neighbor is named Harder, rather than Harker. Using their verbal Irish wit, Phil and his daughter, Josie, soundly defeat the pompous Yankee.

Harker in *Long Day's Journey into Night* and Harder in *A Moon for the Misbegotten* are portraits of Edward Harkness, a Standard Oil millionaire whose property actually abutted the Dolan-O'Neill land. By portraying Harkness as the pro-British Harder in the play and pitting him against the Hogans, O'Neill is writing the final episode in the Irish-Yankee conflict begun earlier in the cycle play *A Touch of the Poet*.* O'Neill never forgave the snobbish Yankee New Londoners who rejected his Irish family, and he gets his revenge on them here. In *A Moon for the Misbegotten* he goes beyond his usual attack on Yankees for the indignities they inflicted on the Irish and assails one of his favorite targets, Standard Oil capitalists. As early as 1914 the author assaulted capitalism in a poem entitled "Fratricide." In it, he raised a question that is relevant today: Should young men be sent to war to portect the interests of wealthy American industrialists? "The army of the poor must fight" such a war the poem states; it asks, "What cause could be more asinine/Than yours, ye slaves of bloody toil?/Is not your bravery sublime/Beneath a tropic sun to broil/And bleed and groan— for Guggenheim,/And give your lives—for Standard Oil!" Phil Hogan expresses the author's revulsion, nearly three decades later, for this company when he tells Harder, "I

*In this play the name Harford, probably another deliberate variation of Harkness, is given to the wealthy Yankee family.

couldn't bring myself to set foot on land bought with Standard Oil money that was stolen from the poor it ground in the dust beneath its dirty heel." O'Neill implies here that men are forced to surrender not only their lives but also their souls in the interests of wealth.

The first title O'Neill assigned *A Moon for the Misbegotten*, "The Man of Other Days," indicates that its initial focal point was, as the original idea states, Jamie's "revelation of self." The person to whom he reveals himself is the fictitious Josie Hogan. Like the Night Clerk in *Hughie*, she becomes in this work "The Good Listener" and the author's persona. In the 1943 draft and the published text of the play, Jim Tyrone describes all the details preceding and following his mother's death, an accurate account of the actual events, which Jamie O'Neill must have narrated to his brother.

O'Neill uses nearly the same words to describe his brother in the two late plays. In the 1912 *Long Day's Journey into Night*, Jamie is thirty-three; here Jim Tyrone is in his early forties. Jim's broad-shouldered, deep-chested, healthy physique "has become soft and soggy from dissipation, but his face is still good-looking despite its unhealthy puffiness and the bags under the eyes." Again the word "Mephistophelian" is used to describe his countenance. Beneath the cocky mask of the cynical "Broadway Wise Guy," "when he smiles without sneering, he still has the ghost of a former youthful, irresponsible Irish charm—that of the beguiling ne'er-do-well, sentimental and romantic." Hogan's youngest son, Mike, sees only the alcoholic failure, the spendthrift and wastrel, and expresses hatred for Jim, "with his quotin' Latin and his high-toned Jesuit College [Fordham] education . . . he's nothing but a drunken bum who never done a tap of work in his life, except acting on the stage while his father was alive to get him jobs." In early notes for the play, Jim attributes his downfall, in part, to his hatred for acting: "It took revenge on him, and made him a bum—on and off, a ham."

Jim uses alcohol for the same reasons his mother used morphine in *Long Day's Journey into Night*: as a way to escape the pain of reality and the knowledge of what he has become. In the earlier play he despaired when he discovered that his mother had started taking morphine again after her supposed cure, identifying with her and saying, "It means so much. I'd begun to hope, if she'd beaten the game, I could, too." Like her, Jim is one of life's tragic, self-destructive wounded, a lonely, frightened outcast.

Josie Hogan, twenty-eight, is another misfit, "so oversize for a woman that she is almost a freak—five eleven in her stockings and weighs around one hundred and eighty." Like Abbie Putnam, Cybel, and Sara Melody, she is given the physical qualities of the ideal O'Neill woman: large, firm breasts, a slender waist, and generous hips and thighs. She has a heavy jaw, high cheekbones, and blue eyes, thick black eyebrows and black hair. "The map of Ireland is stamped on her face." Josie affects the pose of a wicked wanton, the promiscuous "scandal of the neighborhood." Her father is aware of her ruse and, rightly, calls her his "Virgin Queen of Ireland." She pretends to be the whore because she is convinced no man could love her for her "beautiful soul." Loyal, loving, sensitive, "she is all woman."

Phil Hogan, fifty-five, is a wiry little man with a sturdy peasant physique, a fat face, a "big mouth, and little blue eyes with bleached lashes and eyebrows that remind one of a white pig's." He has a pronounced brogue and the verbal skill to sell "doctored up" animals to the uninitiated. Josie calls him the "damndest crook that ever came out of Ireland." With her, he engages in a long-running, good-natured quarrel in an attempt to hide the fact that he adores his daughter and loves her more than anything else in the world.

The assertion may seem incongruous, but Hogan is a partial portrait of the author's father, James. Like him, he is miserly with his sons and carefully hides the whiskey he himself heartily enjoys. He is continually acting and posturing; in the second act he assumes the role of drunkard to trick Josie. Hogan has three sons, with whom he is always in conflict. His wife died giving birth to the third son; similarly, Ella O'Neill experienced a kind of psychological death after her third son's birth. Hogan, outraged because God did not spare his wife, left the Catholic Church, scorning it, its clergy, and its followers. He has a type of father-son relationship with Jim Tyrone, reluctantly sharing his whiskey with him and facilely dispensing words of advice.

Both of the Hogans attempt to cheer the grieving Jim Tyrone, who, like Jamie O'Neill, has an abnormal, obsessive love for his mother. In the notes for *Days Without End*, O'Neill discussed John Loving's Oedipal feelings for his mother and his inability to free himself from guilt and maternal domination. He stated that "Mother worship, repressed and turned morbid, ends by becoming Death love and longing." After Jim's mother dies, he longs only for death, which will reunite them. The circumstances of the fictitious mother's death approximate those of Ella O'Neill's. When James O'Neill died in 1920, Jamie, for his mother's sake, reformed and gave up alcohol. The two traveled to California, where she had a stroke. Fearing that she would die, Jamie went out and got drunk. Later the mother came out of the coma briefly and looked at him reproachfully. Seeing his condition, she closed her eyes "and was glad to die."

In the play, as in real life, the son accompanies the mother's body on the long train trip east. Believing that she has betrayed him by dying, he seeks revenge. He reserves a drawing room on the train, stocks it with a case of bourbon, and hires a fifty-dollar-a-night blonde whore for the trip. Later, after the mother is buried in New London, Jamie is filled with self-loathing whenever he is sober. In the year following her death, which precedes the action of the play, he attempts to alleviate his anguish, as he had on the train, through whiskey and the company of whores. When the play opens, he seeks a total, final oblivion in death.

The son cannot die—yet. As a lapsed Catholic, he is beset by feelings of guilt. He longs for the absolution found only in confession. The need reflects the important role Catholicism played, even unconsciously, in the lives of both the author and his brother. Their early religious training had been provided by their pious mother, even before they were sent to Catholic boarding school at the age of seven, supposedly the age of reason when one is capable of distinguishing between good and evil and of committing a sin. In the following years at school they were taught the catechism and the need to keep the ten laws of God and the six laws of the Church and its teachings. A serious infraction of the laws, mortal sin, supposedly brought spiritual death to the soul. Life was restored only through confession, penance, and absolution. The sin-confession-forgiveness syndrome is an invariable motif in the canon.

Throughout *A Moon for the Misbegotten* death imagery is used to describe Jim Tyrone. He is called "a dead man walking slow behind his own coffin" and a "damned soul" seeking "to confess and be forgiven." He has, he believes, broken the sixth commandment, "Thou shalt not commit adultery," and betrayed God and his mother. Having sinned against the mother, he thinks that forgiveness can come to him only through Josie, the mother figure. Nowhere in the canon is O'Neill's statement that "in all my plays sin is punished and redemption takes place" more effectively illustrated than in *A Moon for the Misbegotten*. In the early scenes of the play, however, Josie, who is deeply in love with Jim, wants a physical as well as a spiritual relationship with him. The memory of too many mornings after wretched nights with whores haunts Jim; he is repulsed by the physical and associates sex only with prostitutes and love only with the mother or maternal figure. When she finally realizes that Jim can accept only maternal love, Josie sacrifices her own desires, saying: "I have all kinds of love for you."

The most developed section in the first scenario, entitled "The Man of Other Days," is the "extraordinary love scene" between Josie and Jim in Act III. In this version he is not repelled by sex. On the contrary, he reveals a physical desire for Josie, making the fulfillment of it a precondition for the Dolans' retaining their farm: "I wouldn't accept if Harder offered a million. Won't sell if—if you don't repulse my advances, so to speak." He alone, except for her father, knows "lots of men haven't had" her as she claims. As Act III evolves and Josie's role in the play expands, the original theme, Jim's revelation of self, becomes part of a larger, more comprehensive plan. The extraordinary love scene shows these two misbegotten creatures to be kindred souls. The new title given the work, "The Moon Bore Twins," indicates a shift in focus to their strange symbiotic relationship. Their explorations of the inner self, which culminate in the confession of opposing dreams and total self-revelation, bring not only self-awareness but love-awareness. Their love is not altogether hopeless here, and Jim even proposes to Josie: "I—I'd like to marry you—but I've nothing to offer." Josie realizes that a future with Jim is impossible. To conceal her sorrow, she says jokingly that she "will accept Mulroy today—he's been begging me to marry him since he tried to seduce me. . . . he'll give me children I can love—the first will be a son and I'll call him Jamie." Later, on November 12, 1941, after he decided to portray Josie and Jim as doomed lovers who are destined to be parted, the dramatist assigned the play its final title, A Moon for the Misbegotten, noting in his Work Diary that it was "much more to the point."

Two weeks later, on November 26, when he began the dialogue and first draft, O'Neill states: "getting great satisfaction [from] this play—flows." He completed this draft on January 20. There is no indication in the early version that O'Neill intended to make this drama an epitaph for his brother; the work became one later in the second, 1943 draft when the author set the play in September 1923, shortly before Jamie's death. From its inception to the completion of the first draft, the drama provided a reminiscent view of the brother, a vehicle designed, as the author states, for "Jamie's revelation of self." Only when O'Neill started the second draft in January 1943 did the major theme of the published version emerge: Jim's attempt to find, through confession, forgiveness for the desecration of his mother's memory and his life of dissipation and to achieve, through the absolution of the mother-substitute and priestess, Josie, moral regeneration and redemption.

Several causes can be cited for O'Neill's decision to change the theme of *A Moon for the Misbegotten* in 1943 by adding a new spiritual dimension to it and to the characterizations of Jim Tyrone and Josie Hogan. As the Work Diary entries indicate, his physical condition had deteriorated; the tremor of his hand became more pronounced. To the man who could express his thoughts only by writing them—as though his arm were the channel, his hand the extension, of his creative mind—this debilitating condition signaled his demise as an artist. *A Moon for the Misbegotten* was important to the dramatist for two reasons. On the personal level, he would never be able to express, in some future play, his own forgiveness, his love, and spiritual wish-fulfillment for his brother. On the creative plane, the ghost of the doomed Mephistophelian-ascetic Jamie O'Neill, which had haunted him and his plays for so many years, would finally be laid to rest.

The final version of the play has many rich levels of meaning. There are several motifs in addition to the forgiveness-redemption theme: the Irish-Yankee conflict, the parent–child conflict, the attempt to reject reality for the comforting world of illusion supported by alcohol and pipe dreams. O'Neill tells his story in a simple, straightforward style; he uses none of the earlier technical devices, save monologues and the protective masks that are removed, layer by layer, act by act.

The play is set on a day in early September 1923 at the Hogan farmhouse. The structure is described as "a fine example of New England architecture," an ugly, dilapidated "clapboarded affair." Windows are broken; shutters and curtains are nonexistent. A one-story addition, Josie's bedroom, "has been tacked on at right." A flight of three unpainted steps extends from the ground to the door leading into this room. Josie, barefooted and wearing a cheap blue cotton dress, comes out of the house and conspires with her brother Mike, twenty, in his effort to run away from his father and the farm. Described as "slyly cunning," "primly self-righteous," and "one of the elite of Almighty God in a world of damned sinners," Mike is "a New England Irish Catholic Puritan, Grade B, and an extremely irritating youth to have around."

Josie gives him a small role of bills taken from their father's purse and advice on how to behave when he arrives at their brother Thomas's home in Bridgeport. The ungrateful youth berates his sister for being a disgraceful loose woman and for concocting a scheme "to hook" Jim Tyrone when he becomes wealthy after his mother's estate is settled. Hogan's great fear when he discovers that the son has run off with his money is that the "pious lump" will "drop it in the collection plate next Sunday, he's that big a jackass." Informed of Mike's suggestion that Josie seduce Jim Tyrone, Hogan points out the merit of the plan: "Sure, you're two of a kind, both great disgraces. That would help make a happy marriage because neither of you could look down on the other." Josie reminds him that Jim gets "drunk every night of his life." Hogan is certain that she has the strength to reform

him; one taste of her club would make him "a dirty
prohibitionist" in a few weeks. Josie says that she would
only conspire against Jim if he broke his promise to allow
her father to buy the farm on "easy time payments."
Hogan admits that no one but their "damn fool" neighbor
Harder would even want the property.

Jim Tyrone enters, showing that he has had "enough
pick-me-ups to recover from morning-after nausea and
steady his nerves." The three engage in witty repartee.
Jim informs the Hogans that they are about to have a
visitor: one of the "Kings of our Republic by Divine Right
of Inherited Swag." Harder, "Standard Oil's sappiest
child," wants to know why Hogan's "fine ambitious Am-
erican-born pigs" are wallowing in his ice pond.

Harder is an immature young man, spoiled and "cod-
dled from birth." His English tweed coat, breeches, and
riding boots inflame the native hatred of the anti-British
Irish. "Ill-equipped for combat with the Hogans," he has
never "come in contact with anyone like them." A hilarious scene follows, which concludes with Hogan's demand
for reimbursement for medical and funeral expenses for
his pigs. "I'll paste your ugly mug on the front page of
every newspaper as a pig-murdering tyrant! Before I'm
through with you, you'll think you're the King of England
at an Irish wake!" The Yankee's "retreat becomes a rout."
The triumphant Hogan plans to return to the Inn with Jim
to celebrate the great Irish victory by getting "drunk as
Moses."

In the following act, at eleven that night, Josie sits on
the steps in her "Sunday best," heart-broken because Jim
failed to return two hours earlier as he has promised. Her
father comes home, pretending to be drunk in an effort to
trick her, and tells her that Jim has agreed to sell Harder
the farm for ten thousand dollars, five times the price the
Hogans were to pay. The father reminds Josie of her vow
that morning to seduce Jim if he reneged on his promise.
Humiliated and seeking revenge, she agrees to play the

whore and "to get him in bed." Hogan vows to return at
sunrise with witnesses. When Jim finally arrives at the
end of the act, he has consumed so much alcohol that he
has "the old heebie-jeebies." He questions the wisdom of
the visit to Josie.

There is no lapse between the second and third acts.
Guilt-ridden, the sodden Tyrone sings, sneeringly:

> And baby's cries can't waken her
> In the baggage coach ahead.

When Josie, who usually abstains from alcohol, pours
generous drinks for both of them, Jim suspects that she is
trying to seduce him. He recalls his nights with prostitutes, the "many dawns creeping grayly over too many
dirty windows." He longs for a night with her "different
from any past night." When she discovers her father's
subterfuge, Josie kisses Jim passionately and suggests that
they go inside. A frightful change comes over him; he
looks at her "with a sneering cynical lust" and addresses
her as if she were a whore: "Come on, Baby Doll, let's hit
the hay." All her adult life Josie has pretended to be a slut;
being treated now like one by the man she loves hurts and
humiliates her. Told that Jamie seeks a higher kind of
love, Josie kisses him now with maternal passion, sacrificing all physical desire and offering him the kind of love
he needs.

All of Jim's defenses crumble. Sorrowfully, he makes
his confession of wrongs against his mother, his cruel act
of revenge on the train. With a "brooding maternal tenderness," Josie assures him that his mother "loves and
understands and forgives." She feels the mother "in the
moonlight, her soul wrapped in it like a silver mantle."
Josie then promises Jim a dawn that "will wake in the sky
like a promise of God's peace in the soul's dark sadness."
The scene demonstrates that the "moon" for the misbegotten is forgiveness, the gift Josie accords Jim. The moon
is associated here with his dead virginal mother. In my-

thology, the moon signifies the chaste Diana; as a Christian emblem, it represents the Blessed Virgin Mary. Josie, as intermediary and priestess, had to be a virgin, for she is identified in Jim's mind with his pure mother. The virgin mystique had to be manifested to sustain the son's belief that he has been forgiven.

The last act takes place at dawn of the following morning. Josie has cradled the sleeping Jim in her arms throughout the night. They make a pieta-like "tragic picture": "this big sorrowful woman hugging a haggard-faced, middle-aged drunkard against her breast, as if he were a sick child." Hogan comes in from the barn where he has been sleeping, wondering what has taken place. Josie informs him that a "great miracle" has occurred: "a virgin who bears a dead child in the night, and the dawn finds her still a virgin." He vows to avenge any wrong done to her, but she assures him that she was the one at fault: "I thought there was still hope. I didn't know he'd died already—that it was a damned soul coming to me in the moonlight, to confess and be forgiven and find peace for a night." Weary of her father's duplicity, Josie vows to leave him: "You can live alone and work alone your cunning schemes on yourself." Docilely, the old man goes into the house when ordered to do so.

Reluctantly, Josie wakes Jim, hoping he will "remember one thing and forget the rest." He assumes, at first, that he is in the arms of a prostitute and that the night has been like all the others. The "dreamy peaceful hangover" perplexes him. He says, "It's hard to describe how I feel. It's a new one on me. Sort of at peace with myself and this lousy life—as if all my sins had been forgiven." The sight of Hogan's "real, honest-to-God bonded Bourbon" jogs his memory. He tries to conceal his shame by pretending that he does not remember what happened the previous evening, but seeing Josie's sorrow, he says, "Forgive me, Josie. I do remember! I'm glad I remember! I'll never forget your love! . . . I'll love you always."

Josie watches Jim's receding figure in the final scene. Her father begs her gently, "Don't darlin'. Don't be hurting yourself." His lying scheme, he tells her, had been concocted not to obtain money but to ensure her happiness. Hogan's overwhelming love comforts Josie, and the two resume their old teasing banter. Before following him into the house, she stares once more at the road and says: "May you have your wish and die in your sleep soon, Jim, darling. May you rest forever in forgiveness and peace."

During the "extraordinary love scene" in Act III in which Josie relinquishes physical, personal love for the spiritual, maternal type, she says, "Maybe this is the greatest of all—because it costs so much." The same point could be made about the play itself. It is not the greatest in achievement, for it ranks in the second category with *Mourning Becomes Electra* and *A Touch of the Poet* after the masterpieces *Long Day's Journey into Night* and *The Iceman Cometh*; it did, however, require the greatest effort to complete. With his health failing, his hand trembling so that he could scarcely write, O'Neill found it difficult to finish *A Moon for the Misbegotten*. In January 1943, while working on the first act of the second draft, he noted in his Work Diary: "What I am up against now— fade out physically each day after about 3 hours—page a day because [I] work slowly even when as eager about play as I am about this—Park[inson's disease]. main cause—constant strain to write." The dramatist completed the second act in March, the third in April, and was still reshaping the fourth on May 3, 1943, when he recorded the last entry on his creative efforts in the Work Diary.

Personal, as well as, artistic considerations motivated O'Neill to undertake the second draft of *A Moon for the Misbegotten* in 1943. In a letter to Dudley Nichols dated December 16, 1942, he points out the major flaw in the 1941–1942 script: "Managed to finish the first draft but

the heart was out of it. . . . There is a fine unusual tragic
comedy in 'A Moon for the Misbegotten' but it will have to
wait until I can rewrite the lifeless post-Pearl Harbor
part of it." O'Neill's primary goal in rewriting the play was
to bestow on Jamie, posthumously, through Josie, the
care he himself denied Jamie in his final months and the
absolution his brother sought. In spite of his disparaging
remarks about Jamie in *Long Day's Journey into Night*,
the dramatist sincerely loved his brother and was distraught by the humiliation and pain he endured in his last
illness, which began long before the date stated in *A
Moon for the Misbegotten*: September 1923. Frances
Cadenas, a friend, in her letter of July 18, 1923, to the
playwright, describes the critical condition of Jamie, who,
because of the pain in his hands, was unable to write.*
Similarly afflicted later as he created *A Moon for the
Misbegotten*, O'Neill could not fail to identify with his
brother. Probably the remembrance that he himself
lacked heart and did not visit Jamie when he was ill and in
need of comfort prompted the dramatist to provide his
brother, in an artistic endeavor, with the personal and
spiritual consolation he lacked in real life, the forgiveness
extended to Jamie, through Josie, in the last line of the
play: "May you rest forever in forgiveness and peace."

Through Josie, one of his most beautiful creations,
O'Neill provides a valuable lesson. She sacrifices her own
desires and gives Jim the spiritual love and forgiveness he
needs. In modern society the individual seems to have
lost the ability to love another selflessly. Josie's actions

*Mrs. Cadenas told O'Neill that after receiving his letter that
morning she went to see his brother at Riverlong in Paterson,
New Jersey. The doctor had diagnosed the illness as "alcoholic
neuritis and that is what is causing the intense pain and possibly
affecting his eyes":

Jim's story is that he does not feel any better, and that the
pain is not only in his limbs but in his hands this week. He
does not like the place, the food is wretched, and that he
cannot sleep during the night or day. The method of treat-

demonstrate that in a world lacking religious certitude one can, through sacrifice, bring a kind of redemption to another. Jim's search to be forgiven and to belong resembles that of every individual. The play takes on universal dimensions. Through his final view of the homeless, alienated Jim Tyrone, O'Neill seems to be saying here, as in other plays, that man can belong only in death. *A Moon for the Misbegotten* is a coda in the canon; it presents O'Neill's final message: before finding release in death, man must be reconciled with God, his fellow man, and himself.

Unlike *Long Day's Journey into Night*, *A Moon for the Misbegotten* was staged before O'Neill's death. The Theatre Guild assembled a company to tour the midwest. Supposedly a pre-Broadway production, it premiered in Columbus, Ohio, on February 20, 1947. The Irish in the audience were repulsed by the coarse shanty-Irish Hogans. In Detroit the company encountered censorship problems, and the play was labeled a "dirty show." *A Moon for the Misbegotten* was not presented on Broadway until May 2, 1957, four years after O'Neill's death and a few months after the success of *Long Day's Journey into Night*. The latter enabled audiences and critics to perceive the autobiographical nature of the late plays. They understood and acclaimed the 1957 production and subsequent revivals in 1968, 1973, and 1984.

A Moon for the Misbegotten is O'Neill's most Irish play. Called a "strange combination comic tragic" work by its author, it reveals the dual light-dark nature of the Irish. The hilarious pigs-in-the-pond incident in Act I

---

ing this neuritis is giving him ten drinks of whiskey during the day and some other kind of a drink before the whiskey which burns like fire and acts as a purgative. . . . He cannot read or write so he asked me to write for him and to tell you about his condition. He also expresses a great desire to see you. . . . If there is any change I shall telegraph you at once. I'm sure a letter from you would be very bracing. He has a male attendant who reads to him.

shows the jocular, light-hearted side of the Celts. As the play unfolds and Jim Tyrone reflects on his past life, the dark introspective nature of the Irish is manifested. It is unfortunate that O'Neill did not retain the scene of "opposing dreams" from the first, 1941–1942 draft. In earlier plays Jamie O'Neill is depicted as a Mephistophelian character. The dual-natured Mephistophelian-ascetic Dion Anthony in *The Great God Brown* is perhaps the most accurate portrait of Jamie in the canon. In "The Man of Other Days" Josie describes man's opposing dreams (actually opposing natures) as "deadly enemies. It's a fight to see which will own your life." Reluctantly, Jamie reveals his first dream, a Lucifer dream, of "the cynic who believes in nothing." His second dream is "kid stuff—dates back to school—catechism—the man who loves God, who gives up self and the world to worship of God and devote self to good works." This identical dichotomy appears in the notes for *Long Day's Journey into Night* in the description of the mother, who in Act III recalls her girlhood desire to be a nun. Her dual nature emerges in this act: the "vain happy chattering girlishness—then changing to a hard cynical sneering bitterness with a bitter biting cruelty and with a coarse vulgarity in it—the last as if suddenly poisoned by an alive demon." Her ascetic-Lucifer dichotomy emerges in her elder son. In the last line of *A Moon for the Misbegotten*, O'Neill truly forgives his tragic brother for all past misdeeds; nowhere in the canon does he absolve his mother, the most miscreated of the misbegotten O'Neills.

The Late Contemplated Plays: 1940–1943

In 1940 O'Neill conceived and developed ideas for three plays that seemed to form a timely antitotalitarian trilogy: "The Visit of Malatesta," "The Last Conquest," and "Blind Alley Guy." The projected dramas represent the author's creative response to the world events of the previous year. On August 31, 1939, he noted in his Work Diary: "up till 3 a.m. listen [to] Hitler's war speech against Poland." Throughout the spring of 1940 he could not shake his "war obsession," which, he admitted, "is becoming neurosis—can't save even myself by not working and despairing about the future of individual freedom" (Work Diary, June 25, 1940). O'Neill had in past plays pointed out the forces that could endanger and enslave man. In the problem plays of the early 1920s, man's chains are forged by economic exploitation and ethnic discrimination. Now his unbridled greed and sense of racial superiority lead him in the 1930s to the threshold of Auschwitz and spawn the master-monsters of political oppression depicted in the three plays O'Neill worked on during his last creative years but unfortunately failed to finish.

On January 4, 1940, the day after he completed *The Iceman Cometh*, O'Neill made his first notes for a comedy, "The Visit of Malatesta," whose hero, the legendary anarchist leader Cesare Malatesta, escapes from Italy in 1923 after Mussolini comes to power and seeks refuge with his former revolutionary friends, the Italian-American Daniellos. Like his historical counterpart, Enrico Malatesta, the protagonist has devoted his life to the anarchist ideals of social, economic, and political equality, ideals forgotten by his Americanized followers. Malatesta brandishes a two-edged sword: against the Fascist despotism of the old country and the enslaving tyranny of materialism in his adopted land. He sets out to reform not only Tony Daniello, who operates a speakeasy, his family, and Italian anarchist friends but also two corrupt Irishmen who frequent the "speak." The play contains many elements found in *The Iceman Cometh*: a barroom setting, the retreat to pipe dreams, political corruption and greed, and, primarily, a focus on anarchism.

In his first 1940 notes O'Neill depicts Malatesta as an ardent believer in the innate goodness of his fellow man. When the Axis dictators unleashed their madness and fury upon the world, the dramatist despaired "about the future of individual freedom." To him, the war was not merely a conflict between countries but a part of the eternal struggle between the powers of good and evil. In Italy Malatesta had witnessed cruelty, injustice, and greed—all sanctioned by a totalitarian government. Now in the United States, a democracy, supposedly advocating justice and equality, he expects but fails to find these principles practiced. What he discovers in the Daniello household pains and dismays him; each person is consumed by greed or a base desire. The central message of the play is summarized in Malatesta's admonition to his materialistic friends: "Utopia is impossible until man outgrows his base greed—his spiritual immaturity—and develops a soul. No Movement can do it—they lead to greed for power—each man and woman strives within himself or herself to conquer own natures."

In his last reference to the Malatesta work, on March 2, 1941, O'Neill stated that he liked the concept but had "lost grip on it—trouble is too many ideas (the war, perhaps)." The next day he outlined "The Last Conquest," which again issues a warning but without the humor that characterizes "The Visit of Malatesta." There is no mere threat of oppression by a Fascist leader thousands of miles away in "The Last Conquest"; man is now enslaved in a World State and persecuted by a brutal dictator. This work shows the consequences of the failure to heed Malatesta's message—O'Neill's favorite Biblical quotation: "For what shall it profit a man, if he shall gain the whole world and lose his own soul?" In "The Last Conquest" modern man is a tragic, damned Faustian creature, having lost not only his freedom and prized acquisitions but even the awareness that he possesses a soul.

O'Neill began "The Last Conquest" on August 30, 1940. He described the plot of this "World-Dictator fantasy of a possible future" as "the attempted last campaign of Evil to stamp out even the unconscious memory of God in Man's spirit." The dictator, called The Savior of the World, believes that he has successfully eliminated the remembrance of God from the minds of his oppressed subjects. A plan is devised to test this assumption by His Minister of Spiritual Affairs, a Magician, who is, in reality, the Devil, the power behind the throne. The Devil fashions a life-size statue of Christ contrived so cunningly that "it seems like a living man who had fainted or had just died." The Devil fears the prophecy that this ancient Redeemer is to appear a second time on earth. "So long as men can remember no matter how dimly and subconsciously the faintest dream of a return of the spirit, they have not been completely conquered." He plans to stage a mock second coming of Christ "in which he will be compelled to repeat his former salvational career on earth for the amusement of all our loyal subjects." Jeering laughter will purge men's minds of the memory of this Savior. The World Dictator will be forced to crucify him not because he is a rival "but simply because under the law of our enlightened realistic State, the mentally disabled are executed." The Devil plans to utilize his experience in creating illusion and disillusion, in hypnotism, and in ventriloquism.

In July 1941 O'Neill decided to have the actual spirit of Christ miraculously infuse the wooden figure. While rehearsing the dialogue, the Devil-Magician is startled when a voice suddenly comes from the figure; he is triumphant: "Knew you must accept this challenge." Christ says, "I accept this drama as you have planned it, O Son of Modern Man." In the eight scenes of the play Christ reenacts the various stages of his passion from his temptation to his crucifixion. In the Epilogue O'Neill devised in December 1942 Christ defeated Satan. The awakened masses vow: "We will not forget this time. The God in us is stronger if we choose. Christ is our refuge and our strength and evil cannot prevail."

Unfortunately, O'Neill found it impossible to continue "The Last Conquest." On December 13, 1942, he stated: "No go—decide will have to quit on this again—or on anything else—one of my old sinking spells is on me—lower than low—mind dead" (Work Diary). Three days later, in a letter to Dudley Nichols, he said that his creative impulse was blocked when he worked on "The Last Conquest" "by the hopeless certainty that it could not be understood now, or its possibilities admitted— more than that, a feeling in myself that, until this war, which must be won, is won, people should concentrate on the grim surface and not admit the still grimmer, soul-disturbing depths."

Ever mindful of Hitler, Mussolini, and Stalin, O'Neill portrayed his World Dictator as the apotheosis and legatee of these modern tyrants: "There is no physical resemblance between him and any of the dictators of totalitarian nations, like Hitler of Germany, who has preceded him," yet the "Savior of the World owes much to these men, whose spiritual heir He is, but of course He can never admit He owes His power to anything but His own Divine Genius and He had decreed that no memory of these men must ever be spoken or written." There are several topical allusions to Hitler and his Nazi regime in

"The Last Conquest": concentration camps, the crowd marching "goose-step up a mountain side," flags in the Amphitheatre of Games "with sickles, hammers, swastikas," the dictator's fear of being seen "consorting with a Jew," and his promise to Christ to manufacture a family tree showing Him to be "the son of an Aryan emigrant to Palestine."

To O'Neill, Hitler was evil incarnate, and he represented the gravest threat to individual freedom in modern times. The specter of the Nazi dictator haunted O'Neill's next project, "Blind Alley Guy." Initially, however, the work was another autobiographical memory play, depicting the complex relationship between the central character and his family. The author began "Blind Alley Guy" on December 16, 1940, exactly two months after completing *Long Day's Journey into Night*, which depicted incidents that occurred in his life in 1912. It appears in the new work that he wanted to take his story beyond this year, into the 1912–1918 period. Traits and attitudes of the dramatist are given to Rickey, the central figure, and those of Ella and James O'Neill are attributed to his parents, Ed and Tess White. The focal point of the early idea for the play is the love-hate family relationships.

In July 1941 O'Neill emerged from another period marked by "war jitters" and devoted to his antitotalitarian play, "The Last Conquest." At this time "Blind Alley Guy" changed from an autobiographical work to a propaganda play. The hero, now called Walter White and resembling Brecht's Arturo Ui, is a Hitler-like gangster. His parents and sister are given new characterizations; they have lost "all ethical and moral values . . . no faith in old religion—government all grafting politicians—sex morality of no meaning, ancient bigotry." O'Neill changed the date of the setting to 1934—"year Hitler's seizing power"—and gave his hero the Nazi dictator's traits and background. The dramatist drew a parallel be-

tween Hitler, whose friends (Röhm and his followers) supposedly planned to "double-cross him," and Walter,
whose wife betrays him. The central motif of the play is
"Recurrence argument of Ed and Tess about Hitler—
opening Acts I, II, & IV—follow same pattern—each
ends on note of affinity to Walt."

Two dominant motifs of O'Neill's work merge in
"Blind Alley Guy": autobiographical memories of the past
and concerns for humanity's present and future social
well-being. Appropriately for our time, the latter takes
precedence in this work. By changing the autobiographical characterizations of the Whites and portraying them as
godless materialists who support the ruthless German
dictator, O'Neill delineated the prototypes of the apathetic Americans who inhabit the totalitarian World State
of "The Last Conquest" and willingly submit to its tyrannical "Hitler-like leader." In his notes for the play, the
author writes, "The spirit is intangible, unseen while
greed and power are realistic facts" and "Imperialism has
reached its final expression, men are spiritually dead."
O'Neill's primary purpose in writing the antitotalitarian
trilogy in the early 1940s was to make modern man aware
of the threat to individual freedom, that his own flawed
nature posed the gravest danger to its preservation. The
message he wished to impart is spoken by the formerly
enslaved people of the World State: "It is good to be
free—to have a soul again—to know there is good and evil
in our hearts and we can choose."

Bibliography

I. WORKS BY EUGENE O'NEILL
(ARRANGED CHRONOLOGICALLY)

PLAYS

The Plays of Eugene O'Neill, 12 vols. Wilderness Edition. New York: Scribner's, 1934–1935.

The Plays of Eugene O'Neill, 3 vols. New York: Random House, 1951.

A Moon for the Misbegotten. New York: Random House, 1952.

Long Day's Journey into Night. New Haven: Yale University Press, 1956.

A Touch of the Poet. New Haven: Yale University Press, 1957.

Hughie. New Haven: Yale University Press, 1959.

"The Ancient Mariner." *Yale University Library Gazette*, Vol. 25, No. 2 (October, 1960).

Ten Lost Plays of Eugene O'Neill. New York: Random House, 1964. This volume contains O'Neill's first five plays, which were published in 1914 by the Gorham Press (*Thirst and Other One-Act Plays*): *The Web, Thirst, Recklessness, Warnings*, and *Fog* and five plays published in 1950 in an unauthorized edition by New Fathoms Press (*Lost Plays of Eugene O'Neill*): *A Wife for a Life, Abortion, The Movie Man, Servitude*, and *The Sniper*.

More Stately Mansions, ed. Donald Gallup. New Haven: Yale University Press, 1964.

Children of the Sea, ed. Jennifer McCabe Atkinson. Washington: NCR/Microcard Editions, 1972. This volume contains "Children of the Sea" (an early draft of *Bound East for Cardiff*), *Bread and Butter, Now I Ask You*, and *Shell Shock*.

The Calms of Capricorn, developed by Donald Gallup. New Haven: Ticknor & Fields, 1981.

NON-DRAMATIC WRITINGS

"Strindberg and Our Theatre." *Provincetown Playbill*, January 3, 1924.

"Memoranda on Masks." *American Spectator*, 1 (November 1932), p.3.

Inscriptions, Eugene O'Neill to Carlotta Monterey O'Neill. New Haven: Privately printed, 1960.

Poems 1912–1942, ed. Donald Gallup. New Haven: Yale University Library, 1979.

Work Diary 1924–1943, ed. Donald Gallup (2 vols.). New Haven: Yale University Library, 1981.

UNPUBLISHED WRITINGS

Beinecke Rare Book and Manuscript Library, Yale University. In 1978 Donald Gallup, curator of the Collection of American Literature, asked me to edit for publication the hitherto restricted material in the Eugene O'Neill collection. Included were four notebooks in which O'Neill recorded his ideas for plays from 1918 to 1938; notes, scenarios, and early drafts for completed plays (*Chris Christopherson, Anna Christie, The First Man, The Great God Brown, Desire Under the Elms, Marco Millions, Lazarus Laughed, Strange Interlude, Dynamo, Mourning Becomes Electra, Days Without End, More Stately Mansions, The Iceman Cometh, Long Day's Journey into Night, Hughie,* and *A Moon for the Misbegotten*); notes, scenarios, and first drafts for unfinished plays ("The Guilty One" [1924], "Career of Shih Huang Ti" [1925], "Squarehead Saga" [1926], "Bantu Boy" [1927], "Life of Aeschylus" [1929], "Philip II–Don Juan of Austria Play" [1930], "Life of Sturgo Nacimbin" [1934], "*Ah, Wilderness!* Sequel" [1934], "Robespierre" [1938]); and copious notes for three fairly well developed plays ("The Visit of Malatesta," also named "Malatesta Seeks Surcease"; "The Last Conquest"; and "Blind Alley Guy," also called "Gag's End" [1940–1943]). I also had access to other miscellaneous documents, including "Cycles," "List of All Plays," and Nietzsche Quotations, and a collection of letters O'Neill wrote to friends, to Kenneth Macgowan and Dudley Nichols, to Lawrence Langner, Theresa Helburn, and Robert Sisk of the Theatre Guild, and others, and letters Carlotta O'Neill wrote to Dale Fern.

Houghton Library, Harvard University. The library holds typescripts of a completed play, "The Personal Equation"; a scenario, "The Reckoning"; correspondence between O'Neill and Agnes Boulton, his second wife; and letters in the Isaac Goldberg Collection.

II. OTHER WORKS CITED

Barnes, Clive. "Quintero's Completion of Play at Broadhurst." *The New York Times*, November 1, 1967, p. 45.

Basso, Hamilton. "The Tragic Sense—III." *The New Yorker*, March 13, 1948, pp. 37–47.

Boulton, Agnes. *Part of a Long Story*. Garden City, N.Y.: Doubleday, 1958.

Brooks, Van Wyck. *The Flowering of New England 1815–1865*. New York: E.P. Dutton Co., 1936.

Clark, Barrett. *Eugene O'Neill*. New York: Robert McBride, 1926.

———. *Eugene O'Neill, the Man and His Plays*. New York: Dover, 1947.

Floyd, Virginia. *Eugene O'Neill at Work*. New York: Frederick Ungar, 1981.

———. *Eugene O'Neill: A World View*. New York: Frederick Ungar, 1979.

Josephson, Matthew. *The Robber Barons—The Great American Capitalists, 1861–1901*. New York: Harcourt Brace & Co., 1934.

Kerr, Walter. "No One Will Ever Live in It." *The New York Times*, November 12, 1967, II, pp. 1, 5.

McKay, Richard. *Some Famous Sailing Ships and Their Builder Donald McKay*. New York: G.P. Putnam's Sons, 1931.

Miller, Perry. *The New England Mind—the Seventeenth Century*. Cambridge, Mass.: Harvard University Press, 1954.

Olsson, Tom J. A. *O'Neill och Dramaten*. Stockholm, Sweden: Akademilitteratur, 1977.

Törnqvist, Egil. *A Drama of Souls*. Uppsala, Sweden: Almqvist & Wiksells, 1968.

Weissman, Philip. "Conscious and Unconscious Autobiographical Dramas of Eugene O'Neill." *Journal of the American Psychoanalytic Association*, 5 (1957), 432–460.

Index